An enlarged, facsimile edition of

The Elements of Astrology

by Luke Dennis Broughton, 1828-1898

Astrology Classics
Bel Air, Maryland

The publisher extends his thanks to Philip Graves, for the use of his copy.

About the Author *taken from Astrological Pioneers of America*, by James H. Holden and Robert A. Hughes. Published 1988 by the American Federation of Astrologers. Used by permission.

Back cover: U.S. Capitol Building, November 16, 1860. Courtesy of the Architect of the Capitol, Washington, D.C., who reminds us their images may not be used in any way that would imply endorsement by the Architect of the Capitol or the United States Congress of a product, service, or point of view. Did you know the dome of the Capitol was built by slaves?

ISBN: 978 1 933303 46 8

This edition published May, 2012

Published by
Astrology Classics
The publication division of
The Astrology Center of America
207 Victory Lane, Bel Air, MD 21014
On line at http://www.**AstroAmerica.com**

Synopsis

Preface iii
To the Student v
Lessons and Books on Astrology xx

Table of Contents xxi

Glossary of Astrological Terms xxv

Elements of Astrology

Introduction 5
Brief History of Astrology 8
Astrology in London, *by Edgar Lee* 45
Letters 50
Pharaoh's Dream 58
Theories of Ancient Astronomers 60
Perihelion Epoch of Jupiter 62
Effect on the Earth of the Near Approach of Mars 66
Meteorology and Planetary Influence 72
The Planet Neptune in Gemini 74
Personal Description Determined by Planets 79
Assassination of President Lincoln 81
Assassination of President Garfield 82
Lizzie Borden Murder Case 85

Elements of Astrology 87
Signification of the Twelve Houses 89
Nature, Quality, Description of the Twelve Houses ... 90
General Appearance, by the Twelve Signs 97
Persons Described by the Eight Planets 99
Planets in Signs 105
Planets in Conjunction 122
Planets in Sextile and Trine 131
Planets in Square and Opposition 135
Practical Astrology 141
To Set a Map of the Heavens 142
How to Calculate the Part of Fortune 151
Rules for Reading Horoscopes 155
Synopsis of Medical Astrology 183
Rules for Marriage and Children 189

How to Judge Fortunate or Unfortunate 191
Mental Abilities 193
Profession and Trade 194
Lords of the Houses in Other Houses 199
Changes in Build and Complexion 224
Planetary Anatomical Rulerships 227
Rectification 228
Division of the Twelve Signs, etc. 233
Table of Essential Dignities 237
Table of Orbs 240
Table of Friends and Enemies 241
Planetary Hours 244
Planetary Hours: Perpetual Tables 255
Elections 287
Horoscope of William McKinley 295
Horoscope of William Jennings Bryan 298
Horoscope of Queen Victoria 310
Horoscope of Lord Byron 324
Horoscope of Charles Dickens 340
Horoscope of Ulysses Simpson Grant 343
Horoscope of George Washington 346
Modern Medication 351
Objections to Astrology Answered 358
The Planet Neptune 363
Horoscopes of Presidents Cleveland and Harrison 365
Horoscope of Kaiser Wilhelm II 375
Horoscope of the Third French Republic 377

Appendix: Why I am an Astrologer

Preface 379
Introductory Remarks 380
The Humbug of Astrology, *by Richard Proctor* 401
Reply to Mr. Proctor 405
Discussion Pro and Con about Astrology 429
Unparalleled Outrages, *by W.H. Chaney* 454
The Tower of Babel 469

Read and Reflect 474
Broughton's Monthly Planet Reader 486

About the Author 487

Synopsis added by the Publisher, 2012

THE

ELEMENTS

OF

ASTROLOGY

BY

L. D. BROUGHTON, M. D.

"To deny the influence of the stars is to deny the wisdom and providence of God."
                                                                TYCHO BRAHE.

"A most unfailing experience of the excitement of sublunary natures by the conjunctions and aspects of the planets, has instructed and compelled my unwilling belief."   JOHN KEPLER.

"Principles built on the unerring foundation of observations and experiments, must necessarily stand good until the dissolution of nature itself."   EMERSON.

Price, $1.50.

NEW YORK:
PUBLISHED BY THE AUTHOR,
68 SOUTH WASHINGTON SQUARE.

ASTRONOMICAL SYMBOLS AND ABBREVIATIONS
OF
SIGNS, PLANETS AND ASPECTS.

SIGNS.

♈	Aries.	♎	Libra.
♉	Taurus.	♏	Scorpio.
♊	Gemini.	♐	Sagittarius.
♋	Cancer.	♑	Capricorn.
♌	Leo.	♒	Aquarius.
♍	Virgo.	♓	Pisces.

PLANETS.

♆	Neptune.	☉	Sun.
♅	Uranus.	♀	Venus.
♄	Saturn.	☿	Mercury.
♃	Jupiter.	☽	Moon.
♂	Mars.	⊕	Part of Fortune.

ASPECTS.

☌	Conjunction,	00°	Sesq. Sesquiquadrate,	135°
⚺	Semi-sextile,	30°	Bq. Bi-quintile,	144°
∠	Semi-square,	45°	☍ Opposition,	180°
✶	Sextile,	60°	P Parallel,	=
Q	Quintile,	72°	☊ Dragon's Head.	
□	Square,	90°	☋ Dragon's Tail.	
△	Trine,	120°		

Degrees,	°	H	Hours.
Minutes,	′	M	Minutes.
Second of Space,	″	S	Seconds of time.

One would think that people would ask the advice of some competent Astrologer who has made thousands of observations, on such as marriages, partnerships, commencing business, or laying a corner stone, etc., before commencing these undertakings, especially when it can be proved by thousands or even millions of instances, that when the planets at these events are in evil positions for such undertakings, in 99 cases out of every 100, prove unfortunate or disastrous to the persons undertaking them, that these people would, in time learn to pay attention to such matters, but such is not the case.

I will here state that I had intended devoting a certain part of this work to "The Elements of Horary Astrology," also "Mundane Astrology," "Medical Astrology," and "Astro-Theology," but I shall have to defer these branches of the science to another volume. I hope to follow the present book with one on nativities, in the same method as the horoscopes commencing on page 295.

Copyright, 1898, by L. D. Broughton. Entered at Stationers' Hall, London, England.

L. D. BROUGHTON, M. D.

CHART OF THE HEAVENS

FOR THE TIME OF BIRTH OF

Dr. L. D. BROUGHTON,

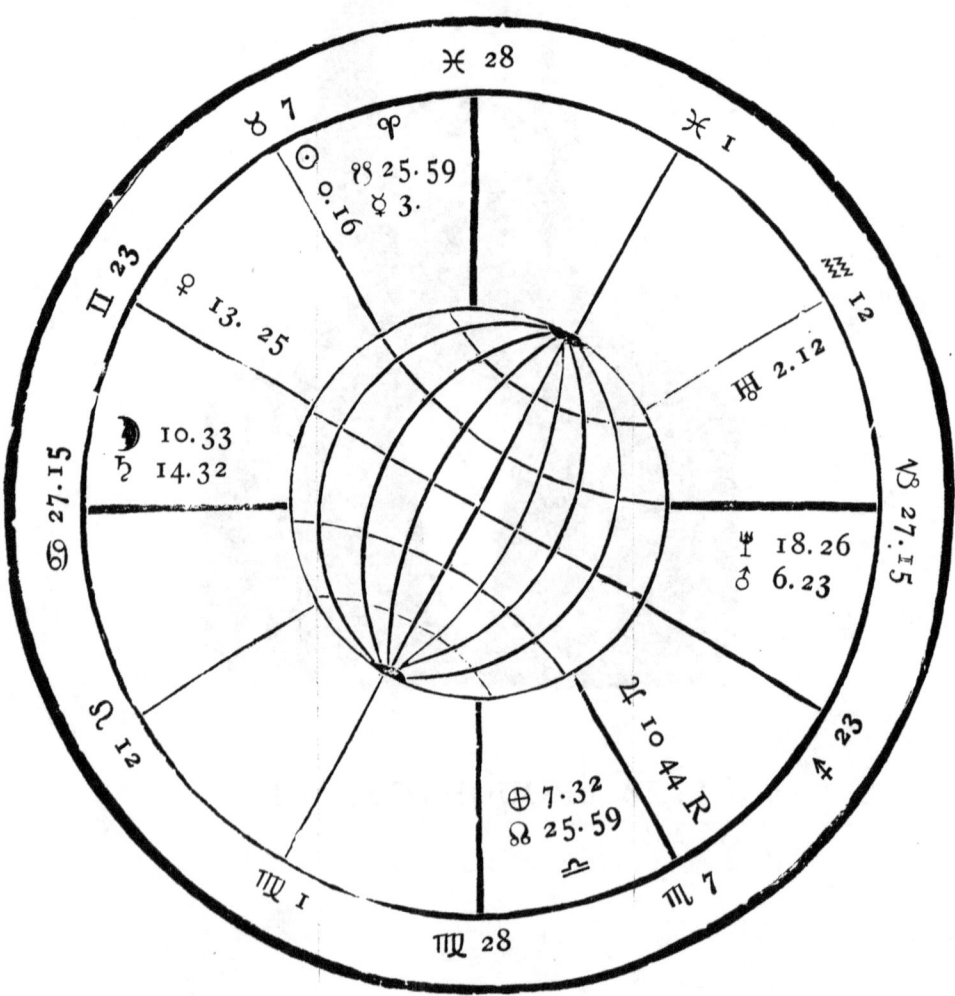

April 20th, 1828, at 10.00 A.M.,
Leeds, Yorkshire, Eng.

PREFACE.

MANY of my readers may think I have devoted too much space in these pages in answering the opponents of Astrology, instead of giving all my attention to the teaching and illustration of the science, but as the opponents are in a great majority in all Christian countries their influence is too important to be slighted.

Some years ago, when the Legislature of a Western State enacted a law to suppress Astrology, the Philadelphia "Ledger," in an editorial stated that the Legislatures would not need to enact such laws if they would teach the people to read and write; therefore the only reason that I am an Astrologer is because I can neither read nor write.

If some kind missionary, instead of going to teach the heathen in China or in the wilds of Africa to read and write, would devote some of his energy in teaching me, he would forever stop me from prating about Astrology; besides, it might be the means of saving my soul.

At the age of eighteen it was my misfortune to lose my father, and I shall never forget how the minister of the Episcopal Church which we attended, devoted a whole afternoon, while my father lay dead in the house, in arguing and trying to persuade my eldest brother to give up the belief and practise of Astrology. There is little doubt that the minister, in his mind's eye, saw my father's soul writhing in all the agonies of the damned, and felt it to be his duty to save my brother, if possible, from such torments.

The same minister, when talking to me afterwards, praised the beautiful language in the forms of prayer in his church prayer book, and said that "we not only ought all to pray alike, and use the same set forms of prayer, but we ought all to think alike on all religious subjects."

In trying to compel every one to think and pray alike, the authorities have tried, convicted, and executed in Europe, within the last four hundred years, *over eleven million heretics and witches, including Astrologers,* and they have not yet succeeded in accomplishing their object. If we estimate the amount of money, time, and energy that it has cost the people of those countries in hunting up, arresting, trying, convicting, and executing these people, even if they had succeeded in their object, would they not have paid too dearly for their whistle? And if the governments and priests had spent the same amount of time, money, and labor in teaching the people useful knowledge, including Astrology, how much further would the world now be advanced in civilization and human happiness? Even if the priests and clergy had succeeded in compelling every person to think and believe alike in religious matters, I should like to know how much better we would be. Should we not, in that case, be taking rapid strides backward to the dark ages, and to the hanging and burning of witches and heretics? Would not human intellect be shrouded in ignorance, superstition and bigotry?

A large number of these heretics and witches, including Joan of Arc, have been placed on the calendar of saints, and the people have built monuments to their memory; but in all history I have never met with a single instance where the judges and persecutors of these witches and heretics have been thus honored and immortalized. From our standpoint the question natturally arises, who were the guilty parties—those who were executed, or the persecutors and executioners?

My father had many friends on account of his Astrological knowledge, and they often came to him for advice, but he did not take money for it; he also taught a number of persons the science, among them the late Frof. Lister, formerly of Boston, afterwards of New York. My father was a man of extensive information, and to my young mind seemed to be a walking encyclopœdia. I do not remember asking him a question on any subject whatever to which he could not give me a lucid and proper answer; but he always had one saying when he got through, which I now repeat: "I am getting old, my memory is failing me; do not take my word for it, but read and study for yourself."

TO THE STUDENT.

Besides writing this book for the student's perusal and guidance, I may possibly be of some assistance in advising him as to other books on the subject which will be of advantage to him while studying, in order to become proficient in Astrology and be able to judge of the merits or demerits of the science for himself.

One of the best books the student should read, and which is most essential, is Claudius Ptolemy's "Tetrabiblos," or four books of Astrology. It is to the Astrologer what the Bible is to the Christian theologian, or the text-book that all students ought to study in order to become well versed in the science. This work is over 2,000 years old, and it is said that Claudius Ptolemy gathered and compiled all that was then known on the ancient science of Astrology. Astrologers of Europe and North America have generally followed Ptolemy's system. We have a number of translations of Ptolemy's Tetrabiblos from the ancient Greek, but Ashmond's translation is recommended as the best for English students. His translation is an exceedingly interesting book. My first reading of this work gave me more pleasure than any novel I have read since. The translation by Mr. Walley is a very good book, but is much smaller than Ashmond's and not so interesting. Cooper's translation is also good, but is somewhat complicated and difficult to understand. Mr. James Wilson, who wrote and published the "Dictionary of Astrology," made a very good translation, but I did not find it as interesting as others. Mr. John Worsdale made a splendid translation, but he appears too dogmatical and positive in many of his assertions; in his translation he often uses the expression, "in all cases whatsoever;" but the student will find when practising Astrology, that he will have to take into account a number of planetary influences in order to arrive at a true conclusion, and it is best not to be too positive in his judgment of the influence of any one particular planet.

Worsdale's translation has never been printed, and those who have the book either had to copy it by hand, as I have done, or else buy it at a very high price, as it is extremely scarce. Sibley's translation is very large, published in three volumes, and goes into many particulars, but he is often unscientific or visionary. I look upon it as the least satisfactory translation of Ptolemy of any that I have read. There are other translations of Ptolemy which I have seen, but the authors' names have slipped my memory.

From the time of Claudius Ptolemy until near the twelfth century, a period of over a thousand years, there appears to have been no progress made in the science of Astrology in western and northern Europe. After Rome conquered England and nearly the whole of northern Europe, about the commencement of the Christian era, Astrology, Astronomy, and nearly all the arts and sciences disappeared in Europe, excepting such as church and monastery architecture, sculpture, painting, working of precious metals to be used in religious rites, etc. The people were shrouded in mental darkness; ignorance and superstition spread everywhere in these countries, and history gives us a period of a thousand years of what are called the "dark ages." The people in those times gave but little attention to anything but relics and saints and the most groveling superstition; all kinds of learning, except such as appertain to religious rites, were extinct, and for hundreds of years there were numbers of priests and bishops who could neither read nor write. In every country where the Christian religion spread, the minds of men became stunted, and the people became effeminate and vassals to the priests and the lords of the manor. According to common opinion, that ought to have been the Elizabethan Age for Astrology; but Astrology, like all other sciences and arts, disappeared from these Christian people in the northern parts of Europe, and in England, Scotland and Ireland.

While the people in the above named countries were either going naked or dressed in wolves' or bears' skins, the un-Christian Moors in Barbary and Spain, and in other parts of Europe and Africa, were making rapid advances in refinement and culture, such as architecture, astrology, astronomy, anatomy, medicine, agriculture, and other arts and sciences, but more especially in the sciences of astronomy and astrology.

Generally speaking, whenever and wherever civilization has advanced in either pagan or Christian countries the science of Astrology has always become popular. During the time that Rome was at the height of its glory, and was said to be the mistress of the world, we are told by the Rev. Thomas Dick that the Romans were so infatuated with Astrology and Astrologers that the Emperors issued edicts to expel them from the capital, but without effect; and even after they were expelled by a formal decree of the Senate, they were so protected by the people that they still remained in Rome unmolested. The same author tells us that this art has been practised in every period of time, and in every country in the world it is still practised; *"And in ancient times Astrology was uniformly included in the list of sciences."*

During the time that Christianity was spreading in England, Astrology was almost forgotten in northern Europe. The Egyptians, Arabians, Chinese, Japanese, and the people of the East Indies and the islands of Greece, were cultivating Astrology and Astronomy along with other sciences, and the advance of learning generally, to a great extent, during this thousand years of the "dark ages" in Christian countries; although but few, if any, of their works on Astrology have been translated into English. I have only been able to read a few translations from other languages.

But few astrologers were known in England after the "dark ages" until near the 13th century. Among those few were Roger Bacon and some monks, who studied Astrology in their monasteries during this period, although but few of their works have been handed down to us.

I can only bring to mind Placidus de Titus, an Italian monk, of whose work I have a good translation by Cooper, who translated Ptolemy's Tetrabiblos. It was published before the Copernican system of Astronomy was known, and it has a very curious description of the seven heavens and the Primum Mobile. Placidus was also a great believer in the "Part of Fortune," it being, according to his theory, in some nativities, the "giver of life." It is a very good book, but expensive. I have several works which were printed in the old English, or black letter, during the 16th century, or soon after the invention of printing; it is hardly likely that students will come across any of these, as they are very rare.

After the discovery of printing and the revival of learning in Christian countries, especially in England during the reign of Queen Elizabeth, a number of astrologers sprang into existence, among whom was Dr. Dee, a very noted English Astrologer, and physician to the Queen, who often consulted him for astrological advice. There were a number of other astrologers who became noted, and among the most learned was William Lilly, who was consulted by Charles the First and the leaders of the Revolutionary Parliament. He gave a great impulse to the science of Astrology and its study. His book on that science, called "Christian Astrology," laid the foundation for what is called "Modern Astrology." It is a very large volume and very expensive, but well worth reading, and the student should procure it if it ever comes in his way.

"Zadkiel" (Lieut. Morrison, of the British Navy) published an incomplete edition about the year 1830. After his copyright expired, Mr. H. G. Bohn of London republished the same edition, and has sold hundreds of thousands of copies.

Henry Cooley, one of Lilly's pupils, published a very good book on that science, called the "Key to Astrology." John Gadbury, near the same time, published a large book on Astrology called the "Doctrine of Nativities." John Gadbury was a very smooth writer, especially in that part of his work which treats on Horary Astrology; he was the first one who calculated a "Table of Houses" for 40 degrees north latitude, answering for New York and Philadelphia. He wrote several other works on Astrology, the names of which I have forgotten. Dr. Saunders near the same time published a remarkably good work on "Medical Astrology," which is one of the best books that has ever been published on that subject; the Introduction was written by William Lilly. Nicholas Culpepper, about the same time published the "British Herbal;" it had an enormous sale, a great many editions having been issued; I have about twenty. The edition published by Dr. Hamilton in two large volumes is the most complete; it gives the astrological description of diseases, and how to cure them with the herbs; each herb is described, and also the name of the planet that governs it. "Culpepper's Herbal" at one time was like the family Bible, in almost every cottage in England. It was the book that first drew my grandfather's attention to the science of Astrology, and induced him to study and make use of it in the practice of medicine. There have been a number of other very good books on Medical Astrology printed, many of which I have read, but the names of the authors I have forgotten. In short, at one time Medical Astrology was the basis of the only legal practice of medicine that was permitted in England, and many countries of Europe—the same as it is at the present time in many parts of Asia.

About the time Culpepper's "British Herbal" made its appearance William Ramsey published an excellent work on "Mundane Astrology;" it is a large volume and very expensive, but one of the best books on that subject ever published in the English language. After the middle of the 17th century there were a great many very good astrological books published by different authors. Among the most noted of these books was "Butler's Astrology," a large volume published on nativities, in 1688, by the Rev. Doctor John Butler, Rector of Litchborough, England, and chaplain to the Duke of Ormond, is a very good scientific book, and the author was a remarkably intelligent man. He is very technical and scientific, and his book is too far advanced for young students. The main reason we are indebted to the Rev. John Butler for his book on Astrology is that some years previously to that time he spent a great deal of his energy publishing articles against Astrology and condemning it, but afterwards came to the conclusion that he could expose Astrology with much more effect if he studied it and became acquainted with its principles, and the result was that he wrote one of the most scientific books on the subject. He also republished a horoscope of Jesus Christ, and calculated that he was born at 12 o'clock at night, on the 25th of December; but Cardinal de Ailly, who died in 1425, had previously calculated and published the horoscope of Jesus Christ. About 1425 there was a great number of cardinals and bishops, and other dignitaries of the Church, who were believers and students in Astrology, and recognized the science; among the number was Calixtus III., Pope of Rome.

Towards the end of the 17th century Dr. Salmon published a very good work called the "Soul of Astrology." Another author, whose name I forget, published a work called the "Marrow of Astrology." Another published the "Spirit of Astrology;" I think it was Mr. John Partridge. Mr. Hayden also published a very good little book on the science. Mr. White's "Astrology" is an excellent work. About the same time a large number of astrological books were published in London. We might designate it the "Elizabethan Age of Astrology," especially during the latter part of the 16th and the early part of the 17th centuries.

In 1723 Richard Ball published a remarkably good book on the science, called "Astrology Improved;" and about the middle of the 18th century there was quite a number of astrological almanacs and ephemerides published. I find no less than nine yearly almanacs and ephemerides published in London in 1768. Probably the one that became most popular was that published by FRANCIS MOORE, physician, called the "Vox Stellarum, or Royal Almanac." The Rev. Thomas Dick said that it attained an annual sale of over two hundred and forty thousand. It was afterwards very popular under the name of "Old Moore's Almanac" for over a century.* The next to that in popularity was the Almanac and Ephemeris of John Partridge; it attained a large circulation, so much so that the Stationers' Company who were engaged in sending gospel missionaries abroad, and who published the "Gentleman's Diary" and the "Woman's Almanac," purchased the right of publication from Partridge's widow, and continued to publish it for nearly a hundred years after.† The next almanac of importance was "Parker's Ephemeris" which attained a

---

* See Appendix, page 437.   † See Appendix, page 445.

a large circulation. The "News of the Stars," almanac and ephemeris, published by William Andrews, student in Astrology, became very popular; Salem Pearse's Celestial Diary or Ephemeris was a great favorite; "Poor Robin's Almanac" became very noted, especially on ccount of its prognostications. Richard Saunders published the "English Apollo," a yearly almanac which became very well known; also the "Speculum Anni," or almanac published by Ennis Season, became very popular; an almanac published by Tycko Wing, "Philomath," became a great favorite. Altogether, these almanacs and ephemerides must have attained a yearly circulation of over a million.

On account of the persecutions against astrologers and Astrology in the latter part of the 18th century, the interest in the science began to decline. The encyclopœdias and other books which mentioned the name Astrology, and also the ministers of the gospel, could not invent too severe epithets against the science and its professors, and during this period but few if any ephemerides, except Partridge's and White's, were published, and the latter was chiefly used by captains of vessels to find the longitude and latitude of their ships at sea. But about 1820 Astrology commenced to revive again, and Mr. Smith commenced publishing "Raphael's Almanac and Prophetic Messenger;" he also published several books on the subject. Raphael's "Manual of Astrology" is a very good book; also Raphael's "Hand Books of Astrology," chiefly "Genethliacal" or nativities, and one volume on "Horary Astrology," and a small volume called the "Key to Astrology." All four books are very good and concise. Raphael's "Prophetic Messenger" and ephemeris is still published in London, and has a an annual sale of near 200,000.

Near the beginning of the present century John Worsdale published his "Genethliacal Astrology." He was the first who revived, or rather discovered, what is termed the long calculations, or the "Arc of Directions" in nativities. Besides translating "Ptolemy's Tetrabiblos," Mr. Worsdale published several books on the science in addition to his "Genethliacal Astrology," and he made a number of discoveries in that science, or at least other astrologers gave him the credit of making them, but he insisted that Claudius Ptolemy made these discoveries and taught them two thousand years before. He also published a pamphlet containing the horoscopes of Napoleon Bonaparte and Arthur Wellesley, who was afterward the Duke of Wellington; in that pamphlet he made a prediction that as Gen. Wellesley had the benevolent planet Jupiter in the mid-heaven in his horoscope, in almost the exact place that Napoleon Bonaparte had the evil planet Saturn, if ever these generals met on the battlefield Napoleon would be vanquished and would never lead another army, which prediction was fulfilled at their first meeting. That pamphlet was published eleven years before the battle of Waterloo.

About 1830 "Zadkiel" commenced publishing his astrological almanac, which has attained over one hundred and sixty thousand yearly circulation. He also published a yearly ephemeris; both continue to the present day. Besides republishing Lilly's Astrology, he published a remarkably good and useful book called the "Grammar of Astrology," and his two hand books on Astrology are equal to anything that have been published on nativities. For a long time he published a monthly periodical called the "Horoscope," and his name has become well known throughout the civilized world. But probably one of the most learned astrologers that has given attention to the subject since Lilly's time, was Joseph W. Simmonite, of Sheffield, England. His "Arcana of Astral Philosophy" is an exceedingly good work, and it has been republished by the Occult Publishing Company of Boston. Dr. Simmonite simplified the long calculations and made many improvements. His Horary Astrology I kept on my desk for reference for over 30 years. His book on Revolutions is one of the best that has ever been published, and his Botanic Practice of Medicine is also an excellent little volume; I carried it in my pocket for years, and committed to memory his descriptions of diseases. Dr. Simmonite published for many years an almanac called the "Meteorologist" and a yearly Ephemeris; also a monthly periodical called the "Messenger."

In addition to Zadkiel's Almanac and Ephemeris and Raphael's Prophetic Messenger and Ephemeris, there has been published in Petersborough, England, for nearly sixty years, "Orion's Prophetic Almanac, Weather Guide and Ephemeris," which is a very good, readable almanac, and has a large circulation. On page 142 of this volume I stated that there was no ephemeris published in the United States, but since I began to write this book, I find that Joseph G. Dalton, of Boston, has commenced publishing "The Boston Ephemeris." The first issue is for the year 1898; but I am sorry to say he has made all the calculations for the longitude of London, England, instead of making them for either the longitude of Boston, New York, Philadelphia, Washington or Chicago; but it certainly is a very useful and correct Ephemeris.

Mr. Dalton has also published a very comprehensive Table of Houses from 22° to 56° north latitude; it is a very good and useful book, and can be had at my office for $2.50. It is the first Table of Houses that has been published for every even degree of north latitude from 22° to 56°. It will also answer for the southern hemisphere from 22° to 56° south latitude by a few slight calculations. Mr. Dalton is one of the most learned mathematicians in the United States, and has taken great interest in Astrology.

The "Star" is a very good work on long calculations, published by Eben Shemaya. A New Illustration of the Science of Astrology, by Sibley, is a very large, voluminous work, of over 1,000 pages, and larger than any ordinary family Bible. Wilson's Dictionary of Astrology is a remarkably good work for a student to have; a new edition is printed by the Occult Publishing Company, of Boston. Mr. James Wilson was a splendid writer on Astrology, and very scientific.

There has been a flood of Astrological books published of late years, both in the United States, and in England, and a great many of the best of the old authors have also been reprinted. The Occult Publishing Company, of Boston, has printed all the works that I have mentioned of J. W. Simmonite, and also published a number of new books on the science. Mr. Bragdon, "Regulus," has written several good works on Astrology; among others a brief Ephemeris of Uranus, Saturn, Jupiter and Mars, from 1701 to 1918; also a "Table of Ascensions," "Signs of the Times," and "Zodiacal Physiognomy." Mr. Allen Leo, the editor of "Modern Astrology," a monthly periodical published in London, England, has issued a useful little work called "Practical Astrology." J. B. Sullivan's "Seven Easy Lessons in Astrology" is a good little book for learners.

"Astrology, Science of Knowledge and Reason," by Ellen H Bennett. I cannot speak of the merits of this book, as I have not read it. Mr. James Hingston, one of the editors of the New York Herald, has lately published a very good readable book, called the "Gospel of the Stars, or Wonders of Astrology." Carl Anderson's "Astrology and the Bible" is a very good work. "Natal Astrology," and the "Soul and the Stars," by G. Wilde and J. Dodson of Halifax, England, is an excellent work on nativities. "Astrology as It Is and Not as It Is Represented," is also a very good readable book. "The Text Book of Astrology," chiefly genethliacal or nativities, in two large volumes by Alfred J. Pearce of London, are remarkably good books for advanced students.

The first book published on Astrology in the United States, was one by Dr. Roeback,* a perfect fraud and an impostor,

---

* See Appendix, page 452.

who knew no more of Astrology than he did about flying; he got a newspaper reporter to compile it for him, who copied it chiefly from John Gadbury's book on Astrology, and called it the "Doctrine of Nativities According to Horary Astrology." For a long time it was the only Astrological book published in this country.*

Of late years there have been several pseudo-Astrological works published on what is called "Solar Biology," by Mr. Butler, Eleanor Kirk and some others, but practically they are not books on Astrology, and the student will lose time in studying them. Besides, they are not reliable.

For over one hundred years nearly all scientific men denied that the Moon and planets had any influence on the weather, but of late years it is astonishing how many almanacs and periodicals are now published on the weather in the United States, by such as Rev. Mr. Hicks, Wiggins, Devoe, and others; and all their predictions on the weather are from the influence of the Moon and the planets and their aspects. We have even arrived at the point now that without aspects of the Moon and planets we have no change of weather.

When I published "Broughton's Monthly Planet Reader and Astrological Journal" 40 years ago, it was the only monthly periodical of the kind in the world, or at least in the English language. I was acquainted with nearly every man in the United States who had any knowledge on the subject, and probably at that time there were not twenty persons that knew enough of Astrology to be able to erect a horoscope, and they were all either French, English or German. There was not an American, either man or woman, in the whole United States who could even erect a horoscope at that time. At the present day there are many thousand American people who are studying Astrology, and some have become quite proficient in the science. The study and investigation of Theosophy has drawn the attention of the American people to the subject of Astrology. They are beginning to find out that Astronomy and Astrology are the foundation of all religions, and there never was a time when there were such a demand for astrological books; also there never was such facilities for studying the science as there are at the present day. Within a few years from now, if the interest

---

* The first monthly periodical ever published on Astrology in the United States was edited by Thomas Hauge, called "Hauge's Horoscope." It commenced about the year 1840, and was continued for a number of years.

The second monthly periodical was issued by my eldest brother, Mark A. Broughton, called "Broughton's Monthly Horoscope." It commenced in 1849, and was published for a number of years. My brother previously published an astrological almanac and ephemeris in Leeds, England.

The above series were very similar to the "20th Century Astrologer," which is published at the present time at 9 Columbus Ave., New York, for which periodical I write the predictions.

continues, any person who shows an ignorance of the subject will be laughed at. There are now numbers of persons who, well-informed on other subjects, still show an ignorance and a remarkably strong prejudice against Astrology, as proof of which I refer the reader to different parts of the book, where I have noticed some of the remarks of the editors of the "New York Sun," the "Times," the "Herald," and especially in my remarks on the "Humbug of Astrology," published in the "World" by Richard A. Proctor. Besides the editors of the above named papers, there are several other persons that I ought to pay some little attention to in this part of my book.

For several years I published "horoscopes" in a number of newspapers and periodicals in different parts of the United States, and sent circulars to editors, asking them if they would like horoscopes in their papers. The following are samples of some of the answers I received:

Youth's Companion, Boston, Mass.,
May 15th, 1895.

Mr. Broughton,
Dear Sir:

The proposition which you make to the *Companion* is one which is entirely out of its scope, and one which we should under no circumstances adopt. We are not ourselves believers in Astrology, and we pity those who are.
Very Truly Yours,
The Editors.

Montgomery St., Jersey City, N. J.,
Feb. 1st, 1896.

Dr. L. D. Broughton,
    68 So. Washington Square,
Dear Sir:

I have no doubt that an increase of circulation among a certain class could be effected by using your horoscopes. I should, however, be very sorry to undertake to secure circulation by fostering such a baleful and ridiculous superstition.
Yours Respectfully,
The Evening Journal Assoc.,
JOSEPH A. DEAR, Treas.

I might here mention that a particular friend of mine, who was studying Astrology, one day went into a large book store in Baltimore, and asked if they had for sale "Wilson's Dictionary of Astrology." The proprietor made answer by saying "No, and I hope for the sake of humanity, that such a book has never been published." My friend quietly asked him, "Do you know anything about Astrology?" "No, and I do not want to know anything about it." There are vast numbers of this kind of people in all Christian countries; I will not attempt to answer them myself, but refer the student to pages 245 and 246 of this book, and let Mr. James

Wilson answer them for me, as I think he can do it in much more forcible and better language than I have at command.

I wish the student to distinctly bear in mind that Mr. Wilson knows what he is writing about, whereas the editors of the "Youth's Companion," Mr. Joseph A. Dear, and the book store man in Baltimore, know nothing about Astrology, consequently do not know what they are talking about. They are simply talking of some undefinable chimera which they have in their own brain, and which has no relation whatever to Astrology. No one could have been more opposed to what he thought was Astrology than Professor W. H. Chaney, before he became acquainted with me. One time he was at a public meeting in Boston, and the speaker, a very intelligent man, happened to mention the word, "Astrology." Mr. Chaney told me afterwards, he looked down with supreme contempt on the gentleman for insulting such an audience by mentioning the word "Astrology." There is no doubt if the above editors did acquire some knowledge of the science, they would work equally as hard in favor of Astrology, and do as much to promulgate its principles, as Mr. Chaney has done since he commenced studying the science. Mr. Chaney has made it a study, day and night, and has published numbers of text books on the science, which he calls "Primers," besides editing a monthly magazine on Astrology, and publishing an ephemeris in this country for a number of years. He also republished White's Ephemeris, extending over 75 years, making a number of calculations for the same, to find or correct the positions of the planets. And as he tells us in his preface to White's Ephemeris, "I will say in conclusion that I have toiled very hard for the last year and a half, and have been setting type and reading proof, with my mind on a constant strain to detect an error. For months in succession, Sunday as well as week days, I have made an average of fifteen hours, daily labor." Mr. Chaney has continued to labor hard in the cause for over thirty years, by lecturing, writing and teaching the science of Astrology at great sacrifice to himself.

To correct as far as possible the wrong impressions that many intelligent people have on Astrology, I have published this volume, so as to disseminate a knowledge of the science.

God appears to have made the world upside down, and things appear inverted to men as well as to babies, the first time they look at them; and men, like babies, have to learn to see things aright. That is the reason why the common people, the first time any truth is presented to them, oppose it with all the vehemence they can possibly command, and persecute the persons who present these great truths, and in doing so these ignorant people think they are rendering God service, for which God will reward them in a future life, and so all the people that die go to the wrong place, and the public afterwards find that those who were persecuted the most have been the best people while living in this world, and ought to have gone to the good place in the next.

We are taught in the Episcopalian creed, that Jesus Christ "suffered under Pontius Pilate, was crucified, dead and buried, descended into hell and rose again from the dead on the third day, and ascended into heaven, and sitteth on the right hand of God, the Father Almighty." And if that is not all true, I do not see why the authorities should imprison people, and burn them alive at the stake for not believing it.

Joan of Arc was burned alive by the English for being a witch, but really for no other reason than that she was a successful leader or general for the French soldiers, and defeating the English armies; but it took over four hundred years for her to ascend into heaven.

In this book I have attempted to accomplish three objects:

First, to make the book interesting to the general reader, although he has no knowledge whatever of the science of Astrology.

Second, to bring forward such an amount of facts and phenomena in their relation to Astrology, and the various events in history, that it will be an impossibility to deny their relation. These phenomena and the coincident events might have been traced back for thousands of years, if it had been necessary to bring further proof, and all of them would have coincided so as to be related or connected one with the other. Emerson says: "Principles built on the unerring foundation of observations and experiments must necessarily stand good until the dissolution of nature itself."

Third, to make "The Elements of Astrology" so simple, easy and plain to an ordinary person, who has received a common school education, that hereafter there can be no excuse for any person that can read and write remaining ignorant of the science of Astrology.

I am aware that there have been numbers of very good text books on Astrology published, the names of most of which I have mentioned in the preceding pages, but they have all been written as if the author expected the student had already become interested in the subject, and had made a certain advancement in the science, or that he had a competent teacher at hand to instruct him in the rudiments and principles of the science; or at least all the students in

Astrology whom I have become acquainted with have made that complaint; and I must admit when I commenced studying Astrology, over fifty years ago, it would have been an impossibility for me to have learned from the books without a teacher, as it is more difficult to learn than any other of the natural sciences.

My long experience and practice has made me so familiar with the science that I hope I have made the "Elements of Astrology" so easy to be understood, that it will answer as a stepping stone to larger and scientific books on the subject.

That such a work is called for at the present day, I might bring thousands of instances to prove, but will only give one:

A lady wrote me from Salem, Massachusetts, Dec. 14th, 1897, and expressed herself in the following language:

"Esteemed Sir:

Will you permit me, an interested reader, and an ardent admirer of all your writings, to intrude upon your valuable time by penning a few lines on a subject on which I know you can assist me, if you will kindly consent to do so. I am very desirous of becoming an Astrologist. I am well educated and a student, and I am willing to work hard to accomplish the object in view. I have procured the "Language of the Stars," which seems beyond my comprehension, and "Raphael's Key to Astrology;" also have the Astrologer's Magazine, but try as I may I cannot get ahead, and I am very much discouraged, yet I am determined to conquer in spite of all obstacles. I felt that you might kindly advise me what is the best plan to pursue, as I am so anxious to succeed. I thought that in writing to you you might kindly suggest to me the "missing link" which I have failed to discover."

I hope and really believe that not only this lady, but every other lady who can read the English language, will discover the "missing link" in the following pages.

Some of my friends think that I have devoted too much space in this book to the general reader; but how shall we reach such people as the Editor of "Youth's Companion," the book store man in Baltimore, or Mr. Joseph A. Dear of the "Jersey City Evening Journal," without addressing them in language which they can understand? Of course if such as they can not become interested in Astrology, they will still go on regarding that science as "baleful, and ridiculous superstition." If every kind of information that Mr. Dear does not know is "laughable and of a low and degrading nature," there must be a large surplus of that commodity in the world, and the only way to reduce it is for him and all persons like him to become better informed.

Mr. W. R. Hearst, editor of the "New York Morning Journal," appears to be of a different opinion to the editor of the "Jersey City Journal," as the former gentleman has offered one thousand dollars to the one who can make the most correct predictions for 1898, either by Astrology or any other method.

Of course if Mr. Hearst had made that offer fifty years ago, there would not have been a minister of the Gospel or a newspaper editor in the country, that would not have condemned him to everlasting torment. As the former gentlemen regarded even the wish or desire to pry into the future as equal in iniquity to "sinning against the Holy Ghost, which is never forgiven, either in this world or that which is to come," Mr. Hearst would even have been treated worse than I was when lecturing on the science of Astrology, thirty years ago.

No one could have been more opposed to the science of Astrology, or have striven more to have laws enacted for its suppression, than the late Charles A. Dana, editor of the "New York Sun," and yet at the end of each year, instead of giving a synopsis of the past events of that year, as was done by all other papers, he went on guessing what would happen in the following year, and in nine cases out of ten he was incorrect in his conclusions.

The offer of $1,000 which the "Journal" has made will give a great impulse to the study of Astrology, especially in the United States, as the people will gradually discover that there is no other method equal to the science of Astrology in predicting future events, either national or individual.

Mr. Emerson says: "Hitch your wagon to a star." The student should constantly bear in mind that when he was born not only his wagon, but he himself, was hitched to a PLANET, and that "there is not a pulse beats in the human frame that is not governed by the stars or planets above us, and at thy birth thy mother's eye gazed not more steadfastly on thee than *did the planet that rules thy fate.*"

It is our duty to learn and study the nature of these planets, and their influence on human beings, and be guided by them, and as John Kepler says: "A most unfailing experience of the excitement of sublunary natures by the conjunctions and aspects of the planets, has instructed and compelled my unwilling belief." If we only will let the conjunctions and aspects of these same planets instruct our unwilling belief they will enable us to make the most of our talents and opportunities while sojourning through this vale of tears.

The man who will insist in remaining in ignorance must suffer the natural consequences, but at the same time he should not try to compel other people to remain in the same condition. The student will find all honest astrologers will aid him to learn the science himself, so as to form his own judgment of its merits or demerits, and after he has become informed on the subject, he will not be like the "fox with the sour grapes," regard everything which he does not know or cannot understand as "fostering to baleful and ridiculous superstition."

There is no doubt that near the end of 1898 other newspapers will make similar offers besides the "New York Morning Journal," if they find it to their interest to do so, even if such men as Mr. Dear think it is " fostering a baleful and ridiculous superstition among a certain class." What class Mr. Dear refers to is difficult to conjecture. I cannot believe that he referred to the class who study and investigate Astrology. I might give a number of illustrations, why I cannot think he refers to the latter "class" but give the following, as one reason:

Some years ago, when my eldest son assisted me in my practice, and I was out visiting patients, and gentlemen or ladies came to my office to consult me in regard to their ailments, he attended them, but if any very intelligent wealthy lady or gentleman came in their carriages, he often made the mistake of asking them if they had not come to consult his father on Astrology, as few, except of that class came to consult me in that science; but of course the above kind of people is not the "class" among which Mr. Dear wishes to "increase the circulation" of his paper, but among that class, who when I was giving lectures on Astrology, came to make disturbance and break up my meetings, and to make night hideous in the room above, where we were living.

In conclusion I will say that if I have succeeded in inducing even one person to become interested in this ancient and long neglected science, who formerly looked on it as "baleful and ridiculous superstition," I shall not have written this book in vain; and as Mr. James Hingston, (a man whom I highly esteem, although he is one of the editors of the New York Herald,) in his Preface to his "Gospel of the Stars, or Wonders of Astrology," says:

"My object in writing this book has been to aid in popularizing the once famous, but long neglected science or art of Astrology. The facts therein contained I have gathered from many sources, but mainly from the works of the great dead star readers, to whom I gladly acknowledge my debt of gratitude; for, even though they be dead, who can say that they are utterly beyond the reach of praise or blame?

"I have aimed rather to interest than to instruct, for which reason instead of a text-book, I give here a picture of Astrology as it was in the past, dwelling to the best of my ability on the glories of its career, and showing why it is as worthy of esteem in our days as it was in the days of

Ptolemy. I know of no book on the subject that has been written from this standpoint. There are some serviceable text-books for students, but there are hardly any astrological books that appeal to the people."

I agree with Mr. Hingston, that we ought, at the present day, to show that Astrology is as worthy of esteem now as it was two thousand years ago.

In the following pages, I have endeavored to combine a text-book with a "picture of the glorious career of Astrology in the past," and at the same time to make it interesting to both the student and general reader. How far I have succeeded in my object, I leave to a kind and indulgent public to decide.

LESSONS AND BOOKS ON ASTROLOGY.

I have endeavored to make Astrology as plain and easy as possible to the learner in the following pages, but still there may be some persons, who cannot possibly learn the science without lessons from a competent teacher; should any of my readers not be able to master the subject without such assistance, to those I offer instruction at $3.00 per lesson of one hour. Sometimes it is necessary for persons to take eight or ten lessons before they are able to calculate horoscopes and read them satisfactorily.

There are some persons so constituted that it is impossible for them to make any headway in studying Astrology, and this can be learned beforehand from their horoscopes; as there are many persons so constituted as never to become good musicians, orators, actors, physicians or lawyers, and it would be advisable before commencing the study of Astrology to have their horoscope calculated, and find if it is favorable for that science, if so, then there is no doubt but what they can become proficient in it, and it will be an advantage to them; for this information I charge from $2.00 to $5.00.

In addition to the "Elements of Astrology," there are numbers of other books published on the science, which it is advisable that the student should purchase, and study as much as possible; some of these books I have mentioned in the previous pages, but there are some that are much easier understood than others, and those mentioned below are of that kind.

It is often very difficult to advise the student which particular book he should read and study first; that depends upon what particular branch of Astrology he is aiming to become proficient in; for instance, if he wants specially to study Mundane Astrology, he should purchase books on that subject, the same in regard to Nativities, Medical Astrology or Horary Questions, etc., but if he wants to become a competent Astrologer, and have a general knowledge of the science, I recommend him to purchase the following, which can be obtained at my office, *No. 68 South Washington Square, New York*, at the prices appended.

"Key to Astrology," by Raphael,.......$0.35
"Horary Astrology,"...................... 1.00
"Raphael's Horary Astrology,".......... 1.00
"Simmonite's Horary Astrology,"....... 1.25
"Seven Easy Lessons on Astrology,".... .75
"Guide to Astrology," Raphael, 2 volumes, 2.00
"Wilson's Dictionary of Astrology,"..... 4.00
"Lilly's Astrology," and "Zadkiel's Grammar of Astrology,"............ 2.00
Table of Houses from 22 to 56 north latitude,........................$2.50
Raphael's Ephemeris for 1898, including Tables of Houses for latitude of London, Liverpool and New York,... .25
Raphael's Ephemerides, back years, (each) .35
"Boston Ephemeris," by J. G. Dalton,... .25
"A Treatise of Natal Astrology,"........ 3.50
"Complete Arcana of Astral Philosophy," by J. W. Simmonite,............ ... 4.50

All other books on Astrology that are in print may be had on application at reasonable rates.

CONTENTS.

	PAGE
Preface,	iii.
To the Student,	v.
Lessons and Books on Astrology,	xx.
A Glossary of Astrological Terms,	xxv.
Elements of Astrology,—Introduction,	5
A brief History of Astrology, by its Friends or Advocates	8
A short History of Astrology by its Enemies,	12
Remarks on Prof. Proctor's "Humbug of Astrology,"	17
Rev. Thomas Dick of England on Astrology, in his "Improvement of Society by the Diffusion of Knowledge,"	18
"Chambers's Encyclopœdia" on Astrology,	19
John Kepler's Discoveries in Astronomy and Astrology,	21
John Dryden, Cardinal Richelieu, and Sir Isaac Newton, Astrologers,	22
The supposed Argument which the Enemies of Astrology, have brought against that Science,	24
Dr. Mesmer and Animal Magnetism, and the French Academy of Science—Benjamin Franklin and the Lightning Rod,	32
Harry Howard, his execution for murder, and Hipnotism,	33
Chinese and Astrology, and their Method of making use of it in their Marriages.	35
Mrs. Maud S., The New York Times, and Astrology,	36
The Author's Criticism on the Editor of the New York Times,	37
Mrs. Maud S.'s Daughter's Horoscope,	38
The Opposition to Lectures on Astrology in New York City	40
The Persecution the Author met with at 814 Broadway, New York.	41
The interference of the Author's Lectures, and the breaking up of the Meetings,	42
The stoppage of the Author's mail in the post-office in New York,	43
Astrology in London, by Edgar Lee,	45
Correspondence with Dr. L. D Broughton, O. D. Bradgen, and A. N. Doerschuk on writings of horoscopes,	50
The Bible and Astrology,	57
Pharaoh's Dream and the Magicians of Egpyt and Babylon.	58
Misrepresentation of Astrology,	60
Theories of ancient Astronomers,	60
Perihelion Epoch of Jupiter coincident with the return of Cholera and epidemics,	62
Action and reaction of one planet on another,	65
The effect on the earth and its inhabitants of the near approach of Mars,	66
Diagram of the Solar System,	67
Mars in opposition to the Sun,	67
The period of the war,	68
The sign Gemini rules the United States,	69
Critical times—stirring periods,	69
Important era in history, (Salem Witchcraft),	70
Meteorology and Planetary Influence,	72
The planet Neptune in Gemini, 1720; South Sea Bubble, and John Law's Banking Scheme,	74
Neptune in Gemini from 1888 to 1902; Panama Scandal, and suspension of Baring Brothers, of London,	76

	PAGE
The sign Taurus rules Ireland,	79
Personal description of man or woman described by the Planets,	79
The afflicting planets describe the assassins in remarkable murder cases,	80
The horoscope of the assassination of President Lincoln, on April 14th. 1865,	81
The horoscope of the assassination of President Garfield. July 2d, 1881,	82
The horoscope of the assassination of Lord Frederick Cavendish and Mr. Thomas Burke, May 6th, 1882,	83
Horoscope of the assassination of Carrie Brown ("Old Shakespeare,").	84
Horoscope of the assassination of Mr. Andrew J. Borden and his wife, August 4th, 1892,	85
Elements of Astrology—Rudiments of the Science,	87
A blank chart of the Heavens, showing the position and number of Houses,	88
The signification of the 12 Houses,	89
The nature, quality and description of the 12 Houses,	90
Advice to students studying Astrology,	93
Remarks on the signs of the Zodiac,	94
Divisions of the signs of the Zodiac,	95
General appearance of persons described by the 12 signs of the Zodiac,	97
Persons described by the 8 Planets,	99
The description of Herschel persons,	99
The description of Saturn persons,	100
The description of Jupiter, Mars and Sun persons,	101
The description of Venus persons,	102
The description of Mercury and Moon persons,	103
General advice to the student in learning the description of persons,	104
Herschel in the 12 signs of the Zodiac,	105
Saturn in the 12 signs,	106
Jupiter in the 12 signs,	108
Mars in the 12 signs,	110
Sun in the 12 signs,	113
Venus in the 12 signs,	115
Mercury in the 12 signs,	117
The Moon in the 12 signs,	119
The effects of the conjunction of Uranus with the 7 planets,	122
The effects of Saturn in conjunction with the other planets,	125
The effects of Jupiter in conjunction with the other planets,	126
The effects of Mars in conjunction with the other planets.	128
The effects of the Sun in conjunction with the other planets,	129
The effects of Venus and Mercury, when in conjunction with the Moon,	130
Of the Sextile and Trine aspects of the significators,	131
The effects of the square or opposition aspect between the significators,	135
Practical Astrology,	141
Rule to set a Map of the Heavens,	142
Horoscope of the Inauguration of Hon. William McKinley,	143
Chart of the Heavens for the time that President McKinley took the oath of office,	146

CONTENTS.

	PAGE
Horoscope erected for the time that the Extra Session of Congress met at Washington, D. C., March 15th, 1897, at 12 Noon,	150
Nativity of Mrs. Maud S.'s daughter,	151
How to calculate the "Part of Fortune,"	151
Chart of the Heavens for a girl born July 2d, 1884, at 8.35 A. M., New York City,	152
Lords or Rulers of the signs of the Zodiac,	153
Table of Lords of the signs or of the Houses,	154
Claudius Ptolemy—reasons for allotting the signs to these planets,	154
Rules for reading horoscopes,	155
Acquire a regular system of reading a horoscope,	156
The giver of Life,	157
Personal description,	158
How to describe a person by the planets and the signs of the Zodiac,	159
Rules to be followed in describing persons,	160
Sickness, diseases and complaints,	161
The financial benefit to the persons in studying Astrology,	161
Riches and Poverty,	162
Mental Abilities,	162
Disposition and Temper,	162
Business and Honor,	163
Friends and Enemies,	163
Morals and Religion—relations and journeys,	163
Marriage,	164
Rules for describing the kind of person, a lady or gentleman will marry; also whether it will be a happy or unhappy marriage,	164
The kind of gentleman Mrs. Maud S.'s daughter will marry,	166
The age when married,	167
Children,	167
Health,	167
The various contingencies and events of life,	167
Rules how to calculate those various events and contingencies of life,	168
Criticism on the New York Times, and other remarks on Astrology,	171
Criticism on Chas. A. Dana, editor of the New York Sun—remarks on Astrology,	174
Horoscope of the Chinese Consul's son,	175
Remarks on the Part of Fortune,	176
How to describe a person born under the planet Mercury in the sign Cancer,	177
Health and Life,	178
Riches and Poverty,	178
Trade and Profession,	178
Friends and Enemies,	176
Marriage and Children,	179
Fortunate and Unfortunate periods, or the various contingencies or events of life,	180
Rules for judging the events and the times that they will happen in nativities,	181
Remarks on Secondary directions,	182
A Synopsis of Medical Astrology,	183
On Professor Draper's ridiculing William Lilly's Astrology,	184
Parts of the bodies ruled by the 12 houses and the 12 signs of the Zodiac,	185
Diseases caused by the planets,	187
Rules to judge the probable time of Marriage of the native—also the number of children,	189
How to judge if a horoscope is fortunate or unfortunate,	191
Mental Abilities,	193
The temper or the animal passions,	194
Profession and Trade—Riches and Poverty,	194

	PAGE
Business or Profession in which the native will be unfortunate,	196
Profession or Business in which the native would be fortunate,	198
The influence of the Lord of the first house in each of the 12 houses,	199
The Lord of the second in the 12 houses,	201
The Lord of the third in the 12 houses,	202
The Lord of the fourth in the 12 houses,	204
The Lord of the fifth in the 12 houses,	205
The Lord of the sixth in the 12 houses,	206
The Lord of the seventh in the 12 houses,	208
The Lord of the eighth in the 12 houses,	210
The Lord of the ninth in the 12 houses,	212
The Lord of the tenth in the 12 houses,	213
The Lord of the eleventh in the 12 houses,	215
The Lord of the twelfth in the 12 houses,	217
Remarks and Explanations,	219
Remarks on the lords of the 12 houses, and explaining how they are used in directions, transits, revolutionary figures, etc.,	223
Remarks on the changes in the personal appearance of the native in the different periods of his life,	224
Rules for judging of the changing of the build and complexion of the native,	224
The planets impress distinct characteristics or marks on the native which can be recognized,	226
The seven planets rule the human system—named in the following order,	227
How to find the time of day a person is born; also how to correct the wrong time of birth,	228
Table of Essential Dignities, and various other tables and information,	231
Planets and other symbols,	231
The signs of the Zodiac and their classification,	232
The division of the 12 signs of the Zodiac,	233
Triplicities or Trigons,	234
The signs divided among the planets,	235
Explanation of the Table of Essential Dignities,	236
Table of Essential Dignities, and debilities of the planets,	237
Remarks on the Table of Essential Dignities of the planets,	238
Joys of the planets,	239
The reason a planet receives its joy in one of its own signs and not in the other,	239
Historical remarks on the Essential Dignities of the planets,	239
Orbs of the Planets,	240
Table of the planet's orbs,	240
The mean motion of the planets,	240
Table of the mean motion of the planets,	241
Sympathy and antipathy of the planets—or friends and enemies,	241
A table of the friendship and enmities of the planets,	241
Aspects of the planets,	242
New aspects discovered by John Kepler,	243
The Dragon's Head or Moon's Node,	243
Good and evil Planetary Hours,	244
Prof. Wilson's criticisms on skeptics of Astrology,	245
Different grades of believers in Astrology,	246
Remarks on the planetary hours,	247
The French and Latin names of days of the week, and explanation why the names of some of those days of the week have been changed	248
Signification of the planetary hours, and what use may be made of them,	249

CONTENTS.

	PAGE
The influence of the planetary hours of the Sun, Moon and the five planets,	229
The hours of Saturn and Jupiter,	249
The hours of Mars, Sun, Venus, and Mercury,	250
The hour of Moon,	251
Remarks on the planetary hours,	251
The reason planetary hours have not been more generally made use of,	252
The hours of good planets and the hours of evil planets may vary in their influence in certain horoscopes,	253
Tables of planetary hours, and the reason why they vary in length,	254
Perpetual table of planetary hours from sunrise, until 2 hours after sunset,	255
Table of planetary hours from sunrise until 2 hours after sunset on every alternate Wednesday of any year,	282
The difference between clock or mean and solar time,	285
Perpetual Table of Equation of Time,	286
Different methods of measuring time by the Heavenly Bodies,	286
Elections or choosing a fortunate time to commence new business, removal or remarkable changes,	287
Election for laying the first stone,	288
Elections for buying or renting a house, lands or tenements, etc.,	288
Elections for removal from one house to another,	288
Election for entering into new business, office or employment,	288
Election for commencing a trade or profession,	289
Election for Marriage,	289
Election for proposing Marriage,	290
Election for introduction to Ladies and Gentlemen,	290
Election for going on a Journey,	291
Election for Navigation or going on a Voyage,	291
Election for Collecting a Debt or Money that is owing,	292
Elections to make friendship to brothers, sisters, kindred, neighbors, etc.,	292
Elections for hiring servants or employees,	292
Some choice rules or aphorisms for election relating to several undertakings,	292
Elections for duels and lawsuits,	293
Remarks on the time that some persons that we know of have got married and the result, especially that of Mr. and Mrs. Langtry.	294
Horoscope of Hon. William McKinley,	295
Chart of the Heavens for the time of birth of Hon. William McKinley,	296
What the Stars Say, from the "Baltimore American,"	297
Hon. William J. Bryan's Horoscope,	298
Chart of the Heavens for Hon. W. J. Bryan's time of birth,	299
The two Conventions,	300
Further remarks on the Horoscopes of President McKinley, and Hon. William J. Bryan, and their nominations,	300
Chart of the Heavens when Hon. William McKinley was nominated for President,	301
Chart of the Heavens for the time of the nomination for President of Hon. William J. Bryan,	301
Horoscope for the sailing of the German Fleet for China,	305
Chart of the Heavens for the time of marriage of Mr. and Mrs. Langtry,	307

	PAGE
Picture of Mr. and Mrs. Lillian Langtry,	308
Horoscope of Victoria, Queen of Great Britain and Ireland, and Empress of India,	310
Remarks on reading Queen Victoria's Horoscope at a public lecture,	311
Remarks on the Horoscope of Prince Albert,	312
The picture of Prince Albert,	313
The portrait of Queen Victoria at 20 years of age,	314
Picture of Queen Victoria at the age of 79,	315
The Revolutionary Chart of Queen Victoria from May 24th, 1898, to May 24th, 1899,	316
Remarks on the Revolutionary and Secondary Directions of Queen Victoria,	316
Queen Victoria's Secondary Directions from May 24th, 1898, to May 24th, 1899,	317
Horoscope of Lillian Russell,	319
Chart of the Heavens for the time of birth of Lillian Russell,	319
Pictures of Lillian Russell's first and second husbands,	320
Picture of Lillian Russsll and her third husband,	321
Picture of Lillian Russell and reported fourth husband,	322
Horoscope of Lord George Gordon Byron,	324
Chart of the Heavens for Lord Byron's birth,	324
Picture of Lord George Gordon Byron,	325
Marriage of Lord Byron,	326
"Byron's Farewell to England,"	330
Horoscope of the Young King of Spain,	332
Chart of the Heavens for the time of birth of the Young King of Spain,	332
Picture of Alphonso XIII., King of Spain, his Mother, and his two Sisters,	333
Heredity and Planetary Influence,	334
Horoscope of the multi-millionaire, Jay Gould.	336
Portrait of Jay Gould,	337
Seven concise reasons why everyone should have a reading of their lives,	339
Horoscope of Charles Dickens,	340
Chart of the Heavens for the time of birth of Charles Dickens,	340
Portrait of Charles Dickens,	341
Horoscope of Gen. Ulysses Simpson Grant,	343
Picture of Gen. Grant,	344
Chart of the Heavens for Gen. Grant's birth,	345
Horoscope of President George Washington,	346
Chart of the Heavens for the time of Gen. George Washington's birth,	346
Picture of Gen. George Washington,	347
Prof. Draper on William Lilly's Astrology,	349
Sickness and Allopathic treatment of Gen. George Washington.	349
The physician's report of Gen. Washington's last illness,	350
Modern medication, or the Allopathic treatment of Mr. Maybrick,	351
Dr. Brown-Sequard's Elixir of Life,	351
Dr. Koch's remedy for Consumption,	351
Mr. Pasteur and Prof. Verneuil's remarks on Dr. Koch's remedy for Consumption,	352
A cure for the bite of a rattlesnake,	352
"Who are the regulars and who are the quacks?"	352
The ingredients and prescriptions sent by Allopathic doctors to Samuel Boyer for the cure of dyspepsia,	353
Dr. Trumbull W. Cleveland's prescription for Mrs. James L. Carhart's baby,	354
The second prescription of Dr. Cleveland and his treatment of Mrs. Carhart's baby,	355
Persecution of Homeopathic and Botanic Practitioners,	356

XXIV CONTENTS.

	PAGE
Allopathic physicians endeavoring to suppress patent medicines by having laws enacted against their manufacture	357
The objections to the science of Astrology answered,	358
The planet Neptune,	362
Neptune in the 12 houses,	363
The aspects of Neptune,	364
Horoscope of President Cleveland and of Ex-President Harrison,	365
Horoscope of Grover Cleveland,	366
Horoscope of Benjamin Harrison,	367
Chart of President Harrison's birth,	368
Further remarks on the horoscopes of Ex-President Harrison,	369
A few remarks on the horoscope of President Cleveland,	370
Esther Cleveland's nativity,	371
The Baby's horoscope,	373
The horoscope of Emperor William III of Germany,	375
The horoscope of the third French Republic,	377
Why I am an Astrologer,	378
Preface,	379
Introductory remarks,	380
Sentence of Mr. Romain to 18 months imprisonment by Judge Gordon, of Philadelphia, Pa.,	380
1—Why I undertook to write this pamphlet,	381
2—The object I wish to accomplish by the present publication,	383
A letter to the editor of the New York World, by the Author	384
An introduction to the Reader,	387
A letter of introduction,	388
The Author's extensive acquaintance,	388
Remarks on Charles A. Dana's periodical fits of insanity,	391
How the innocent suffer by corrupt laws,	392
If Charles A. Dana had lived 300 years ago he would have advocated laws to prevent people from reading the Bible,	393
The Author's persecution at 814 Broadway,	394
Astrological Society,	395
How Israel Holdsworth came to republish White's Ephemeris,	395
The reason Mr. Chaney republished White's Ephemeris in the United States,	396
Why I came to have the planet Neptune's longitude calculated,	397
The scarcity of Astrologers and Astrological Ephemerides in the United States,	397
An account of both my grand fathers,	398
Why I came to lecture on Astrology at 814 Broadway,	400
Professor Richard A. Proctor, on Astrology,	401
The Humbug of Astrology,	401
The New York World refused to publish my answer to Richard A. Proctor,	404
Reply to Mr. Proctor which the New York World refused to publish,	405
The Author's criticism on Mr. Proctor and the New York World,	407
Riots in London caused by the repeal of tyrannical laws in 1778,	408
Astrology and Astronomy in ancient times,	409
The diseases of the body supposed to be caused by evil spirits or devils,	410
Comparing Astrology with Music,	411
The persecutions by the Catholic Church and the burning of John Huss,	412
The assumptions of Richard A. Proctor,	413
First:—The christian religion,	413
Second:—Reformation and witchcraft,	415
A miracle is Legitimate witchcraft, and witchcraft is an Illegitimate miracle,	416

	PAGE
Bayard Taylor's comparison of Christianity and Mohammedism,	417
Third:—The change from the Ptolemaic to the Copernican system of Astronomy,	418
The reason I have not produced any facts in regard to Astrology, is that Richard A. Proctor ignored them,	419
Every science is gradually built up from facts which are gathered from observation and experiment,	420
Dr. Caldwell's remarks on Dr Salmon,	420
Had Mr. Proctor been acquainted with any Astrologers, it no doubt would have changed his opinion on Astrology,	421
Dr. Cox and Homeopathy,	421
Mr. Proctor convicts himself, after being his own judge and jury,	422
The influence of planets on the stature and build of individuals,	423
The influence of the planets on happy and unhappy marriages,	423
The change of opinion in regard to Astrology by the editors and persons connected with the New York World, since they published Proctor's "Humbug of Astrology,"	424
Herbert Spencer's epitaph on Proctor's tomb,	425
To the Reader,	427
Discussions in favor of Astrology and assertions against it,	429
First:—arguments in favor of Astrology,	429
The Pastoral Letter,	431
Second:—Assertions of those who oppose Astrology,	432
Chambers in their Information for the People on Phrenology,	433
Third:—Chambers's Encyclopedia on Astrology,	433
John Partridge's Almanac published by the Missionary Society of London	433
Changing of the opinion in regard to William Lilly and Astrology, in Encyclopedias,	434
Thomas Dick on the Absurdity of Astrology,	435
Rev. Thomas Dick puffing Astrology,	436
Astrologers in Rome and their persecution,	438
Penny Magazine's Refutation of Astrology,	439
The ridiculous conclusions of the Penny Magazine,	441
Quotations from a number of Astrological books proving it,	441
The Author of the Penny Magazine and their Refutation of Astrology,	443
The minister of the Gospel—remarks on the wickedness of Astrology,	444
All the writings against Astrology are generally shallow and nonsensical,	444
Extracts from Francis Moore's almanac,	445
The eclipses for 1768,	446
The impostor Dr. Roeback of Philadelphia,	452
Death of Amee Smith in the Hotel Victor, New York,	453
"Unparalleled outrages" against Astrology and Astrologers. W. H. Chaney	454
"The Gospel of the Stars or the Wonders of Astrology," Mr. James Hingston,	462
Laying the corner stone of the School of Theosophy,	464
Rules for laying corner stones,	466
Theosophists all Awry,	467
Picture of the Tower of Babel,	468
Description of the Tower of Babel,	469
Scientists all agree that Astrology is a debasing superstion, but they all disagree among themselves,	470
"Azrael" on the harmony of all Astrologers,	471

A GLOSSARY OF ASTROLOGICAL TERMS.

Affliction. A planet, or the cusp of a house, being in evil aspect to any planet, or in Conjunction with a malefic.

Airy Signs. Gemini, Libra and Aquarius.

Ambient. The whole canopy of the heavens, when spoken of in a general way.

Angles. The 1st, 4th, 7th and 10th houses.

Application—to apply. These terms mean the approach of any planet to the body or aspect of another, or the cusp of any house.

Ascential Difference. (A. D.) This, added to its right ascension (A. R.) if it have *south* declination, but subtracted therefrom if it has *north* declination, gives its oblique ascension.

Ascendant. The eastern horizon, or the cusp of that house which represents the party; as the cusp of the 5th is the ascendant for a child of the querent.

Ascending, a term denoting any planet or sign, which are between the 4th and 10th houses, more especially when rising above the eastern horizon.

Aspect. The being placed at certain distances from a planet, or the cusp of a house, as, if Jupiter be 60 degrees from the Moon, then they are both said to be in sextile aspect to each other.

Barren Signs. Gemini, Leo and Virgo.

Benefics The two planets Jupiter and Venus, and sometimes Herschel.

Bestial Signs. Aries, Taurus, Leo, Sagittarius, (the first half excepted) and Capricorn.

Besieged is when a planet, *fortunate* by nature, is situated between two malevolent planets as Venus, in 12 degrees of Cancer, Saturn in 15 degrees, and Herschel in 10 degrees of the same sign; where she is in a state of "siege," and highly unfortunate. He whose significator it was, would be denoted thereby to be in "a great strait," and particularly "hemmed in" or surrounded with ill fortune.

Bicorporeal Signs. Gemini, Sagittarius and Pisces.

Cadent. So called, because they are fallen from the angles. These are the weakest of all the houses.

Cardinal Signs. Aries, Cancer, Libra and Capricorn.

Cazimi. The heart of the Sun, or being within 17 minutes of the exact longitude of the Sun; which is considered a strong position, but, we think, erroneously.

Circle of Position. An astronomical term used in calculating the polar elevation of any planet. They are small circles bearing the same relation to a meridian circle which the paralells of latitude do to the equator

Collection of Light. In Horary questions when a planet receives the aspects of any two others which are not themselves in aspect. It denotes that the affair will be forwarded by a third person, described by that planet; but not unless they both receive him in some of their dignities.

Combustion, is when a planet is posited within 8 degrees 30 minutes of the Sun, either before or after the Sun's body. In horary questions, unless the Sun is chief significator, this is deemed unfortunate. The Moon is singularly weak when so elongated.

Common Signs. Gemini, Virgo, Sagittarius and Pisces.

Conjunction. Two planets being in the same longitude. If they be exactly in the same degree and minute, it is a partile conjunction, and very powerful; if within the half of the sum of their two orbs, it is a platic conjunction, and less powerful.

Converse Motion. Is that which is caused by the diurnal rotation of the Earth on its axis, which makes the Sun, Moon, etc., appear to rise, approach the meridian, set, etc. It applies particularly to the Sun and Moon, when they are carried towards the promittors or their aspects.

Culminate. To arrive at the midheaven, or the cusp of the 10th house.

Cusp. The beginning of any house, and the cusp extends 5 degrees on each side of the line.

Debilities. A planet in a weak and afflicted position, as fall, detriment, etc.

Declination. The distance any heavenly body is from the equator.

Decreasing in Light. When any planet is past the opposition of the Sun, decreases in light; this is a testimony of weakness.

Decumbiture. A lying down; the figure erected for the time of any person being first taken ill, and taking to their bed.

Degree. The 30th part of a sign in the Zodiac; or the 360th part of any circle.

Descendant. The 7th house, or that space from the western horizon to one-third of the distance towards the meridian above the earth.

Descension. The going down of any body from the meridian above the Earth to that below it; for though the Sun is lost sight of at sunset, he still *descends* till he reaches the anti-meridian at midnight.

Detriment. The sign opposite the house of any planet; as Venus in Aries is in her detriment. In horary questions it is a sign of weakness, distress, etc.

Direct. As applied to planets denotes their moving in the true order of the celestial signs, as from Aries to Taurus, etc.

Direction. The measuring the space between the bodies of any two planets, or that between any two parts of the heavens, to ascertain at what period of life the promised effect will appear. Their distance is a certain number of degrees of the A R. of the Sun, which, when he has passed over the direction is complete. It is called the *Arc of Direction.*

Direction, Secondary The aspects formed by the Moon in the days immediately succeeding the birth. Each day between the birth and the time the aspect is formed is equal to one exact year of life; thus, if the Moon form a good aspect with Jupiter exactly 21 days to the hour and minute after birth, the native will feel its effects about his 21st birthday.

Direct Motion. This is in reality converse motion, but is so called to distinguish the case of the promittors being carried towards the bodies or aspects of the Sun or Moon, which directions are considered somewhat less powerful than those by *converse motion.*

Diurnal Arc. Is the length of time that part of the heavens in which any planet is at birth above the Earth; and it is usually measured by degrees.

Dispose, Dispositor. A planet disposes of any other which may be found in its essential dignities. Thus, if the Sun is in Aries, the house of Mars, then Mars disposes of the Sun, and is said to rule, receive, or govern him. In horary questions when the dispositor of the planet signifying the thing asked after is himself disposed by the lord of the ascendant, it is a good sign. To dispose by house is the most powerful testimony; then by exaltation, then triplicity, then term, and lastly, face, which is a very weak reception.

Double-bodied Signs. Gemini, Sagittarius and Pisces.

Dragon's Head. Is the north node of the Moon, or when she crosses the ecliptic into north latitude. It is always a good symbol, denoting success, a good disposition, etc.

Dragon's Tail. Is where the Moon crosses the ecliptic into south latitude, or her south node. It is very evil, and in all things the reverse of Dragon's Head; it diminishes the power of good, and increases that of evil planets.

Earthy Signs. Taurus, Virgo and Capricorn which form the earthy triplicity.

Ephemeris. An almanac of the planets' places. The best is Raphael's *Ephemeris*.

Equinoctial Signs. Aries and Libra.

Exaltation. An essential dignity, next in power to that of house.

Face. The third part of a sign, or *ten* degrees *deconate*.

Fall. A planet has its fall in the opposite sign to that in which it has its exaltation. In horary questions, a planet in its fall denotes a person unfortunate, despised, degenerated, mean, insolvent or helpless; and the thing signified by it is in a helpless state, except some good aspect by application, or some translation of light happen, which will relieve it quite unexpected.

Familiarity. Any kind of aspect or reception.

Feminine Signs. Taurus, Cancer, Virgo, Libra, Capricorn and Pisces.

Fiery Signs, or Fiery Triplicity. Aries, Leo and Sagittarius.

Figure. The diagram which represents the heavens at any time; it is also called a scheme or horoscope.

Fortitudes. Influences of the planets made stronger by being well posited.

Fortunes. Jupiter and Venus and the Sun; Moon and Mercury, if aspecting them, and not afflicted, are considered fortunate planets.

Fixed Signs. Taurus, Leo, Scorpio and Aquarius.

Fruitful Signs. Cancer, Scorpio and Pisces.

Frustration. The cutting off, or preventing anything shown by one aspect by means of another. Thus, if Venus, lady of the ascendant, were hastening to the trine of Mars, lord of the 7th in a question of marriage, it might denote that the marriage would take place; but if Mercury were to form an opposition to Mars before Venus reached her trine of that planet, it would be a frustration, and would show that the hopes of the querent would be cut off; if Mercury were lord of the 12th it might denote that it would be done by a secret enemy, if of the 3d by means of a relation, etc.

Geniture. The moment of time an infant is brought into the world.

Horary Question. So named from the Latin word *hora*, an hour, because the time of their being asked is noted, and the chart of the heavens for that time is taken to judge of the result.

Horoscope. The ascendant is sometimes so called; but it is more generally a term for the figure of the heavens used by Astrologers for predicting by nativities, mundane Astrology, and horary questions.

Houses. The twelve divisions or compartments into which the circle of the heavens is divided; also the signs in which any planet is said to have most influence.

Human Signs. Gemini, Virgo, Aquarius, and the first half of Sagittarius. Any person's significator therein shows them to be of a human disposition.

Hyleg. Sun, Moon or the ascendant is the giver of life.

Hylegiacal Places. The 1st house, from 5 degrees above to 25 degrees below its cusp; 7th house, from 5 degrees below to 25 degrees above its cusp; the 9th house, from 5 degrees outside its cusp to 25 degrees below the 11th house. If the Sun is in any of those places it is "hyleg;" if not, then if the Moon is in any of these places it is "hyleg," if it is not, then the ascendant is "hyleg."

Impeded. This signifies being afflicted by evil planets. The Moon is impeded in the highest degree when in conjunction with the Sun.

Ingress. A planet's transit over a place, the Sun, Moon, mid-heaven or ascendant, or has arrived at any point in the Zodiac.

Increase in Light. When any planet is leaving the Sun, and is not yet arrived at the opposition; after which it decreases in light. The former is a good, the latter an evil testimony, especially as regards the Moon.

Increasing in Motion. When any planet moves faster than it did on the preceding day.

Inferior Planets. Venus, Mercury, and the Moon; so called because their orbit is inferior to that of the Earth.

Infortunes. Uranus, Saturn and Mars; also Mercury when he is much afflicted.

Intercepted. A sign which is found between the cusps of two houses, and not on either of them.

Joined to. Being in any aspect.

Latitude. The distance any star, etc., is north or south of the ecliptic. The Sun never has any latitude. Latitude on the earth is the distance any place is north or south of the equator.

Lights. The Sun and Moon.

Light of Time. The Sun by day and the Moon by night.

Longitude. On the Earth is the distance from any place east or west of Greenwich, England; in the heavens, it is the distance of any body from the first point of the Zodiac, Aries, 0 degrees 0 minutes, measured on the ecliptic.

Lords. Planets which have the most influence or powerful effects in particular signs. Thus, if Aries ascend in any chart, Mars, which rules that sign, is the lord of the ascendant.

Lunation. The conjunction, square or opposition of the Sun and Moon, also the length of time in which the Moon appears to move around the Earth; the time from new Moon to new Moon.

Malefics. Uranus, Saturn and Mars.

Malefic Aspects are the Semisquare, Square, Sesquisquare, Opposition and Conjunction of evil planets. When planets are found at the distances which constitute these aspects, they act very evil for the native.

Masculine and Feminine. Saturn, Jupiter, Mars and Sun are masculine, and Venus and Moon are feminine. Mercury is masculine or feminine according as he aspects the former or the latter.

Masculine Signs. Aries, Gemini, Leo, Libra, Sagittary and Aquarius. The others are feminine.

Matutine. Appearing in the morning; that is, those stars or planets which rise before the Sun.

Mean Motion. That of Saturn is 2 minutes; Jupiter, 4 minutes 59 seconds; Mars, 33 minutes 28 seconds; the Sun, 59 minutes 8 seconds; and Moon 13 degrees 10 minutes.

Mundane Parallels are equal distances from the meridian.

Nativity. The birth of any one. It is the instant that the infant first draws breadth. It also signifies the map of the heavens at that instant.

Nebulæ. Clusters of stars that look like clouds.

Neomenium. The new Moon or change of the Moon.

Nocturnal Arc. The space through which any body in the heavens passes while under the horizon.

Northern Signs. Aries, Taurus, Gemini, Cancer, Leo and Virgo.

Oblique Ascension. A part of the equator that rises in an oblique sphere, when one pole is elevated and the other depressed.

Oblique Sphere. One in which all circles parallel to the equator are oblique to the horizon, and form acute angles with it.

Occidental. Western.

Orb of a Planet. The distance within which a planet continues to operate. The orbs are Saturn 9 degrees, Jupiter 12 degrees, Mars 7 degrees 30 minutes, Sun 17 degrees, Venus 8 degrees, Mercury 7 degrees, the Moon 12 degrees. The orb of the fixed signs is 5 degrees. The angles also are effected by any star or planet within 5 degrees of the cusp.

Oriental. Eastern. If a star is to the east of the M. C., it is oriental; if otherwise, it is occidental. But the Sun is said to be oriental only when he is applying to or approaching the meridian, and occidental when leaving it.

Parallels. The zodiacal parallel signifies having the same declination or distance from the equator, north or south. This is a very potent familiarity.

Parents. The Sun and Saturn signify the father. The Moon and Venus signify the mother. Their condition is shown by the strength and condition of these in the native's nativity.

Partile. An exact or perfect aspect agreeing to the very minute.

Part of Fortune. The point in the heavens which is equally distant from the ascendant as the Moon is from the Sun in longitude.

Perigee. The part of a planet's orbit where it is nearest to the Earth.

Peregrine. A peregrine planet is one having no kind of essential dignity. He usually signifies a thief in all questions of theft.

Periodical Lunation. The time required by the Moon to return to her own place, viz., 27 days 7 hours and 41 minutes.

Planets. These are Saturn, Jupiter, Mars, Sun, Venus, Mercury Moon and Uranus. We may now say Neptune also. The asteroids we do not consider.

Planetary Hours. Hours ruled by the planets. These hours are counted from the outward planet Saturn inward to the Moon. The hours of the day are counted from sunrise to sunset and of the night from sunset to sunrise.

Platic. This means *wide* It is used to signify some aspect within half the sum of the orbs of the two bodies or planets.

Promissor. The planet which promises to produce the event. The planet applying to the significator, or to which the latter applies. In nativities that planet to which the Sun, Moon, M C., or the ascendant applies is the promissor, they being significators.

Proper Motion. That which is direct through the Zodiac, in contradiction to the mundane motion, or that caused by the daily rotation of the earth on its axis.

Prorogator. The planet which upholds life.

Quartile. The square aspect of 90 degrees in the Zodiac; and of three houses in the map or figure of the heavens.

Querent. The person who enquires or asks a horary question.

Quesited. The thing or person enquired about.

Quintile. An aspect of 72 degrees, not very potent.

Radical. That which belongs to the radix or figure of the birth.

Radical Elections. Times chosen or elected for commencing undertakings. They chiefly depend on the aspects then forming to the Sun, Moon, M. C. or ascendant at birth. Thus if Jupiter is on the ascendant, or in trine thereto, it is a good time to elect for any change to restore health.

Rapt Motion. The daily motion of the heavens from east to west.

Rapt Parallels. Equal distances from the meridian formed by rapt motion and measured by the semi-arcs of the bodies moved.

Rays. Beams of influence, constituting aspects.

Reception. The disposing of one planet by another, in consequence of receiving it into its dignities.

Rectification. The discovery of the true moment of the birth by comparing the periods of events in life with the aspects that produce them.

Refranation. Is when two planets are approaching an aspect, one of them falls retrograde before the aspect is complete. This shows that the event promised by the aspect will come to nothing.

Retrograde. When a planet appears to move backward, or contrary to the regular order of the signs, it shows that nothing promised by that planet can be relied upon. In nativities it shows that the planet will do very little or no good by his aspects, unless he is otherwise extremely well dignified, etc.

Revolutions. The return of the Sun to its place at birth. The aspects then formed, especially those to the radical places, denote the general influences during the year.

Right Ascension. An arc of the equator, reckoned from the first point of Aries.

Right Distance. The distance of any point from another, measured by right ascension.

Right Sphere. One in which all the circles are parallel to the equator form right angles with the horizon.

Satellites. Minor bodies which move about others; as the Moon above the Earth.

Scheme. A map of the heavens.

Semi-arc. Half a diurnal or nocturnal arc.

Semi-quartile. A half a square, or half of 90 degrees; viz., 45 degrees. It is an evil aspect.

Separation. When two planets having been in partile aspect to each other begin to move away therefrom. If all the significators are separating in a question of marriage, it shows that no marriage will occur. So in other things.

Sesqui-square. A square and a half, or 135 degrees. It is evil, but less potent than a square.

Significator. The planet ruling the ascendant is always the significator of the querent.

Signs of Long Ascension. Cancer, Leo, Virgo, Libra, Scorpio and Sagittary.

Signs of Short Ascension. Capricorn, Aquarius, Pisces, Aries, Taurus, Gemini.

Southern Signs. Libra, Scorpio, Sagittary, Capricorn and Pisces; they being to the south of the equator.

Speculum. A table comprising the chief data from which directions are to be worked or calculated in a nativity. It contains the latitude, declination, right ascension, meridian distance (in right ascension) and semi arc of each planet.

Stationary. When a planet appears to stand still in the heavens in consequence of the earth's motion being different from the planet's motion.

Succedent. Those houses which follow the angles. They are the second, fifth, eighth and eleventh.

Superior Planets. Uranus, Saturn, Jupiter and Mars.

Sympathy. Where the significator in one nativity, is in the same place in the Zodiac that it is in another nativity, then there is a mutual sympathy found between those persons. The strongest is where the Sun in one nativity is on the place of the Moon in another; if the Moon is found in the same position in each nativity, it causes love between the sexes, and a feeling of sympathy between those of the same sex. If the two ascendants are opposed, or if an evil planet in one nativity is on the place of the Sun or Moon in another, there is no sympathy and possibly antipathy or hatred. If all the planets agree or are in good aspect in two nativities, there is a very strong sympathy, which generally lasts until death; and in the case of a male and female causes "Love at first sight."

Table of Houses. A table giving the longitude of the signs for each house.

Term. An essential dignity, less potent than any other except the face.

Testimony. Any aspect, or position of a significator in a horary question, bearing on the matter by being in configuration with some other significator. In nativities, the positions of the several planets, as regards the Sun, Moon, M.C., and ascendant, are testimonies of good or evil to the native.

Transits. The passages of the planets over the places of the Sun, Moon, M.C., or ascendant, of the horoscope at the birth.

Translation of Light. When one planet separates from the conjunction or aspect of another, and soon after forms a conjunction or aspect with a third, he is said to translate the light of the one he leaves to the one which he approaches. It denotes aid or assistance in bringing some matter to a conclusion by a person described by the planet so translating the light.

Travelling. The luminaries, or Mars, falling away from the angles, chiefly if into the ninth house, cause travelling. This will be more so if the Moon aspect Mercury, and they are in moveable signs.

Trigons. These are the four triplicities, viz.: Fiery, Aries, Leo, Sagittary; Earthy, Taurus, Virgo, Capricorn; Airy, Gemini, Libra, Aquarius; Watery, Cancer, Scorpio, Pisces.

Triplicity. See *Trigon.*

Tropical Signs. Cancer and Capricorn.

Under the Sunbeams. Within 17 degrees of the Sun. A planet so situated is weak, but more so if combust, within 8 degrees 30 minutes.

Void of Course. When planets form no aspect before they leave the sign. It is noticed chiefly in regard to the Moon in horary questions. It usually shows that nothing will come of the matter in question. It often shows that the question is not radical.

Zenith. The point exactly over head.

Zodiac. The belt of the heavens, in which the Sun and all the old planets move.

Zodiacal Aspects. Those aspects, or angles, in the heavens, measured by the degrees of the Zodiac. See *Aspects.*

Zodiacal Paralells. The parallels of declination, or points in the heavens at equal distances from the equator. These have great and lasting power in nativities, especially when formed at the birth.

ALPHABETICAL INDEX.

In addition to the contents the author has inserted an Alphabetical Index, which is more convenient for students, enabling them to readily find any special rule or principle in this science that they may wish to use in their practice.

	PAGE
A Glossary of Astrological Terms	xxv
A Brief History of Astrology by its Friends or Advocates	8
A Short History of Astrology by its Enemies	12
Astrology in London, by Edgar Lee	45
Action and Reaction of One Planet on Another	65
A blank chart of the Heavens, showing the position and number of Houses	88
Advice to Students studying Astrology	93
Acquire a regular system of reading a Horoscope	156
A Synopsis of Medical Astrology	183
A table of the Friendship and Enmities of the Planets	241
Aspects of the Planets	242
A cure for the bite of a rattlesnake	352
Allopathic physicians endeavoring to suppress patent medicines by having laws enacted against their manufacture	357
A few remarks on the horoscope of President Cleveland	370
A letter to the editor of the New York World by the author	384
An introduction to the reader	387
A letter of introduction	388
Astrological Society	395
An account of both my grandfathers	398
Astrology and Astronomy in ancient times	409
A miracle is Legitimate witchcraft, and witchcraft is an Illegitimate miracle	416
Astrologers in Rome and their persecution	438
All the writings against Astrology are generally shallow and nonsensical	444
"Azrael" on the harmony of all Astrologers	471
Business and Honor	163
Business or Profession in which the native will be unfortunate	196
"Byron's Farewell to England."	330
Bayard Taylor's comparison of Christianity and Mohammedism	417
"Chambers' Encyclopœdia" on Astrology	19
Chinese and Astrology, and their Method of making use of it in their Marriages	35
Correspondence with Dr. L. D. Broughton, O. D. Bradgen, and A. N. Doerschuk on writing of horoscopes	50
Critical times—stirring periods	69
Chart of the Heavens for the time that President McKinley took the oath of office	146
Chart of the Heavens for a girl born July 2d, 1884, at 8:35 A. M., New York City	152
Claudius Ptolemy—reasons for allotting the signs to the planets	154

	PAGE
Children	167
Criticism on the New York Times, and other remarks on Astrology	171
Criticism on Chas. A. Dana, editor of the New York Sun—remarks on Astrology	174
Chart of the Heavens for the time of birth of Hon. William McKinley	296
Chart of the Heavens for Hon. W. J. Bryan's time of birth	299
Chart of the Heavens when Hon. William McKinley was nominated for President	301
Chart of the Heavens for the time of the nomination for President of Hon. William J. Bryan	301
Chart of the Heavens for the time of marriage of Mr. and Mrs. Langtry	307
Chart of the Heavens for the time of birth of Lillian Russell	319
Chart of the Heavens for Lord Byron's birth	324
Chart of the Heavens for the time of birth of the young King of Spain	332
Chart of the Heavens for the time of birth of Charles Dickens	340
Chart of the Heavens for Gen. Grant's birth	345
Chart of the Heavens for the time of Gen. George Washington's birth	346
Chart of President Harrison's birth	368
Comparing Astrology with music	411
Chambers in their Information for the People on Phrenology	433
Changing of the opinion in regard to William Lilly and Astrology, in Encyclopœdias	434
Dr. Mesmer and Animal Magnetism, and the French Academy of Science	32
Benjamin Franklin and the Lightning Rod	32
Diagram of the Solar System	67
Divisions of the signs of the Zodiac	95
Disposition and Temper	162
Diseases caused by the planets	187
Different grades of believers in Astrology	246
Different methods of measuring time by the Heavenly Bodies	286
Dr. Brown-Sequard's Elixir of Life	351
Dr. Koch's remedy for Consumption	351
Dr. Trumbull W. Cleveland's prescription for Mrs. James L. Carhart's baby	354
Dr. Caldwell's remarks on Dr. Salmon	420
Dr. Cox and Homeopathy	421
Discussions in favor of Astrology and assertions against it	429
Death of Aimee Smith in the Hotel Victor, New York	453
Description of the Tower of Babel	469
Elements of Astrology—Introduction	5
Elements of Astrology—Rudiments of the Science	87
Explanation of the Table of Essential Dignities	236

	PAGE		PAGE
Elections, or choosing a fortunate time to commence new business, removal or remarkable changes..	287	How to describe a person born under the planet Mercury in the sign Cancer	177
Election for laying the first stone....	288	Health and Life	178
Elections for buying or renting a house, lands or tenements, etc...	288	How to judge if a horoscope is fortunate or unfortunate	191
Elections for removal from one house to another	288	How to find the time of day a person is born; also how to correct the wrong time of birth	228
Election for entering into new business, office or employment	288	Historical remarks on the Essential Dignities of the planets	239
Election for commencing a trade or profession	289	Horoscope of Hon. William McKinley	295
Election for Marriage	289	Hon. William J. Bryan's Horoscope.	298
Election for proposing Marriage	290	Horoscope for the sailing of the German Fleet for China	305
Election for introduction to Ladies and Gentlemen	290	Horoscope of Victoria, Queen of Great Britain and Ireland, and Empress of India	310
Election for going on a Journey	291	Horoscope of Lillian Russell	319
Election for Navigation or going on a Voyage	291	Horoscope of Lord George Gordon Byron	324
Election for Collecting a Debt or Money that is owing	292	Horoscope of the Young King of Spain	332
Elections to make friendship to brothers, sisters, kindred, neighbors, etc	292	Heredity and Planetary Influence...	334
Elections for hiring servants or employees	292	Horoscope of the multi-millionaire, Jay Gould	326
Elections for duels and lawsuits	293	Horoscope of Charles Dickens	340
Esther Cleveland's nativity	371	Horoscope of Gen. Ulysses Simpson Grant	343
Every science is gradually built up from facts which are gathered from observation and experiment	420	Horoscope of President George Washington	346
Extracts from Francis Moore's Almanac	445	Horoscope of President Cleveland and of Ex-President Harrison	365
Friends and Enemies	163	Horoscope of Grover Cleveland	366
Friends and Enemies	176	Horoscope of Benjamin Harrison	367
Fortunate and Unfortunate periods of the various contingencies or events of life	180	How the innocent suffer by corrupt laws	392
Further remarks on the horoscopes of President McKinley and Hon. William J. Bryan, and their nominations	300	How Israel Holdsworth came to republish White's Ephemeris	395
Further remarks on the horoscope of Ex-President Harrison	369	Had Mr. Proctor been acquainted with any Astrologers it no doubt would have changed his opinion on Astrology	421
First:—The Christian religion	413	Herbert Spencer's epitaph on Proctor's tomb	425
First:—Arguments in favor of Astrology	429	Important era in history (Salem Witchcraft)	70
General appearance of persons described by the 12 signs of Zodiac.	97	Introductory remarks	380
General advice to the student in learning the description of persons	104	If Charles A. Dana had lived 300 years ago he would have advocated laws to prevent people from reading the Bible	393
Good and evil planetary hours	244	John Kepler's Discoveries in Astronomy and Astrology	21
Harry Howard, his execution for murder, and Hypnotism	33	John Dreyden, Cardinal Richelieu and Sir Isaac Newton, Astrologers	22
Horoscope of the assassination of Carrie Brown ("Old Shakespeare")	84	Jupiter in the 12 signs	108
Horoscope of the assassination of Mr. Andrew J. Borden and his wife, August 4th, 1892	85	Joys of the planets	239
Herschel in the 12 signs of the Zodiac.	105	John Partridge's Almanac, published by the Missionary Society of London	433
Horoscope of the Inauguration of Hon. William McKinley	143	Lessons and Books on Astrology	xx
Horoscope erected for the time that the Extra Session of Congress met at Washington, D. C., March 15th, 1897, at 12 Noon	150	Lords or Rulers of the signs of the Zodiac	153
How to calculate the "Part of Fortune"	151	Lord of the first house in each of the 12 houses	199
How to describe a person by the planets and the signs of the Zodiac	159	Lord of the second in the 12 houses..	201
		Lord of the third in the 12 houses...	202
		Lord of the fourth in the 12 houses...	204
		Lord of the fifth in the 12 houses	205
Health	167	Lord of the sixth in the 12 houses	206
Horoscope of the Chinese Consul's Son	175	Lord of the seventh in the 12 houses.	208
		Lord of the eighth in the 12 houses..	210
		Lord of the ninth in the 12 houses...	212

	PAGE
Lord of the tenth in the 12 houses...	213
Lord of the eleventh in the 12 houses	215
Lord of the twelfth in the 12 houses.	217
Laying the corner stone of the School of Theosophy.............	464
Mrs. Maud S., the New York Times, and Astrology...................	36
Mrs. Maud S.'s Daughter's Horoscope	38
Misrepresentation of Astrology	60
Mars in opposition to the Sun.......	67
Meteorology and Planetary Influence	72
Mars in the 12 signs................	110
Mercury in the 12 signs.............	117
Mental Abilities	162
Morals and Religion—relations and journeys.........................	163
Marriage...........................	164
Marriage and Children..............	179
Mental Abilities....................	193
Marriage of Lord Byron.............	326
Modern medication, or the Allopathic treatment of Mr. Maybrick...........	351
Mr. Pasteur and Prof. Verneuil's remarks on Dr. Koch's remedy for Consumption.....................	352
Mr. Proctor convicts himself, after being his own judge and jury....	422
Neptune in Gemini from 1898 to 1902; Panama Scandal, and Suspension of Baring Brothers, of London..	76
Nativity of Mrs. Maud S.'s daughter.	151
New Aspects discovered by John Kepler...........................	243
Neptune in the 12 houses...........	363
Of the Sextile and Trine aspects of the significators..................	131
On Professor Draper's ridiculing William Lilly's Astrology........	184
Orbs of the planets..................	240
Preface.............................	iii
Pharaoh's Dream and the Magicians of Egypt and Babylon......	58
Perihelion Epoch of Jupiter coincident with the return of Cholera and epidemics...................	62
Personal description of man or woman described by the Planets,...	79
Persons described by the 8 Planets..	99
Practical Astrology.................	141
Personal description................	158
Parts of the body ruled by the 12 houses and the 12 signs of the Zodiac	185
Profession and Trade—Riches and Poverty...........................	194
Profession or Business in which the native would be fortunate........	198
Planets and other symbols..........	231
Prof. Wilson's criticisms on skeptics of Astrology......................	245
Perpetual table of planetary hours from sunrise until 9 hours after sunset............................	255
Perpetual Table of Equation of Time............................	286
Picture of Mr. and Mrs. Lillian Langtry................................	308
Picture of Queen Victoria at the age of 79..........................	315
Pictures of Lillian Russell's first and second husbands..................	320
Picture of Lillian Russell and her third husband....................	321
Picture of Lillian Russell and reported fourth husband................	322

	PAGE
Picture of Lord George Gordon Byron................................	325
Picture of Alphonso XIII, King of Spain, his Mother and his two Sisters............................	333
Portrait of Jay Gould................	337
Portrait of Charles Dickens.........	341
Picture of Gen. Grant...............	344
Picture of Gen. George Washington.	347
Prof. Draper on William Lilly's Astrology...........................	349
Persecution of Homeopathic and Botanic Practitioners............	356
Preface.............................	380
Professor Richard A. Proctor on Astrology...........................	401
Penny Magazine's refutation of Astrology...........................	439
Picture of the Tower of Babel.......	468
Queen Victoria's Secondary Directions, May 24th, 1898, to May 24th, 1899.............................	317
Quotations from a number of Astrological books proving it........	441
Remarks on Prof. Proctor's "Humbug of Astrology"................	17
Rev. Thomas Dick, of England, on Astrology, in his "Improvement of Society by the Diffusion of Knowledge.".....................	18
Remarks on the signs of the Zodiac.	94
Rule to set a Map of the Heavens....	142
Rules for reading horoscopes........	155
Rules to be followed in describing persons..........................	160
Riches and Poverty..................	162
Rules for describing the kind of person a lady or gentleman will marry; also whether it will be a happy or unhappy marriage. ...	164
Rules how to calculate the various events and contingencies of life.	167
Remarks on the Part of Fortune....	176
Riches and Poverty..................	178
Rules for judging the events and the times that will happen in nativities...............................	181
Remarks on Secondary directions...	182
Rules to judge the probable time of marriage of the native—also the number of children..............	189
Remarks and Explanations..........	219
Remarks on the lords of the 12 houses, and explaining how they are used in directions, transits, revolutionary figures, etc.......	223
Remarks on the changes in the personal appearance of the native in the different periods of his life..............................	224
Rules for judging of the changing of the build and complexion of the native............................	224
Remarks on the Table of Essential Dignities of the planets..........	238
Remarks on the Planetary hours....	247
Remarks on the Planetary hours....	251
Remarks on the time that some persons that we know of have got married, and the result, especially that of Mr. and Mrs. Langtry.	294
Remarks on reading Queen Victoria's Horoscope at a public lecture...............................	311
Remarks on the Horoscope of Prince Albert...........................	312

	PAGE
Remarks on the Revolutionary and Secondary Directions of Queen Victoria	316
Remarks on Charles A. Dana's periodical fits of insanity	391
Reply to Richard A. Proctor, which the New York World refused to publish	405
Riots in London, caused by the repeal of tyrannical laws in 1778	408
Rev. Thomas Dick. Puffing Astrology	436
Rules for laying corner-stones	466
Saturn in the 12 signs	106
Sun in the 12 signs	113
Sickness, diseases and complaints	161
Sympathy and antipathy of the planets – or friends and enemies	241
Signification of the planetary hours, and what use may be made of them	249
Some choice rules or aphorisms for election relating to several undertakings	292
Seven concise reasons why everyone should have a reading of their lives	339
Sickness and Allopathic treatment of Gen. George Washington	349
Sentence of Mr. Romain to 18 months imprisonment by Judge Gordon, of Philadelphia, Pa	380
Second:—Reformation and witchcraft	415
Second:—Assertions of those who oppose Astrology	432
Scientists all agree that Astrology is a debasing superstition, but they all disagree among themselves	470
To the Student	v
The supposed Argument which the Enemies of Astrology have brought against that Science	24
The Author's Criticism on the Editor of the New York Times	37
The Opposition to Lectures on Astrology in New York City	40
The Persecution the Author met with at 814 Broadway, New York	41
The interference of the Author's Lectures, and the breaking up of the Meetings	42
The stoppage of the Author's mail in the Post-office in New York	43
The Bible and Astrology	57
Theories of Ancient Astronomers	60
The effect on the earth and its inhabitants of the near approach of Mars	66
The period of the war	68
The sign Gemini rules the United States	69
The planet Neptune in Gemini, 1720; South Sea Bubble, and John Law's Banking Scheme	74
The sign Taurus rules Ireland	79
The afflicting planets describe the assassins in remarkable murder cases	80
The horoscope of the assassination of President Lincoln, on April 14, 1865	81
The horoscope of the assassination of President Garfield, July 2, 1881	82
The horoscope of the assassination of Lord Frederick Cavendish and Mr. Thomas Burke, May 6, 1882	83

	PAGE
The signification of the 12 Houses	89
The nature, quality and description of the 12 Houses	90
The description of Herschel persons	99
The description of Saturn persons	100
The description of Jupiter, Mars and Sun persons	101
The description of Venus persons	102
The description of Mercury and Moon persons	103
The Moon in the 12 signs	119
The effects of the conjunction of Uranus with the 7 planets	122
The effects of Saturn in conjunction with the other planets	125
The effects of Jupiter in conjunction with the other planets	126
The effects of Mars in conjunction with the other planets	128
The effects of the Sun in conjunction with the other planets	129
The effects of Venus and Mercury, when in conjunction with the Moon	130
The effects of the square or opposition aspect between the significators	135
Table of Lords of the Signs of the Houses	154
The Giver of Life	157
The financial benefit to persons in studying Astrology	161
The kind of gentleman Mrs. Maud S.'s daughter will marry	166
The age when married	167
The various contingencies and events of life	167
Trade and Profession	178
The temper or the animal passions	194
The influence of the lord of the first house in each of the 12 houses	199
The planets impress distinct characteristics or marks on the native which can be recognized	226
The seven planets rule the human system—named in the following order	227
Table of Essential Dignities, and various other tables and information	231
The signs of the Zodiac and their classification	232
The division of the 12 signs of the Zodiac	233
Triplicities or Trigons	234
The signs divided among the planets	235
Table of Essential Dignities, and debilities of the planets	237
The reason a planet receives its joy in one of its own signs and not in the other	239
Table of the planet's orbs	240
The mean motion of the planets	240
Table of the mean motion of the planets	241
The Dragon's Head or Moon's Node	243
The French and Latin names of days of the week, and explanation why the names of some of those days of the week have been changed	248
The influence of the planetary hours of the Sun, Moon and the other five planets	249
The hours of Saturn and Jupiter	249
The hours of Mars, Sun, Venus and Mercury	250

	PAGE
The hour of the Moon	251
The reason planetary hours have not been more generally made use of	252
The hours of good planets and the hours of evil planets may vary in their influence in certain horoscopes	253
Tables of planetary hours, and the reason why they vary in length	254
Table of planetary hours from sunrise until two hours after sunset on every alternate Wednesday of any year	282
The difference between clock or mean and solar time	285
The two conventions	300
The picture of Prince Albert	313
The portrait of Queen Victoria at 20 years of age	314
The Revolutionary Chart of Queen Victoria from May 24, 1898, to May 24, 1899	316
The physician's report of Gen. Washington's last illness	350
The ingredients and prescriptions sent by Allopathic doctors to Samuel Boyer for the cure of dyspepsia	353
The second prescription of Dr. Cleveland and his treatment of Mrs. Carhart's baby	355
The objections to the science of Astrology answered	358
The planet Neptune	362
The aspects of Neptune	364
The Baby's horoscope	373
The horoscope of Emperor William III. of Germany	375
The horoscope of the third French Republic	377
2—The object I wish to accomplish by the present publication	383
The Author's extensive acquaintance	388
The Author's persecution at 814 Broadway	394
The reason Mr. Chaney re-published White's Ephemeris in the United States	396
The scarcity of Astrologers and Astrological Ephemeris in the United States	397
The Humbug of Astrology	401
The New York World refused to publish my answer to Richard A. Proctor	404
The Author's criticism on Mr. Proctor and the New York World	407

	PAGE
The diseases of the body supposed to be caused by evil spirits or devils	410
The persecutions by the Catholic Church and the burning of John Huss	412
The assumptions of Richard A. Proctor	413
Third—The change from the Ptolemaic to the Copernican system of Astronomy	418
The reason I have not produced any facts in regard to Astrology is that Richard A. Proctor ignored them	419
The influence of planets on the stature and build of individuals	423
The influence of the planets on happy and unhappy marriages	423
The change of opinion in regard to Astrology by the editors and persons connected with the New York World since they published Proctor's "Humbug of Astrology."	424
To the Reader	427
The Pastoral Letter	431
Third—Chambers' Encyclopedia on Astrology	433
Thomas Dick on the Absurdity of Astrology	435
The ridiculous conclusions of the Penny Magazine	441
The Author of the Penny Magazine and his Refutation of Astrology	443
The Minister of the Gospel—remarks on the wickedness of Astrology	444
The eclipses for 1768	446
The imposter, Dr. Roeback, of Philadelphia	452
"The Gospel of the Stars, or the Wonders of Astrology," Mr. James Hingston	462
Theosophists all Awry	467
"Unparalleled Outrages" against Astrology and Astrologers, W. H. Chaney	454
Venus in the 12 signs	115
What the Stars Say. (From the Baltimore American)	297
" Who are the regulars and who are the quacks?"	352
Why I am an Astrologer	378
1.—Why I undertook to write this pamphlet	381
Why I came to have the planet Neptune's longitude calculated	397
Why I came to lecture on Astrology at 814 Broadway	400

ADVERTISEMENT.

Dr. L. D. Broughton is a regular college graduate in medicine, also president of the Astrological Society of New York. Having had over fifty years practice in medicine and astrology, his long experience in both these sciences enables him almost to guarantee satisfaction to those who may favor him with their confidence. He can be consulted either personally or by letter, at his office, 68 South Washington Square, New York.

Office hours from 9 a. m. to 3 p. m., and from 5 p. m. to 8 p. m.

OPINIONS OF THE PRESS.

From Cincinnati Enquirer, of Nov. 17, 1898.

"The Elements of Astrology" is a new work just published by the Author, Dr. L. D. Broughton, of 68 South Washington Square, New York.

The horoscopes that appeared in the columns of the *Enquirer* some years ago were edited by Dr. Broughton, and those who paid any attention to these readings will be enabled to judge for themselves what amount of faith to place in the teachings of astrology after reading the elements of that science.

From New York Herald, of Nov. 13, 1898.

Students of the so-called occult sciences will be glad to learn that a new and excellent work on astrology has just been published in this city and London, the author and publisher being L. D. Broughton, M. D. The book, which is entitled "Elements of Astrology," is a comprehensive and lucid text-book on this most ancient science. Several books on this subject have been published during the last few years both in this country and in Europe, but it would be difficult to find one which is more instructive or more interesting than the present work. As a rule modern astrological text-books are mere compilations of earlier works, and contain little or nothing that is original. Dr. Broughton's book, however, is not of this sort. True, it contains much that may be found in Lilly's "Christian Astrology," and other old books on the subject, but it also contains much that will be new even to the trained student. This will not surprise those who know that Dr. Broughton's father and grandfather were firm believers in astrology: and that he himself has been studying it all his life. It is doubtful if there is any man living now who has cast more horoscopes than he has, or is more skilled in this fascinating science. In the present work, Dr. Broughton not only lays down clear and simple rules for the guidance of students, but he also gives us some notable horoscopes of prominent persons, and some interesting reminiscences of his career as a teacher and champion of astrology. Altogether this is an admirable book, and one which deserves to be welcomed by all those who are interested in this curious, old, predictive science.

From New York Sunday News, October 30, 1898.

Astrology still has its attractions, and probably thousands of **persons resort to** its professors every year to have their horoscopes cast. It is a curious study, and the fact that its devotees are not diminishing is shown by the number of books dealing with it that are constantly issued, both here and abroad. One of the latest of these is a curiosity in its way. The author is Dr. Broughton, of this city, whose horoscopes in the Sunday News some time ago will doubtless be remembered.

The title of this work is "The Elements of Astrology," but, apart from giving instruction in the subject, it is full of really interesting information. The future of persons now living is forecast with frank confidence, as for instance, that of the boy King of Spain, Alfonso XIII, of whom it is said that he is very liable to meet with accidents, "particularly to the head, face and abdomen;" and, further, that, "as he gets older he will become quite stout, similar to Queen Victoria, as he is born under the same planet in the same sign, and then he will look much shorter, but will have a gentlemanly appearance, and, like the Queen, he will be very ambitious."

Further, we are told that this youth will, when he comes of age, "often be at war with other nations, but will generally come off victorious and gain much renown. * * * Spain will be very prosperous under his reign, and it will become one of the leading nations of the earth before his death." The world will evidently have to keep an eye on him if this horoscope of his is correct, for we are also told surely that Spain will be equally as fortunate under the reign of King Alfonso XIII. as Great Britain during that of Queen Victoria.

Another wonderful and timely prediction is that as to the fate to befall the German fleet which gave Admiral Dewey so much anxiety at Manila a short time ago. On this point Dr. Broughton says:

"There is no doubt that Prince Henry's expedition will prove disastrous. It will be strange, indeed, if the voyage does not prove disastrous to Emperor William, as well as to his brother, and also to the whole German nation, and that within a short time they will be like the French, who sent their navy to seize and possess Tonquin in China. They were soon very glad to get back to France, and when they did get back they took the cholera germs with them, which ravaged Marseilles and Toulon, and that epidemic spread over a great part of France and carried off many thousands of its inhabitants. The expedition also came near making another revolution in France.

Of the present French Republic it is interesting to be told that, having survived up to November of last year, there is nothing very threatening ahead of it until next February, when it will meet with severe afflictions, that will continue until 1901.

ELEMENTS OF ASTROLOGY.

INTRODUCTION.

Astrology is taken from the two Greek words, Astron, a star, or constellation of stars, and Logus, a discourse; meaning a discourse on the influence of the stars.

Astronomy is from Astron, a star or constellation of stars, and Nomos, law, meaning the knowledge or science of the laws of the stars. In former ages astrology and astronomy were twin sciences and astronomy was studied solely for astrologers to make astrological predictions. Indeed, the priest, physician, the astronomer and the astrologer were generally one and the same person, and the priest and the physician spent as much time in studying astrology and astronomy, as they did in studying theology and the science of medicine. [Further on I expect to prove that both theology and medicine are offsprings of astrology.]

But as science and learning advanced, it gradually became too laborious for any one man to be proficient in all the four sciences or professions, and in the course of ages they became separated, and one man studied astrology, another astronomy, another medicine, and another studied to be a priest, and as it often happens that when neighbors or relations fall out they become the bitterest enemies, and as the astrologers were always, in olden times, at the head of these professions, or "the power behind the throne," and controlled or guided the kings, emperors and Pharoahs, the other three professions became jealous and combined against the astrologer, and have done everything possible to degrade him and destroy his science and profession.

Even at the present day the students of medicine in some parts of the world, such as Thibet and other countries, spend nine years in the study of medicine, the last three they spend altogether in the study of astrology, as they deem that the most important or essential part of medicine, hence they study it the last, after having mastered or got through studying the elementary branches, such as anatomy, physiology, chemistry, materia medica, etc.

Dr. Lambert of London, England, has lately published a book on the practice of medicine, and in it attempts to prove the great advancement that science has made within the last 200 years, and gives as an illustration, that formerly when a student came up for his final examination previous to getting his diploma, he was generally asked the following question: "If you are called to the bedside of a sick person, where would you look for the disease?" The student is made to answer: "*In the sixth house.*" In the latter part of this Elements of Astrology, I shall treat more especially on the science of medicine and astrology, and shall often have occasion to refer to the sixth house.

It may be news to the reader to learn that Doctor Saunder, of London, England, published a large volume on the "sixth house," and William Lilly, the celebrated Astrologer, wrote the introduction to it.

I shall endeavor to prove that the old school physicians, or what are called the allopaths, on account of not giving attention to the sixth house, and by their method of treating diseases, actually destroy over 100,000 people every year in the United States alone. But more on this subject afterwards.

It is just about fifty years since my special attention was drawn to the science of astrology, and I made up my mind to study that science, cost what it would in labor or time.

I may here state that I was brought up in the atmosphere of astrology and kindred sciences, as my father, grandfather and relations for several generations had all given attention to these subjects, and were adepts in them.

My father did not practice astrology for a living, but he had a number of friends who came to consult him and ask his advice. I was often in the room when he was giving such advice, and was very much interested in what was going on, and in the manner he read the horoscopes. My eldest brother studied astology, and had a large practice, and became an expert.

For reasons which I need not mention, my brother when he was about three weeks old was removed to my father's sister's, and he never afterwards lived at home, consequently he knew little of my private life.

One time on a visit to my aunt's my brother offered to read my horoscope, and after giving him my time of birth he made a map of the heavens and read it off in such a manner and with such accuracy of detail, that, to put it mildly, I was astonished. From that time I made up my mind that I would study the science at any cost.

The system of astrology that I shall call the reader's attention to, is the Egyptian system, which was taught and practiced by Claudius Ptolemy (the great Egyptian astrologer and astronomer), in his work called "Ptolemy's Tetrabiblos" or Four Books of Astrology. Claudius Ptolemy lived about 2,000 years ago. He collected and published all that was then known on that science. He also published a book on astronomy called "The Ptolemaic Astronomy," which system has, since the invention of the telescope, been exploded, and the Copernican system of astronomy now prevails at the present day. Ptolemy's two books, the one on astrology, and the other on astronomy were often bound in one volume. In those days and long before navigation had become a science, those two sciences (astronomy and astrology) were always closely associated, and but few persons studied astronomy except those who studied astrology, with the sole view of making predictions.

When Ptolemy's system of astronomy was exploded it was taken for granted by ignorant persons that his system of astrology was also exploded, which idea is altogether erroneous. Ptolemy also published a Geography, but it was not exploded any more than his system of astrology, and both his geography and astrology are studied even to the present day.

Besides Ptolemy's system of astrology there is also an Arabian system which I have given some attention to, and the Chinese astrology, which I have not been able to investigate, as it has not been translated into the English language, that I am aware of.

Ptolemy's Four Books on Astrology are to the European and American student what the Bible is to the student of Christian Theology, consequently we have had a great number of translations of "Ptolemy's Tetrabiblos." I have some six or eight translations myself; for instance, Sibley's, Whalley's, Wilson's, Ashmand's, Coopers's, Worsdale's, and a few others that I cannot bring to mind. In short, when a person succeeded in studying astrology, and also had a knowledge of the Greek language, he must needs commence the translation of "Ptolemy's Tetrabiblos," similar to a person who is excelling as a painter, in order to become celebrated, he must paint a Madonna; also a person excelling in the Greek and Hebrew language, if he is a devout Christian, thinks he must commence translating the Bible, hence, there are many translations of the Bible and many Madonnas. Ashmand's translation of Ptolemy is counted the most perfect by English astrologers, and I think I cannot do better than give a short extract from his preface to the translation of Ptolemy. Ashmand says on page 5:—

"Of all sciences which have at any time engaged the attention of man, there is not one, the real or assumed principles of which are less generally known in the present age, than those of astrology. Out of a thousand persons who now treat the mention of this ancient science with supercilious ridicule, there is scarcely one who knows distinctly what it is he laughs at. Such contented ignorance, in persons, too, sufficiently informed in other respects, is the more extraordinary, since astrology has maintained a most conspicuous part throughout the history of the world, even until comparatively recent days. In the East, where it first arose, at a period of very remote antiquity, it still even now holds sway. In Europe and in every part of the world, where learning had impressed the human soil, astrology reigned supreme until the middle of the seventeenth century. It entered into the councils of princes, it guided the policy of nations, it ruled the daily actions of individuals, and physicians who were not well versed in this science were not deemed competent to practice their profession. All this is attested by the records of every nation which has a history."

In the brief history of astrology which I present to the reader, I have endeavored to be as impartial and as unbiassed as possible. He will find extracts from both the works of the enemies of astrology and astrologers, and also extracts from those authors who have written favorably on that subject.

Solomon in his Proverbs, says: "Let thy neighbor praise thee, yea, a stranger, and not thine own self." This advice of Solomon, I think, is without sense or reason, because a stranger could have very little knowledge of the party he intended to praise, and in so praising, it could only be called flattery or appealing to one's vanity. If Solomon had said: "Let thy neighbor praise thee, yea, thine enemy and not thine ownself," he would have spoken to the point, and more sensible than in the above Proverb. When an enemy praises either a science or an individual, it is evident that there must be some good or truth in that science or that person.

I shall commence by naming the authors who have written the most savagely against astrology. They are the Rev. Thomas Dick, of England, and the late Richard A. Proctor, also of England, and William and Robert Chambers, of Scotland. I shall quote from each of these authors as they are printed in their works. I might here state that it would have been much pleasanter for me, not to have had to refer to the enemies of astrology in any form or manner, but only to have written a book explaining its principles, and the best and easiest method of learning and practising that science. But astrologers have been so persecuted and imprisoned, and often put to death, in all Christian countries, that I think it is nothing but right that I should draw the reader's attention to the fact that astrology still continues to exist as a science, in spite of all those persecutions and imprisonments of its professors, which proves beyond a question, that there is truth in the science. Had any other profession met with the same amount of persecution, the professors who practised it would have been crushed or exterminated ages ago; although there might have been some little truth in those so-called sciences which those professors practised or followed.

Whenever the time arrives when the science of astrology shall become well known and understood, similar to arithmetic and astronomy, then all the persecutors will disappear, or at least they will be so ashamed of themselves, that they will be afraid to open their mouths, for fear of being held up to public scorn and ridicule, similar to what we should regard a person at the present day who can neither read nor write, and cannot tell the time of day when looking at the hands on the face of a clock or watch that keep correct time. If these ignorant persons should commence to persecute and imprison all those who can read and write, or can tell the hour and minute of the day by looking at the face of a clock they would then place themselves in the same position as the persecutors of astrology, and those persecutors being at the same time ignorant of that science.

A BRIEF HISTORY OF ASTROLOGY, BY ITS FRIENDS OR ADVOCATES.

In tracing the antiquity of astrology, we are directed back to the remotest periods on record. The Jewish historian, Josephus, who wrote nearly two thousand years ago, asserts that the Antediluvians were acquainted with astrology, and the same author states that it was understood by Seth, who was taught the science by Adam, his father; so that by taking this authority, we are carried back for the commencement of this knowledge to our first parents. Josephus further states that Seth, foreseeing the flood, in order to preserve a knowledge of this science to posterity, engraved the rudiments thereof upon two permanent pillars of stone, which endured through many generations, and were not entirely effaced till some time after the deluge. We are also told by the same authority, that the science was taught by Enos and Noah, who preserved it to the days of Abraham, who extended the knowledge of it by divine aid, teaching it to the Chaldeans and Egyptians. Joseph also patronized and taught it in Egypt; and Origen, Diodorus Siculus, and other ancient historians, supposed him to have been the author of an astrological work called: "The Aphorisms of Hermes the Egyptian."

The prophets and seers acquired a knowledge of this science from Moses, and it was afterwards taught among the tribe of Issachar, who are on that account, called in Scripture, "Men who had understanding in the times," and were expert in resolving all questions concerning futurity, and as this tribe were neither priests nor Levites, nor endowed with the spirit of prophecy, it follows that their understanding in the times, and the ability in foretelling future events, arose entirely from an acquired knowledge of the signs and influences of the heavenly bodies. The Persian astrologers were called Magi, or wise men, who were skilled in the times; and the Chaldeans termed their astrologers men skilled in wisdom and cunning sciences, who learned the learning of the Chaldeans. And after their method of studying their science of astrology, Daniel, Shadrach, Meshech and Abednego were instructed by their tutor, Melzer, and became ten times more learned in all matters of wisdom and understanding than all the astrologers of the realm, in consideration of which, they were elected members of the public schools of Babylon, which were founded for the study of this science; and Daniel was made by the king's decree master over all the Chaldean astrologers.

It was a common custom in the days of Samuel, to go to the seers or men of understanding in the times, to be informed concerning future contingencies and other matters, and we find Saul consenting to the proposal of his servant, to go to the seer and inquire respecting the strayed asses of Kish, Saul's father, which they were sent out in search of. Also we find that David when in Keilah, having heard that Saul was coming to beseech him, was desirous of knowing the truth of the matter and if he were coming as reported; and whether the men of Keilah would be true to him, or would betray him, and being informed they would betray him into the hands of the enemy, who were seeking his life, he fled into the wilderness of Kiph, and escaped the danger impending over him.

Space will not permit detailing minutely the progress of astrology in Egypt, Babylon, Persia, Greece, Arabia, China, India and the nations of Europe; we must therefore content ourselves with a few particulars. The first Egyptian astrologer of importance was Hermes, who lived at a period anterior to Moses. Dr. Cudworth observes that beyond doubt there was among the Egyptians such a man as Thoth, Theuth or Tauth, who was called the first Hermes, who together with letters, was the inventor of arts and sciences, as arithmetic, geometry, astronomy, and of the hieroglyphic learning. The Egyptians also had among them another eminent advancer or restorer of learning who was called the second Hermes, who composed books on several arts and sciences, which books were said to be carefully preserved by the priests in the inmost recesses of the temples. The same author observes that in the religious processions of the Egyptians the precentor goes first, carrying two of the books of Hermes with him. After him follows the Horoscopus, who is particularly instructed in astrological books, which are four. These four books might have been the Tetrabiblos of Claudius Ptolemy, before mentioned, and which are studied at the present day.

Diodorus informs us that the "Chaldeans in Babylon, were a colony of the Egyptians, and they became famous for astrology, having learned it from the priests of Egypt."

In Persia, the names of Zoroaster and Gjamasp stand on record as eminent astrologers; the former lived about 520 years before Christ, and the latter in the reign of King Gushtasp.

In Greece flourished the famous astrologer, Anaximander, who was born 610 years before Christ; also Anaxagoras, Thales, Euripides, Socrates and Pericles; after these, followed Pythagoras, Plato, Porphyry, Aristotle, Proclus, Conon, Democritus, Hippocrates and other famous astrologers too numerous to particularize here.

In Rome, we find Virgil, Cicero, Prepertius, Macrobius, Horace and Gellius, as devoting themselves to the study of astrology; also Manillus, whose astrological treatise is still extant. The "Universal History" also mentions some learned men among the Arabians, who studied and wrote on this science. Among Europeans, may be mentioned Cornelius Agrippa, Jerom, Cardan, and Placidus de Titus. In the fifteenth century, Regiomontanus published his "Ephemerides" for astrological purposes, containing the planets, longitudes, aspects, etc., for thirty years, and so eager were persons of all nations to obtain this work, that all the copies were soon bought up at the price of twelve Hungarian pieces of gold each.

In the English nation, if we go back to the learned men of former days, we find them all consenting to the belief in planetary influence. We may commence with the noted astrologer, Oliver, of Malmsbury, in the year 1060; and near to him, Herbert, of Lorraine, 1095; John, of Hexam and Simeon, of Durham; Aegidius of St. Albans, Roger Bacon, Robert Grouthead, John Holyhood, Michael Scot, Duns Scotus, William Grizaunt, Clinton Langley, John Killingsworth, Geoffrey Chaucer, John Waller, the Duke of Gloucester, Robert Recorde, and many others.

In the seventeenth century, may be noticed the names of Dr. Mead, Blagrave, Flamstead, Ramsey, Dr. Goad, Partridge, Elias Ashmole, William Lilly, John Gadbury, Richard Ball, Dr. Saunders, Dr. Dee the physician to Queen Elizabeth, and numbers of others who were famous for their learning and knowledge of astrology. During this period the science of the stars shone forth in the refulgent splendor of a noonday sun, and again its grandeur declined before the baneful influence of prejudice, and scepticism which caused cruel and unjust laws to be enacted to suppress it, which laws have continued their effect till the latter part of the present century. But the discerning public are now beginning to reason on the subject, and say that these learned, great, and good men, whom we have here enumerated, could not have all been deluded, but that they must have had sufficient grounds to have supported their belief, and which the writings, calculations and experiences of astrologers of the present period daily prove.

No other science that I am aware of has such an honorable and ancient record as that of astrology. Even if we except that part of the history of the Jews, by Josephus, where he says that God taught Adam astrology by inspiration, and Adam taught his son, Seth, yet there is enough left of the history of the Jews and of astrology to show that the science originated at a very early period in the history of mankind; not only that, but astrology has an honorable history in every nation or race of people on the face of the earth that has attained any degree of civilization. Even the enemies of astrology cannot deny that fact. In the above short sketch of the history of astrology, I have only given the account of that science as published by persons who were not prejudiced against it, but even in giving the history of astrology as published by its most bitter enemies, the reader will be astonished at the amount of praise given to it, although they have tried to say everything they could against it and its professors; yet in spite of their enmity, it has been impossible for them to speak the truth and not praise it; and really their praise is more worthy of notice than the unbiassed history of the science that we have from the astrologers themselves, or its historians who have lived in almost all ages and in every nation, since civilization began. If our enemies praise us, there must be some truth in their praise, or they would not bestow it.

In the remainder of this history of that science, I shall quote only from persons who have written against it, and who have done everything possible to crush it, either by fair means or foul. I shall now let the enemies of astrology speak for themselves on this subject.

The first author I shall refer to, is the late Richard A. Proctor, of England, who became quite noted on account of his popular lectures on astronomy. Probably no author has been so bitter against astrology, or appeared to be more afflicted with that peculiar disease which might be termed *astrophobia*. Once I heard him lecture on astronomy in Chickering Hall, New York. He there stated, that even if we could predict epidemics of diseases, plagues, earthquakes, etc., by the aid of astronomy, it would degrade that science to do so. For my part, I cannot understand how a science or human beings can be degraded by being useful in warding off or in any way mitigating those fatal epidemics or calamities which often afflict the human race.

After the New York *World* had succeeded in having John De Leon, an astrologer, sent to Sing Sing for fifteen years, in order to justify itself in the eyes of the public, it employed Richard A. Proctor to write an article on the "Humbug of Astrology," which was published in the New York *World*, on Sunday, Feb. 6, 1887. In that article he gives a

SHORT HISTORY OF ASTROLOGY

and says:

"Can it be (many have said to me), that all the wise men of past ages, those to whom we attribute so many of the beliefs that to this day we hold sacred, can in this matter of astrology have been wholly decived? Not only among all the leading races of antiquity, and in all the chief civilized nations, but during periods of time such as no other faith can boast of having swayed, men held firmly to the belief that the stars in their courses foretell, nay rule the fortunes of men. The cuneiform inscriptions of Assyria, the hieroglyphs of Egypt, the most ancient records of Persia, India and China agree in showing that of old, all men believed the sun and moon, the planets and the stars to be as 'Radiant Mercuries, carrying through ether in perpetual ound decrees and resolutions of the gods.' Nay, throughont the long period, to be measured by thousands of years, when all men held this belief, the most part held *what anciently had been the belief of all*, that the sun and moon and all the host of heaven are not merely the exponents of the will of the gods, but are actually as gods themselves. To this day, are not only all languages permeated by the expressions belonging to the old astrological teachings, but all the feasts and fasts of the religions of our age, purified though they have been from Sabaistic beliefs, attest in the clearest way, to the astronomer, their origin in Sabaistic observances. To this day Christians and Jews, Buddhists and Mahommedans, regulate their yearly ceremonials by the solstices and equinoctial passages of the sun, and the weekly renewals of religious observances were derived originally from the moon's motions, and were determined by the moon, 'when new' in her first quarter, 'full' in her third quarter, and 'new' again. Among the Jews and Mahommedans, indeed, the 'new moon' observances and those which formerly attended the rising and setting of the sun, are still retained. Astrology, the outcome of those Sabaistic beliefs which were once universally prevalent, had a most respectable origin, and if common opinion could prove any doctrine just, astrology it seems should have been based on truth. Why then should it now be held only worthy of belief by the ignorant and silly and be maintained as true only by rogues and charlatans?"

If it be true, as Mr. Proctor states, and those statements can be verified by the history of nearly all civilized nations, in all past ages, that in ancient times all the learned men studied, and all were believers, in astrology—so much so, that even at the present day, all languages are permeated by old astrological teachings,—it appears to me a very bold assertion for Mr. Proctor to make, and without a particle of proof, when he says that "belief in astrology now is only maintained by the ignorant and silly, and the rogues and charlatans."

In the latter part of this volume, I shall bring enough facts to prove to any reasonable mind, that "it is only the ignorant and silly, the rogues and charlatans," *who do not believe in astrology* except in a few cases similar to Trilby before she met Svengali, and was hypnotized, she being tune-deaf, and therefore could not enjoy harmony or music. There are also others who cannot enjoy the beauties of nature on account of being what is termed color-blind. But I shall refer to this subject in the latter part of this volume, and will only add here, that it is not good reasoning or good law for any person to say that because he is blind all others who can see ought to be sent to prison, or because he is deaf that all who say they can hear are ignorant and silly, or rogues or charlatans, and yet this is Professor Proctor's logic and law, and I defy any one to prove the contrary. It is this kind of reasoning and law that has often caused our judges and juries to fill our prisons with convicts.

I shall now illustrate what Mr. Proctor means when he says that throughout the long period, to be measured by thousands of years, when all men held this belief, that the most part held what anciently had been the belief of all, and which was not only proved by the cuneiform inscriptions of Assyria, the hieroglyphs of Egypt, the most ancient records of Persia, India and China, all agreeing in showing that of old all men believed the Sun, Moon, the planets and stars "ruled the fortunes of men."

In addition to the above statements, all of which are true to the letter, we have a remarkable illustration in the names of the days of the week, and the hours of the day, which have been adopted by almost every civilized nation. There are but few people at the present day who know how we came to call the days of the week by the names that are given them, and why they came to be so named, and why we have *seven* and not any other number, and why they run in the present order—Sunday, Monday, Tuesday, Wednesday, Thursday, Friday and Saturday. Some people might think that if they had been named after the planets they would be named in the order that the planets run. That is, counting from the outer planet Saturn, then Jupiter, Mars, Sun, Venus, Mercury and the Moon; or, in other words, they would have run Saturday, Thursday, Tuesday, Sunday, Friday, Wednesday and Monday.

In order to make the reader understand the principles of the arrangements of the days of the week, I will state that we have the twelve hours of the day and the twelve hours of the night from the twelve signs of the Zodiac; in short, twelve was reconized as a sacred number by the ancients; even Christ had his twelve apostles. Formerly the hours were reconed from sunrise to sunset, instead of 12 o'clock midnight to 12 o'clock midnight, but that was during the time when most of the civilized people dwelt near the equator, and the days and nights in those parts are nearly of equal length all the year round. But afterwards when people began to migrate to both the northern and southern latitudes and to settle there, they reckoned the hours from the middle of the day, or when the sun arrives in the midheaven or highest point to the middle of the night, or when the sun is at the lowest point, the days varying so in length in the higher latitudes that the people could not measure time so accurately by the rising or setting of the sun. The ancients not only allotted a planet to rule or govern each day in the week, but a particular planet also ruled or was alloted to each hour of the day, and those hours were called planetary hours and were numbered or recorded from the outer planet Saturn, inward to Jupiter, Mars, Sun, Venus, Mercury and the Moon.

What is termed the *planetary hour* is the unit by which the names of the days of the week are controlled or regulated, or, in other words, it is the unit which causes the first day to be Sunday, second Monday, third Mars' day, fourth Mercury's day, fifth Jupiter's day, sixth Venus' day, and the seventh Saturn's day. The ancients allotted or gave the first day to the Sun, and the hour that commenced that day, counting from sunrise, was allotted to that luminary; the second hour to the planet Venus, the third hour to Mercury, the fourth hour to the Moon, etc. It is not to be wondered at that in very ancient times, or rather in the prehistoric period, the people recognized the Sun as the cause of all earthly blessings, such as light, heat, and the cause of the growth of plants, fruit and grain of every kind which nourishes animals and man; that those ancient people should have allotted the first day of the week to that most conspicuous of the heavenly bodies, and that the Sun's day should have the first hour of the day appropriated to it. Then Venus the second, and Mercury the third, Moon the fourth, Saturn the fifth, Jupiter the sixth, and Mars the seventh, counting from the farthest planet to the nearest. The Sun likewise governs the 8th, 15th and 22d; Venus governs the 23d; Mercury the 24th, and the Moon governs the first hour of the next day; therefore it is called Moon's day, and so on; Saturn governs the second hour, Jupiter 3d, Mars 4th, Sun 5th, Venus 6th, Mercury 7th, Moon 8th. The Moon also governs the 15th and 22d, Saturn 23d, Jupiter 24th, and Mars the first hour of the following day, which is called Tuesday, and so on each day, commencing at sunrise, according to the following table:

SUNDAY.

Sun	Ven.	Mer.	Moon	Sat.	Jup.	Mars
1	2	3	4	5	6	7
8	9	10	11	12	13	14
15	16	17	18	19	20	21
22	23	24				

MONDAY.

Moon	Sat.	Jup.	Mars	Sun	Ven.	Mer.
1	2	3	4	5	6	7
8	9	10	11	12	13	14
15	16	17	18	19	20	21
22	23	24				

TUESDAY.

Mars	Sun	Ven.	Mer.	Moon	Sat.	Jup.
1	2	3	4	5	6	7
8	9	10	11	12	13	14
15	16	17	18	19	20	21
22	23	24				

WEDNESDAY.

Mer.	Moon	Sat.	Jup.	Mars	Sun	Ven.
1	2	3	4	5	6	7
8	9	10	11	12	13	14
15	16	17	18	19	20	21
22	23	24				

THURSDAY.

Jup.	Mars	Sun	Ven.	Mer.	Moon	Sat.
1	2	3	4	5	6	7
8	9	10	11	12	13	14
15	16	17	18	19	20	21
22	23	24				

FRIDAY.

Ven.	Mer.	Moon	Sat.	Jup.	Mars	Sun
1	2	3	4	5	6	7
8	9	10	11	12	13	14
15	16	17	18	19	20	21
22	23	24				

SATURDAY.

Sat.	Jup.	Mars	Sun	Ven.	Mer.	Moon
1	2	3	4	5	6	7
8	9	10	11	12	13	14
15	16	17	18	19	20	21
22	23	24				

In a number of languages, for instance, the French and the Latin, and some others, the people still retain the names of the planets for the names of the days in the week. But some four hundred years after England had been conquered by the Romans, the English and other nations were left to take care of themselves; they were invaded or conquered by pagans called Goths, from Gothland, and the Norsemen from the North, who came from Norway and Sweden. Among those noted generals was one named Thor; his wife's name was Frea. When he died, Jupiter's day, or Thursday, was named in honor or remembrance of Thor, and Frea, his wife, had Venus' day or Friday named in honor of her. Even at the present day travelers in Sweden have the tombs of Thor and Frea pointed out to them. Another noted general was named Woden, or the man of the woods, and when he died they named Wednesday or Mercury's day in honor of him. Another famous general was Twi, and when he died, Tuesday or Mars' day was named after him; and no doubt if those wars had continued and the generals had gone on conquering the nations, each day of the week would have been named after some great commander of some noted army which came to invade England and other barbarous countries; as we have the eighth month of the year named after the Roman Emperor Augustus, and the seventh month in honor of Julius Cæsar.

The Quakers and Shakers have done everything they could to change the names of the days of the week, as they had an impression that they were all named after the pagan gods and thought it wicked to call days after those heathen deities, so they called Sunday the Lord's day or first day, Monday the second day, Tuesday the third day, and the fourth, fifth, sixth and seventh days.

During the French Revolution, the Revolutionists not only abolished all religion and worshipped the Goddess of Reason, but they began a new calendar and changed the names of the days of the week, and broke up the weeks entirely, and made each week ten days long, and three weeks in a moon or month.* But this system of reckoning

---

* THE REPUBLICAN CALENDAR OF FRANCE.

In 1793 the National Convention of the First French Republic decreed that the old era should be abolished in all civil affairs and that a new era should commence from the foundation of the Republic.

The commencement of the year was fixed at the autumnal equinox, which nearly coincided with the epoch of the foundation of the Republic. The names of the ancient months were abolished, and others substituted having reference to agricultural labors or the state of nature in different seasons of the year.

Beginning 22 September, 1792, the year was divided into 12 months of 30 days, each with 5 complementary days at the end to be celebrated as festivals, and were dedicated to Virtue, Genius, Labor, Opinion, Reward. Every fourth or Olympic year was to have a sixth complementary day to be called "revolution day," and every period of four years was to be called a Franciade.

The first, second and third centurial years, viz , 100, 200, 300, were to be common years, the fourth centurial year, 400, was to be a leap year, and this was to continue till the fortieth centurial, 4000, which was to be a common year. *The months were to be divided into three parts of ten days each,* called decades. The names of the months and the days of the Gregorian Calendar, to which they corresponded were as follows :

time was so artificial and contrary to all the laws of nature that it was soon discontinued. The French people, like all other Christians, and I might say all other civilized nations, call the names of the days of the weeks after the names of the planets, which govern those days, and also have the seven days of the week similar to other nations.

Indeed in every civilized or half civilized nation on the face of the earth they have the names of the days of the week called after the planets and have them arranged according to the planetary hours, commencing the first hour after midnight with the name of the planet that rules that day.

The planetary hours are not all of equal length, and they are reckoned from sunrise to sunset, and not from 12 o'clock at night, when the day really commences, but at sunrise. In summer the planetary hour of the day is much longer than the planetary hour of the night. The way to calculate the length of the planetary hours for any particular day in the year is to find out what time the Sun rises and what time it sets on that particular day, then add the number of hours together, afterwards reduce the number of hours from sunrise to sunset into minutes by multiplying them by 60 and adding the odd minutes to that sum, and then dividing it by 12, which gives the length in hours and minutes of the planetary hour of that particular day. When the planetary hour is more than 60 minutes long in the day it is less than 60 minutes in the night, but near the 21st of March and the 21st of September the planetary hour in all latitudes is the same length—that is, 60 minutes for both night and day.

I propose further on to prove that the planets still rule and always did rule the days of the week that they are named after, and also each hour of the day is ruled by its own particular planet, and in the order of their distance from the earth, commencing with the most distant planet, Saturn, then Jupiter, Mars, Sun, Venus, Mercury and the Moon,

Probably there is nothing more convincing of the general belief in Astrology throughout the whole civilized world in former ages than the names of the days of the week, and the planetary hours governing the same, and which we continue to make use of even to the present day.

Vendemaire	Vintage	Sept. 22 to Oct. 21.
Brumaire	Foggy	Oct 21 to Nov. 20.
Frimaire	Sleety	Nov. 21 to Dec. 20.
Nivose	Snowy	Dec. 21 to Jan. 19.
Pluviose	Rainy	Jan. 20 to Feb 18.
Ventose	Windy	Feb. 19 to Mar. 20.
Germinal	Budding	Mar. 21 to April 19.
Floreal	Flowery	April 20 to May 19.
Prairial	Pasture	May 20 to June 18.
Messidor	Harvest	June 19 to July 18.
Thermidor	Heat	July 19 to Aug. 17.
Fructidor	Fruit	Aug. 18 to Sept. 15.

Floreal (the "flowery") the eighth month in the Republican Calendar of France, which from Nov. 24. 1793 to Sept. 9, 1805, was used in place of the Gregorian. Floreal began April 19-22 and ended May 18-21.

In Roman days the festival of Flora, the Goddess of Flowers, was between 28th April and 3d of May.

By Napoleon's command this new system was abolished and the era of the Gregorian Calendar resumed on Jan. 1, 1807. (See note on page 248.)

It is an utter impossibility for those days to have been arranged in the order in which they are by chance, or without a knowledge of the planetary hours, therefore those learned men who first arranged the days in the week must have had a practical knowledge of Astrology, and such as but few learned men at the present day possess, and there must have been thousands of Astrologers in every nation and in all parts of the world which claimed to be at all civilized, to have had such an influence on mankind as to have made the names of those days to become universal, or to be adopted by all civilized nations on the face of the earth. There is nothing to be compared to it, even in religion science, politics, or even fashion; and as Professor Proctor says:

"Astrology had a most respectable origin, and if common opinion could prove any doctrine just, astrology must, it would seem, have been based on truth."

Professor Proctor goes on to say in his

"HUMBUG OF ASTROLOGY":

"Having thus decided on the special influence of the seven planets, the ancients readily formed a system by which, as they supposed, the action of those influences on the fortunes of men and nations might be determined. When they had also learned how to calculate the position of the planets for any length of time in advance, they believed that they had obtained full power of predicting the fortunes of each man as soon as having calculated the aspects of the heavens at his nativity they had learned which planets were most potent in their influences of his fortune.

"And with this power of prediction came some power of favoring good fortune and preventing evil; in other words, in ruling as well as reading the planets."

I think that astrologers in all parts of the world ought to thank Professor Proctor for praising up Astrology as he has done, and for having laid the principles of that science on such a solid and firm foundation.

When Mr. Proctor says: "The ancient Astrologers having thus decided on the special influence of the seven planets" and "their influences on the fortunes of men and nations," etc., he does not tell his readers that the ancients had observed the influences in the horoscopes of men and in the horoscopes of nations for thousands of years, and that those influences were unfailing in their effect, and that the effects of the planetary influences are observed in hundreds of thousands of horoscopes, even up to the present day, by astrologers in all parts of the world.

I have myself observed the effects of the planetary influence in over two hundred thousand horoscopes, and continued to observe their effects in some horoscopes over 40 years, and every man who studies and practices Astrology becomes convinced of the effects of the "seven planets on the fortunes of men and nations" and must agree with John Kepler, the greatest Astronomer that ever lived, when he says: "A most unfailing experience of the excitement of sublunary nature by the conjunction and aspects of the planets has instructed and compelled my unwilling belief."

If Richard A. Proctor had spent some time in making calculations of the seven planets and observing their effect in horoscopes as the great Astronomer, John Kepler, had spent years in doing, it is possible that instead of writing an article for the New York *World* helping the editors to justify their conduct in the eyes of the public for being the means of sending an innocent man to Sing Sing prison for fifteen years for the sole purpose of booming their paper, as the chief editor afterwards wrote a letter, over his own signature, acknowledging such to be the case,—I say, if Mr. Proctor had followed the example of John Kepler instead of calling all Astrologers "lying knaves, silly charlatans and unscrupulous rascals," etc., he might have been like Bishop Butler, who, after writing and doing all he could to expose Astrology, undertook to study it so that he could condemn the science with more effect, and wound up by writing and publishing one of the best text books on Astrology we now have.

The next author who has written against Astrology and to whom I shall call the reader's attention is the Rev. Thomas Dick, of England. In a work which he published there, and was republished by Harper Brothers, of New York City, and called the

"IMPROVEMENT OF SOCIETY BY THE DIFFUSION OF KNOWLEDGE."

It was republished about the year 1830 and went through a great many editions, both in England and this country. Mr. Dick says on page 32, when referring to Astrology:

"This art has been practiced in every period of time. Among the Romans the people were so infatuated with it that the Astrologers, or, as they were then called, the *mathematicians,* maintained their ground in spite of all the edicts of the Emperors to expel them from the capital; and after they were at length expelled by a formal decree of the Senate, they found so much protection from the credulity of the people that they still remained in Rome unmolested. Among the Chaldeans, the Assyrians, the Egyptians, the Greeks, and the Arabians, in ancient times, *Astrology was uniformly included in the list of sciences* and used as one species of divination by which they attempted to pry into the secrets of futurity. The Brahmins of India at an early period introduced this art into that country, and by means of it have rendered themselves the arbiters of good and evil hours,* and of the fortunes of their fellow-men, and have thus raised themselves to great authority and influence among the illiterate† of the multitude. They are consulted as oracles, and like all other imposters, they have taken great care never to sell their answers without a handsome remuneration. In almost every country in the world this art is still

---

* Or, in other words, the Brahmins calculated the times of the good and evil planetary hours for the people.

† The Rev. Thomas Dick should not entirely have lost his head in the excitement of writing against Astrology; he infers that it was only the illiterate who believed in Astrology, and in a few lines further on he tells us that all the Kings, Queens, and the learned and scientific men of the world believed in Astrology at that period of the world's history.

practiced, and only a short time has elapsed since the princes and legislators of Europe were directed in the most important concerns of the state by the advice or predictions of Astrologers. In the time of Queen Catharine De Medici, Astrology was so much in vogue that nothing, however trifling, was to be done without consulting the stars. The Astrologer Morin, in the seventeenth century, directed Cardinal Richeleu's motions in some of his journeys, and Louisa Marie de Gonzaga, Queen of Poland, gave 200 crowns to carry on an edition of his astrological Gallicoa; and in the reign of Henry the Third and Henry the Fourth, of France, the predictions of Astrologers were the common theme of court conversation. Even in the present day and in the metropolis of the British Empire this fallacious art is practiced, and its professors are resorted to for judicial information, not only by the vulgar, but by many in the higher spheres of life.* The extensive annual sale of more than 200,000 copies of Moore's Almanac, which abounds in such predictions, and of similar publications, is a striking proof of the belief which is still attached to the doctrines of Astrology in our own age and country."

In spite of the venom which the reverend gentleman has tried to heap on the science of Astrology and its professors, and probably no man has tried harder to crush that profession than the Rev. Thomas Dick, the reader can see for himself that it was impossible for him not to praise the science, and prove that it has been practiced in every age and nation on the face of the earth, and believed in by the learned men, the nobility, and kings and queens.

The next persons whom I shall refer to as having written and published works condemning Astrology are William and Robert Chambers, of Edinburgh, Scotland.

In Chambers' Encyclopedia, published at Edinburgh, Scotland, and republished by J. B. Lippincott & Co., of Philadelphia, in 1872, under the word Astrology, the following is said:

"Astrology meant originally much the same as Astronomy, the knowledge of the stars, and was at length restricted to the science of predicting future events, especially the fortunes of men from the position of heavenly bodies. *This was considered the higher or real science*, while the mere knowledge of the stars themselves, their places, and motions, or Astronomy, was, till a very recent period, cultivated mostly with a view to judicial Astrology. Astrology is one of the most ancient forms of superstition, and is found prevailing among the nations of the East, Egyptians, Chaldeans, Hindoos, Chinese at the very dawn of history. The Jews became much addicted to it after their captivity. It spread into the West and to Rome about the beginning of the Christain era. Astrologers played an important part at Rome, where they were called *Chaldeans* and *Mathematicians*, and though often banished by the Senate and Emperor under pain of death, and otherwise persecuted, they continued to hold their ground. The Roman poet, Manilus, author of an astronomical poem still extant, was addicted to Astrology, and even Ptolemy." [The writer here refers to Claudius Ptolemy, the author of the Ptolemaic System of Astronomy and "Ptolemy Tetrabiblos," or Four Books on Astrology. These books have

---

* In the Lives of Necromancer, by William Goodwin, on page 253, he says : "That Robert Dudley, Elizabeth's chief favorite was sent to consult Dr. Dee, a famous Astrologer, as to the aspects of the stars, that they might fix on an auspicious day for celebrating her coronation."

stood the test of over 2,000 years, and are text-books on that science at the present day.] "The Astronomer did not escape the infection which in his time had become universal. It accorded well with the predestinarian doctrines of Mohammedanism, and was accordingly cultivated with great ardor by the Arabs from the 7th to the 13th century. For centuries the most learned men continued devoted to the delusive science. Regiomontanus, the famous mathematician; Carda, even Tycho Brahe and Kepler, could not shake off the fascination of Astrology. Kepler could not deny a certain connection between the position of the planets and the qualities of those born under them."

The Astrologers who lived in the era of the above scientific and learned men were certainly in very good company, to say the least, and the law makers and senators must certainly have been an ignorant and prejudiced class, similar to what they are at the present day. In all ages and nations, especially in Christian countries, it has been the custom for legislators to enact laws to suppress everything that was not popular with the masses, as they say the rights of the few must give way to the majority. If it was religion, the professors were imprisoned or executed for being heretics; if it was science, its advocates were imprisoned or executed for being witches or wizards. If the intelligence of the people of any country were such that they rebelled against such fanatic laws, so that they could not be enacted, or if such laws were enacted and the legislatures were compelled to repeal them, yet in all such countries there has always been invented traps or snares to catch these persons advocating any new doctrine or science, or in some way compelling such persons to break or violate some law that had no relation to, and was never intended to oppose that science or new religion which the professors were teaching or advocating.*

In the days of Christ we read in Matthew, 22d chapter, from 15th to 23d verses, that the Pharisees took counsel to entrap Christ in his talk, and on a subject that had nothing whatever to do with the religion he was teaching, but related to the subject of tribute or taxes which the Jews had to pay. Judea previously having been conquered by the Romans, the people of that country were compelled to pay tribute to their conquerers; and they knew if they could get Christ to say that the Jews were not to pay tribute, then the authorities would have Christ arrested, and if he said the Jews were to pay tribute then the Jews would condemn him. But Christ said, "Why tempt me, ye hypocrites? Show me the tribute money. And they brought unto him a penny, and he said, Whose is this image and superscription? And they said unto him, Cæsar's. Then said he unto them, Render unto Cæsar

---

* After the election and inauguration of Grover Cleveland in 1893, business came almost to a standstill and banks were failing daily. Vast numbers of the unemployed commenced marching from Ohio to Washington, D. C. to urge Congress to do something to relieve the distress of the unemployed. They went by the name of Coxey's Army. That individual and his followers having arrived in Washington, were marching up the Capitol grounds, and the crowd was such that Coxey could not pass, neither could he retreat, and in order to pass he stepped on the grass. The moment he did so he was arrested, although there were thousands of others walking on the grass. He was tried, not for any criminal act he had committed, but because he did not "*keep off the grass.*" Of course the trial was a farce, yet I believe he had to suffer imprisonment for several weeks.

the things that are Cæsar's and unto God the things that are God's." And Matthew goes on to say, " they went their way."

"A KNOWLEDGE OF ASTROLOGY DOES NOT COUNT, EXCEPT SO FAR AS IT PROVES A PERSON INSANE OR AN IMBECILE."

Chambers' Encyclopedia states that John Kepler was the greatest Astronomer of all ages. He was born near Stuttgart, Germany, December 27, 1571. It was he who discovered what is known as the first three great laws in Astronomy. "The first law is that the planets move in elipses, with the Sun in one of the foci. The second, that the Radius-vector sweeps over equal areas in equal times. The third, that the square of the periodical time is proportional to the cube of the same distance." He made other great discoveries in Astronomy, and was also a noted mathematician.

Kepler also made many discoveries in Astrology, among others what is called Kepler's Aspects; these are the semi-sextile, the semi-square, the quintile, and the sesquiquadrate and the biquintile.

Robert G. Ingersoll, in one of his popular lectures, praises John Keplar on account of his knowledge of Astronomy and states that the scientific world is indebted to that great man for wonderful discoveries in that science, but at the same time Ingersoll condemns Astrology and compares it to the superstitions of the Christian religion, and he entirely ignores John Kepler's discoveries in Astrology, or at least they do not count with that popular infidel. In some respects Robert G. Ingersoll may be compared to the people in England and other Christian nations. Some years ago, when Lord Dufferin was British Ambassador at Constantinople, he one day heard a number of cannons firing in the street or public square, and went out to make inquiries as to what was the cause of the celebration. One of the Turkish officers whom he asked told him that the government had been making reforms for the Christians in the Turkish dominions, and said this was the day these reforms took effect. The officer also said : "By the way, we have also made reforms for the Mohammedans, and they also go into effect to-day, but you know reforms for the Mohammedans do not count with you Christian people." It appears that discoveries in Astrology do not count with either Christians or infidels.

> "Strange such a difference there should be
> 'Twixt tweedledum and tweedledee."

Is it any wonder John Kepler " could not shake off the fascination of Astrology?" For in addition to proving the "connection between the position of the planets and the qualities of those born under them," he also states that he had had " an unfailing experience of the influence of the planets by the conjunction and aspects, which had instructed and compelled his unwilling belief."

In a small work called " The Uses of Biography," by Edwin Paxton Hood, London, England, published in 1853, in Chapter VII., the writer gives an account of the foibles and vices of great men, and on pages 116 and 117 we have the following sentences:

"Cardinal Richelieu, the minister of a great Empire (France) believed in the calculation of nativities. Even Sir Isaac Newton gave credit to the idle nonsense of judicial Astrology; he who first calculated the distances of the stars and revealed the laws of motion by which the Supreme Being organizes and keeps in their orbits unnumbered worlds; he who had revealed the mysteries of the stars themselves. Dryden, Sir Isaac Newton's contemporary, believed in the same absurdity."

[Is it not strange that a man may excel in all the modern sciences, and even make wonderful discoveries in such as Astronomy and mathematics, and be counted sane and sensible, and even a very learned man, but the moment he touches Astrology, by some legerdemain, he is said instantly to become insane or a scoundrel? There is no doubt but Sir Isaac Newton was an excellent Astrologer, and even calculated his own and probably most of his friend's horoscopes. Cardinal Richelieu no doubt understood Astrology, but probably he employed eminent Astrologers to do the most of the calculations for him in his judicial Astrology, as had Queen Elizabeth.]

"It is published by William Congreve, an English actor, and the same was also published in the Encyclopedia Britanica, and a number of other publications) that John Dryden calculated his son Charles' horoscope, and the predictions were fulfilled to the letter. Mr. Congreve states 'that when Mrs. Dryden commenced in labor of her son Charles, Dryden left his watch in charge of one of the ladies in attendance with a strict injunction to notice the exact moment of the child's birth. In about a week after her confinement Mr. Dryden took the occasion to tell his wife that he had calculated the child's horoscope and observed with grief that the child was born in an evil hour. That Jupiter, Venus and the Sun were all under the earth, and the Lord of the ascendant was afflicted with a hateful square of Saturn and Mars. He went on to tell her that if he lives to arrive at his 8th birthday he will come near a violent death, but if he escapes that, and I see but small hopes that he will, in his 23d year he will again be under the same evil direction, and if he escapes that also, the 33d and 34th years will, I fear— There he was interrupted by the grief of Lady Dryden, who could no longer hear one calamity after another prophesied for her new born son.'

"When young Dryden arrived near his 8th year, it was arranged that Lady Dryden should spend the Summer vacation with her Uncle Mourdant, and Mr. Dryden was invited to the country seat of the Earl of Berkshire, his brother-in-law, to spend his vacation." [It appears from the account published that Dryden had two sons, John and Charles; it was arranged that each of them should take one of the boys. Lady Dryden wished her husband to take John, as she desired to have Charles with her, feeling that he would be safer under her maternal care than in his father's company, "but Dryden insisted on taking Charles, and they parted in anger."

"On the child's 8th birthday it was arranged by the Earl of Berkshire that his guests should go hunting, and Dryden, to keep the child out of mischief, set him a double lesson in Latin, with a strict injunction that he should not go out of the house. Charles was performing his duty in obedience to his father, but as ill-fate would have it the stag made towards the house, and the noise alarming the servants they hastened out to see the sport. One of the servants took young Dryden by the hand and led him out to see it also; when just as they came to the gate, the stag being at bay with the dogs, made a bold push and leaped over the court wall, which was low and very old, and the dogs following threw down a part of the wall ten yards in length, under which Charles Dryden lay buried. He was immediately dug out, and after six weeks languishing in a dangerous way he recovered. In the 23d year of his age, Charles fell from the top of an old tower belonging to the Vatican at Rome, occasioned by a dizziness with which he was seized, the heat of the day being excessive. He again recovered, but was ever after in a languishing, sickly state. In the 33d year of his age, being returned to England, he was unhappily drowned at Windsor. He had, with another gentleman, swam twice across the Thames, but returning a third time, it was supposed he was taken with a cramp, because he called out for help, though too late. The father's calculation proved but too prophetical."

Some persons will say, what is the use calculating horoscopes when the fate is inevitable and cannot be avoided, or in any way warded off, even when the nature of the accident and the time of the event has been predicted? But the reader ought to bear in mind that the aspects in this nativity are what are called marked. The mere expression of Mr. Dryden's, that "the child was born *in an evil hour* (meaning an evil planetary hour); *Venus, Jupiter and the Sun were all under the earth, the ascendant being afflicted with a hateful square of Mars and Saturn,*" alone proves that he was an Astrologer, and also that the child had a marked horoscope and that it would die a violent death. It also shows that the ascendant was what is termed the "Giver of Life," and being so afflicted it was almost impossible for the native to die a natural death. Therefore in horoscopes of this kind, the stars are said to rule or govern the native, and the native does not rule the stars, but he is *controlled by them.*

Horoscopes, like that of Charles Dryden, are the exception and not the rule, but when we meet with them there is nothing more convincing of the truth of Astrology. Indeed, in this kind of nativities *Astrology becomes a positive or exact science,* and in such cases it is almost useless fighting against fate. In the case of young Dryden, although he had wealthy, kind and indulgent parents, also servants to take special care of him, yet those servants went and led him into the very evil they were charged to guard him against. With such "unfailing experience" no wonder when such men as Sir Isaac Newton, John Kepler, Cardinal Richelieu and John Dryden could see such convincing proofs of the truth of Astrology that they should look upon the science of Astronomy only as an elementary branch of the science of Astrology, as we look upon A, B, C, or the English alphabet, as merely the elements of language. But the real science of language only begins when we associate these letters into syllables and words, and associate meanings to words, and then associate words into sentences, and those sentences into paragraphs, etc.

William and Robert Chambers, in their Encyclopedia, say that:

"Astronomy or the knowledge of the stars was till a very recent period cultivated mostly with a view to judicial Astrology," and that "this (Astrology) was considered the *higher or real science,*" and as Richard A.

Proctor says: "That throughout the long period, to be measured by thousands of years, when all men held this belief, the most part held what anciently had been the belief of all," and "to this day are not all languages permeated by the expressions belonging to the old astrological teachings?"

The reader ought to bear in mind that those men who held to this "belief" were at that time the most learned men on the face of the earth, and were all able to calculate nativities, and to prove the truth of their observations, and no doubt they were all similar to John Dryden and John Kepler, who had had "a most unfailing experience of the excitement of sublunary nature by the conjunctions and aspects of the planets" in those horoscopes which they calculated.

Thus far I wish the reader to understand that in this section I have only been giving the evidence of witnesses against Astrology. If I were a lawyer and were pleading the cause of Astrology before a judge and jury, I think I should be justified in requesting the judge to throw the case out of court if the opponents of that science had no further evidence to offer, as the proof against Astrology so far is not valid or proved beyond a reasonable doubt. But on the contrary the evidence has gone altogether in favor of the truth of that science. But as a vast number of authors who have written against Astrology during the past two hundred years have employed what they term arguments against the science, and which they deem very conclusive, I think I ought to give some, if not all, of those arguments, and then let the readers judge for themselves. If the reader has been surprised at the testimony already brought by the witnesses against Astrology, I think he will be much more surprised with their arguments; as these arguments could not possibly stand a moment against any other science, no matter how ridiculous or nonsensical that science might be, and the only reason that I can account for these arguments having been brought against Astrology is that the people at large must be more or less insane and incapable of judging fairly in the matter. Possibly I am like the man who was confined in an insane asylum. When his friends went to see him they inquired why such a sensible man as he was thus confined. He made answer by saying: "It was only a matter of opinion which caused my confinement; I said that all the world was crazy, and they said I was crazy, and the majority ruled."

THE SUPPOSED ARGUMENTS WHICH THE ENEMIES OF ASTROLOGY HAVE BROUGHT AGAINST THAT SCIENCE.

One of the main arguments those professors always bring against Astrology is the law of gravitation. They argue that "as the Sun, Moon, planets and Stars are so far away from the earth, and man being such a small body, that the law of gravitation or attraction must have such a very insignificant effect on him that it is impossible to be felt or calculated, or that it can have any influence whatever." If it could be proven that the law of gravitation was the only law, force, or influence in the heavens above, or on the earth beneath, or in the water under the earth, and that the planets and signs of the Zodiac or the Sun or Moon could not act on the earth and its inhabitants in any other manner, then that argument might have some weight, but until that is proven no person but one perfectly ignorant of the laws of nature would think of making use of such a plea; yet I have known graduates and professors of colleges to bring it forward, deeming themselves very learned and wise in being able to urge such a weighty consideration against the science of Astrology, and in their wisdom they laughed at me for stating my belief in that science, and at my proofs of such belief.

Any person having a knowledge of modern science, I think, must admit that there are other influences and laws at work in nature, besides the law of gravitation. Take, for instance, the science of electricity. There are laws and principles in that science that are altogether at variance with the laws of gravitation, so far as we understand them at the present day, or are ever likely to understand them.

The rapid progress that is now being made in electrical science is simply astonishing. It looks at the present time that electricity is going to supersede steam and coal gas, and that before long our machinery, ships, railways and mills will be run by electricity, and that our houses will be lighted and warmed by that method.

Only compare electricity at the present day with what it was a hundred years ago, and the reader must admit that it is simply marvelous. Even if the professors of colleges could have had proofs at that time that there was no other force or influence in existence but the law of gravitation, such proofs would have very little weight at the present day; besides, there are other new forces constantly cropping out; we need only to look at photography at the present day, and look at it fifty years ago and compare the difference. The discovery of the X-Ray is another remarkable proof of forces and laws existing in nature that were previously never thought or dreamed of.

In the early part of the present century, Professor Faraday, of England, in studying the galvanic cells, discovered that two electric currents are in motion, and he named one "Cathode," the other "Anode." The first name was applied to the current entering the cell and the latter to the one leaving. These currents when passing through glass tubes produce a spark or glow. Other electricians and chemists have made investigations in that direction until Professor Roentgen, of Germany, in the latter part of 1895, was able to photograph through a plank of wood a foot in thickness, and various other substances which formerly it was believed that light never entered. Aluminum is very susceptible of having light transmitted through it. This light is believed to be the quintescence that the old philosophers tried to discover and make use of for thousands of years. Professor Edison has improved on those experiments by the use of electric light, and what is termed the X-Ray; and there is no telling at the present day what may be accomplished in that direction at some future time in the arts and sciences.

The ancient philosophers and Astrologers divided everything on the earth into four divisions, which they styled the elements or *essences*, and which four elements they named fire, earth, air and water; they also divided the heavenly bodies into those elements or essences, especially the signs of the Zodiac, and the planets, and the Sun and the Moon. The signs of the Zodiac were called the trigons or triplicities. The fiery signs were Aries, Leo, Sagittary; the earthy signs were Taurus, Virgo and Capricorn; the airy signs were Gemini, Libra and Aquarius, and the watery signs were Cancer, Scorpio and Pisces. The signs of any particular triplicity are in trine aspect to each other. The fiery signs were termed hot and dry; the earthy signs, cold and dry; the airy signs were hot and moist, and the watery signs were cold and moist. They also divided the nature or qualities of planets into these four elements or essences. The planet Saturn is cold and dry; Jupiter is hot and moist; Mars is hot and dry; the Sun is called temperate; that is, neither hot nor cold, and neither dry nor moist. Venus is cold and moist. Mercury is termed changeable, and it depends on what aspect it has to other planets, and is so controlled by *their* natures whether those planets are cold or moist, hot or dry, etc. The Moon is cold and moist.

Besides these four elements or essences of nature, the ancients were confident that another essence existed, which they called the quintessence, from the Latin quinti, five, and they believed that this quintessence pervaded all nature by a peculiar *ether*, that penetrated all nature, both animate and inanimate, on the same principle that the X-Ray discovered by Professor Roentgen penetrates or is transmitted through all bodies, especially animal and vegetable. And the ancients also believed that it even extended from one planet to another, and from the Sun to the Moon and the earth.

The ancients spent much time and labor in trying to get at and understand the quintessence by all kinds of chemical experiments and processes, and these philosophers were afterwards called alchemists. Hence we have the word chemistry derived from "alchemist."

I have a number of large volumes that were written and published hundreds of years ago by those alchemists, which treat altogether on this quintessence; they believed that in some way this influence or quintessence of the planets acted on the earth and its inhabitants, and ruled, controlled or influenced the earth and its inhabitants. And those passages in the Bible referred to in a former part of this work referred to the Astrologers who were possessed of that belief.

At the present day it is generally believed by most learned men that all light and sound and other phenomena of nature are produced in some way by this universal principle and all-pervading ether or quintessence. Mr. Keeley, of Philadelphia, has been working on this quintessence most of his life, and hopes to produce a substance that he thinks will revolutionize all motive power, as steam power superseded hand or manual labor, and which will eventually do away with steam or electricity as a motor. But no matter how the planets act on the earth and its inhabitants, there is one thing that is certain and absolute, that is, that they do act in one way or another. Any person giving the subject a thorough investigation cannot deny that fact. The young student of Astrology may have to calculate and look through a number of horoscopes before he can bring one positive fact to bear in proving the science absolutely true, on account of the influence of the planets, one operating on and against another, and presenting conflicting testimony, as it is termed. As an illustration, the chemists may have to search through material nature a long time to find a piece of pure iron, or gold or silver, or of other substance not in combination with any other substance or metal. But when he can find the pure article he knows it has certain qualities or properties which it always retains when in a pure state; so when we can get any particularly clear aspect, or planetary influence, the effect is always certain, but the effects may not always be exactly the same. For instance, I will mention that the signs of the Zodiac, besides being divided into fiery, earthy, airy and watery signs, are also divided into what is termed "tall" and "slender" and "short" and "stout" signs, and "light" signs, and "dark" signs, and so are the planets also divided into "tall," "short," "dark," "light," "slender" or "stout" planets; persons born under them are tall, short, light or dark, etc., and when we can find a tall light sign on the ascendant, and the planet which rules or governs that sign is in another tall light sign, or in the same tall or light sign in the ascendant, and the Moon is in a similar tall light sign, the person born at that time is always tall and light complexioned, and even if he is a negro he is much lighter complexioned than negroes generally are or either of his parents, and is also tall. When there is a short, stout sign on the ascendant, and the planet which has the most influence in the ascendant, or is lord of that sign, is in a short, stout sign, or in the same sign in the ascendant the Moon also in a short, stout sign, that person is always short and stout, no matter how tall and slender both his parents are. Also in marriage there are certain rules in Astrology which I might state never can be overcome, as they always have an effect. For instance, if he marries, he always marries a lady described by the planet that the Moon first applies to by aspect, if he marries at all, and if the Moon makes an evil aspect of an evil planet, say, for instance, the square or opposition of Saturn or Mars, and particularly if there are evil planets in the seventh house (the house of marriage) he is always unhappy in his married life. But if the Moon makes a good aspect of a good planet, and there are good planets in the seventh house, that person always lives happily in married life, no matter how vile or vicious he may be himself, he gets a good, affectionate wife, she almost worships him, and is very much affected at his death. Also in a woman's horoscope; she marries a gentleman described by the planet that the Sun first applies to by aspect, and if the Sun makes an opposition or square of Saturn and Mars, and particularly if there are evil planets in the seventh house, she always has a very unhappy married life, but if the Sun makes a good aspect of a good planet, and there are what are termed good planets in the seventh house, that woman invariably lives a happy married life, and her husband cannot see a fault in her. These facts are absolute, and the reader will readily see that it would be impossible for such influences to be produced by what are termed the laws of gravitation or attraction, or by the law Sir Isaac Newton is said to have discovered. There are similar rules or laws in Astrology in regard to scars, marks or moles. These marks or moles are governed by particular planets in the various signs which rule the human body. Also in regard to diseases or ailments of any particular part of the body, and the time of life they are likely to be affected by evil planets, when transiting through these signs or in evil aspect to planets in them. Whenever a person is sick these parts are always most affected. I shall treat more fully on this subject later on in this work.

If the enemies of Astrology had been sincere in their endeavor to explode the science, they would have stated certain facts in particular horoscopes, especially of noted persons, contradicting the statements which I have made, instead of going off into generalities and talking about the laws of gravitation and centripetal and centrifugal forces, which have nothing to do with Astrology, and Astrologers have nothing to do with those laws.

The Rev. Thomas Dick, of Scotland (instead of disproving the facts which I have stated, and which may be found in text-books on Astrology), in his book called "Improvement of Society by the Diffusion of Knowledge," says on page 31:

"The planetary bodies, indeed, may in certain cases have some degree of physical influence on the earth by virtue of their attractive power, but that influence can never affect the operation of moral causes or the qualities of the mind. Even although it were admitted that the heavenly bodies have an influence over the destinies of the human race, the principles and rules on which Astrologers proceed in constructing horoscopes and calculating nativities are nothing else than mere assumptions, and their pretensions nothing short of criminal impositions upon the credulity of mankind."

Did Mr. Dick write this sentence in pure ignorance, or was it a deliberate falsehood on his part? He must have known that there were thousands of astrological works published in England and in different parts of Europe, which gave the *data* and *formula* for making the *calculations* and *predicting the fate of men*. In other words, did he think that because he had never read and studied these books no one else had ever done so, and that every person was ignorant of the existence of such books? There are a great many persons in Europe and the United States who have read and studied these works if he has not; and the "cuneiform inscriptions of Assyria, the hieorglyphs of Egypt, the most ancient records of Persia, India and China" prove beyond a question that the science of Astrology has been known, studied and practiced in all Eastern countries almost since Adam's time.

To afford an idea of the ridiculous arguments which the Rev. Thomas Dick, William and Robert Chambers and others have brought against Astrology, I will here give one or two special illustrations.

Let us suppose that a man has been engaged all his life in studying and teaching the English grammar, his father and grandfather for hundreds of years having been thus engaged; that this man and his forefathers and all their friends and relations have learned and taught it almost ever since the language has been spoken, and never discovered that this science had been exploded, but on the contrary their experience had gone to prove that English grammar is a true science and firmly based on the laws of language and that it could not be exploded so long as the laws of nature remained unchanged. On the other hand, suppose that all persons who did not know the first elements of English grammar, and had had no practical experience in teaching it, had been told and believed that that science had been exploded. Would those latter persons' arguments or evidence be sufficient proof to convince any sane person that the rules of English grammar were false, and its teachers and professors were frauds; or to use Professor Proctor's words that "they were all ignorant and silly knaves or rogues or charlatans," simply because the former taught and practiced something which the latter had never learned?

To take another view of the case, let us suppose that another set of men and their forefathers had been engaged in learning, practicing and teaching arithmetic for hundreds of years, and that they had equal confidence in their science, but those persons learning, teaching and practicing arithmetic are not satisfied with bringing proofs and facts that their science is true and founded on the laws of nature, but must bring the rules of arithmetic to bear on English grammar. Let us suppose that they commenced by first stating their sums, and by adding a noun and a verb together to make an exclamation, or they tried to take a verb from an adverb and wanted a participle to remain, or they took a noun from a pronoun and wanted a verb to remain, or they tried to state a sum by saying as a verb is to an adverb, so is a noun to a pronoun, and so on. Or again, suppose the grammarian wanted to explode arithmetic by his science and commenced by trying to parse the multiplication table, and try to see what mood and tense any particular number or figure was in, or whether it was in the nominative, possessive or objective case, and so on to the end of the chapter. Any science or learning could be exploded by such a method, and yet these are the only kinds of arguments that have been brought against Astrology; or, in other words, the only arguments I have ever seen published, except those from the Bible, and they so Herod out Herod that it is not worth while referring to them.

There are other sciences or professions besides Astrology that have been assailed in almost a similar manner, and by parties trying to explode or refute one science by another. We have a remarkable instance in the science of homeopathy, and the allopathic physician trying to explode that science by the allopathic practice of medicine.

I must say that for a long time in my youths I was very much opposed to homeopathy and its principles, and thought it altogether contrary to common sense or the laws of chemistry or physiology. I was brought up to believe that the more we got any medicine or drug concentrated, the more wonderful its curative effects became; or, in other words, the more we could get rid of the extraneous matter of a drug, the stronger it became, and the more efficiently it acted on the complaint or diseased part. For instance, a chemist would distill and redistill any particular liquid or spirit, to get it as pure as possible. He would sublimate and resublimate any particular drug also to get it as concentrated as possible; or, in other words, the doctor or chemist would try to get at what is termed the *quintessence* of the drug. The ancient chemist or alchemist thought that if they could once get the universal solvent they might discover the "Elixir of Life," and they would then have a remedy for all diseases, and the people would die only of extreme old age. But the professors of the homeopathic practice of medicine have gone on the other tack; they commence by diluting a medicine, and constantly diluting the pure drug or remedy, believing at the same time that the drug will become more *potent* or stronger by constant dilution, or by adding extraneous matter, such as sugar of milk, or water or alcohol to the original drug, and at the same time triturating or shaking it.

The homeopathic physician claims that a drug or medical plant has two principles or actions when administered to a sick person; that it has a primary action, and afterwards a secondary effect. For instance, a person may take a dose of castor oil. The first action is that of a cathartic; its secondary action is as an astringent, and a person continuing to take the same drug, it will have a tendency to cause constipation. When the patient again takes the oil he has to increase the dose, and each time has to do so to produce the same effect; or, in other words, the patient gradually becomes more and more constipated the more castor oil he takes. It is the same with any other cathartic medicine. The same principle applies in the liquor habit, also in the morphine, tobacco, or snuff habits. They have either to make the whiskey or drug stronger or increase the quantity from time to time to produce the same effect.

For instance, I once read of a certain judge who had to take a whole box of cathartic pills every morning, in order that he might have an evacuation during the day.

In my early years I remember a cousin of mine. Dr. William Broughton, who made great fun of the homeopathic practice of medicine. In short, it was a regular standing joke or butt with him, and yet every day he was practicing or doctoring on the homeopathic principle, but did not know it. In giving an account of a case of diarrhœa which he had cured after all the other doctors had failed, he stated that his remedy was a very small quantity of castor oil, only half a teaspoonful, every day, and the astringent property of the oil had entirely cured the diarrhœa. To make this matter a little plainer to the reader, I will state that the human constitution is so organized that when any extra action of any part of the body is produced, nature not only repairs that loss or injury received, but adds a little more to it, or makes the parts stronger so as to be better prepared for the next over-exertion or special action. For instance, if a man who has very delicate or soft hands should commence working with a shovel or crowbar, his hands for the first day or so will get very sore and tender, but afterwards, if he continues that work, nature makes the skin thicker and harder, and the more he uses or wears those parts of the hands, the harder, thicker and tougher the skin becomes. Therefore, the next time he commences shoveling or working with a crowbar, he can work longer before his hands become tender or sore. It is the same in the lining of the intestines. When a person takes a dose of castor oil or anything which produces a special action of those parts, nature not only repairs the damage done, but also adds to the thickness of the inner coating or lining of the intestines, so that the next dose of medicine will not have such an injurious effect as the first, and it is found by experience that the secondary action (as it is sometimes called) or the tendency of nature to more than repair the effect or damage done to the human system by any particular cause or drug is more to be relied upon in its curative effects than any primary action of a drug or remedy; and the point to be aimed at is to get as small a primary action as possible, and the secondary action is not reduced in its effect in proportion to the small primary action of a drug, but in many cases the secondary *reaction* is even stronger or more *potent* when the primary cause is reduced or weakened by trituration with sugar of milk, or any unmedicinal substance. It is certain that homeopathic doctors make a great many wonderful cures, and if we can judge by past experience it appears that in the course of time homeopathy will be the main if not the only practice of medicine throughout the whole civilized world, and it is the only science of medicine that has yet been discovered which is governed by or in accord with nature's laws and is to be relied on in almost all cases. But still homeopathic doctors go a little too far in stating that there never has been and never can be a cure made of any disease or derangement of any part of the human system which has not been and is not cured on the homeopathic principle, or the law of "similia similibus curantur," or "like cures like." There is no doubt that there have been some cures made by assisting nature and using remedies that have acted on the principle of the primary effect of a drug, similar to the primary action of castor oil relieving constipation for the time being, even if it does not cure permanently. But generally the primary effect of a remedy or drug has a tendency to confirm or establish the disease and causes it to be incurable; hence so many allopathic doctors' patients become confirmed invalids, and has a doctor all the time until death comes to their relief.

Samuel Hahneman has the credit of discovering the principle of "similia similibus curantur," and its action in the human economy, and which principle had been overlooked or neglected, if not entirely ignored, by the doctors of the allopathic school. Thousands if not millions of lives of human beings have been saved by homeopathy, and the lives of those patients would have been destroyed by the old-school practice of medicine. Yet the allopathic doctors have done everything possible to crush homeopathic and all other kinds of practitioners of medicine out of existence. They have been abused by the old-school physicians similar to the manner in which Richard A. Proctor abused Astrologers, by calling them all kinds of vile names, such as quacks, imposters, frauds, humbugs, etc. But the allopaths ought to bear in mind that abuse is the weakest of all arguments. I shall again refer to this subject further on in this volume.

It is impossible to prove or disprove the science or practice of homeopathy by allopathy, or to prove or disprove allopathy by homeopathy. They each work or travel on different lines, and I might say in opposite directions, to accomplish the same result, and each must stand on its own merits, and prove its truth by its success in practice; or, in other words, "The proof of the pudding must be in the eating of it." But the persecution and imprisonment of homeopathic physicians and calling them vile names does not prove the allopathic practice of medicine to be the only true and correct practice, neither does it disprove homeopathy.

We have other remarkable illustrations of the folly of professors of one science trying by their rules and laws to explode another science that is governed by altogether different principles and laws in the instances of electricity and mesmerism. During the time of Benjamin Franklin, over one hundred years ago, the science of electricity was not in the developed condition that we find it in at the present day; probably if it had been, the professors of that science would have attended to their own business, and would have left mesmerism alone to explode itself. But in those days the scientists must try their hand at exploding animal magnetism by the science of electricity. So the French Academy of Science appointed a committee of savants, and among that committee was Benjamin Franklin, to examine into the theory and practice of Doctor Mesmer's animal magnetism, but instead of investigating what was then termed mesmerism, and now called hypnotism, they brought what knowledge they had of the science of electricity to bear on the subject, and, of course, they could not help exploding it. Dr. Mesmer was declared to be a fraud and an impostor, and was driven out of Paris, and I believe out of France altogether — as the allopathic doctors drove Samuel Hahnemann out of Germany. How much more the science of electricity might have been advanced at the present day had those learned men or savants given their whole attention to it and let mesmerism explode itself; in that case they might have discovered some method or law by which Benjamin Franklin's lightning rod would not have been discarded at the present day, and which has been proved perfectly useless in preventing buildings from being struck or set on fire by lightning. It did not require any committee of French savants to explode the lightning rod, as it exploded itself, and the Yankee peddlers no longer travel all over the United States and other countries boring and frightening almost to death the poor old farmers, and almost compelling them to have lightning rods put upon their stables, barns and houses: which expense is now saved, and the poor farmer is not swindled out of his earnings by swindlers called lightning-rod peddlers.

In those days the general belief was that all tall buildings, as church steeples and other high structures, were more likely to be struck by lightning than low buildings. Therefore such buildings had to have lightning rods extending beyond the highest part of the structure or the owners could not get them insured; and yet we are having buildings put up at the present day from 20 to 30 stories high (called sky-scrapers), and none of the owners of these buildings ever dream of protecting them from lightning by Benjamin Franklin's lightning-rod. On the other hand, in spite of Franklin and the savants of France, mesmerism or hypnotism still lives and is growing, and is likely to grow and spread.

Benjamin Franklin and the French savants were either deluded or mistaken in their investigation of mesmerism, or else the people of the present day are entirely mistaken in their notions on hypnotism. We have a remarkable instance of this in a murder trial in a Western State, where it was proved and admitted that a man murdered a young lady for the insurance money on her life, yet he was not executed but confined in prison as an accomplice. Another man, who had witnesses to prove an alibi, and also proved that it was impossible for him to have committed the deed, as he was miles away at the time of the murder, was brought in guilty by the jury, sentenced to death by the judge, and executed, because it was believed by the jury that he had mesmerized or hypnotized the man who had committed the murder. I refer to the case of Harry Hayward, who was hung at 2:10 A.M. on December 11th, 1895, in Minneapolis, Minn.*

"When the innocent is convicted, the judge is condemned."

---

* STORY OF THE CRIME.

The crime for which Harry Hayward was hanged was one of the most remarkable of this century.

On the night of December 3, 1894, the body of Miss Catherine Ging was found in a tamarac swamp on the further shore of Lake Calhoun, a few miles from Minneapolis, Minn. About the same time a horse, drawing an empty buggy, with blood besmeared over the cushions and sides, walked into Gossman's livery stable, where it had been hired early in the evening by Miss Ging.

Rigid and searching inquiry was at once instituted by the authorities. It developed that Miss Ging had her life insured for $10,000, the policies being made payable to Harry Hayward.

This directed suspicion toward him, and after being under surveillance for a few days, he was, together with his brother Adry, taken in custody.

As Hayward was at the theatre on the night of the murder, it was shown conclusively that he did not do the actual killing.

Then Adry told a remarkable story. He said that Harry had plotted to kill Miss Ging for the life insurance money and wanted his assistance, which was refused. Some days before the murder Adry had told the story to L. M. Stewart, an old and respected citizen and long-time friend of the family.

Mr. Stewart dismissed it as an idle yarn, and only recalled it when the dead body of Miss Ging was found in the lonely tamarac swamp. Further investigation by the police developed the

How much more creditable it would have been to Dr. Franklin and how much higher he would now stand in the estimation of the learned world if he never had been colleagued with those French savants in exploding mesmerism it is very difficult to say, but being interested with them in assailing what is now a very interesting science under the name of hypnotism, he proved himself a dupe, even if his lightning-rod had not been a failure.

His biographers who wrote his life nearly one hundred years ago, take particular notice of his being interested with the French savants, and state particularly the great amount of good he did to the community by exposing Dr. Mesmer and his system of treating or curing disease. But at the present day Franklin's biographers, like Mr. Parton and others, whose works I have read of late, have all skipped over that part of Benjamin Franklin's life and do not even mention it, as they know it was a dishonor to Franklin and the savants of France to have been mixed up in any such disgraceful proceeding.

I might go on giving hundreds of other illustrations of the folly of the professors of one science trying to explode another science by rules and laws which do not belong to the latter, similar to the professors of the science of Astronomy attempting to explode the science of Astrology by principles and laws which have no reasonable application.

But Astronomers ought to bear in mind that Astrology is not a new science similar to Mesmerism or Phrenology, etc., but has been taught and practiced in all ages, as well as the present day.

Outside of Europe and the United States there are more than three-fourths of the inhabitants of the globe who are firm believers in Astrology, and the more intelligent people who are living in those parts, such, as Turkey, the East Indies, China, Japan, and other nations, apply it in their everyday business, and in those countries the Astrologers are as they were in ancient times, mentioned in the Bible and other ancient histories, where the Kings, Emperors and Pharoahs consulted them in all important matters. In like manner to-day the Eastern Kings, Emperors and rulers never think of going to war or undertaking any business of importance without first consulting the Astrologers; not only that, but no marriage of wealthy or noted

---

fact that Hayward met Miss Ging that night and drove out as far as Thirteenth Street, where he was met by Claus Blixt, the janitor in the employ of his father. Blixt drove Miss Ging out Calhoun road and shot her. He then came into town on foot, going to several places where he was known for the purpose of establishing an alibi.

Hayward after leaving Miss Ging hurriedly retraced his steps and took a young society lady to the theatre, sitting through the performance apparently unconscious of the tragedy which was then being enacted. Blixt was afterwards arrested and confessed to the actual killing. He was given a life sentence in the Stillwater Penitentiary. In telling his story he claimed that *Hayward had him in his power, exercising an influence over him that it was impossible to resist.* Hayward himself was placed on trial, and despite the best legal talent that money could buy, was found guilty of murder in the first degree and sentenced to death. The usual appeal to the higher courts was made and overruled.

A petition for clemency or commutation of the death sentence was denied by the chief executive of the State Medical experts agree that the man was abnormal and totally devoid of all moral sense and signed the petition simply upon that point.

The condemned refused all spiritual advice during his stay in jail and spent most of his time reviling and cursing his brother and others whom he charged with being responsible for his conviction.—Copied from the New York *Morning Journal*, December 11, 1895.

See appendix page 453.

persons is ever celebrated or consummated without consulting an Astrologer, who by comparing their horoscopes determines whether the parties to be married will agree or live happily; in other words, if it will be a fortunate marriage. Those who write on the subject of marriage in India and China, and who make use of Astrology in relation to marriage, and emigrants who come to this and other western countries, especially to Europe to lecture on these subjects, state that there is not *one in a thousand of such marriages* which is not successful and happy. In contrast to those marriages in India, China and Persia, I will simply give one instance or illustration, it is that of the Rev. Mr. Peters, who preached two sermons in a prominent church in New York City in the latter part of 1895. In the forenoon he preached on the evils and miseries that attended war, and pictured very vividly the distress and suffering which war caused. In the evening he preached on marriage and stated that the next thing to war in causing misery in this life was unhappy marriages. He stated that he had married over one thousand couples and scarcely one of that thousand were really happy marriages. He advised women not to get married, but devote themselves to charity and church duties instead.

The New York *Sun* in an editorial made fun of the Rev. Mr. Peters by stating that a great many women who get divorces get them for no other purpose but the pleasure of getting married again, and they generally marry a second husband shortly after getting rid of the first.

To give one proof of the importance that the Chinese place on the position of the planets at the time of birth in a child's horoscope, I will state that on the 25th of July, 1895, at 1 A.M., there was born at No. 26 West 9th Street, New York City, a male child, the son of the Chinese Consul to New York; the event and the time of the birth was of so much importance that the Consul went to the expense of cabling the news to China, to be sent at once to an Astrologer for its horoscope to be calculated. He did not wait for the news to travel by the fast mail. There is no doubt the Consul paid about $2.50 a word for the cablegram, which would appear a large sum in China. After the horoscope had been calculated the friends and relatives of the child living in China would take the horoscope to a number of their friends who had a girl born near or within a few years of the boy's time of birth, and they would compare the position of the planets in each of the horoscopes to see whether if they got married they would agree and be happy, or if it would turn out what is termed a happy marriage. For instance, the first thing they would look at in the male's horoscope would be to observe what aspect the Moon first made after the time of the child's birth, and they would see in this case it first made a conjunction of Venus in the sign Virgo, which is what we call a fortunate aspect for marriage. Then they would find what aspect the Sun made in the female's horoscope, whom they wish to negotiate with in regard to marriage. If the Sun made a good aspect of a good planet in a good house, that would be a favorable indication that she would live happy in her married life. They would also see whether the female would answer to the description of the planet Venus in the sign Virgo, which describes the future wife of that particular male's horoscope. For instance, the planet Venus in the sign Virgo would describe a rather tall, slender and slightly dark-complexioned person, with dark hair, oval face, round forehead and soft, expressive eyes; she would be very refined, also intelligent, fond of music and the fine arts. In this manner they would go from one friend's house to another until they met with a female's horoscope near the same age that did agree in every particular with the one in hand, and when they did meet with a horoscope which agreed in almost every point they would then know that the couple would live happy when married, and in such cases it is generally decided in their infancy that they shall become man and wife when they come to their proper age or maturity.

This line of study and investigation and consulting Astrologers on marriage has been practiced in China and in the East Indies and other countries for thousands of years, or from time immemorial, and with almost uniform success. In this work I shall insert the horoscope of the Chinese Consul's son and give the rules and principles which the people of China and the East adopt in arranging these marriages.

These laws and rules are more thoroughly understood in those countries than even the principles and laws of breeding animals are understood in the United States and Europe at the present day, and the people there have continued this method of arranging marriages by the principles and rules of Astrology for a much longer period than the Western world has continued the breeding of domestic animals, such as horses, cows, sheep, dogs, etc. The people of Europe and America have by such methods of breeding and training brought these animals almost to perfection in their various departments of animal culture within the last two or three hundred years. What an evolution in horses, both in the speed of running and trotting, and in their perfect form, and also in their handsome appearance can be noticed in the thoroughbred horse, to say nothing about improvement in the breed of cows, sheep, dogs, pigeons, poultry, etc. I question whether the people in China and parts of Africa and the East Indies would treat the method that we employ in breeding and training and bringing to such perfection the various animals that are used in America and Europe with the same contempt that the Western world treats Astrology and Astrologers at the present day.

To give an illustration to prove this remark, I need only refer to an article which appeared in the New York *Times* on March 9th, 1895, as follows :

" *To the Editor of New York Times:*

" DEAR SIR :—Please cast my daughter's horoscope ; she was born at 8:35 A.M. on July 2d, 1884, in New York City, and oblige
Yours respt.,   MRS. MAUD S.

" This letter is an exact copy of one that came to the *Times* office a few days ago ; it gives some idea of what strange problems are constantly and confidently propounded for the journalist's solution. There is no reason to suspect that Mrs. Maud S. wrote otherwise than in perfect good faith, or that she does not really believe the data submitted to be sufficient basis for calculations of practical value. It would be easy to concoct a 'horoscope' more or less humorous and to connect it with the day and year she gives, but it would be rather dreary fooling at best. The letter makes so plain the mournful incompleteness of modern civilization, it betrays so clearly the persistent survival here and to-day of debasing superstitions, and it makes so terribly manifest the immeasurable harmful influences to which not a few children are subjected by well-meaning parents in the metropolis of an enlightened nation, that comment other than serious seems wholly out of place."

From the tenor of the above letter it is evident that the editor of the New York *Times* is not a first-class Astrologer; if he had been he would have either calculated the girl's horoscope or said nothing about it, therefore he is not qualified to give an opinion on the science. Had he lived in Babylon during the reign of Nebuchadnezzar he certainly would not have been elected member of the public schools of that nation for being "ten times better than all the magicians and Astrologers in the realm." Neither would he have " been made master of all the magicians and Astrologers for his wisdom and understanding of Astrology " (see Daniel, Chapter I., verse 20, and 5th chapter, verse 11). But on the contrary, his " debasing superstition " and his "immeasurable, harmful influence" would have caused him to be put at the foot of the class in those schools, or confined in a dungeon, if he had not had the sense to keep silent. "Therefore, it depends on the time and place, or on history and geography" whether any science or learning is a " debasing superstition " and subjects its advocates to persecution and imprisonment, or its professors are elevated to the highest positions in the realm, immediately under the king or emperor.

How different the editors of a newspaper in any part of India or China, or in any other Eastern country would have treated the letter of Mrs. Maud S. if the time of birth had been sent to them to have the horoscope calculated. As an instance of the importance the Chinese attach to the horoscope of a child and to the time of birth, I need only refer to the Chinese Consul, living at No. 26 West 9th Street, New York City, referred to on page 35.

Had the editor understood Astrology, instead of exposing his ignorance as he did, he might have inserted the horoscope of Mrs. Maud S.'s daughter and given the mother some very good advice, what line of business or what profession she was best adapted for, or any special talents she possessed, and he might have warned the mother of certain contingencies or misfortunes which would befall the child, and which she might have guarded the child against if the mother could have obtained such information.

As an illustration of what I mean I will here insert the horoscope of the above time of birth, which is written similar to thousands which I have published in daily and weekly newspapers,—The New York

Sunday News, The Illustrated American, Pittsburg (Pa.) *Dispatch,* Cincinnati *Euquirer, Sunny South,* Harrisburg *Telegram,* Louisville *Courier-Journal,* Manchester (N. H.) *Mirror,* etc.

It is likely Mrs. Maud S. intended writing to the *Sunday News,* a paper I had been writing for about two years.

Mrs. Maud S.'s daughter was born July 2d, 1884, at 8:35 A.M., N. Y. According to the time given above this young girl was born under the Sun in the sign Cancer, with Leo on the ascendant, Jupiter, Sun and Venus rising, and Saturn, Mercury and Neptune in the midheaven.

When she comes to her full growth she will be near the medium height, rather slender when young, but will gradually become quite full built, and will at the age of 40 weigh 180 pounds; rather light complexion, light brown or almost flaxen hair (her hair will have a slight yellowish tinge when a child), slightly full face, round forehead, full, expressive eyes, rather prominent nose, have a straight, proud walk, fond of dress and decoration, and always have a very neat, tidy appearance. The rules of Astrology say that she will be harmless, cheerful, pleasant, but at times indolent and not fond of employment or hard work, but inclined to dancing and recreation, and very fond of the company of the opposite sex.

On the whole she has a rather fortunate horoscope, and will never come to very low circumstances, or poverty, but will often be annoyed by treachery from secret enemies or near neighbors.

She will generally enjoy fair health, and there is every probability of her living to be quite old. She will at times be troubled with some weakness of the back, kidneys and bladder, and palpitation of the heart, and danger of indigestion and tightness of the chest. She will have to avoid strong tea, coffee and stimulants and high-seasoned food; if not, she will suffer from nervousness, indigestion or weakness of the stomach and liver.

She is a person of very good intellect, will learn rapidly and be fond of the fine arts; also will excel in mathematics or anything that requires deep thought; also be fond of Astrology, spiritualism, mesmerism, etc. She will have a fluent tongue and would succeed either as a public speaker or writer for newspapers or magazines. She will find it very difficult to retain money; it will easily get out of her fingers, and she will be unfortunate in regard to lending or assisting friends with money. She will marry to rather good advantage, but will not live over-happy; she will keep company with a gentleman for a length of time who will be near or above the medium height, well built, rather light complexion, oval face, high forehead, hair receding from the temples, rather prominent nose and full expressive eyes; great danger of disgrace or unhappiness caused by that gentleman, and it is impossible for her to marry him.

Her husband will be above the medium height, rather slenderly built, will never become stout, thin face, high forehead, sharp nose, quick, penetrating eyes, dark complexion, with dark brown or black hair, will have a particularly straight or proud walk, be fond of dress and decoration, but likely to soon become jealous and cause her much unhappiness on that account, yet it is not probable they will separate, but he will not be long lived.

She marries a second time and is much more fortunate. Her second husband will be near the medium height, slightly full built, rather pale complexion, roundish face and forehead, soft brown hair, rather sharp nose and soft expressive eyes, very gentle in his manners, and agreeable, fond of music and the fine arts. She will only have a small family of children, not more than three or four, chiefly boys, and they will often have poor health and not be much good to her.

She has already had several evil aspects to pass by, which caused her health to suffer; one of those times was when she was a little over one year old, likely to have had a fever. Another at two years of age, but that was more likely to have been an accident or another fever, or some derangement of the stomach and intestines. Evil again at four, seven and eight. Had an evil time in November and December, '92, and during February, March, May, June, July, August and September, '93—very likely sickness for herself or unhappiness in her family. Another marked evil time commenced in January, '95, and continued to April. Unfortunate again in October and November, '95. Then more fortunate to January 1st, '98, then marked evil to July 1st, '98; likely to have severe sicknesses or meet with some accident. Evil again in October, November and December, '98; a particularly evil time from February 1st to the end of December, '99; then fortunate to June 1st, 1900; then evil to September 1st, 1900. The year 1903 will be evil, but more fortunate then until she is 21. She will be keeping company and may possibly marry, but doubtful at 21, but more likely to have the unhappiness connected with the light complexioned, full built gentleman at that time and not marry until she is near or a little over 23.

Further on I will insert the map of the heavens at the time of birth of Mrs. Maud S.'s daughter and give the rules and principles that govern in calculating this and other nativities; then the reader will be able to see what the principles of Astrology are and judge " how plain the mournful incompleteness of modern civilization" is and which " betrays so clearly the persistent survival here and to-day of the debasing superstition, and how terribly manifest the immeasurable, harmful influence, to which not a few children are subjected by well-meaning parents in the metropolis of an enlightened nation."

When the reader comes to study the science of Astrology, which I hope to make very plain and easy to learn in this volume, he will be equally astonished at the ignorance and debasing superstition of the editors of the New York *Times*. If these editors are so ignorant and superstitious, what must be the condition of their readers? It must be deplorable in the extreme. " The stream never rises higher than its source." If these newspaper editors went no further than calling the Astrologer and his science improper names and only wrote about the debasing superstition of the science of Astrology, I might let the matter pass, but every Astrologer knows by dear bought experience the amount of persecution he has had to go through on account of the ignorance and superstition of newspaper editors, but more especially the ignorance and superstition of editors of religious periodicals and ministers of the Gospel. The Astrologer in nearly all Western countries is not only consigned to everlasting torment in another world, but he has to go through all kinds of persecution and imprisonment in this world, and nearly all those countries have laws enacted for the special purpose of suppressing Astrology. I will here give a few facts as illustrations of the above statement. When my father died, about the year 1847, I was then a little over 18 years old. The minister of the church we attended, as soon as he learned of the death of my father, came to the house to talk to my oldest brother; he spent a whole afternoon trying to convince my brother of the wickedness of the practice of Astrology, and even stated that my father's soul was burning in hell fire at that moment for the wicked act of having practiced that science, and that my brother would have to suffer the same torments if he did not reform and be converted.* A few years after the death of my father my sister being in poor health, went as a patient to Leeds Infirmary. [The institution referred to in the note below.] While there she became acquainted with a young girl who had formerly lived as a servant with William Seed, an old friend of my fathers, and who had published an astrological almanac for many years in Leeds, England.† When the servant knew that my sister was acquainted with Mr. Seed, and that he had often visited our house, they became very good friends.

One of the ladies who visited the infirmary to pray with and convert the patients, in some way found out that the servant had lived at the house of William Seed, and the lady spoke to the girl in this manner: "How was it that you lived with such a wicked man as that?" The girl made answer by saying: "Mr. Seed was a very good man, and he read his Bible and said his prayers every night and morning." The lady made answer by saying: "If he did pray, he prayed to the devil." I might give a number of other illustrations similar to the above of the ignorance, prejudice and superstition of religious communities and of newspaper editors, but will only mention a few instances of my own persecutions.

In 1866 I rented an entire floor for a lecture hall and residence at 814 Broadway, opposite 11th Street, New York; there I gave lectures four or five times a week on Astrology, Phrenology, etc., and on Sunday afternoons and evenings I lec-

---

* I ought to state here that my father did not practice Astrology publicly, but simply did it for his friends and acquaintances, and solely for their benefit and without pay. In his early years he had studied Astrology and medicine with his father, and was of much assistance to his neighbors and friends in giving them advice in case of sickness and trouble. He was for several years an assistant house physician in Leeds Infirmary with his eldest brother, but later left that institution. His elder brother practiced medicine afterwards and continued in that profession all his life and was remarkably successful, while my father went into the manufacturing business of linen and woolen cloth, he having a dye house and dyed his own goods.

† My eldest brother also published an astrological almanac similar to that of Mr. William Seed, and of Raphael's of London, also for many years he published a monthly periodical called *Broughton's Monthly Horoscope*, besides other publications.

tured' on Natural Theology and other sciences, and also on moral or religious subjects. While giving these lectures I met with all kinds of persecution which the enemies of Astrology could possibly invent; not only were the people who came to the meetings insulted in the passage way, but all other kinds of annoyances that could possibly interfere with the meetings were practiced. They even turned off the water, so that we had to get a supply from the neighbors. While I was lecturing, rowdies who were hired for that purpose, would go into the room above and raise heavy benches as high as they could and let them drop on the floor right over our heads, so as to confuse me in my lecture, and every other kind of disturbance they could think of or invent was practiced. This was continued for nearly two years. Finally, on account of my wife's delicate health, she being near confinement, I was compelled to move out of the building to save her life; the child died within three days after her confinement in similar spasms that she suffered from while the noise and disturbance was going on. My wife often became unconscious and flighty on account of the noise over our heads. One night it was all I could do to prevent her from tearing the hair out of her head and committing other violence. She never fully recovered from the suffering and distress which she endured in that building, and was never herself again afterwards. On the night above referred to, the police came from the street on account of hearing such noise and disturbance and asked me what was all that noise about. I told them I did not know, so they went up to the room and arrested the whole party on their own responsibility and took them to the Police Court. My wife being very ill, it was impossible for me to leave her, therefore I requested Mr. W. H. Chaney, who was at that time assisting me in my lectures, to go and make complaint of the misconduct of the rowdies in the room above. The rowdies were discharged the next morning, and a day or two afterwards Mr. Chaney was arrested for false imprisonment* and he lay

---

* It was James McDermott, a son-in-law of the landlord, Alexander Eagleson, mentioned above, who got the order of arrest for Mr. Chaney, and James McDermott accompanied the officers and Mr. Chaney to Ludlow Street jail, tantalizing him all the way. While Mr. Chaney was in jail he was tried by a judge and jury who awarded James McDermott $100 damages. Mr. Chaney or his lawyer knew nothing about the trial or judgment until long afterwards. When Mr. Chaney was discharged from jail he made application to the Court to have the case reopened. After his lawyer had made the plea for a new trial, he stated that Mr. Chaney also wished to say a few words. The judge said he "hoped he would make them very short, as he knew all about the case." Mr. Chaney put this question to the judge, "Did you know when you impanelled the jury and had the witnesses sworn in this case that the complainant had me locked up in jail and I knew nothing about the trial?" The judge made answer by saying that he did not know. It is evident that the judge told a deliberate falsehood on the bench, as he just stated before that "he knew all about the case." There is no doubt that a vast number of other trials conducted as that of Mr. Chaney's has occurred in New York and other cities. Mr. Chaney could never get a new trial and a judgment of $100 stands against him to-day.

Previous to the disturbances above related, Mr. Chaney made the remark to me that while he was district attorney in Bangor, Maine, also in Iowa, and when he owned and edited daily papers, that he often had prayed to be sent to prison and yet be innocent. This was a case in which a *prayer was answered*. Mr. Chaney went to make the complaint at my request, and did so solely to oblige me.

I never could find out whether that was a trap set by the police, they going into the room and arresting the rowdies on their own responsibility, then afterwards getting us to make charges against them, so that those rowdies could have us arrested for false imprisonment. The attention of the police was attracted by the large crowd in the street, which the noise on the floor above us had been the means of collecting. See appendix page 453.

in Ludlow Street jail over six months. I was also arrested for publishing an account of the outrage, which the lawyers construed into a libel and sued me for $10,000 damages. After a great deal of worry and anxiety, and one delay after another, the trial at last came off after several years, and the landlord who sued me and whose name was Alexander Eagleson, got six cents damages. I might here state that all the parties who attended the meetings were very well pleased and satisfied with the lectures, and they could not understand why the persecution was continued against me, but it was the religious community, chiefly the Catholics, who no doubt believed that if it became known that the events of life were governed by fixed laws, it would in some way interfere with their answers to prayer and divine providence and their religious services. On account of the misrepresentations of the New York *Herald's* reporter, one Sunday night, the Sergeant of the Police Station in Mercer Street came with a large number of police officers in citizens' clothes, to arrest all parties who attended the meeting, along with the lecturer, and take them to the Mercer Street Station. That night Mr. Charles Stewart, of Newark, New Jersey, was lecturing on Natural Theology, chiefly in its relations to the heavenly bodies and the goodness of God. After the meeting the Sergeant told me the reason they came was that they were sent by the authorities of the city to arrest all parties in the hall, but as the lecture was such a good one, and its moral influence was also so good, they had their journey for nothing, and that he would do all he could to influence the authorities to prevent us from being disturbed in the future. He stated that he wished there were hundreds of lectures of that kind in the city every Sunday night; it would be a good thing for the people.

Detectives were employed for years to follow me; they even followed me into the houses when I visited my patients under the pretense of asking the lady of the house questions, but with all their skill, ingenuity and perseverance they were never able to get any charges against me. Some years afterwards I loaned some furniture to a person on Long Island; that furniture was seized for debt incurred by the party to whom it was loaned. When I went to obtain it the sheriff told me I could not have the furniture unless I replevined it, and that it would cost me as much as it was worth. But after looking at me a short time he said, "I know you; did you not once live at 814 Broadway, New York?" I told him I did. He then went with me to the man who had seized the furniture and said, "I know this man; he is all right." They gave up the goods without another word, and even carted the furniture to the railroad station. This sheriff told me he had been employed for a long time to follow my steps when he was a detective in New York, and he said he knew me well and had been in my house numbers of times.

Not only was I persecuted as above related, but my mail was intercepted and opened by those detectives to try and get evidence against me, and the money in letters sent to me was extracted and the letters destroyed, and when it was only a few dollars they quietly put the money into their pockets and thus destroyed my business and my reputation.

A gentleman whom I became acquainted with while I was living in Philadelphia, an old patient of mine, who resided in New Jersey, and had read my publications a number of years, sent me a letter containing a $50 bill to pay for some goods I had purchased for him and sent him. The letter was opened and destroyed and the money taken out and returned to the writer with the following letter, written in backhand, so as to disguise the handwriting:

"NEW YORK, March 31, 1866.

"SIR:—There is an old saying that a fool and his money are soon parted.

"Fortunately the $50 sent by you to Dr. Broughton fell into the hands of an honest man, who now returns it to you with the advice that you will keep your money and not send it to any Quack of an Astrologist, who can no more nor as well tell you what will happen to you, as you can guess at it yourself. If you don't need the money give it to some one that does, and not to any 'Star Gazer' or 'Planet Reader' who makes his money by gulling ignorant people out of their hard earnings. No humbug of a fortune teller can do yon five cents' worth of good, nor tell you anything except what he may guess or invent. Your letter was sent to me by mistake or your $50 would have been thrown to the dogs. See if you can't put the money to a better use. A FRIEND."

The writer of the above letter said the $50 was sent to him by mistake. That person told a deliberate falsehood; it was sent to my address, and had it not been intercepted like other letters it would have reached me, as it was directed plainly to Dr. L. D. Broughton, 814 Broadway, New York City, and at that time there was not another Dr. L. D. Broughton in New York, or for that matter, in the whole United States. The man who had sent me the money re-inclosed the $50 in another envelope, and also the letter of the man who had intercepted my mail, but who was "too honest a Friend" to put his name and address to the letter, so as to let my correspondent know who that "Friend" was, so that he might write to him and thank him for his kindness and the interest he had taken in his welfare.

If the letter had only contained two or three dollars this "Friend" would have put the money in his pocket and not said a word about it, the same as he had done with scores of other letters, but he thought there might possibly be some inquiry about the $50 and he might get into trouble if he was found out, or the $50 bill was traced to the thief. Besides the "Friend" evidently knew all about me and my business and knew exactly where I lived, and could have forwarded the letter to me if so disposed. But no doubt this friend had authority from the New York Post Office and the police authorities in the city to intercept all my mail so as to get evidence to convict me of some crime and thus send me to prison if it was possible.

For many years, both before and after 1866, I received letters from parties scolding me and using all kinds of rough language, stating that they had sent money to me; but as I had not received their former letters or the money, of course I could not write their horoscopes or answer their questions or send them instructions. I always wrote to the parties to that effect. My letters being stolen in the post office was a great damage and loss to me in my business.

Even as late as May, 1895, when I was writing horoscopes for the Louisville *Courier-Journal* to be published free in that paper, for any person who would send time and place of birth to the editor, the *Courier-Journal* had to discontinue publishing horoscopes. The managing editor, Chas. B. Pierce, wrote to me May 16, 1895, the following:

"The postal authorities gave us very decided notice that if we accepted any remuneration for the service, either by way of furnishing private horoscopes or advancing their publication, they would stop the transit of our paper in the mail. We did not care to make an issue of the question with the postal authorities, so discontinued publishing the horoscopes."

In the United States we are said to live in a free country, where we have free speech, free discussion and liberty of the press, and yet newspapers like the Louisville *Courier-Journal* are not allowed to publish horoscopes free to their readers without having their paper stopped from going through the mail. Is it not time that the subject of Astrology was investigated by the light of reason and science, and the people permitted to find out whether the science is true or false? For years whenever I went to the post office to lay a complaint of my mail being intercepted and the money taken out, I got nothing but insults from the postmasters or those I spoke to, and I was told that no such letter had ever been sent to me. In Philadelphia, before I moved to New York, my letters were rifled, the money taken out, and when I went to the post office and stated the facts, I got nothing but rebuffs. Shortly after I moved to New York the letter carrier in that district was arrested for opening other parties' letters and taking money from them; as he had acquired the habit of opening my mail and taking the money out, he continued the habit and opened other persons' mails. He was arrested, prosecuted and sent to prison for ten years.

Possibly there is not a country in the world where Astrologers have been more persecuted than they have been in England, especially within the last hundred years. If a person went to consult an Astrologer and paid him a sixpence or a shilling, which was marked so that he could swear to it, he could have the Astrologer's house broken into and searched, and have him arrested with no other evidence than the marked sixpence or shilling found on the Astrologer, just the same as if the Astrologer had stolen the shilling from the party. In short, they hunted Astrologers down as we read in history they formerly hunted witches and wizards. There were detectives and police especially employed to prosecute them. A gentleman, an Astrologer, whom my eldest brother knew well, and who resided in Manchester, England, was arrested and sent to prison on no evidence than the fact that there were several respectable ladies who were waiting for their turn to see him in his parlor. But of late years the tide is turning and it looks as if

Astrology is going to be as respectable, if not more so, than any other profession, and similar to what it was in ancient times, as we read in history and the Bible, especially in Daniel.

I copy the following from the *Arena* of January, 1893, published by B. O. Flower, Boston, Mass., and it tells the story about the change going on in London, England. I will here state that the *Arena* is the most liberal and fair-minded periodical that I know of in the United States, and I would advise all my readers to subscribe for it, and they will find it to their advantage by so doing:

ASTROLOGY IN LONDON.
By Edgar Lee.

"As a proof that in Enlgand there is some disposition being shown to deal in a more broad-minded way with those who practice Astrology, I will instance the following: At the beginning of the past year the somewhat popular and largely circulated organ, Society, began to devote a certain portion of its space every week to Astrology. Articles appeared not always by the same hand, but under the same nom de guerre of 'Jupiter,' and in a short time the paper was simply overwhelmed with correspondence from every part of the three kingdoms. A contemporary of undeniable cleverness, which has, like most of the so-called 'smart' journals of the epoch of no very ancient pedigree, attacked Society, and particularly 'Jupiter,' and called seriously upon the public prosecutor to enforce the law upon this person; and when that functionary was perverse enough to be imperturable to the somewhat ferociously worded advice, it followed up the attack by fierce personalities, more suggestive of editorial amenities in California twenty years ago than Fleet Street and the Strand in 1892. Well, the criminal authority at Queen Victoria's treasury remained passive, and the reason is not far to seek. Public opinion on the subject of Astrology in England has undergone a startling change; and a prosecution by the State at the present juncture, and more especially immediately before the elections, would have been a trifle too daring for the most reckless government to indulge in. The professors of Astrology in England are legion and they include an immense number of charlatans; indeed, it may be broadly stated that the charlatans outnumber the genuine Astrologers in the proportion of three to one; hence it is so desirable that some authoritative organ which could write on astrologic topics without fear of making itself amenable to the law should be established, if only for the purpose of acting as a finger-post to those who are seeking the truths of astral lore.

"Among the genuine Astrologers one must again distinguish between those who may be termed intuitive and those who base their predictions on absolute mathematics. The latter are the more numerous section and to the reasonable mind the more reliable; the former, on the other hand, probably possess a larger following, since their deductions are far more rapid and always more startling than their slower brethren.

"Among the intuitive Astrologers I rank in the first flight the seer of the Charing Cross Road, whose predictions for the past forty years approach the marvellous.* This man practically of independent means, is the scion of an illustrious name in the annals of London's civic history, and is the son and grandson of two men who both practiced as Astrologers back into the last century, and were accounted as the leaders of the cult. This old gentleman has been consulted by peer and peasant; the late Prince Consort bore

---

* Henry J. Dukes, who has since died.

witness to his skill; the first Lord Lytton, Charles Dickens, George Eliot, and the late Lord Beaconsfield, when Mr. Disraeli, frequently interviewed him, and to this day his house is visited by many of our leading ladies and gentlemen in society, while more than one of our commercial magnates and stock exchange speculators seek his advice on personal matters.

"Then again, in the Caledonian Road, close to King's Cross, is to be found another 'intuitional.'* One of our chief lady novelists, whose works are well-known to the American public—I refer to Florence Marryat—can bear witness to the astonishing power of prognostication possessed by this hoary wizard whose fame extends far beyond the metropolis of England.

"In the month of June, 1887, another famous Astrologer within sound of Bow Bells was consulted by a journalist on a subject of considerable import to himself. Queen Victoria's jubilee ceremony was to take place the following day, and the journalist had received instructions from his editor to be present in Westminster Abbey to describe the event at length. In view of the enormous number of tickets issued by the Lord Chamberlain to view the splendid spectacle, hundreds of workmen had been employed for several days in rigging up seats in the interior of the sacred edifice, and the vast quantity of timber employed suggested to the anarchists a ready means of bringing about a perfect holocaust of victims. The threats of these gentry to destroy at one fell blow the heirs apparent of several European dynasties were overheard in a low Soho cabaret by the detectives who are ever lurking about that notorious quarter. The whole conspiracy soon got wind and found its way into the newspapers, with the result that certain feeble folks who had obtained tickets became alarmed, and the press loudly demanded extra police precautions, so that a horrible catastrophe might be averted. The particular journalist of whom I speak was among the alarmed ones, and his wife, a believer in Astrology, insisted on his consulting with the 'intuitional' of her choice. The oracle replied (the minute of interrogation was his guide): 'There is not the slightest fear of anything happening to-morrow. Jupiter, who rules Her Majesty, is in his full dignity, and nothing sinister could possibly occur. There is, however, likely to be an accident to some one, who, though not royal, is in some way connected with the royal house, and it would appear as though it were a horse accident.' It will be remembered by many that on the morning of the ceremony the Marquis of Lorne, while in the park en route to join the procession, was thrown from his charger and sufficiently injured to prevent his taking part in the proceedings.

"That same night while the journalist was making this inquiry, two other querents applied to the Astrologer, both asking a question as to the safety of the Abbey on the morrow. The reply given by the Astrologer was naturally a repetition of his previous answer, whereupon the younger of the two visitors, who spoke English imperfectly, asked for a forecast of his own career. After ascertaining minutely the hour of birth and the latitude and longitude of the birthplace, the Astrologer inquired if he were by profession a soldier, and the reply was that he held rank in a foreign army. 'Your end will be sudden and by lead,' said the Astrologer, 'and, so far as I can see, the end is so near that it is not worth while casting the nativity.' The

---

* Thos. Wilson, a watchmaker of London, was called upon by Princess Victoria, accompanied by her guardian—her aunt—and requested him to erect and read her horoscope, which he did to her satisfaction. Mr. Wilson came to New York some years ago and did business at 28th Street and Third Avenue, but returned to London the latter part of 1866, and died only a few years ago. Some six or seven years ago Mr. Wilson was arrested in London for practicing Astrology. He told the judge that he had been in practice over fifty years and this was the first time he was ever molested. The judge said that "if you are ever brought before me again I shall have to hold you;" then discharged him. Mr. Wilson was at that time nearly eighty years of age.

young man laughed at the time, but it afterwards transpired that he was the Archduke Rudolf of Austria, whose melancholy and tragic demise will be still fresh in the memory of the reader.

"I could record many other instances of the abnormal development of the intuitive faculty in the astrologic seers, but I will now come to an example of what purely mathematical Astrology can accomplish. An Astrologer, long resident in London, and who was alive until very recently, belonged to that section which regards prediction by astral calculation as an exact science. He received a mysterious visit from a stranger in September of 1869, who asked him whether, in view of the complications then arising in Central Europe, he could fix on a date when Prussia might advantageously quarrel with France. At this time the Luxemberg Sucession had assumed a perilous aspect, while the aspirations of the Hohenzollern family to the Spanish crown had already been the subject of serious diplomatic uneasiness to more than one foreign minister. 'I must 'first,' said the Astrologer, be placed in possession of the actual birth moments of King William of Prussia, Count Bismarck, Count von Moltke, the Emperor of the French and his consort and Marshal Leboeuf. It would be as well, too, that I should have the dates of the coronation of the first King of Prussia, of the Hohenzollern dynasty, and the coronation day of Napoleon I.'

"'And supposing,' returned the stranger, 'that these are supplied you, how long will it be before you arrive at a decision?'

"'It may possibly take me a week or more,' rejoined the other, and the inquirer on this left him abruptly. In due course the necessary particulars were supplied, and after an immense amount of labor the Astrologer reported that the best moment for the Prussian King to flount France would be some hour in the afternoon, as nearly as possible midway between the 9th and 14th of July, 1870. The stranger paid nothing for this advice at the time, but preserving his incognito, disappeared from the Astrologer's ken. Who does not know the exact date when France heard with indignation that William had turned on his heel in Unter den Linden when approached by M. Benedetti, the emissary of the Tuilleries? Is not the 11th and 12th of July graven on every Germany memory? While as for the result of the alleged snub, do not millions of Frenchmen remember to their cost the result of this strangely astral calculation? In the February of 1871, when the iron-girt city of Paris was in its last throes, the Astrologer receive a letter passed through the German military lines containing Berlin billets de banque to the amount of two hundred pounds sterling, with the simple words on a plain sheet of paper, ' With thanks of Germany.'

"From 1879 to 1888 palmistry was the dominant occult attraction of the majority of our West End ' At Homes.' No hostess could be deemed to have filled up her evenings satisfactorily unless a cheiromant of the first quality formed part of the entertainment. Heron Allen's books on the fascinating study had obtained a somewhat wide circulation, and the amateur cheirosophist was everywhere *en evidence*. Sometimes these interesting reunions would be diversified by the appearance of a physiognomist who after a short lecture on the wonderful index to character which the features provide would entertain the assemblage by practical illustrative experiments on the subjects present, many of which, as may be imagined, were very amusing. Sometimes—but these occasions were rare—a calligraphist would appear on the scene—Madame Volski, for example, whose remarkable delineations of character from handwriting have excited the wonderment of more than one European crowned head. Lesser lights than Madame Volski would often try their more 'prentice hands in the same direction, but of late years this class of entertainment has fallen into desuetude, and a *demand for a science which shall have more of the elements of exactitude* has become general. During the present London season I, myself, personally know one Astrologer numbering his votaries by the thousand, who has been invited to at least twenty social gatherings of the upper ten, and who has been offered large fees for his attendance. I need scarcely say the absurd act of Parliament, which prevents his taking money in the exercise of his astrologic vocation, has hindered his acceptance of these calls on his time, and as a consequence has resulted in a loss to him of considerable emolument.

"Now as to works on Astrology, which are becoming rarer every year, it may astonish the reader to learn that there are at least one hundred and fifty authors of all sorts and conditions who have penned volumes during the last two centuries to be found in many a collection owned by the richer class of Englishmen. The prices now of most of these books are prohibitive, but there are certain well-established Astrologers to whom stocks of such cooks have been handed down by their forefathers, and who do a thriving trade by their sale. It may be noted as a singular fact—and I think that the celebrated society of 'Odd Volumes,' as well as one of their principal members, M. Quaritich, the biggest book buyer in the world, will bear witness to the truth of my assertion—that at nearly all great book auctions, works on Astrology are conspicuous by their absence. The reason for this is that your astrologic enthusiast scarcely ever permits them to come into the market if he knows of their existence, and even as the whereabouts of the valuable picture or etching is known to the dealers, and is generally snapped up before coming under the hammer, so also is the whereabouts of most esoteric books, especially those appertaining to the movements of the planets in their relation to man. In connection with Astrology another point has lately cropped up; it is true that it is only a side issue, but it is so interesting to the world at large that I cannot close this paper without mentioning it. There are first sight repulsions between certain people for which there is no accounting by any fixed rule. A enters a ball-room or the coffee-room of a hotel for the first time and sees B. Neither had ever seen the other before; neither knows anything of one another. They are both well-dressed, respectable-looking people, so that no repugnance can possibly spring up on either side on the score of appearance; yet in both their minds has lodged a dislike for each other, which can sometimes never can be wholly eradicated.

"The new Saturnian theory on this subject is a little abstruse, but it is equally remarkable. These people are positives and negatives, brought about through their being born under different conditions of Saturn's light, i. e., the positives will be born when the light is shining on the earth direct from the nucleus, the negatives when the light is shining through or being intercepted by the ring. Astronomers will raise their hands in pious horror at such superstitious teachings, but let the Astronomer shut himself up in his observatory and be for the nonce forgotten, while the reader tests the matter for himself. Imagine the dial plate of a clock and let the figures from one to twelve be taken to represent January to December. It is a cycle without beginning or end, i. e., November and January are not nine months away from one another, but only one month intervenes. This is the threshold of the theory. A is born in January, B in June; A and B will have a repugnance for one another, or if not an actual repugnance each will intentionally or unwittingly always injure the other. So will other months, February and July, October and April, July and December. To quote briefly from this singular and novel hypotheses after its creator had exhausted his scientific reasons for the light of Saturn, exercising so direct an evil effect on mankind, goes on to say: "Men have talked on the theory of repulsion by electro-biology, magnetism, and tried to account for it in that way. It is something in the air, say others, but there is nothing satisfactory in these suggestions, and the fact that some people are without apparent reason distinctly repellent to other people exists and remains. The reason is purely and wholly Saturnian; and although the demonstration until now is not very perfect, as it has only been discovered quite recently, it is sufficiently perfect to suggest patient inquiry to render it more so. You will always or nearly always find when this feeling of repulsion comes over you that the birthday of the object of your dislike is four, five or six months away from your own, and the farther away it is the more certain and intense the dislike. The year matters little unless it be seven, fourteen and a half, twenty-two or twenty-nine years from yours, these being the dates of Saturn's squares. Two individuals born in the same month, if they come together in business, get along swimmingly. In the case of husband and wife they are indeed too fond, and such a match frequently produces jealousy, but let the husband be born in May and the wife in November, and the result will be disastrous. Let any one who reads this and disbelieves it cast his or her memory back and try to remember the person who brought them the most harm, either with intention or by accident. They will be surprised at the corroborative evidence such inquiry will produce. Naturally there are exceptions, but these exceptions prove the rule, etc.

"Later on the same writer quoted the divorce court in support of his theory and gives numerous instances from history of positives and negatives, who had destroyed one another, cites curious facts connected with the regard borne by the Queen for her various relations, and altogether furnishes a very pretty array of facts. The theory, however, requires a convention of Astrologers to sit on and analyze it before it can hope to be accepted, and meanwhile Ptolemy, pure and simple, with the addenda of Uranus and Neptune, to correct some of his unavoidable errors, with the sometimes vexed question of the influence of the asteroids—these will remain faith and gospel of the English student of Astrology for the present."

If all writers who had written either for or against Astrology had been as liberal minded as Mr. Edgar Lee, I should not have had to write and publish this book, and Astrology would have been recognized throughout the Christian nations as one of the established sciences, but through some fatality which is difficult to understand the people in all Christian countries have followed the injunctions of the Bible to the letter where it says, "*Thou shalt not suffer a witch to live,*" and in their ignorance the people have included Astrologers in the class of witches and wizards, and they have been condemned unheard and convicted without trial and even without evidence. It is generally supposed, and it is even a theory in law, that a person is innocent until he is convicted; but Astrologers do not come under that class. Even in the case of Mrs. Fleming, of New York City, who was indicted by the Grand Jury for the murder of her mother, a judge of the Supreme Court decided that she was an innocent woman until convicted, and that she had a perfect right to inherit a certain amount of property which was to come to her by will, through the death of her mother, and for the murder of whom she was just going to be tried. Should it ever come to be known throughout the whole civilized world that Astrology is as much a science and no more wicked than the practice of the science of arithmetic, the people will then begin to open their eyes and wonder whether the whole community in Christian countries are not practically insane, and the man that was confined in a lunatic asylum was more than half right in his answer when asked how it was that such a sensible man was confined in such an institution. When people come to think of the millions of dollars that have been wasted by the judiciary in hunting down and bringing to trial and convicting innocent people called Astrologers, also the money that has been spent in confining those innocent people in prisons, and often in hanging them and burning them alive—if all that money, time and effort had been spent in advancing civilization and human happiness, how much better it would have been for the whole people of those countries? And when it comes to be found out that Astrology is the most useful of sciences, and of more real practical benefit to humanity at large than any other science that was ever known, they will be ready to exclaim in the words of Shakespeare, "What fools these mortals be."

It may be asked by the reader, if I am a qualified person to write on the subject of Astrology, and understand that science sufficiently myself to be able to teach it to others. I will let the following correspondence speak for itself. I make it public without any scruples of conscience, as there was nothing in these letters understood to be private when written, and which passed through the mail to the different parties whose names are mentioned below. The first letter that I shall call the reader's attention to is one from Mr. O. D. Bragdon, Boston, Mass., which reads as follows:

BOSTON, MASS., March 9th, 1894.

DR. L. D. BROUGHTON,

DEAR SIR:—Some days since I received a copy of "Planetary Influence," published by yourself, with nothing to indicate positively from whom the publication came. I have taken the liberty of inferring that you were the sender, and take this opportunity of thanking you, and at the same time of assuring you of my high estimation and appreciation of the sentiments and opinions you therein set forth. I have for many years been an admirer of yours, particularly when I have been able to catch a glimpse of your "fine Italian hand" in some press contribution, or in perusing some of the older productions of yours of the war times. I trust that at some time I may have the pleasure of meeting and thanking you personally.

I am just in receipt of a letter (copy of which I inclose you) from a Mr. A. N. Doerschuk, of Kansas City, Mo., dated February 2, which purports to have been addressed by Mr. T. E. Wilson, librarian to the New York *World*, making a peculiar kind of request, and I have taken the liberty of advising him that I have referred his letter to you, as being more properly *one of the best*, if not the foremost man in the science in America. I do this because I believe your wide experience and evident long researches in our beloved science have best fitted you to become the American champion in such questions, provided this inquiry is made in good faith. If it is not, your acquaintance with the constitution and pulse of the New York *World* makes you better able to treat the disease from which it suffers. Whatever your course in the matter may be, I feel fully assured it must be the best one that could be adopted, and if there is anything I can do to aid you for best results to our science, you may command me. My recollection is that the New York *World* has avowed itself the enemy of Astrology, whether its writers are ignorant of or acquainted with the laws of the science I know not. Perhaps you are better able to judge of the genuineness or good faith of the request of Mr. Doerschuk. Certainly February 2d was a peculiar day from which to date or inaugurate such an investigation if it was really done in good faith.

I shall be pleased to learn your conclusions as to the matter and stand ready to assist you in any way I can.

Thanking you again for your courtesy in forwarding the little pamphlet, I am
Very sincerely yours,
O. D. BRAGDON.

P. S.—On second thought I inclose original letter of Mr. Doerschuk. Possibly the handwriting may be of consequence to you. See also copy of my letter to Mr. D.
B.

The following is Mr. A. N. Doerschuk's letter to Mr. O. D. Bragdon and forwarded to me, and which speaks for itself:

KANSAS CITY, MO., Feb 2, '94.

DEAR SIR:—Through the kindness of Mr. T. E. Wilson, librarian to the New York *World*, I have the great pleasure of this informal introduction to you. Mr. Wilson kindly addressed this letter for me, and its subject can best be stated in a few words. Recently I, with several of my intimate friends, have been deeply interested in Astrology. To satisfy our friends and ourselves of the actual science in the matter, we have decided if possible to have three distinct horoscopes cast by one of the foremost men in the science. Any actual expense connected with this matter will be gladly refunded by us. Hoping that you will kindly consent to accommodate us, and that we shall have the pleasure of an early reply, I remain
Very truly yours,
A. N. DOERSCHUK.

The next letter is Mr. Bragdon's letter to Mr. Doerschuk, of Kansas City, in reply to his first letter:

BOSTON, MASS., March 10th, 1894.

MR. A. N. DOERSCHUK,

DEAR SIR:—Your favor of February 2d, addressed to me by Mr. T. E. Wilson, has just been received, and its contents considered.

I appreciate the compliment that Mr. Wilson pays me but fear he has overlooked better talent nearer home, and in the belief that I may be better furthering your desires to have satisfactory evidence of the genuineness of the science, I have taken the liberty of forwarding your letter to Dr. L. D. Broughton, of No. 68 South Washington Square, New York City. This gentleman has wide experience in the science and his judgment and opinion will perhaps go as far to convince you of the actual science as could those of any man outside of yourselves. I would suggest that perhaps you might better convince yourselves of the truth of Astrology by each investigating his own nativity by the light of the rules of Astrology, which are easily obtained by any one from published works on the subject rather than to make your belief dependent upon the success or failure of any other human being in judging the details of your private lives. I judge you would not find it a very laborious task and think it would be far more satisfactory to you in the end.

Trusting I have acted for your best interests, and have best served the honesty of your purpose by referring your note to Dr. Broughton,

I remain, yours respectfully,
O. D. BRAGDON (Regulus).

The following is the first letter of Mr. A. N. Doerschuk to me, in reply to a short note to him stating that I had received his letter directed to Mr. O. D. Bragdon, of Boston, and that I wished further information about the horoscopes in question, and whether they were for individuals, or to be published in some newspaper or periodical. I also stated that I had sent him two or three pamphlets, etc.

KANSAS CITY, Mo., March 13, '94.

DR. L. D. BROUGHTON,

DEAR SIR:—Your favor of the 12th inst. inclosing the pamphlets on "Planetary Influence" and "Why I am an Astrologer" are at hand, also a letter from Mr. O. D. Bragdon, of the Regulus, of Boston, Mass., stating that our letter forwarded to him had been forwarded to you, in hope of obtaining better satisfaction of our desires.

We beg to thank you for your kindness as above mentioned and hope that we may have the extreme pleasure of your assistance in furthering to our satisfaction our knowledge of astrological matters, in which you are so well versed.

We desire to know what consideration must be offered to induce you to cast for us three separate and distinct horoscopes, giving a full description of the three persons, their past and present lives and their future possibilities; also what would be in your judgment the proper vocation of each individual; in short, we desire a complete nativity of each person cast by your own hands. We are not prompted in this by any morbid curiosity since we firmly believe in the science of your profession.

Our object has been to gain access to the most thoroughly learned authority on the subject, since we desire the riper judgment of others on matters concerning our own nativity. We sincerely hope that it may be within your province to be of service to us in this matter. We hope to receive an early reply stating what facts will be necessary and convenient in forwarding our ends. Hoping that we may have the benefit of your ripe knowledge and awaiting an early reply, we remain Truly yours,

Represented by A. N. DOERSCHUK.

The following is my reply to Mr. Doerschuk:

NEW YORK, March 20, 1894.

MR. A. N. DOERSCHUK,

DEAR SIR:—Yours of the 13th inst. came to hand on Saturday, but I have been too busy to answer it until to-day. I also received a letter from Mr. Bragdon, of Boston, stating that he had received one from you and that he had referred you to me.

If you had stated in your letter whether you wanted those horoscopes for publication or for private individuals, I should have understood better what to do. To make a complete horoscope, such as you desire, I will charge $20 each. But possibly you may get sufficient proof of the science of Astrology to satisfy yourself for five or ten dollars each. I shall require the name of the place where the party was born, so as to get the longitude and latitude of the place of birth, and also the exact time of birth, or as near the exact time as possible. That is, you must give the year, the month, day of month, hour and minute. If they do not know the minute, they had better send a short description of themselves, such as color of hair and eyes, weight, height, complexion, etc, and if there are any special marks on their person I should like to know them. But if they are satisfied of the exact time and place of birth, all the other information is not necessary.

If you want to convince yourself of the truth of Astrology the best plan is to take lessons in that science, the same as if you wanted to convince yourself of the truth of arithmetic.

I have had a great many pupils in my time, so have my brothers, my father and grandfather; and in all these years there has never been a pupil of any of our family that has discovered that Astrology was not a true science. Enclosed you will find a copy of a horoscope of Mr. David H. Reid, of 81 East 125th Street, New York.*

This gentleman sent his time of birth to the New York Sunday *News*, a paper that I have been writing for off and on for about 30 years, but I have contributed about three columns every Sunday for the last year and a quarter. You will also find inclosed three columns cut out of that paper of February 4th, 1894. In it you will find the horoscope marked and also find a copy of his letter. I have had hundreds of similar letters from persons who have had their horoscopes published in the Sunday *News*.

During last Summer Mr. Ruthiel, one of the editors of the Baltimore *News* sent his time of birth to the New York Sunday *News*, and in due course of time his horoscope was published. Afterwards my son, in writing to Mr. Ruthiel, asked him for his time of birth, and noticing that it was the same as had been published in the *News*, my son cut it out and sent it to him. Mr. Ruthiel, in writing to my son in reference to his own horoscope, made the following remarks: "The reputation of your father being the best in the country, if not in the world, I find is not misplaced. He has hit me exactly, the only difference is that I am fair; the time of marriage is exact (38 years); I do not see how he did it, and also the favorable and unfavorable periods mentioned are correct in every particular."

Possibly Mr. Ruthiel would be a more suitable person than myself to satisfy you of the truth of Astrology, as he has been in practice as a writer for over twenty years, has published much on the science, especially in the Baltimore Daily *News*, the Pittsburg *Dispatch*, and the *Capitol* at Washington, and he also has a good knowledge of Astrology.

Forty years ago I probably stood alone in this country as the champion of Astrology. Certainly I was the only one who was publishing anything advocating that science. I published *Broughton's Monthly Planet Reader and Astrological Journal* for many years, but since then it is astonishing how many people have given attention to that subject, and I think there must be scores in the country now that could convince you of the truth of that science, who have nearly all been taught by my father, my brothers, or myself. Probably the fairest test to prove the truth or falsity of the science would be to let me choose a number of times and places of birth out of those that I think I could handle best, and would prefer those that a few minutes out of the exact time would not make much differerence. For instance, the inclosed horoscope will convey the best idea of what I mean. It is what we term a plain horoscope and one that can be easily read without making any mistakes. Now had I to choose twenty or thirty of them, and if the whole came out perfectly correct, the same as an example in arithmetic, I think that ought to convince any skeptic who was ever likely to be convinced.

I am writing from six to ten columns each week for the Pittsburg *Dispatch*, similar to what I am writing for the New York Sunday *News*, and I

---

* I intended publishing Mr. David H Reid's horoscope, but I find I had not space.

might as a test pick out eight or ten of those times of birth and let the people whose horoscopes have been published report to the editor whether they are correct or not, their answers to be printed in the following Sunday's *Dispatch*. Even that would not be a perfect test, as the persons sending their time of birth to the *Dispatch* might not be absolutely certain of their exact moment of birth. As an illustration I will here state that when I lectured in 1866 and 1867 at 814 Broadway, New York, there was a gentleman handed in his time of birth and gave it at three o'clock in the afternoon; after I was through reading off his horoscope he stated that it was nearly all wrong. As soon as I saw the man standing up I told him he had not given me the correct time of birth, but he was absolutely certain that he had. He attended the lecture the following week and handed in his time of birth a second time. Remembering the date, I did not cast the map of the heavens, but made the remark at the close of the lecture that the gentleman whose horoscope was read last Tuesday night, had handed in his time of birth a second time and it is written three o'clock in the morning instead of three in the afternoon. I told the gentleman that he was still in error, that he could not have been born at three o'clock in the morning, but he might have been born at five o'clock A.M. He stated that he asked his parents and they had told him that the last statement was the correct time of birth. However he went home and told them what I said and they all hunted up the family Bible and it stated that he was born at five A.M., as I had informed him. He came to consult me on business and other matters a number of times afterwards. I will give one more instance. A gentleman who was formerly one of the editors of the New York *Herald*, who does not wish his name to be made public, since I published "Planetary Influence," has taken quite an interest in Astrology and has commenced studying it, and wishing to have the horoscopes of all his friends, he asked Mr. H., a private secretary of Mr. C. D., and he gave his time of birth as nine o'clock in the morning; after the map of the heavens had been erected this friend called on Mr. H. and told him he could not have been born at nine A.M. as his personal appearance would not answer to a man born under Leo. Mr. H. stated that it was the time his mother had given him. This friend then set to work to find out the time of birth from Mr. H.'s personal appearance and hit on 10:30 A.M. as answering his description, he then wrote the horoscope and took it to Mr. H. On his entering the office Mr. H. stated that he had since seen his father who had told him that he was born at 10:30 A.M. When Mr. H. read the horoscope he was somewhat surprised. The gentleman who employed Mr. H. had also taken some interest in this science and has had his horoscope cast, which has proved correct and is likely to be published shortly in some New York newspaper.

Astrology would have been much further advanced if it had not been for the persecution it has met with in all Christian countries. The Astrologers have been classed as witches and wizards and have been imprisoned and executed just the same as those imaginary beings; as the Bible states, "Thou shalt not suffer a witch to live," and the authorities have tried their best to fulfill that injunction.

Probably no science can be made as useful as Astrology if it is cultivated similar to Astronomy at the present day. If all boys and girls were taught the trades and professions that they are most suited for according to their horoscopes, as indicated by the science of Astrology, the amount of distress and misery that could be avoided would be astonishing. Often the unhappiness that married people suffer might be alleviated if not avoided by this science, if their horoscopes were compared previous to marriage.

It is published in books on marriage and stated by travellers from India that nearly one-half the people on the face of the earth at the present day are governed by this science in regard to choosing a partner for life. In India and China when a child is born they take the horoscope of that child and go to various friends and acquaintances to compare it with the horoscope of a child of the opposite sex, and keep on comparing until they meet with one that harmonizes with the horoscope then in hand. Then the friends or relations make arrangements for the marriage to take place when the parties become of a suitable age.

There was a Hindoo who gave a lecture on the manners and customs of the Hindoos a short time ago at the Liberal Club in New York City, and he made the statement that there was not one marriage in a thousand but what were successful and happy by following this method of comparing horoscopes of the opposite sex before becoming engaged or getting married. They do not ask the question in those countries, "Is marriage a failure?"

I have made this letter longer than I had intended, only I thought from the tenor of your letter that you wished to become interested in the science of Astrology.   Yours respectfully,

L. D. BROUGHTON.

The above letter was the last of the correspondence I had with Mr. A. N. Doerschuk, of No. 1201 Grand Avenue, Kansas City, Mo. He never even wrote to let me know that he had received my letter. Why he and his friends dropped the matter, I am unable to say; I can only conjecture. One of the editors of the New York *Herald*, to whom I read this letter, told me that it was a trap which they had deliberately planned, and that they would send the wrong time of birth of some person so as to expose Astrology in the New York *World* and thus boom the circulation of that paper. I am sorry that newspaper editors have such a bad opinion of each other, but they know one another better than I do. I am aware that there is nothing too low, mean or contemptible for the editors of the New York *World* to stoop to in order to increase their circulation. I need only refer to the sensation that they made in having John De Leon, an Astrologer, living in East 4th Street, New York, sent to Sing Sing fifteen years for no other reason than to boom their paper, as the editor, Col. John Cockerill, afterwards stated over his own signature, and then afterwards getting Prof. Richard A. Proctor to write the article called "The Humbug of Astrology," in which he called all Astrologers "silly, ignorant charlatans, rascals and lying knaves." The ex-editor of the New York *Herald* stated that I had made the best move that I could possibly have made in referring Mr. A. N. Doerschuk to one of the editors of the Baltimore *News*. He said it was a very good bluff and that it would end the matter, because the New York *World* would never attempt to fight one of the editors of the Baltimore *News*, who had a newspaper to back him.

I may be mistaken altogether in the above remarks, and it is possible that Mr. Doerschuk and his friends may have reconsidered the matter in regard to getting proofs of the truth of the science of Astrology, and did not care to go through the same kind of persecution that I and my family and friends have had to go through in advocating that science, and probably they may have thought that it would lower their standing in the community if it was found out that they were investigating the science of Astrology.

I will here state and try to prove in the latter part of this book that Richard A. Proctor deliberately told a falsehood in that article called the "Humbug of Astrology." I shall also republish *verbatim* Mr. Proctor's article from the New York *World* in the latter part of this volume, with my comments on the same, which the New York *World* refused to publish. Probably no other man stooped so low as to vilify, for a few dollars, persons who were utter strangers to himself as Richard A. Proctor did in that article.

I do not know whether the reader observed in Mr. O. D. Bragdon's letter, when speaking of myself, that he never even mentioned that I was silly, ignorant, a rascal, charlatan or lying knave. Possibly he does not know me as well as the New York *World* knows me.

I will here state that there is no learning, science, profession, trade, or secret order that forms a fellowship so binding and lasting as the knowledge of Astrology. Go where he will, if he meets any persons who have a knowledge of that subject he is always welcome and receives the greatest attention; at least that has always been so in my experience and with those persons whom I have known. It is only those persons (and chiefly the religious communities) who have no knowledge of Astrology who are the Astrologers' bitterest enemies. One more point which the reader should bear in mind, and that is once an Astrologer always an Astrologer. I have never known, and I don't believe that any other person has ever known a man or woman who having studied Astrology has afterwards discarded it; they may on account of the ignorance and prejudice of others around them not let it be known that they know anything about that science. In all other professions there are some back sliders, and who afterwards become skeptics or unbelievers.

In the foregoing pages I have endeavored to give some very strong proofs of the influence of the planets, the Sun and Moon on the earth and its inhabitants. The planetary influences can be recognized and calculated by their revolutions, their perihelion and aphelion and in their aspects or relations to each other.

Lord Bacon in his Organum, if I remember right, states that when any effect always follows any particular cause, and if that cause is increased the effect is also increased, and when the cause is decreased the effect is also reduced in proportion, and when the cause is entirely removed the effect also entirely ceases, then he says: "You may always attribute that particular effect as being produced by that particular cause."

I have quoted a sufficient number of instances from both profane and sacred history, and also an equal number of astronomical calculations of the positions of the planets, their various aspects to each other, when transiting any particular sign of the Zodiac to warrant a further investigation of this subject by any intelligent reader. Also I have every reason to believe that similar calculations and observations have been made by Astrologers in nearly all civilized countries, and those calculations reach back to a very remote period, if we can believe history and inscriptions on ancient buildings and the deductions of learned men.

The Bible contains much Astrology, if properly interpreted, especially in what is termed the Old Testament.

Job, which is one of the oldest books now in existence, in Chapter 38, verses 31, 33 says: "Canst thou bind the sweet influences of the Pleiades or loose the bands of Orion? Knowest thou the ordinances of Heaven? Canst thou set the dominion thereof in the earth." Isaiah, 47th Chap., 13th verse says: "Let now the Astrologers, the star-gazers, the monthly prognosticators stand up." And we also read in Daniel, 5th Chap., 11th verse, "That Daniel was made by the decree of Nebuchadnezzar master of all the magicians, Astrologers and Chaldeans in Babylon." I might go on making extracts from the Bible, Josephus, and other ancient books to prove that the science of Astrology antedates all ancient written history. They certainly prove that Astrology is no recent upstart, and that it has been known, studied and practiced from time immemorial.

All sciences are begun by accumulating facts and by observations and experiments; afterwards these facts, observations and experiments are compared and arranged in regular order. Hence it is said that *science* is knowledge methodically arranged and classified; it is then much easier to be learned, as the most simple part can be acquired first. Afterwards the more complicated parts can be learned, and so on. I hope I have succeeded in so arranging the various parts of the science of Astrology that any one who has acquired a common school education can study Astrology and prove its truth or falsity.

Before commencing the "Elements of Astrology," the reader may desire to know whether we have any facts to prove that the planets the Sun and Moon have any influence on the earth and its inhabitants, as he may think that if we cannot furnish some proof before commencing studying that science, it might be all a waste of time attempting to learn it; also it may be advisable to give some proof that in all ages and in all countries Astrology has in some way been mixed up in people's minds with other things, and other so-called learning, such as dreams, witchcraft, etc., that have no connection whatever with it. We have a remarkable illustration in the Bible where Pharoahs and kings believed that dreams were in some way associated with Astrology, and that Astrologers had some supernatural knowledge of interpreting dreams and other occult powers.

I give the following as proof of what I here state, and also proof of planetary influence on the earth and its inhabitants.

PHARAOH'S DREAM AND THE MAGICIANS OF EGYPT AND BABYLON.*

GENESIS XLI, 8.—"And it came to pass in the morning that his spirit was troubled, and he sent and called for all the magicians of Egypt, and all the wise men thereof, and Pharaoh told them his dream, but there was none that could interpret them unto Pharaoh."

14, 16. "Then Pharaoh sent and called Joseph, and Pharaoh said unto Joseph, I have dreamed a dream, and there is none that can interpret it, and I have heard say of thee, that thou canst understand a dream and interpret it."

According to the Bible it appears that Pharaoh was very much troubled about his dreams, and wished to have an interpretation of them, and no doubt he thought the Magicians and Wise Men were the most capable of interpreting them.

We also read in Daniel, chapter II, that Nebuchadnezzar had a dream which troubled him very much, but he did not remember it; he not only wanted the wise men to interpret the dream, but to tell him what he had dreamt, as we read in verses 2, 5, and 10:

"Then the king commanded to call the Magicians and the Astrologers and the Sorcerers and the Chaldeans, for to shew the king his dream; so they came and stood before the king."

"The king answered and said to the Chaldeans, The thing [dream] has gone from me; if you will not make known unto me the dream and the interpretation thereof, ye shall be cut in pieces. and your houses shall be made a dunghill."

"The Chaldeans answered before the king and said, There is not a man upon the earth that can show the king's matter; therefore there is no king, lord, or ruler that asketh such a thing of any Magician, or Astrologer, or Chaldean."

But Daniel made up a fine story, and told the king that he had been dreaming about a wonderful image, and gave the interpretation of the fictitious dream, which pleased the king. Had either Pharaoh or Nebuchadnezzar known anything about Astrology, they would not have sent for the Astrologer to interpret dreams, as that science has nothing to do with such matters. Pharaoh might as well have called together his land surveyors, or the builders of the pyramids and catacombs of Egypt to interpret his dreams as to call the Astrologers for that purpose.

Both in ancient and modern times people have had strong impressions or dreams when heavy calamities were hanging over them. The dreams of Pharaoh and Nebuchadnezzar are instances of ancient times,

---

* In ancient times people believed that the Lord spoke to persons in dreams and told them what to do, as we read in Matthew, chapter 2, verse 13, The angel of the lord appeared to Joseph, in a dream saying, "Arise and take the young child and his mother, and flee into Egypt."
We also read in Joel, 2d chapter, 28th verse : "Your sons and your daughters shall prophesy, your old men shall dream dreams, and your young men shall see visions."
Some of these dreams seems to have been so plain as to interpret themselves, but other dreams required what was called an interpreter, and some persons became very noted on account of their special gift in interpreting dreams, and were often in great demand.

and I might instance Lizzie Borden and President Lincoln of modern times. In the trial of Lizzie Borden it came out that she had told a lady friend, on the evening previous to the murder of her father and mother, that she was afraid something was going to happen to her father. We have another instance in that of President Lincoln, who the night before his assassination was troubled with an unpleasant dream. On the following morning he was very much depressed, and while at the Cabinet meeting he told those present about it, and said that he had similar dreams before the battle of Bull Run and other disastrous events of the Union army, and he was afraid that some other unfortunate event was about to take place that would in some way affect the Government. I need not remind the reader that on the same evening President Lincoln was assassinated by Wilkes Booth in Ford's Theatre, Washington, and the whole Cabinet came near being murdered that night by a band of conspirators.

In ancient times people paid more attention to dreams than they do now, and a good interpreter was in great demand. According to Bible history Joseph paid great attention to the interpretation of dreams. No doubt he had a particular gift for interpreting them, as is shown by the interpreting of the Butler's and Baker's dreams while they were in prison. In both cases the interpretation was true.

Joseph's gift as an interpreter is no argument for or against Astrology; yet I have heard scores of sermons on Pharaoh's dream and Joseph's successful interpretation, after the Magicians and Wise Men had failed, and it was noted as a forcible argument against the science of Astrology. The interpreters of dreams, clairvoyants, mind readers, Gypsies, fortune tellers, etc., although commonly classed under the name *Astrologers*, have no connection whatever with the science of Astrology.

Astrology is purely a science of observation and inductive philosophy, which has been continued for thousands of years, and by people who have made it their special business to make these observations, even in spite of the opposition and persecution which the votaries of this science have had to endure.

In ancient times all the civilized nations had their *wise men* and Astrologers on hand so as to be ready whenever the kings or Pharaohs wished to consult them, and, as Richard A. Proctor said, "The cuneiform inscriptions of Assyria, the hieroglyphs of Egypt, the most ancient records of Babylon, Persia, India, and China, agree in showing that of old *all men believed the Sun and Moon, Planets and Stars in their course foretell, nay, rule the fortunes of men.*"

In ancient times, and even of late years, everything of a mysterious nature was classed under the head of Astrology, and even Astronomy came under the same class, as all the calculations in that science were made solely for the use of Astrologers, and to enable them to make their predictions, before the science of navigation came into general practice.

Why Nebuchadnezzar, the king of Babylon, should have called the Astrologers to tell him his dream, is difficult to understand, as the most ancient books we have on Astrology in use at the present day, which were written more than two thousand years ago by one of the Pharaohs of Egypt, called Claudius Ptolemy, the author of the Ptolemaic system of Astronomy, does not mention anything about interpreting dreams by Astrology in his Four Books on that science.

MISREPRESENTATION OF ASTROLOGY.

The reader can judge how much Astrology has to do with the interpreting of dreams, clairvoyance, fortune-telling, etc., after he has read what follows, which I give as a sample of the observations which Astrologers have made of late years in that science, and also to prove for themselves whether or not Astrology has any foundation in the laws of nature.

THEORIES OF ANCIENT ASTRONOMERS.

HOW PLANETS ARE SUPPOSED TO AFFECT THE EARTH AND ITS INHABITANTS—JUPITER'S PERIHELION COINCIDENT WITH THE RETURN OF CHOLERA.

It is an axiom of modern philosophy that nothing occurs by chance; every event is the effect of the action of some law. Often the occurrence may be clouded so that its primary cause is not apparent, and some minds will consider it of the nature of a miracle, but investigation will always prove the existence of the motive power.

The periodic visitation of epidemics of disease is one of the occurrences to which many possible causes have been assigned, but medical men are far from giving a satisfactory explanation of their appearance. In some years cholera has started from its birthplace in India, and traveled over most of the world. In other years it has remained about its home, and we have heard little of it. It may be said that the circumstances which permit of its being carried to different places in the years of its greatest prevalence are the causes of its spreading; but this is not entirely true. The methods of prevention are never relaxed, as the people always regard it as a public enemy which has to be kept at a distance.

The passage of cholera from one place to another seems to be often more rapid than the means of communication by ordinary travel. That it is dependent upon and aided in its spread by atmospheric conditions is recognized; but that its germination is also dependent upon a vitiation of our atmosphere has not been admitted by the medical faculty.

It was the accepted theory of the old astronomers that the earth was influenced by the other planets of our solar system. Since the change from the Ptolemaic system of astronomy, which was based upon the theory that the earth was the centre and all the other planets revolved around it, the modern theories have accepted the sun only as the source of all power and life, and the influence of our sister planets upon mundane life has been denied.

That the ancient astronomers could have followed their theories blindly for so long a time, without some basis in fact, seems hardly probable, and that the evidences upon which their theories were based were not altered by the discovery that the groundwork of their structure was wrong, leads a few men to-day to accept some of their teachings as true. It was their belief that certain positions of the planets so influenced our earth that epidemics, earthquakes, and often changes in our social relations, were the result. That it has some basis in truth is evidenced by circumstances which may be easily verified.

In our solar system the planets, including the earth, revolve around the sun in regular periods. The orbits, or paths, of the journeying spheres do not form a perfect circle, however, and each planet at some part of its path is nearer to the sun than in other portions of its orbit. The great Kepler proved that these orbits take the form of an ellipsis or oval, of which the sun forms the central point of one end. When a planet passes that portion of its circle where it is nearest to the sun it is technically considered in its perihelion, from the Greek peri, about or near, and helios, the sun. In the opposite segment of its circle it is said to be in aphelion.

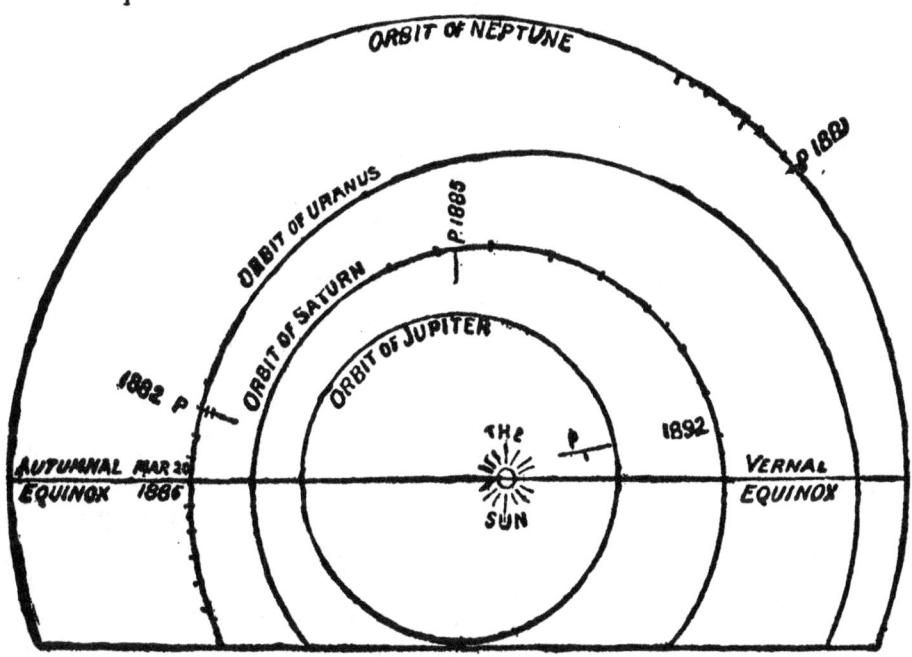

The periods when the superior planets, Jupiter, Saturn, Uranus and Neptune are in their perihelia seems to be coincident with the appearance of epidemics of disease, and particularly with the return of Jupiter and Saturn to that portion of their orbits does the earth and its inhabitants seem to suffer.

Jupiter makes the circuit around the sun in a little less than twelve years. Owing to the ovoid form of his orbit, he is near the sun about one-quarter of the time, and away from the central orb three-quarters.

Saturn makes his revolution in about twenty-nine and one-half years, and, therefore, is in perihelion several years. Two of these periods of Saturn occupy about fifty-nine years, and correspond to five of the periods of Jupiter; and both planets reach their nearest point to the sun together every fifty-nine years, and are at that time many millions of miles nearer to the great central orb than they are in aphelion.

The article on cholera in the August number of the New York Medical Journal for 1871 asserts that cholera had broken out in Hudwar, India, every twelfth year since 1783, and notably in 1867. This seems to correspond with the perihelion epochs of Jupiter, and a study of a few of these epochs may be interesting.

PERIHELION EPOCH OF JUPITER.

The years 1892 and 1893 is one of the times when Jupiter is passing the central point of his perihelion. That the earth has felt some disturbing influence is easily proven. The prevalence of cholera, which threatened to invade this country, after making itself felt so disastrously in Hamburg and different parts of Germany, France, Russia, Spain, and Italy, and the great mortality which it produced in those countries, besides the large number of cases and deaths at New York Quarantine in the summer and fall of 1892; also the return of typhus fever to New York in the spring of that year, and the large number of cases and deaths from that disease. It is a remarkable coincidence that we have not had a single case of typhus fever either in New York or any part of the United States since the last perihelion of Jupiter in 1881, and typhus cases are likely to occur until Jupiter gets out of his perihelion.

Regarding the prospects of cholera visiting the Unite States in the year (1893), the following is from the New York Sunday News of July 16th, 1893:

"Cholera Prospects.—What is the outlook for cholera? asks a correspondent of the Philadelphia Times. Latest advices from United States consular and medical officers abroad are gloomy. The disease prevails all over France. It is at Nantes, Quimper, Narbonne, Montpelier, Niemes, Toulouse, and Cette. There are several cases at Marseilles, from which great port vessels are sailing every day for America. In the district of Lorient and Vannes the plague is widespread. Meanwhile it is raging in Galicia, Austro-Hungary, and in several provinces of Southwest Russia. However, it is well-nigh impossible to get any definite information as to the progress of the complaint in the Czar's dominions, owing to a secretive official policy. Complaining of this, our Minister at St. Petersburg asks that a physician under the Marine Hospital Service be attached to the legation for the purpose of gathering medical news.

"The plague has just broken out at Mecca with alarming virulence. The holy city is only two days' journey by caravan from the nearest Red Sea port. At the same time the United States Minister at Constantinople reports that the disease is spreading rapidly westward from Bagdad across Mesopotamia toward the Mediterranean. There is much commerce directly between this country and the ports of the Mediterranean and Red Sea. When it is considered that such news is far from reassuring, it is some comfort to know that there is no cholera in Germany. At Hamburg, which no longer gets its water supply from the infected River Elbe, only one case has appeared since March 1."

Great credit is due both to the authorities at Washington and the Board of Health of New York in preventing cholera from getting a foothold in this city in the fall of 1892; and if Jupiter were only further along in his perihelion, we might venture to hope that the same vigilance will prevent its access here in the summer and fall of 1893.

As one of the effects of the present perihelion of Jupiter, I might mention the visits of La Grippe, which has *traveled twice around the world* in the last few years, and carried off hundreds of thousands of its victims, and left its lasting effects on millions of others which it attacked, but which survived after a lingering illness.

The large number of earthquakes, volcanic eruptions, cloudbursts, and floods, in all parts of the world, seems to give rise to a belief in the existence of some super-mundane cause. As Jupiter will be in his perihelion for nearly two years yet, it is probable, judging from past events, that we shall suffer more or less during that time.

Twelve years ago was the period of Jupiter's last passage around the sun, and for a couple of years previous, as well as in the years immediately following, there were diseases in epidemic form. In the years 1878, 1879, 1880, and 1881, yellow fever was epidemic part of the time in New Orleans, Memphis, and Vicksburg; the black pest in Russia and Turkey, where diphtheria was also prevalent; a severe epidemic of cholera existed in India, which spread to Egypt and invaded France, being epidemic in Marseilles and Toulon, carrying off thousands of the inhabitants of the two cities, and crossing into Italy. There were many cloudbursts, cyclones and earthquakes in those years. Typhus fever was prevalent in 1881 in New York, and there had not been any cases of that disease here for a number of years previous.

In 1868 Jupiter was in perihelion, and as early as 1866 cases of cholera occurred in the United States, and the disease was prevalent from that time till 1873. Perhaps the most serious time was in the year 1866. In 1867 it was very violent in India.

The next previous perihelion of Jupiter was in 1856. Saturn also reached his nearest point to the sun in that year, and diseases were prevalent for several years before and after that time. Cholera broke out in this country in 1851, and lasted several years. Yellow fever was more virulent than usual in the South; in New Orleans in 1853, and again in 1856, and in Norfolk in 1855. During the French, English, and Russian war in 1854 and 1855, cholera and low fevers carried off thousands of soldiers in the Crimea. The number of deaths was so great as to attract the attention of the whole civilized world.

Jupiter made his next previous perihelion in 1845. In that year cholera commenced in India and traveled to every part of Europe, and notably severe in Russia. In England it was particularly virulent. In that part of England where I then resided there was scarcely a house in which cholera did not exist, and in some families every member died. The mortality was so great in some neighborhoods that one person out of every seventeen died of the disease; and the atmosphere there was so vitiated that perishable food became putrid in much less than the usual time. A piece of meat elevated on the tail of a kite became putrid in little over an hour. I remember in the summer and fall of 1848 when walking out evenings, that the atmosphere was so heavy and oppressive that at times it was very difficult to breathe, and it had a very oppressive effect on me. The cholera reached this country in 1848, and was epidemic in New York and Philadelphia. Mars was in his perigee in 1847, and probably assisted in the vitiation of the atmosphere.

In 1833 Jupiter was once more near the sun. That year and the year previous are known in the history of the country as the cholera years. The disease commenced in India in 1829, and in 1830 spread over Europe with great virulence and rapidity. The disease made such great inroads into our population that it will probably be remembered for generations to come. Most of our oldest citizens refer back to that time as the cholera year. Mars was in perigee in 1832, and probably lent his influence to the destruction of life. Saturn was in perihelion in 1826, and his deteriorating power was probably the starting of the epidemic so early in Europe.

In 1797 Jupiter and Saturn reached their nearest point to the sun about the same time, and Uranus made the visit in 1798. Noah Webster, the compiler of the dictionary which bears his name, collected the data of epidemics in past centuries, in two volumes, and published them in 1799, under the head of "A History of Pestilential Diseases." His account of the events of these years is startling.

Yellow fever was prevalent in every seaport of the United States as far north as Portland, Me. In Philadelphia it was very severe, and the accounts written by Dr. Rush of his experience then may be read with interest by those who desire to investigate. Winters were very severe at that period, and the Delaware river was frozen over for months at a time; and for this reason, as well as the unhealthy summers and the yellow fever in that city continuing until the frost set in, Philadelphia received its great fall and New York its rise. From that time the Pennsylvania metropolis lost its prestige as a seaport, and New York was the gainer.

Many theories have been advanced to account for the influence of planets in their perihelia. That immense bodies like Jupiter and Saturn are likely to affect the other planets of our solar system by their approach to the central power, is reasonable. The means by which this influence is transmitted to the earth is, of course, a matter for speculation.

A very ingenius theory is, that the presence of these great orbs near the sun interferes with the operation of the law of gravitation upon the earth, the lessening of the sun's influence permitting the exudation of vapors, and reducing the vitality of the earth's inhabitants. That there are many eruptions of volcanoes and earthquakes, cloudbursts and cyclones at such times would seem to give force to the idea that some of the sustaining power is taken from the earth's crust.

Noah Webster finally arrived at the theory that comets were the cause of the atmospheric disturbance which produced epidemics and pestilential diseases, and instances the cosmic visitor of 1797.

Mr. Webster afterwards gave up that theory, and adopted another one, which was, that volcanoes and earthquakes were the causes of epidemics, by permitting large quantities of noxious gases and impure or poisonous air to escape from the bowels of the earth during their operation, and instances the effect of "the great volcanic eruption in Iceland in 1783, by which the atmosphere was rendered pestilential by discharges of fire and lava from the earth, so much so that the rain which fell was *acid* and *corrosive*, destroying *cattle and men*, covering the bodies of cattle with pustules and sores, and excoriating the hands and faces of men when it fell on them. It also killed vegetables. The effects were felt not only in Iceland, but in Norway and other parts of Europe."

Mr. Webster appears sometimes to get confused while writing his two volumes of "Epidemics and Pestilential Diseases," and is at a loss how to account for the *causes of these diseases*. Yet, as he says, it can be proven by history that one-fourth of the deaths have been caused by epidemics, and there must be some cause which produces them. His motive in writing the history of those epidemics was to try and find out what was their cause. His theory of earthquakes and volcanic eruptions being the cause, does not appear to meet the case. As he gives instances where people were driven out of cities by epidemics, and afterwards driven back by earthquakes that occurred in the country. Therefore, according to his theory, the effect came before the cause.

Is it not possible that when a number of superior planets are in their perihelion at the same time, and those planets, which are a thousand times larger than the earth, and they at that time being millions of miles nearer the sun than when at their aphelion, that those planets when near the sun may so act on it, and that orb may react on our atmosphere, so as to produce earthquakes, volcanic eruptions, and other disturbances of the atmosphre, such as cloudbursts, tornadoes, etc., which in their turn may cause pestilential diseases, and epidemics naturally to follow, or at least be more prevalent at those periods than at other times?

Sometimes very heavy floods spread over a large tract of low lands, carrying mud and vegetation with it; the sun, acting on it, decomposing the vegetation and producing fermentation, will often produce chills and fever, bilious and, at times, typhoid fever. These fevers may so debilitate the constitution of the inhabitants as to make them liable to contract other diseases, the germs of which may exist in the atmosphere.

An extensive overflowing of the Nile in Egypt has been known to produce typhus fever and the plague, which has extended into other countries.

Even famine has been known to produce epidemics, an instance of which is in Genesis xli, 54, when the Nile did not overflow for seven years.

ACTION AND REACTION OF ONE PLANET ON ANOTHER.

That one planet has an effect on another I think cannot be questioned. We have a remarkable instance in the discovery of the planet Neptune by Mr. Leverrier in 1846. For a long time astronomers noticed that the planet Uranus did not always proceed at its uniform motion in its orbit, and they came to the conclusion that there must be an undiscovered planet whose orbit was outside that of Uranus. Mr. Leverrier, by his calculations, not only predicted in what part of the heavens Neptune must be at that time, but said that the planet must be equal to a star of the tenth magnitude to produce the disturbing effect in the motion of Uranus that had been noticed by himself and other astronomers.

If two planets, Neptune and Uranus, which are A THOUSAND . MILLION

MILES APART, have a perceptible effect on each other, that can be noticed by our astronomers with their telescopes, why may not some of the nearer planets to the earth, as Venus, Mars, and Jupiter, have a marked influence on the earth and its inhabitants which may be noticed without a telescope?

The effect of the sun and moon on our tides is a convincing proof that one planet has an influence on another, to say nothing about the seasons of the year produced by the sun's rays striking the earth at differents angles, which cause summer and winter.*

THE EFFECT ON THE EARTH AND ITS INHABITANTS OF THE NEAR APPROACH OF MARS.

Let us examine the effect of one of the nearest planets to our earth—*Mars*, termed a superior planet, as its orbit is outside that of the earth, and ascertain whether it has had any effect upon the earth's atmosphere and its inhabitants.

Mars, when it makes one of its periodical visits near the earth, called its perigee, and when the earth is between the sun and Mars, the full disc of the God of War is presented to us as the moon is when at its full. Then Mars appears to us much larger than at other times.

Very little knowledge of astronomy is necessary to understand the relation of this planet to our earth, and the reasons for the changes in its apparent size when viewed from mother earth. The rapidity of motion of the planets around the sun is in proportion to their distance from the sun. Although there is believed to be a small planet closer to the sun, the nearest that we recognize as of sufficient importance to name is the God of Messengers, Mercury, which makes a revolution around the celestial centre in about eighty-eight days.

Next to Mercury is Venus, whose revolution is two hundred and twenty-four and two-thirds days. The planet in which we all have a vital interest, is next to Venus. The earth makes the journey around the sun in three hundred and sixty-five days, five hours, forty-eight minutes and forty-eight seconds, or one revolution in one year. Mars lies outside of the earth's circle, and completes its circuit around the sun in one year, ten and one-half months. Jupiter is next in the group, and occupies nearly twelve years in the circuit. Saturn takes twenty-nine and a half years, Uranus, or Herschel, as the older astrono-

---

* It has been observed by astronomers that when Jupiter is in his perihelion, that a great number of spots appear upon the sun; they are sometimes formed in a few hours, and are thousands of miles in diameter, and are even so large that our earth could be dropped into one of them without touching either side; also, cloudbursts, tornadoes, etc., are more frequent on the earth during the time the sun spots are most numerous and larger than usual. The spots disappear when Jupiter is in his aphelion. This proves almost beyond question that the planets react on each other. Also, it has been noticed that the Aurora Borealis, or Northern Lights, are brighter and more numerous when Jupiter is in his perihelion, and when there are spots on the sun. We have had no Northern Lights to speak of since Jupiter was last in his perihelion in 1881, until within the last two years.

Is it not reasonable that when the sun's envelopment is so disturbed by electricity and magnetism that the electricity coming from the sun to our earth and other planets should so disturb the earth's electricity as to cause cloudbursts, cyclones, tornadoes, and other atmospheric disturbances and at times even so disarrange the gases of our atmosphere sufficient to produce epidemics and other diseases? ☞ See note, page 62.

mers called him, eighty-four years and twenty-seven days, and Neptune, the most distant yet discovered, consumes one hundred and sixty-five years in his passage from any given point in his orbit around the sun and back to the same place.

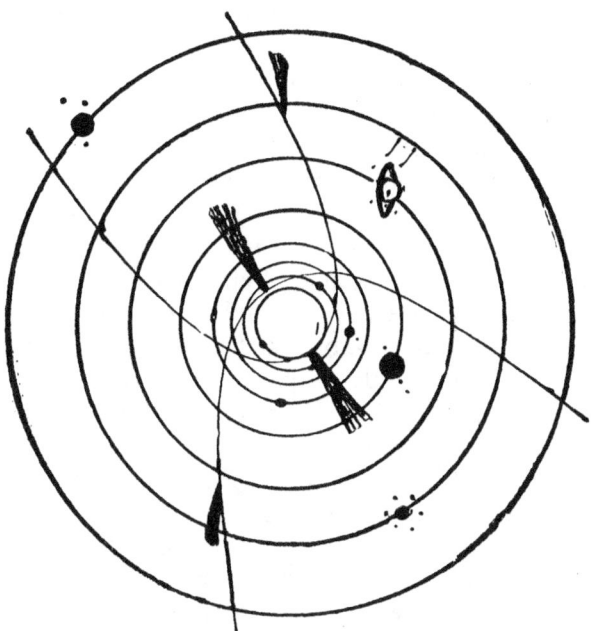

DIAGRAM OF THE SOLAR SYSTEM.

The above diagram is a representation of the Solar System, with the sun in the center, and the planets revolving around it. The large dot on the outer circle, in the upper left hand, represents Neptune, which is calculated to be 2,850 million miles away from the sun. The dot on the next inner circle, opposite Neptune, is Uranus, which is 1,828 million miles from the sun. On the next inner circle, on the right upper side, or the dot with the ring around it, is the planet Saturn, which is 909 million miles from the sun. The large dot on the next inner circle, below Saturn, is Jupiter, which is 495 million miles from the sun. On the next inner circle, on the lower portion, is Mars, at the distance of 145 million miles from the sun. The next dot, just on the line toward the sun from Jupiter, is the planet we are all interested in, the Earth, and it revolves around the sun at the distance of 95 million miles. On the next inner circle, on the upper right hand side, is the planet Venus, which revolves around the sun at the distance of 68 million miles. The little dot on the smallest circle, and opposite the planet Venus, is Mercury, which is 37 million miles from the sun. The ovals, with the dots and the long tails to them, are comets coming toward and receding from the sun. They always come toward the sun with the head or nucleus foremost, but when they get near that orb they commence to turn around, with their tails away from the sun, and back away tail foremost, with the head or nucleus still toward the sun. The comet on the lower portion is represented as approaching the sun, and the one on the upper part represents a comet receding or going away from the sun. The very small dots around the larger ones represent the moons of the planets.

MARS IN OPPOSITION TO THE SUN.

The approach of Mars to our earth was always viewed by the old astronomers as a period to be dreaded. They believed that wars, famines, volcanic eruptions, and earthquakes would be the result, and certainly there were many curious coincidences to give coloring to their fears. That this position of Mars does affect our atmosphere cannot be disputed; whether by an interference with the supply of vital fluid from the sun, the robbing of us by the attractive power of the visitor of our magnetism from the sun, or simply by disturbing the equilibrium of our gases and changing the relations of the elements which form our atmosphere, is not known. That some disturbance occurs is a fact.

In the case of Mars, it is an easy matter to refer to the period when he approaches nearest to our earth, and, though he does so once in every revolution, yet the greatest occurrences are at the time when our earth lies between the sun and Mars, and Mars is in his perigee at the same time, which is once in about fifteen years. Mars is then said to be in perigee, and at the same time in opposition to the sun, as the old astronomers termed it, the earth in those days being considered the centre of our planetary system.

The planet Mars was, in August, 1892, in this unfavorable position, and whether his presence was the cause of the labor strikes in Pennsylvania, Western New York, and Tennessee or not, it is strange that the two should occur together. Mars passes on, and as it began to pass its perigee the labor troubles at Carnegie's and other parts of the United States were gradually adjusted, and the excitement subsided. And we may thank the God of War for his departure and the peaceful settlement of the labor troubles.

The last time that Mars paid the earth a similar visit was in 1877. It does not require a very good memory to recall the stirring incidents of that memorable year in the history of labor troubles. Pennsylvania has been much stirred by the Homestead troubles, but the Carnegie strike was nothing compared to the Pittsburg riots of that year. Business was stagnated, and the whole country was aroused by the scenes which transpired in 1877. And had it not been for Wm. H. Vanderbilt offering a premium to the employees of the New York Central and Hudson River Railroad, it is more than likely that there would have been a general strike of railroad employees throughout the United States. As it was, there was a large number of the militia called out to put down riots in different States. The moons of Mars were discovered at that time.

THE PERIOD OF THE WAR.

From 1877 it requires but slight thought to carry every citizen back another fifteen years. War and strife darkened our country in 1861–'65, and from the perils of that period we are only now recovering. That visit of Mars was intensified by another influence, which we will refer to further on.

In 1847–8 the next previous approach of Mars to the earth brought war with Mexico and this country, also exciting political times in Europe, where every government felt some disturbing element. Louis Phillippe met his downfall in France, the Pope was forced to seek safety in flight from Rome, all were a strange series of coincidences.

Fifteen years previous to that time carries us back to 1832. Few persons are alive to-day to tell of the scenes of the cholera epidemic. It was the greatest infliction this country ever suffered from the dread disease, and business was nearly at a standstill.

In 1832 England was on the verge of a revolution, and only the passage of the Reform bill prevented serious disturbances and cruel war.

CRITICAL TIMES.

It may be asserted that wars, riots, disease and other troubles have come when Mars was far from the earth, and it is not to be denied. But Mars is not the only planet whose visits have seemed to be coincident with mundane disturbances. All life insurance companies agree in the statement that the twenty-ninth year is the most critical period in the lives of individuals. More deaths occur at this age, or immediately preceding or following it, than at any other time, except in early infancy. This period corresponds exactly to the revolution of Saturn, whose journey around the sun is completed in twenty-nine and a-half years. The older astronomers paid more attention to that evil planet than our present students of astral science.

The most remarkable coincidences, though, are to be found by a study of the revolutions of the distant orb Uranus. Most stirring scenes have followed his return to certain positions in the Zodiac, and though it cannot be explained why, or by what means these phenomena are brought about, yet they are easily seen to be quite nearly allied in time.

According to the writings of ancient astronomers, such as Claudius Ptolemy and other ancient Astrologers, each country was said to be ruled by a particular sign of the Zodiac; for instance, Aries was said to rule England, Taurus Ireland, and the celestial sign Gemini has been considered by students of astral science to be the constellation which rules the United States. The incidents which have led to the adoption of this theory are worthy of study; particularly those phenomena which have seemed to follow the advent of Uranus and other planets into this constellation. Uranus is at present in the sign of Scorpio. He remains in a sign seven years, traveling through the twelve signs of the Zodiac in his circuit around the sun in eighty-four years. Uranus entered the constellation of Gemini the last time in 1859, and occupied seven years, or until 1865, in transiting through it.

A STIRRING PERIOD.

This period, commencing with the Harper's Ferry incident, and followed by the firing on Fort Sumter, the bloody battles of an awful rebellion was one of the most trying times the Federation of our Union has ever passed through.

In the January number of "The Monthly Planet Reader and Astrological Journal"* of 1861, published in Philadelphia at that time by the author, referring to the then anticipated Civil War, I said :—"Uranus does not pass out of Gemini until 1865, and I do not look for any peace for this country until that time." This period was also made critical by the perigee of Mars. I remember distinctly in reading the newspapers at the time the account of the capture of the arsenal at Harper's Ferry, Va., the arrest, trial and hanging of John Brown; the bombardment and surrender to the rebels of Fort Sumter; the secession of the Southern

---

* The back numbers of the above named Journal, bound in one volume, containing a number of predictions relating to the Civil War, also horoscopes of the leading Generals in the United States at the time, mailed to any address for $1.00.

States; the battles of Bull Run and Ball's Bluff; the surrender of New Orleans and Vicksburg and a number of Southern forts to the Union army; the battles of Chancellorsville and Petersburg; the battles in the Wilderness, Spotsylvania, and Cold Harbor; also the battles of Shiloh, Lookout Mountain, and of Gettysburg, Sherman's march to the sea, and the surrender of General Lee to General Grant, at Appomattox Court House, on April 9th, 1865, just as the planet Uranus was approaching the end of the sign Gemini. Uranus entered the sign Cancer on the 25th of June, when the war came to an end.*

Let us go back to the next previous transit of the planet Uranus through Gemini, which carries us back eighty-four years, and we arrive at another exciting period when Uranus and war were coincident visitors. It is just eighty-four years from 1859 to 1775, and from that year till 1782 our country passed through fire and devastation, or, as Thomas Paine said, "these were the times that tried men's souls."

There is not a schoolboy who has not read about the "War of the Revolution," and knows all about the throwing of the tea into Boston harbor, the battles of Bunker Hill and Lexington, the retreat of Washington through New Jersey and his recrossing the Delaware, the trying winter months at Valley Forge, the battles of Bennington and Schuylerville, the treachery of Benedict Arnold, and the surrender of Lord Cornwallis to General Washington.

Uranus entered the sign of Gemini in the spring of 1775, and left that sign in the spring of 1782. Hale's "History of the United States" says: "Early in the spring of 1782 pacific overtures were made to the American Government, and both nations desisted from hostile measures."

IMPORTANT ERA IN HISTORY.

Eighty-four years previous to the time of the American Revolution was not so serious a period for the country, but from 1691 to 1698 was sufficiently marked to be considered an important era in history. The Salem witchcraft horrors were during that period, and the semi-insanity

---

* Some of my critical readers may be disposed to say that as the war came to an end before the planet Uranus left the sign Gemini, therefore that planet had nothing to do with the war of the Rebellion. At the time of Gen. Lee's surrender to Gen. Grant, April 9, 1865, Uranus had less than four degrees to travel to get out of the ruling sign of this country. Even then the excitement of the Rebellion was not quite over, as President Lincoln was shot after that time. And when the last of the Rebels surrendered on May 26th, Uranus was over twenty-eight degrees and eleven minutes in Gemini. All Astrologers agree in their writings that when a planet is over twenty-eight degrees in a sign, it then takes on the influence of the sign following. Therefore Uranus's influence over the United States was ended at the time when the war came to an end.

When I predicted in the "Monthly Planet Reader" of January, 1861, "that until Uranus gets out of the sign Gemini," which would not be "until June, 1865, we do not look for any peace for this country," the people of Philadelphia had many a good laugh at my expense, as nearly everybody came to the conclusion that the excitement would soon blow over; and even Abraham Lincoln was of the same opinion, as he said in his speeches "that there was nobody hurt." In the April number of 1861 I said: " I look for warlike preparations during the middle of April, or some decided blow being struck either by the General Government or the seceding States." I need not remind the reader that the Rebels commenced firing on Fort Sumter on April 13th. Also, in the April number of 1865 I made the following prediction: "Some noted General or a person in high office dies or is removed about the 17th or 18th. President Lincoln died on April 15th, after being shot by Wilkes Booth on the 14th. I mention these as remarkable coincidences made by the calculation of the motions of the planets and their influence on mundane affairs.

which seemed to fill the minds of learned judges was enough in itself to indicate that the same disturbing influence was operating. Uranus entered Gemini in the spring of 1691, and the first accusation of bewitching occurred in Salem in February, 1692, and the first trial for witchcraft in June of that year. Hale's History says "the war with the French and Indians, which began in 1690, was not yet terminated. For seven years were the frontier settlements harassed by savages, and the English employed in expeditions against them. A history of these would consist only of repeated accounts of Indian cunning and barbarity, and of English enterprise and fortitude. Peace between England and France, which took place in 1697, was soon followed by peace with the savages."

The next previous period of Uranus's visit to Gemini was during the seven years commencing in 1607. Captain John Smith with Captain Christopher Newport reached Chesapeake Bay, ascended the James River, and founded the village of Jamestown, the first permanent settlement in the country, in April, 1607, the time that Uranus entered the sign of Gemini. The unsettled conditions which followed are very easily remembered by students, and the troubles of the early settlers did not cease until 1614, when the immigrants made up their minds to embark from Jamestown, and distribute themselves among the fishermen on the banks of Newfoundland. With this intention they embarked, but just as they drew near the mouth of the James River Lord Delaware appeared with immigrants and supplies. Sir Thomas Dale, who ruled with vigor and wisdom, made several valuable changes in the laws of the colony.

Uranus left the sign Gemini in 1614. Hale, in his "History of the United States," when describing the condition of the people at Jamestown from 1607 to 1614, says: "The latter part of this period of suffering and gloom was long remembered with horror, and was distinguished by the name of '*the starving time.*' In six months at one time want, sickness, anarchy, and vice had *reduced the number of the colony from 490 to 60.*"

I have given the historical effect of one planet in the ruling sign of the United States, extending from 1607 to 1865. The events that took place in each of the seven years, or during the time that Uranus remained in the sign Gemini, may be said to be the epochs in the history of this country. In short, if the events that occurred in the seven years that Uranus remained in Gemini, in the four revolutions, were to be left out of the history of the United States, we should have a history of the country which would be similar in every respect to the play of Hamlet with Hamlet left out.

In the foregoing pages I have pointed out the influences or the effects of the planets on mundane affairs, when acting separately, and proved from history the events which have occurred near the same time. To say the least, it must strike the reader as something very remarkable, and it is somewhat strange that the attention of the learned professions, especially astronomers, has not previously been drawn to those remarkable coincidences.

But these gentlemen have been so engaged in ridiculing everything that had any resemblance to investigating the laws of nature, that they have not been able to look any further than the end of their noses.

Mr. B. G. Jenkins, of London, England, said in a paper read by him before the Dulwich College Geological Club, in the summer of 1888, on

METEOROLOGY AND PLANETARY INFLUENCE:

"From the lofty heights of modern science we have been accustomed to look down with pity and contempt upon the Astrologer of the Middle Ages—the weak dabblers in science, who were foolish enough to believe that the stars had an influence upon man. An allusion to Astrology was always good to raise a laugh at a science meeting, and the Astrologers and Alchemists were classed together as either dreamers or charlatans. Of late years, however, a reaction has set in. The Astrologer is becoming habilitated very rapidly. The influence of the planets upon the earth is now admitted to be very distinct, and fresh proofs of their disturbing influences are constantly cropping out."

If the planets Mars, Jupiter, and Uranus, the first in its perigee and in opposition to the sun, the second in perihelion, and the third while transiting through Gemini, the ruling sign of the United States, have produced such marvelous effects, both in this country and in other parts of the world, and their influences have been so conspicuous as to become almost landmarks in the history of those nations, is it not possible, reasoning from analogy, that the effect may be even more marked on the earth and its inhabitants when there are two or more planets operating at the same time? This can only be proved or disproved by making astronomical calculations and referring to pages of history for facts.

Jupiter's perihelion occurs every eleven years and ten months; Mars, when in opposition to the sun and in his perigee at the same time, occurs about every fifteen years. Sometimes these phenomena coincide or occur near the same time; at other times they occur a number of years apart.

We will only notice those periods when the perigee and perihelion of these planets occur near the same time, and refer to pages of history for corroboration of their influence. But before doing so let us refer to another remarkable coincidence. Is it not singular that the first time cholera broke out in its native home, Hudwar, India, and spread to other countries in 1783; also the time when the great volcanic eruption in Iceland, which caused such sad havoc to animal and vegetable life, should both occur in the same year? Noah Webster, in his first volume, was of the opinion that comets were the cause of epidemics, as he had noticed in history that either during or just previous to epidemics, comets made their appearance, and that but few if any exceptions to this rule had ever occurred; but in his second volume, his attention having been called to the destructive effects to animal life of the great volcanic eruption in Iceland, and of volcanoes in other places, he came to the conclusion that volcanic eruptions and earthquakes were the causes of epidemics and pestilential diseases.

The first perihelion of Jupiter which I shall call attention to occurred in 1785, or within two years of the great volcanic eruption in Iceland, and the first perigee of Mars, which occurred near that time, was in 1787, two years afterwards. In 1789 the French revolution broke out, which lasted many years, and which deluged the greater part of France in blood, and plunged the whole civilized world into war, and over one million soldiers were slain.

In 1832 Mars was again in perigee, and Jupiter in perihelion in 1833. This planetary influence was intensified by the perihelion of Saturn in 1826. Then occurred the greatest epidemic of cholera ever known; also there was a great commotion in England, which lasted several years, and came close to a civil war, as the people demanded and got the extention of the franchise. In 1845 was another perihelion of Jupiter, and in 1847 Mars was in his perigee, when cholera again spread over nearly the whole world. The United States was at war with Mexico, and all Europe was in political convulsions, which continued for several years. In August, 1892, Mars was again in his perigee, and in October Jupiter was in perihelion. I need only to refer to the epidemic of La Grippe. It has been estimated that over three hundred thousand persons died of that disease in the United States in its two visits of 1889–'90. It is reported that other countries in Europe and Asia suffered more in proportion to their population than the United States did. In short, there is not a part of the earth where La Grippe did not visit in its two voyages around the world. To say nothing about the epidemic of cholera in Europe and Asia in the summer and fall of 1892 and during the present summer (1893); also yellow fever is prevalent this summer. In Brazil it was reported that three hundred a day were dying of the fever. Small pox in Norway is so epidemic that the Emperor of Germany did not touch at any of the ports on his voyage in the North Sea in July, 1893.

There is no doubt but that these evil influences will produce the most dire effects in France and Germany, and that both those countries will be deluged in blood. I shall dwell more on this subject in the latter part of this volume, in which I shall publish the horoscope of William II. of Germany and the horoscope of the time when the third Republic of France was formed.

The effect of the perihelion of Jupiter and the perigee of Mars occurring within two months of each other in 1892, will certainly be more disastrous than that which occurred before the French Revolution, and will be more lasting, but not quite so disastrous in causing epidemics, on account of three superior planets, Saturn, Uranus and Neptune, each getting out of his perihelion and going into aphelion. But there is no doubt but that before Jupiter gets out of his perihelion, which will not be before the end of 1894, we shall have enough cholera and other epidemics, both on this continent and in Europe and Asia, to satisfy any reasonable person.

If the planet Uranus had entered the sign Gemini seven years later, or in 1783 instead of 1775, or if the perigee of Mars or the perihelion of Jupiter had occurred seven years earlier, the war of the Revolution would have been more destructive of human life than it was. Even as it was, the United States felt the disastrous effect of Jupiter and Saturn in their perihelion in 1797 and of Uranus in 1798, when yellow fever was epidemic from New Orlaans to Portland, Maine, during 1793, 1794 and 1795.

If there had been a perihelion of Jupiter near the time of the breaking out of the war of the Rebellion, that war would have been more destructive to human life; but one of the perihelions of Jupiter occurred several years before the war broke out, the other several years after it was ended. Even as it was, the Union soldiers suffered greatly with fever while camping out in the Southern States, which I attribute to the perigee of Mars in 1862.

Had the perigee of Mars occurred in 1860 or 1861, when the planet Uranus was in the early degrees of Gemini, the war would have been more bitter and fierce than it was. Neither the North or the South appeared to get up sufficient steam or to be in real earnest about the war until Mars entered his perigee in the spring of 1862. After that the North and South were in earnest until the war ended.

What made the Crimean war so destructive to the health and lives of the English and French soldiers in 1854 and 1855 was the perihelion of Jupiter in 1856, and what made the Franco-Prussian war so destructive to the health and lives of the German and French soldiers, caused by an epidemic of small pox, in spite of vaccination and revaccination, was the perihelion of Jupiter in 1868–69.

THE PLANET NEPTUNE IN GEMINI.

In the foregoing pages attention has been called to the effect on this country of the planet Uranus in the sign of Gemini. I might have given a number of other times when planets were transiting through the sign Gemini, and noted their influence on this country; but in doing so I was afraid the subject would become too complicated for the general reader to follow. Perhaps it will not be uninteresting to notice the effect on this and other countries of another planet in Gemini, viz., *Neptune*.

Neptune has only transited through Gemini once since Captain Christopher Newport and his followers entered the James River and founded the village of Jamestown. It takes Neptune one hundred and sixty-five years to go once around the sun, or to make one revolution, and fourteen years to go through one sign.

Neptune entered Gemini in 1720 and left it in 1734. In 1720 England was at war with Spain, and the American colonies suffered much on that account, especially in the Carolinas. The Spaniards in Florida incited the Indians against the inhabitants of the South, and harassed them for a number of years, until the Indians were conquered and they emigrated to New York, where they joined the Five Nations in 1722.

South Carolina was in open rebellion, and refused to recognize the royal governor, and in 1720 they elected James Moore governor, who was afterwards recognized by England.

In 1729 the King of England purchased for twenty-two thousand and five hundred pounds, seven of the eight proprietors. Carolina was afterwards divided and called North and South Carolina, each receiving a royal governor.

In 1727 the Count De Los Terres laid siege to Gibraltar, but all his efforts to plant the Spanish flag on that Rock were unavailing. Spain also fitted out a large fleet to invade England, but failed, partly on account of the storms at sea, which disabled and separated the war ships, two being captured in the Orkney Islands, Scotland.

In England the South Sea Company had been formed with the object of trading on the Pacific coast of South America. Afterwards this company bid against the Bank of England, and succeeded in buying up the British annuities, and National debt, they to collect certain taxes. These annuities could be changed into South Sea shares at the option of the holder. Within six days thousands of the annuitants had exchanged their certain income for the boundless imaginary riches of South America. The company circulated the report that the English and Spanish nations were going to trade Gibraltar for Peru, where there was reported to be so many gold and silver mines. The stock rose rapidly from one hundred pounds per share to one thousand pounds, when Robert Walpole and others sold out, clearing one thousand per cent. In August, 1720, the delusion was at its height, but when the crisis came thousands of persons who had deemed themselves wealthy awoke to the fact that they were reduced to beggary. Great distress was caused throughout England; almost all trades were stopped, which also affected this country. King George of England was in Hanover, Germany. Express after express was forwarded to him, urging his instant return to England to call Parliament together to devise means to restore confidence. Parliament resolved to strip the plunderers of their ill-gotten riches. In 1724 there was collected the sum of nine millions and four hundred and seven thousand two hundred pounds to be used to relieve the distress of those who had suffered from the gigantic fraud; but the distress was felt for many years afterwards.

On account of the rapid rise in the stock of the South Sea Company the people became insane on the subject of companies. There were Water, Fishery, Manufacturing, and Foreign Trade Companies; also companies for fattening hogs and importing jackasses from Spain. All ordinary business was neglected. As money was rushed in one big flood towards London to invest in these companies, all other business came to a standstill.

John Law's Banking and Mississippi Scheme, or "The Company of the West," also came to grief in the memorable year of 1720, when Neptune entered the sign Gemini, and brought terrible distress to all parts of France. Like the South Sea Bubble in England, the John Law's Banking Scheme was going to pay off the national debt of France in a few years, and at a time when they could not pay one-quarter of the interest by the collection of all the taxes.

The vision of having the sole trade of a fertile empire, with its plantations, manors, cities, and busy wharves on the Mississippi in North America—the certain product of the richest mines and mountains of gold were blended in the French mind into one boundless promise of treasure. Ingots of gold from the mines of Louisiana were to be seen in Paris. John Law became a Catholic, and was appointed Comptroller of Finance in France, and had a decree made that no person or corporation should have on hand more than five hundred livres (a livre is about a franc) in specie. All taxes were to be collected in paper, and paper was made the legal tender in all payments.

Law's Bank became, by negotiation with the Regent, the Bank of France, and its stock rose a thousand per cent. The new city of New Orleans and the valley of the Mississippi inflamed the imagination of France, and John Law's company obtained sole control of the commerce of Louisiana and Canada. The Regent's mother wrote to a friend "that the king's debts were all paid."

Law might have regulated at his pleasure the interest of money, the value of stocks, the price of labor and produce. The Legislature enacted laws which forbade certain corporations to invest money in any thing but Mississippi stocks. All circulation of gold and silver, except for change, was prohibited. The public enthusiasm now arose to absolute frenzy, and Law's house and the street in front of it was daily crowded. As the stock rose in value, many wary speculators (contrary to law), foreseeing a crisis, had secretly converted their paper and shares into gold, which they transmitted to England or Belgium. Gold and silver becoming scarce, a general run was made on the bank; it stopped payment, and Law was compelled to flee the country. Much of the paper was cancelled, and the rest converted into "rentes" at an enormous sacrifice.

The downfall of Law abruptly curtailed expense for Lousiana. Instead of large and opulent cities people could now only see unwholesome marshes, which were the tombs of immigrants. Its name in France was a name of disgust and terror. Years afterwards there were only two hundred huts among the canebrakes where the city of New Orleans now stands. The loss to the community in France was enormous. The bank notes and stock of Law's bank, or the Bank of France, for which the people had paid hard cash, were worthless, and they had no money to carry on their business. The depression was felt for years afterward.

NEPTUNE IN GEMINI FROM 1888 TO 1902.

Neptune entered Gemini for the second time in the history of our country on the 27th of May, 1888. For a parallel to the Mississippi Company, or Law's Bank, I need only remind the reader of the Panama scandal, which has attracted the attention of the whole civilized world for the last few years. The effect of those scandals on France has been in every respect similar to John Law's Bank scandal; also the South Sea Company in England. In all these cases numbers of people who stood high in the community had to flee the country; some committed suicide, and some were expelled from Parliament both in England and France; others suffered imprisonment and disgrace.

It must appear to the reader a remarkable coincidence that when any special planet in its passage around the heavens comes to the same sign it previously occupied, and which sign rules any particular country, that history almost appears to repeat itself. At least, if we are to judge by past history and present events, such is the case.

For instance, when we read in the history of France the account of the breaking up of John Law's Bank and the collapsing of the Mississippi Scheme, the trials which followed, and the uproar and recrimination in the French Parliament at that time, if we could only change the date and names, we might think that we were reading the history of France in the years 1891–'92–'93. The accounts published in the papers of the trial, conviction, and imprisonment of the Count de Lesseps and his son, and those who were associated with them, for corruption, bribery, and defrauding the public; also the suicide of Renach and the running away of Dr. Herz, the parallel is complete.

In England, in 1890 and 1891, they had almost a parallel to the South Sea Bubble in the Argentine Republic Scheme. The Baring Brothers, Bankers of London, suspended and came near failing on account of their investments in that country in building railways and other improvements before they were really needed. Had it not been for the timely assistance of the Rothschilds, the Bank of France, and other rich corporations, there is no doubt but that one of the richest banking firms in the world would have gone under, and carried scores of other banks and business houses with them. Even as it was, it made a noted tightness in the money market, which was felt all over the civilized world. In the Argentine Republic money was so scarce for two years afterwards that gold remained at about three hundred per cent. premium.

We are apt to smile when we read the accounts of the people in England during the excitement of the South Sea Bubble rushing with their annuities, from which they were certain of a safe and permanent income, to be exchanged for shares in the South Sea Company; a company, as Shakspeare says, which had neither a "local habitation or a name," and that the rush was so great that the bank where the annuities were exchanged for shares was compelled to set tables and clerks in the street to accommodate the crowd. Yet at the last Presidential election, on Nov. 8, 1892, a large majority of the working classes in the United States were equally anxious to *reduce their own wages over fifty per cent.* by voting that the "Federal Government has no constitutional power to impose and collect tariff duties except for the purpose of revenue only."* Not only did they vote to reduce their own wages, but also to throw a large number of employees of workshops and factories out of

---

* The "New York Sun" of August 16, 1893, in an editorial, said:—

"Last year, in a season of general prosperity such as never blessed a nation living in the light of civilization, the prevailing industrial system was condemned with almost a revolutionary show of disapproval. All visible facts argued for a popular verdict directly opposed to that deliberately recorded by the immense majority. . . . Either the American public are a set of summer fools unparalleled in fairy tales, or the election a year ago was the most colossal uprising of a populace socialistically inflamed, against the representatives of prosperity, against the alleged robbery of the tariff that the world has seen. . . . The people of the United States went crazy on the 8th of November, 1892."

The above paragraph shows emphatically that there was some super-mundane influence in operation, similar to the Salem witchcraft. That workingmen should cast their votes to take the bread out of their own, their wives' and their children's mouths, shows that there has been an epidemic of insanity; and, as the ancients said, "whom the gods wish to destroy they first make mad."

employment altogether; which will so overcrowd the farm hands and labor market, as to compel those laborers to work for a mere pittance, or remain unemployed and starving.

Before the election last November it was asserted that the high tariff and the McKinley Bill made the hard times; since the election it has been the Sherman Silver Purchase Bill that is to blame for so many banks failing and the depression and stagnation in trade and business.

It may appear singular to some of my readers that the four "schemes" that have produced such widespread distress in France and England were all *true Americans*. It is true that the first was represented as being in South America; the second in what is now known as New Orleans, Louisiana; the third in Central America, and the last again in South America.

That some super-mundane influence has been in operation of late in the United States, which has in some way affected the mentality of man, I think cannot be denied. The stagnation in business is phenomenal, and the failing of banks and the breaking up of business houses, which first commenced in Australia, and which is now spreading over almost all parts of the United States, is certainly remarkable.

Things will continue to remain in this unsettled condition, or at least no permanent improvement in business, until Neptune leaves the ruling sign of this country.

The stagnation of business and the tightness of the money market is in some respects equal to the panic of 1873, when the United States Government demonetized silver, which had a marked effect in depressing business throughout this country and other parts of the world.

On September 16, 1893, Neptune (before turning retrograde) stands at 13° 34' in Gemini. On July 28, 1893, the President of the United States called an extraordinary session of Congress to meet on the 7th of August, the hottest part of summer, to devise means to relieve the stagnation of business and the panic in the money market, which has caused so many failures of banks and business houses.

As Neptune gets further into Gemini (after it turns direct) things will grow worse instead of better, more especially during the first four months of 1894, when Saturn will be in square to Mercury's place in the horoscope of this country. I look for more business houses and banks failing than there have been during the spring and summer of 1893. From May 1, 1894, to April, 1895, Jupiter will be in the ruling sign of the United States. Business then will be better than it has been for several years past. Afterwards things will continue unsettled until Neptune arrives to 28° of Gemini.

In the year 1900 Saturn will come to the opposition of Neptune in Gemini. Then I look for another *epoch* in the history of the United States, in many respects similar to the one from 1861 to 1865. In the latter part of this volume I shall treat of the events of the United States.

THE SIGN TAURUS RULES IRELAND.

In the forepart of this volume I mentioned that Aries rules England and that Ireland was ruled by Taurus; and whenever there has been an evil planet in that sign, or in evil aspect to it, Ireland has suffered more or less. The planet Neptune entered the sign Taurus in the spring of 1875, but did not get far into the sign until the summer of 1876, when the disturbances commenced to be felt in Ireland. In 1879 it arrived at 10°, when the Irish Patriots organized the *Land League,* and riots and evictions multiplied. But the most serious *boycotts* occurred in that country when Saturn also entered Taurus in 1881, when Charles Stewart Parnell, John Dillon, and hundreds of other prominent Irishmen were arrested, and trial by jury was practically abolished. But in the spring of 1882 Saturn and Neptune began to approach each other, and in May they both formed a conjunction with the Sun and Mars in the ruling sign of Ireland.

At that time I was expecting some serious commotion or riots to occur in Ireland, when Lord Frederick Cavendish was murdered along with his Secretary, Thomas Henry Burke, on May 6th, 1882. Saturn continued to afflict Ireland's ruling sign until May 21, 1883, but Neptune did not leave that sign until the spring of 1888, when there was more peace and fewer evictions and imprisonments than there had been for many years.

Is it a coincidence that now while there are no evil planets in the sign Taurus, but on the contrary the benevolent planet Jupiter is there, that Ireland is more peaceful than it has been for many years, and the British Parliament appears likely to grant it its own government, now while Jupiter is in its ruling sign? This is certainly very singular. Jupiter entered Taurus in the early part of this year, and will remain in that sign (except during the month of September) until April, 1894.

After Jupiter gets out of Taurus and when Saturn and Uranus are both in the sign Scorpio, in opposition to Taurus, I look for serious disturbance and riots in old Ireland. The years 1895, 1896, and 1897 will be particularly unfortunate years for that country. No doubt we shall have another exhibition of the Kilkenny cats in that island, which will continue until both Saturn and Uranus get out of the sign Scorpio, or from an opposition of Taurus.

THE PERSONAL DESCRIPTION OF A MAN OR WOMAN DETERMINED BY THE PLANETS.

Persons can almost always be described in their personal appearance, even without the Astrologer seeing them, by the sign on the eastern horizon and the planet having the most influence in the sign rising at their time of birth. This may be discredited by a number of my readers, as they will say that a child has always a similar personal appearance to either his father or mother, and that the signs and planets have nothing to do with it.

If a child has a sign rising at the time of its birth which will describe a person like its father or its mother, then, as the physiologists say, "it takes after its father, or is like its mother." But if the sign rising at birth describes a person different to its father or mother, then the child does not resemble them, or, in other words, it does not take after them.

I have known this remarkable coincidence to be verified in my own practice in thousands of instances, and without any exception, and all other Astrologers have had a similar experience. For instance, if a child is born with what Astrologers term a "tall sign" rising, and the planet having the most influence in that sign be in another tall sign, that child so born will be tall, no matter how short both its parents are. It is the same if a child is born under what is termed "short," or "stout," or "slender signs." The child always follows in its personal appearance the description of the sign and the planets it is born under, and when the man or woman does not coincide in personal appearance with the sign rising and the planet having the most influence in that sign, we always know the time of birth given is not correct.

I could give thousands of instances to verify this statement, but will give only one, which occurred in my own family.

My brother's son, who resides in England, came on a visit to New York, and he requested me to cast his horoscope. He stated that his mother had told him that he was born on a given date at 12 o'clock at night. After the map of the heavens was erected for the time given I told him it was impossible for him to have been born at that time, as the sign rising would describe a tall, slender, light-complexioned person, and he was short, thick-set, and dark. On his return to England he asked his father for the exact time he was born. His father stated that it was at 6 o'clock in the evening. The son wrote to me, giving his corrected time of birth, and wishing me to write his horoscope. After the figure was set I wrote back that the time he had sent was also wrong, as it did not describe him. The son then visited his sister, who resided in another part of England, and who had the family Bible. He found it written in the Bible that he was born at 7:10 P. M. The sign then rising and the position of the planets described him correctly in every particular.

I might go on filling a large volume with such facts were it necessary, and yet people who have no knowledge of the science of Astrology tell us that there is nothing in it, and some of them have repeated the falsehood so often that they have come to believe it themselves.

THE AFFLICTING PLANETS DESCRIBE THE ASSASSINS IN REMARKABLE MURDER CASES.

There is another remarkable coincidence which I have noticed, and for a long time: that is, that when anything occurs in mundane affairs which attract widespread attention, such as murders or any serious accidents, there is always a remarkable configuration of the heavenly bodies. Generally, if not always, the persons having committed such murders, etc., can be described by the afflicting planets.

I have examined a number of charts of the heavens for the time that a remarkable murder or other crime has been committed, and I have often been astonished at the striking configuration of the planetary system at those times, and how clearly the heavens portrayed the person or persons who committed the deed.

Possibly a few horoscopes of some of the assassinations or murders which have occurred in the last twenty or thirty years may not be uninteresting to the general reader. They certainly will be interesting and instructive to the student of Astrology, if he examines them carefully. The first I shall notice is the assassination of President Lincoln.

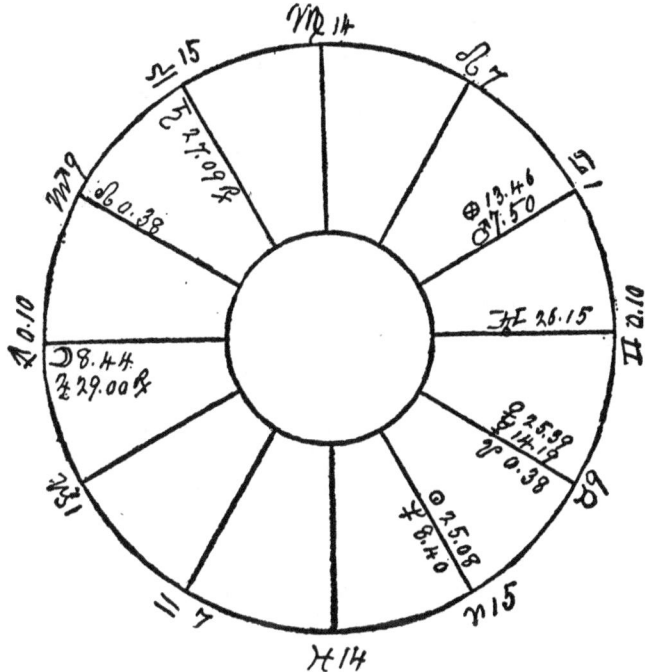

The above chart of the heavens represents the position of the planets at the time of the assassination of President Lincoln on April 14, 1865, at 9:30 P. M., Washington time. If the Astrological student inspects the position of the planets in the above figure, he will see that the afflicting planets are Mars in Cancer in the 8th house (the house of death), in exact square to Neptune, on the cusp of the 5th house, in Aries. Also, he will notice Saturn in the 11th house in opposition to the Sun, also in the 5th house in Aries.

The assassin is indicated by Mars in Cancer and Saturn in Libra. The books say : " It describes a person above the medium height, slender, with comely dark hair, oval face, prominent nose, large eyes, dark but clear complexion, and good looking; one opinionated of himself, prodigal of expense. Also, Saturn in opposition to the Sun, if Saturn be significator; the person is ambitious, overbearing, hating control, subject to the frowns of people in power, and often meets a violent death."

It may appear singular that Saturn in the house of friends indicated that a false friend did the deed: also the 5th house (where the President's planet was situated) indicates a theater or some place of amusement, etc. The Sun and Neptune are both in Aries (which sign rules the head), indicating that the President would be injured or wounded in the head. [*President Lincoln was shot in the head in a theatre.*] The close square of Mars to Neptune from the 8th house (the house of death), indicated certain death, and that the assassin shot with the deliberate intention to kill.

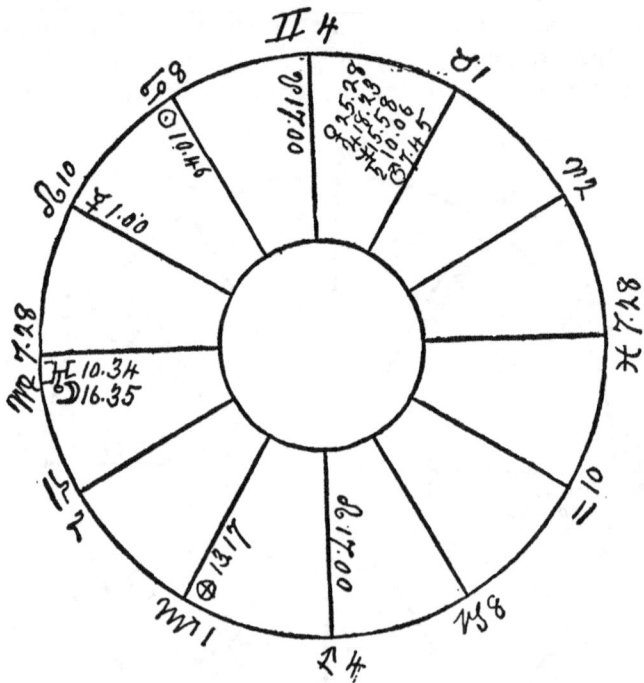

The above map of the heavens was set for the time President Garfield was shot by Charles Jules Guiteau, July 2, 1881, at 9:25 A. M., Washington time.

The student will notice that the Moon and Uranus are in the ascendant, also that Neptune in Taurus is in mundane square to the Moon, and the evil planet Saturn in conjunction with Mars, in mundane square to Uranus. The assassin is indicated by Neptune and Saturn.

The books say : "Saturn in Taurus describes a person of middle stature, but in no wise comely, one who has an awkward appearance, not well made, rough in carriage, sordid, and vicious. Saturn in conjunction with Mars denotes a rash, turbulent disposition, one who is generally unfortunate, engaged in some calling of a low order, and frequently ends his days in prison."*

The Moon and Uranus in Virgo, in the ascendant denotes where President Garfield would be injured or wounded, as Virgo governs the lower part of the body and the intestines.

Saturn and Neptune in the 9th house (the house of long journeys), indicates that Garfield was on a journey. [N. B. The President was just going to the train, intending to travel with his wife and family, whom he expected to meet in New York, throughout the greater part of the Eastern States.]

---

* No doubt Mars in conjunction with Saturn caused Mr. Guiteau to be much lighter in complexion and thinner than what is regularly described as a Saturn in Taurus person.

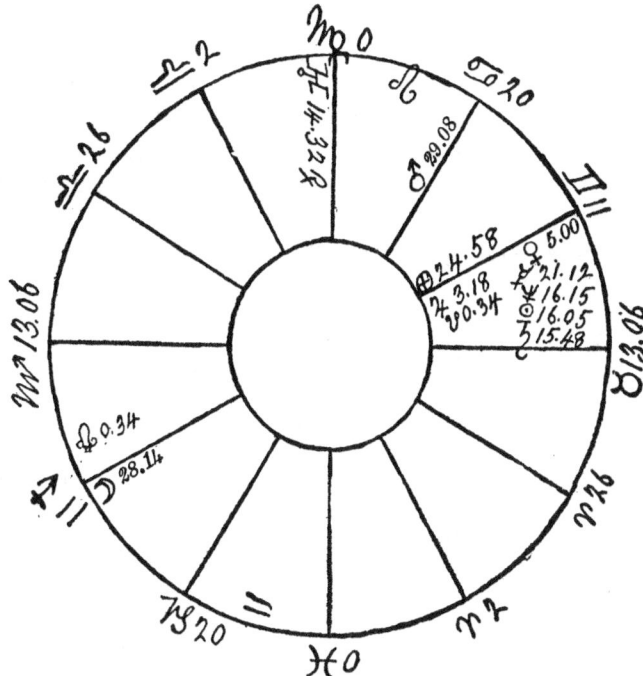

This chart of the heavens was calculated for the time when Lord Frederick Cavendish and Mr. Thomas Henry Burke were found assassinated in Phœnix Park, Dublin, Ireland, on May 6, 1882, at 7:10 P. M., Dublin time.

The assassins are indicated by the Sun, Saturn, Neptune, and Mercury, all in conjunction in Taurus in the 7th house, in close opposition to the ascendant. Of the four assassins indicated by the four planets, the two principal ones are described by Saturn and the Sun in close conjunction in Taurus.

The books in desribing a person indicated by Saturn in Taurus, say: "He is of medium stature, rather heavy, with a rough carriage, dark hair, one who is awkward, with a lumpish appearance, not well made, sordid and vicious." Saturn in conjunction with the Sun indicates losses by men in power, who persecute him, and confine him within the walls of a prison for some contempt of law·" He is seldom healthy, or of long life.

The other principal assassin is described by the Sun in Taurus in conjunction with Saturn. The books say: "It denotes a short, well set, rather ugly person, with a dusky complexion, brown hair, large, broad face, wide mouth, and great nose. A confident, proud, and bold man, fond of opposition, proud of his physical strength, and generally vicious.

The Sun in conjunction with Saturn denotes "a disagreeable, deceitful, unmerciful, unfortunate man, who loses his property by some speculation, which in the end often brings him to ruin; particularly if he has anything to do with the government or people connected with the State."

The other two assassins are indicated by the two planets, Neptune and Mercury in Taurus, but it is not worth while to give their description in these pages.

It may appear singular that the parts of the murdered men's bodies injured, and the kind of death should be described by the heavens. The books say "that Taurus rules the throat," and these murdered men met their death by having their throats cut; also, they were wounded in the upper part of the chest; and their planets being in fixed signs in angles shows that they were all near home, or not on a long journey, as in President Garfield's case.

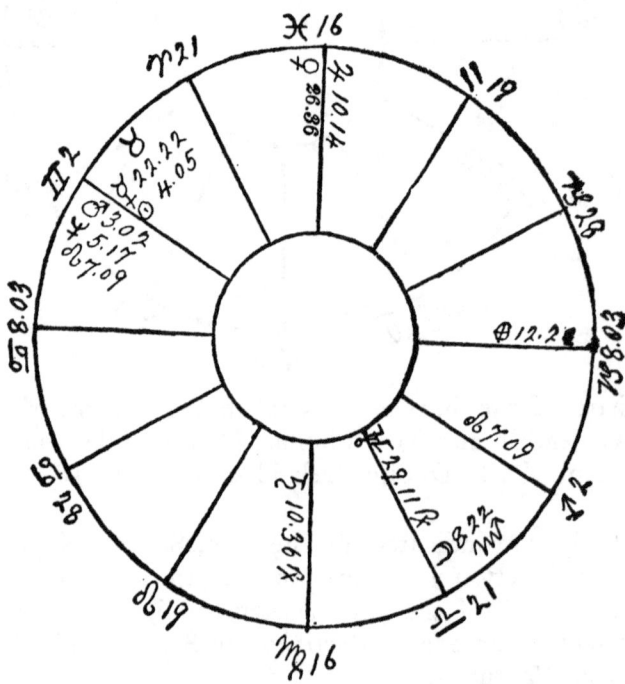

This figure of the heavens shows the position of the planets when Carrie Brown (Old Shakespeare) was found murdered in a hotel in the lower part of the city of New York, on the morning of April 24, 1891, at 9 o'clock.

The afflicting planet is Saturn (there was only one murderer in this case) in Virgo, just leaving the cusp of the 4th house, retrograde, and in opposition to Jupiter on the cusp of the 10th house.

The books say: "Saturn in Virgo describes a rather tall person with a spare body and swarthy complexion, dark brown or black hair, and a sordid countenance; one unfortunate, inclined to melancholy, and retaining anger.

As Saturn is retrograde, and just going into the 3d house (the house of journeys), it is evident that the murderer went away on a journey immediately after committing the deed, and did not return.

Saturn in Virgo indicates the parts injured, that is the abdomen and lower part of the body.

The Moon in Scorpio, in the 5th house, in opposition to the Sun, in aspect to Saturn and Jupiter, indicates that both the murderer and victim belonged to the degraded class; also the kind of place the murder was committed in is indicated by the Moon in Scorpio in the 5th house; that is, a place of low resort, also a public house or a place of amusement.

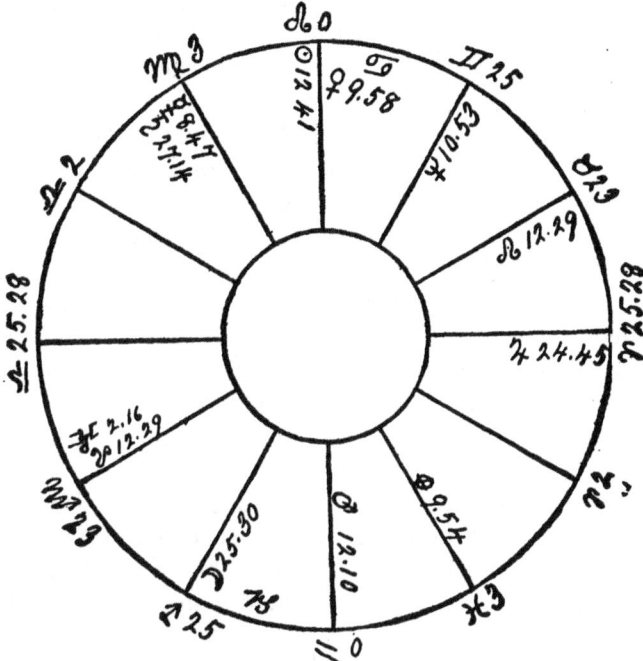

The above chart shows the position of the signs and planets when the bodies of Mr. Andrew J. Borden and his wife were discovered on the 4th of August, 1892, at 11:13 A. M., in Fall River, Mass.

The afflicting planet in this figure is Mars in Aquarius in the 4th house, in close opposition to the Sun in Leo in the mid-heaven. It also shows beyond a question that it was a man, and not a woman, who did the deed, and he had no one with him.

Mars in Aquarius, the books say, "gives a well composed body, rather corpulent, inclined to be tall, although frequently not above the medium height [I should say about 5 feet 8 inches], with a fair or sanguine complexion, sandy or auburn hair, mustache is yellow or sandy, round face, high forehead, quick, sparkling eyes, and has a straight and proud walk." Mars, in opposition to the Sun, "denotes a man of great ambition and violence, but his fortune is too evil to allow him to succeed."

Mars in the 4th house in a fixed sign, indicates that the Bordens were murdered in their own house, also that the muderer did not go away off, as in the case of Carrie Brown's murderer. Therefore the murderer in this case is still in the neighborhood of the murder, or not very far away.*

---

* The student of Astrology will notice that in all these five charts of the heavens, the afflicting planets are masculine and evil, which denotes that they were men who committed the murders. The last chart is more marked in this respect than any of the others. The reason that the man got away unnoticed and unsuspected, is also indicated by the planet Jupiter in the 7th house, and falling cadent, and the Moon in the 3d house leaving a trine or good aspect of it.

The parts of the bodies injured are indicated by Sun in Leo, which rules the heart and upper parts of the body, and Mars rules all sharp tools or instruments.

I have been very particular in giving the description of the murderer in this case, and if this publication has any effect in leading to his conviction and clearing an innocent woman from even suspicion, I shall deem myself amply rewarded for my labor.

I was interested in reading the trial of Lizzie Borden, and could not help thinking that Mr. Knowlton, the prosecuting attorney, ought to have lived two hundred years ago. He would then have won everlasting fame as a persecutor of witches, and so overshadowed Cotton Mather that the reverend gentleman would have dropped into obscurity.

When reading Mr. Knowlton's speech, describing how Lizzie Borden had first killed her step-mother, and then her father, I could not help believing that had he been addressing a Salem jury two hundred years ago, he could in that case have easily convinced them that the devil stood between her and her victims and caught every drop of blood, so that not a particle could reach her; and that it was his Satanic Majesty who instigated her to the deed, and gave her the strength of a giant to accomplish the fiendish work. In those days all warrants for the arrest of criminals read: "That the person had committed the deed with malice aforethought, being instigated thereto by the devil."

But in these days the only way to convict an innocent person is to get some noted expert to show a chemical test before the jury, of which they are entirely ignorant (the more ignorant the better), and which may be proven entirely erroneous in the very next trial.

As Mr. Knowlton was so anxious to convict Miss Borden, if he had only sent for a Philadelphia doctor to bring his microscope to examine that small drop of menstrual blood that was found on her skirts (not half the size of a pin head), and that doctor had also stated before the jury, after examining it, that he would *stake his life* that the small particle of dried blood was part of the identical blood found saturating the floor and the bodies of the murdered victims, then he could have easily convinced the jury of her guilt, and had the pleasure of seeing an innocent woman swinging from the gallows.

One would think the affliction bad enough when any person, either man or woman, has a relative assassinated in their own house, and without a moment's notice, and also come near being murdered themselves, without being dragged off to prison and put to the trouble and expense of a trial, and have to fight for their life against all the power and influence of the State, moving heaven and earth for their conviction and execution.

Another case of persecution occurred in the city of New York, in the supposed murderer of Carrie Brown. It has since been shown, almost beyond a question, that nearly all those vile women perjured themselves, yet that poor man, a stranger in a strange country, is unpardoned and undischarged. The last I read about him, he had become insane, and was confined in an insane asylum.

ELEMENTS OF ASTROLOGY.

Astrology may be divided into five divisions or parts, and each can be learned separately, similar to arithmetic. In arithmetic we first learn numeration, then addition, afterwards subtraction, multiplication and division, so Astrology can be divided into parts and learned in like manner. First the houses and their qualities, or what belongs to them. Second the aspects of the houses, or their relations to each other. Third the signs of the Zodiac and their relations or aspects to each other and their significations. Fourth the nature of the planets, their motions, revolutions and their significations, and their aspects to each other. Fifth their strength in the various houses and in the different signs of the Zodiac. It is easiest to learn one part thoroughly and understand it before the learner commences another part. It is impossible for a learner to get the proof of Astrology until he has become somewhat advanced in its study, but when he is advanced the proof comes of itself. I have never known a person who has learned Astrology that was not a thorough believer in it, the same as a person who has learned arithmetic is a firm believer, no matter how skeptical he may have been before he had learned it. The science of Astrology is unique, and there is no science to be compared with it in one respect, that is, that all those persons who are the most ignorant of it appear to have some kind of intuition that tells them that it is utterly false or wicked, but those persons who have studied the subject always speak of it as a heavenly science or truth itself, and there is no other science that I know of that is like it in that particular. In short, it generally happens that the persons who are the most ignorant of any one of the other sciences have generally the greatest confidence in it and its professors. For instance, a person who is ignorant of chemistry imagines that the chemist can anyalyze and know all about the elements of every material substance, and believes that the chemist can recombine or put together all the elements of matter so as to form any chemical substance that he chooses, and so on of any other natural science. But when he comes to study chemistry he finds that he has had altogether wrong notions on the subject.

RUDIMENTS OF THE SCIENCE.

The circle of the heavens is divided into four equal parts, and each part is composed of 90 degrees, making in all 360 degrees in the circle. The commencement of each one of these quarters is called an angle. These angles are the Eastern horizon, or where the sun rises; the Western horizon or where it sets; the mid-heaven, or where the sun is at mid-day, and opposite the mid-heaven is called the Nadir, and it is that point directly under where we stand. Each of these quarters is divided into three parts of 30 degrees, which are called houses, and there are 12 houses in all.

The ancient writers named them mansions. These 12 houses are counted from the Eastern horizon, and they continue round the circle from the East to the North, then to the West and so on round to the East again, or in the opposite direction to the rising, culminating or setting of the sun. The first house commences at the Eastern horizon and extends 30 degrees below; the second house commences at that point, or at the end of 30 degrees, and extends to 60 degrees below the horizon; the third house commences 60 below the horizon and ends at the fourth house, or that point opposite the mid-heaven; the fourth house extends 30 degrees to the next, or the fifth house, which extends 30 degrees from that point to the sixth house, which extends to the western horizon or seventh house, which commences at the Western horizon and extends 30 degrees to the eighth house, which commences 30 degrees from the Western horizon and extends 30 degrees to the ninth house; and the ninth begins at 60 degrees from the Western horizon and extends to the tenth house or meridian, which commences at the mid-heaven and that extends to 30 degrees from the mid-heaven to the eleventh house; the eleventh house commences 30 degrees from the mid-heaven and extends 60 degrees or to the twelfth house; and the twelfth house commences at that point and terminates at the commencement of the first house, making in all 12 houses round the heavens, as shown by the accompanying figure.

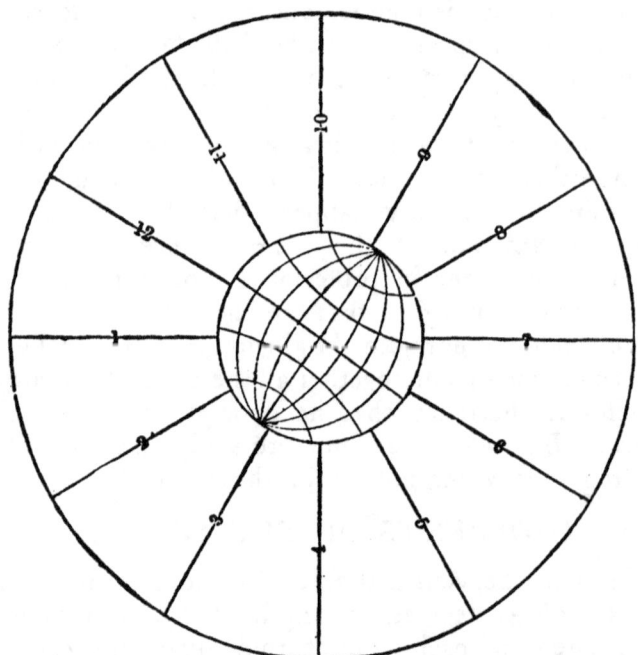

The reader will see by the numbers in the chart that the houses are reckoned in the contrary direction to the rising, culminating and setting of the sun. The houses are divided into good and evil. The good houses, counting them in the order of their strength or importance, are the first, tenth, second, seventh, fourth, ninth, eleventh, fifth and third. The evil houses, counting them in the order of their strength for evil, are the eighth, twelfth and sixth. These houses are termed evil because they have no aspects to the ascendant or first house. When a planet is in an evil house, and a person is born under that planet, that person is weak, or he is subject to misfortunes, sickness or trouble of some kind; but when a planet is in a good house and strong and unafflicted, it is said to be well dignified and causes the person born under it to be fortunate, if other good influence concur. The house that is the most fortunate or of the highest importance is the first; the next in importance is the tenth house, and then follows the second, and so on.

The heavens, besides being divided into what are termed four quarters and then into houses, are also divided into what are termed aspects, and those aspects are called mundane aspects to distinguish them from what are termed zodiacal aspects, which I shall speak of further on.

These aspects are certain geometrical figures and are reckoned by the number of degrees from one point to another point. For instance, the angles are 90 degrees apart and are said to be in square aspect to each other. The heavens are also divided into three equal parts, termed triplicity, which are 120 degrees apart and are in trine aspect to each other. When the heavens are divided into six equal parts or 60 degrees, that is termed a sextile aspect. But that part of the heavens which is opposite to the other is called an opposition. The trine aspects are said to be the strongest for good, the sextile are the second in strength for good, the semi-sextile or 30 degrees are the least strong for good; the most evil aspect is the opposition, and next to that the square, and then what is termed a conjunction, or when two evil planets are of the same longitude that is said to be an evil aspect with evil planets, and a fortunate aspect with good planets. The ascendant is in square to the mid-heaven and the fourth house and in opposition to the seventh house. The ascendant is in trine to the ninth and the fifth, and is in sextile to the eleventh and the third houses, therefore when any planet is in the seventh it is in opposition to the ascendant; in the mid-heaven and the fourth it is in square to the ascendant, or in the ninth or fifth it is in trine to the ascendant, in the third or eleventh it is in sextile to the ascendant, and so on of the other houses.

These aspects must be thoroughly committed to memory, and also the houses and their significations, or what they are said to govern.

The houses are also divided into angles, succeedent and cadent. The angles said to be the strongest are the first, tenth, seventh and fourth; the succeedent are the next in strength, that is, the second, fifth, eighth and eleventh. The cadent houses are the weakest of all; they are the third, sixth, ninth and twelfth; yet when a planet is in the ninth house it is said to be sometimes quite strong, provided it is not too near what is termed the eighth house; if it is near the mid-heaven all the better.

THE SIGNIFICATION OF THE TWELVE HOUSES.

The first house is said to rule the life and health of the native; the second his money or personal property; the third his relatives and short journeys; fourth, the father and landed property; fifth, children and pleasure; sixth, sickness and small cattle; seventh, marriage and public enemies; eighth, death, legacies and wills; ninth, religion, law suits, and long journeys; tenth, mother, business and honor; eleventh, friends, hopes, etc.; twelfth, secret enemies and imprisonment.

One old author has summed up the twelve houses in the following verses; it would be well for the reader to commit them to memory:

> First house shows life, the second wealth doth give;
> The third, brethren, fourth, how parents live;
> Issue the fifth, sixth diseases bring;
> The seventh wedlock, and the eighth death's sting;
> The ninth declares man's pious faith and zeal;
> The tenth the glory of a common weal;
> Our friendship from the eleventh house is known;
> And sorrow from the twelfth to every one.

A student must be well informed in the houses and their significations before he ventures to go any further in the study of this science, therefore I give below the main significations of all the houses.

The following more important parts of this volume will be printed in larger type, and each paragraph numbered for easy reference.

THE NATURE, QUALITY AND DESCRIPTION OF THE TWELVE HOUSES.*

1 FIRST HOUSE.—This house signifies the life of man, stature, complexion and shape of the querent or native, because when the sun or any other star comes to that point they arrive and become visible in our horizon. It rules the head or face. If Mars be afflicted in this house in a nativity or question it gives, one time or other, a wound or scar in the face or head. If Saturn or dragon's head be there, it gives a very coarse countenance and slovenly behavior. Of colors it has the white, that is if a planet be in this house which has signification of white, the complexion of the party will be very pale, white and wan. His apparel also will much incline to a white grey or very light color. So for cattle, when their significators or planets are found in this house, it denotes them to be of a light color. This house is masculine.

2 SECOND HOUSE.—Signifies the neck and throat, the wealth, poverty, movable goods or money of the native or querent; loss or gain by commodity or money lent, profit or loss, or damage in law suits. It signifies the querent's monied friends or assistance. Of color it denotes green. Jupiter and Venus rejoice in this house, and if Jupiter or Venus be strong, either in a question or nativity, it makes a man rich and fortunate; but Saturn and Mars weak in this house, and the dragon's tail there, makes him a beggar, or at least he wastes his estate, though it was never so considerable, by riotous living, fires, or losses. It is feminine.

---

* The significations of the twelve houses given here, answers both for nativities and horary questions.

3 THIRD HOUSE.—Rules the chest and arms and gives judgment concerning brothers, sisters, cousins, or kindred neighbors, short or inland journeys of the querent; also about letters, rumors and news, messengers, etc., and removing from place to place. Of colors it has the red, yellow and sorrel. The planet Mars is not so fortunate in this house as some think, unless he be joined to Saturn by good aspect. This house is the joy of the Moon; for if she be posited therein, especially in a movable sign, it is an argument of much travel to the native and that to advantage, too, if she be there strong and friendly beheld by the fortunes. But if afflicted there without reception, the native will be always trudging and trotting about to little purpose; and if the dragon's tail happens to be there, he will be cheated if not robbed and abused in his travels. It is a masculine house.

4 FOURTH HOUSE.—Signifies old people in general, the native or querent's father, lands, houses, tenements and inheritances; tilling the earth, hidden treasure and mines of all kinds; the end or conclusion of any design, project or undertaking; ancient dwellings, gardens, orchards, fields and pastures; the quality and nature of the ground the querent is about to purchase; whether they are vineyards, corn-fields or chases, or whether the ground be barren, strong or woody. It is the north angle and rules in man's body the breast and the lungs and is feminine. Color, red or yellow. The Sun and Venus, if in this house in good aspects with the lord of the ascendant, or second house, the native or querent will inherit or have an estate fall to him from or by means of his father, especially if the lord of the eighth house behold either of them with a benevolent aspect.

5 FIFTH HOUSE.—This house rules the stomach and liver, and we give judgment concerning children, ambassadors, of the state of a woman with child, whether it be male or female, as also of banquets, plays, games, dancing, music, pleasure, delight and merriment; of the health or sickness of the querent's son or daughter; it also denotes ale-houses, taverns, messengers and agents, for merchants or others trading at sea; the wealth or poverty of the father. Of color, black, dark or honey. Leo and Venus joy in this house, because Venus is the fifth planet and Leo is the fifth sign of the Zodiac. Saturn is wholly unfortunate when it is in this house; all authors agree that Saturn or Mars in the fifth house never fails to give the native or querent cruel, stubborn, obstinate, rebellious and disobedient children; and also unfortunate in speculation. It is masculine.

6 SIXTH HOUSE.—Governs the abdomen; and men and maidservants, day laborers, galley slaves, all manner of small cattle, such as deer, goats, hares, conies, loss or gain from them, the sickness of the querent or native, whether long or short, curable or not; likewise

farmers, tenants, and it also denotes uncles and aunts by the father's side. This house, having no aspect to the ascendant, is therefore called mala fortuna, the house of evil fortune; yet if Jupiter, Venus, dragon's head or Mercury be well placed and aspected in this house, and Mars behold Mercury with a friendly ray, it makes the native or querent an able physician if he undertakes that employment. Of colors it governs black. Mars rejoices in this house, but the chief consignificators are Virgo and Mercury. It is a feminine house.

7 SEVENTH HOUSE.—Rules the kidneys and the lower part of the back, and gives judgment concerning marriage; it describes the person inquired after, whether it be man or woman; all sorts of love questions or public enemies; all men whom we have common dealings with, all quarrels, lawsuits and duels. In Astrology and medicine it signifies the artist himself; it also signifies grandfathers, thieves and theft, the persons stealing, whether man or woman; wives or sweethearts, their shapes, descriptions, and conditions, whether nobly or ignobly born; fugitives or runaways or outlawed men. Saturn or Mars in the seventh or the Moon ill-placed in this house shows very unfortunate marriages. Of color, dark or black. This is the angle of the west and is masculine.

8 EIGHTH HOUSE.—Signifies death, sadness and sometimes riches never thought of; wills, deeds and legacies of the dead, the estate of the debtor, of querent's wife, or whom he deals with, portion of the maid, whether much or little, easy to be got or with difficulty. In duels it denotes the adversary's second, in lawsuits the defendant's friends, what kind of death a man may die. It signifies fear and anguish of mind, and the heir to the querent; it rules the privy parts. Of colors, green and black. Of diseases, the piles, stone, strangury, poisons, etc. Feminine house.

9 NINTH HOUSE.—Signifies religion, learning, books, art and science; judgment is given of voyages and long journeys by sea or land; clergymen in general, as bishops and inferior ministers; dreams and visions, news or letters from foreign parts, the kindred of the husband, wife or sweetheart. Of colors it has the green and white, of man's body the hips and thighs. If Jupiter be herein well placed it naturally signifies a devout man, or one modestly given; the dragon's tail, Mars or Saturn are very unfortunate in this house and make a man an agnostic or infidel, and also unfortunate as a minister, lawyer or in law suits. It is masculine.

10 TENTH HOUSE.—Personates kings and princes, dukes, earls, judges, commanders-in-chief in armies and towns, all sorts of officers in authority, mother of the querent, honors, preferment, dignity, office, the pro-

fession or trade any one uses; it signifies kingdoms, countries, empires, dukedoms. Colors, red and white. It rules the knees and hams. Configurators of this house are Capricorn and Mars; it is called the mid-heaven and is feminine. Jupiter or the Sun well placed in this house gives great honor to the native or querent, but Saturn, Mars or dragon's tail usually denies honor to persons and little success in their employment or calling.

11 ELEVENTH HOUSE.—From this house we acquire judgment concerning friendship and friends, their qualities and conditions, the querent's or native's hopes, a harbor or relief to voyagers, the assistance of princes, their money and allies; it signifies the exchequer, the king's council, ammunition and soldiers. In a commonwealth, governed by a few nobles and commons, it shows their assistance in council, as in New York the tenth house denotes the mayor, the eleventh the common council, the ascendant or first house the generality of the commoners of the city. Of members it rules the legs to the ankles. Of color it rules saffron or yellow. Aquarius and the Sun are cosignificators of this house. Jupiter in this house gives good and faithful friends. And it is as strong in this house as in either of its signs, (♐ or ♓) in the other houses. It is a masculine house.

12 TWELFTH HOUSE.—It has signification of private enemies and evil tongues, as also great cattle, as horses, cows or oxen. It also signifies sorrow or tribulation, prisons, imprisonment, jails and jailers, treason and all manner of villainy, chronic diseases, with all other torments and afflictions. It is the house of self undoing, for if the lord of the ascendant be afflicted in this house, it denotes the querent will be the occasion of his own misfortunes. It has for cosignificators Pisces and Venus. Saturn does much joy in this house, for naturally Saturn is author of mischief. It rules in man's body, the feet. Of colors it rules green, and is a feminine house.

Before the reader proceeds any further he ought to get the twelve houses and their significations committed to memory, and should commence learning the first house and then the second house, and so on until he knows them all, and can repeat the houses and their significations from memory. He should also learn to be able to change the ascendant, either in his own horoscope or any other person's horoscope. For instance in the chart of the native his father's ascendant is the fourth house, and then the father's second house, or the house connected with his father's money matters is the fifth house, the sixth is his father's brother or his neighbors; the seventh house, his land or property; the eighth house is his father's children; the ninth house is his father's sickness; the tenth house is his father's wife or his own mother, or his public enemies; the eleventh house is his father's house of death; the twelfth house is his father's house of long journeys, religion or lawsuits, The first house is his father's house of business or honor; the second house is his father's house of friends; and the third house is his father's house of secret enemies, imprisonment, and so on. He also takes the seventh house for the first house of his wife or lover, etc.; in like manner the tenth house is the first house for his mother, and then the eleventh house would be the house of her money or movable property, etc., and so on all round the heavens. The student must get these houses and their significations thoroughly committed to memory. He must be able when any question whatever comes up to refer it to its proper house without any hesitation and not have to guess at it, and unless he learns the houses thoroughly he will never make a good Astrologer. He must learn them the same as he ought to learn his multiplication table, and never mind being laughed at by persons who are ignorant of Astrology. He must be able to treat them as John Foster advised persons who wanted to learn "Decision of Character" Mr. Foster advised his students to reply in this manner: "You will laugh or smile, will you; much good may it do you. I do not care if the whole neighborhood laugh in a chorus; of course I should be sorry to see such a number of fools altogether, but glad to think that you do not consider me one of your number. What should I think of my science if it required the aid of vain and shallow minds who cannot understand it, or what should I think of myself if I should shrink at your sneers?" After you have once mastered thoroughly the science of Astrology, you will not laugh at those persons who are ignorant of that science—you will simply pity them.

The reader ought to bear in mind that the houses should always be learned first, as they are the foundation of Astrology, and like other foundations they never change but always remain fixed in their various places in the heavens, only so far as we may change them, as the fourth house being the first house for the father; the seventh house being the first house for the wife; and the tenth house being the first house for the mother, and so on. After the student has thoroughly learned the houses, he then proceeds to learn the twelve signs of the Zodiac, namely: Aries ♈, Taurus ♉, Gemini ♊, Cancer ♋, Leo ♌, Virgo ♍, Libra ♎, Scorpio ♏, Sagittary ♐, Capricorn ♑, Aquarius ♒, and Pisces ♓.

The signs are constantly changing their position in the heavens, and do not remain fixed like the houses, one sign rises on the average every two hours, as there are twelve signs in the Zodiac and twenty-four hours in the day, the earth turns on its axis once in twenty-four hours, each sign passes the midheaven every day. Like the houses they are divided into four different parts, and the first is what is termed the cardinal or movable signs, and those are Aries, Cancer, Libra and Capricorn; the second are fixed signs, and are Taurus, Leo, Scorpio, and Aquarius; the next are common signs, that is, neither movable, cardinal nor fixed, but between the two; they are Gemini, Virgo,

Sagittary and Pisces. For instance, if a person is born with a fixed sign on the ascendant, or his planet in a fixed sign, that person is apt to be more fixed and determined in his natural disposition and cannot be easily changed, but if a person is born with a movable sign on the ascendant, or his planet is in a movable sign, then he is apt to change and be very changeable and likely to move around a great deal. The movable signs, like the cardinal houses, are in square aspect to each other. The fixed signs are also in square aspect, and the common signs are in square aspect to each other. The signs are also divided into what are termed the trigons or triplicities; they are called the fiery triplicity, the earthy triplicity, the airy triplicity, and the watery triplicity. These triplicities are in trine or good aspect to each other. The signs of the fiery triplicity are Aries, Leo and Sagittary; the earthy triplicity is Taurns, Virgo and Capricorn; the airy triplicity is Gemini, Libra and Aquarius; the watery triplicity is Cancer, Scorpio and Pisces. The fiery triplicity is termed hot and dry; that is, when a person is born with a sign of the fiery triplicity on the ascendant, and his planet is also in a fiery sign, that person is more liable to fevers and fires, or suffers from heat, and is generally what is called hot-tempered or quick and active. The earthy triplicity is cold and dry, and persons born under the earthy triplicity are of a cold and dry nature. When born under the airy triplicity they are hot and moist and generally good natured and kind-hearted. The watery triplicity causes persons to be phlegmatic and generally fond of the water or liquids, and are often successful connected with both, provided their planets are not afflicted in watery signs.

They are also divided into the Eastern, Southern, Western and Northern signs. The Eastern signs are the fiery triplicity and are Aries, Leo and Sagittary; the Southern signs or earthy triplicity are Taurus, Virgo and Capricorn; the Western signs or airy triplicities are Gemini, Libra and Aquarius, and the Northern signs or watery triplicity are Cancer, Scorpio and Pisces. The signs are also divided into fruitful and barren signs. The fruitful signs are Cancer, Scorpio and Pisces, and the barren signs are Gemini. Leo and Virgo. Those persons born under planets in a fruitful sign are apt to have a number of children. Those born under planets in barren signs are likely to have but few or possibly no children. They are also divided into the signs of voice, that is, those persons born with their planets in the signs of voice are apt to be very good speakers or writers; these signs are Gemini, Libra, Sagittary and Aquarius; they are sometimes also called human signs. Persons born under those signs are generally more humane and kinder hearted than persons born under planets in other signs, or under planets in what is termed beastial signs. The beastial signs are Aries, Taurus, Leo, Capricorn and the last half of Saggittarius.

The mute signs are Cancer, Scorpio and Pisces. Those persons born with their planet in these signs are apt to have an impediment in their speech or are very poor talkers or public speakers. The signs are also divided into Equinoctial, which are Aries and Libra, that is, when the Sun is in either of these signs it is said to cross the line of equinox. The tropical signs are Cancer and Capricorn. These signs are also divided into masculine and feminine. The masculine are reckoned from Aries, then every other sign is called masculine, that is, Aries, Gemini, Leo, Libra, Sagittary and Aquarius. Those (whether men or women) born with their planet in masculine signs are generally more masculine than other persons. The feminine signs are Taurus, Cancer, Virgo, Scorpio, Capricorn and Pisces. The signs are also divided into dry and moist signs; the dry signs are Aries, Taurus, Leo, Virgo, Sagittary and Capricorn. Those persons born with their planets in these signs are more dry in their nature and apt to be more feverish when ill than other persons. The moist signs are Gemini, Cancer, Scorpio, Libra, Aquarius and Pisces, and persons born with their planets in those signs partake of their nature. They are also divided into the Northern and Southern signs. The Northern signs are Aries, Taurus, Gemini, Cancer, Leo and Virgo. The Southern signs are Libra, Scorpio, Sagittary, Capricorn, Aquarius and Pisces. The Northern signs are always in opposition to the Southern signs and are always on opposite houses. For instance, if the sign Aries is on the ascendant or rising, the sign Libra will be on the seventh house or setting, and so on of all the other Northern and Southern signs.

The fiery signs, Aries, Leo and Sagittary are in trine aspect or 120 degrees apart, the earthy signs are the same or in trine aspect, and so is the airy and watery signs ; all the signs in a triplicity are in trine aspect to each other. The fiery and airy signs are in sextile to each other, that is, Aries is in Sextile to Gemini, Leo is in sextile to Libra, and Sagittary in sextile to Aquarius, so is the earthy and watery signs in sextile to each other, that is, 60 degrees apart: Taurus is in sextile to Cancer, Virgo to Scorpio, and Capricorn to Pisces.

All the movable or cardinal signs are in square aspect to each other or 90 degrees apart, that is, Aries in square to Cancer, Cancer in square to Libra, and Libra in square to Capricorn, and Capricorn is in square to Aries. The fixed signs are in square to each other; Taurus is in square to Leo; Leo in square to Scorpio, and Scorpio in square to Aquarius. The common signs are in square to each other ; Gemini is in square to Virgo ; Virgo in square to Sagittary, and Sagittary in square to Pisces, and *vice versa*.

The student should commit all these aspects and divisions of the signs to memory, so that he can repeat them without a single mistake, the same as the multiplication table. He may not see the benefit of it at present, and think it may all come to him afterwards when he begins practicing Astrology, but he will find that he has a great deal to learn besides these signs and their various triplicities and aspects, and therefore it is best for him to be as perfect as possible in this part of Astrology before he proceeds any further. After he has mastered this part of the science then he must learn how to describe a person by the twelve signs of the Zodiac ; it will also be advisable for him to commit this part to memory so that he can repeat the whole from beginning to end.

GENERAL APPEARANCE OF PERSONS DESCRIBED BY THE TWELVE SIGNS OF THE ZODIAC.

ARIES ♈.

13 Describes a person not exceeding in height or very tall, but lean or spare, large bones, and his limbs strong, the visage long, black or reddish eyebrows, a long scraggy neck, thick shoulders, the complexion dusky, brown or swarthy.

TAURUS ♉.

14 It represents one of short stature, but full, strong and well set, a broad forehead, great eyes, large swarthy face and broad strong shoulders, great mouth and thick lips, large hands, black or coarse reddish hair.

GEMINI ♊.

15 An upright, tall, straight, thin or well built body, either in man or woman; the complexion sanguine, not clear but obscure and dark; long arms, yet many times the hand and feet short and fleshy; dark hair, almost black; a strong active body, a good piercing eye, and of perfect and quick sight, of excellent understanding and judicious in worldly affairs.

CANCER ♋.

16 Generally a low and small stature, the upper parts larger than the lower, a round face, sickly pale and white complexion, the hair brown, little eyes, prone to have many children, if a woman.

LEO ♌.

17 Great round head, large prominent or staring eyes, quick sighted; a full and large body, and more than of middle stature; broad shoulders, narrow sides, yellow or dark flaxen hair, and it curling or turning up; a fierce countenance, but ruddy high sanguine complexion; strong, valiant and active, step firm and mind courteous.

VIRGO ♍.

18 A slender body, rather tall, but well composed; a ruddy or brown complexion, black hair, well favored or lovely, but not a beautiful creature; small, shrill voice, judicious and exceedingly well spoken, studious and given to history, whether man or woman. It produces a rare understanding if Mercury be in this sign, and Moon in Cancer, but somewhat unstable.

LIBRA ♎.

19 It personates a well formed body, straight, tall and more

subtle or refined rather than gross; a round, lovely and beautiful face; a pure sanguine color; in youth no abundance or excess in either red or white, but in age pimples or a very high color; the hair is yellowish, smooth and long; eyes generally blue and temper even.

Scorpio ♏.

20 A corpulent, strong, able body, somewhat broad or square face; a dusky, muddy complexion and dark hair, much and crisping; a hairy body; somewhat bow-legged; short necked; a stout, well-trussed person.

Sagittary ♐.

21 It represents a well-favored countenance, somewhat long face, but full and ruddy or almost like sunburned, the hair light chestnut color, the stature somewhat above the middle size, a conformity in the members, and a strong able body; inclined to baldness, and one fond of horses.

Capricorn ♑.

22 Usually a dry body, not high of stature, long, lean and slender face, thin beard and black hair, a narrow chin, long small neck and narrow chest. I have found many times Capricorn ascending the party to have light hair, but in the seventh, or setting, dark.

Aquarius ♒.

23 It represents a thick or stout corporature, or one of a strong plump, well-composed body, not tall; a long visage, sanguine complexion; if Saturn, who is lord of this sign, be in Capricorn or Aquarius, the party has dark or black hair and in complexion sanguine, with prominent teeth, otherwise I have observed the party is of clear, light or fair complexion, and of sandy colored hair or very flaxen, and a very pure skin.

Pisces ♓.

24 A short stature, not very well made; a good large face, pale complexion, the body fleshy or swelling; not very straight, but stooping somewhat with the head when walking; inclined to lean forward.

The student had better learn to memorize the general description of the 12 signs of the Zodiac, and he ought to bear in mind that whatever planet may be in any of these signs, it is always more or less tinged by the description of the signs above named. For instance, if either Saturn, Mars or Jupiter or any other planet be in the sign Aries, the person is generally near the middle height, rather large bones, strong limbs, longish face &c. Also if the planet be in the sign Taurus, no matter what planet it is, it has a tendency to make the person born under that planet, inclined to be short and stout, and so on. He had also better learn to associate in his mind the "short" and "tall" signs, and "stout" and "thin" signs. For instance, Aries, Gemini, Virgo, Libra and Sagittary and sometimes Aquarius will describe a tall person, and he will be but seldom stout, more apt to be slender or thin. The short signs are Taurus, Cancer, Leo, Scorpio, Capricorn and Pisces, and sometimes Acquarius. The persons born with their planets in those signs, are very likely to be below the medium height, although sometimes Pisces will describe a tall and stout built person; it depends what planet is in that sign. For instance Mercury in the sign Pisces, will describe a person short, and Jupiter or the Sun in the sign Pisces, the person is almost certain to be tall and stout. The stout signs are Taurus, sometimes Cancer, Leo, Scorpio and Pisces, and sometimes Aquarius; but after the student once becomes familiar with those signs and their general description, he can instantly form an opinion by the aspects of the planets of what description the person is; and in that manner correct the time of birth, if the person does not know the correct time, or has given the wrong time of birth.

The student will next learn the description of persons born under the various planets, and also their signification. He must bear in mind that the planet, no matter what sign it is in always has a certain characteristic belonging to itself, and he can generally tell whether a person is a Jupiter or Venus person by their personal appearance, no matter what sign that planet is in; also he can distinguish between a Saturn and a Mars person, and so on, in regard to any other planet. He had best read and then commit to memory, if possible, the kind of persons described by the eight planets.

I will here state that it has not yet been fully learned how to describe the appearance of persons born under Neptune in each of the twelve signs of the Zodiac, as sufficient time has not elapsed since its discovery to have made proper observations. I shall have something to say on this subject in the latter part of this book; the student and also the professors of Astrology, should be very careful, and not give special descriptions of persons born under what is called the new planet, until we become more familiar with it, both in its characteristics and the kind of *persons it describes.*

PERSONS DESCRIBED BY THE EIGHT PLANETS.

I will here preface what is meant by a planet being well dignified, or ill dignified. A planet is said to be well dignified when in good aspect to good planets, or in a sign in which it is said to be strong and not afflicted, or in its own sign. A planet is said to be ill dignified when in evil aspect to evil planets, or in a sign in which it is said to be weak, or what is termed in its "detriment" or "fall."

THE DESCRIPTION OF HERSCHEL.

25 It indicates a person above the medium height, more apt to be well built or slender and wiry, than stout, especi-

ally if that planet is in the ascendant; has a tendency to be dark complexioned rather than light, but if light, a very light blonde, with yellow hair. High forehead, rather full face and that somewhat distorted, and generally a wide mouth; rather small, restless, grey, brown or hazel eyes, but seldom blue or black eyes, spare beard and likely to become bald before middle age. Active in manner, fond of study, also fond of science, inventive and fond of the occult or mysterious. He is seldom of a pleasant appearance, and generally odd or eccentric in his behavior. This is the description of Herschel persons when not in aspect to other planets, but when in aspect to other planets, the native partakes very much of the nature or quality of those planets.

26 When well dignified it describes a person well built, and nearly six feet high, of a commanding appearance and of great energy and perseverance. He will probably make some invention or discovery that will cause him to become famous or very wealthy. Has a great liking for astrology, astronomy, chemistry, etc., and will easily become an adept in those sciences.

27 When ill-dignified it describes a person rather slender, and but seldom above the medium height, disagreeable and odd in his manner, with some deformity, either in his personal appearance, walk or actions; also restless and unsettled.

28 Herschel naturally describes old persons, especially old maids or batchelors, recluses or hermits, and those who but seldom go into company. It rules furnaces, labatories, wild, unfrequented places, old, desolate buildings, antique furniture, statuary, old books and old pictures.

Of Saturn.

29 He naturally represents one of a middle stature, dark or swarthy complexion, little eyes, lowering eye-brows, flattish nose, thick lips, and stoops forward with his head when walking; large ears, dark or black hair, thin beard, and sometimes none at all; in short, a very peevish, melancholy and clumsy person, when in no aspect, but in aspect to other planets, you must mix their significations accordingly.

30 When Saturn is well dignified the persons signified by him are grave and sober, performing all their actions with judgment and discretion, having a searching fancy, and much given to study.

31 When he is ill dignified he signifies a malicious, envious, covetous, jealous, lying, dissembling, thievish person, not regarding his word or reputation.

32 Saturn naturally signifies old men, as grandfathers and fathers, as also persons who dig in mines or pits of the earth, husbandmen, day laborers, clowns, beggars, brickmakers, colliers, gardeners, sextons, tanners and curriers of leather, monks and jesuits.

Of Jupiter.

33 Jupiter naturally describes one of a tall stature, of a ruddy complexion and smiling countenance, an oval visage, high forehead and comely grey eyes, the hair soft and auburn, or of a light brown; much beard and the body every way handsomely formed; of a prudent and commendable carriage; sober and grave in his speech and just and upright in all his actions.

34 But when this planet (though a fortune) is ill dignified, he denotes the persons signified by him to be a mere dissembler, a hypocrite in matters of faith and religion, ignorant and careless and of a dull capacity, and instead of doing good he contrives ways and tricks to cheat his friend under a pretense of doing him a kindness.

35 He signifies clergymen and civilians, bishops, priests, judges and senators, young scholars and students in the law, clothiers and woolen drapers and all sorts of trades that deal in wool or woolen clothing.

Of Mars.

36 He represents a person of a middle stature, big-boned, and a strong able body, of a ruddy brown complexion and round visage, his hair for the most part red or of a sandy flaxen (unless in an earthy sign) and curling, a piercing sharp hazel eye, of a bold, lofty spirit, and a confident and undaunted countenance.

37 When he is well dignified he represents a person of a prudent behavior, though bold and confident, excellent in war, taking all the feats of honor upon himself, a boaster of his own acts; in fine he is really valiant and scorns to be overcome.

38 When ill dignified he delights in quarrels, murder and thievery and all evil actions, a traitor, and of a rash, inhuman, turbulent spirit, neither fearing God nor man.

39 Mars represents conquerors, usurpers, tyrants, or pretended kings, ruling by oppression and usurpation, colonels, captains and soldiers, physicians, apothecaries, surgeons, gunners, bailiffs, marshals, butchers, bakers, smiths, cutlers, barbers, watchmakers, cooks and carpenters.

Of Sun.

40 He represents a person of a plump, corpulent body, large face, broad, high forehead, a saffron or honey colored

complexion, great full eyes, yet a sharp sight, the hair yellow or light flaxen, much beard, generally of a great spirit, though honest, humane and courteous and of a healthful constitution.

41 When well dignified he inclines a person to honorable and great undertakings, for the most part high-minded, faithful and generous, very prudent and desirous of rule or sovereignty, of a very noble and majestic spirit, yet is very punctual and just to his friends and keeps his promise, even to his enemies, a mortal hater of all base and dishonorable actions.

42 When ill dignified he gives a proud, domineering, troublesome, vaporing person, using neither gravity in his words nor sobriety in his actions, always boasting of his pedigree, a mere spendthrift, careless of his family or estate, a hanger on and depender upon other men's charity.

43 The Sun signifies persons of the highest degree of men, as emperors, kings, princes, dukes, marquises, earls, barons, courtiers and magistrates of all sorts, as also gentlemen in general. In trades he denotes goldsmiths, minters of money, coppersmiths, braziers and pewterers.

Of Venus.

44 Venus describes one of a comely, middle stature, round or oval face and handsome visage, a whitish or clear complexion, curious lovely eyes, fair smooth hair, most commonly of light brown; red and cherry cheeks, with little becoming dimples in them or in the chin, the face fleshy, smooth and amiable, the person, whether man or woman, every way exceedingly handsome and delightful, and well shaped, going neat and decent in every part, both in clothes and person.

45 When she is well dignified the person described is of a pleasing disposition, a lover of pleasure and delighter in music and the fine arts; one who goes very cleanly and neat in apparel, zealous in affection, often entangled in love matters, nothing mistrustful or suspicious, a right virtuous person, be it either man or woman.

46 If ill dignified she signifies a person given to incestuous habits, to rioting and lewdness, not regarding his or her reputation, a hunter of concert-halls and saloons, carelessly wasting his money and estate, using neither faith nor conscience in conversation; and if Venus be in square or opposition to Mars in any woman's nativity or question, it denotes her a vile drunken creature, as also a notorious thief and liar.

47 She signifies all sorts of maids, wives and widows, musicians, painters, players, gravers, jewellers, silkdealers,

gamesters, perfumers, embroiderers, seamstresses, drawers of pictures, artists, glovers, and allssuch commodities that adorn women.

Of Mercury.

48 He represents a person medium tall and straight of body, a long visage, high forehead, long nose, thick brown or black hair, but little beard; his face of a dark or swarthy complexion, long arms and hands. If in aspect to Saturn, more dull and heavy; if with Jupiter more temperate; with Mars, rash and passionate; with the Sun, more generous; with Venus, merry and jesting; with the Moon, a mere shifter and deceiver. Mercury is much influenced by any or all the planets he is in aspect with.

49 When well dignified in a question or nativity the person signified by him is of a pregnant wit, desirous of learning; attaining anything with ease, eloquent in his speeches, aiming at the perfection of the arts; he is often desirous of travel into foreign countries, and is the author of many curious and notable inventions.

50 If weak or ill dignified then he signifies one given to boasting, prating and lying, a pretender to all manner of knowledge, but not capable of any, a mere conceited coxcomb, a thievish, cheating person, given to strife, contention and unreasonable disputes, a troublesome wit, with which he employs his pen and tongue against every man and generally without any just cause or reason.

51 Mercury generally signifies philosophers, astrologers, mathematicians, schoolmasters, poets, advocates, merchants, secretaries, accountants, solicitors, clerks, stationers, printers, booksellers, tailors, usurers, carriers and messengers.

Of Moon.

52 She denotes one of a large stature, round, pale or whitish face, grey eyes, and sometimes one bigger than the other; the hair brown or light brown, an abundance of hair and beard; the body plump, having thick fleshy hands and fingers.

53 When well dignified she denotes a lover of all honest arts and inventions, delights in novelties, and naturally inclined to remove and shift from place to place; a very timorous and easily frightened person, but a soft and tender and well-disposed creature.

54 When ill dignified she denotes vagabonds, an idle, lazy, drunken companion given to sottishness, delighting to live careless or beggarly, one of no spirit or forecast, a perfect hater of labor, a mutable, unsettled and inconstant person.

55 She signifies the common people, as also queens, duchesses, ladies, and all women in general, pilgrims or travellers, sailors, fishermen, and such as go long voyages by sea or land, barrelers, brewers, coachmen, letter carriers, milliners, messengers, bar-tenders, malsters, mid-wives, nurses, hackneys, charmen and water-bearers, charwomen and washerwomen.

After the student has thoroughly committed to memory the description of persons born under the eight planets, regardless of what signs they may happen to be in, and also the description of the persons born under a planet well dignified, or ill dignified, and also the persons, professions or trades signified by the various planets, he can then proceed to learn the description of persons indicated by the planets in each of the 12 signs of the Zodiac, and it would be advisable to learn by heart as many of these descriptions as possible. Even if he could commit to memory the whole, it would be best to do so, similar to his learning any latin lesson, or rules in the English grammar, but any way he should be able to remember what might be termed certain landmarks, of persons described by the planets in particular signs. For instance, he should commit to memory the description of persons indicated by the planet Venus in the sign Libra ; of Jupiter in the sign Sagittary ; of Saturn in the sign Aquarius : of the Sun in the sign Leo: of Mercury in the sign Virgo, and so on. These will serve as guide-posts or landmarks, for most of the planets in the different signs.

Astrology is a science and also an art ; we might compare it to music. A person studying mnsic may know all the notes and may be able to give expression to any of them at any moment on any instrument or by the voice, but the musician is known or appreciated chiefly by his skill in associating these various notes together, to produce tunes or harmony, and the more successful he is in that respect, the better musician he is. It is the same in the practice of Astrology, the more successful an Astrologer is in delineating the personal description, and also the mental qualities, temper and the various traits or characteristics of the persons and their liking or inclination to any particular science, trade or profession, the more successful does the Astrologer become, and the better he becomes known as a person qualified for his profession. It is astonishing how skillful the Astrologer can become in describing persons both bodily, mentally, and physically, by the planets in the different signs, by constant trial and long practice : particularly if the Astrologer has a special gift in acquiring a knowledge of that science, similar to a person having a particular gift for learning music, painting, etc.

The following is a description of persons born under the eight planets, in each sign of the Zodiac, and *which the student ought* to commit to memory if possible.

HERSCHEL IN THE TWELVE SIGNS.

We can generally recognize a ♅ person by their unsettled eyes, which are often hazel, and cannot look at any one object long; they are generally above the middle height, sometimes very tall; they are but seldom stout. They are always fond of discoveries and inventions, and the occult. ♅ makes more old maids and old bachelors than all the other planets put together, especially if it is in the ascendant.

♅ in ♈

56 Rather tall stature, lean, and well made, light hair, hazel or grey eyes, ruddy or sun-burned complexion: strong constitution, ambitious, and quick in anger.

♅ in ♉

57 Short, thick-set person, dark hair and eyes, deep-set; rather fleshy, muddy or swarthy complexion, short neck; passionate, boasting, and revengeful; a person to be avoided, conceited and luxurious.

♅ in ♊

58 Produces a tall, thin stature; brown hair, and grey eyes, well made, quick step, active and nimble; fond of science, of a rather good disposition, eccentric in behavior, generous and inventive.

♅ in ♋

59 Produces a short, thick-set, corpulent body, pale complexion, brown hair and grey eyes; conceited, bigoted, fond of drink, violent, eccentric, and ungovernable.

♅ in ♌

60 Makes a full-sized stature, broad, strong shoulders, light brown hair, and sandy beard; firm walk. In disposition, generous and free; eccentric, fond of military display, rather proud, and self-conceited.

♅ in ♍

61 A short stature, dark hair and eyes, lean body, small limbs; of an eccentric turn of mind, fond of curiosities and novelties, studious, scientific but mean and close in worldly affairs.

♅ in ♎

62 Produces a full stature, well-made body, oval face, light hair, and sanguine complexion; of a scientific, ambitious turn of mind, soon angered, and eccentric in behavior.

♅ in ♏

63 Short and thick-set body, broad shoulders and often ill-made; dark, swarthy complexion, dark or black hair and

eyes, a malicious, deceitful, cunning person, given to drink and pleasures, and a most despicable person when ♅ is afflicted in this sign by an evil aspect of ♄ or ♂.

♅ in ♐

64 Describes a person of tall stature, light hair and eyes, lofty forehead, good complexion. In disposition generous and free, fond of all sports, and enthusiastic.

♅ in ♑

65 Denotes one below the middle stature, well-made, short neck, high forehead, dark hair and eyes; proud, austere, and conceited, and possessing but few laudable proclivities.

♅ in ♒

66 Produces a person above the middle stature, brown hair and eyes, well-made, and handsome broad face; very ingenious, fond of science and novelties, eccentric, and of good disposition.

♅ in ♓

67 Medium stature, sickly, light or pale complexion, dark hair and eyes, ill-made hands or feet, bad walk; in disposition sottish and dull, dejected and despised.

SATURN IN THE TWELVE SIGNS.

A ♄ person can generally be recognized, no matter what sign of the Zodiac it may chance to be in, by his thoughtful and studious appearance; he is generally careful and saving, and has a down look when walking; he is but seldom lively or cheerful, or inclined to pleasure, and he is more inclined to be slender than stout. ♄ generally gives bad teeth, and in ♓ they are discolored and rotten.

♄ in ♈

68 Gives a ruddy complexion, a spare, raw-boned person, full face, often dark hair, not much beard, addicted to boasting, resolute, quarrelsome and very ill natured.

♄ in ♉

69 Gives a person in no wise comely, but a heavy, clumsy, awkward appearance, dark hair, middle stature, not well made, rough in carriage, sordid, vicious, etc.

♄ in ♊

70 Represents a person of rather tall stature, dark, sanguine complexion, oval visage, dark brown or black hair, ingenious but unpolished, perverse and generally unfortunate in most of his undertakings.

♄ in ♋

71 Denotes a person of middle stature, rather short than tall, sickly and feeble, meagre face, dark hair, languid eyes, the body sometimes crooked; jealous, malicious and deceitful in his dealings.

♄ in ♌

72 Gives a person of moderate large stature, broad, round shoulders, wide chest, lightish hair, large boned, surly aspect, eyes sunk, apt to stoop. Qualities tolerably good, generous but passionate, not over valiant or courageous when put to the test.

♄ in ♍

73 Represents a person of a tall, spare body, swarthy complexion, dark or black hair, and that plentiful; a long head, solid countenance, generally unfortunate, inclined to melancholy, retaining anger, a projector of curious matters to little purpose, studious, subtle, reserved, inclined to pilfering and indirect dealings.

♄ in ♎

74 Describes a person above the middle stature, soft brown hair, oval face, large nose and forehead, clear complexion, one opinionated of himself, prodigal of expense. They are given to debate and controversy and seldom leave any wealth at their death.

♄ in ♏

75 Represents a person of a mean stature, stout, thick-trussed body, broad shoulders, black or dark hair, which is usually short and thick; quarrelsome, mischievous, one who will undertake violent and dangerous actions, though often to his own detriment.

♄ in ♐

76 Gives a large body, brown hair, good make, tolerable complexion, obliging disposition, not covetous, moderately frugal, rarely profuse, but somewhat choleric. One who will not bear an affront yet willing to do good to all; a lover of his friends and merciful to an enemy

♄ in ♑

77 Personates a lean, raw-boned body, dark or black hair, middle stature, dark complexion, small, leering eyes, long visage, and a stooping, awkward posture in walking. One who is peevish, discontented, melancholy, covetous, of few words, fearful, retains anger, and is of great gravity.

♄ in ♒

78 Gives a reasonable full-bodied person, a large head and face, rather inclined to corpulency, middle stature, sad brown hair, a clear complexion, sober, graceful deportment, affable, courteous disposition; of an excellent, searching fancy, and generally very proficient in what they undertake in arts and sciences; a person of a pregnant genius, yet liable to be conceited.

♄ in ♓

79 Describes a middle-statured person, pale complexion, sad or dark brown hair, a large head and full eye, sometimes the teeth are distorted; a person not very comely; active to do mischief, malicious and given to contention and dissimulation; an uncertain, fickle person in everything, though often presenting a good outside, yet fraudulent and deceitful in the end. They are not talkative but deliberate, and do evil with malice aforethought. They are said to improve as they grow older.

JUPITER IN THE TWELVE SIGNS.

Jupiter persons are generally known by having a straight walk, but not really proud, like a ♂ person; they are above the medium height, inclined to be full built, and often stout; they are known by having an oval face, high forehead, and hair receding from the temples, and sometimes they become bald before middle age; they are often persons of great ambition, and like to rule others; they make poor servants.

Jupiter usually gives good teeth, and frequently an apparent mark in the front teeth. In an airy sign, he gives broad front teeth; in a fiery sign, crooked; in earthy they are discolored; and in a watery sign, the teeth decay suddenly, and grow black and rotten, especially if he be in ☌ with ☋, or in any evil aspect of ♄ or ♂. If he be in a watery sign, in □ or ☍ to ☿, the party has some defect in his delivery or speech. Jupiter in an airy sign, the body is more strongly built and corpulent; in a fiery sign more square and strong; in an earthy, a well composed body, and in a watery, more fat and often comely.

♃ in ♈

80 Describes a middle stature, but not stout, rather lean than corpulent, a quick penetrating eye, high nose, oval visage, generally with pimples or a peculiar redness in the face. They are of a free, noble, generous disposition, very obliging, polite and complacent, especially to their friends.

♃ in ♉

81 Gives a middle stature, stout, well-set body, but though compact not handsome; hair brown, rough and curling, complexion swarthy, and frequently the skin looks shiny and oily. The disposition reasonably good, judgment

sound, deportment good, behavior free and charitable, fond of the female sex, and very humane and compassionate to the distressed.

♃ in ♊

82 Represents a well-made, compact body, plump, yet above the middle stature, sanguine complexion, though rather dusky, brown hair and full expressive eyes, the deportment graceful, affable, courteous, gentle, mild, obliging and good-natured. An admirer of the female sex and a lover of learning. But if ♃ be near Occulus Taurus in ♊ 6° 47′ with 2° 34′ south lat., he will be addicted to women. And if near Aldebaran in ♊ 8° 7′ with 5° 28′ south lat., he will be rash and unstable, inimical to himself and disagreeable to others. If with the bull's north horn in ♊ 20° 54′ with 5° 22′ north lat., he will be rash and violent.

♃ in ♋

83 Gives a person of middle stature, a pale, sickly and unwholesome complexion, oval face, hair dark brown, body rather plump but disproportioned. A busy, talkative character, very conceited and apt to intermeddle with other people's concerns. A lover of women and fond of the water whereon he is usually fortunate. Unless Mars throws a good aspect to Jupiter he is not courageous.

♃ in ♌

84 Represents a strong and well-proportioned tall body, the hair is light or yellowish brown and curling; complexion ruddy, eye full and fiery; person rather handsome. The disposition is noble-minded, courageous and magnanimous, but lofty and proud and ambitious, one who delights in warlike actions, is a terror to his enemies, and who scorns to bend to them; fond of contending for honors, etc., and full of daring and enterprise.

♃ in ♍

85 Gives a person of a reasonable full stature, well built, and what may be termed handsome; sad brown or black hair, ruddy complexion, but not clear or fair. One who is choleric and given to boasting, studious, yet covetous, and by his rashness often meeting serious losses; he is not easily imposed or wrought upon by any person.

♃ in ♎

86 Renders the body complete and elegant, a handsome form, and inviting face, upright, tall stature, rather slender, clear complexion, a full eye, oval face, light brown hair, subject to have pimples or a rash in the face. Disposition and

temper mild; behavior winning and obliging to all, partial to exercise and recreation; much esteemed and honored.

♃ in ♏

87 Gives a middle stature, stout compact body, coarse hair, fleshy and full face, muddy or dull complexion. Manners proud and lofty, one who is ambitious, and desires to bear rule over his equals; resolute and covetous, ill natured and selfish, very subtle and crafty, therefore to be very warily dealth with.

♃ in ♐

88 Gives a fine, tall, upright body, good form and make, oval face, ruddy complexion, brown chestnut colored hair, full beard and whiskers, but the hair falls off early in life, especially about the temples, a good eye, and much expression in the face. The mind is just and noble, disposition courageous, humane, affable and agreeable; manners polite and accomplished. One fond of horses and hunting.

♃ in ♑

89 Describes a small stature, pale complexion, thin face, little head, not much beard, weakly person, dark brown hair, said to be darker than the beard. The mind is ingenious, but peevish, inactive, helpless and indolent.

♃ in ♒

90 Personates a middle stature, well set, brown hair, clear complexion, rather corpulent, compact make, and of a cheerful, obliging disposition, hurtful to none; well conducted, and moderate in recreation; just and merciful, good humored, industrious, communicative, inclined to be scientific, and but little inclined to extravagance.

♃ in ♓

91 Describes a person of middle stature, obscure complexion, plump, fleshy body, lightish brown hair. Disposition harmless, studious, and possessed of excellent talents and good acquirements; friendly, kind, and inoffensive. They delight in good company, and to be upon the water, where if ☽ throw not an evil aspect to ♃, they are very fortunate.

MARS IN THE TWELVE SIGNS.

A Mars person is generally known by having either red, or auburn, or yellowish hair, but sometimes he has black hair, and if a man, his mustache is generally lighter than his hair; has a proud, military walk, fond of dress and decoration, and often a boaster, or blows his own trumpet; he easily gets into quarrels or fights, but generally comes off conqueror; he speaks quick and is generally very decisive in his language and actions.

If ♂ be in ☌, □ or ☍ of Saturn, or with ☋, the disposition is very evil, especially if they be in angles, then the person he describes is very fierce and violent. He is the giver of courage and resolution, but if ♂ be weak and afflicted he is very deficient. If Mars be in fiery signs, he is hasty and choleric, and there is generally observed to be a falling in of the cheeks, and a lightness of features, with an angry look; in earthy signs, a sullen dogged temper; in airy signs, more free and obliging; in watery, sottish dull and stupid, unless Mars be well aspected by Jupiter, Sun or Moon.

♂ in ♈

92 Represents a person of middle stature, well set, large boned; swarthy complexion, light hair, and curling, frequently red; austere countenance, and, if ♂ be oriental, ruddy, and smooth; bold and undaunted, confident, choleric, and proud; fond of war and dispute; one who often gains by those means.

♂ in ♉

93 Gives a middle stature, well set, rather short; dusky complexion, dark or black hair, which is rough and coarse; broad face, and wide mouth; he will generally have some scar or other mark in the face, which is often ruddy, but never fair. He will be gluttonous, debauched, given to drinking and wenching; also a gambler, and very quarrelsome, treacherous, and illnatured. He is generally unfortunate, but if ♂ be near the Pleiades, remarkably so.

♂ in ♊

94 Gives a tall person, with black or dark brown hair, (although if ♂ be in the first seven degrees of ♊, the terms of ☿, it will be light,) sanguine complexion, and well proportioned body. He is restless and unsettled, but ingenious; unfortunate in most things, living in a mean way, generally shifting here and there, leaving his debts unpaid, and exercising his wits for a livelihood; in short, a *chevalier d'industrie*, or mere swindler. But if ♂ be in good aspect to ☉, ♃ or ♀ it will mitigate these evil propensities.

♂ in ♋

95 Describes a short figure, and a bad complexion, with brown hair and not much of it; the body is generally ill made, and crooked. The temper is sour and bad; one who is given to sottishness, a mean servile unfortunate creature; usually he is employed in some low business, being incapable of better.

♂ in ♌

96 Shows a well proportioned body, rather tall, light brown hair, oval face, sanguine or sunburnt complexion,

large eyes, stout limbs, and a brisk, cheerful aspect. A lover of women, given to boasting, fond of robust sports, as hunting, riding, shooting, etc., and ready for warlike occupation at any time. He dresses well and is a favorite with the ladies, but it is generally to his prejudice.

♂ in ♍

97 Produces a middle sized body, well made, and proportioned, black hair, or very dark brown; the first seven degrees gives lighter hair than the rest of the sign, being the terms of Mercury, the complexion is swarthy or darkish, and generally some scar, mark or blemish in the face. A hasty, proud, revengeful and spiteful mind; one who remembers an injury, is hard to please, conceited, and generally very unfortunate in all he undertakes.

♂ in ♎

98 Gives a neat made, rather tall person; his face oval; complexion sanguine, and hair light brown and soft, but, if in the last six degrees, (his own term,) it is more wiry and reddish. The disposition is brisk and cheerful, but fond of boasting, and very conceited, one who is fond of dress, effeminate in appearance, much attached to women, by whom he is also much beloved and frequently ruined.

♂ in ♏

99 Produces a well set form of middle stature, rather corpulent, swarthy complexion, black, curling hair, broad and plain face. The temper is very unsociable, and rash; they are generally revengeful, ungrateful, quarrelsome and wicked; yet of good genius and ready apprehension, excelling in mystery, etc.

♂ in ♐

100 Denotes a tall person, with a well proportioned body, compact, and well made, sanguine complexion, oval visage, a quick, penetrating eye; the mind is cheerful, merry and jovial, but disposition hasty, passionate, high minded and lofty; courageous, loquacious, and fond of applause: on the whole a good character.

♂ in ♑

101 Represents a mean or small stature, thin, lean body, little head, thin face, bad complexion, being sallow and obscure; black, lank hair. An ingenious mind, witty, shrewd and penetrating, generally fortunate and successful in his undertakings.

♂ in ♒

102 Gives a well composed body, rather corpulent, and inclined to be tall, (though frequently not above the middle

size), fair or clear complexion, sandy hair, a turbulent disposition, and addicted to controversy, etc.; not very fortunate in general.

♂ in ♓

103 Represents a mean stature, rather short and fleshy, a bad complexion, far from handsome; a debauched look, light brown hair, sottish and stupid; a great lover of women, if in his own terms or those of Mercury, sly and artful, deceitful, idle and worthless, not friendly to any one.

THE SUN IN THE TWELVE SINGS.

A Sun person is generally known by having a particularly straight or proud walk, as if he was a man of great consequence. He often has a full face, full prominent eyes, and broad forehead; is generally a go-ahead person, and wishes to show off, especially in having a fine house, or wanting to become a leading politician; he has generally good health, or if sick, readily recovers.

☉ in ♈

104 Decribes a rather tall stature, strong and well made; a good complexion, though not very clear, light hair, flaxen or yellowish, and large eyes. The man is noble, valiant and courageous, delighting in warlike actions and enterprises; he gains victory, is famous, and a terror to his enemies, etc.

☉ in ♉

105 Gives a short, well set, rather ugly person; dusky complexion, brown hair, large, broad face, wide mouth and great nose. A confident, proud and bold man, fond of opposition, proud of his physical strength, and one who generally is victorious.

☉ in ♊

106 Represents a well proportioned body, above the middle stature, sanguine complexion, brown hair. He is affable, courteous and kind, not very fortunate, as he is so meek and mild tempered, often controlled and imposed on by others.

☉ in ♋

107 Gives a mean, ill formed body, deformed in the face, with a very unhealthy aspect; the hair brown. A harmless, cheerful person, but indolent, and not fond of employment; one who spends his time in sports and pastimes, dancing, etc., and is greatly addicted to women.

☉ in ♌

108 Gives a strong, well proportioned body, and a very portly person, sanguine complexion, light brown or yellowish hair, a full face, and large staring eyes, and very prominent;

there is generally a mark or scar on the face. A very just, upright and honorable man, who scorns to do any meaness; punctual and faithful to friends, and magnanimous even to his enemies, in short a right royal disposition; a very ambitious man, withal, fond of rule and authority, and given to war and dominion, conquest, etc.

☉ in ♍

109 Makes a person inclined to be tall of stature, and slender, but very well proportioned, good complexion, dark hair, and much of it, but not black; the mind ingenious and cheerful, fond of honest recreation, especially agreeable at convivial parties, etc.

☉ in ♎

110 Produces an upright, tall and slender body, full eyes, oval face, ruddy complexion, light hair, and frequently a rash or pimples in the face. The mind is honorable, and disposition good, but the party is always unfortunate, especially in all matters of war or ambition.

☉ in ♏

111 Gives a remarkably square built, full fleshy person, broad face, cloudy complexion, dun or sunburnt, brown hair; mind ingenious, but the temper rugged and overberaing, manners disagreeable, disposition ambitious, one who will not admit of an equal; they are fortunate upon the seas, or as surgeons, physicians, etc.

☉ in ♐

112 Makes a tall, handsome, well proportioned body, oval face, sanguine complexion, or rather brown or sun burnt; light brown hair, but in the first eight degrees of the sign it is darker; one who is very lofty and proud spirited, aiming at great things, austere and severe, and one who performs some honorable exploits, and often becomes ennobled, or receives titles, honorary distinctions, etc.

☉ in ♑

113 Represents a mean stature, ill made, spare thin body, oval face, sickly complexion, soft brown hair, not curling, and if in the first six degrees of the sign, it is light brown; the party is just and honorable in his principles, a tolerably fair temper, and gains love and friendship by his agreeable conversation; one who is very hasty at times, and much given to women.

☉ in ♒

114 Describes a person of middle stature, well made, corpulent body, round, full face, clear complexion, and light

brown hair, (in the term of Saturn, it is dark brown),. The disposition tolerably good, free from malice or deceit, but yet vain, proud, desirous of bearing rule and ostentatious.

☉ in ♓

115 Gives a stature rather short, body plump and fleshy; a round, full face, and indifferent complexion, light brown hair, in the first eight degrees of the sign it is flaxen, and very soft; the party is extremely partial to female society, very effeminate, fond of pleasure, etc., and though harmless to others, ruins himself by extravagance, debauchery, gambing, intemperance, feasting, etc.

VENUS IN THE TWELVE SIGNS.

A Venus person is generally full built, near the medium height, has a pleasant countenance, fond of music and the fine arts; generally has an oval face, round forehead, soft, expressive eyes, and a rather small nose; He takes delight in music, fine arts and decoration, and if a man, has an effeminate appearance, and is fond of female society.

♀ in ♈

116 Describes a middle stature, rather tall and slender, light hair, (if in the term of Jupiter, dark); good complexion, a pensive aspect and usually a mark or scar in the face, (may be marked more or less with small pox, according as Venus is afflicted or not). They are generally unfortunate both to themselves and others, unless Venus have a ✶ or △ of ♃, ☉ or ☽.

♀ in ♉

117 Gives a handsome person, though the stature is not great, the body is extremely well made, plump but not gross; and if Venus be well aspected, they are very handsome, the complexion is ruddy, but not fair; generally females are handsome brunettes, and have much the form and figure of the Venus de Medicis. The hair is generally brown, and if Venus be in her own term, it is very soft and luxuriant; if in the term of Jupiter it is a shining black. The eyes are generally black, and very expressive; the temper is mild and winning, the disposition, kind, humane, obliging, etc. They generally gain much respect from those with whom they converse, and are generally fortunate.

♀ in ♊

118 Describes a person above the middle height, slender, upright, and well made. The complexion, clear and fair, with soft brown hair; frequently brown or hazel eyes. They

are good humored, loving, liberal, just and charitable, and rarely guilty of anything dishonorable.

♀ in ♋

119 Represents a short person, a fleshy body; round, pale and sickly face, with light hair, and if the Moon be with Venus, and they are in the ascendant, the face will be quite white and wan, and the hair very light colored; but if Venus be in the term of Mars, the hair may be reddish, and a tinge of color appear in the cheeks. They generally have small grey or greenish eyes. The disposition is idle and dull, they are fond of low company, and vicious pleasures and pursuits, if it be a female of the poorer classes, she is a frequenter of spirit shops, etc. They are fickle and timid, put the best side outwards, and seem to be in earnest when they are not; ever mutable and inconstant.

♀ in ♌

120 Gives a person reasonably tall of stature, well composed body; clear complexion, round face, full eyes, freckled and fair skin; hair, reddish, or if in the term of Venus it may be flaxen. They are petulant and passionate, soon angry and soon pleased again: free, generous, sociable and good humored, but rather proud and frequently indisposed, though not seriously.

♀ in ♍

121 Shows a tall, well proportioned figure, oval face, dark hair, or if in her own term, sad brown, and a dusky complexion. They are ingenious, eloquent, active and clever, of an aspiring turn, but rarely successful in their pursuits; generally unfortunate.

♀ in ♎

122 Describes an upright tall, elegant person, extremely well made, with a genteel carriage. The face is oval and rather beautiful, having pleasing smiles and beautiful dimples; but they are frequently freckled. The hair is brown and soft, and rather grows long than plentiful. They are kind, affectionate and very obliging, and generally well beloved by all with whom they have any dealings. If Venus be in the ascendant, and there be no afflicting aspects, and Jupiter, cast a △ from ♒, the party, if a female, will be a perfect beauty.

♀ in ♏

123 Denotes a short, stout, well set, corpulent body, broad face, and dusky complexion, and dark or black hair, (unless Venus be in the terms of Mars or her own); one who has nothing very pleasant in the countenance. They are envious,

debauched and vicious; given to contention: and if Venus be afflicted by Saturn or Mars to very disgraceful actions; and if both Saturn and Mars, afflict and there be no assistance by good aspect of Sun or Jupiter, they are possèsed of very evil propensities.

♀ in ♐

124 Represents a person rather tall than otherwise, well made; clear or sanguine complexion, fair oval face, brown hair. They are generous, spirited, aiming at no mean things, rather proud and passionate, yet are generally good tempered, kind and inoffensive. They delight in innocent recreations, and are in short very obliging, fortunate persons.

♀ in ♑

125 Describes a small sized person, short stature, a pale face, thin and sickly; with dark hair, (but if Venus be in her own term, sad brown). They are generally persons who love their belly, fond of enjoyment; not fortunate, subject to sudden changes in life and strange catastrophes.

♀ in ♒

126 Gives a handsome well formed person, clear complexion, rather corpulent or large body; brown hair, if she be in her own term, flaxen. A good disposition, quiet and affable, courteous, not at all inclined to vicious actions, peaceable, obliging to all: fortunate in his affairs and respected by his friends and acquaintance in general.

♀ in ♓

127 Personates a middle stature, a fleshy plump body, a round, full face, with a dimple in the chin, good complexion, between pale and ruddy. Good humored, just, kind, mild and peaceable; ingenious, but somewhat unstable, yet moderately fortunate in the world.

MERCURY IN THE TWELVE SIGNS.

A Mercury person is inclined to be slim, often above the medium height, active, talkative, fond of learning and studying; he generally makes a good orator, editor or author, and often has some light occupation, such as being a book-keeper, or being a clerk in a store; has generally a thin face, high forehead, sharp nose, dark hair, and rather dark complexion. These remarks are only intended for persons described by ☿ when it has no aspect to any other planet, but when in aspect to other planets, it takes more of the nature of those planets that it is in aspect to, and the person has to be described accordingly.

☿ in ♈

128 Gives a mean stature, spare and thin body, oval face, light brown and curling hair, dull complexion. A mind rather ill disposed; addicted to dispute, to lie, steal and many tricks, and unworthy actions; in short, a mere knave.

☿ in ♉

129 Gives a middle sized, corpulent, thick person, strong and well set; swarthy and sun burnt complexion, dark, short and thick hair. He is idle, slothful; one who loves ease and gluttony, and who ruins himself among the female sex.

☿ in ♊

130 Shows a straight, upright, tall body, well formed; brown hair, good complexion, and a very intelligent look. An ingenious, pregnant fancy, a good orator, a cunning lawyer, or a clever book-seller: one who perfectly understands his own interest, and (if Mercury be not afflicted) one who is a subtle politician, not easily deluded by the most cunning knave he may encounter.

☿ in ♋

131 Personates a low, short stature, an ill complexion, a thin, sharp face, small eyes, sharp nose, dark hair; one who is given to drink, light fingered, ill natured, dishonest, and very deceitful and changeable; a very mean little wretch, if Mercury be afflicted.

☿ in ♌

132 Gives a full, large body, and good stature, dull, swarthy sunburnt complexion; light brown hair, round face, full eyes, a broad or high nose. A hasty, proud, conceited, ambitious, boasting, contentious and troublesome character.

☿ in ♍

133 Denotes a tall, slender, well proportioned person; dark brown hair, (or if Mercury be in the terms of Jupiter or Saturn, black hair); not a very clear complexion, a long visage, and austere countenace. A very witty, ingenious, talented mind, and if Mercury be free from affliction, a profound scholar or linguist and capable of any undertaking which requires great ability.

☿ in ♎

134 Personates a tall body, well made, but not thin; light brown, smooth hair, a ruddy or sanguine complexion. A just, virtuous, prudent man, a lover and promoter of learning, and having great natural abilities and many acquired accomplishments.

☿ in ♍

135 Gives a short or low stature, full and stout built, but ill made body, broad shoulders, swarthy dark complexion, brown curling hair. Not any way elegant or pleasing, yet ingenious and studious, very careful of his own interest, fond of the female sex, and partial to company and merry making.

☿ in ♐

136 Denotes a person of tall stature, well formed, not corpulent, but rather large boned and spare; an oval face, a large nose, and a ruddy complexion. A man who is hasty but soon reconciled, rash in many things to his own injury, yet well disposed, striving after honorable things, but seldom attaining them, not very fortunate.

☿ in ♑

137 Gives a mean or small stature, often crooked or ill made and bow-legged; a thin face and figure, dusky complexion, and brown hair. A very peevish, discontented, dejected, sickly feeble person, yet active; one who is unfortunate to himself, and disagreeable to others, owing to his suspicious nature, and ill temper.

☿ in ♒

138 Shows a person of middle height, rather fleshy and corpulent; a good complexion, and clear skin, with brown hair, and full face. An ingenious, obliging character, inclined to study, fond of arts and sciences, very inventive, and remarkable for his talent, as well as being a humane, kind, charitable person.

☿ in ♓

139 Gives a short, dumpy figure, though if in his own term or that of Saturn, rather thin, pale face, brown hair, sickly look, and very hairy body. A very peevish, repining, foppish person, addicted to wine and women, very effeminate and contemptible.

THE MOON IN THE TWELVE SIGNS.

Persons described by the Moon are inclined to be full built or stout, rather phlegmatic, are generally slow in motions, and do not care for active business, they like to take things easy, and if a female, she is generally indolent or slovenly; they are more likely to be light complexioned than dark. The above remarks are intended for Moon persons, when that planet is not in aspect to any other planet.

☽ in ♈

140 Describes a person of indifferent stature, rather fleshy, or plump round face, tolerably good complexion; light brown

or flaxen hair. The mind is rash, angry, ambitious and aspiring, often changing, and he undergoes, various mutations in life, and is seldom fortunate.

☽ in ♉

141 Gives a strong, corpulent, well set body, rather short; rather good complexion, dark brown or black hair. A gentle, obliging, kind, sober, just and honest man; one who gains esteem, is much respected, and attains perferment according to his station in life.

☽ in ♊

142 Describes a tall, well formed, upright, comely person; brown hair, good complexion, between pale and sanguine. The mind is ingenious, yet crafty and subtle to excess, not of the best disposition, nor very fortunate, unless other good testimonies by aspects of Jupiter, Sun or Venus concur or corroborate.

☽ in ♋

143 Represents a middle stature, well proportioned and fleshy person, a round, full face, pale and dusky complexion, sad brown hair. The mind is flexible, given to change; a merry, easy, pleasant, disposition very harmless and peaceable, fond of good company; one who is generally well beloved and fortunate in most affairs; unsteady but free from passion or rash actions.

☽ in ♌

144 Denotes a person above the middle size, well proportioned, strong and large boned, sanguine complexion, light brown hair, large and prominent eyes and full face. A lofty, proud, aspiring person, very ambitious and desirous to bear rule, one who abhors servitude, or dependence, and is generally unfortunate.

☽ in ♍

145 Describes a rather tall person, dark brown hair, oval face, rather ruddy but tolerably clear complexion. An ingenious, reserved, covetous, melancholy, unfortunate person, not in general very well disposed, and one who seldom performs any very commendable actions.

☽ in ♎

146 Gives a tall, well composed body, with smooth, light brown hair; handsome and pleasant, cheerful countenance, fine red and white complexion. They are merry, jocund and pleasant, and much admired by the female sex; very fond of amusements; and if a female she is courted by numbers, yet

☽ in ♏

147 Denotes a thick, short and ill shaped person, rather fleshy; of an obscure complexion, dark hair, often black, especially if Moon be in the term of Jupiter or Saturn. They are sottish and vulgar, malicious, brutish and treacherous, and if it be a female she is generally infamous in her desires, and if Moon be afflicted by the □ or ☍ of Saturn or Mars, she is openly scandalous.

☽ in ♐

148 Represents a handsome, and well proportioned, rather tall person; oval face, sanguine complexion, rather bronzed and bright brown or shining chestnut hair. The disposition is good, open and generous, but hasty and passionate, yet forgiving; one who aims at great things, is fortunate and much respected by those with whom he associates.

☽ in ♑

149 Gives a person of low stature, a thin, small, weak body, bad health and feeble, especially about the knees; small features, black hair and dull complexion; one who is inactive, dull not ingenious, generally very debauched in his conduct. and held in low esteem by his companions, etc.

☽ in ♒

150 Represents a middle sized person, well made, and rather corpulent; brown hair, clear skin and sanguine complexion. They are ingenious, affable, courteous and inoffensive; a lover of curious and scientific studies, having much invention, and a person rarely guilty of unworthy actions.

☽ in ♓

151 Describes a person of a mean or low stature, but plump or fat; pale and bloated face, light brown hair and sleepy eyes; one not inclined to action, unless of the worse kind; unfortunate both to himself and others, given to drink.

N. B.—If Moon be well aspected, and in a good house, the disposition is much improved.

After the student has become well acquainted with each of the planets in the twelve signs of the Zodiac, he will then have to learn the conjunctions and aspects of the planets. This part of Astrology becomes much more complicated than that which he has already learned, as in each case, he has two or more factors to deal with, and these factors are liable to changes or variations, and it is sometimes very difficult to tell which planet has the predominating influence; there are no special rules for him to be guided by, and which are not liable to changes. This part of Astrology can only be learned by constant practice and experience in investigating horoscopes and horary astrology.

THE EFFECTS OF THE CONJUNCTIONS OF URANUS WITH THE SEVEN PLANETS.

♅ is never the only significator in a nativity or in horary Astrology. There is no question but that ♄ is lord of both ♑ and ♒. Nearly one hundred years ago, when ♅ was discovered by William Herschel, a number of Astrologers in England and other parts of the world, allotted ♑ for ♅'s signs, and let ♄ only have the sign ♒ for its sign. But afterwards the Astrologers changed it about and gave ♅ the sign ♒, and ♄ the sign ♑.

The ancients have allotted both ♑ and ♒ to ♄, as their ruling planet; and as ♄ has been recognized as lord of those two signs, and it has been proved by the experience of thousands of years, that they are the signs that ♄ rules, it is not advisable to be re-arranging the signs and planets, every time a new planet is discovered.

There is no doubt but that ♅ has a great influence in the sign ♒, especially when that sign is on the ascendant or 10th house, or ♅ is in that sign, or in aspect to it; also ♅ has great influence in the sign ♏. As remarkable events takes place when ♅ is transiting that sign. These two signs and ♊ are the only signs that ♅ has much influence in or while transiting them, that I have been able to observe. I will speak further on this subject in the latter part of this volume.

♅ ☌ ♄

152 If ♅ is in ☌ with ♄, especially in the sign ♈ or in the ascendant, it causes a disfigurement or deformity of the face. The parties are also very liable to accidents or narrow escapes, especially if ♅ is afflicted by an evil aspect in the midheaven. ♅ ☌ ♄ in any sign causes the native to be liable to many misfortunes or accidents, especially if they are in angles; every seven years brings some misfortune or calamity.

If ♄ be significator, it makes the person very fond of inventions and discoveries, especially connected with large constructions, such as engines, bridges or large buildings, and it is more than likely that he will make some great invention or discovery by which he will accumulate a large fortune. The native may spend his whole life in establishing some new society or new religion, and is willing to undergo much persecution to accomplish that object; as in the case of William Q. Judge trying to establish Theosophy. He had the ☉ ☌ ♄ and ♅, all in the sign ♈ in the ascendant, in his horoscope.

♅ ☌ ♃

153 If ♅ be in ☌ with ♃ in any prominent position in a horoscope, either the ascendant, midheaven, 11th or 7th house, the native will gain by unlooked for events or legacies, and may

become rich by means of wealthy friends, or by associating with prominent people, such as governors, etc. He will have great magnetism in controlling others; will be fond of new discoveries or inventions of all kinds, and is certain to be a leader of society, or be in some way prominent.

If ♃ be significator, he meets with much treachery and deceit from false friends or secrect enemies, especially from the wealthy, the clergy and lawyers, and is likely to suffer through his efforts in getting up some new religion, which will clash with Orthodoxy and Old Fogyism. Madam H. P. Blavatsky had ♅ ☌ ♃ in the midheaven, and both in opposition to ♂ in the 4th house in her horoscope, although she was born under the planet ☿ in the sign ♋ in ☌ with the ☉.

♅ ☌ ♂

154 If ♅ be in ☌ with ♂ in ♈, it makes the native hotheaded, malicious and blood-thirsty, and inclines him to commit some criminal act during some part of his life, by which he suffers imprisonment or death. If ♅ is in ☌ with ♂ in any other sign, it makes him willful, stubborn, and often vindictive, especially in the ascendant or midheaven or 7th house; but at the same time he will be a person of good abilities, given to daring deeds, often liable to accidents, misfortune and injuries.

If ♂ be significator, he will be very fond of inventions and discoveries, and make a good carpenter or builder, but will often be unsettled, and not remain long in one place, yet he may be a good machinist, and make a reputation connected with fire-arms, sharp instruments and inventions that other people never thought of.

♅ ☌ ☉

155 If ♅ be in the ascendant or midheaven, in ☌ with the ☉, it makes the person very ambitious and persevering, and willing to suffer much to carry out any special hobby; he wants to be a governor or manager, or hold some high position.

If ☉ be significator, he will be a person of great ability, fond of deep study and inventions, will take great delight in the occult and mysterious; and will care but little for women or female society; his ambition is to get up some new form of government, etc.

♅ ☌ ♀

156 If ♅ is in ☌ with ♀ in the ascendant, midheaven, or 7th house, it makes the party indifferent to females, eccentric and odd in dress and manners, and care but little for fashion:

he will be fond of the odd or curious, and if an artist, will draw pictures, showing the oddities of human nature; will care but little for money, and liable to meet with heavy losses and disappointments.

If ♀ be significator, the native receives benefits from very wealthy or prominent persons, and if she be strong in ♉ ♎ or ♒, he is likely to make some great invention or discovery that will immortalize his name, and cause him to become famous and prominent, especially if these planets be in the ascendant, 9th, 10th or 11th houses.

♅ ☌ ☿

157 If this aspect occurs in the midheaven or ascendant, especially in the signs ♊ ♍ ♎ or ♒, it makes the native a great scholar, very fond of studying the occult sciences, especially such as Mesmerism and Astrology, and is likely to become prominent as a writer on those subjects.

If the ☌ occurs in ♈ ♋ ♏ or ♑, the native is likely to be given to making frivolous discoveries or inventions, such as perpetual motion, etc., and waste his time on useless subjects that will bring him but little profit. It would also make him addicted to speculation and games of chance.

If ☿ be significator, and it occurs in movable signs ♈ ♋ ♎ or ♑, he is very unsettled, discontented, and dissatisfied with almost everything, and very probable that he will travel in foreign parts. If the ☌ occurs in ♊ ♍ ♎ or ♒, he is likely to be talented, and a great investigator of occult sciences; also, it makes him liable to accidents or narrow escapes of being killed, or unlooked for events, and at times very serious misfortunes.

♅ ☌ ☽

158 This ☌ in a man's horoscope often makes him an old bachelor, and if he does marry, he very seldom marries to advantage, and generally leads an unhappy life, or they separate, especially if the ☌ occurs in the ascendant, midheaven or 7th house. Is very likely to travel a great deal, especially on water, yet if ☽ and ♅ be strong in a good house, he may at times become very prominent and wealthy, but great danger of poverty overtaking him again. In a female's horoscope, they are apt to never marry; be cranky, or have odd ways, and not care for fashions.

If the ☽ be significator, the native is liable to travel a great deal, will be like a rolling stone, and even if married, will change his residence a number of times. The native is fond of studying occult sciences; has a great liking for spiritualism, and everything connected with the mysterious. They are very seldom practical people, and often live unhappy married lives. They have queer, odd ways, and few people get along well with them. If married, either male or female, they are very likely to separate. A male cares very little for women, and a female is happier being an old maid, than being married and having a family.

♄ ☌ ♃

159 If ♄ be significator, he gives the native inheritance of estates, and profit by means of agriculture; his disposition is extremely moral and grave; he may gain a fortune by merchandise, or possibly by preaching.

160 If ♃ be significator, the disposition is not so good. The native seldom meets with much success in the world. He is very niggardly, and generally acquires property by some selfish and unusual means, though he seldom enjoys it like other persons. He generally lives hated by every one for his mean and deceitful ways, and dies in obscurity.

161 If ♂ be in square to the significator, and in aspect with Mercury, he is generally duped of his property, and dies a miserable death.

♄ ☌ ♂

162 If ♄ be significator, the native is of a rash, turbulent disposition, and generally very unfortunate; very often engaged in some public calling of the lowest order, and frequently ends his days in prison.

163 If ♂ be significator, the disposition is equally bad, but not quite so rash, being more sly and cowardly. Sometimes he gains favor from elderly persons, who assist him with their property, which he generally loses in the end, and becomes very unfortunate, especially if the significators be under the earth.

♄ ☌ ☉

164 If born under ♄, it signifies losses to the native by fire (especially if they be in a firey sign), or by men in power, who persecute him, and confine him within the walls of a prison for contempt of the law; and he is seldom healthy or of long life.

165 If ☉ be significator, the native is generally very disagreeable, deceitful, mistrustful and unfortunate, always losing his property by some speculation, which, in the end, often brings him to ruin, particularly if the native has anything to do with the government or persons connected with the state.

♄ ☌ ♀

166 Shows gain to the native, if signified by ♄, by means of ladies, and to a considerable extent, he is attached to them. Greatly addicted to pleasure, and very fortunate where females are concerned. If he is a man of property, he often wastes most of it by gambling or pleasure.

167 If ♀ be significator, the native is very artful, sly, unfortunate, destitute of friends, often disappointed of benefits by death, and he loses considerably by persons older than himself, especially if he be in trade.

♄ ☌ ☿

168 If ♄ be significator, the native is subtle and crafty, fond of researches into antiquity; one of much gravity and considerable learning, though not always of the most agreeable personal manners.

169 If ☿ be significator, he is dull, suspicious, mean, cowardly, calculating and covetous. Should he turn his attention to literature, he may gain some knowledge, although with great labor; and should he become an author, his writings may bring him into lawsuits or imprisonment.

♄ ☌ ☽

170 If ♄ be significator, the person is restless and unsettled in his purposes, and often changes his residence. He is not very fortunate, though he may sometimes benefit by the lower order of females.

171 If ☽ be significator, he is poor, miserable and dejected, of an unpleasant and sullen disposition, extremely unfortunate, and uncommonly covetous, though possessing scarcely any property. With much suspicious caution, he frequently commits the most unaccountable errors in affairs of the greatest consequence; as through excess of prudence, he is very likely to doubt and deliberate in the moment of action.

♃ ☌ ♂

172 If ♃ be significator, the native is bold, proud, and ambitious; fond of martial exploits and enterprises; a good soldier or surgeon, though he may lose much by strife and contention, and sometimes receive wounds in quarrels.

173 If ♂ be significator, he is good, pious and just. He is eminently successful in the law and the church, and often makes a fortune by those means.

♃ ☌ ☉

174 If ♃ be significator, the native is weak, servile and credulous. He incurs the displeasure of men in power, by whom he is much oppressed, and often ruined. He has bad health; and is generally a vain, talkative character, indulging in fanciful speculations about religion and other matters, for which he is totally unqualified.

175 If ☉ be significator, the power of Jupiter is so much destroyed by the power of the Sun, that he has but very little effect; though the party will, in general, be very much given to religion, which, if Jupiter, be well dignified in other respects, and not ill aspected will be sincere; otherwise he is fanatical or hypocritical.

♃ ☌ ♀

176 If ♃ be significator, it promises the greatest happiness. The native is highly favored by the female sex, by whose means he gains great advancement. He is rich, prosperous, and fortunate; very healthy, and greatly admired and respected. It shows great personal beauty.

177 If ♀ be significator, it denotes great beauty of person (unless Venus be in Scorpio or Capricorn), also riches, honors, ecclesiastical preferment, tne person so represented is truly virtuous, pious, kind and beneficent to all, with the greatest goodness of heart, and a disposition that will command universal love and esteem.

♃ ☌ ☿

178 If ♃ be significator, it denotes a person of great learning, a good lawyer or divine of excellent abilities and much information.

179 If ☿ be significator, he is mild, humane, religious, fond of literature, possessing an elegant mind, and a gentle, engaging disposition; he is raised to eminence and protected by powerful patrons. He accumulates great riches, and is in general extremely fortunate.

♃ ☌ ☽

180 If ♃ be significator, the person so represented is restless and changeable and seldom sufficiently settled to procure much wealth. He is, on the whole, very fortunate; often gains considerably by marriage, and is a general favorite with the fair sex. He is a great traveller, and is eminently successful in maritime affairs and among seamen, shipping, etc.

181 If ☽ be significator, he is fortunate, in ecclesiastical affairs or among mercantile men, magistrates, etc. He obtains great wealth, though he is liable to losses, frequently by canting or hypocritical persons who impose upon his natural kindness and generosity of disposition. He has, however, too much good fortune to be injured by those persons to any serious extent.

♂ ☌ ☉

182 If ♂ be significator, the native is in danger by fire, lightning, or infectious fever. It has been said in this case, with great truth, he has the favor of kings and princes, and it may be their frowns too, to his utter undoing. He may rise hastily, but perhaps to a great precipice where he meets a fall.

183 If ☉ be significator, the native is brave, but headstrong and violent. He will probably attain some considerable rank in the army or navy; but he will be frequently wounded, and most probably die in battle or be killed by some accident or fall, or be a victim to some contagious fever.

♂ ☌ ♀

184 If ♂ be significator, the native is kind and gentle; upon the whole, though at times rather hasty, he is moderately fortunate, extremely fond of women, and not always very particular as to their respectability.

185 If ♀ be significator, he is wicked and debauched, a companion of prostitutes, from whom he generally receives great injury; a drunkard, frequently brawling in taverns or low public houses, though he may sometimes meet with good fortune, he will quickly dissipate whatever property he may possess in the company of the most worthless of mankind.

♂ ☌ ☿

186 If ♂ be significator, it represents the native as possessed of considerable ability, a skilfull mechanic, or a good mathematician, one of an acute sarcastic wit. If he be in the army or navy, for which he is well qualified, he obtains great reputation for his bravery, and is distinguished still more for the policy of his measures. He is never very scrupulous as to the means he employs, and will pay but little respect to persons or possessions of others, when he can gain any advantage by sacrificing them to his own interest.

187 If ☿ be significator, he makes a cheat or swindler, a thief, robber or treacherous miscreant, a frequenter of gambling houses, rash, furious and blood-thirsty.

N. B.—Any evil aspect of Saturn increases these evils, and a good aspect of Sun, Jupiter or Venus will much diminish them.

♂ ☌ ☽

188 If ♂ be significator, it shows one of an unsettled life and temper, and a favorite of females; he is frequently a wandering adventurer, more remarkable for the variety of his fortune than his success or abilities. He is likely to die in a strange country.

189 If ☽ be significator, he is a bold, enterprising character; frequently in great danger of a violent death, quarrelsome and given to dueling, etc. He may be a good surgeon or soldier, and is seldom noted for much humanity. If a female, she is extremely likely to be seduced.

☉ ☌ ♀

190 If ☉ be significator, it denotes one of soft and effeminate manners, a pleasing address, a great admirer of the ladies. He is too much given to extravagance and dissipation.

191 If ♀ be significator, he is of short life, unfortunate and oppressed, too sickly to make much exertion, very proud and extravagant.

☉ ☌ ☿

192 If ☉ be significator, it gives some ingenuity, but not much sound judgment.

193 If ☿ be significator, he represents a person of mean and shallow abilities, one addicted to fraud and deception, incapable of learning anything which requires memory or judgment, and extremely superstitious. He may succeed well in trade or business, but for study he is wholly unqualified.

☉ ☌ ☽

194 If ☉ be significator, it represents a restless and changeable person, who aims at great things, but seldom accomplishes them.

195 If ☽ be significator, the native is extremely unfortunate, and generally sickly and unhappy, dejected and oppressed by men in power. He is rash and violent, subject to burns and scalds, and has frequently some defect in the eyes; and if the ☌ happen near the Hyades, Pleiades or

Praespe, he is likely to be nearly blind. If the Moon be applying, he is in danger of death, especially if it happens in the 8th house, or Sun be lord of the 8th house; but if Moon be separating, the danger is not so great.

♀ ☌ ☿

196 If ♀ be significator, it represents one who is polite, mild and courteous, fond of the elegant branches of literature, a pleasant companion, a favorite of females, and one of an excellent disposition.

197 If ☿ be significator, he excels in any pursuit that requires taste, a good painter, an excellent poet or musician; of a very humane disposition, and of the most prepossessing appearance.

♀ ☌ ☽

198 If ♀ be significator, it renders a man very mutabale and uncertain; often promising, through goodness of disposition, much more than he is capable of performing.

—199 If ☽ be significator, he is of an easy, happy, disposition, with little care beyond the enjoyment of the present moment; a great proficient in all elegant amusements, and of an easy and genteel address.

☿ ☌ ☽

200 If ☿ be significator, the native is possessed of great abilities, though generally very unsteady in his pursuits. He frequently travels in some literary capacity.

201 If ☽ be significator, the effects are not very different; his intellectual powers are of the first order; he is much attached to learning, and gains great reputation by his abilities.

202 N. B.—It must be most carefully observed, whether these planets have any other familiarity at the same time, for should Herschell, Saturn or Mars be in square, it will make a most remarkable difference. Indeed, this must be scrupulously attended to in all cases, but especially when Venus, Mercury or Moon may be significator.

After the student has learned well the ☌ of the planets, he must also learn the ✶ and △ aspects. This part of Astrology is more abstruse, as there are not only the qualities of two or more planets, but also the qualities of two signs to be learned, which often makes it quite complicated and conflicting. The same remarks apply to the □ or ☍.

OF THE ✶ AND △ ASPECTS OF THE SIGNIFICATORS.

203 As I have stated before, I cannot conceive of any person being born entirely under the planet ♅, yet if that planet is in the ascendant, it has more influence over the native than any other planet in the first house, or even the lord of the ascendant. In the following mental qualities and disposition, I shall only give the indications of ♅ being in aspect to the other planets, significator or significators.

♅ ✶ or △ ♄

204 This aspect makes the native inclined to be cunning and inquisitive, and apt to over-reach others, he is also fond of the occult and deep studies; will make a good civil engineer, but is somewhat eccentric and reserved.

♅ ✶ or △ ♃

205 The native is very ambitious to become in some way prominent before the community; he is generous, noble-minded, and often successful by being appreciated and assisted by those strongly influenced by ♃ in their horoscopes. He generally is striving to establish some new religion, or in some way to better the condition of the community, either socially or morally, and he sometimes does much good in that way; as he is a man of extensive knowledge and influence, and of a broad liberal mind.

♅ ✶ or △ ♂

206 Makes the native subtle, witty, highly ingenious, penetrative and active. Is fond of great constructions, such as large buildings, machinery; also very fond of mechanics of all kinds, particularly inventions. Likely to make some invention that will cause him to become renowned, especially fire-arms or destructive implements.

♅ ✶ or △ ☉

207 Causes a person to be very domineering, has very little feeling for others, is inclined to go on the principle of rule or ruin. Yet the native is inclined to be at times generous and of extraordinary abilities. He will excel in the occult and mysterious, such as Astrology, Astronomy and Chemistry; is also likely to make some new discovery or invention.

♅ ⚹ or △ ♀

208 Makes the native very artistic, but eccentric and conceited. Has a strong admiration for the beautiful; is also fond of the occult sciences, and likely to be a teacher of those subjects, or a writer on the same, and, if a female, may have very good clairvoyant powers.

♅ ⚹ or △ ☿

209 Causes the native to be very ingenious, studious, inquisitive and an observer of human nature; with remarkable talent for science. He possesses original ideas, and if ☿ and ♅ are in airy signs it causes the native to be quick in intellectual culture, and excel as an educator, and is very penetrating into the mysterious or occult.

♅ ⚹ or △ ☽

210 Causes the native to be changeable, fond of traveling, inclined to be wayward and eccentric, very fond of curiosities. Likely to take up what are called abstruse sciences, such as Magic, Astrology, Theosophy, etc.; and, at the same time, he is a person of remarkably good intellect.

♄ ⚹ or △ ♃

211 If ♄ be significator, it gives riches by means of agriculture, and the native is of a sedate and religious disposition.

212 If ♃ be significator, he is extremly grave, and frequently gains riches by legacies or mining.

♄ ⚹ or △ ♂

213 If ♄ be the significator, it increases the courage of the person so signified, and renders him more open in his resentment.

214 If ♂ be significator, he is prudent and cautious, bigoted in religion, and should other aspects befriend Mars, he may gain an estate.

♄ ⚹ or △ ☉

215 If ♄ be significator, the native is generous and noble, though somewhat austere in his behavior.

216 If ☉ be significator, he is ostentatious, boastful and conceited; he may be expected to gain by legacies, or to be successful as a farmer.

♄ ✶ or △ ♀

217 If ♄ be significator, he is prodigal and extravagant, wasting his money among females.

218 If ♀ be significator, he is modest, shy and retired in his manners; he gains the favor of elderly people, and sometimes inherits their property.

♄ ✶ or △ ☿

219 If ♄ be significator, it gives ingenuity and subtlety, though such talents are generally employed to little purpose.

220 If ☿ be significator, he is very cautious and prudent, and is addicted to the study of arts and sciences.

♄ ✶ or △ ☽

221 If ♄ be significator; the native is changeable, jealous and mistrustful.

222 If ☽ be significator, he is vain and conceited, mean in his actions, though without the excuse of rashness, as he does nothing without much deliberation.

♃ ✶ or △ ♂

223 If ♃ be significator, it gives bravery, and the spirit of military adventure; he is a good soldier, surgeon or chemist.

224 If ♂ be significator, he is noble, generous, and ambitious, and will rise rapidly in the army.

♃ ✶ or △ ☉

225 If ♃ be significator, it makes one extremely fortunate and very noble and courageous in his disposition.

226 If ☉ be significator, he gains money rapidly, is always respected, and possesses a most excellent disposition.

♃ ✶ or △ ♀

227 If ♃ be significator, it causes beauty, love, riches, and real goodness of heart; this is the most fortunate aspect that can be formed.

228 If ♀ be significator, the person is virtuous, aimable, of a noble disposition, incapable of fraud or malice.

♃ ✶ or △ ☿

229 If ♃ be significator, it gives great learning, sound judgment and excellent abilities.

230 If ☿ be significator, he possesses solid sense, an open generous disposition and real good fortune.

♃ ✶ or △ ☽

231 If ♃ be significator, it makes a man very fortunate, beloved by females and respected by the poorer classes of society.

232 If ☽ be significator, he is just and charitable, sincere in his friendships, and generous to the full extent of his means.

♂ ✶ or △ ☉

233 If ♂ be significator, it gives a very noble disposition and great mind, it causes one to rise rapidly in the army; he is uncommonly successful in war, and will gain much by the patronage of men in power.

234 If ☉ be significator, it confers great bravery and a high spirit; he rises to granduer by means of his courage, and is invincible in military talents.

♂ ✶ or △ ♀

235 If ♂ be significator, it causes lewdness and dissipation; his disposition is not radically bad, but he is extremely thoughtless and improvident; he may gain by females, for he possesses a fascinating influence, which he never fails to exert to the utmost with the female sex.

236 If ♀ be significator, he is handsome but proud, rash and inconsiderate; and neither remarkable for prudence nor principle.

♂ ✶ or △ ☿

237 If ♂ be significator, this aspect gives great acuteness, penetration and learning, the native, however, is crafty, rather hasty, and extremely confident.

238 If ☿ be significator, he possesses great courage, is very ingenious in any mechanical trade, a good engraver or mathematician, and will succeed in anything that requires presence of mind and a quick intellect.

If Mercury receive any aspect of Herschell, the native is extremely fitted to become a good astrologer, especially if Moon assist Mercury by ✶ or △ aspect, but a □ or ☍ is better than no aspect of ☽ and ☿.

♂ ✶ or △ ☽

239 If ♂ be significator, it makes one restless and changeable, servile and talkative; he travels much, and receives much assistance from females.

240 If ☽ be significator, he is very passionate and changeable, with a high spirit and good abilities.

☉ ⚹ or △ ☽

241 If ☉ be significator, it confers riches and honor; the native is fortunate with women, and is much respected by the multitude.

242 If ☽ be significator, he is proud and aspiring; he is generally successful, but his fortune is not permanent, unless both Sun and Moon be in fixed signs.

♀ ⚹ or △ ☿

243 If ♀ be significator, this aspect gives ingenuity, subtlety and good nature.

244 If ☿ be significator, the native possesses a refined and accomplished mind; he is neat in his person and elegant in his manners; a lover of music and the fine arts in general.

♀ ⚹ or △ ☽

245 If ♀ be significator, it is a very fortunate aspect, it shows a person who is much assisted by female friends, and one who, though unstable, often obtains considerable property.

246 If ☽ be significator, the native is gentle, obliging, amiable and genteel in his manners, and is much admired by females; whose condition in life depends on the strength or debility of Venus.

☿ ⚹ or △ ☽

247 If ☿ be significator, the person signified, is witty, ingenious, subtle, easily learning anything to which he applies, and frequently acquiring many sciences without assistance. He is somewhat reserved and a little melancholy, but from his extensive knowledge is always a useful, and sometimes a pleasant companion.

248 If ☽ be significator, this is the most favorable aspect for learning or scientific speculation.

THE EFFECTS OF THE □ OR ☍ ASPECTS BETWEEN THE SIGNIFICATORS.

♅ □ or ☍ ♄

249 It makes the native crafty, malicious, wayward, stubborn, and often very eccentric, and fond of uncommon subjects and mysteries. If the planets be in angles or cardinal signs it makes him an enthusiast; he often commences rash undertakings, which are likely to lead him into disaster, and may

land him in prison or disgrace. He will be fond of the occult, and may make a good clairvoyant.

♅ □ or ☍ ♃

250 Causes the native to be an enthusiast in reforms in politics, religions or creeds, and is likely to often come to grief through them; meets with much opposition and many crosses and disappointments; he is likely to be grave, serious and thoughtful, especially if his planet be in cardinal signs, angles or fixed signs; he is also likely to meet with much treachery.

Samuel J. Tilden had ♅ □ ♃ in his horoscope, which no doubt caused him to be cheated out of the Presidency after he was elected by the people (as ♅ was in the 12th house, the house of secret enemies, and ♃ on the cusp of the 9th house, the house of law).

♅ □ or ☍ ♂

251 Makes the native precipitant, irregular and impulsive; he is eccentric, rash, daring and ambitious, and fond of the occult, also of electricity and chemistry. It sometimes causes the native to be full of hatred and destructive vehemence. These qualities are particularly strong if they occur in either the 1st, 3rd, 9th or 10th houses, or in cardinal or fixed signs; they are likely to cause the native to be a great inventor, especially in fire-arms, or destructive implements, large engines or constructions of any kind.

♅ □ or ☍ ☉

252 Causes the native to meet with many obstacles and difficulties; he is also eccentric and liable to heavy losses and disappointments, and have opposing influences to contend with; he may become famous and renowned, but it will be after much opposition, and after having overcome many obstacles and difficulties. Sometimes he becomes famous on account of his opposition to established creeds or religions, or old fogyism, and sometimes he rises by other people's misfortunes, especially if this aspect occurs in cardinal or fixed signs, or in angles. Robert G. Ingersoll has ♅ in his horoscope in the midheaven in close ☍ to the ☉ in the 4th house in fixed signs. Jay Gould had ♅ in the midheaven in close □ to the ☉ rising. Charles Dickens had ♅ in ♏ in □ to the ☉ in ♒ both in fixed signs. Horace Greely had ♅ in ☌ ♂ in the sign ♏ in the midheaven, and both in □ to the ☉ rising in the ascendant in ♒ all in fixed signs. In my own horoscope ♅ is in the 7th house in ♒ in □ to the ☉ in the midheaven in ♉, both in angles and fixed signs, which aspect has caused me to have many powerful and bitter enemies.

♅ □ or ☍ ♀

253 Causes the native to have a keen appreciation of natural beauty. Is apt to be jealous in love affairs, fond of the opposite sex, often to his own ruin. If a male, is not successful in dealing with females. Has a keen appreciation of grace and delicacy of form. Is very fond of the occult and mysterious, and may become noted as a public lecturer or teacher on those subjects. The natives are very liable to be old maids or bachelors, or if married not continue to live with their partners, or if they do, it is under protest.

♅ □ or ☍ ☿

254 The native is eccentric, imaginative, instinctive, and often possesses good judgment, especially if those planets be in airy signs, cardinal signs or in angles, but if either of them are in weak or watery signs, it causes the native to be erratic, and have but indifferent ability. Is likely to try to discover perpetual motion, or want to become famous as a rain maker; and lacks intuitive observation and instinctive judgment. He believes in some of the most absurd dogmas, and be skeptical of some of the simplest and demonstrative problems. He is likely to have curious notions on government, marriage, financial, political or domestic life, and may try to establish communities.

♅ □ or ☍ ☽

255 Makes the native mutable, fond of change, often wayward and impulsive; generally becomes a wanderer, or a great traveller, and but seldom remains in one place or position. But if either of these planets be in ♒ ♎ or ♊ it causes the native to have considerable ability, and be fond of obstruse sciences, and sometimes excelling in learning or discoveries, or receiving new ideas. If either of these planets be in cardinal or fixed signs, or angles, he may become prominent, or in some way noted on account of his odd and eccentric manners, and be at times almost regarded as a lunatic. Emporer William II, of Germany, was born under the Moon, in ♏ in close ☍ to ♅ in ♉ both fixed signs.

♄ □ or ☍ ♃

256 If ♄ be significator, it shows much trouble by lawyers or the clergy.

257 If ♃ be significator, he is always wretched and miserable, idle, unfortunate and beggarly.

♄ □ or ☍ ♂

258 If ♄ be significator, it is the aspect of cruelty and murder, and the person so signified, is extremely unfortunate;

he generally lives a most dejected life, and dies a violent death.

259 If ♂ be significator, the person shown by him is very malicious, treacherous and blood-thirsty; one delighting in the most evil deeds, yet very cowardly, sly and inclined to suicide, and secret revenge, and has a cruel disposition

♄ □ or ☍ ☉

260 If ♄ be significator, it is the aspect of infamy and contempt, the person is prodigal, ambitious, overbearing, hating control, very disagreeable in his manners, extremely unfortunate, subject to the frowns of persons in power, and often meets a violent death.

261 If ☉ be significator, the person is cowardly, spiteful, treacherous, malicious, unfeeling, covetous, repining, always despising anything of kindness and humanity; one who generally leads a life of wretchedness, and frequently meets with a bad end, and sometimes dies in prison.

♄ □ or ☍ ♀

262 If ♄ be significator, it shows dissipation, and the person leads a most detestable life, connected with the lowest order of prostitutes, by whom he is eventually brought to ruin and disgrace.

263 If ♀ be significator, the person is generally of an evil disposition, and not very handsome, is sly, artful, full of mischief, and much addicted to dissipation, though not suspected; but generally unfortunate.

♄ □ or ☍ ☿

264 If ♄ be significator, it indicates a thief, cheat or swindler, a low, cunning fellow, sly, envious, treacherous and malicious; one who is always planning some scheme to deceive his most intimate friends; generally forming a bad opinion of every one, and not at all particular as to speaking the truth.

265 If ☿ be significator, the person is very artful, always involved in strife and contention, and much given to vilify the character of others, by whom he is tormented with law-suits; it also indicates pettifogging attorneys, who seldom act honestly towards their clients.

♄ □ or ☍ ☽

266 If ♄ be significator, it shows a wandering, unsettled and changeable person, not of a genteel form, but one who is down-looking and inclined to stoop forward, always very fretful and appearing full of trouble, not a good disposition,

not to be depended on. He seldom attains any high situation, but if he does, he soon falls into disgrace again.

267 If ☽ be significator (which in some measure she always is of the native), the person is extremely unfortunate, always in trouble with the lower order of mankind, from whom he receives many inquiries; he is mean, cowardly and very dejected, is rather unhealthy, seldom living a long life, and generally dying a a miserable death.

♃ □ or ☍ ♂

268 If ♃ be significator, it denotes violence, ingratitute, a furious temper, and danger of death by malignant fevers.

269 If ♂ be significator, it shows pride, ingratitude, insolence, and the hatred of the clergy on account of theological opinions.

♃ □ or ☍ ☉

270 If ♃ be significator, it gives arrogance, prodigality and much vanity, with a great desire to be distinguished, which is but very rarely gratified.

271 If ☉ be significator, the person represented wastes his property by riotous living and all kinds of extravagance.

♃ □ or ☍ ♀

272 It ♃ be significator, it shows extravagance, dissipation and all kinds of debauchery and intemperance.

273 If ♀ be significator, the person has many enemies among the clergy and legal profession, magistrates, etc., and he is equally void of virtue and prudence.

♃ □ or ☍ ☿

274 If ♃ be significator, it gives trouble, contention, perplexities, lawsuits, and in consequence, indigence.

275 If ☿ be significator, the person is frequently persecuted for his singular religious opinions; his understanding is weak, and he is often involved in strife and contention.

♃ □ or ☍ ☽

276 If ♃ be significator, it shows one of many words, though of poor abilities; he is weak and foolish, and if in a public capacity, is execrated by the multitude.

277 If ☽ be significator, he is injured by faithless friends and deceitful relatives, and his property is impoverished by hypocritical fanatics.

♂ □ or ☍ ☉

278 If ♂ be significator, he is a man of great ambition and violence, but his evil fortune will not allow him to succeed.

279 If ☉ be significator, he is restrained by no principle of honor or gratitude, his affairs are always deranged, and he makes use of the most violent means to retrieve them. Such a one frequently becomes a footpad, murderer or housebreaker, and is either killed in some contest, or falls a victim to the laws of the country.

♂ □ or ☍ ♀

280 If ♂ be significator, these aspects cause lust, excess, prodigality and injury by loose women, and complete waste of fortune.

281 If ♀ be significator, he is very treacherous, mischievous, base and inconstant; or if it be a female, she is a prostitute or very shameless.

♂ □ or ☍ ☿

282 If ♂ be significator, it shows one of some ability, but his talents are applied to the most dishonorable purposes.

283 If ☿ be significator, it denotes a thief or assassin; one whose most solemn protestations are not to be believed; who will desert his benefactors at their utmost need; he is violent, furious, contentious, and despised by every one for his infamous life.

♂ □ or ☍ ☽

284 If ♂ be significator, the native, described by him, is a fit companion for the lowest and most unprincipled of mankind; he is very unfortunate, and is probably a wandering vagabond, who travels over the earth without a friend or a home.

285 If ☽ be significator, he is excessively abusive, malicious and treacherous. He may travel into foreign countries as a sailor or soldier, amidst innumerable dangers and hardships, and die by pestilence, dysentery, or the sword.

☉ □ or ☍ ☽

286 If ☉ be significator, the person suffers losses, trouble and much anxiety.

287 If ☽ be significator, he is obstinate and quarrelsome; he is exceedingly ambitious and prodigal, and is sometimes marked in the face, or his eyes are affected; the latter is especially the case if the Sun be afflicted by Mars, or either Sun or Moon are with the nebulous stars.

♀ □ or ☍ ☽

288 If ♀ be significator, it shows a changeable, unsettled life, great trouble in marriage, and much ill fortune.

289 If ☽ be significator, it shows a dissolute, extravagant life, attended with indigence and poverty, and much trouble from females.

☿ □ or ☍ ☽

290 If ☿ be significator, it no doubt gives some abilities, but such persons are too unsettled to apply very closely to any subject; they are continually shifting their situations (especially if Mercury be in a movable sign), nor are they very sincere in their professions of friendship, nor very scrupulous in the method by which they may attain their ends.

291 If ☽ be significator, they have a defect in their utterance, have but little ability, except a kind of low cunning, which they apply to dishonest purposes. But as Mercury is acted on by every planet having an aspect to him, it will be necessary to observe each aspect and allow for its influences, for if Mercury or the Moon have a trine of Jupiter, the square of Mercury to Moon will not be near so evil, though the person will be far from sensible, notwithstanding, that they are tolerably honest and well-meaning.

OBSERVATION.—The student must always remember, that the true character and condition of the person signified, can only be correctly learned by noticing all the aspects the significator may receive, as well as observing the nature of the sign and house it is in, and the degree of strength or weakness it possesses, as well as those planets which aspect it. Thus if the significator be Mars, and he receive the opposition of Sun, yet if Sun be weak, and Mars have also a trine of Jupiter, this benefic planet being strong, he may judge that the native will suffer by the evil influence of Sun, by receiving a severe wound in a duel, or in honorable warfare; whereas, if instead of the trine of Jupiter, the square of Mercury occurred, there would be little doubt, that he would be killed by police officers, or die by the hand of the public executioner; the latter especially, if Sun was in the 10th house.

PRACTICAL ASTROLOGY.

Having in the foregoing pages given an outline of Astrology, which outline the reader should read over and over until he knows it by heart, or can repeat any passage without looking in the book similar to a minister of the Gospel, who can repeat almost any passage in the Bible without looking at the chapter and verse.

After the student is able to repeat any of the foregoing rules in Astrology as ♃ in the sign ♐, or ♂ in the sign ♈, he should then try to mix or combine these rules, as a painter mixes the different colors of his paints until he knows the particular shade or tint that any two colors when so mixed will produce, when painting any special object or likeness; so the young student of Astrology should know the effect that the various aspects of the planets, either good or evil will produce. He should also learn the different signs and the kind of persons they will describe; if on the ascendant or first house, and not occupied by any planet; also the characteristic of the planets themselves when they are in any sign or house, and notice whether they are angular, succeedent or cadent, and whether the planet is weak or strong in that sign or house.

But before the reader can make much headway in learning the various combinations, it will be necessary for him to learn how to erect a map of the heavens, nativity or horoscope, as it is at times called, for any particular hour and minute of either day or night and for any longitude or latitude on the globe.

In order to do this he will require a table of houses for the place or latitude for which he wishes to set the map of the heavens; he will also require an ephemeris or astrological almanac which gives the longitude, latitude and declination of the Sun, Moon, and different planets referred to in the preceding pages, for the year he wishes to cast the horoscope.

Raphael's Almanac and Ephemeris published in London, England, is considered the best. I do not know of any astrological ephemeris published in the United States.

RULE TO SET A MAP OF THE HEAVENS.

FIRST.—Having procured the ephemeris for the year desired, then learn in the same ephemeris what was the right ascension of the Sun, at the noon previous to the required time,* in hours, minutes and seconds. To this right ascension add the number of hours and minutes that have elapsed since that noon. The sum of both will be the right ascension in time of the meridian or midheaven. Then procure a table of houses for the latitude of the place for which the student wishes to erect his map of the heavens.

SECOND.—Find the longitude answering to this right ascension (or sidereal time) in the first column of the table of houses for the latitude required, and opposite in the next column he will find the number required, and on top of page the number 10, meaning the 10th house, which longitude is to be marked over the line on top of the blank map which denotes the midheaven or 10th house, together with the sign in the column under the figure 10.

THIRD.—In a line with this on the top of the column will be found the 11th, 12th, 1st, 2nd and 3rd houses, which he must copy on the same horizontal line as the 10th house, and enter over the lines which have those numbers in the blank map of the heavens and on the lines, which denote those respective houses.

---

* In the ephemeris published of late years the right ascension of the Sun is given in the third column of the ephemeris headed sidereal time (or star time), and the student does not have to add when the clock is too slow, or subtract when too fast, according to the Sun, as he had to do in the old ephemeris.

Horoscope of the Inauguration of Hon. William McKinley.

Take the time President McKinley took the oath of office on March 4th, 1897, at 1:18 P. M., Washington, D. C., for an example.

In Raphael's Ephemeris for 1897, if the reader turns to March 4th, on a line with that in the next column under the heading Sidereal Time, he will find 22 hours, 50 minutes and 2 seconds. If he adds the 1 hour and 18 minutes that have elapsed since noon to that sum he will get 24:08. As 24 hours complete a day, he rejects the number 24, and turns to the table of houses for New York*, which is near the latitude of Washington, in the first column on first page, he will find under the Sidereal Time, 0 hours, 7 minutes and 20 seconds, and on a line with that, the figure 2 in the column, and on the top of the column the figure 10 which means the 10th house, and immediately under it the sign Aries ♈.

The sign ♈ and the number 2 he copies in the blank map, over the line marked 10. Go to the next column and find, on the top, 11 and Taurus (♉.), which means the 11th house, and the sign ♉ and on the line with 0-7-20 he will find the figure 8, copy the sign ♉ and figure 8, over the line marked 11, in the map on page 144. And on the same line he will find 17 and on the top of the column 12 Gemini (♊), he enters the sign ♊ and 17 over the line marked 12 in the blank map. In the next column he finds on the top the words "Ascend," meaning the Ascendant or first house, and underneath the sign Cancer (♋) he copies the sign ♋ and 20:22 over the line marked 1, or first house. On the next column the figure 10 and on the top of the column the figure 2 and the sign Leo (♌), the figure 2 means second house. Copy the sign ♌ and figure 10 on the end of the line marked 2 in the blank map. In the next column he will find the figure 3, and top of the column 3, and under it the sign Virgo (♍). Copy ♍ and number 3 at the end of the line in the blank map marked 3.

These six houses are called the Eastern houses, and he copies what are termed the opposite signs or the six Western houses, which are the 4th, 5th, 6th, 7th, 8th and 9th. The student must learn what signs are always opposite each other.

The Eastern and Northern signs are ♈, ♉, ♊, ♋, ♌, ♍.

The Western and Southern signs are ♎, ♏, ♐, ♑, ♒, ♓.

Therefore the student will copy Libra (♎) and number 2 on the line marked 4 in the blank map, and Scorpio (♏) and number 8 at the end of the line marked 5 in the map, and Sagittary (♐) and number 17 on the end of line marked 6 in the map. And Capricorn (♑) 20:22 on the end of line marked 7 in blank map. And Aquarius (♒) and 10 at the end of line marked 8, and Pisces ♓ and number 3 at the end of line marked 9.

After the signs of the Zodiac are put in their proper positions and the number of degrees and minutes put with each sign, so as to show how many degrees of that sign has ascended or descended beyond what is termed the *cusp* of any given house. Then proceed to calculate the

---

* In Raphael's Ephemeris for each year, on pages 30 and 31, the student will find a "Table of Houses" for Latitude 40° 43' north, it being the latitude of New York City.

position of the planets and place them in the blank map. There is no Astrological Ephemeris calculated for New York or Washington; therefore we have to use the Ephemeris calculated for London, England, and as there are five hours and eight minutes difference in time between London and Washington, we have to allow for that difference. Therefore the longitude of the planets that are calculated for twelve noon in London, we reckon as though they were calculated for seven o'clock in the morning for Washington, D. C.

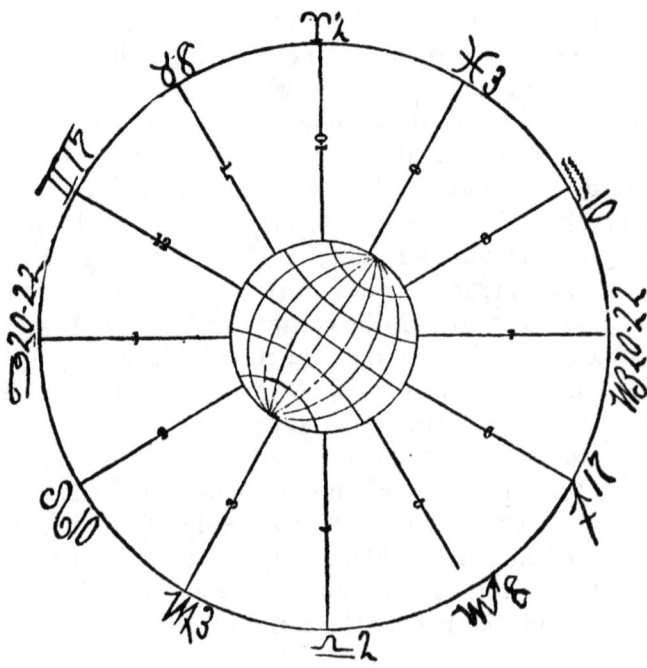

Map of the Heavens showing the signs of the Zodiac for the time President McKinley was inaugurated, March 4th, 1897, 1 h. 18 m. P.M.

In calculating the time for putting the signs of the Zodiac in the blank map, we always reckon from twelve o'clock at noon, and add the hours or minutes that have elapsed since that time, to the hours and minutes given in the column under Sidereal time in the Ephemeris.

But if the time is before twelve o'clock, we subtract the number of hours and minutes that will elapse before noon, from the Sidereal Time in the third column in the Ephemeris for that day.

If we wish to set a chart of the heavens for London, England; after calculating the longitude of the signs and writing them in the blank chart, we then add the number of degrees and minutes that a planet will travel from twelve o'clock noon to the hour and minute we are setting the chart for, to the planet's longitude marked in the column in the Ephemeris for that day. But if for Washington, D. C., we add the number of degrees and minutes that a planet travels from seven o'clock in the morning to the hour and minute we set the chart of the heavens for to the degrees and minutes marked in the planet's longitude column in the Ephemeris for that day.

The time Mr. McKinley took the oath of office was one hour and eighteen minutes in the afternoon, therefore reckoning from seven o'clock in the mor ing, to that time is six hours and eighteen minutes. We have to find out how fast each of the planets and Sun and Moon are traveling that day, and then find how far they will travel in the six hours and eighteen minutes and write the degree and minute, of the planets in the signs in the blank chart on that day.

In the fourth column of Raphael's Ephemeris for March 5th, 1897, the Sun is 15 degrees, 12 minutes and 29 seconds. And on the 4th of March it is 14 degrees, 12 minutes and 25 seconds. Therefore if we subtract one from the other we find that the Sun in a day had traveled one degree, no minutes and four seconds. Then the Sun will travel fifteen minutes in six hours, being one fourth of a day. If we add the fifteen minutes to 14 degrees, 12 minutes and 25 seconds, it will amount to 14 degrees, 27 minutes and 25 seconds. Add one minute more to the Sun for the extra twenty minutes in time it makes 14 degrees and 28 minutes, dropping the seconds. In the sign Pisces, place the ☉ 14:28 just a little above the line marked 9 in the blank map in the sign ♓.

The student should look at the map of the heavens when he has placed the Sun in it, and notice from the time of day whether the Sun is in its right position. If it is not, then he has made some mistake in placing the signs of the Zodiac in the blank map, and must correct that mistake before he goes any further. For instance, in the chart he sets for noon, the Sun must be in the midheaven, near the line marked 10, if near sunrise, the Sun must be near the line marked 1. If near sunset, must be near the line marked 7, and midnight the Sun must be near line marked 4. He will see the Sun is in its right position in the chart on page 146, at 1:18 P. M.

In the column number 6 of Raphael's Ephemeris the student will find on March 4th, that the Moon is 25 degrees and 39 minutes and 19 seconds in the sign Pisces. Therefore, omitting the seconds, the Moon has 4 degrees and 21 minutes to go before it is out of the sign Pisces, and on March 5th, the Moon is 7 degrees and 53 minutes in the sign Aries. Therefore if we add 4 degrees and 21 minutes to 7 degrees and 53 minutes, we find the Moon travels at the rate of 12 degrees and 14 minutes in twenty-four hours. In six hours the Moon will travel 3 degrees and 4 minutes, or one fourth of 12 degrees and 14 minutes. Add 3:04 to 25:39 makes in all 28:43, and add 11 minutes in longitude for the 26 minutes in time, makes altogether 28:54 in the sign Pisces. Place the Moon 28:54 in Pisces, just over the Sun, above the line marked 9.

On the opposite page of the Ephemeris, on March 4th the planets Neptune, Uranus and Saturn do not travel any distance on that day, so enter them on the map, as they are marked in the signs in the Ephemeris. Neptune (♆) is 17:32 in Gemini (♊), so place ♆ just below the line marked 12, and in the sign ♊. Enter Uranus (♅) just above the line marked 5 in Scorpio (♏), 29:03, put an R, to show that Uranus (♅) is retrograde. Place Saturn (♄) just below the line marked 6 in the sign ♐, 0:45.

146   ELEMENTS OF ASTROLOGY.

The planet Jupiter (♃) is retrograding 8 minutes per day; take **one** minute from 4:06 and place ♃ just below the line marked **3**, in Virgo (♍), 4.05 and an R, to show that that planet is retrograde.

In the next column Mars (♂) is 22:28, in ♊, and on the 5th day ♂ is 22:52, showing that in 24 hours ♂ has traveled 24 minutes in longitude; therefore Mars would have traveled 6 minutes or one fourth of 24 minutes in six hours; add the six minutes to 22:28 and enter ♂ in the blank map, just below the planet Neptune, in the sign ♊, 22:34.

On March 4th, Venus (♀) is 29:43 in Aries (♈), on the 5th it is 0:34 in Taurus (♉). Thus ♀ has traveled 51 minutes in 24 hours. Add 13 minutes to 29:43 and enter ♀ left of the line marked 10 in the sign ♈, 29:56.

In the next column, Mercury (☿) is 22:08 on the 4th, and on the 5th 23:38, showing that in 24 hours ☿ has traveled 1 degree and 30 minutes, and in six hours it travels 22 minutes. Enter ☿ a little above the line marked 8 in the blank map, in the sign Aquaries (♒) 22:30.

On the right hand column on top of second page of Ephemeris for March, the student will find "Moon's Node" and on the 3rd day he will find 13:53 in ♒. Enter the Moon's North Node (☊) in the blank map on the line marked 8. The opposite sign, of the map being ♌ enter the South Node (☋), 13:47.

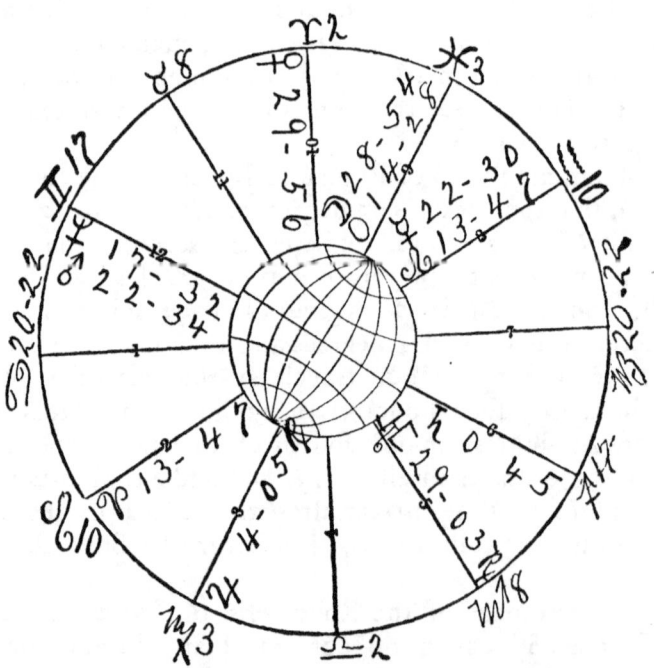

Chart of the heavens for the time President McKinley took the oath of office, March 4th, 1897, at 1:18 P. M., Washington, D. C.

The above Chart is what is termed an Astrological Map of the heavens all complete, (except the [⊕] part of fortune, which I shall show the reader how to find when I explain to him how to calculate the next chart following). We sometimes look for what are termed the aspects, both good and evil, and place them below the figure, in the following manner:—

Good Aspects.			Evil Aspects.		
☿	△	♂	☉	□	♆
☽	△	♅	♃	□	♄
☽	△	♄	♃	□	♅
♀	△	♃			

We also sometimes copy the Latitudes and Declinations of the Sun, Moon and planets for that day, and place them in a similar manner, below the figure.

I shall defer what is termed reading the foregoing chart until the student is further advanced in his studies, and will only add that if a child was born in or near Washington, D. C., on March 4th, 1897, at 1.18 P. M. the foregoing chart would be that child's Horoscope or Nativity, and we would read it as we read all other Nativities, according to the rules of *"Genethliacal Astrology."* But as this chart was calculated for the time the President took the oath of office, we have to read it according to the rules of *" Mundane Astrology,"* which I shall treat of in the latter part of this volume.

It is very important that the student should learn to set a figure or chart of the heavens correctly, for any part of the day or night. Therefore I cannot do better than give another example how to erect a map of the heavens. I will erect the next chart for the time that the Extra Congress met in Washington, D. C., 1897, being the first Congress under President McKinley.

The *New York Evening Sun*, of March 15th, 1897, in its Washington news, states:—"That precisely at 12 o'clock (noon) the clerk called the house to order." Therefore we will calculate the chart for 12 o'clock (noon) that day. The student must read again carefully the rules how to set a map of the heavens on page 142.

In Raphael's Ephemeris on March 15, 1897, in column 3, marked on the top of the column Sidereal Time, you will find 23:33 and as it is neither before nor after 12 noon, we neither subtract nor add, but take these figures and look in the Table of Houses, for New York. On the first column on the left hand side and under Sidereal Time, find the nearest number to the above which is 23 degrees, 34 minutes and 18 seconds, and on a line with that in the next column on the top, you will find number 10, meaning 10th house, and underneath the sign ♓. Enter the sign ♓ and 23 on the end of line marked 10, in blank map. On the top of next column you will find number 11 and ♈ underneath, and on a line with 23.34 you will find 29: enter ♈ 29 on end of line marked 11 in blank map. On the top of the next column find number 12 and down the column the sign ♊, and on a line with 23:34 the figure 9: place ♊ and 9 on the end of line marked 12, in blank map. In the next column find ascend., which means the ascendent or first house, and down in the column find the sign ♋, and on a line with 23:34 find 13.37: place ♋ 13:37 on end of line marked 1, in blank map.

On top of next column find 2, and below in same column find ♌, and on a line with 23:34 find 3, place ♌ 3, on end of line marked 2, in blank map. On top of the next column find figure 3, and immediately below the sign ♌, and on a line with 23:34 find 25 : place ♌ 25, on end of line marked 3, in blank map.

On page 143 the student will find what signs are opposite each other, as ♈ is opposite ♎, and ♍ is opposite ♓, etc. Therefore place ♍ on end of line marked 4, in blank map, and always place the same number that is with the opposite sign; as ♓ in this blank map is 23 degrees, place 23 along with ♍; and copy ♎ and 29 degrees on end of line marked 5, in blank map; and ♐ 9 on end of line marked 6; and ♑ 13.37 on end of line marked 7; and ♒ 3 on end of line marked 8, also ♒ 25 on end of line marked 9.

After the student has gone around the chart in this manner, then he must look and see that all the twelve signs of the Zodiac are on the chart. Commence counting ♈, ♉, ♊, etc.; the student will notice in this chart the sign ♉ is left out; therefore insert the sign ♉ just under the line of outer circle between ♈ and ♊, and directly opposite place ♏ just within the line of the circle, between ♎ and ♐. Then all the signs and number of degrees are put in their correct places in blank map.

We now commence to calculate the longitude of the Sun, Moon and each of the planets, and insert them in their proper places or the signs where they belong, and with their degrees and minutes marked along side of them.

(If the chart of the heavens was calculated for 12 o'clock noon, London, England, we should then copy the number of degrees and minutes into the blank chart that are affixed to the Sun and Moon and the planets in the Ephemeris for 12 o'clock noon on the 15th of March, 1897.)

But the reader will remember that in the former chart of the heavens that we calculated, that there is a difference of 5 hours and 8 minutes in time between London, England, and Washington, D. C.; therefore we have to add the number of degrees and minutes that a planet has travelled from 6.52 o'clock in the morning to 12 o'clock noon to the number of degrees and minutes that the planet is marked in the Ephemeris.

The student will find that the Sun on the 15th of March is 25 degrees and 11 minutes, on the 16th, is 26 degrees and very nearly 11 minutes, therefore the Sun is going one degree a day; in that case it goes 12 minutes in longitude in 5 hours; we in this case mark the Sun in the sign ♓ 25:23 and to the left of the line marked 10 in the blank chart. The moon in Raphael's Ephemeris is 10 degrees and 23 minutes on the 15th, and on the 16th, 24 degrees and 5 minutes, therefore it is going 13 degrees and 42 minutes in 24 hours, or 2 degrees and 50 minutes in 5 hours, we add the 2 degrees and 50 minutes to the 10 degrees and 23 minutes, which makes 13 degrees and 13 minutes, we enter the Moon and that number a little below the line marked 2 in the blank chart in the sign ♌. ♆, ♅ and ♄ travel very little in the 24 hours between the 15th and 16th; therefore we enter these planets and the degrees and minutes as we find them in the Ephemeris. ♆ 17 degrees and 37 minutes in ♊, a little below the line marked 12 in the blank chart, ♅ in the sign ♏ 29 degrees and 0 minutes; between the 2 lines numbers 5 and 6 R; also enter ♄ 0.45 in ♐ a little below the line marked 6 R; ♃ is Retrograding 7 minutes in the 24 hours, therefore we subtract 2 from 2:46, making it 2 degrees and 44 minutes, and enter it to the left of the line marked 4 in the blank chart, in the sign ♍ R. Mars travels at the rate of 26 minutes in the 24 hours, therefore we add 5 minutes to the 27:5, marked in the Ephemeris, and enter it 27 degrees and 10 minutes in the sign ♊, a little below ♆. Venus is going at the rate of 40 minutes in the 24 hours, therefore we add 8 minutes to the 8 degrees and 12 minutes marked in the Ephemeris, and enter it between the line 11 and 12 in the blank chart, in the sign ♉, 8 degrees, 20 minutes. Mercury is travelling at the rate of nearly two degrees a day; therefore it will go 24 minutes in the 5 hours, we add the 24 minutes to the 9.33 which makes 9.57, and enter it to the right of the line marked 10 in the blank chart in the sign ♓. The Moon's Node is 13 degrees and 15 minutes in the sign ♒; therefore we enter that number a little below the line marked 9 in the blank chart in the sign ♒, and we enter the ☋ and 13:15 a little above the line marked 3 in the blank chart. The figure is now complete, except the "Part of Fortune" which I shall explain to the student how to calculate it in the next chart of the heavens that we erect. We shall defer reading this chart until we come to treat on the subject of *Mundane Astrology* in the latter part of this volume. (See page 150.)

It will be advisable for the student, in order to perfect himself in erecting the charts of the heavens, to calculate a chart for the same time of day, for each day in succession. Possibly it may be the best for the learner if he lives in, or near New York City, to calculate it for 7 o'clock in the morning; in that case he will look in the Ephemeris for the Sidereal Time for that day at 12 o'clock noon, which he wishes to calculate the chart of the heavens; and from that sum marked there he will subtract 5 hours, and with the remainder, he will then look in the Table of Houses for New York City, for the nearest to that sum in the first column, or Sidereal Time, or the nearest number corresponding to the Sidereal Time in the Ephemeris for that day; after he has deducted the 5 hours before noon. Then copy the signs and figures on a line with the Sidereal Time, belonging to the 10th, 11th and 12th, the Ascendant or First House, and the 2nd and 3rd house, in a blank chart. After the student has copied all the Northern signs, he must look for the Southern signs, or for the signs that are opposite each other; also write the degrees and minutes that are along side the Northern signs, along side of the Southern signs. Afterwards he will copy out of the Ephemeris the Sun, Moon, and the planets just as he finds them marked for that day, and their degrees and minutes along side of each.

Then he will have a chart of the heavens for 7 A. M. for that day, and will by looking at it know what aspects the Moon is going to make during the day.

Below the student will find chart of the heavens for the time that Congress met in Washington, D. C., March 15, 1897, at 12 noon.

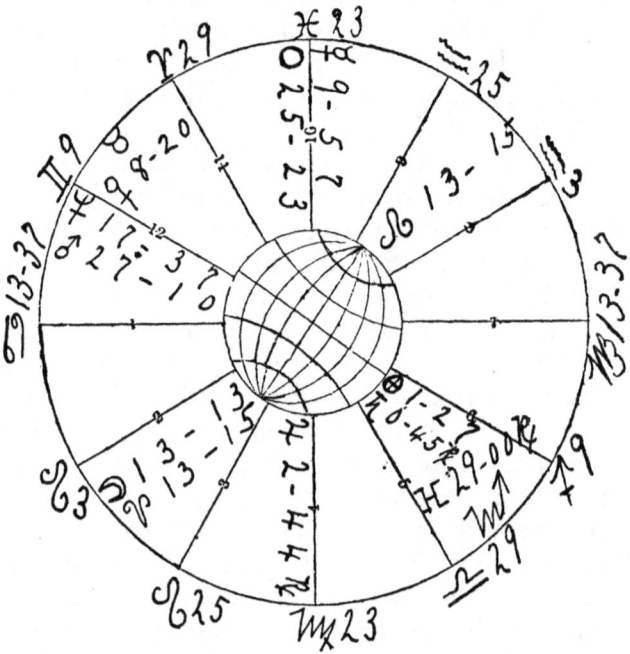

I shall explain how to read the above chart in the latter part of this volume.

I calculate the positions of the signs and of the planets for 12 o'clock noon, for every day of the year, in order to find out what aspects the Moon forms with the other planets and the Sun; I also notice what aspects the Sun and Moon form with the positions of the planets, in my horoscope, for that day. The student will find it good practice, if he follows the same method, and he will find by doing so, that he is learning something every day, and when he has learned it, he would rather part with any other knowledge that he may possess, than that knowledge.

After the student has learned to set the chart of the heavens for any day at 7 A. M., it would be advisable for him next to learn how to calculate a map of the heavens for 1 P. M. By looking in the Ephemeris for the Sidereal Time, and then adding one hour to that sum, and to look in the Table of Houses for the "Sidereal Time" and copy the 6 Northern signs on the houses, 10th, 11th, 12th, 1st, 2nd and 3rd, and the degrees and minutes along side; also after placing the Southern signs in the blank chart opposite the Northern signs, then in order to get the longitude of the planets, he must see how far they travel in the 24 hours, and take one quarter of that sum and add to the longitude of the planets marked in the Ephemeris, and enter them into the proper signs in the blank chart, but if the planet is Retrogade, then he must see how much it is retrograding in the 24 hours, and subtract one quarter of that sum from the number of degrees and minutes, marked in the Ephemeris, and enter the remainder with the planets in the blank chart in its proper sign and house.

THE HOROSCOPE OF MRS. MAUD S's DAUGHTER.

The next chart of the heavens that we propose to erect is that of the daughter of Mrs. Maud S., born July 2, 1884, at 8:35 A. M., New York City.

In order for the student to follow me in the calculation of this horoscope, he will have to procure an Ephemeris for 1884, and if he looks in the 3d, column under the words "Sidereal Time," on the 2d of July, for that year, he will find 6 hours and nearly 44 minutes, and as this time of birth occurred before noon, he will deduct the number of hours and minutes that will elapse from 8:35 A. M. to 12 noon, which is 3 hours and 25 minutes, he will subtract that sum from 6 hours and 44 minutes, which will leave 3 hours and 19 minutes, he will then look for the nearest to that number of hours and minutes in the "Table of Houses" for New York, and he will there find 3 hours, 18 minutes, and on a line with these figures he will find the longitude of the 10th, 11th, 12th, 1st, 2d and 3d houses, which he will enter in a blank chart; he will then place in the same chart the opposite signs and their degrees and minutes. Then the student will look in the Ephemeris for July 2, 1884, and there find the longitude of the Sun, Moon and planets for 12 noon calculated for London, which is equivlent to 7 A. M. in New York. He will then calculate how much each planet travels from 7 A. M. to 8:35 A. M., and place the planets and degrees and minutes in their proper signs and houses in the blank figure.

HOW TO CALCULATE THE PART OF FORTUNE.

292 In this chart of the heavens I have also calculated the "Part of Fortune," and this is done by adding the longitude of the Ascendant to the longitude of the Moon, and from that sum subtract the longitude of the Sun; the remainder is the longitude of the "Part of Fortune" in signs, degrees and minutes. We always commence to count from Aries, and count to the sign next to that in which the Sun and Moon is located; we count the same way for the Ascendant. In this case we find that in counting from Aries the

Ascendant is	4 signs,	28 degrees,	4 minutes,	
the Moon is	7 "	6 "	33 "	add.
	11 "	34 "	37 "	
the Sun is	3 "	11 "	00 "	subtract.
	8 "	23 "	37 "	

293 In this case the Sun is 8 signs, 23 degrees and 37 minutes, and if we count from Aries we will find that the 8th sign is Scorpio; therefore the "Part of Fortune" is 8 whole signs,

and 23 degrees and 37 minutes into the 9th sign, which is Sagittarius; and enter accordingly in ♐ just below the line marked 5 in the blank map.

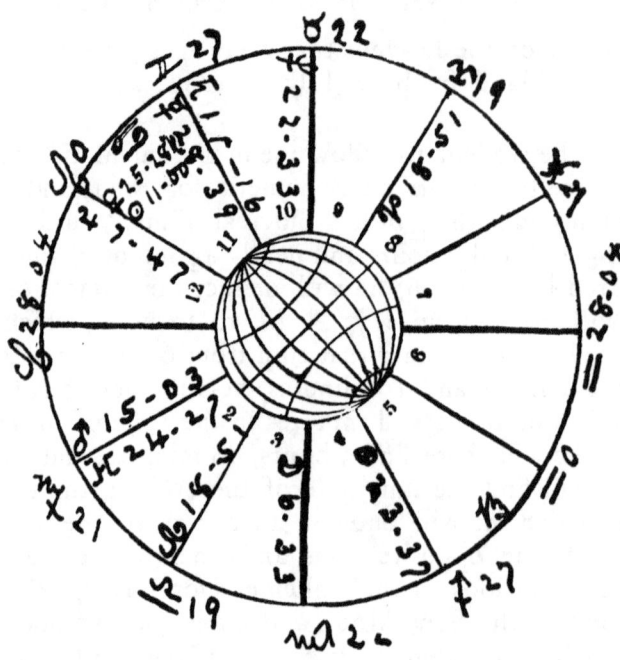

CHART OF THE HEAVENS FOR GIRL BORN JULY 2d, 1884, at 8:35 A. M., NEW YORK CITY.

Chart of the heavens for the above named time of birth all complete, ready for the Astrologer to commence what we call reading.

No doubt the chart appears to the student like a wagon wheel, with 12 spokes, and a large hub in the centre, with certain hieroglyphics on the outside rim, and on a number of spokes; these hyeroglyphics may appear to the student like insects crawling on the spokes and on the rim, and he will probably be equally puzzled as to what they mean, as the editor of the "*New York Times*"; but possibly he may be like Mrs. Maud S. and have "perfect good faith, and really believe that the data submitted is sufficient basis for calculations of practical value." I shall not "concoct a horoscope for the day and year here given," neither shall I do "any dreary fooling," I leave that for the editor of the "*New York Times*," but I expect to make the horoscope interesting. If the student ever becomes a good Astrologer, he will be able to see the picture of the young lady in this "hieroglyphic diagram" as she appeared as a baby, at 2 or 3, at 8 or 10, also at 18 or 20 years old, or at any other period of her life, not only as she will look when a young lady of 25 or 30, or whether fat, slender, tall, or short, dark or light, but also he could give color of hair and eyes, and her varied physique and general appearance. Also as she will appear when a woman of 50 or 60 or more years old.

I shall explain to the student how to describe her mental qualities, and tell what business she might succeed in, if any, what kind of men she should avoid, in order to guard against disgrace or special unhappiness, and a particular description of the gentleman she will marry, and the gentleman she will meet with who is likely to cause her much unhappiness, and whom she will not marry, and which party she ought to try to avoid; also I shall explain to the student what diseases she will suffer from, and in what parts of her life they will occur, and what parts of the body will be most afflicted, and a number of other things which it is advisable for every person to know to guard against misfortunes.

The student must not expect to learn every thing at once (Rome was not built in a day); he must be satisfied at first by being able to tell whether the horoscope is a fortunate or an unfortunate one, and afterwards he must learn why it is unfortunate, and what particular aspects and positions of the planets make it unfortunate, and why it is fortunate and what particular aspects or positions of the planets make it fortunate. For instance, in the horoscope of Chas. Dryden, John Dryden told his wife "that the child was born in an evil hour, that Jupiter, Venus and the Sun were all under the Earth, and the Ascendant afflicted with an hateful square of Mars and Saturn." These remarks indicated that the child had a very unfortunate horoscope, and that all the evil directions during its life, or what are sometimes termed aspects, would tell with a vengeance; and that he would not feel much good from what are called the good aspects or directions.

The above horoscope is what is termed a rather fortunate one, still it would have been much better if the Sun did not make an aspect of Mars for her first marriage, especially as Mars is an evil planet and in evil aspect to Saturn in the midheaven.

LORDS OR RULERS OF THE SIGNS OF THE ZODIAC.

294 Before the student can begin to learn to read a nativity or horoscope properly, in addition to learning the houses and the signs of the Zodiac and their signification, also the planets, and their various significations, he will have to learn what are termed the lords and ladies of the houses, or rather lords or rulers of the signs of the Zodiac. The seven planets which the ancients were acquainted with, were Saturn, Jupiter, Mars, Sun, Venus, Mercury and the Moon. The old Astrologer allotted two of the signs of the Zodiac to each one of these planets, as they found by experience that those old Astrologers alotted two of the signs of the Zodiac to each them, than they had in any other of the signs of the Zodiac; but they only allotted one sign each to the Sun and Moon; and no matter what sign each of the five planets and the Sun and Moon may happen to be in, they are still said to be lords and ladies of the signs that have been allotted to them, as those old astrologers found by long experience and practice,

that what are sometimes called the seven planets have great influence or sympathy with the particular signs that they are lords or ladies of, and which they retain, whether they are in these signs or not. For instance, Mars is lord of Aries and Scorpio; Venus is lady of Taurus and Libra; Mercury is lord of Gemini and Virgo; Moon is lady of Cancer; Sun is lord of Leo;* Jupiter of Sagittary and Pisces; and Saturn of Capricorn and Aquarius.

295 I have generally been the most successful in getting students to commit to memory what are termed the lords or ladies of the houses or signs of the Zodiac, by his learning them in the order in which I have here given. Some students learn them easiest one way, and some another. I will give below four different methods of committing them to memory, and the student may choose whichever method he finds the easiest to learn, but whichever method he learns them by, he must bear in mind he must commit them to memory before he can read a nativity or horary question successfully.

Signs	Lords of Signs	Signs			Planets	Signs	Lords of Signs	Signs		Planets
♈	♂	♈ and ♏	allotted to		♂	♋	☽	♋		☽
♉	♀	♉	"	♎	"	♀	♌	☉	♌		☉
♊	☿	♊	"	♍	"	☿	♍ and ♊	☿	♑ and ♒		♄
♋	☽	♐	"	♓	"	♃	♎	"	♉	♀	♐	"	♓	♃
♌	☉	♑	"	♒	"	♄	♏	"	♈	♂	♏	"	♈	♂
♍	☿	♋			"	☽	♐	"	♓	♃	♎	"	♉	♀
♎	♀	♌			"	☉	♑	"	♒	♄ †	♍	"	♊	☿
♏	♂									
♐	♃									
♑	♄									
♒	♄									
♓	♃									

* Claudius Ptolemy in his Tetrabiblos, as translated by Ashmond, tells us that the reason the old astrologers allotted the sign Leo to the Sun, was that the Sun had the most power or influence over vegetation, etc., when he was in the sign Leo, that is from the 22d of July to the 22d of August; and as the Sun has the most power in the sign Cancer (from the 22d of June to the 22d of July), in causing rain and wet weather, they allotted the sign Cancer to the Moon, it being a moist or watery planet. Then as Saturn was a cold and dry planet, it being the furthest away from the Sun, they allotted it the two signs furthest away from Cancer and Leo, or the signs in opposition to those two, that is Capricorn and Aquarius, as the two houses or signs of Saturn; then as Jupiter was the next nearest to Saturn, coming towards the Sun and Moon, and being a warm and moist planet, they allotted it the next two signs to Capricorn and Aquarius, that is Pisces Sagittary; then they allotted the next two signs coming towards Cancer and Leo, to Mars, that is Scorpio and Aries; then they allotted the next two signs, that is Taurus and Libra to Venus; then the next two signs, that is Gemini and Virgo they allotted to the planet Mercury; then Cancer was allotted to the Moon and Leo to the Sun.

† Zadkiel, of London, tells us in one of his books on Astrology, that there is a stone in the British Museum, which was brought from Egypt with the above arrangement of the Planets and Signs of the Zodiac engraved on it, and the Astronomers and savants of Europe have been puzzling their brains how it was that the ancient Egyptians so arranged the signs and the planets, and whether in some prehistoric age the signs of the Zodiac followed in the order above shown. If those savants had looked into any Astrological text book, they would have had the whole thing explained in a nut shell; but it would have lowered their dignity to have consulted an Astrological book. There is no doubt but that some ancient Astrologer so arranged them and had them engraved, so that his students could more easily learn them; or he might have done it, so as to keep them constantly in his own mind.

296 The student cannot have the lords of the various signs too thoroughly committed to memory. If he does not know them well, he will commit a number of mistakes in his reading of horoscopes. He can choose whichever of the four tables given that he thinks he can commit easiest to memory.

297 In order to make the student understand what is meant by the lords and ladies of the different signs or houses, and at the same time understand the above tables, I will say that after the chart of the heavens is cast, the student will first see what sign is on the Ascendant or first house, and if ♈ is on the ascendant then ♂ is said to be lord of the ascendant or first house. If ♉ is on the ascendant, then ♀ is lady of the first house. If ♊ is on the ascendant then ☿ is lord of the first house. If ♋ is on the ascendant, then the Moon is lady of the Ascendant or first house, and so on through the whole signs of the Zodiac; in the same manner if ♈ is on the midheaven or 10th house, then ♂ is said to be lord of the 10th house, or if ♉ is on the midheaven, then ♀ is lady of the 10th house. The same if ♈ is on the 7th house, then ♂ is lord of the 7th house, and if ♉ is on the 7th house, then ♀ is lady of the 7th; and so on through the 12 signs of the Zodiac, and through the different houses of the heavens.

RULES FOR READING HOROSCOPES.

When we commence to read a horoscope we generally divide it into what are termed parts or divisions:

1st. As to whether the native may live or not, and the probable length of life.

2d. The description of the party, whether light or dark, tall or short, etc.

3d. The diseases that he will be afflicted with, or is most liable to.

4th. Whether the person will be wealthy or poor, or have various changes in life, sometimes up or down.

5th. The mental qualities, or what line of studies to pursue.

6th. The disposition or temper, whether high tempered or of an easy disposition.

7th. What line of business the native may succeed in, and his natural inclinations

8th. We examine in regard to friends or enemies, whether much benefitted by the former, or much afflicted by the latter, and which will be the most injurious or beneficial, males or females.

9th. We examine in regard to moral character, whether religious or skeptical, vicious, or inclined to be honorable.

10th. We look in regard to relations and near neighbors, and long and short journeys.

11th. In regard to marriage, whether happy or unhappy, and a description of the person the native will marry; also a description of the persons they will keep company with previous to marriage.

12th. The probable time of life the party will marry.

13th. Children; whether few or many, beneficial or injurious.

14th. Whether the native will enjoy fair health or be sick most of the time, or whether they will ever be troubled with sickness.

15th. The various contingencies and events of life.

HAVE A REGULAR SYSTEM OF READING A HOROSCOPE.

It is always advisable for the student to acquire a certain method or system of reading a horoscope, as in that case he is less liable to become confused or leave out some important part of the nativity, but there are times when it will be advisable to deviate from one particular method; for instance, on one occasion I was consulted by a lady, mother of a leading New York actress; after giving her age and where she was born, I calculated a chart of the heavens for the time of birth. The first words I said to her were, "You did not live with your husband three months." She answered by saying, "Well, I managed to murder it out with him a whole year." The reader will easily see that I made a mistake to begin with, but the lady discovered there was something in Astrology. When the student sees a striking feature in a horoscope, it is often advisable to touch upon that feature at once, as in that case he will often get the confidence of his client at the outset, but as I previously remarked, it is generally advisable to acquire a certain method and stick to it as near as possible; even when he has everything down to an almost perfect system, he will find plenty to confuse him, on account of horoscopes differing so much from one another. I shall never forget, while studying Astrology, a remark made by my brother, which was, "Throw as much overboard as you possibly can, and judge by the remainder, and even then you will have plenty to confuse you." The student often acquires the bad habit of actually trying to confuse himself; he gets everything mixed by trying to judge from too many combinations, when on the contrary he should try to acquire the habit of separating the science into parts, and in that way simplify it as much as possible, and in course of time will begin to make good headway, and gradually master the science.

Astrology, like music, may be divided into a science and an art. For instance, a person may understand the science of music almost to perfection, and yet may not be able to play a single instrument, and only an indifferent singer; in like manner a person may be well versed in the science of Astrology, and not be able to read a single horoscope correctly. The former is called the science, and the latter the art of Astrology, but no person can be an artist in either music or Astrology unless they have some knowledge of the science.

The first thing I generally look at in a horoscope is to see whether the person is likely to live ; sometimes I look at the persons themselves, and then at the horoscope, and if the horoscope does not describe a person like the client, I know then that there has been a mistake made in the time or place of birth, and I go no further uutil that mistake is rectified.

1st.—*Giver of Life.*

After the chart of the heavens is calculated, I generally see how strong the giver of life is, because that decides the length of life, other influences or aspects being equal. To find out which is the giver of life, we first see where the Sun or Moon is, whether either of them is in what are termed "Hylegiacal Places" in the horoscope. These places of the heavens are divided into three parts : the first is from 5 degrees above the cusp of the ascendant to 25 degrees below; the next is 5 degrees below the cusp of the 7th house to 25 degrees above ; the next is 5 degrees below the cusp of the 9th house to 25 degrees below the cusp of the 11th house.

If the Sun is in any of these places, it is said to be the giver of life, and if unafflicted, then the person will live to an old age, unless some remarkably evil positions of the planets indicate the contrary ; even then the native will not die in infancy, and may live beyond middle age. If the Sun is not in any of the positions above named, then the Moon is giver of life, if she is in any of these places referred to above. But the Moon is not as strong for long life, when the giver of life, as the Sun, and the person who has the Moon "Hyleg" seldom enjoys the best of health. When neither the Sun nor the Moon is the giver of life, then the ascendant is said to be "Hyleg," which is that part of the heavens from 5 degrees above the cusp of the ascendant to 25 degress below, and if the ascendant is afflicted by the presence of an evil planet (either Saturn or Mars), it is then very doubtful of the native living to middle age ; but if Jupiter and Venus be in the ascendant or within 25 degrees below the cusp, then the chances of life are much more in favor of the native.

In the horoscope of the young lady born July 2, 1884, at 8.35 A. M., the student will find that the Sun is the giver of life, as there are 27 degrees of Gemini on the cusp of the 11th house, and the Sun is 11 degrees in Cancer ; therefore the Sun is within 14 degrees of the cusp of the 11th house, consequently it is the giver of life in this horoscope, and it is unafflicted—that is, no evil planet afflicts the Sun, and the Moon is applying to a trine of the Sun, and the Sun is making a sextile of Mars rising; therefore, it is said to be well fortified, and the native is almost certain to live to old age, or between 60 or 70 years old.

The Moon is always co-significator in all horoscopes, unless it be the planet that the native is born under, and in those cases Cancer is on the ascendant, and the Moon is then the ruling planet, it being lady of that sign.

If the Moon had not been afflicted in the sign Scorpio in this horoscope, and so near a square of Jupiter, in the 12th house (an evil house), and Jupiter being lord of the 8th house (the house of death), she might in that case live to be over 70.

2d.—*Personal Description.*

In order to describe the native by the horoscope, we first notice the sign in the ascendant, also see if there are any planets in the ascendant, and if so, we notice the signs that they are in, and also see if they have any aspects to any other planets; then we go to the lord of the ascendant and see what sign it is in, and if it has any aspects to any other planets; then we go to the Moon and see what sign it is in, and what aspect it has to any other planets, and *judge by the combination of the whole.*

In the horoscope of Mrs. Maud S.'s daughter, the sign Leo is on the ascendant, therefore the student must read what kind of person the sign Leo describes (see 17).* There is no planet in the ascendant, therefore we go to the Sun in the sign Cancer, and read the Sun in Cancer, 107; then we notice the Sun is in sextile to Mars, we read the kind of person the Sun in sextile to Mars describes, 234; then we turn to the Moon and read the kind of person the Moon in Scorpio describes, 147. In this horoscope the Moon is in close square to Jupiter in Leo, and being so near the square, we read 84, what kind of a person Jupiter in Leo will describe, also the description of the Moon in square to Jupiter, 277, and by the combination of the whole we describe the native. The student must not notice any other *planets in the horoscope in describing the native,* unless they are in opposition, or in square, trine, or sextile aspect to the ascendant, as for instance, a planet in the 7th house in opposition to the degree and minute rising, or in close square from the 10th or 4th, or in trine to the ascendant from the 9th or 5th, or in sextile from the 3d or 11th; and as I said before, you must notice very particularly any planet or planets that may be in the ascendant and what signs they are in. In the nativity of Mrs. Maud S.'s daughter, we find that there are over 28 degrees of the sign Leo on the ascendant; therefore nearly all that sign has risen, and in this horoscope there is a great part of the sign Virgo in the ascendant. In this case we have to read 18, giving the description of the sign Virgo, and then go to the lord of Virgo, which is Mercury, and notice what sign it is in, which is Gemini, and what aspect it has to any other planet (it is in square to Uranus); we first read the description of Mercury in Gemini, and then read the description of Mercury in square to Uranus, and by mixing the whole, we can get at a very close description of the native; but this part of Astrology requires considerable skill and practice to become proficient in.

In order to simplify the method of describing a person by the horoscope, or by the position of the planets at the time of birth, I will, in this case, reprint the descriptions of the signs Leo and Virgo on the ascendant; also, the lord of the ascendant, which is the Sun in Cancer in sextile aspect to Mars; also a person described by the Moon in Scorpio,

---

* Refers to paragraph 17 on page 97, which describes a person born with Leo in the ascendant or 1st house. This explanation will answer for all other numbers which follow. All those paragraphs which are numbered are printed in large type.

and the description of Jupiter in Leo; also of a person described by the Moon in square to Jupiter; also a person described by Mercury in Gemini, and by Mercury in square to Uranus.

For practice, the student must see how near he could come to writing off a personal description of the native, by the combination of the whole, as indicated by the above horoscope. It will be good practice for him to try and do it over a number of times, and then read the description that I give of Mrs. Maud S.'s daughter, on page 38. There is one thing that the student should distinctly keep in mind, that is, he should condense the personal description as much as possible, so that any person acquainted with the young lady who reads it, would say, "that is her exact description," just the same as if looking at a good photograph or oil-painting of the lady.

Here follows the quality and description of the signs Leo and Virgo, also of the Sun, Jupiter, Mercury and the Moon.

Leo gives a great round head, large, prominent, or staring eyes, quick sighted, a full and large body, and of more than middle stature; broad shoulders, narrow sides, yellow or dark flaxen hair, curling or turning up; a fierce countenance, but ruddy, high, sanguine complexion; strong, valiant and active; step firm and mind courteous.

Virgo gives a slender body, rather tall but well composed, a ruddy brown complexion, black hair, well favored or lovely, but not a beautiful creature, small, shrill voice, judicious and exceedingly well-spoken, studious and given to history, whether man or woman.

Sun in Cancer gives a mean, ill-formed body, deformed in the face, with a very unhealthy aspect, the hair brown. A harmless, cheerful person, but indolent and not fond of employment.

Sun Sextile to Mars confers great bravery and a high spirit; he rises to grandeur by means of his courage and invincible military talents.

Moon in Scorpio denotes a thick, short, and ill-shaped person, a fleshy, obscure complexion, dark hair, often black.

Moon in Square to Jupiter he is injured by faithless friends and deceitful relatives, and his property is impoverished by hypocritical fanatics.

Jupiter in Leo represents a strong and well-proportioned, tall body; the hair is a light or yellowish brown and curling; complexion, ruddy; eye, full and fiery; person, rather handsome.

Mercury in Gemini shows a tall, upright, straight body, well formed, brown hair, good complexion, and a very intelligent look.

Mercury in Square to Uranus, he lacks intuitive observation and instinctive judgment; is skeptical, etc.

After the student has read all the above, of a person being described by the signs and planets, no doubt, to his mind, it will appear all confusion, and it would puzzle a Philadelphia lawyer to straighten the matter out, but after a while he will find that it will all come plain and easy to him; experience will teach him what to rely on in almost all cases, and what is only of secondary importance. It is very difficult to describe this young lady by her horoscope, on account of what is called conflicting testimony; but in some nativities which we shall read further on, the student will find it then very plain and easy describing the natives by their horoscope. There are no special rules that never vary and that can be relied upon in all cases, but generally he must give:

1st.—Prominence to the signs on or in the ascendant.

2d.—To planets in the ascendant.

3d.—To the lord of the ascendant and its aspects.

4th.—To the Moon and its aspects.

Whenever there is a planet in the Ascendant, especially if it is a superior planet, it generally has the most influence in describing the native. In the nativity of the Rev. Henry Ward Beecher, Jupiter is in Leo in his ascendant, and if the student reads Jupiter in Leo, on page 109, he will find that it comes very close to Mr. Beecher's description. General Grant had Saturn, Sun and Jupiter in the sign Taurus in the Ascendant, and if the Student reads all those planets in the sign Taurus, he will find that they come very close to giving an accurate description of him.* In the horoscope of Mrs. Maud S's daughter, if there had only been the sign Leo in the ascendant and the Sun in Cancer, it would have been much easier to describe her, and she would also have been much lighter complexioned (a regular blond), and much fuller built, even as a child or young lady, especially as the Moon is in the sign Scorpio, a stout sign; but there being a part of Virgo in the ascendant, and it being a tall, dark sign, and Mercury in another tall, dark sign (Gemini), those influences make her quite slender when young, and above the medium height, and also will gradually cause her hair to become a light brown as she gets older. But the Moon being in a stout sign, and the Sun being in Cancer, a stout sign, and a stout sign on the cusp of the ascendant makes her full built; after middle age, or at 40 or 45, she may reach the weight of near 200 pounds, chiefly caused by the Moon being in the sign Scorpio, and in square to Jupiter in Leo.

After a little practice, this part of Astrology will become very plain and easy, besides being very convincing of the truth of the science. It will be advisable for the student at first, whenever he attempts to read a horoscope, in describing the native, to copy out of this volume, on a sheet of paper, the kind of person described by the sign in the ascendant, and of any planet in the ascendant; the description of the lord or lady of the ascendant in whatever sign it may happen to be in, the aspects of the lord of the ascendant; and then the person described by the Moon, in whatever sign it may be in, and its aspects; by so doing the student will be surprised how easy it becomes.

To give an illustration, a homœpathic physician may have to read over a number of large pages in his Homeopathic Materia Medica, in order to arrive at the proper remedy, to meet all the symptoms that his

---

* These two horoscopes will be published further on in this volume.

patient may at the time be afflicted with. After a while, by experience, he appears to arrive at the proper remedy as if it were by instinct. So the student in Astrology, after he has read a number of horoscopes knows what aspects and what planets and signs to rely on, and he will arrive at a right conclusion, as if it were by intuition; but Astrology, like music and a number of other sciences and professions, is largely dependent on experience and practice. I might say practice is everything.*

I shall condense the remainder of the horoscope for Mrs. Maud S.'s daughter, and only give an outline as a guidance, and let the student enlarge on it from his own study and investigation.

3d.—*Sickness and Diseases and Complaints.*

The diseases this young lady is most liable to suffer from, are indicated by the Moon in Scorpio, which governs the lower part of the body and back, such as the kidneys, bladder, uterus and lower part of the intestines; the Moon being in square to Jupiter in the 12th house (the house of sorrow and trouble), in the sign Leo, which governs the heart and back, and Jupiter also being lord of the 8th house (the house of death), Saturn in Gemini, which governs the chest and arms, being the lord of the 6th house (the house of sickness), and in square to Mars, lord of the

---

* Unless the student takes great pleasure in the science of Astrology, regardless of any worldly benefit that it might be to him, it is impossible for him to become a learned or scientific Astrologer. It is like all other sciences or professions in that respect. The musician, artist, or sculptor who does not take pleasure in his particular line of art, will never arrive at the head of his profession.

There are some people in this world who can never see any good in anything unless it brings them wealth. Money is their God, and if they can only see and reach the glittering gold at the final goal, they are ready to endure all kinds of hardships, of either heat or cold, and put up with all kinds of privations to attain their object. We have an illustration or object lesson in proof of this, in the thousands of persons who have heard of the discovery of gold near the Klondyke River in Alaska, and who are going in crowds to that god-forsaken country, and are ready to relinquish everthing—their wives, families and friends, and endure the inclemency of an arctic climate—to put up with all kinds of inconveniences, both in regard to food, lodging and clothing, and even run the risk of destroying their health and their lives, by such exposure.

To those persons who make wealth their god, I have to say that there is money to be made by the practice of Astrology, without having to endure all the above enumerated hardships, and without having to leave family or home; on the contrary, it will be a continued source of pleasure and happiness. But money cannot be acquired by Astrology, without working for it. In course of time the student will become so proficient in the science as to have clients come to consult him, and pay him fees for his services, and which often amounts to quite a sum in a week; besides, he may get orders to write horoscopes, for from $2 to $5, $10 or $20 each; there are also a number of people who wish to have each day written off; called "Fortunate or Unfortunate day," and remarks for each month, for which they pay $5. I have written those days off for some parties for nearly 30 years. I have also written off predictions of the stock, mines, and produce market, for which clients pay $5 per week, and those parties often come to consult me besides, for which they seldom pay less than $5 per visit. He may also, in time, get orders to write horoscopes for daily newspapers, which sometimes, in my case, has amounted to $200 per week; and at times it was impossible to supply the demand, the editors of the papers writing and telegraphing almost daily, "Can you send us more horoscopes? We want to get out a larger Sunday edition, and insert 4 pages of horoscopes," when they were publishing two or more columns, three times per week besides the Sunday editions, and they paid me $5 per column, and seven columns to a page.

The people are becoming hungry for this kind of literature, called the Occult; they devour it, whenever it comes in their reach. I need only mention such works as H. Rider Haggard's "She," F. Marion Crawford's "Mr. Isaacs," and a number of other books which have large circulations, but more especially works on Theosophy, which are all running into Astrology, and which works are now extensively read; in short Theosophy, Astrology, etc., are in the air. People breathe it, especially in the Western States. It is astonishing how many book stores have sprung up in the last few years, which deal altogether in what are termed Occult Publications, and new works are published almost weekly. The demand for such publications is becoming almost universal, and within a few years there will scarcely be a respectable newspaper in the United States or Canada, which will not have an Astrological or Horoscope column. And experts and reliable Astrologers who are first in the market, will receive the most benefit.

Further on in this volume I shall refer to the Astrological influence which is operating in the heavens at the present time, and which is causing this craving in the human mind for Astrology, **Theosophy, and kindred science**; also for works of fiction which treat on Occult subjects.

4th and also of the 9th. The native will at times be seriously afflicted by a tightness of the chest, and palpitation of the heart, and will also suffer from some weakness of the stomach and intestines, especially the lower part. Mars being lord of the 9th, which indicates science, and lord of the 4th (the end of all things), and Saturn lord of the 7th house, which indicates the physician, and Saturn and Mars being in square aspect to each other, shows that there is great danger of the native having her life shortened by her physician. She must never employ a tall, slender, dark complexioned doctor, especially if he has a thin face, high forehead, small dark eyes, and black hair (indicated by ♄ in ♊, and ♂ in ♍), unless she wants to die young. But the Sun "the giver of life," unafflicted and strong by being in good aspect to Mars and the Moon, indicates that possibly by some good luck or by means of friends, she may avoid those misfortunes referred to above, especially as the Sun is in the 11th house (the house of friends), and in good aspect to Mars, lord of the 4th house (the house of the native's residence). It is possible she may be so guarded by her friends, that she may live to old age, but, at the same time, there will often be danger, especially when she has evil aspects in operation in her nativity.

4th.—*Riches and Poverty.*

This young lady will have many changes in life on account of Mars being on the cusp of the 2d house, in square to Saturn in the midheaven, and Mercury lord of the second in square to Uranus in the second. I will state the various periods when those unfortunate events will occur, when I come to treat on the various contingencies and events of life; will only state here that her first husband will generally be the cause of of her low circumstances, on account of his own misfortunes and extravagance.

5th.—*Mental Abilities.*

The mental qualities are chiefly governed by Mercury, and the propensities and passions are chiefly governed by the Moon, Mercury being in the sign Gemini, its own sign, indicates that she will be of very good intellect and will learn rapidly, and make a very good scholar, although she will be eccentric, and it will be very difficult for her to apply her mind long at a time to any one subject, yet she will be a good speaker and writer, and would succeed as an authoress, especially writing books similiar to those of F. Marion Crawford and H. Rider Haggard. This is indicated by the square of Mercury and Uranus, which will make her very fond of such subjects. She will maintain a good moral reputation, this is indicated by the Moon making a trine aspect to the Sun, and the Sun being her ruling planet; even the Moon in square to Jupiter would give her good moral tendencies, but at times make her gloomy and despondent on account of Jupiter being in the 12th house (the house of sorrow), and also lord of the 8th house, (or house of death.)

6th.—*Disposition and Temper.*

She will generally have a good natured disposition, but at times of a domineering tendency, as those born under the Sun always want to control others; will but seldom get into bad tempers, on account of the Sun being unafflicted in the 11th house (the house of hopes); she will generally be of a cheerful and hopeful tendency, but at odd times slightly gloomy and despondent.

7th.—*Business and Honor.*

It is doubtful about her succeeding in business, except writing or teaching, as Saturn being in the 10th house (the house of business), and in square to Mars on the cusp of the second; she would lose money by any business she would undertake. She will be particularly unfortunate in keeping a restaurant, hotel, store, or boarding-house, this is indicated by Saturn lord of the 6th and 7th, and also lord of the intercepted sign in the 5th, afflicting the midheaven and being in square to Mars, afflicting the 2d house; and also by Jupiter, lord of the 5th being in the 12th in square to the Moon. The Moon is always co-significator, if not the only significator.

8th.—*Friends and Enemies.*

Mercury lord of the 11th house in the 11th in Gemini; the Sun and Venus also there, indicates that she will have many prominent friends, but they will seldom continue to be good friends long, as Mercury is in square to Uranus, which makes them fickle and uncertain; also the Moon being lady of the intercepting sign Cancer, being in the sign Scorpio which is naturally a treacherous sign, being in square to Jupiter in the 12th house (the house of sorrow and trouble), indicates that a number of her friends will turn into secret enemies, also she is liable to lose a number of her friends by death, as Jupiter is lord of the 8th house (the house of death). She will have more enduring friends of the female sex, rather than the male sex; as Venus is in the 11th, in Cancer, in good aspect to Neptune in Taurus in the midheaven, and Venus is also in good aspect to Uranus in the 2d. Her male friends are much more likely to be treacherous than her female friends, and also she is more liable to lose money by her male friends, on account of Mercury, a masculine planet in the 11th house, being in square to Uranus in the 2d house (the house of money).

9th and 10th.—*Morals and Religion—Relations and Journeys.*

This lady will be of rather skeptical turn of mind, especially on religious subjects, as Mars is lord of the 9th, and is afflicted by a square of Saturn; but the Sun, her planet, being in good aspect to Mars, causes her to be of a good moral tendency, and not any way vicious, but inclined to be honorable in her dealings: as all persons born under the Sun are, especially when the Sun is not afflicted. This lady will be very fortunate in regard to near relations, and also neighbors; Venus is lady of the 3d house (the house of relations and neighbors), unafflicted in the 11th house, and in good aspect to Neptune and Uranus, indicates that her neighbors and near relations will generally be her best friends, it also indicates that she will be fortunate in short journeys, but not fortunate in long journeys, especially in money matters, as Mars lord of the 9th is afflicting the 2d, and is in square to Saturn in the midheaven. This aspect will make her very unfortunate in lawsuits, especially anything connected with church matters; her enemies will generally be of a religious tendency or very pious.

11th.—Marriage.

This lady will be unfortunate in her first marriage, and great danger that she will separate from her husband, or he leaves her, any way it is not a fortunate marriage, and it will cause her much unhappiness.

298 In all female horoscopes, we first see what aspect and what planet the *Sun* first applies to, and whether that aspect is a fortunate aspect, and that planet a fortunate planet. If the Sun first makes an evil aspect of an evil planet, say to a conjunction, square or opposition, of either ♄ or ♂, then that female, if she marries, will have an unhappy married life, especially if there are evil planets in the 7th house (the house of marriage), or evil planets aspecting the 7th house, or if the lord of the 7th house is an evil planet, and is any way afflicted by evil aspects, especially by being in square or opposition to ♄ or ♂.

299 But if the *Sun* applies to a good aspect of a fortunate planet, say to a conjunction, sextile, or trine of ♀ or ♃, especially if ♃ or ♀ be in the 7th house, or in good aspect to the 7th house, or a fortunate planet is lord of the 7th house, then that female lives happy in her married life with her first husband.

300 We judge male horoscopes, in regard to marriage, by the aspect the *Moon* makes, and not the aspects of the Sun, as in female horoscopes. If the Moon in a male horoscope makes a good aspect of a fortunate planet, say ♃ or ♀, especially if there are any fortunate planets in the 7th house (the house of marriage), or ♃ or ♀ is lord or lady of the 7th house, then that male, if he marries, lives happily in married life. But if the Moon first makes an evil aspect of an unfortunate planet, say ♄ or ♂, and if ♄ or ♂ is lord of the 7th house, or in evil aspect to the 7th house, or if the lord of the 7th house is afflicted by an unfortunate planet, then that male, if he marries, is unfortunate in married life, or they separate soon after marriage; but sometimes the wife dies shortly after marriage, or they do not have any children, and much unhappiness in the family is caused on that account.

301 Those aspects in a female's nativity which the Sun makes either good or evil, to either ♆, ♅ or the ☽ are not to be noticed, as she never or hardly ever marries the person described by those planets; she will probably keep company

with persons described by those planets; and if the Sun makes evil aspects to them, either conjunction, square, or opposition, the native may meet much unhappiness, if not disgrace by the persons described by those planets. The same rule applies in male horoscopes when the ☽ is making aspects of either ♆, ♅, or the ☉; but the native does not marry the lady described by those planets.

302 To find out the personal description in a female's horoscope of the parties that the native will keep company with, and not marry, in addition to those already mentioned, see what aspect the Sun is leaving in a female's horoscope, and that planet in the sign describes the parties she keeps company with and does not marry; also see whether any evil planets be in the 7th house, or the Moon is making or separating from any aspect of any planet, and those planets describe the gentleman she keeps company with and does not marry.

303 To find out the description of the ladies in a male's horoscope that the native will keep company with, see what aspect and what planet the Moon is separating from, and those planets will describe the ladies the native keeps company with but does not marry; also notice what planets, especially evil ones, are in the 7th house.

304 When the Sun in a female's horoscope, or the Moon in a male's horoscope, makes a square or opposition of evil planets, especially if lord of the ascendant be making a square or opposition of the lord of the 7th, very often the native never marries, or if he or she does, they are very likely to separate soon after marriage.

305 The first planet that the Sun applies to, by aspect, in a female's horoscope, describes the first husband of the native. If the native marries a second time, then the second planet that the Sun applies to by aspect, describes the second husband. The third planet the Sun applies to describes the third husband of the native, if she marries so many times, and so in regard to the fourth planet, etc.

306 The first planet that the Moon applies to by aspect describes the first wife of the native in a male's horoscope. And the second planet that the Moon applies to by aspect describes the second wife, if he marries a second time, and so on.

307 The same rules apply in regard to the aspects and planets that the Sun or Moon applies to in female or male horoscopes, in reference to fortunate and unfortunate planets, and good or evil aspects, etc., in regard to the second or third marriage, that it does in the first marriage, and whether they live happy or unhappy in the second or third marriage, etc.

308 When nearly all the planets are rising or oriental, especially ☉, ♃ and ♀, the native generally marries early in life, but if nearly all the planets are setting or occidental, the native is almost certain to marry late in life, if they marry at all, or to persons much younger than themselves.

309 If in a lady's horoscope the Sun makes a good aspect of an evil planet, or in a gentleman's horoscope the Moon makes a good aspect of an evil planet, or *vice versa*, then the parties may not separate, but often have much unhappiness, or in some cases what are termed love spats; and by seeing what house the planet is lord of that afflicts, it can often be pointed out from what cause the unhappiness will arise, whether jealousy, mother-in-law, sister-in-law, brother-in-law, religion, poverty, etc.

In this lady's horoscope the Sun makes a good aspect of an evil planet (Mars), and Mars is afflicted by a square of Saturn, and also Saturn is lord of the 7th house (the house of marriage); therefore, although the Sun makes a good aspect, yet Mars being an evil planet and so afflicted, it will not be a happy marriage, as he will be very jealous, suspicious, unfortunate, and often commence rash or unreasonable undertakings. He will be very willful, stubborn, and generally keep her poor. He may be killed, commit suicide, or die of some violent fever; they will be far from being happy. She marries a second time, and the Sun next makes a conjunction of Venus in the 11th house, and that being a fortunate planet and a fortunate aspect, she will live happy. He will be refined, intelligent, and of a good-natured disposition, as Venus is in good aspect to Neptune in the midheaven, and also Uranus in the 2d house (the house of money); therefore, she will improve her circumstances by her second marriage. But before the Sun makes the conjunction of Venus, it makes a sextile of Neptune in the midheaven, and also a sextile of Uranus in the 2d house. She will keep company with gentlemen described by Neptune in Taurus in the midheaven, and Uranus in Virgo, during her widowhood, but will not marry either, as neither a man nor woman hardly ever marries a person described by either Neptune or Uranus, but keeps company with those persons; but if they do marry them, which is very seldom, they always make short, unhappy marriages. In a lady's horoscope, they keep company with parties before marriage, that the Sun is separating from and not applying to, but never marry them; the Sun is not separating from any planet except the Moon. In this nativity the Moon is making a square of Jupiter in the 12th house, she will keep company with the gentleman described by Jupiter in Leo, previous to her first marriage, and will have much sorrow and unhappiness caused by that gentleman, and he is very likely to die early in life, or possibly before the lady marries her first husband, as Jupiter is lord of the 8th house (the house of death) and is in the 6th house (the house of sickness), from the 7th house; there is great danger of this lady meeting with disgrace from this gentleman described by Jupiter in Leo, as he will pretend to be very pious and religious; this threatened disgrace is indicated mostly by Jupiter being lord of the 5th house (the house of children and pleasure), afflicting the Moon in Scorpio, which governs the sexual organs. Her friends may possibly prevent the disgrace, especially if they are forewarned.

12th.—*The Age when Married.*

This horoscope does not indicate an early marriage, although she will be engaged at 19, and will come near marrying, but it will be a serious disappointment; this is indicated by the Sun being in aspect to Mars; she will meet with another serious disappointment at 21; that gentleman may die and cause her much unhappiness, she is almost certain to marry when 23. I may refer to this matter again in the "various contingencies and events of life."

13th.—*Children.*

This horoscope is unfortunate for children, and she will only have a small family; it is extremely doubtful about her having more than one or two children, or three at the most, and the probabilities are, that she may not have any to live to maturity. Jupiter lord of the 5th house and also lord of the 8th (an evil house), and in square to the Moon, her co-significator, and the Moon is afflicted in the sign Scorpio (which governs the lower part of the body), also Saturn lord of an intercepted sign in the 5th house is in square to Mars, which will cause her to suffer in health when carrying children, and also cause miscarriages, as Virgo rules the abdomen. Should she have any children to grow up, they will be a world of sorrow and trouble to her.

14th.—*Health.*

This lady will generally enjoy fair health, but will at times have severe attacks of sickness, especially during gestation, on account of Saturn being in square to Mars in Virgo; and the Moon in Scorpio in square to Jupiter; but the "giver of life" unafflicted, indicates that she has a good constitution, and will readily recover from sickness, or at least will not remain sick for a long period at one time.

15th.—*The Various Contingencies and Events of Life.*

These are judged, first, by examining closely all the positions of the planets in the horoscope, and seeing which evil aspects will have the most effect in the person's life and on their constitution, and also seeing what fortunate aspects we can rely on to benefit the native in the different periods of her life.

There are three kinds of aspects or *directions*, as they are sometimes called, which control the various events of a person's life. The first are the transits, the second are secondary directions, and the third are the primary directions. The planets Saturn and Jupiter are the main planets to rely on for transits in most horoscopes, and especially when Saturn is afflicted by an evil aspect of an another planet, and when that other planet is an unfortunate planet, as it is in the horoscope of Mrs. Maud S.'s daughter. She has Saturn in the midheaven in square to Mars, on the cusp of the 2d house; therefore, Saturn in passing around the heavens in its revolutions, will every $7\frac{1}{2}$ years form an evil aspect to its own place and to Mars' place. Saturn takes 29 and nearly one-half years to make one revolution around the heavens. Therefore, when she is $7\frac{1}{2}$ years of age, it will be in conjuction with Mars' place and in square to its own place; at $14\frac{1}{2}$, it will be in opposition to its own place and in square to Mars' place; at 22, it will be in square to its own place and in opposition to Mars' place; at $29\frac{1}{2}$ years it will be transiting over its own place, and also in the midheaven and in square again to Mars' place; at the same time forming evil aspects to all the four angles of the horoscope, which is equivalent to striking four blows at one time, and as it will be in conjunction with Mars and afflicting the ascendant, in opposition to the 7th house, and in square to the midheaven and the 4th house; therefore, besides afflicting Mars' place and in square to its own place, it is afflicting all four angles of the horoscope at the same time. These are termed very evil aspects.

The effect of these transits as they are termed, and also their influence on the native's life and health, are beyond our power to explain. Although all these planets and the Sun and Moon, at 7 years of age will be millions and millions of miles away from the positions they were in when Mrs. Maud S.'s daughter was born; yet whenever those planets in their revolutions come in evil aspect to the radical places of those planets, she is *bound to feel their evil influence in some way*, especially if there are no good aspects of fortunate planets in operation at the same time.

Sometimes an evil direction or transit of Saturn will cause the native to be very ill; at another time will cause an accident; at another time a near relation or parent will be very sick or die; another time losses in money matters; another time it may bring lawsuits, domestic unhappiness, quarrels with relations or separation of man and wife.

Saturn afflicting its own place and Mars' place, when it forms those evil aspects, will also in a short time after each of those periods afflict Mercury's and Uranus' places, every $7\frac{1}{2}$ years, and also what is termed the "Part of Fortune," which influences her money matters; as the planet Uranus is afflicting the 2d house, and is in square to the "Part of Fortune," on the cusp of the 5th house, and is also in square to Mercury in the 11th house (the house of friends).

In addition to those evil influences which Saturn causes every $7\frac{1}{2}$ years during its revolution around the heavens, there will be evil aspects to other planets which it will form; for instance, it will make a conjunction of Jupiter's place in the 12th house (the house of sorrow), and be in square to the Moon, the co-significator, when she is $4\frac{1}{2}$ years old, and then every $7\frac{1}{2}$ years after that age, it will form the conjunction, square and opposition of those places again. For instance, at 12, $19\frac{1}{2}$, 27 and so on, as long as she lives.

In addition to the evil aspects of Saturn to those various planets mentioned above, we shall have to notice particularly in this horoscope, the evil aspects of Mars to its own radical place and to the various other planets, in its revolutions around the heavens, on account of it being in evil aspect to Saturn in the midheaven at birth, and on account of Mars afflicting the 2d house. For instance, Mars came to a square of its own place on September 12, 1896, and to a conjunction of Saturn's place on September 17th, and then to an opposition of "Part of Fortune" on October 1st, a square of Uranus' place on October 5th, and a conjunction of Mercury's place on October 20th, and it continued near a conjunction of Mercury's place until November 13th. It turned retrograde on November 3d, and really continued to afflict all those positions of the planets until March 20, 1897. During all this time, if she had been a woman, she would have had serious mental trouble, losses of money, and treachery of false friends, or some kind of evil reports circulated; but as she is only a girl of about 12 years old at this time, it is more than likely that her parents might have had much trouble and worry. Also, if Uranus or Neptune afflicts any of those places of the planets at the time of birth, she is bound to feel the evil effects, and even if Jupiter remains any length of time (on account of its retrograde motion), in evil aspect to the Moon's or its own place, she will feel the evil influence.

This young lady's good fortune will be caused chiefly by the good aspects of Jupiter, Venus and the Sun, on account of those planets all rising, and also by Neptune in the midheaven being in good aspect to Venus and Uranus. To calculate those directions and transits all out, would take up too much space in this volume, therefore, I leave it for the young student to practice on.

The student should bear in mind that Jupiter takes nearly 12 years to go around the heavens; therefore, when she is one year and three months old, it was in conjunction, which is a good aspect, to the Sun's place, which would be a benefit; and within a few months afterward it was in conjunction with Mars' place. Uranus takes 84 years to go around the heavens, and 7 years to travel through one sign. Neptune takes about 160 years to go around the heavens, or 14 years to travel through one sign.

Besides the revolutions of the planets, we also notice what are termed the Secondary Directions; these are the aspects which the Sun and Moon and planets form with each other; and each day after birth is reckoned a year in time of the native's life. For instance, on July 6, 1884, or four days after the child's birth, Mars came to a square of Saturn's place, therefore, at 4 years of age, it was a very evil time for that child, especially in regard to sickness, and also evil to the father, as Saturn always indicates the father. On July 7, 1884, the Sun came to a sextile aspect of Mars by secondary direction, and, therefore, at 5 years of age it would be a fortunate period for that child; its health would be good, and something favorable would occur for its parents, particularly the father, as the Sun also indicates the father in a child's horoscope, and so on for the other planets. In addition to those aspects, there are what are termed Primary Directions, which we have to notice. These are reckoned by every degree in the longitude of the planets, as being equal to one year in the child's life. For instance, Uranus is 4 degrees from a square of Mercury's place, therefore, at 4 years of age it would be an evil period for the child, and there being an evil secondary direction that came up for that year, it would intensify that secondary evil direction. Those primary directions are reckoned both by what are termed Direct, and also what are termed Converse Directions, that is, they are both noticed when the planets are applying to the aspect, and also when they are leaving any aspect. For instance, Jupiter is one degree past a square of the Moon, and by converse directions, it would be an evil period for the child at one year of age, as Jupiter will come to a square of the Moon, the co-significator, by converse directions, it being very near one degree from that aspect.

Besides those unfavorable periods mentioned on page 39, I will mention that at 19 years of age, ♄ will be transiting in her 6th house in square to the moon and in opposition to Jupiter; it will produce poor health for herself, sickness or death for her mother or for some female relation; also, as ♂ is in aspect to the Sun at birth, she will have some serious unhappiness in love affairs at that time, as 19 years is what is termed the period of ♂. (I shall refer to these periods further on in this volume.) She will also have another unhappy time at 21, and another serious unpleasantness in love matters, very likely some disaster in her money affairs, or may meet with very heavy losses, or serious law trouble that will threaten poverty, and possibly death of an old relation or a near friend. It will be a very unfavorable time for her to marry then, and the marriage would bring her much unhappiness. This is shown by ♄ coming to a square of its own place, in opposition to ♂, and then in oppoition to ♅ and to a square of ⊕. If she takes a long voyage, she will suffer from stormy weather and be threatened with shipwreck or some serious disaster. At 27 years of age ♄ will be transiting near the midheaven in opposition to the Moon, and in square to ♃. This period will bring poor health and much unhappiness, and if married, domestic unhappiness and great danger of separation. Marked evil periods at 29 and 30, as ♄ will then be transiting over its own place in the midheaven, in square to ♂ on the cusp of the 2d, and also coming to a square of ♅ in the 2d (the house of money), and in opposition to ⊕. This will be the most disastrous period she will have until she gets to be near 59 years old; during this period her health will be poor, sickness, if not death in her family, heavy losses, and much domestic unhappiness, probably connected with a lawsuit, or might be a divorce, if married, she is almost certain to be parted in some way from her husband.

In addition to transits, primary and secondary directions, there are what are termed parallels, that is, when two planets have the same declinations, it is called a parallel, the same as if one planet has the same declination of either the Sun or the Moon. These parallels are like conjunctions, that is, they are good with the good planets, and evil with the evil ones. In some horoscopes these declinations or parallels have a marked influence on the native's life, but when the declinations are not within orbs at birth, they do not have much influence in that particular nativity. In the horoscope of Mrs. Maud S.'s daughter, Jupiter was 18 degrees and 56 minutes in north declination on July 2, 1884, and Venus was also 18 degrees and 28 minutes in north declination; therefore, we call that a very close parallel, and they being the two most fortunate planets that are known, they would have a marked influence on the native's life, in producing good friends, especially female friends who would be of great benefit to her. These parallels would make this young lady much more sociable, pleasant, and agreeable in her manners than she would have been, if Jupiter and Venus had been wide apart in their declinations at her birth. The parallel is much stronger when both the planets have north declinations, or when both have south declinations, but even if one planet is north and the other is near the number of degrees and minutes south declination, it is still called a parallel; but it is not as strong as when both planets have north or both south declinations. The most evil parallels are Saturn and Mars, and when they have near the same declinations at birth, it makes much unhappiness for the native all through life, and their influence would be similar to a conjunction of these two evil planets. In this horoscope, the declinations of Saturn and Mars are over 5 degrees apart. Saturn 1 degree and 24 minutes south, and Mars is 6 degrees and 50 minutes north; therefore, they are not in what are termed orbs, and they have but little influence in this child's horoscope.

In the second volume of this work, I shall give special direction by the rules of Trigonometry and Logarithms, how to calculate what are termed the primary directions, parallels, etc.

The remainder of the transits and aspects in the horoscope of Mrs. Maud S.'s daughter, that I have mentioned on page 39, I leave the student to try and trace out himself by the rules already given, as I think it will be good practice for him.

I will conclude this horoscope by mentioning a curious circumstance which occurred lately at Scranton, Pa., and which was told to me by Mr. E. T. Sweet, the night editor of the Scranton Tribune. He said: "They wrote up and published in their paper a number of fictitious horoscopes of leading politicians of their town, and associated them with those individuals' time of birth." These horoscopes attracted much attention, and were read extensively, but in order that the writer might become familiar with certain Astrological names, or what are called technical terms, he borrowed Lilly's Astrology, by Zadkiel, out of the Public Library, and commenced reading the book with that object in view, never dreaming that there was any truth in the science; but as he went on reading, he began to find out that Astrology was a true science and instead of "concocting horoscopes," as the editor of the *New York Times* calls it, he commenced to study Astrology in a systematic manner, and wrote to me to procure for him a number of Astrological books, in addition to those I had already published. I cannot but think, that if the editor of the *New York Times* was to commence studying Astrology, he would soon find that what he called a "debasing superstition," was, in reality, one of the most beneficial and useful sciences that is known to man, and that he was speaking a greater truth than he was aware of in regard to himself, and other christian editors, when writing about the "mournful incompleteness of modern civilization and education."

I have gone more into particulars in the foregoing horoscope than I had intended, and it is much longer than any others in the following pages; but as the editor of the *New York Times* appeared to think there was nothing whatever in Astrology, only what the Astrologer concocts, I thought it best to give a few of the principles and rules that Astrologers go by in calculating horoscopes. And should Mrs. Maud S. ever read this horoscope of her daughter, I cannot but think that she will admit that every paragraph that I have published is absolutely correct, and that if she follows the directions and advice herein given, it may save her daughter and herself much unhappiness, if not disgrace. Although in some respects her daughter's horoscope is somewhat marked, yet those evil influences pointed in the girl's nativity are not entirely inevitable, as those directions and aspects were in the horoscope of Charles Dryden, as calculated by his father.

We sometimes meet with horoscopes where the position of the planets in relation to each other, or what are termed aspects, are so striking or marked that the native becomes almost like inert matter, that is, entirely controlled by natural laws, or like a cork on water subject to the wind and tides, and has no will of his own. In such cases, the rules and principles of Astrology become like the laws of the Medes and Persians, which cannot be altered.

I cannot impress too strongly on the mind of the student the importance of being familiar with the nature and description of the houses, signs and planets, and their relation to each other. If he has all these well impressed upon his mind, he will find his work comparatively easy in studying Astrology. At first he will find some difficulty in tracing the transits or revolutions of the planets through the signs of the Zodiac, and through the different houses, especially to the angles; and also to the aspects and conjunctions of the radical positions of the Sun, Moon and planets at birth; and, at the same time, calculate the secondary directions, also the primary directions, and combine the whole; predicting correctly their effects on the events and contingencies of the native's life. In addition to the above, he will have to know how to calculate Revolutions. This is done by first calculating the exact degree, minute and second that the Sun was in at birth; then calculate when it arrives in any particular year, in the same sign, and the same degree, minute and second; then erect a chart of the heavens for that time; that is called the Revolution for that year.

If the student does not become familiar with all the elements of the science, he is very similar to a person making calculations in arithmetic who has not become familiar with the elementary branch of that science.

For instance, if he wanted to multiply a row of figures by any particular number, and every time he attempted to multiply a figure by another figure, he had to commence with the multiplication table—twice 1 is 2, twice 2 is 4, until he arrived at the multiplication of those two particular figures, he would be a long time getting through, and the chances are that it would not be correct, even after he thought he had completed the example.

I once heard of a woman who received a love-letter when a girl, and she preserved it until she was over 70 years old, and it became yellow with age, and soiled with handling, still she would put on her spectacles and read it, and commence, " M-y, my ; d-e-a-r, dear, My dear, l-o-v-e, love, My dear love," and so she kept on until she got through the whole letter, and never learned to read it right along. Had this woman learned to spell, read and write properly when she was young, she would have then commenced reading and gone right on without any hesitation until she got to the end ; and would have read it with more satisfaction, than having to spell each word and repeat each word and sentence. So any person who learns the elements of Astrology properly, that is, the nature of the houses, the signs, the planets, and the aspects, will commence reading a horoscope with the same facility that a person reads a page in a book in a known language; not only that, but if he knows absolutely that the time of birth is correct, or that the time he has set a horoscope for, on special business, is the correct time, he knows then that what he is reading will be all true and correct, as the planets do not lie—whereas the page in the book might be all fiction or untruths from beginning to end.

As the student progresses, he will be astonished at the exact truth and correctness of Astrology, and wonder how the ancients could have collected so many facts and rules, especially when he comes across horoscopes that are not what is termed complicated. For instance, a horoscope of a person born under Jupiter in Saggittary, with Jupiter and the Moon both in the same sign in the ascendant, and not in aspect to any other planet, or any other planet aspecting the ascendant. When the student meets with a horoscope of that kind, he not only can describe that person accurately, either verbally or in writing; but if the student is anything of an artist, he can draw almost an exact picture of that person; describe how he will look when a young man at the age of 24 ; give the color of the hair and eyes, or any particular striking features, and the height and build, even before the native is a month old ; not only that, but he can give a correct description of the lady that he will marry, or whether they will live happy or unhappy, also the kind of business that he would succeed in. and the various talents and inclinations ; his disposition and temper, the special diseases that he will be liable to ; length of life, and manner of death, etc.

But in those horoscopes where what is termed the lord of the ascendant is in a tall, light sign. and the sign ascending is a stout, dark sign; and the Moon in a tall, light sign, it is much more difficult to become familiar with all these variations. But by constant study, he will be able to describe a person under such conflicting testimonies; but it cannot be done without a great deal of practical experience in the science.

But the first thing to be done, and which is very important, is that the student should always find the correct positions of the signs of the Zodiac, and calculate the longitude of the planets correctly, and never make a mistake; because if he should have the position of the planets wrong in a horoscope, it is impossible for him to proceed without committing errors. The student must know already that it takes considerable knowledge to even calculate a map of the heavens correctly. Mr. Charles A. Dana, editor of the *New York Sun*, advises all his readers never to pay an Astrologer more than 25 cents, for reading or writing a nativity. The reader must see that it is worth 25 cents to calculate the horoscope, without reading or writing the same; and the question is, would Charles A. Dana like to give up his position as editor of the New York Sun to calculate horoscopes and write them at 25 cents each.

It is evident that Charles A. Dana looks on Astrology in the same light as the editor of the *New York Times*. It is strange that such men who are generally well informed in many respects (indeed if they were not, they could not hold their positions), look on every kind of learning which they do not understand, or was not taught them in college, as "debasing superstition," and all those persons who do not think and believe as they do, they regard as "ignorant and superstitious," and they bewail the "mournful incompleteness of modern civilization and education," and think those persons' knowledge and learning to be entirely harmful in their influence on the rising generation, and that any person practicing or teaching those sciences should be subject to all kinds of persecution, and the public should be taught to rob and injure them all they possibly can. Even ministers of the gospel, judges and legislators, entertain similar ideas.

As the student advances in the noble science of Astrology, he will gradually begin to find that those persons who stood so high as learned and scientific men in his estimation, will be gradually lowered from their high pinnacle of scientific attainments, and the public will no longer send "strange problems" to be "confidentially propounded" by those "journalists," especially when the readers find that the editors themselves do not know half as much on the subject as the reader himself. See p. 47c.

The next horoscope is that of the Chinese Consul's Son, referred to on page 35. I insert this on account of it being especially good for first marriage, but it is also good for several marriages in succession, if he is so disposed. Some of my readers may think that I picked this out of several thousand Chinese times of birth, but this is the only one I had; so I had "Hobson's Choice." I insert it to show the effect that Astrology has produced in the nativities of successive generations by comparing horoscopes before marriage.

The one following is Queen Victoria's. She has no patience with a divorced woman, and it is said she will not receive one at Court. No doubt she thinks it is every married woman's own fault if they do not have the Sun apply to a good aspect of the planet Jupiter, in its own sign and lord of the 7th house (the house of marriage) as she has. I shall endeavor, as I proceed, to make every horoscope either "point a moral or adorn a tale."

HOROSCOPE OF THE CHINESE CONSUL'S SON.

He was born July 25, 1895, at 1 A. M., No. 26 West 9th Street, New York City. See pages 35 and 36 of this volume.

To calculate this child's horoscope, the student will require Raphael's Ephemeris for 1895, and he will see in the Ephemeris for July of that year, in the 3d column the heading "Sidereal Time," and on a line with the 25th day, 8 hours 11 minutes and 47 seconds. If he adds 12 hours from noon of the previous day up to 12 o'clock night, and then 1 hour for 1 o'clock in the morning, he will find that it amounts to 21 hours and nearly 12 minutes. If he looks in the Table of Houses for New York City, he will find under the heading "Sidereal Time," the nearest figures to that amount is, 21 hours 13 minutes and 52 seconds, and on a line with that number in the Table of Houses, he will find the various signs to be written on the 10th, 11th, 12th, and the ascendant or 1st house, the 2d and 3d houses, which he will copy in the blank chart, with their degrees and minutes along side, and then copy the opposite signs which are shown on page 143. He will also copy the degrees and minutes which are along side the northern signs in the chart.

Then the student will commence to insert what are called the planets' places; and he will find that 1 o'clock in the morning is just 6 hours before 7 o'clock; therefore, he will deduct one-fourth of the degrees or minutes from what are marked in the Ephemeris on the 25th, which the planets have traveled from the 24th to the 25th at 7 o'clock in the morning, and the remainder is the positions of the planets in the signs and houses. In the horoscope he will also insert the ☽'s (North) Node (☊), which he will find on the 2d page of the Ephemeris near the top on the right hand, and the ☽'s (South) Node (☋) he will place in the opposite sign, giving it the same degrees and minutes.

After the student has calculated the longitude of all the planets, and written them in the blank chart, then he will proceed to calculate the "Part of Fortune" (⊕). (See 292–293.) This is done by adding the longitude of the ascendant to the longitude of the Moon, and then from that subtract the longitude of the Sun, and the remainder is the longitude of the "Part of Fortune" (⊕).

In making these calculation, we always count from the beginning of the sign ♈, and when we insert ⊕ in its proper place in the horoscope, we also count from the beginning of the sign ♈. In this horoscope ♈ is on the cusp of the 12th house, and ♉ is intercepted in the 12th house, this makes the ascendant 2 signs, 9 degrees and 23 minutes If we count again from ♈ to the sign next to the one that the Moon is in, we shall find it to be 5 signs, and the Moon is 14 degrees and 25 minutes in the 6th sign:

Ascendant,	2 signs,	9 degrees,	23 minutes,
Moon,	5 "	14 "	25 "
Add	7 "	23 "	48 "

Again, if the student counts from ♈ next to the sign that the Sun is in, he will find it is 4 signs; and the Sun is 2 degrees and 0 minutes in the 5th sign; if he subtracts 4 signs 2 degrees and 0 minutes from 7 signs 23 degrees and 48 minutes, he will find the following result:

	7 signs,	23 degrees,	48 minutes,
Subtract	4 "	02 "	00 "
	3 "	21 "	48 "

He will find that ⊕ is 3 signs 21 minutes and 48 seconds, and if he counts from the beginning of ♈ to the end of the sign ♊, he will find that it is 3 whole signs, therefore, the ⊕ is 21 degrees and 48 minutes in the 4th sign, which is ♋, and near the cusp of the 3d house.*

The following chart is a map of the heavens for the time of birth of the Chinese Consul's Son, born July 25, 1895, 1 A. M., New York City.

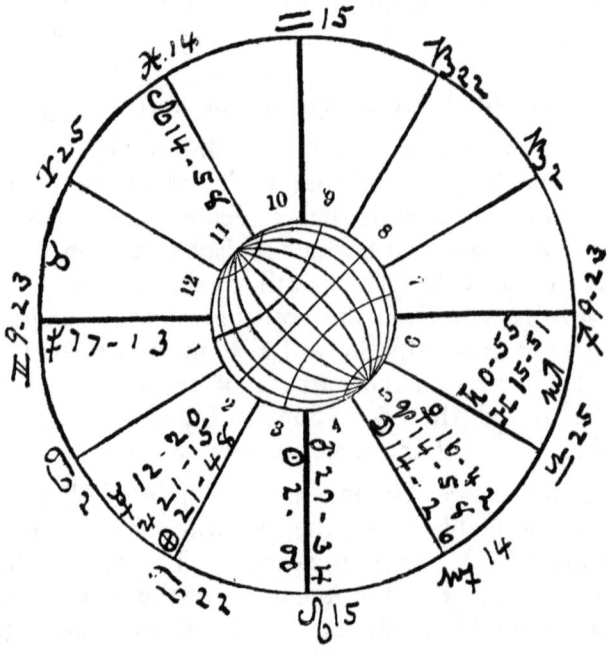

* In this volume I shall avoid, if possible, entering into any discussions or arguments with other Astrologers, or taking sides with those who differ among themselves, and will only train my guns on the public enemies of Astrology. I shall be the last one to discharge any ammunition on the professors of this science. But there is one part of Astrology which is technically called the "Part of Fortune," and which has been a bone of contention among Astrologers for hundreds, if not thousands, of years, that I cannot pass without giving to it a few words of explanation, and seeing if I can reconcile those differences of opinion on that point.

Mr. James Wilson in his "Astrological Dictionary," calls the "Part of Fortune" a "bunch of nothing hatched in the brain of Claudius Ptolemy," and he goes on to ridicule the idea with much sarcasm. But other Astrologers, such as Sibley, and several others whose names I have forgotten, attach much importance to the "Part of Fortune," and regard it and its influence very much in a similar light to what we regard the influence of what are termed the seven planets. They not only attribute to its good or evil influence (according to its aspects) of the native's financial affairs, or what is termed money matters, but they also give it the power to determine the length of life of the native, the same as the Sun or Moon, when either of them are "Hyleg," or when these luminaries are not posited in the "Hylegical Places," and the Part of Fortune happens to be so posited that is from 5 degrees above the cusp of the ascendant to 25 degrees below; or from 5 degrees below the cusp of the 7th house to 25 degrees above, and from 5 degrees below the cusp of the 9th house to 25 degrees below the cusp of the 11th house.

[I wish to inform the student that I have written this horoscope without once referring to the text books giving the rules and principles of Astrology. Similar to writing a letter without referring to the dictionary to see whether I have spelled each and every word correctly, or whether I have expressed the exact meaning of each and every word which I have made use of in writing the letter. It is advisable that the student become equally familiar with the principles and rules of this fascinating science, so that he can adopt the same method in reading a horoscope, and scarcely ever make a mistake, unless he happens to come across a nativity where the position of the planets and signs of the Zodiac are such that he has never seen anything like them before. In that case, he will then have to refer to the rules and principles of Astrology that have been laid down in the numerous text books that have been published on this science; as he might refer to an English dictionary to find the exact spelling or meaning of a word that he had never met with.]

This child was born under the planet Mercury (☿), in the sign ♋ (131), just commencing to rise, in sextile to the Moon (247) and the planet ♀ (244), both in the sign ♍ (121–145) in the 5th house, and also in trine to ♅ (209) in the sign ♏, in the 6th house, with ♊ (15) and ♆ on the ascendant. All the planets are under the earth, which causes it to be a weak horoscope, both for health, life, and arriving at prominence.

If the Part of Fortune should happen to be in any of these positions above-named, and neither the Sun or the Moon are in these places, they say that in these cases the Part of Fortune is Hyleg or the "Giver of Life," and these Astrologers have given a number of illustrations of horoscopes to prove their assertion. I must say that I disagree with these Astrologers, and believe, from my own experience, that the Part of Fortune has only reference to the native's money matters or his financial standing. In all horoscopes which I have carefully examined whenever the Part of Fortune has been much afflicted by the conjunctions or evil aspects of the unfortunate planets, although the native may be wealthy in the common sense of the term, yet he is generally very hard up for ready cash, and often meets with serious disaster or misfortune on account of not being able to command money on short notice. But when the Part of Fortune is in good aspect to fortunate planets and in what are termed good houses in the native's horoscope, I have found that he generally keeps in easy circumstances, and has a comfortable income, and is enabled to pay his debts. If the Part of Fortune is very much afflicted by evil planets, or on the contrary it is in good aspects with the fortunate planets, and also in fortunate houses, these conditions of the native's money matters may have much influence on the native's life, and in some cases when very much afflicted, may have a tendency to shorten it. It should always be borne in mind, that when the native is young or in infancy, these evil aspects to his money matters generally fall on the parents or guardians, and so afflict the native indirectly.

When the Part of Fortune is in cadent houses and has no aspects to any particular planet, either good or bad, I find that it is not worth while taking any notice of it, as in these instances it has very little influence in the condition of the native's life, or even in his money matters or worldly circumstances.

It is only these persons who have had but little experience or practice in Astrology who wish to discard entirely the Part of Fortune. Although in some horoscopes it has but little influence, yet the student will find in others that it has a very great influence on the native's money affairs. I sincerely hope that the student will find in his own horoscope that the Part of Fortune is either in the ascendant, 2d, 11th, midheaven, 7th or 5th houses, and that it is in good aspect to Jupiter, Venus, the Sun and Moon. If such is the case, he will certainly find his path through life very much smoother and happier than the majority.

In the horoscope of the daughter of Mrs. Maud S., her Part of Fortune is very much afflicted by an opposition of Mercury, and a square of Uranus, and she will certainly feel the effect of these afflictions all through life. In the horoscope of the Chinese Consul's Son, the Part of Fortune is in conjunction with the planet Jupiter, in the sign Cancer, and Jupiter is in its exaltation; also the Moon disposes of the Part of Fortune; and the Moon is in conjunction with Venus, and both are in good aspect to Mercury, Jupiter and the Part of Fortune. We say in this case that the Part of Fortune is very strong, and well dignified by having so many good aspects, even if cadent.

The Part of Fortune is a point which is the same distance from the ascendant that the Moon is from the Sun, and it is called the luminary to the ascendant. It is always under the earth, from New Moon to Full Moon, and above the earth from Full Moon to New Moon again.

Those positions of the planets will describe a person near or above the medium height, stands about 5 feet 7 or 8 inches; rather well built, but will never become stout, and will be rather slender during his early years; have a rather thin or oval face, slightly high forehead; sharp nose, small, dark eyes; dark brown or black hair, and rather dark or muddy complexion. He will not be handsome, but will be rather good looking, somewhat prepossessing and talkative. The rules of Astrology say (131): "He will be deceitful, changeable, and at times ill-natured and dishonest." But ☿ in close sextile to the Moon (247) and ♀ (244) improves his disposition, and makes the native have a refined and accomplished mind; will be neat in his person and elegant in manners; a lover of music and the fine arts; ingenious, subtle, easily learning anything to which he applies his mind; inclined to be reserved, but on account of his extensive acquirements, he will be a pleasant companion.

Health and Life.

He has a rather good constitution, but will never be strong or robust, as the ascendant is the "Giver of Life" (see page 157), and his planet ☿ is in a weak sign (16); still there is a chance of his living to be rather old, but not to a great age, as the evil planet ♄ is in the 6th house (6) (the house of sickness), and in the sign ♏ (20), and in square to the Sun. This aspect will make him liable to weakness of the kidneys, bladder, and lower part of the body, and also palpitation of the heart, on account of the Sun being in ♌, which governs the heart, and he will be liable to derangement of the stomach and liver, and nervousness on account of ☿, which rules the nervous system, being weak in the sign ♋, which sign rules the stomach and liver.

Riches and Poverty.

This native will never be in very low circumstances, but will always be rather well to do, and have wealthy relations, as ♃ is on the cusp of the 3d house, near a sextile of the ☽ and ♀ (231–227) in the 5th house, and both in sextile to the native's planet ☿, in the 2d house (the house of money). He will be fortunate with speculation, and any property and stocks, or values he may possess, is likely to advance.

Trade and Profession.

This native will never work for his living, and doubtful about his learning any particular trade. He would be very successful as a musician, actor (245 and 199), or being connected with places of amusement or entertainments, on account of the 5th house being so well aspected and fortified by fortunate planets. He would also be fortunate in any kind of traveling, or being engaged on railroads, or being a traveling agent, or in any business that cause him to take short journeys; as the ☽, lady of the 3d house, is in good aspect to ☿, ♃ and the Part of Fortune (⊕), in the 3d house, and the ☽ in ☌ with ♀ in the 5th house. He would also be successful in keeping a store, especially selling anything appertaining to women's apparel, such as silks, satins, fancy articles, or jewelry, on account of the ☌ of ♀ and ☽, and both in ✶ to ☿. He would be fortunate as a stock broker, especially railway stocks, and, in that respect, might become very wealthy. He would be unfortunate in keeping a boarding-house, practicing law, or being a minister, as ♄ is lord of the 9th house, afflicting the 6th house, and in □ to the ☉; also unfortunate in taking long journeys, or in lawsuits.

Friends and Enemies.

He will be very fortunate with friends, they will be of benefit to him, especially near relations, as ♃ lord of the 11th house is in his exaltation on the cusp of the 3d house in ☌ with ⊕, and in good aspect to ♀ and also ☽ is lady of the 3d house. He will scarcely ever have any poor relations, or persons that he will have to assist. He will have very few secret or public enemies, as ♀ is lady of an intercepted sign ♉ in the 11th house in ☌ with the ☽. Would be unfortunate with servants, especially elderly or poor people, and also unfortunate with small animals, as the 6th house is afflicted by ♄ in □ to ☉.

Marriage and Children.

He will be fortunate in marriage, and will live happy ; but previous to marriage, he will have two or more disappointments in love affairs; one is indicated by a lady described by the planet ☿ in ♋ (131), as the ☽ is leaving a ✶ of ☿ (303), and the other by a lady described by the planet ♅ in ♏ (63). The first will be similar in appearance to himself, but not so tall or heavily built and lighter complexioned. The second will be rather thick-set, dark complexion, broad face and forehead, and older than himself. He marries a person indicated by the planet ♀ in ♍ (121). She will be nearly as tall as himself, slender build, have an oval face, round forehead, slightly dark complexion, with clear skin, and dark or black hair. She will be very prepossessing and agreeable in manners, polite and accomplished. She will also be ingenious, active, eloquent, and aspiring, as ♀ is in ☌ with ☽ (198), and both in ✶ to ☿ (243 and 244). They will live very happily (300). Should he take a second wife (306), it will be very fortunate, and they will live happily. She is described by the planet ♃ in ♋ (83) She will not be near as tall as the first one, and will be slightly full built, rather pale skin, dark brown hair, rather plump, or round build, high forehead, and slightly full face, and prominent eyes. She will be very agreeable, wealthy, and most likely a realative, as ♃ is in the 3d house (the house of relatives).

His wives are very likely to have six or more children, as his horoscope is very fortunate for children, especially as ☿, lord of the 5th house, is in a fruitful sign, and the ☽ and ♀ are both in the 5th house, in good aspect to ☿, his ruling planet. His children will be very fortunate, and arrive at eminence. They are more likely to be girls than boys, on account of two feminine planets being in the 5th house (the house of children). He will probably marry when about 22 years of age, if not, then at 26, but it is more likely that he will be married a second time, when he is 26, as it is customary in China for the wealthy to have more than one wife.

Fortunate and Unfortunate Periods, or the Various Contingencies and Events of Life.

In addition to learning what to rely on in describing the native, and also to find out the mental qualities, or the profession, trade, business or occupation that a person is best adapted for, together with the description of friends or enemies, or whether fortunate or unfortunate marriage, and description of the person that the native will marry, etc. The student must acquire the habit of instantly finding out in particular horoscopes, what kind of aspects or directions he can rely on, which causes the various contingencies and events in that person's life. He will find by practice and constant observation, that there are certain aspects in certain particular horoscopes, that he can always rely on in causing these changes or events, and which will have a marked effect in different periods of that person's life.

310 If a number of the superior planets are in square or opposition to each other, especially Mars, Saturn and Uranus, and particularly if the Sun and Moon are in square or opposition; the student can always depend on what is called the transits for producing the unfortunate events in that person's life.

311 When the superior planets, and particularly the Sun and Moon, and Jupiter and Venus are in trine or sextile to each other, the student can always depend upon the transits of Jupiter, and sometimes even of Venus or the Sun for producing marked fortunate periods of that person's life.

312 If, at any time, in a horoscope of that kind, when a fortunate transit occurs of Jupiter, and an evil aspect of Saturn or Mars occur near the same time, it is very difficult to tell which will have the preponderance, but generally in such cases, if there are two good ones to one evil one, then the good influence will predominate, but if there are two evil ones to one good one, and particularly if these evil ones are either Saturn or Uranus, then you can depend upon the evil one predominating at that particular period of the native's life, and he will be afflicted by some particular evil, although sweetened by some slight favorable event.

313 When there is no particular aspect, either sextile, trine, square, conjunction or opposition in the native's horoscope, then the secondary directions have the most influence in causing the various events in the different periods of the native's life, either good or evil.

314 When a number of superior planets at a time of birth are applying by aspect to either a square, opposition, sextile,

trine or conjunction, then the primary directions have generally the most marked influence on that native's life.

315 But when the aspects of sextile, trine, conjunction, square or opposition are past, at the time of birth, the primary directions, have but little influences in that particular horoscope, or on the native's life.

316 The student must always bear in mind that Jupiter takes very near 12 years to go around the heavens, or one year to transit through one sign; therefore, these aspects, either good or evil, reckoned by the transits can easily be calculated, either to the angles or to particular planets; the aspects to the Sun and Moon are particularly to be noticed.

317 Saturn takes a little over $29\frac{1}{2}$ years to go around the heavens, or $2\frac{1}{2}$ years to transit through one sign, and the conjunctions, squares or opposition of Saturn must generally be noticed; the trine or sextile aspects of Saturn have but little effect; but sometimes they will bring marked good, especially if the nativity indicates benefit by wills or legacies.

318 Mars takes 1 year and 10 months to go around the heavens, or it averages over 7 weeks to transit through one sign. Uranus takes 84 years to go around the heavens, or 7 years to transit through one sign. Neptune takes nearly 14 years to transit through one sign.

319 The transit of Venus, Mercury and the Moon can scarcely be noticed in a horoscope for either good or evil, but the transits of the Sun are very often important, especially if the native has the Sun in good aspect to Jupiter, Venus or the Moon in the midheaven or ascendant, then near the birth-day it generally brings some good fortune to the native. For instance, I have the Sun in the midheaven at birth; when ever the Sun comes around to its own place, unless some prominent evil aspects are in operation at the time, it generally brings me some slight good fortune.

320 Primary directions are aspects which occur either before or after birth, and the number of degrees that the planets have to go in order to form the aspects, correspond with the same number of years of the native's life. These directions which occur after birth, are termed direct directions, and those which occured before birth, and when calculated backwards, are called converse directions. When a planet is in a sign of short ascension, when making an aspect either direct or converse, we must reckon a little less than a year in time for a degree in longitude, and when a planet is in a sign of long ascension we reckon a littlet more than a year for a degree. It is easy to find or notice these

aspects within a few years after birth, but when the native gets beyond 60 or 70 years of age, it takes an experienced astrologer to pick these aspects out and calculate them correctly.

321 Secondary directions are those aspects which occur from day to day after birth, and each day is reckoned a year. For instance, the secondary directions for the *first year* are those aspects that occur in the horoscope in the first 24 hours of the native's life. The secondary directions for the *second year* occur in the horoscope in the second 24 hours of the native's life. In order to calculate them correctly, the student will find it easier to place the signs of the Zodiac in a blank chart the same as they were at birth, and place the original number of degrees and minutes along side of each sign the same as they were in the horoscope, and then calculate the position of the planets for that day, for the same hour and minute that the child was born, and place them on the chart the same as if the child had been born on the 2d or 3d day, etc. For example, the second year of the child's birth, he will calculate the position of the planets as they are 24 hours after birth, and place them in the chart. That is the secondary directions for the second year, and so on for the other days corresponding to the years all through life.

In the horoscope of the Chinese Consul's Son, the primary directions and the transits will have the most marked effect in the events of his life, on account of Saturn being so near a square of the Sun, and the Sun lord of the 4th house, and Saturn in the 6th; also Mars' primary directions or transits will have a marked effect on account of it being in an angle at birth. The transits of Jupiter will have the most marked effect for good in this horoscope, whenever it is either in conjunction, square, opposition, sextile or trine to its own place, it will form good aspects to Venus and the Moon, and, also, generally to the planet Uranus. At one year old this child would have severe attacks of sickness, as the Sun would come by converse direction to a square of Saturn, which is one degree apart, also Saturn would transit over Uranus' place at birth near that time, but at three years of age it would have a good transit of Jupiter in sextile to its own place and of Mercury's place (his own planet), also it would be transiting over the Moon's and Venus' places, and in good aspect to Uranus' place. Every 7 years this child will have an evil period, as it will always feel, in a marked degree, the square, opposition and conjunction of Saturn to its own place, and in this horoscope it would be in evil aspect to the Sun's place, and would soon afterwards form an evil aspect to Uranus' place and to a square of Mars' place. The most critical times for the native were when one year old, and again when 14 years old; in the latter case, Saturn will be in opposition to its own place and in square to the Sun's place, and the Sun will come by primary direction to a conjunction of Uranus' place; in the 6th house (the house of sickness), and **Saturn lord of the 9th house**, shows danger of death by a mistake of the doctor. I will leave the remainder of these aspects of the native's life to be calculated by the student, and would advise him to read over again the last paragraph on page 167, and the whole of page 168, and the first paragraph on page 169.

When giving judgment on a weak horoscope like the above, in order to assist the student to decide whether the child will live, Claudius Ptolemy tells us to procure the time of birth of both parents, and if they both have evil horoscopes for children, then, if the child has a weak horoscope, it generally dies; but if they both have good horoscopes for children, then that child with a weak horoscope generally lives, unless the horoscope is very weak or afflicted.

A SYNOPSIS OF MEDICAL ASTROLOGY.

In order to simplify the study of Astrology as much as possible, it was my original intention, when I laid out the plan of the parts of the *Elements of Astrology*, to have deferred mentioning, or in any way describing any of the ailments that the human system is subject to, until the latter part of the volume, where I intended bringing the whole subject of diseases or ailments caused by planatery influence to the attention of the student, but, at the same time, not with any intention of making doctors or practitioners of medicine of the student of Astrology. But if he had any knowledge of medicine or had attended a medical college, he would find Astrology, in that case, of infinite advantage in his practice of medicine.

As I progressed, I found it difficult to proceed without noticing, to some extent, the various ailments of the native, and impossible to describe them, without giving some general information and rules on the matter. Yet I shall enter more fully into Medical Astrology near the close of this volume. The most difficult part to overcome in this branch of Astrology is to modernize it, as there has been few, if any, works published for many years on that subject.

Some two or three hundred years ago, there were a great many books published by numerous authors, treating on this subject, and some of them were exceedingly good, and evinced an extensive knowledge of Medical Astrology, and such that I cannot help but believe that had the medical professors at the present day an equal knowledge, the death rate of the people would become encouragingly less within a few years. I have quite a number of these works in my library. But they are too voluminous to be made use of in a work of this kind, where I intend giving only an outline of Medical Astrology, and have no intention of writing specially for the medical profession only in an indirect manner.

Some twenty years ago, Prof. Draper, of New York, published a long article in *Harper's Magazine*, which was said to have been delivered as a lecture before the students of a popular medical college of New York City, in which he took special pains to ridicule Astrology in connection with medicine, and gave that lecture to convince the students what rapid strides the science and art of medicine had made within the last two hundred years. Of course he took it for granted that all the students he was lecturing to were equally as ignorant on the subject as himself, and had he not published the lecture in a popular periodical, it is possible that no further attention would have been given to the matter, but as he laid himself open to criticism by publishing the lecture, I think I ought not to let the matter pass without giving it some notice.

Had Prof. Draper, instead of ridiculing William Lilly's Astrology before his students, looked into almost any book on the sciences, arts or professions that were published two or three hundred years ago, he would not have found the subjects they treated of as perfect as we find them at the present day. Therefore, why did he single out Astrology as a target above all other sciences and hold it up to public ridicule? It is true, that the professors of Astrology were influenced or hampered by medical absurdities two or three hundred years ago, the same as the doctors are at the present day hampered by similar absurdities. If Prof. Draper had examined Astrology as taught and practiced in William Lilly's time, it would have compared very favorably with anatomy, physiology, chemistry, materia medica, surgery or obstetrics, as taught two or three hundred years ago.

If he had examined medical books in those days he would have found the authors writing about the wind in the veins and arteries, and other similar complaints and diseases, and remedies recommended for such diseases (indeed the word arteries is derived from the word air, as the doctors in those days believed that nothing but air circulated in the arteries). Chemists would have told him all about the division of the elements into four, earth, air, fire and water, and also into phlogistics and anti-phlogistics; besides numbers of other things too numerous to mention.

Even the Astrologers were hampered by the absurdities of the Astronomers, as in those days they nearly all believed that the earth was in the centre of the universe, and that the whole of the heavenly bodies revolved around it once in twenty-four hours, which caused day and night.

Indeed, if we except mathematics, architecture, sculpture and painting, all other sciences, arts or professions were in the same boat with Astrology. Only that the science of Astrology was much further advanced than any other of the sciences, arts or professions, if we except the few above-mentioned, as there had been much more attention and study devoted to it than any of the other sciences, by astrologers and physicians Therefore, had Prof. Draper wished to turn the medical college into a comic opera house for the amusement of his students almost any other science or profession that was in vogue or popular two or three hundred years ago, would have answered his purpose much better than that of Astrology. If he had looked into almost any medical or surgical book during the time of William Lily, he would have found material for laughter that would have far surpassed that in Lily's Astrology. But if he had wanted material connected with the practice of medicine to compose a farce or comic opera, he need not have gone so far back as the early part of the seventeenth century. Neither would he have had any occasion to go out of the United States for his material. Not one hundred years ago, he could have gone to Mount Vernon, Virginia (if the matter had not been too serious for jest), and have found all that he needed in the last sickness and death of General Washington, as published on page 349 in this volume.

It may be asked why has not Astrology advanced within the last two or three hundred years as the other sciences? We answer, it has advanced, and if it has not kept pace with the sciences above alluded to, the reason is that Astrology and Astrologers have endured more persecution than all the other sciences and professions combined. When the public became crazy on the subject of witch-craft, the professors of Astrology were classed with witches and wizards, and they had to endure similar persecution. They were betwixt the upper and nether mill stones, for if they predicted correctly they had dealings with the devil and were executed as witches, and if they were wrong in their predictions they were persecuted for being frauds. In short, they were betwixt the devil and the deep sea. Those persecutions are now dying out, and the people will see Astrology make as rapid advancement as any of the other sciences, as the public are waking up to the truth and importance of that science.

Parts of the Body Ruled by the 12 houses and the 12 signs of the Zodiac.

322 The 12 houses govern the various members of the body, the same as the 12 signs of the Zodiac govern them. The 1st house and ♈ govern the head; the 2d and ♉ the neck; the 3d and ♊ the shoulders, arms and hands; the 4th and ♋ the breast and stomach; the 5th and ♌ the heart and back; the 6th and ♍ the intestines, uterus and abdomen; the 7th and ♎ the lower part of the back, kidneys and bladder; the 8th and ♏ the generative organs, both male and female; the 9th and ♐ the hips and thighs; the 10th and ♑ the knees and legs; the 11th and ♒ the ankles and lower part of the legs, the 12th and ♓ the feet.

Diseases of ♈ when Afflicted by Evil Planets.

323 Denotes neuralgia of the head or face, headache, toothache, baldness, swelling or pimples on the face, small-pox, gumboils, hair-lip, polypus of the throat or ear, ringworm on the head, fits or apoplexy, and all injuries to the head or face.

Diseases of ♉, etc.

324 Sore throat, diphtheria, mumps, quinsy, abscesses in any part of the throat or neck, scrofula, especially when located in the neck, tumors, discharge of phlegm or rheums, inflammation of the throat or falling of the pallette, etc.

Diseases of ♊, etc.

325 Governs all diseases and accidents or infirmities of the arms, shoulders or hands, scrofula or impure blood, deranged imagination, and nervous diseases generally.

Diseases of ♋, etc.

326 It signifies imperfections or injuries of the breast, nipples or stomach, weak digestion and dyspepsia of all kinds, cosumption or phthisic, all coughs or colds, and what are termed stomach coughs; dropsical humors, tumors or cancers of the stomach or breast.

Diseases of ♌, etc.

327 All diseases of the ribs, side, back, or heart, such as palpitation, trembling or pain of the heart, pleurisy, convulsions, also violent burning fevers, weakness of the heart, or as if it were going to stop beating, sore or inflamed eyes, also plagues, pestilences, yellow fever and yellow jaundice.

Diseases of ♍, etc.

328 Rules all infirmities or weakness of the intestines, such as worms, wind-colic or obstructions of the bowels, diarrhœa, dysentery, and injuries to the intestines or abdomen; it also rules the womb, and sometimes the generative organs, of both men and women, when any unfortunate planet is afflicted in this sign, especially in the 6th house.

Diseases of ♎, etc.

329 Governs the back or kidneys, pain or injury to the head, or pain of the loins, ulcers or sores, stone or gravel in the kidneys or bladder, and all weakness or injuries of the lower part of the back.

Diseases of ♏, etc.

330 Governs all diseases of the generative organs, gravel or stone in the bladder, ruptures, fistulas or piles, and all afflictions of the private parts, either men or women; all unnatural discharges, such as gonorrhœ or leucorrhœ, or private diseases, or injuries of the womb, or spermatic cord; also pain in the groin, ruptures, etc.

Diseases of ♐, etc.

331 Indicate the thighs or hips, and all diseases appertaining to that part of the body. It also rules fistulas, tumors, and all injuries affecting those parts, such as piles or hemorrhoids, heated blood, fever, pestilence, falls from horses, or hurts caused by four-footed beasts; also injuries caused by fire, heat, and intemperance, or by any sports, such as injuries from hunting, riding, etc.

Diseases of ♑, etc.

332 Governs the knees and all diseases incident to those parts, either sprains or fractures. Is also denotes leprosy, itch, and cutaneous complaints, and rheumatism affecting the lower limbs, especially the knees.

Diseases of ♒, etc.

333 Governs all injuries or ailments connected with the legs or ankles, and all manner of infirmities incident to those parts, such as swollen feet and ankles, and all weaknesses of the ankles, also spasmodic and nervous diseases, cramps caused by wind, etc.

Diseases of ♓, etc.

334 Rules all diseases of the feet, such as gout and lameness, pain or weakness of the feet, swollen feet, mucous discharges, itch, blotches and breakings out, boils, ulcers, proceeding from impure blood; colds, and disease caused by living in moist or damp places; also bowel complaints, caused by wet, damp or cold feet.

DISEASES CAUSED BY THE PLANETS.

Diseases of ♅.

335 Uranus rules all sudden diseases, such as sudden deaths, cramps, fits, etc., and affects those parts of the body ruled by the sign that the planet happens to be in at birth; also, it generally governs all accidents which befall the native, especially if that planet happens to be in the ascendant, midheaven, the 3d or 9th houses at birth.

Diseases of ♄.

336 All diseases of the bones, complaints, ailments of the right ear or teeth, fever and ague, all fevers arising from cold or dampness, leprosy, consumption, jaundice, palsies, and all weaknesses and trembling; vain fears and fantasies, dropsy, rheumatism, gout and pains in the bones, apoplexy, hemorrhoids and ruptures, especially if ♄ be in ♏ or ♌ or in evil aspect to ♀.

Diseases of ♃.

337 All infirmities or obstructions of the liver, pleurisies, inflammation of the lungs or pneumonia, or tightness of the chest, bronchitis palpitation and trembling of the heart, cramps, pains in the spine; all diseases of the veins, also scrofula or impure state of the blood, or fevers proceeding from too great an abundance thereof, such as apoplexy, etc., or complaints brought on by too high living or intemperance.

Diseases of ♂.

338 All kinds of fevers, plagues, inflammations, such as pestilential fevers, burning fevers, carbuncles, all plague sores, burnings, ringworms, blisters, insanity produced by rush of blood to the head, tendency to flightiness or high tempers, jaundice, diarrhœa or dysentery, hemorrhoids or fistulas, and all diseases of the gall, or of the genital organs of either men or women, or of the kidneys or bladder, almost all kinds of breakings out of the skin, and of wounds caused by sharp instruments, burns, scalds or fire-arms, small-pox or measles.

Diseases of ☉.

339 All infirmities of the eyes, palpitation and trembling of the heart, nervous prostration, pimples or breaking out of the face, nervousness, sudden swooning, cramps, diseases of the mouth, impure breath, catarrh, putrid fevers and fevers generally, and inflammations of almost all kinds. The ☉ governs in man the heart and brain, and in woman the emotional nature, such as hysteria, etc.

Diseases of ♀.

340 Venus chiefly rules the kidneys, navel, abdomen, lower part of the body, and all the unnatural discharges of those parts, such as gonorrhœa, leucorrhœa, etc., and all diseases arising from inordinate lust, impotency, hernias, diabetes, dropsy, Bright's disease, or any involuntary discharge of the urine, etc.

Diseases of ☿.

341 All nervous complaints or giddiness in the head, vertigo, lethargies, insanity, fligthiness, and all complaints caused by diseases of the brain, stammering and imperfection of speech, vain and flighty imagination, and all defects of memory, hoarseness, dry coughs or great abundance of spittle, and all sniffling in the nose, gout of the feet, foul or diseased tongue, and all imperfectness of the fancy or intellectual parts; also mutes or the deaf and dumb, and impediments of speech.

Diseases of ☽.

342 Diseases of the left side, the bladder or generative organs, periods of women, dropsy, diarrhœa, and all cold rheumatic diseases, indigestion produced by taking cold, weakness or lameness of the feet, worms, injuries to the eyes, fits of long standing, or what is termed falling sickness; scrofula, convulsions, abscesses, small-pox, measles, etc.

I have only inserted so much of Medical Astrology as would enable the student when reading a horoscope to get a general knowledge of the diseases the native would be liable to; and also, the diseases he would be liable to die of. The complaints caused by the aspects of the planets to each other, and the aspects in the various signs, I defer to the latter part of this volume, where I treat more fully on medical astrology.

343 In that particular sign or house, the evil planets ♄, ♂ or ♅, are, in the horoscope, the native is certain in some part of his life to be afflicted in that part of the body that is governed by that sign and house, if the sign and house that the planet is in, agree; for instance, in ♈ and in the 1st house, then the head is certain to suffer more or less when the native is taken sick, or during evil aspects, etc.; or if in ♍ and the 6th house, then the abdomen and the intestines and lower part of the body is the most affected when sick. If the planet is afflicted by an evil aspect in the sign or house by another evil planet, the native may be subject to that ailment or disease most of his life. But if afflicted by two evil planets, especially if the planet is in an unfortunate house (in either the 6th, 8th or 12th house), then it is very doubtful about the native ever being cured of that complaint. In my own horoscope, I have ♂ in the sign Capricorn, in the 6th house in □ to ☿ in the 10 house, and in ☍ to the ☽ (my ruling planet) in the 12th house, and also applying to an ☍ of ♄ in the 12th, which has caused me to suffer from pain or rheumatism of the knees most of my life, especially if my health becomes poor; also to meet with several accidents to the knees. Had my father and I not understood Astrology, it is more than probable that the doctors in trying to cure me of rheumatism of the knees, would have so treated me that I should have been a cripple and going on crutches over thirty years ago. Yet in spite of those evil aspects, I am now as active on my feet as most men of my age.

Rules to Judge the Probable Time of Marriage of the Native, also the Number of Children.

344 It is very important that the student should learn some special rules in regard to the time of marriage of the native, although there are no rules that will hold good in all cases, as the individual horoscopes vary so much, still, with practice, it is astonishing how perfect an experienced astrologer can become in predicting the time of marriage of either a man or woman from their horoscope.

345 Claudius Ptolemy gives us one special rule which generally can be relied upon, that is "when most of the planets are rising or oriental, they generally produce early marriages."

346 "Most of the planets, occidential or setting, produce late marriages," and those rules are generally correct, but there are a number of aspects of both the Sun and Moon which causes variation to these rules, in both male and female horoscopes.

347 When Saturn or Mars are in the 7th house (the house of marriage), especially if they have evil aspects, marriage is generally delayed, as they cause treachery and deceit in the lovers, and this may be one reason why the planets, when occidental, especially if either Saturn or Mars, produces late marriages.

348 Jupiter or Venus or both in the 7th house, especially in good aspects, generally hastens marriage, and causes the native to have a number of lovers and sweethearts, and he generally has to marry one to get rid of all the others. It is especially so in female horoscopes.

349 The Sun in a female's horoscope making an evil aspect to a retrograde planet, or sometimes making a good aspect to a retrograde planet, will often delay marriage until near 40 years of age.

350 In a male's horoscope, the Moon making an evil aspect to a retrograde planet, especially Saturn or Mars, will often delay marriage, and even cause the native to die an old bachelor.

351 The Sun in a female's horoscope making an evil aspect to a retrograde planet, often causes the native to be engaged a number of times, and each time the marriage is broken off, which sometimes delays marriage until late in life.

352 But sometimes the Sun in a female's horoscope making an aspect, either good or evil, to a retrograde planet, she sometimes marries early in life, especially if these planets are rising, but she generally separates soon after marriage.

353 The rule which I have generally adopted to find out the time of marriage, is by looking carefully at the position of all the planets on the face of the horoscope, and judging by their positions and aspects as close as possible about what age the native will marry, and then calculate what particular fortunate aspect will come near that age, in any particular year or month, and often the time of marriage can be predicted in that way very correctly.

354 But when a horoscope is particularly evil for marriage, it is very seldom that they marry under what we call fortunate aspects or directions for marriage; and, therefore, that

rule cannot always be applied, but by practice and experience the student will generally be able to judge very close to the time of marriage, and also the number of marriages, by the above rules and those which have previously been given on pages 164, 165 and 166.

Children.

355 In judging the number of children that the native is likely to have, the student must always see whether there are fruitful signs on the ascendant, the 5th, 7th or 11th houses; the 11th house is the house of children, of the husband or wife.

356 If there are evil planets in either the 5th or 11th house, the native has either few children or else if he has a large family, most of them die early in life. It generally indicates a world of trouble caused by children. If the lord of the 5th house is in the 6th, 8th, 12th or 2d house, especially if it is an evil planet, it causes unhappiness in some way with children, or most of them will die.

357 If lord of the 5th house is in a fruitful sign and in a good house, and in good aspects, then most of the native's children will live; especially if the sign of the 11th house is a fruitful sign, and lord or lady of the 11th is in a fortunate house in a fruitful sign; in that case, sometimes the native will have 10, 12 or more children, and most of them, if not all, will live, and be of benefit to the native.

In the horoscopes that follow, I shall endeavor to point out examples both in regard to fortunate and unfortunate marriages and the time of marriage and the number of times of marriage; and also in regard to the number of children, and whether fortunate or unfortunate with children. If the student makes a number of observations of horoscopes, he will be able to apply the rules which I have given in almost any individual horoscope that he may meet with. I might have given a number of other rules, but in doing so, there would be danger of complicating the matter, instead of making it plainer and easier to be learned.

HOW TO JUDGE IF A HOROSCOPE IS FORTUNATE OR UNFORTUNATE.

358 When the student commences to judge a horoscope, it is often advisable for him to write down all the good aspects of the planets, Sun and Moon in one column, and all the evil aspects of the planets, Sun and Moon in another column, and after comparing them to strike a balance. But he must give preponderance of influences, either good or evil, to the surperior planets, and notice particularly whether the evil planets are lords or ladies of the evil houses, and the good planets are lords or ladies of fortunate houses, and judge

accordingly. By a little experience, he will gradually become so familiar with horoscopes as to judge at once whether a horoscope is what is termed a fortunate or an unfortunate one, and by noticing the following rules he can judge from what house or direction the good or evil will come.

359 Whenever the fortunate planets are cadent, or under the earth, and the evil planets are high up in the heavens, or in angles, you can always judge that the horoscope is more or less unfortunate, and the native will have a great many misfortunes to contend with all through life; but more especially in his early years.

360 When the fortunate planets are in angles or high up in the heavens, and the unfortunate planets are cadent, or under the earth, then you can judge that the native has a fortunate horoscope, and will be generally successful through life.

361 When the lord or lady of the ascendant and the Sun and Moon are high up in the heavens at birth, especially if they are in good aspect to fortunate planets, and the lord of the 7th or 12th house are weak and afflicted, then that horoscope is a fortunate one, because the native can always overcome his enemies and triumph in the end.

362 When a horoscope has Jupiter, Venus, or both in the 2d house unafflicted, then the native is generally fortunate, as they acquire money or this world's goods, or that which conquers the world.

363 But when Saturn, Mars and Uranus are in the 2d house, the native is generally unfortunate, because he wastes his substance and is often in poverty, no matter how intelligent that man may be.

364 If the student notices what houses the afflicting planets are lords of, he can generally tell the native from what quarter or parties the affliction may come, and by knowing that, it can often be more or less avoided.

365 For instance, if the affliction comes from the 3d house, he can avoid having dealings with neighbors or near relations, also any business which causes him to take short journeys, etc.

366 If from the 9th house, avoid wife's or husband's relations, and their near neighbors; also lawsuits and religious disputes, and long journeys.

367 If from the 11th house, then be especially guarded against false friends.

368 If from the 12th house, avoid as much as possible making secret enemies, and so on, of the other houses.

369 Also notice what houses the planet is lord of, where the good influences are, and make the most of them. If the planet promising the good influence is lord of the 10th house, then advise the native to follow some regular business indicated by that fortunate planet, or get associated with governors or prominent people, etc.

370 If lord of the 11th house, then friends will benefit.

371 If lord of the 5th house, then either children, speculation or keeping a place of amusement, etc.

372 If lord of the 6th house, then small cattle, servants, or keeping a boarding-house, etc., and so on of the other houses.

Mental Abilities.

373 We judge of the native's mental faculties chiefly by the planet Mercury, and its aspect to the Moon.

374 If Mercury be in its own house, either Gemini or Virgo, it confers considerable intellect on the native, especially if it happens to have any aspect to the Moon, even a square or opposition of the Moon, is better than no aspect.

375 But a sextile or trine aspect of Mercury and the Moon, if Mercury is in its own house, confers the highest order of abilities on the native, especially if Mercury be in the midheaven, the 9th, 11th or the ascendant.

376 If Mercury be in Aries, Libra, Sagittary or Aquarius, it confers considerable ability on the native.

377 If Mercury be in Cancer, Leo, Scorpio, Capricorn or Pisces, unless it has some good aspect to a fortunate planet, or has some aspect to the Moon, the native is of very inferior abilities, and likely to lead a plodding or servile life.

378 If Mercury be in sextile or trine aspect to Jupiter, Mars, Sun or Venus, it sharpens the intellect very much, and the native is generally of rather good abilities.

379 When Mercury is in Cancer, Leo, Scorpio, Capricorn or Pisces and in a cadent house, and no particular aspect to the Moon, or any of the superior planets, the native is then only fit for a common, plodding life, and will never amount to much, unless he should happen to have Jupiter in the ascendant or high up in the heavens, then he might be helped by some of his friends or surrounding circumstances.

380 In all horoscopes the student should bear in mind, that he must look more to the planet Mercury for the native's mental abilities, than to the Moon or lord of the ascendant.

I shall refer to the derangement of the mind, when I come to treat of the diseases of the body, in the latter part of the volume.

The Temper or the Animal Passions.

381 We judge of the temper or passions of the native chiefly by the Moon and Mars; Mercury controls the intellectual nature of man, and the Moon and Mars the animal or passionate nature.

382 If the Moon is in square or opposition to Mars or Saturn, the native will then give way to his passions, and is very likely to be of a violent temper and may even become vicious, and often get into misfortunes or even prison by his bad temper, unless Mercury is very well dignified and in good aspect.

383 The Moon in square or opposition to the Sun, makes the native very stubborn and willful, and he will not take advice, especially if the aspect occurs in fixed signs.

384 The Moon in square or opposition to Uranus, makes the native erratic, changeable, and generally he does the right thing at the wrong time, and the wrong thing at the right time, and thus goes blundering along.

385 The Moon in square or opposition to both Saturn and Mars, especially from the 8th, 12th or 6th houses, the native is likely to have serious misfortunes, and meet with a violent death, or often be sick, or end his days in prison, unless the good influence of Jupiter, Venus and the Sun intervene.

386 The Moon in sextile or trine aspect to Venus, Jupiter or the Sun, makes the native benevolent, kind hearted and affectionate, and is much opposed to causing pain to others, even to animals

387 The Moon in good aspect to the Sun or Jupiter, especially if they are high up in the heavens, or in the ascendant, makes the native honorable minded, and he cannot be tempted to do wrong.

388 Jupiter in the 9th, 10th, 11th houses or the ascendant, unless it is afflicted, causes the native to take great pride in his reputation, and he will not do anything that will endanger or injure it, in any shape or manner, if he can help it.

Profession and Trade—Riches and Poverty.

389 Claudius Ptolemy tells us in his Tetrabiblos, that a man's profession or trade is controlled by the planet which rises the next above the Sun, but that rule has not generally been verified in my own experience in the practice of Astrology, still it might have been true two thousand years ago.

390 The native's profession or trade is chiefly governed, at the present day, by his mental abilities and not by the planet that rises above the Sun.

391 If Mars be well dignified and strong, or in his own house, especially in the ascendant, 9th, 10th or 11th house, or even the 7th, the native is likely to excel in, or follow some kind of mechanical pursuit, or be connected with military affairs, and is also fond of inventions, and generally wants to be in a business of his own, and dislikes to be engaged under others.

392 Mercury strong in its own house or in good aspect to the Moon, either in the ascendant, 9th, 10th, 11th or 7th house, or even the 5th house, makes the native inclined to writing and studying, and he either becomes an author, newspaper editor, or is some way mixed up with writings or printing; and very often causes the native to be a minister or lawyer, and he always takes delight in literary pursuit, and may be a public speaker or politician.

393 Venus well dignified in a horoscope, makes the native take delight and even excel in such as painting, sculpture or the fine arts and music, especially if Venus be strong in its own house, and in good aspect to the Moon, or is in the ascendant, 2d, 5th, 9th, 10th and 11th houses.

394 Jupiter in good aspect to superior planets, and high up in the heavens, in a horoscope, makes the native inclined to become religious, or want to hold some political position, or become a judge, member of the legislature or governor, especially if Jupiter is either in the ascendant, 2d, 9th, 10th or 11th house. Sometimes Jupiter in the 7th house causes the native to be very fortunate in political pursuits, as it generally gives him very powerful friends; but if Jupiter is afflicted in the 7th house, it sometimes causes him to have powerful enemies.

395 The Moon strong in either the ascendant, 9th, 10th, 11th, 2d, 3d, 5th or 7th house, generally causes the native to travel much, and be engaged either on the sea or become a traveling agent, or be in someway engaged in traveling.

396 The Sun strong in the 9th, 11th, midheaven or the ascendant, causes the native to be very ambitious and persevering, and generally he has other people working under him, than working himself, and he is generally ambitious to be a judge, governor, or hold some high position.

397 Saturn strong in a horoscope or the midheaven, causes the native to be inclined to farming or agricultural pursuits, unless Mercury is strong, then it causes the native to become

very thoughful, quiet and industrious; although of a plodding nature, he is generally fond of literary pursuits, and is a plodder in that line.

398 Uranus strong in a horoscope, causes the native to be very fond of inventions and discoveries; he very seldom follows any regular employment. When Uranus is strong in the ascendant, 9th, 10th, 11th, 2d or 7th house, he is very often poor the greater part of his life, yet afterwards may acquire great wealth by some discovery or invention.

399 In a horoscope where most of the planets are cadent or weak, the native generally spends most of his life working for others, or as a menial or servant.

400 When there is no special aspect of the planets, especially of the superior planets, then the native is generally a drudge or follows some menial employment.

Business or Profession in which the Native will be Unfortunate.

401 The student in advising the native what particular employment he ought not to follow, should always look well to the house in the horoscope that governs that employment he advises the native not to engage in. For instance, the native would be unfortunate as a minister, lawyer or sea captain, or any business connected with long journeys if there are evil planets in the 9th house, especially if they have evil aspects, or if the lord of the 9th house is afflicted by a square or opposition of Saturn or Mars, or indeed of any planet.

402 It is unfortunate for the native to be engaged in any business connected with the 6th house, if that house is afflicted by evil planets, or its lord is in square or opposition to other planets. He would, in that case, be unfortunate in keeping a boarding-house, engaging servants, breeding small animals, or being a physician or nurse, etc.

403 If the 5th house is afflicted, the native would be unfortunate in all kinds of speculation, theatres, places of amusements, keeping a hotel, or being an actor or public speaker.

404 If the 4th house is afflicted, the native would be unfortunate in farming, mining, owning property or being a real estate agent, and his real estate will depreciate or meet with misfortunes or some kind of bad luck.

405 If the 3d house is afflicted, then he wonld be unfortunate in taking short journeys, railway traveling, being a traveling agent, or any business connected with neighbors or near relations.

406 If the 2d house is afflicted, the native is more fortunate working for others than being in business for himself, and is less liable to meet with serious losses and misfortunes in his money matters.

407 When the native has Saturn in the midheaven, especially if it is afflicted by an evil aspect of an evil planet, he is always unfortunate in business for himself, and is likely every seven years to fail or break up in business, or at least to meet with very heavy losses; he is more fortunate engaged under others, or less liable to meet with heavy losses

408 The native is unfortunate in any public business or where he deals much with others, who has evil planets in the 11th house in his horoscope, as his friends are very apt to prove treacherous, and often swindle him; but if the native has fortunate planets in the 11th house, especially if they are in good aspect to the other planets, he will be very successful in any public business, such as keeping a store, hotel, or anything of that kind, providing the 5th and 6th houses are not afflicted.

409 The native having evil planets in the 12th house, especially if they have evil aspects to other planets, his acquaintances and neighbors will put themselves about to do him an injury, even if it is no benefit to themselves.

410 Unfortunate planets in the 7th house, or the lord of the 7th house afflicted, the native is then unfortunate in any partnership, and should always avoid partners, if he does not, he will often come to grief, not from his own misfortune or bad conduct, but from his partner's misfortunes.

411 It is better to have squares and oppositions of planets in a horoscope than to have no aspects, as the squares and oppositions certainly cause the person to have great energy and perseverance, and makes him determined to overcome obstacles and difficulties; and sometimes a person becomes successful with evil planets in the ascendant; yet he is generally beset by oppositions most of his life, especially in his younger years, but he may partly overcome them after middle age.

412 In any horoscope look well to the Moon before deciding whether it is a fortunate or unfortunate nativity; as all the old authors on Astrology agree in saying, "that it is better for the native to have the lord of the ascendant (or ruling planet) afflicted than the Moon."

Profession or Business in which the Native would be Fortunate.

413 Fortunate planets in the ascendant cause the native to be successful as a superintendent or business manager. He is generally fortunate in business for himself and rises to prominence, and becomes quite wealthy. He dislikes working for others, but he generally brings good fortune to his employer.

414 Fortunate planets in the second, cause the native to become quite wealthy, especially if Jupiter and Venus are there, and they are in good aspect to other planets. He would succesd as a speculator, banker, money lender or merchant, or in any business which causes him to handle money.

415 Fortunate planets in the third, cause the native to be very successful in taking short journeys, working on railroads, stage-coaches, as conductor or motorman; also fortunate as a traveling agent or letter carrier, or in any business connected with short journeys.

416 Fortunate planets in the fourth, make the native fortunate in mining, real estate or as a real estate agent, farmer or in any way connected with lands or fruits of the earth; he generally has money left him by the death of his father or relations, and his estate increases in value, and he generally becomes wealthy.

417 Fortunate planets in the fifth, cause the native to be successful with theatres, places of amusement, as an actor or actress, keeping a hotel or store, stock or produce broker, and he often derives benefit from his children.

418 Fortunate planets in the sixth, cause the native to be successful in keeping a boarding-house, hiring servants, or keeping an intelligence office; he would also be fortunate as a nurse or physician, or breeding small cattle.

419 Fortunate planets in the seventh, cause the native to be successful in partnership, or dealing with friends; is often very successful as a politician, as his friends will assist him; he is also fortunate in marriage, or his wife brings him wealth.

420 Fortunate planets in the eighth, cause the native to be fortunate in the management of wills; as executor or conveyancer of property; or being engaged as an undertaker.

421 Fortunate planets in the ninth, cause the native to be successful as a minister, lawyer, embassador, or travelling agent, sailor, telegraph operator, or taking long journeys on railroads, or long voyages.

422 Fortunate planets in the tenth, make the native very successful as a politician; he is likely to rise to prominence and become very wealthy; he is also generally successful in

business, and should always be engaged in some business of his own, and never work for others, but, if he did, he would bring good fortune to his employer.

423 Fortunate planets in the eleventh, give the native many friends, and he will be successful dealing with friends and they often benefit him, and he generally succeeds as a politician, or in any business in which he deals with the public.

424 Fortunate planets in the twelfth, cause the native to succeed in anything connected with the mysterious or supernatural, such as a clairvoyant, spiritualist, or as an astrologer, or in electricity or magnetism; he generally makes a good physician.

---

425 The student ought to take particular notice, whether the fortunate planets are lords or ladies of good houses or evil houses, because if the planets are lords or ladies of the 6th, 8th or 12th house, and they are in the ascendant or midheaven, or in other houses that we call good, the native may receive injuries instead of benefits from the good planets, even if it is either Jupiter or Venus; but if they are lords or ladies of good houses, strong and in good aspect, then the native generally succeeds in any business indicated by the planets, signs or houses marked in the horoscope.

426 As this is so important a matter, I think I cannot do better than give a synopsis of the influence of each of the lords of the 12 houses, as they affect each of the 12 houses when posited therein at birth.

The influence of the lord of the first house in each of the 12 houses.

427 The lord of the ascendant in the 1st house denotes long life, general good health and peace of mind, but if afflicted there by an evil aspect of an evil planet, or by the lord of the 6th, 8th or 12th house, it denotes the contrary, or much unhappiness through life.

428 The lord of the 1st in the 2d house, the native grows rich by his own industry; but if weak, retrograde or afflicted there, it denotes want and poverty.

429 If in the 3d house, the native will be inclined to travel, and often be unsettled and generally lives with his near relations; but if afflicted there, his brethern and kindred will be very unkind to him and cause him most of his trouble, and generally be his enemies; he is also unfortunate in short journeys.

430 If in the 4th house, the native is born to good position and inheritance from his father or near relations, he is likely to become very wealthy, but if afflicted there by either lord

of the 11th, 12th, 7th or 10th house, he will either die in prison or become very poor.

431 If in the 5th house, the native will be benefitted by his children, be successful in speculations; but if weak or afflicted by Saturn, Mars or Dragon's Tail, he will have but few children, or they will die young, and they will cause him unhappiness, or they will be disobedient, and he will generally be unfortunate in his speculations and with places of amusement.

432 If in the 6th house, it denotes sickness to the native, and he generally lives in a mean and uncomfortable manner, or often lives in a boarding-house; but is likely to make a good physician, or be fortunate in breeding cattle if not afflicted, but if afflicted there, it denotes short life, and a great deal of vexation, trouble, sickness and poverty.

433 If in the 7th house, the native loves the company of women, and goes a great deal in company, and is generally fortunate or benefitted by marriage, especially if well dignified there; but if afflicted, his wife or sweetheart will be the cause of his ruin, and if the sign on the 7th be Scorpio, and evil planets afflict the 7th house, let him beware of poison; or his wife, or lovers are likely to put him in prison, and his partners or wife swindle him.

434 Lord of the 1st in the 8th house, weak or afflicted, the native is always pensive, meloncholy, and likely to attempt suicide, or is often in much trouble or sorrow. It generally causes the native to be of short life, unless the giver of life is very strong.

435 If in the 9th house, the native is fortunate with clergymen, law or long voyages; he is benefitted by strangers, and generally travels most of his life, or he may hold some position in a foreign country; but if afflicted in the 9th, it denotes danger of thieves or being shipwrecked; he is unfortunate in law matters, or connected with religion, and is likely to be an infidel or skeptic.

436 If in the 10th honse, the native is born to great honor, and often arrives at eminence, and is generally successful in almost all kinds of business; but if afflicted in the 10th, the wealthy and prominent, also judges will generally injure him, and he is deprived of his rights, and may gain several fortunes, and then be defrauded out of them.

437 If in the 11th house, the native will bring his hopes and expectations to perfection, and generally acquire a great many friends; but if afflicted there by evil aspects or is weak or retrograde, there is but little hope from his friends or acquaintances, and they often do him much harm.

438 If the lord of the ascendant be in the 12th house, the native will have many enemies, and likely to be partly the cause of his own misfortunes; if it be weak and afflicted there, then there is great danger of his dying in prison, unless the lord of the ascendant is in its own sign, in that case he may escape imprisonment, but will suffer much sorrow and trouble through life, chiefly caused by secret enemies.

Lord of the second in the 12 houses.

439 The lord of the second in the 1st house, denotes that the native will become rich, and easily obtain wealth without much labor, unless it is very much afflicted in the 1st house, then he is liable to meet with heavy losses.

440 The lord of the second in the 2d house, the native gets money by his own skill and industry; but if afflicted there, he squanders money, and it easily passes through his fingers, and he is often threatened with poverty.

441 Lord of the second in the 3d house, the native suffers losses from his brothers, neighbors or near kindred, especially if Saturn, Mars or the Dragon's Tail are in the 3d house; but if in good aspect to the lord of the 1st or 3d, then he is benefitted by his neighbors and relations, and in taking short journeys.

442 If in the 4th house, it gives the native an estate from his parents, and he is generally fortunate in dealing in lands, mines, or being a farmer; when afflicted there, then it indicates the contrary.

443 If in the 5th house, he receives profit or benefit from his children; is successful in speculation, keeping a hotel, being a public speaker or actor, or being connected with places of amusement; but if afflicted in the 5th house, then he is unfortunate, both in speculation, children and with places of amusement, or public speaking.

444 If in the 6th house, the native's servants will rob him, run away with his goods, his cattle will be unfortunate or die, and he will suffer loss from his estate; but if in good aspect, he may gain a fortune by the practice of medicine, breeding cattle, keeping a boarding-house, or derive benefit from his uncles and aunts.

445 If in the 7th house, the native is likely to gain an estate through his wife or by partnership, by trading or dealing with others; the native's wife or husband may die and leave them property; but if the lord of the ascendant is afflicted in the 7th, there is danger of being swindled out of it, even if left to them.

446 If in the 8th house, the native is likely to be extravagant, and easily parts with his money, but if in good aspect, he may gain by death or legacies, especially if the lord of the 8th house is in good aspect to the lord of the second or first.

447 If the lord of the 2d is in the 9th house, he will gain by merchandise or taking long journeys, or trading in foreign parts; he would also be fortunate as a clergyman, dealing in books, or being connected with science, law or religion; he is also likely to be benefitted by his wife's kindred; but if afflicted in the 9th house, danger of misfortunes and losses in law and by accidents in long journeys, and of being persecuted, or lose money on account of his religion, science, or learning.

448 If in the 10th house, the native gains by being employed by some nobleman, or by a person in high office; he is also benefitted by his mother or mother's relations, or his wife's father; if unafflicted in the 10th house, he becomes very wealthy, but if afflicted, he loses money by law or judges, wealthy people, or his mother's relations.

449 If in the 11th house, the native gains considerable by means of his friends, or by accidental fortune or good luck, selling or dealing in wheat, or by speculation, or anything connected with the fruits of the earth, or by yearly rents; but if afflicted in the 11th house, the native is terribly swindled by false friends, who will rob and keep him in poor circumstances most of his life.

450 If in the 12th house, the native is subject to losses by thieves, and being swindled by lawyers threatening imprisonment, but if in good aspect to fortunate planets, he will gain by cattle or horses, and will be fortunate in horse-racing, or in such as inventions, especially with electricity or mesmerism, clairvoyance or astrology; and he may acquire money by medicine.

Lord of the third in the 12 houses.

451 If the lord of the 3d house is in the ascendant, the native will be wealthier or better off than his brethren, or else he has none living, but if he has, they will receive advantages from him, and he will also be a benefit to his neighbors, but if the lord of the 3d house is afflicted in the ascendant, then his neighbors and brethren will cause him a world of trouble, and he will be unfortunate in traveling on short journeys.

452 If in the 2d house, the native's brethren will be at strife with him, on account of money and property, and he is,

likely to lose heavily by them, especially if it is afflicted in the 2d house.

453 If in the 3d house, the native's brethren will assist him; he will take a great many short journeys, probably will be engaged in traveling most of his life; but if afflicted in the 3d house, he will be in low circumstances, lead a plodding, careful, industrious life, but often be poor.

454 If in the 4th house, the native's brethren will endeavor to cheat him out of his parent's estate, especially if the lord of the 8th house be in the 4th house, but he is likely to accumulate property by traveling or dealing with his neighbors.

455 If in the 5th house, the native's near relations go into strange countries or emigrate, and he is likely to be happy with his children, or they will be a benefit to him; he also will be fortunate in speculation unless afflicted there.

456 If in the 6th house, the native will live unhappily with his brethren, and receive injuries and damages by them.

457 If in the 7th house, unafflicted, the native will be fortunate in partnership, and is likely to speculate, also travel a great deal, and probably become very wealthy; but if afflicted in the 7th house, his neighbors will make much trouble between him and his wife or his partners, and very likely to get into law difficulties, or they separate.

458 If in the 8th house, the native is likely to bury all his brethren, and he will take a journey to avoid trouble and false accusations.

459 If in the 9th house, the native's brethren will travel into strange countries, and probably hold some prominent positions under the government in foreign parts, by being consuls, etc.; they are also likely to become lawyers, ministers, or travel a great deal on land or on long voyages.

460 If in the 10th house, the native's brethren will not live to old age, but some of them are likely to become very prominent; and the native will gain some office under the government by means of a long journey.

461 If in the 11th house, the native's brethren will be his friends and be of much advantage to him, and through them he will be very prosperous and fortunate; but if afflicted in the 11th house, the native's brethren are likely to make him much worriment by becoming false friends, and probably will cost him a great deal of money and possibly sorrow and trouble.

462 If in the 12th house, the native's brethren or neighbors will be great enemies to him and plan for his downfall, and very likely he will have to leave his native country on that account; he will be unfortunate in traveling.

Lord of the fourth in the 12 houses.

463 If the lord of the 4th house be in the ascendant, it denotes good for the native by tilling of land, farming, husbandry, or connected with buildings, mines, or speculating in mines, and he will become more eminent than any of his brethren; but if afflicted in the ascendant, it indicates the contrary.

464 If in the 2d house, the parent's estate will fall to the native, especially if the lord of the 5th house be in the 2d house; the native will become honorable and buy and sell houses or lands; he will also be fortunate in speculation.

465 If in the 3d house, it denotes that the native's father will suffer damage by the native's brethren, if not imprisonment; and if afflicted in the 3d house, the native will have much trouble with his brothers and sisters and near neighbors, as they are likely to become his secret enemies.

466 If in the 4th house, it denotes good fortune by ancient men and things; the native's father will live to be old, and be of great assistance to him. The native is likely to become quite wealthy by dealing in lands, mines or houses, etc.

467 If in the 5th house, strong and well aspected, the native's father will become very wealthy, and the native will inherit from his father, especially if the lord of the 5th house is in the second; also the native will be happy and fortunate with children, unless it is an evil planet or afflicted.

468 If in the 6th house, the native will be prosperous as a physician, or breeding small cattle, hireing or engaging servants, but if afflicted in the 6th house, there is great danger that the native will not live to old age, or that he will often suffer from sickness or poor health.

469 If in the 7th house, the native will gain an estate by his wife, and generally be fortunate with women, also with partners, or with tilling the land, or with mines or farming; but if the lord of the 4th house is afflicted in the 7th house, then the native suffers much on account of his wife, and she may reduce him to poverty or put him in prison.

470 If in the 8th house, the native's father will not live to old age; it also denotes benefit, or the receiving of an estate by legacies or wills, unless it is afflicted, if so, the contrary.

471 If in the 9th house, it denotes profit to the native by religious matters, lawsuits, taking long journeys, merchandise or trading in foreign parts; but if afflicted in the 9th house, the native is likely to lose his possessions or real estate from treachery connected with law or corrupt judges.

472 If in the 10th house, the native will gain an estate by being employed by the government, or one who stands high in position, or a person in power, or else by having some public employment.

473 If in the 11th house, the native will generally be much respected and benefitted by his neighbors, or persons who live near him, and is likely to gain some political position on account of their good will or friendship.

474 If in the 12th house, the native will take long journeys, caused by crosses and disappointments, or the native's parents will have to emigrate, and he will suffer misfortunes on that account, and great danger of the native's father not living to be old, or die in prison.

Lord of the fifth in the 12 houses.

475 If the lord of the 5th house is in a fruitful sign in the ascendant, unless afflicted, the native will have many children; they will also love him and be of advantage to him. He will also be very fond of speculation, and very likely to be engaged in some business of that kind, or being an actor, or in some way connected with places of amusement. There is danger of his becoming a gambler.

476 If in the 2d house, the native's children will become well off, especially if there are fortunate planets in the 2d house, and the native will have comfort in them and rejoice in their prosperity.

477 If in the 3d house and well dignified, it causes profit to the native by short journeys, and he is very likely to travel much.

478 If in the 4th house and well dignified, the native will inherit an estate from his parents, and he is very likely to become quite wealthy, and will also be fortunate in speculations.

479 If in the 5th house, he will delight in music and places of amusement, and his children will be prosperous; he will also be very successful as a speculator, or a stock or produce broker; but if afflicted in the 5th house by evil aspects of unfortunate planets, it indicates the contrary.

480 If in the 6th house, the native will be prosperous in dealing in small cattle, or as a physician, boarding-house keeper, etc., and also he will be of a mild, patient disposition, and will endure sickness without murmuring or discontent; but there is great danger that his children will suffer much from sickness, even if they do not all die in infancy.

481 If in the 7th house and unafflicted, the native will live very happily with his wife, but may have some trouble or vexation caused by his children; he will also be prosperous in partnership, and very likely to become quite wealthy, but if afflicted there, he loses by speculation, etc.

482 If in the 8th house, the native is benefitted by legacies or wills, but his children are likely to die early in life, and he will have but few children to live, especially if it is afflicted by the lord of the 8th house.

483 If in the 9th house, the native will have beautiful children, he will take much pleasure and profit in traveling and in long journeys; he will also be given to scientific and political pursuits, and receives advantages from his wife's relations.

484 If in the 10th house, the native gains honor and respect from people in high position, and also comfort and happiness from his mother or his wife's father; he is also likely to become very wealthy on account of being fortunate in speculation, or an estate coming to him from his father.

485 If in the 11th house, the native will be fortunate and enjoy prosperity, but there is great danger that his children will become his public enemies, or in some way injure him, especially if Saturn, Mars or the Dragon's Tail are in the 11th house.

486 If in the 12th house, his children will cause him much anger and sorrow, but he will be very fortunate with cattle, horse-racing and horses; but if afflicted there, it may get him into serious trouble on account of gambling or speculation.

Lord of the sixth in the 12 houses.

487 The lord of the 6th house in the ascendant, the native generally has poor health, and is seldom strong and robust, especially in his early years; the nature of the sickness is indicated by the sign on the 6th house, and the planets in the 6th house, and also by its lord   He is generally unfortunate or loses by small cattle or fowls; either they die or are unprofitable to him; he is also unfortunate with servants.

488 If in the 2d house, the native will generally be poor, often going from bad to worse; if the lord of the 2d house is retrograde, and in square or opposition to the lord of the 6th house, so much the worse; he is also unfortunate in keeping a boarding-house, as a physician or keeping small animals. Unless the lord of the 6th house is a fortunate planet, strong or in good aspect to the other planets, then it is not so evil.

489 If in the 3d house, the native's near relations will have poor health, and generally die early in life, and he will suffer sickness and misfortunes himself in traveling on short journeys, and his neighbors will not be his friends.

490 If in the 4th house, the native's father will be unfortunate and sickly, and often in poor circumstances, and the native is liable to injure himself by taking improper medicine.

491 If in the 5th house it indicates affliction to the native's children; and he is likely to injure his own health by feasting and inordinate or lustful pleasure; he will also be unfortunate in speculation, or connected with places of amusement, or keeping a hotel.

492 If in the 6th house it denotes good health to the native, unless it is much afflicted, and he is generally successful as a physician, keeping boarders or dealing in cattle; but if afflicted, it indicates the contrary.

493 If in the 7th house, the native is liable to meet with injuries from women, and often injures his health and pocket by them, especially if Mars is in the 7th house, in square or opposition to Venus; it sometimes causes the wife to die shortly after marriage, and shows her to be of low extraction and to have been in poor circumstances.

494 If in the 8th house, the native is likely to bury both his enemies and his servants; also, it brings losses and misfortunes with his wife's or partner's money; if the lord of the ascendant apply by a square or opposition to the lord of the 6th house, it denotes death to the native or his mother; neither of them will live to old age, and the native is likely to commit suicide.

495 If in the 9th house, the native will live unhappily with his wife's relations and their neighbors, and the wife's brothers and sisters will be very much opposed to him, and there is danger that the native will often be sick while traveling on a long journey, and is likely to die when traveling, especially on a long voyage.

496 If in the 10th house, misfortune, sorrow and affliction will come to the native's mother, or his wife's father, and there is great danger that the native will meet with some serious disaster or be sent to prison, unless the lord of the 10th house is a fortunate planet or in good aspect to fortunate planets, then he may escape being sent to prison.

497 If in the 11th house, the native is likely to be often despondent and gloomy, and have but little hopes, especially if the lord of the 11th house afflicts the lord of the ascendant;

his friends will generally be of low extraction, and is more liable to injure him than be of any benefit, and he is likely to be poor most of his life.

498 If in the 12th house, the native will be hated or disliked by many persons, especially by the lower class, yet without power to injure him very seriously; if in square or opposition to the lord of the 4th house or ascendant, or lord of the 8th house, he is very likely to be killed by large animals or die in prison, or spend most of his life in prison.

Lord of the seventh in the 12 houses.

499 If the lord of the 7th house is in the ascendant, it indicates success in the practice of astrology and medicine, and the native will be beloved by women, and they will be his friends and assist him in his business; if the lord of the 7th house is an evil planet, then it indicates that they will be his enemies, and often bring him trouble or losses, especially if the lord of the 4th house afflicts by evil aspect the lord of the 7th house; it will also cause the native's wife or husband to be a tyrant, jealous and ill-natured.

500 If in the 2d house, the native will marry for love rather than for money, and there is great danger that his wife will not live to be old, and he may marry several times. The native's enemies will not live long, or he is likely to be robbed or in some way swindled by women; if the lord of the 7th house is an evil planet, he will often be cheated or swindled, if not robbed.

501 If in the 3d house, the native's near relations will often be at variance with him, and he cannot get along with them; he is likely to marry some one of his own kindred, and will live at variance with her relations, and not get along well, neither with his own relations nor with his neighbors.

502 If in the 4th house, the native is very likely to follow the profession of his father and be successful in business; he will marry a virtuous wife, unless the lord of the 7th house is an evil planet. He is also likely to have some contention with his relations about his father's estate, especially if the lord of the 8th house is an evil planet, and afflicted by evil aspects.

503 If in the 5th house, the native will marry a very young wife of good behavior, and she is likely to be an actress or musician, or be in public life; he is likely to receive injuries, crosses or unhappiness from his children, or they die young, especially if the lord of the 7th house is an evil planet.

504 If in the 6th house, the native will marry a servant or person of low extraction, and she is likely to be much beneath him, or else she will be a menial or have some scandal or blemish to her reputation; if the lord of the 7th house is afflicted or an evil planet, he will meet with much unhappiness and trouble on account of servants or employees, or persons boarding in his house, and it is very unfortunate for him to be a physician or a breeder of small cattle or fowls, keeping a boarding-house, etc.

505 If in the 7th house, the native will marry a person of good family, but she is not likely to love him, and will cause much unhappiness, strife and contention by reason of other men, especially if it is an evil planet; but if it is a fortunate planet and unafflicted, it indicates the contrary, and that he will live happily with his wife.

506 If in the 8th house, the native will wed a high-born wealthy wife; he will enjoy her estate, but is likely to have some trouble or lawsuit connected with a death of some friend about a legacy; if the lord of the 7th house is an evil planet, his wife is likely to squander both her own and his patrimony, and there is great danger that they will come to poverty through her extravagance.

507 If in the 9th house, it indicates that the native will marry a stranger or a person coming from abroad, or he marries while on a long journey; he is also likely to suffer much on account of religious persecutions, but will gain by his wife's relations, unless the lord of the 7th house is an evil planet, then he will have serious trouble with his wife's relations, lawsuits, religious quarrels, or while on long journeys, caused by thieves, etc.

508 If in the 10th house, the native will marry a very honorable wife or husband, and will gain an estate by him or her, unless the lord of the 7th house is an evil planet, then it will cause much trouble and strife concerning some honorable office or employment, and the native's wife (or husband) is likely to be defrauded of her or his estate, or it will in some way be squandered.

509 If in the 11th house, the native will marry a widow or widower, who is likely to have children living, but he or she will live comfortable with their partners, but danger of difference arises on account of the children, or friends will make trouble on account of the children, especially if the lord of the 7th house is an evil planet, and is in evil aspect to the lord of the 5th house.

510 If in the 12th house, the native will be in danger of dying by the hands of his enemies, either by poison or being killed; his secret enemies are likely to try and do him much harm, and cause him much unhappiness, or try and keep him confined in prison or in an insane asylum; especially if the lord of the 7th house is an evil planet. The native's wife or husband generally suffers by poor health, or is often quite sick, and he or she will not live to be old.

Lord of the eighth in the 12 houses.

511 If the lord of the 8th house is in the ascendant, it makes the native gloomy, despondent and melancholy, and he is likely to be of short life, especially if it is an evil planet; but he is likely to be fortunate in legacies or receive advantages from his wife's income, especially if the lord of the 2d house is in good aspect to the lord of the ascendant or the lord of the 8th house, and the lord of the 8th house is a fortunate planet.

512 If in the 2d house, the native is likely to receive a fortune from his wife, or he may recover debts that he little thought he would ever get, unless the lord of the 8th house is an evil planet, then his wife will squander his money and he loses heavily by bad debts, but if it is a good planet, then he will gain by wills and legacies.

513 If in the 3d house, the native's brothers and sisters will be very unfortunate and generally of short life; he is likely to be unfortunate in taking short journeys, and in his relations with neighbors; and the native is in danger of being killed, or in some way injured in traveling.

514 If in the 4th house, it indicates that the native's parents will not live to be old, especially if the lord of the 8th or 11th house is in square or opposition to the lord of the 4th house (the 11th house being the 8th from the 4th); as for the native, he will die in his own home, unless the lord of the 8th house is in conjunction with the lord of the ascendant in the 9th house, then he dies in a strange country.

515 If in the 5th house, it indicates that the native will bury his children or they come to a violent death, and if they live, they will be very wicked and rebellious, and cause him a world of trouble.

516 If in the 6th house, the native's servants will be unfaithful to him, and his small cattle or fowls will not prosper, but in some way meet with misfortune or die. The native is very likely to suffer from poor health, and may die a violent death or be ill-treated, or he may be poisoned by his physician.

517 If in the 7th house, it causes the native to marry a rich wife or husband, or a fortune will come to the native through his wife (or her husband) unexpectedly; especially if the lord of the 8th house is strong and a fortunate planet, or in good aspect to the lord of the 1st or 2d house, or planets in the 7th house. But if the lord of the 8th house is an evil planet and afflicting the 7th house, the native is likely to marry several times, and his or her wives or husbands will be of short life.

518 If in the 8th house it indicates that the native will die a natural death, and have but little sickness through the whole course of his life, only he may at times be slightly threatened with illness; but if the lord of the 8th house is an evil planet and afflicted by the lord of the 6th or 12th house, then there is great danger that the native will die a violent death, or in some way be killed by an accident or secret enemies or servants, especially if the lord of the ascendant or the giver of life is also afflicted by evil aspects.

519 If in the 9th house, it indicates that the native's wife's (or husband's) relations will deprive him of part of his property, and that there will be a strife and debate between the native and them, especially if the lord of the 9th house or ascendant is in square or opposition to the lord of the 8th house.

520 If in the 10th house, it denotes a violent death, especially if the lord of the 10th house is in square or opposition to the lord of the 8th house, or if the lord of the 8th house is an evil planet; in that case, there is danger that the native will die by the sentence of a judge, especially if the lord of the 8th or 10th house is in square or opposition from fixed signs to the lord of the ascendant.

521 If in the 11th house, the native's friends are short lived, and he is liable to die before middle age, unless the giver of life is strong, or the lord of the 1st house is in sextile or trine to the ascendant.

522 If in the 12th house, the native will be very much troubled, annoyed and worried by his enemies, and there is great danger that he will die in prison, unless the lord of the ascendant is strong or in its own house, or Jupiter or Venus are in the 12th house; but if the lord of the 8th house is strong in the 12th house, and afflicting the lord of the ascendant, then the native is likely to die either in prison or by secret enemies.

Lord of the ninth in the 12 houses.

523 If the lord of the 9th house is in the ascendant, the native is likely to be of a religious disposition, also of a scientific turn of mind and a great traveler; his wife will be prudent and very much respected by strangers and her relations; the native will be fortunate in long voyages or journeys, unless the lord of the 9th house is an evil planet and is afflicted by evil aspects, then it denotes the contrary, and he suffers by his wife's relations.

524 If in the 2d house, the native will gain a fortune by merchandise or trading in foreign parts; he is also likely to gain some position as an embassador or consul to some foreign country, and thus become wealthy and prominent, unless it is an evil planet and afflicted, then he loses by law, religion, long journeys and his wife's relations.

525 If in the 3d house, the native is likely to be unsettled, move from place to place, and he is almost certain to emigrate to foreign countries, probably on account of his brothers and sisters or his near relations.

526 If in the 4th house, the native will gain some position by means of his wife's relations, and will travel on account of his father or mother's relations, or some money will come to him from foreign countries, unless the lord of the 9th house is an evil planet and afflicted.

527 If in the 5th house, the native is likely to have children born to him by other women than his wife, especially if the lord of the 5th house is in evil aspect to the lord of the ascendant, and he may travel or go abroad on that account. If the lord of the 9th house is in the 5th, and a fortunate planet and in good aspect, he may acquire a large estate by speculating in foreign countries, or in some way connected with foreign goods or stocks.

528 If in the 6th house, the native will marry a servant or a person in low circumstances, and he will gain by means of servants or small cattle, especially if the lord of the 2d house is in sextile or trine aspect to the lord of the 6th house.

529 If in the 7th house, the native will marry a stranger or a person born in a foreign country, and one who will be very well educated, and her relations will be kind to her, although they may often be at strife with the native.

530 If in the 8th house, the native will gain considerable by traveling or going on long journeys, and his wife will gain by legacies or wills.

531 If in the 9th house, the native will be religious and very fond of traveling; he may be successful as a preacher or lawyer. His dreams will generally come true, unless the lord of the 9th house is an evil planet, and in evil aspect to the lord of the ascendant.

532 If in the 10th house, the native will gain honor by long journeys, and the wife's kindred will honor the native, especially if the lord of the 9th house is in good aspect to the lord of the ascendant and is strong; but if the lord of the 9th house is an evil planet and in evil aspect, then the native will have a world of trouble with his wife's relations, lawsuits, religious persecutions, and the ill-will of judges, etc.

533 If in the 11th house, the native will suffer on account of religion and often to his utter undoing, unless the lord of the 11th is in sextile or trine aspect to the lord of the ascendant or to the lord of the 9th house, and, in that case, he is likely to gain advantage by friends, especially those living abroad in a foreign country, or he may hold some high position.

534 If in the 12th house, the native will be fortunate in the first part of his life, but in the middle or declining age, his enemies are likely to cause him much trouble, especially if the lord of the 9th house is an evil planet, and in evil aspect to the lord of the ascendant or the 10th house, then there is great danger that the native may be in prison most of his life, or have much suffering on account of lawsuits, or by his wife's relations.

Lord of the tenth in the 12 houses.

535 If the lord of the 10th house is in the ascendant it indicates that the native will attain great dignities, especially if it is a fortunate planet, and in good aspect to the lord of the 1st or 2d house; but if an evil planet and has an evil aspect, though he does rise ever so high, he will fall again, especially if the lord of the 4th house is in square or opposition to the Sun or the lord of the 1st or 10th house.

536 If in the 2d house the native will gain an estate or considerable advantage by gift or office, or from some person in high position, and he will be esteemed for his wealth.

537 If in the 3d house, the native will have few, if any brothers or sisters, but he will gain honor and advantage from his wife's relations, and enjoy it until death; but if the lord of the 10th house is an evil planet, and has an evil aspect in the 3d house, his relations will plot against him, and will endeavor to confine him in prison, or have him sentenced by a judge.

538 If in the 4th house, the native is likely to become a farmer or real estate agent, and will also be fortunate in mines and in any business in which he would have to deal in the fruits of the earth, especially if it is a fortunate planet and in good aspect to other planets, his property will advance in value; but if the lord of the 10th house is an evil planet and afflicted by the lord of the ascendant, 2d or 9th house, then the native will lose his property by lawsuits, etc.

539 If in the 5th house, the native's children will be sickly and but few live; he will be fortunate in marriage and enjoy the property of his wife, but very likely he will not live long, as he is liable to injure his health by feasting, pleasure or too much indulgence and improper living.

540 If in the 6th house, the native is generally poor or in low circumstances, and leads a plodding or drudging life; if the lord of the 10th house is a fortunate planet and in good aspect to other planets, then he is likely to gain honor and wealth by the practice of medicine, or discover some medicine by which he will make a fortune.

541 If in the 7th house, the native will gain by lawsuits and his wife, and acquire credit and reputation by her and her friends and relations; if the lord of the 10th house is an evil planet and afflicted in the 7th house, the native's wife or his partners will bring him sorrow and trouble, there is great danger that he will lose his credit and reputation, or become poor.

542 If in the 8th house, the native will, before middle age, attain wealth and honor by inheritance, wills or legacies; but there is danger that his mother will die early in life, especially if it is an evil planet or afflicted, in that case, he is swindled out of his legacies, or his wife s or mother's estates.

543 If in the 9th house, the native will be prosperous in taking long journeys or sea voyages, but is liable to die in some foreign country; he will also gain profit by learning or scientific pursuits, or being a lawyer or judge, or a member of the legislature, unless it is an evil planet or afflicted, in that case, he is then unfortunate in all the occupations and professions mentioned..

544 If in the 10th house, the native will be prosperous in trade, and likely to become very wealthy and noted on account of the large business that he will transact, and is almost certain to hold some high position under the government; but if it is an evil planet, then he loses it again, and is in danger of disgrace.

545 If in the 11th house, the native will be honored by his friends, and he will be very beneficial and helpful to his acquaintances, and will gain wealth and become prominent and noted, unless it is an evil planet, then he is unfortunate with his friends, and they do him harm instead of good.

546 If in the 12th house, the native will be very unfortunate, and will lose his office and dignity by the treachery of his pretended friends, who will prove to be private enemies; if the lord of the 10th house is afflicted in the 12th house, great danger that the native wll be sentenced by a judge, or have to spend many years in prison on account of his politics, or advocating some unpopular religious dogma, or being a socialist or anarchist, etc.

Lord of the eleventh in the 12 houses.

547 If the lord of the 11th house is in the ascendant it enables the native to overcome his enemies by means of his friends and acquaintances, and enables him to gain his hopes and expectations, and be fortunate in most of his engagements and undertakings; but if the lord of the 11th house is an evil planet or in evil aspects, especially to the lord of the ascendant, 4th or 10th house, then it produces the contrary, and his friends prove treacherous and deceitful, and cause him many losses and misfortunes.

548 If in the 2d house, the native gains riches by his friends and acquaintances, and he gradually becomes well off, as his friends will assist him; but if the lord of the 11th house is either Saturn or Mars and they are afflicted, then he loses money by his friends, who will be constantly borrowing or getting him to go security, and thus cause his ruin.

549 If in the 3d house and a fortunate planet, then the native's brothers and sisters and near relations will be very prosperous and attain prominence, and be of much advantage to him; he will also be very successful in his journeys, and make friends while traveling; but if the lord of the 11th house is an evil planet and afflicted in the 3d house, then his friends prove treacherous, especially while traveling or on journeys. He is also likely to be banished on account of his religion or politics, and meet with accidents and misfortunes while traveling.

550 If in the 4th house, the native's parents will be well off and have a large estate, but will not live long, especially if it is an unfortunate planet, but if a fortunate planet, then the native's estate will increase in value, and his friends remain with him until his death.

551 If in the 5th house, the native will be happy most of his life, and enjoy his friends and be prosperous, and he will also be fortunate with his children; but if the lord of the 11th house is an evil planet and afflicted in the 5th house, then his friends will rob him, and his children will prove treacherous and be a misfortune to him, or they die early in life, or in some way cause him much unhappiness, or he has none born to him

552 If in the 6th house, the native will have to work nearly all his life, or be a servant or lead a plodding life; he will generally have poor health, and he will not live to be old.

553 If in the 7th house, the native will marry a rich and good wife or husband, and they will live lovingly and happily together; but he is likely to be poor in his early years, but becomes well off in middle age; but if the lord of the 11th house is an evil planet and afflicted in the 7th house, then his pretended friends become his public enemies, and bring him to ruin and misfortune, and involve him in many lawsuits or quarrels.

554 If in the 8th house, the native will be unfortunate in trading, but will gain by wills and legacies; but if it is an evil planet and afflicted in the 8th house, the native loses most of his friends by death, or they nearly all die before him.

555 If in the 9th house, the native will be fortunate most of his life, and will have good success, and take many long journeys, and almost certain to hold some high office in a foreign country, such as embassador, consul, etc.; but if the lord of the 11th house is an evil planet and afflicted in the 9th house, then he easily quarrels with his friends and has lawsuits with them, or quarrels on account of religious dogmas, politics, etc.

556 If in the 10th house, the native will rule and become very powerful, and will rise to fortune; his friends will be of great advantage to him, and he may hold one of the highest political positions in the land, especially if the lord of the 11th house is a fortunate planet and in good aspect to the lord of the ascendant or 2d house; but if it is an evil planet and afflicted, then his friends turn against him, and help to bring him to misfortune or ruin.

557 If in the 11th house, the native will have many and very prosperous friends and acquaintances, and will have a good reputation; he is likely to be an adviser to a Governor or President, similar to being one of the cabinet, etc.; but if the lord of the 11th house is an evil planet and afflicted, he will afterwards come to disgrace.

558 If in the 12th house, the native's friends will prove treacherous, and always be plotting for his ruin, or trying to put him in prison, and he is likely to injure himself by leading an improper life, unless the lord of the 11th house is a fortunate planet, in that case it will not be quite so evil; but he must not expect any good from his friends.

Lord of the twelfth in the 12 houses.

559 If the lord of the 12th house is in the ascendant, the native will have many enemies, and they will cause him much perplexity and trouble, especially before middle age or in his early years, and if the lord of the 12th house is an evil planet and in evil aspect to other planets, then there is danger that his enemies will confine him in prison most of his life, and it will cause him to be poor, gloomy and dispondant up to middle age, and not well off even in the latter part of his life; but if the lord of the 12th house is a fortunate planet, then he may avoid being imprisoned, still he will be an unfortunate person and generally poor.

560 If in the 2d house, the native will have a great many lies reported to injure and damage his reputation, and he will be envied for his money or property; the native is likely to be confined in prison or in an insane asylum so that his enemies can get his money or property, but if the lord of the 12th house is a fortunate planet and has good aspects, then he may overcome his enemies, and gradually become well off, especially after middle age.

561 If in the 3d house, the native will have many crosses, misfortunes and much unhappiness caused by his brothers and sisters or near relations, and he will also be unfortunate in any business that causes him to take short journeys; and if it is an evil planet and has evil aspects, his kindred will try to get him into prison, or they die long before his old age.

562 If in the 4th house, the native's father will afflict him and become his enemy, and he will get but little benefit from his parents, or he and his family will have an unhappy home in his early life, and he is likely to leave his home before he becomes of age; his wife's mother will be his enemy, and he will know what it is to have a mother-in-law, but if the lord of the 12th house is a fortunate planet, then his father will not afflict him so much, and he may possibly get along with his relations, and gradually become well off by hard work.

563 If in the 5th house, the native's children will be very disobedient, and cause him much sorrow and trouble, and they are likely to get him into prison; he will also be very

unfortunate in all kinds of speculation, or his secret enemies may lead him into speculation in order to ruin him; but if the lord of the 12th house is a fortunate planet, then he may get along rather comfortably with his children, but they will still cause him unhappiness, or they die early in life.

564 If in the 6th house, the native will be very unfortunate with servants, small cattle and keeping boarders; he will also be unfortunate as a physician, and he is likely to lead a plodding, servile life, and have many hardships to endure, or he will suffer from poor health. But if it is a fortunate planet or in good aspect to fortunate planets, then the native may succeed in the practice of medicine or keeping a boarding house or with servants, etc., but will at times have trouble with them.

565 If in the 7th house, the native will be very unfortunate in his relations with women; they will get him into trouble, or cause him sorrow or misfortunes; and his wife will prove to be his enemy, and very likely get him into prison; he will also be very unfortunate in all kinds of partnerships or dealing with others; his partner will become his enemy and rob him, unless the lord of the 12th house is a fortunate planet and has good aspects, then it is not quite so unfortunate.

566 If in the 8th house, the native will see the death of nearly all or most of his enemies, and his enemies will come to trouble and misfortune; he is likely to get an estate by means of legacies or wills, but with much difficulty; his wife is also likely to be cheated out of her money or estate, or he gets no good from it.

567 If in the 9th house, the native will be troubled and annoyed by his wife's relations, and they will involve him in lawsuits and many difficulties; he will also be unfortunate in taking long journeys, and is likely to suffer much by religious persecution or the clergy, and religious people are almost certain to be his enemies, but if the lord of the 12th house is a fortunate planet, then he is likely to be very pious, or what the people call fanatical or a religious crank, or an advocate of some new dogma or unpopular theology.

568 If in the 10th house, magistrates or people in high office will persecute him, and cause the native much trouble and misfortune; he is likely to be banished or put in prison on account of corrupt judges, or his enemies swearing falsely against him; if the lord of the 12th house is a fortunate planet, then he may escape most of the above difficulties or misfortunes.

569 If in the 11th house, the native will have only pretended friends, and they will act deceitfully and treacherously towards him, and very likely become his secret enemies, and he will be unfortunate in most of his undertakings; he will generally be gloomy, despondent and discontented with his condition in life, especially in the early part of it; but if the lord of the 12th house is a fortunate planet, then he may retain some of his friends, but they will never do him much good.

570 If the lord of the 12th is in the 12th house, the native will have many enemies, and they will have much power to annoy him, and make his life miserable; he is liable to have lies or false reports circulated about him to his injury, and if the lord of the 12th house is an evil planet and in evil aspect to the lord of the ascendant or 4th house, they will bring him to ruin, and probably he will end his days in prison; but if the lord of the 12th house is a fortunate planet, then the evil will not be so great, unless it is afflicted by a square or opposition of an unfortunate planet, and that planet is either the Moon or lord of the 1st house, then he brings his misfortunes on himself, and he ends his days in prison.

REMARKS AND EXPLANATION.

On formulating the foregoing rules we sometimes meet with confusion or conflicting testimony on account of most of the planets being rulers of two houses, and one may be a good house, and the other evil, but if the lord of a house, say the first house, is alone and not in any evil aspect to any planet in that house, and not lord of any evil house, and is not perigrine or very weak, and the said lord is neither Saturn nor Mars, in that case the foregoing rules will be strictly correct, and always prove true in their indications of good fortune. But if it is Saturn or Mars, then it is an indication of evil fortune for anything belonging to that house.

For example, when the lord of the ascendant is alone in the second house, and that lord is neither Saturn nor Mars, and it is not the lord of any evil house, then the indications of riches for the native by his industry and ingenuity is almost certain to come true; but if it is in the second house, and is strong and well aspected by fortunate planets, who are lords of good houses; or if Jupiter or Venus, or both are in the 2d, house unafflicted, then the indications for riches are very marked. But if the lord of the ascendant is weak in the 2d house, and is in conjunction, square or opposition to Saturn, Mars or the Dragons tail, or if either of the unfortunate planets is also lord of an evil house, besides being lord of the ascendant, and is in the 2d house, especially if lord of the 2d, is in an evil house and afflicted by unfortunate planets, from evil houses, then the native will be poor throughout his whole life, and will die in poverty.

I should here remark that the Sun or Mars in the 2d house, is evil for saving money, as they are said to burn up the native's money or he spends it in a lavish and extravagant manner.

When a planet is lord of a good house, and at the same time lord of an evil one; for instance if it is lord of the 10th house, and also lord of the 6th house, then its influence is modified or weakened a great deal when in any good house, as the 2d, 10th, or 11th houses.

If Mercury is in the 2d house, and Gemini is in the 6th house, and Virgo in the 10th, in that case although the native will make money and be generally successful in business, yet he is likely to lose it again on account of sickness either for himself, or his family or relations; but if Mercury receives good aspects in the 2d house, and is lord of the 6th, and 10th houses, then he would be very successful as a physician or in any way dealing in medicine as a business, or keeping a boarding house, engaging servants etc., especially if there are fortunate planets in the 6th or 10th houses.

If the student has studied carefully the last paragraph on page 93 and continued on page 94, he will have a key to the meaning of many of the expressions in the foregoing remarks in relation to the "lords of the 12 houses."

For example, the 4th house in the native's horoscope is the first house or ascendant of the native's father, and the 5th is the father's house of money; the 6th is the father's house of brothers and sisters; the 7th, is the father's house of property or real estate; the 8th, is the father's house of children; and so on of all the other houses in the horoscope. The 10th house is the mother's ascendant or 1st house, the 11th, her house of money, the 12th, her house of near relations, neighbors, journeys, etc.

In paragraph 496 on page 207 where it says: "If (the lord of the 5th house is) in the 10th, misfortune, sorrow and affliction will come to the native's mother or his wife's father, and there is great danger that the native will meet with some serious disaster, or be sent to prison." The explanation of the above paragraph is that the 10th house, although a good house for the native, is in this case an evil house for the native's mother or wife's father, as it is in the 6th house (or the house of sickness,) from the 5th house, and it is the house of the native's mother and of the native's wife, (or husband's) father; and the 10th house is also the house of judges or magistrates, and being in evil aspect to the 5th house, they might cause him much trouble. This will serve as an explanation for other houses of the "lords of the 12 houses," which the student can study himself.

In a few cases of the lords of the houses, I have stated " he or she " or " husband and wife," etc.; but it would be a round about way of expressing my meaning to have continued that method for all the lords of the houses; besides it would have taken too much space.

The student can change the reading for females so as to read "she" for "he," and "husband" for "wife," and read as if the houses and their influence had been intended only for females.

Also in paragraph 527 the student can change the reading altogether, and read it in this manner for females ! "If the lord of the 9th, is in the 5th house, the native will have children to other men than her husband, especially if the lord of the 5th house is in evil aspect to the lord of the ascendant, and she may have to travel or go abroad on that account."

The astrological explanation is that the 9th house is the 5th house, (*or house of pleasure from the 5th house,*) and if the lord of the 9th house, or the 5th house from the 5th, is in the 5th house of the horoscope, then there is danger that the man or woman will go abroad, or go to strangers or persons living at a distance for their pleasure rather than going to his or her own home for the same end or object.

I think I have made the subject quite plain, but for fear the student does not fully comprehend the matter I give one more illustration. If the student turns to paragraph 550 on page 215, where it says: " If (lord of the 11th) is in the 4th house, the native's parents will be well off and have a large estate, but will not live long, especially if it is an unfortunate planet; but if it is a fortunate planet, then the native's estate will increase in value, and his friends will remain with him until his death " (as the 4th house is the end of all things.)

The explanation is that the 4th house is the house of the native's parents, and if the lord of the 11th, which is a fortunate house for the native, is in the 4th house of the horoscope, it indicates that the parents will be well off; but at the same time the 11th house, is the 8th house, or the house of death, reckoning from the 4th house, or house of the parents, also the 4th house, is the 6th, or the house of sickness from the 11th, indicating that the parents will either have very poor health, and not live long, as lord of the 8th, and the 6th, from the 4th house, will both be afflicting the 4th house, or the house of the parents; but if it is a fortunate planet, then they are likely to live long, and also the native will have many friends, as the 4th house is his home or his property, and as it is the end of all things, his friends are very likely to remain by him until his death, and not only that, but his father's friends, or friends of the family are very likely to continue to be the native's friends, and a fortunate planet in the 4th house improves the native's property, or makes it increase in value.

When the student understands all the various meanings of the houses as explained in the last paragraph on pages 93 and 94, he will be able to find out the true meaning of all the lords of the 12 houses, and can even make rules for himself, or extend the remarks in regard to his own or his friends horoscopes.

One thing the student should constantly keep in mind is that *Saturn and Mars are evil planets*, and afflict any part of the horoscope, wherever they are posited, no matter if they are lords of good houses ; and that *Jupiter and Venus are fortunate planets* and they benefit any house in the horoscope, wherever they may be posited, **if not afflicted,** even if they are in evil houses, but in these cases they are of but slight benefit, and may not do the native much good, still they prevent or modify what would otherwise be great harm or serious injury to him.

(For example, a particular friend of mine, who had in his horoscope Jupiter, lord of the 7th and 4th houses, in the 8th house, or house of death, and in square to Mars lord of the 8th, in the 11th house; often made the remark that Jupiter never did him any good, and he did not feel any benefit from its directions or transits through good houses, etc : but still it did him good in an indirect manner; although he did not appear to appreciate it. Once he stated that when at a fire in Manchester, N. H., he was holding the hose, and in order to get the water into the building, they had to break the windows, and while standing there, the whole side of the factory fell outwards, and when the smoke cleared away, to the surprise of everybody he was found to be uninjured; the wall having fallen in such a manner that the window just reached the place where he stood. He had a number of escapes of death in a similar manner. He died a natural death many years afterwards, Jupiter in the 8th, (or house of death), saved him from a violent death. What caused him frequently to be in danger of those accidents was that he had Saturn in his ascendant, and the Moon there also in close square to the Sun in the midheaven.)

In a horoscope it is always best to have a planet that is lord of a house in the same house, even if it is not in the same sign that it is lord of, it makes that planet much stronger, unless it is otherwise afflicted, even an unfortunate planet, if lord of an evil house, and in the house it is lord of, makes it much stronger for the native's good in every way. For example, lord of the 6th house in the 6th, makes the native's health much stronger, and he is better able to endure sickness, than if the lord of the 6th house, is in any other house than the 6th. Lord of the 8th, house in the 8th, even if it is an evil planet, unless afflicted, the native is almost certain to die of old age, and suffer but little sickness, unless the giver of life or the Moon or lord of the ascendant is much afflicted. But there is one exception to this rule, and that is the 12th house,. If lord of the 12th, house is in the 12th, it is very unfortunate for the native, as it causes the native's enemies to be very strong and powerful and able to do him much injury, but if lord of the 12th, is in its own sign and house, then it makes the native's enemies inclined to be rather generous, if such an anomaly can occur as *a generous secret enemy.*

If lord of the 11th, house is in the 11th, it makes the native have very good friends, and they are likely to be of much benefit to him all through life. [In my own horoscope I have Taurus on the cusp of the 11th house, and Venus in ♊ in the 11th house. It has always made me have a large number of good friends, especially females, but to offset these good influences, I have Mercury lord of the 12th, in the 10th house, near a square of the Moon, and also in square to Mars in the 6th, and Saturn, lord of the 7th house, afflicting the Moon in the 12th house; also Mars is lord of the 5th house, and of an intercepted sign in the 10th, and in square to Mercury in the 10th, and in opposition to the Moon, (my ruling planet,) in the 12th house, which aspects have caused me to have as many secret enemies as any person in my circumstances, but as Saturn is weak or in its detriment in Cancer, they have never been able to seriously injure me, but they have caused me a world of trouble and annoyance.]

There is one more idea that I wish to impress upon the student's mind, and that is when the lord of a sign is in its own house, even if it is not in its own sign, it is very strong; and by counting from that house it is lord of, it has its own relations, and signification in the horoscope, the same as if that house was the ascendant of the chart of the heavens.

For instance in paragraph 532, page 213, which says, ("If the lord of the 9th) is in the 10th house, the native will gain honor by long journeys, and the wife's kindred will honor the native, especially if the lord of the 9th is in good aspect to the lord of the ascendant, and is strong." The explanation is that the 10th house is the 2d house, or the house of money, from the 9th house, or house of long journeys, and the wife's kindred, etc. In the same paragraph it says: "but if the lord of the 9th house is an evil planet, and in evil aspect, then the native will have a world of trouble with his wife's relations, law suits, religious persecutions, or ill will of judges, etc." The explanation is, that an evil planet afflicting the 2d house, or house of money from the 9th, is a very great affliction connected with travelling, and law suits, or wife's kindred, etc., as it may cost the native considerable money, if afflicted by an evil planet, as the 10th house, is a house of great importance in the horoscope, and in lawsuits the judge may be very much prejudiced against the native, as the 10th house is in square to the 1st house of the horoscope, and if an evil planet is in the 10th, it afflicts all the more, as it would also be in square to the ascendant.

The 11th house is the 3rd house from the 9th; the 12th house is the 4th from the 9th; the ascendant is the 5th house from the 9th, and it being in trine aspect to the 9th, causes it to be a good house, especially if the lord of the 9th is a fortunate planet, and in the 1st house; but the 2d house is the 6th from the 9th, and it being an evil house, although a good house in the horoscope, it is an affliction to any business connected with the 9th house, especially if lord of the 9th is an evil planet, and in the 2d house; as the native is very likely to be taken sick or die on a journey, or probably he may lose considerable money on account of lawsuits or long journeys. And so on of all the other houses in the horoscope.

Remarks on the Lords of the 12 Houses, and explaining how they are used in Directions, Transits, Revolutionary Figures, etc.

571 By becoming well posted as regards the lords of the different houses in a horoscope, a person can predict how a particular direction or aspect, either Secondary, Primary or Transits, etc., will affect the native in different parts of his life, when those aspects come up, or are completed; for ex-

ample an evil aspect of Saturn, transiting over an angle, in the horoscope, or in square, opposition or conjunction of the Sun, Moon or any of the planets, by knowing what house Saturn is lord of at birth, or in what house it is posited in the horoscope, and from what house it afflicts in its transits, the Sun, Moon or lord of the ascendant, etc., the student can come very close to predicting how it will affect the native during the influence of its transit or evil direction, etc. The same in regard to good aspects, or directions of Jupiter, Venus, Moon or the Sun, he can generally tell when he knows what house it is lord or lady of; from what quarter or what kind of person the benefit is likely to come, and can also give a description of the man or woman who will aid or benefit the native, etc., and also in what particular manner it will affect or benefit him. In the horoscopes which follow, I give a number of illustrations of the lords of the different houses, affecting the native by directions, aspects and transits, and also how to apply them in Revolutions.

Remarks on the Changes in the Personal Appearance of the Native, in the Different Periods of His Life.

572 It is very important to give a few additional remarks as to the personal description of the native. On pages 158, 159 and 160, the student will find rules how to describe the native by the positions and aspects of the planets at the time of birth, and in a general way these rules will hold good in almost all cases, but there are a few exceptions which the student in his experience will learn. By constant observation the student will find that some persons are very light complexioned when young, or have light or yellowish hair, and a fair skin, but as he approaches maturity, his hair will sometimes change to be quite dark or almost black, and his skin becomes much darker; also there are instances where the native is very slender in early life, probably up to 24 years of age, then becomes quite full built, or stout, etc. I might give a number of other instances of the native changing in personal appearance in the different periods of life, and it may be well for the student to know what is the cause of the various changes of the build and complexion of the native.

Rules for Judging of the Changes of the Build and Complexion of the Native.

573 First, if the student observes very closely he will find that when there is a *stout sign on the ascendant*, and the lord of the ascendant is a slender sign, and especially if the Moon

is also in a slender sign, then the native will be slender in early life, or until he gets to be a man, and afterwards he will become of the nature of the ascendant, that is stout, or full built.

574 Second: If the lord of the ascendant, is in a light sign at birth, and particularly if the Moon is also in a light sign, and the sign on the ascendant is a dark sign, then the native is quite light complexioned when young, with light or flaxen hair, but as he grows older the influence of the sign on the ascendant has its effect on the native, and he becomes dark complexioned, and his hair gradually becomes darker as he he comes to maturity.

575 Third: If a slender sign is on the ascendant, and the lord of the ascendant is in a stout sign, especially if the Moon is in a stout sign, then the native is full built in early life, and becomes slender as he arrives at maturity; and if the Moon is in a stout sign he becomes stout after middle age or over 40 years old.

576 Fourth: If a light sign is on the ascendant, and the lord of the ascendant is in a dark sign, particularly if the Moon is also in a dark sign, then the native is slightly dark complexioned when young, and he becomes lighter as he grows to maturity, but in these cases the hair does not change as much as it does when he has light hair when young, and it becomes darker, on account of havng a dark sign on the ascendant.

577 Fifth: If Jupiter has much influence over the native in a horoscope, and he is slender when young, then he begins to fill out, or becomes stouter, when Jupiter performs its second revolution around the heavens, that is when the native is 24 years of age; but if Saturn has any influence in the natives personal description, then he generally begins to get stout when he gets to be 36 years of age, or when Jupiter has performed its third revolution, but if Saturn has much influence in a natives personal description, then he does not begin to grow stout until Jupiter forms his fourth revolution round the heavens, that is from 45 to 48 years of age.

578 Sixth: When there is a slender sign on the ascendant, and the lord of the ascendant, or the Moon are in stout signs, and particularly if they are in fixed signs, the native then sometimes will be slender when young, and become full built when he comes to maturity, and he grows slender again as he gets older, especially if Mars or the Sun is in the ascendant, or has any special aspect to the lord of the ascendant or the Moon, as the Sun and Mars dry up the watery humors of the system, as the native declines in life. This remark is

especially true if the lord of the ascendant or the Moon are in fixed signs. As for example Queen Victoria has Gemini on the ascendant, a slender sign, and the Sun and the Moon in the ascendant, but she has Mercury lord of the ascendant in the 12th house in a fixed and stout sign (Taurus.) She was slender when young, but afterwards became quite full built, but if she lives by this coming winter and through the year 1898, she will become more slender, as the Sun in the ascendant will dry up the watery humors of her system. She would have become slender years ago, if the Moon had not also been in the ascendant with the Sun, as the Moon is a watery planet, and tends to keep her of a phlegmatic nature.

579 Seventh: When a person is born under the planet Mars, especially a man, he will sometimes have quite dark hair and his beard or mustache will be quite light, sandy or yellowish. Whenever the student sees a person with dark hair, and light beard, he can always depend on it that Mars has something to do with his personal appearance, as no other planet produces the same effect. The Sun will sometimes cause a man's beard or mustache to be lighter than his hair, but not to the same extent that Mars does.

The Planets Impress Distinct Characteristics or Marks on the Native, which can be Recognized as follows:

580 Eighth: A Mars person is always straight and proud in his walk, and stamps his heels on the ground when walking and is also fond of dress and decoration and military display.

581 Ninth: A Jupiter person is known by having a prominent nose, and full eyes, rather large forehead; hair receding from the temples, etc.

582 Tenth: A Venus person is known by having a dimple in the cheek or chin, and generally has light soft expressive eyes, and soft brown hair and delicate skin.

583 Eleventh: A Sun person is known by having a full face, proud walk, and appears to be a person of consequence.

584 Twelfth: A Moon person is known by being mild and gentle, and is rather light complexioned and slightly full built.

585 Thirteenth: A Saturn person is known by being slow and deliberate in his actions and motions, and generally has some defect either in his walk, build, or personal appearance.

586 Fourteenth: A Mercury person is generally slender, talkative and active, and always wants to be doing something.

587 The seven planets not only govern the outward personal appearance, build, complexion, temperament, etc., of the native, but there are certain distinct parts of the human system which certain planets rule or have special government of, and which it is well for the student to learn, in addition to those rules mentioned on pages 187 and 188, and to remember them, as it will be useful to him in finding out what special disease or ailment, also what particular parts of the body will be affected or the native will suffer the most from, and also what he will die off.

The Seven Planets Rule the Human System, Named in the Following Order.

588 ♄ Governs the spleen, the right ear, bones, teeth, and retentive faculty, throughout the whole body.

589 ♃ Rules the lungs, liver, ribs, sides, veins, blood and digestive functions.

590 ♂ Rules the gall, left ear, the taste, the face and the testicles.

591 The ☉ rules the heart and back, also the right eye of a man and the left eye of a woman.

592 ♀ Rules the womb, and organs of generation, the kidneys, the throat, women's breast, milk and semen.

593 ☿ Governs the tongue, brain, rational faculties, imagination, hands, feet, and other moving parts of the body.

594 The ☽ rules in the body, the bowels, bladder, the right eye of a woman, and the left eye of a man.

595 The reason I have inserted this synopsis of the influence of the planets on the personal appearance, build, complexion, temperament and their various effects, and also the influence of the seven planets on the different parts of the human system, in this part of the Elements of Astrology, is, that in trying to find out the time of day that a person is born, by looking at the gentleman or lady you can often detect at once under what planet he or she was born under, before asking them any questions, and by changing the horoscope around so as to get different signs on the ascendant, you can often come very close to the hour and minute of birth. Then by asking several questions in regard to their ailments or what they suffer from most, whenever they are taken sick, and then noticing what planet afflicts that particular planet which rules that special ailment or disease and from what sign or house it afflicts, you can often get at the exact time of birth. For instance, if a person suffers most from rheu-

matism, especially of the bones, or neuralgia of the teeth, and is inclined to constipation, it is very probable that he is either born under Saturn or has Saturn in some way aspecting the ascendant, or in evil aspect to the lord of the ascendant or the Moon.

596 The same if a person is born under Jupiter, he generally has some defect in the lungs, or digestive organs, or bad circulation.

597 A Mars person is apt to have some breaking out on the face or skin, or pain in the left ear, or weakness of the generative organs.

598 A Sun person suffers from some weakness of the back, or heart, and if it is a man you can ask him whether he has any defect of the right eye, but if it is a woman the left eye is defective.

599 A Venus person suffers from the lower parts of the body, kidneys or throat.

600 A Mercury person is more apt to suffer from headache, or some affection of the head or nerves.

601 A Moon person suffers from the bowels, and if a woman you can ask her if there is any defect in the right eye, but if a man the left eye is defective.

602 By asking a number of questions that way, the student can generally find out the planet that they are born under, and also come very close to the correct time of birth.

603 In my extensive practice of astrology, I have made a number of other observations of a similar nature to the above, but I am afraid that if I had to put the result of all my experience on paper, it would become too complicated, and too tedious and confusing for the student to easily grasp, and make use of. But if the student continues to make constant observations himself, he will be able to notice a number of similar anomalies of planetary influence which he may use as guides in correcting and reading other horoscopes.

How to find the Time of Day a Person is Born, also how to Correct the Time of Birth.

604 It is advisable for the student never to attempt to find out the time of a person's birth, without seeing him, because a verbal or written description of the native is very often incorrect, but if he has the native himself to look at, he can judge much better what sign and planet he was born under. The student must notice first, the person's height, build, complexion, color of hair, eyes, etc., and try and find out what sign to place on the ascendant, or the sign which will come nearest describing him; then notice what particular sign the lord of

the ascendant is in, and whether it will describe a person similar to the native, also notice the Moon and what sign it is in, and the kind of person it will describe in that sign; afterwards notice the aspects, both of the lord of the ascendant and the Moon; and by changing the different signs on the ascendant, until the student comes to the one nearest answering to the personal description of the native. Then he must ask the native a number of questions in regard to the various events of his life, etc., and if he will not answer these questions then in that case do not bother any further with him. If you can get a direction of a square or opposition of Saturn, Mars or the Sun to the degree and minute on the ascendant, and reckoning a degree for a year in time, and can learn from the native what particular accident, sickness or misfortune befell him at any special time or year of his life, the student can generally find the right degree of the sign on the ascendant at the time of birth. But he must also notice the aspects of Saturn, Mars or the Sun and planets in the 4th house, to find out any particular sickness, accident or misfortune to the father; the same to the 10th house, or to the Moon and Venus, to find out any particular accident, sickness or misfortune to the mother, and when these aspects come up they generally produce some misfortune, sickness or death to the father or mother; and by noticing a number of these things, and should they all correspond and prove true, and the native admits it, then the student can set it down as a fact, that he has got very close to the time of the native's birth.

605 Notice also if there is an evil planet in the ascendant, and whether the planet is low down in the ascendant, or high up, or near the degree ascending, and also notice whether the native has any mark, mole, scar or blemish on the head or face, and see whether the mark or blemish on the head, is high up in the face, near the middle of the face or low down on the face, or on the neck· If the mark or blemish is high up on the face, or on the head, then the evil planet is near the degree or a little above the degree rising; if it is near the middle of the face, then the evil planet is lower down in the ascendant, but if on the lower part of the face or on the neck, then it is low down in the ascendant, or near the second house.

606 If the native has an evil planet in the ascendant, notice whether any other planet is applying to a conjunction, square or opposition to that planet, and notice how many degrees it is from the aspect; then find out from the native what particular year or time of life the native has received an

injury or blemish to the face or head, or had any serious illness, and by reckoning for each degree it has to go to complete the square, opposition or conjunction, one year of the native's life; the student can come very close to the hour and minute of the time of birth.

607 If an evil planet is rising, and the native has no mark or scar on the face, head or neck, then the student can set it down as a fact that the planet had risen above the ascendant before the native was born, but in such cases, the native has generally to suffer sickness or some accident when the planet comes to a conjunction of the degree of the ascendant by direction, and by reckoning a degree to complete the conjunction to the ascending degree for each year of the native's life, the student can come very close to the exact time the native was born

608 The same rule applies to the evil planets, either in square or opposition to the ascendant, and by noticing how many degrees the planet has to go to complete the square or opposition to the degree on the ascendant, and by reckoning a degree of longitude for a year of the native's life, the student can often come very close to the time of birth, by these aspects, even if there is no planet in the native's ascendant.

609 There are other parts of the body, and limbs, besides the head and face, where they may have injuries, marks, moles or blemishes, which we can often make use of in correcting the time of birth. For instance, a person having the sign Pisces on the ascendant, will often have some weakness, or injury, or mole on one or both of his feet, especially if Saturn, Mars or Uranus are in that sign, or in evil aspect to a planet in it.*

610 The same remarks apply to all the other signs being on the ascendant, or even the lord of the ascendant, being in the various signs of the Zodiac.

611 A person having Capricorn on the ascendant, generally has some weakness of the knees, or is very liable to rheumatism of those parts, especially if the planet Saturn is afflicted, and

---

* Judge Kenny who was Governor of Utah, "Whenever he came to Washington on official business of the territory, he would take a trip to New York to have a talk with me on astrology. He used to tell his friends in Washington, D. C., that there was no astrologer in these northern or eastern states that he could have a talk with, except Dr. Broughton. On one of his visits to New York he gave an account of being in a large hotel in Salt Lake City where there was an astrologer who was looking at the horoscope of a man's time of birth, and who was also present; the astrologer told the gentleman that he had a mole on a particular part of his foot, and the man emphatically denied it, so much so, that he bet a heavy wager, *that he had no such mark or mole.* After the wager was laid the man took off his boot and stocking in the parlor of the hotel, and found the mole, which he had never previously noticed, simply because his attention had never been directed to it, but the heavenly bodies and the laws of nature had been directed to it, and *impressed it there*, and the astrologer knew that it was an impossibility for that man to have been born with that peculiar configuration of the heavenly bodies, without that mole being impressed on that particular spot of his foot.

if he has an evil planet in Capricorn, then he has a mole or mark on one of the knees; we can often make use of these weaknesses, moles or marks on the different parts of the body, in correcting the time of birth.

612 When I come to treat on Medical Astrology, I shall enter more fully into these marks, scars, moles, etc., of different parts of the body; but I only refer to them in this place in order to make use of them in correcting the time of birth.

613 When a person applies to me to have their horoscope read, and they do not know their exact time of birth, I generally calculate a chart of the heavens for noon, for the year and the day of the month the native was born, and notice particularly all the signs and aspects, and positions of the planets at that time, and then change it around from one position to another, and at the same time keep looking at the native, until I gradually come to the supposed time of birth, and when I think I have come near the right time, then I calculate another chart of the heavens for that supposed time, and see how the marks, scars, moles, etc., agree, and all the events of the native's life; also his personal appearance must correspond with it; but it is almost impossible to find the hour and minute of birth by the various events of life, such as sickness, accidents, marriage, death of father or mother, etc., unless the native has some particular mark, scar, or injury as a guide, or he is particularly tall, short, stout, thin, or there is something marked in his personal appearance.

TABLE OF ESSENTIAL DIGNITIES AND VARIOUS OTHER TABLES AND INFORMATION, WHICH IS ADVISABLE FOR THE STUDENT TO KNOW AND UNDERSTAND, EVEN IF HE DOES NOT COMMIT THEM ALL TO MEMORY, BEFORE HE COMMENCES READING HOROSCOPES.

In order as far as possible to avoid any repetition of anything published in the first part of this volume, I refer the student to the Rudiments of the Science of Astrology on pages 87 and 88 for the inspection of a blank chart, showing the various positions of the houses of the heavens and their different numbers. I also refer to pages 89, 90, 91, 92 and 93 for the signification of the 12 houses, their natures, qualities and descriptions.

We here commence with the Signs and Symbols of the Planets.

PLANETS AND THEIR SYMBOLS.

♆ ♅ ♄ ♃ ♂ ☉ ♀ ☿ ☽
Neptune, Uranus, Saturn, Jupiter, Mars, Sun, Venus, Mercury, Moon

232   ELEMENTS OF ASTROLOGY.

I refer the student to pages 60, 61, 62, 63, 64 and 65 for the historical account of the planets, Jupiter, Saturn and Uranus, affecting the earth and its inhabitants; and to pages 66, 67 and 68 for the influncee of the near approach of Mars to our Globe, and its influence on the earth and its inhabitants; and on pages 69, 70 and 71 for the influence of the planet Uranus on the United States, while transiting through the sign Gemini; and on pages 74, 75, 76, 77 and 78 for the influence of Neptune on the earth and its inhabitants, while transiting through the sign Gemini; and on page 79 for the influence of the planets on Ireland, while transiting through the sign Taurus; and on pages 99, 100, 101, 102, 103, 104, 105, 106, 107, 108, 109, 110, 111, 112, 113, 114, 115, 116, 117, 118, 119, 120 and 121 for an account of persons described by the eight planets in the signs of the Zodiac; and on the commencement of page 122 to the end of page 141 for the effect o the eight planets on the native, when they form the conjunction, sextile, trine, square or opposition in his horoscope or in Horoary Astrology. Further on the student will find mention made of the planets being in their own sign or house, exaltations, triplicities, and in their terms, faces, detriment and fall; also mention will be made of the various planets being in what is called their joy or highest dignities; and an explanation of the effect or influence of these various essential dignities on the native when they occur in his horoscope.

On pages 185, 186, 187 and 188 is given the various diseases which each of the eight planets govern, and which effect the native.

The Signs of the Zodiac and their Classification.

The signs of the Zodiac, and their symbols are as follows:
Northern Signs, are:

♈   ♉   ♊   ♋   ♌   ♍
Aries, Taurus, Gemini, Cancer, Leo, and Virgo.

They are opposite the Southern signs, which are:

♎   ♏   ♐   ♑   ♒   ♓
Libra, Scorpio, Sagittary, Capricorn, Aquarius and Pisces.

The first six are called Northern Signs, because they decline from the Equinox towards the North Pole.

The second six are called Southern Signs, as they decline from the Equinox to the South Pole.

On pages 97, 98 is given the general appearance of persons described by the 12 signs of the Zodiac, and on pages 185, 186 and 187 is given the various diseases which are ruled by the 12 signs of the Zodiac; but there are several other matters connected with the signs of the Zodiac which ought to be further explained, and which the student should, as far as possible, commit to memory, and especially that part called *Essential Dignities of the Planets*, when they are in certain signs and degrees which it is advisable for the student to know.

The Division of the 12 Signs of the Zodiac.

These signs are divided into Fixed, Moveable and Common signs.
Fixed signs are : ♉, ♌, ♏ and ♒.
Moveable signs are : ♈, ♋, ♎ and ♑.
Common signs are : ♊, ♍, ♐ and ♓.

The Fixed signs are called such partly on account of the position of the Sun, as each year when it enters each of these signs, the weather is said to be more fixed, and not so changeable. For instance when the Sun enters Aries, a moveable sign, the climate or condition of the weather changes, but having got one whole sign into that season or quarter of the year, or over the change, the weather becomes fixed or more settled. So when a number of planets are in fixed signs, or the Sun or Moon are in fixed signs, and there are fixed signs on the angles of the horoscopes, then any business commenced at these times is likely to last or endure; also if a person is taken sick with the planets in a fixed sign, or fixed signs are on the angles, that sickness will not be easily removed or cured. Also, if a person is born with fixed signs on the angles in their horoscope or a number of the superior planets are in fixed signs, they are more stubborn and determined in their nature and disposition, than if they were born with moveable signs on the angles, and their planets also in a moveable sign. As an example, Gen. Grant had Taurus, a fixed sign, on his ascendant, and three of the superior planets, Saturn, Sun and Jupiter, all in that sign in the ascendant, and he had the planet Mars also in a fixed sign. Mrs. Grant once said: "The General is a very stubborn man," and his saying which became famous, "that he would fight it out on that line, if it takes all summer," was very characteristic of a man who had fixed signs on the ascendant, and so many planets also in fixed signs.

Gen. Washington had Taurus, a fixed sign on the ascendant, in his horoscope, and he also had Mars setting in Scorpio, another fixed sign, but Venus, his ruling planet, was in the sign Aries, a moveable sign, and he did not "fight it out on that line if it took all summer," but often retreated and adopted other lines of attacking his enemies.

A person born with moveable signs on the ascendant, or their planets in moveable signs, or any business commenced under moveable signs, especially if they are on the angles, is likely to change or vascillate the same as the weather in Spring, Fall, and the Tropics. Common signs are between the two, that is neither moveable nor fixed, and any business commenced under them is neither fixed nor is it easily changed.

These signs are also divided into Human Signs, which are : ♊, ♍, ♎ and ♐, (the first part of which is human shape).

Persons born with these signs on the ascendant, or most of their planets in these signs, are likely to be humane, kind and good natured in their disposition and temper.

Persons born with their planets in Bestial signs which are ♈, ♉, ♌, ♐ (the latter part,) and ♑, are likely to be more or less Bestial or coarse in their manners or take after animals which these signs are named after, if they are born with any of these signs on the ascendant, or their planets in these signs.

Double Bodied signs are ♊ ♓ and the first part of ♐.

Persons born with these signs on the ascendant, or on the 7th house, or their planets or the Moon in these signs, are likely to marry more than once and also liable to have twins.

Fruitful signs are ♋, ♏ and ♓.

Persons born with these signs on the ascendant, or on the 5th or 11th houses, are likely to have a number of children or be what they call fruitful in regard to children.

Barren signs are ♊ ♌ and ♍.

Persons born with these signs on the ascendant, or on the 5th house, or the Moon or lord of the ascendant in one of these signs, have very few children, if any. For example, Gen. Washington had Leo on his 5th house, which caused him to have no children.

Signs of Voice are ♊, ♍, ♎ ♐ and ♒.

Persons born with these signs on the ascendant or their Moon or lord of the ascendant in any of these signs, are likely to be talkative, have good language and make good speakers.

Mute signs or signs without Voice are ♋, ♏ and ♓.

Persons born with these signs on the ascendant, or their Moon or lord of the ascendant in these signs are not good speakers, they hesitate when talking, and seldom make good orators.

Cardinal signs are ♈, ♋, ♎ and ♑.

Persons born with these signs on the ascendant, or have many planets in any of these signs, become prominent or noted, or they are likely in some way to make a name in the world. They are called Cardinal because the season of the year changes when the Sun enters any of those signs.

Equinoctial signs are ♈ and ♎.

The Equinox occurs when the Sun enters either of those signs.

The 12 signs of the Zodiac are also divided into masculine and feminine. The Masculine signs are every other sign, viz: ♈, ♊, ♌, ♎, ♐, and ♒.

Persons born with any one of these signs on the ascendant are more Masculine and manly than if born under feminine sign; even females have a more masculine tendency when born under them.

Feminine signs are ♉, ♋, ♍, ♏, ♑ and ♓.

Persons born with any of these signs on the ascendant or the Moon or lord of the ascendant in any of these signs are generally feminine; they do not care to fight the world, and are more quiet and easy in their manners.

Triplicities or Trigons.

These signs are also divided into Eastern or Fiery signs, called the Fiery Triplicities or Trigons, which are ♈, ♌ and ♐.

These signs are called hot and dry. That is any person born under any of those signs, or if they are on the ascendant, or the Moon or lord of the ascendant, is in any of them, when they are taken sick, their illness is of a hot and dry nature; when well they are generally of a warm tendency and of a quick temper, and inclined to be of a dry nature; that is they do not retain much watery humor in their system.

Southern or Earthy signs or Triplicty are ♉, ♍ and ♑.

They are cold and dry. Persons born with any of these signs on the ascendant, or if lord of the ascendant, or the Moon is in any of these signs are more of a cold and dry nature; they seldom are afflicted with hot or burning fevers, but their diseases are generally of a cold kind.

Western or Airy signs or Triplicity are ♊, ♎ and ♒.

They are said to be warm and moist. Persons born under any of these signs are generally of a rather warm and moist tendency, and they are generally kind hearted and inclined to be effeminate.

Northern or Watery signs or Triplicity are ♋, ♏ and ♓.

They are cold and moist. Persons born with any of these signs on the ascendant, or the Moon or lord of the ascendant posited in any of them, are likely to be cold and of a moist tendency, and their complaints whenever sick are of that nature.

The signs are also divided into Dry and Moist.

Dry signs are ♈, ♉, ♌, ♍, ♐ and ♑.

Moist signs are ♊, ♋, ♎, ♏, ♒ and ♓.

These signs are also divided into signs of long and short ascension.

Long Ascension signs are ♋, ♌, ♍, ♎, ♏ and ♐.

Short Ascension signs are ♑, ♒, ♓ ♈, ♉ and ♊.

Any aspects from any sign of Long Ascension are likely to be longer before they are felt, but any aspects in signs of Short Ascension their influences are more quickly felt.*

The signs are also divided among the planets in the following order, and these planets that are on the line with the signs, are said to be lord or lady of the signs or houses, and are said to rule the signs they are lords or ladies of whether they are posited in them or not.

♑	♄	♒
♐	♃	♓
♈	♂	♏
♉	♀	♎
♊	☿	♍
♋	☽	
♌	☉	

Besides the planets being lords or ladies of the houses or certain signs, there are other signs in which a planet is said to receive its exaltation or be almost as strong as being in its own house, and even retains the

---

* William Lilly and a number of other old Astrologers, state in their works on astrology, that a square aspect in signs of long ascension is equal to a trine aspect; and a trine formed in signs of short ascension is equivolent to a square aspect, in their influence on the native or in Horary Astrology. I believe all modern Astrologers have given up that theory entirely, and that a square aspect is a square, and a trine aspect is a trine, no matter whether they occur in signs of long or short ascension.

In making calculations to find when any Primary Direction will be complete in a horoscope; reckoning a year for the degree in signs of short ascension, the event occurs about a month less than one year; but in signs of long ascension it is about a month over a year when the event takes place, reckoning a degree for a year in the native's life.

influence of that sign that it has its exaltation in, whether it be posited in that sign or not.

The signs are also divided into what is termed triplicities or trigons which have been mentioned, and which are also called Fiery, Eearthy, Airy and Watery signs on pages 234 and 235. Particular planets are said to rule or control these triplicities. The Sun and Jupiter rule the fiery triplicity; Venus and the Moon rule the Earthy triplicity; Saturn and Mercury rule the Airy triplicity, and Mars rules the Watery triplicity.* Also particular parts or divisions of the signs, are ruled by certain planets called the terms. Jupiter rules the 6 first degrees of Aries; Venus from 6 to 14; Mercury from 14 to 21; Mars from 21 to 26, and Saturn from 26 to 30. Also the signs are divided into three equal parts, and certain planets said to rule these divisions which are called the Faces. Mars rules the first 10 degrees of Aries; the Sun from 10 to 20 degrees, and Venus from 20 to 30 degrees. Venus on account of being in its own house in Libra, is said to be in its detriment in the sign opposite, which is Aries, or it is very weak in that sign. Saturn receives its exaltation in the sign Libra, and its fall in the sign Aries, and in that sign Saturn is very weak, and so on of all the other planets which can be noticed and learned in the table on the opposite page.

Explanation of the Table.

Every planet has two signs for its houses, except the Sun and Moon; they have but one each. ♂ has ♈ and ♏; ♀ Venus has ♉ and ♎; ☿ has ♊ and ♍; ♃ has ♐ and ♓, and ♄ has ♑ and ♒. The planets have their exaltations, as the third column points out: thus ☉ in 19 ♈; ☽ in 3 ♉; ☊ in 3 degrees ♊, etc., are exalted. But the student must bear in mind that the Sun is exalted in any of the degrees of Aries, only it has its highest exaltation in the 19th degree, and so on in regard to the planets being exalted in their respective Signs. These twelve signs are divided into Four Triplicities. The fourth column tells you which planet or planets govern each triplicity; as over against ♋, ♏ and ♓, you find ♂, who governs that triplicity; and over against ♈, ♌, ♐ you find ☉ and ♃ and so on of the other triplicities. The first six degrees of Aries are the terms of ♃, from six to fourteen, the terms of ♀ etc., etc. Over against ♈, in the tenth, eleventh and twelfth columns, you find ♂ 10, ☉ 20, ♀ 30; viz. the first ten degrees of ♈ are the Face of ♂; from ten to twenty, the Face of ☉; from twenty to thirty, the Face of ♀, etc.

In the thirteenth column, over against ♈ you find ♀ detriment, viz.: ♀ being in ♈, is in a sign opposite to one of her own houses, and so is said to be in her detriment. In the fourteenth column, over against ♈ you find ♄, over his head "Fall," that is, ♄ when he is in ♈ is opposite to his exaltation, and so is very unfortunate, etc. Though these things are expressed in the nature of the planets, yet this table makes it more evident to the eye, and is useful for reference.

---

* I refer the student to Ptolemy's Tetrabiblos translated by Mr. Ashmond, for the reason or explanation why certain planets were alotted to rule or govern certain triplicites; as Mars ruling the Watery Triplicity, and the Sun and Jupiter the Fiery, etc.

A TABLE OF THE ESSENTIAL DIGNITIES AND DEBILITIES OF THE PLANETS.

Signs of the Planets.	The Planets.	Exaltations of the Planets.	Triplicities of the Planets.	Terms of the Planets.					Faces of the Planets.			Planets' Detriment.	Planets' Fall.	Planets' Joy.
									First	Second	Third			
♈	♂	☉ 19	☉ ♃	♃ 6	♀ 14	☿ 21	♂ 26	♄ 30	♂ 10	☉ 20	♀ 30	♀	♄	
♉	♀	☽ 3	♀ ☽	♀ 8	☿ 15	♃ 22	♄ 26	♂ 30	☿ "	☽ "	♄ "	♂		♀
♊	☿	☊ 3	♄ ☿	☿ 7	♃ 14	♀ 21	♄ 25	♂ 30	♃ "	♂ "	☉ "	♃	☋	
♋	☽	♃ 15	♂ ♂	♂ 6	♃ 13	☿ 20	♀ 27	♄ 30	♀ "	☿ "	☽ "	♄	♂	☽
♌	☉		☉ ♃	♄ 6	☿ 13	♀ 19	♃ 25	♂ 30	♄ "	♃ "	♂ "	♄		☉
♍	☿	☿ 15	♀ ☽	☿ 7	♀ 13	♃ 18	♄ 24	♂ 30	☉ "	♀ "	☿ "	♃	♀	☿
♎	♀	♄ 21	♄ ☿	♄ 6	♀ 11	♃ 19	☿ 24	♂ 30	☽ "	♄ "	♃ "	♂	☉	
♏	♂		♂ ♂	♂ 6	♃ 14	♀ 21	☿ 27	♄ 30	♂ "	☉ "	♀ "	♀	☽	♂
♐	♃	☋ 3	☉ ♃	♃ 8	♀ 14	☿ 19	♄ 25	♂ 30	☿ "	☽ "	♄ "	☿	☊	♃
♑	♄	♂ 28	♀ ☽	♀ 6	☿ 12	♃ 19	♂ 25	♄ 30	♃ "	♂ "	☉ "	☽	♃	
♒	♄		♄ ☿	♄ 6	☿ 12	♀ 20	♃ 25	♂ 30	♀ "	☿ "	☽ "	☉		♄
♓	♃	♀ 27	♂ ♂	♀ 8	♃ 14	☿ 20	♂ 26	♄ 30	♄ "	♃ "	♂ "	☿	☿	

REMARKS ON THE TABLE OF THE ESSENTIAL DIGNITIES OF THE PLANETS.

The exact method of judging in Astrology is, first, by being perfect in the nature of the planets, and signs; secondly, by knowing the strength, fortitude, or debility of the significators, and well poising or ballancing them, and their aspects, and the several mixtures in your judgment; thirdly, by rightly applying the influence of the chart of the heavens erected, and the planets aspects to one another at the time of birth, according to natural and not enforced maxims of art; for by how much you endeavor to strain a judgment beyond nature, by so much do you augment your error.

A planet is then said to be really strong when he has many essential dignities, which are known by his being either in his house, exaltation, triplicity, term, or face at the time of birth. As, for example, in any scheme of the heavens, if you find a planet in any of those signs we call his house, he is then essentially strong, as ♄ in ♑, or ♃ in ♐, etc.

ESSENTIAL DIGNITY BY HOUSE.—In judgment, when a planet or significator is in his own sign, it represents a man in such a condition, as that he is lord of his own house, estate and fortune; or a man who has a good share of the goods of this world; or it tells you the man is in a very happy state or condition; this will be true, unless the significator be retrograde, or afflicted by any other malevolent planet or aspect.

EXALTATION.—If he is in that sign wherein he is exalted, you may consider him essentially strong; whether he be near the very degree of his exaltation, or not; as ♂ in ♑ or ♃ in ♋.

If the significator is in his exaltation, and no ways afflicted, and in an angle, it represents a person of haughty condition, arrogant, assuming to himself more than his due; for it is observed, the planets, in some part of the Zodiac, do more evidently declare their effects than in others.

TRIPLICITY.—If he is in any of these signs which are alotted him for his triplicity, he is also strong, but in a less degree.

A planet in his triplicity shows a man moderately endued with the goods of this world and rather fortunate; one well descended, and the condition of his life to be good; but not so much as if in either of the two former dignities.

TERM.—If any planet is in these degrees we assign for its terms, we allow it to be slightly dignified, but in rather low circumstances.

A planet fortified, only as being in its own terms, rather shows a man of the corporature and temper of the planet, than any extraordinary abundance in fortune, or eminence in the commonwealth.

FACE.—If any planet is in its decanate, or face, it has the least possible essential dignity; but being in its own face, it cannot then be called peregrine or out of all dignities, but a person indicated by it, is generally in very low circumstances, unless in good aspect, or otherwise strong by house, etc.

A planet being only in its face, describes a man ready to be turned out of doors, having much to do to maintain himself in credit and reputation; and in genealogies it represents a family at the last gasp, even quite decayed, hardly able to support itself.

A planet in its detriment or in opposition to its own sign, as Venus in Aries, is said to be very weak, similar to a person who is at the point of being turned out of doors. A planet in its fall or in opposition to its exaltation as Saturn in Aries, is compared to a person who has met with some misfortune, or has got down in the world, or is in poverty.

The planets may be strong in other ways; viz., accidentally, as when direct, swift in motion, angular, in △ or ✶ aspect with ♃ or ♀ the ☉ or ☽, etc., or in ☌ with certain notable fixed stars, as shall hereafter be related. ☞ When reading a horoscope or nativity, always notice what essential dignity, weakness or imbecility any planet has.

Joys of the Planets.

A planet may sometimes be more exalted in one sign, or have higher essential dignities, than only being in its own house or exaltation, and whenever a planet is in that particular sign, it is said to joy or be specially dignified, and which indicates that the person signified is in very good circumstances, or has nearly all the goods that this world can afford.

Joys or High Exaltations of the Planets.

♄ Rejoices, or is best fortified in ♒.
♃ Joyeth, and is best dignified in ♐.
♂ Takes pleasure most, or rejoices in ♏.
☉ Joyeth most in ♌.
♀ Is best of all dignified in ♉.
☿ Is highly exalted, and pleased in ♍.
☽ The only joy of Moon is in ♋.

The Reason a Planet Receives its Joy in one of its own Signs, and not in the Others.

Saturn rejoices in Aquarius, and not in Capricorn, because it is not only in its own sign, but it is also in its triplicity which makes it more exalted, consequently more potent.

Jupiter rejoices in Sagittary, rather than in Pisces, because in Sagittary it is in its triplicity, besides being in its own sign.

Mars is the same, it is also in its triplicity, besides being in its own sign, in the sign Scorpio.

The Sun is also in its triplicity, besides being in its own sign, in Leo, which causes it to be highly exalted.

Venus is also in her triplicity, besides being in her own sign, in Taurus, which causes her to rejoice in that sign.

Mercury is exalted in Virgo, rather than in Gemini, because it is in its exaltation, besides being in its own sign, in Virgo.

The Moon is in her highest dignities in Cancer, her own sign.

Historical Remarks on the Essential Dignities of the Planets.

There has been much difference between the Greeks, Arabians and other Eastern nations concerning the essential dignities of the planets as to the disposal of the several degrees of the signs suitably to any planet. After many ages had passed and before the time of Claudius

Ptolemy, the astrologers were not entirely settled in the matter; but since Ptolemy's time the Greeks unanimously followed the method he left, and which the other Christians of Europe to this day have since retained as most rational; but the Moors of Barbary at present, and those astrologers of their race who lived in Spain, somewhat vary from us in certain numbers of the degrees of the essential dignities of the planets, etc.

Orbs of the Planets.

All the planets are said to cast an influence of several degrees around themselves when they are near or approaching an aspect of another planet, and getting within a certain number of degrees, they are then said to be within orbs. The following are the orbs of the planets; both when approaching an aspect or when separating.

Table of the Planet's Orbs.

			Degrees.	Minutes.
Saturn's	Orbs	are	10	00
Jupiter's	"	"	12	00
Mars'	"	"	7	30
Sun's	"	"	17	00
Venus'	"	"	8	00
Mercury's	"	"	7	00
Moon's	"	"	12	30

Here you see Saturn's Orb is 10 degrees no minutes, the half of which is 5 degrees. Jupiter's Orb is 12 degrees, half of which is 6 degrees. Mars' Orb is 7 degrees 30 minutes, the half of which is 3 degrees and 45 minutes. Hence it results that the platic aspect (or remaining within Orbs) of Saturn and Mars remain until they are about 9 degrees distant from their Partial (or exact) aspect. The same when two planets are approaching an aspect. Jupiter and Saturn are in aspect as soon as they get within 11 degrees of the aspect.

EXAMPLE.

Suppose Satutn be in 15 degrees of Aries, and Venus in 10 degrees of Gemini, they are then in platic sextile of one another, for the Orb of Saturn, as you may see by the Table is 10 degrees, the half of which is 5. The Orb of Venus is 8, take half of that which is 4, and added to half the Orb of Saturn makes 9, so that they are within Orbs of a sextile aspect, when they are 9 degrees distant from their exact sextile in their respective signs.

The Mean Motions of the Planets.

The planets have certain motions in the Zodiac, when they are direct and the following is what is termed the mean motion of the planet, but sometimes they are Retrograde, and the mean motion includes both the Retrograde and their direct motion.

The Sun and the Moon never have any Retrograde motion. The Sun has very near the same motion each day, but the Moon varies very much in its motion on account of its apogee and perigee, that is, being far away or near the Earth.

Of the Mean Mot... ...lanets.

	Degrees.	Minut...	...onds.
Saturn's	0	2	1
Jupiter's	0	4	59
Mars'	0	31	27
Sun's	0	59	8
Venus'	0	59	8
Mercury's	0	59	8
Moon's	13	10	36

The use which may be made of this, is to know when a planet is swift or slow in motion, for if it moves more in 24 hours than is allowed for its mean motion, it is said to be swift, and if it moves less than its mean motion, it is said to be slow in motion. When a planet is swift in motion and making an aspect, that aspect is stronger for good or evil according to the aspect, than if the planet is slow in motion.

The Sympathy and Antipathy of the Planets. Or Friends and Enemies.

There are certain planets that are said to be friendly to other planets and there are planets which are said to bear enmity to other planets. Venus and Mars are said to be the greatest enemies of all the planets, but for all that they both take sides against their old and common enemy Saturn, as Venus and Mars are both enemies of that planet. The following is the table of friendships and enmities of the different planets, which the student ought to remember if possible, as he will find it of much advantage in his practice of astrology.

A Table of the Friendships and Enmities of the Planets.

PLANETS.	FRIENDS.	ENEMIES.
Saturn's	♃ ☉ ☿ ☽	♂ ♀
Jupiter's	♄ ☉ ♀ ☿ ☽	♂
Mars'	♀ only	♄ ♃ ♀ ☿ ☽
Sun's	♃ ♂ ♀ ☿ ☽	♄
Venus'	♃ ♂ ☉ ☿ ☽	♄
Mercury's	♄ ♃ ☉ ♀ ☽	♂
Moon's	♃ ☉ ♀	♄ ♂

By this table you may perceive that the friends of Saturn are Jupiter Sun, Mercury and Moon, his enemies are Mars and Venus.

In the above table it is said that Venus is a friend of Mars, but Mars is an enemy of Venus. Indeed Venus is friendly to nearly all the planets, except Saturn, but for all that the student will find in his practice in astrology that when it comes to the Human family that Venus and Mars get along very badly together. For instance: If a person is born with either, Aries or Taurus, or Libra or Scorpio on their ascendant, in these horoscopes they have the opposite signs on the 7th house, and if Mars is lord of the ascendant, then Venus is lady of the 7th, or if Venus is lady of the ascendant, then Mars is lord of the 7th house. In all nativities which I have seen with any of these signs on the ascendant, unless there are some special good aspects for marriage in these horoscopes, they nearly all separate. Certainly they are very jealous of each other, and make each other very unhappy.

The student when examining two horoscopes if he finds one of them has Mars lord of the ascendant, and the other has Saturn lord of the ascendant, he can depend upon it that those two parties cannot agree well in any kind of partnership, or business undertaking, or even if one of them has the Sun lord of the ascendant, and the other has Saturn lord of the ascendant, those parties will not agree either in marriage, or partnership, as Saturn's house is in opposition to the Sun's house. The same remark may be applied to other planets which are at enmity with each other. The reason Mars' and Venus' men and women, cannot agree in marriage or partnership, is that these two planets are of opposite natures; that is Mars is hot and dry, quick tempered, full blooded and evil. Venus is cold and moist, phlegmatic and fortunate and good; besides each have their sign opposite to each other, that is Aries is opposite to Libra, and Taurus is opposite to Scorpio. Besides these signs do not agree in temperament, as Aries is hot and dry, and Libra is hot and moist Taurus is cold and dry, and Scorpio is cold and moist. The same kind of reasoning applies to all the planets and the signs that they are ladies or lords of.

Aspects of the Planets.

If the student refers to page 89 of this volume, he will find there the various aspects mentioned and explained, and which he ought to have committed to memory. The various houses of the heavens are in aspect to each other, and also the signs are in aspect to each other, and the planets in their revolutions round the heavens form these various aspects when transiting through these signs.

These aspects have been known and recognized for thousands of years. They are:

☌ Conjunction.		☍ Opposition. 180°
✶ Sextile.	60°	⊕ Part of Fortune.
☐ Square.	90°	☊ Dragon's Head or ☽ Node.
△ Trine.	120°	☋ Dragon's Tail.

The Sextile and Trine are what is termed fortunate aspects, the Conjunction is a fortunate aspect with good planets, and an unfortunate one with evil planets; the square and opposition are the evil aspects, and show a state of enmity between these planets that are in opposition or square to each other. Besides these aspects which were known to the ancients, John Keppler one of the greatest astronomers that ever lived, discovered other aspects that have come into general use with astrologers; although they are not so important as the ones that the ancients knew. In short when we have either the squares, oppositions or conjunctions, sextiles or trines, we pay but slight attention to these new aspects; but when there are no special aspects of the planets formed by what is termed the old aspects, then we notice the new aspects and they are the following.

The New Aspects Discovered by John Kepler.

Semi-sextile	30°	apart.
Semi-square	45°	"
Quintile	72°	"
Sesqui-quadrate	135°	"
Biquintile	144°	"

Parallel of declination, i. e., when two planets are the same number of degrees distant from the Equator, whether one is North and t e other South or both are North or South.

The student ought to understand that the Semi-sextile aspect is only about half the strength of the sextile aspect, and the same with the Semi-square; also these aspects formed by dividing or adding to the good aspects, are fortunate aspects. These that are made up out of the evil aspects of the ancient, such as squares, oppositions, etc., are evil aspects.

The Part of Fortune and what is called the Moon's Node, or Dragon's Head, or Dragon's Tail, are not strictly speaking aspects, still they are positions that astrologers make use of in their predictions. The Part of Fortune is a point of equal distance from the ascendant that the Moon is from the Sun, and is called the luminary to the ascendant, and it has much to do with money matters, when in a good house or in good aspect to good planets, the native is generally fortunate in money matters, unless he has otherwise a very evil horoscope. Also when afflicted by evil planets, or being in evil houses, the native is generally unfortunate in money matters, and if he has an unfortunate horoscope, he is poor most of his life. If the Part of Fortune is cadent and has no aspect, I rarely notice it, or regard it as of little account.

The Dragon's Head, or Moon's Node, is that point where the Moon crosses the ecliptic, and it is generally where the eclipses occur. The Dragon's Head is counted fortunate; the Dragon's Tail is unfortunate. Dragon's Head is of a similar nature or influence to Jupiter, only not so strong, and Dragon's Tail is similar in nature or influence to Saturn, but not so evil.*

---

* All modern astrologers are not agreed nor of the same mind as to the effect or influence on the native of the planets when in their "Essential Dignities," or as to the influence of the "Dragon's Head" and "Dragon's Tail," or the effect of the "Part of Fortune." Some astrologers wish to discard all of them; and of that number was Mr. James Wilson as evinced in his Dictionary of Astrolgoy. He would not admit that any planet can have any effect in any other sign than the one in which it is posited in the horoscope. But nearly all astrologers of the present day admit that the planets are lords or ladies of certain signs; as Mars is lord of Aries and Scorpio, Venus is lady of Taurus and Libra, etc., whether they are posited in these signs or not; but some modern astrologers question the efficacy of the "Terms" and "Faces" of the signs and are at variance as regard these minor influences.

My own experience has led me to believe that each and every planet is stronger in certain signs and in certain degrees of signs than in others. I always feel sorry for any person born with his ruling planet out of all Essential Dignities and in cadent houses, and in no good aspects to fortunate planets, and the Moon, and the Part of Fortune afflicted; such persons are drudges or menials nearly all of their lives and generally die in poverty. I should have been more fortunate if the Dragon's Tail had not been in my midheaven, and the Part of Fortune had not been so afflicted by Mercury applying to an opposition of it from the tenth house, and Mars making a square from the sixth house, and the Moon my significator in the twelfth house just leaving a square.

There are some persons so dull or obtuse as not to be able to distinguish any of these finer influences in astrology, or indeed in any other art or science; as there are persons that cannot take pleasure in music on account of their inability to distinguish between the tunes "Old Hundred" and "Yankee Doodle," and there are others who cannot understand anything that is not hammered into them as if by a sledge hammer.

GOOD AND EVIL PLANETARY HOURS.

"The lucky have whole days, and these they choose:
The unlucky have but hours, and these they lose."—DRYDEN.

"There is a tide in the affairs of men, which taken at the flood, leads on to fortune."—SHAKESPEARE.

"To every thing there is a season, and a time to every purpose under the heaven: a time to be born and a time to die; * * * a time to kill, and a time to heal; * * * a time to get, and a time to lose."—SOLOMON.

The meaning of the above is, that fortunate persons when they intend to transact any particular business, or make any special changes in their lives, choose "fortunate hours" or "lucky times" for that purpose, such as getting married, removing, taking journeys, going into any new business, performing surgical operations, beginning treatment of patients, changing the medicine, etc.

The unlucky persons not knowing these fortunate hours, and having no intuition or knowledge to guide them, often choose "unfortunate hours" to commence important undertakings, which cause these undertakings to generally end in disaster; and although they may have short periods of good fortune, not knowing when these "fortunate hours" occur they do not succeed, and their "Lives," as Shakespeare says, "are bound in shallows and in miseries."

In ancient times, or before the Christian Dispensation it was customary to ascertain the good and evil times by calculating the movements of the heavenly bodies, and all important business was commenced under fortunate "Planetary influence," and in "fortunate hours," such as turning the first "sod," laying the first "stone," or driving the first "pile" on which to erect an important building or structure. (See note on page   of the Appendix.)

It is just possible that choosing these "fortunate" times for the commencement of large constructions may have had something to do with the duration of these ancient buildings, as for example, the Catacombs and Pyramids of Egypt, the ruins of Babylon, and the numerous Temples of Greece and Rome, and other ancient structures referred to by Volney, and other writers in their account of the ruins of ancient cities. Mr. Volney in his book on "Ancient Ruins" furnishes substuantial proof of the attention which our forefathers gave to Zodiacal and Planetary influence in relation to the time of commencing their buildings and large constructions.

It is impossible to explain why the time for the commencement of any new business, or the erection of any important building, should have anything to do with the future prosperity of that business, or the long duration of these buildings, any more than it is possible to explain why the time when the child draws the first breadth of life, and the aspects of the heavenly bodies, and the positions of the signs of the Zodiac, should have anything to do with the life, death, sickness, health, prosperity or adversity of that child; but such are the facts, and which facts can be proved in thousands and even millions of instances. We have to take these facts as we find them, as we take thousands of other facts or occurences, without any proof beyond the facts themselves. We cannot reason on them, until we have enough to formulate a science, after being arranged into methodical order.

Astrologers like other persons in the various conditions and walks of life, have had differences; some have believed certain parts of astrology which others have not. Astrologers might be compared to the two classes of homœpathic physicians, one of them being high potency and the other low potency. There are artrologers who do not believe in the high potency of Astrology, or in anything they cannot calculate, and get positive or ponderable proof of; they do not believe in any of the imponderables in Astrology; For instance, these Astrologers take but little stock in the "Part of Fortune," the "Dragon's Head" and the "Dragon's Tail," the "Planetary Hours," and the "Essential Dignities of the Planets," etc. Some will even deny the special influences of each of the "twelve houses" as they are termed, and will only believe or notice the angles, or the points of the heavens of the rising, setting, and the culminating of the Sun, Moon and planets; and the nadir, or that point opposite the midheaven.

Professor Wilson was one of the latter kind of Astrologers, and yet no one was more emphatic in his belief of Astrology, and had less patience with the unbelievers in that science. In his Dictionary of Astrology in answer to the objectors and sceptics in Astrology, he makes use of the following language:

"As to the common place objections against Astrology, they are too superficial to be worth a moment's attention, much less to deter an active mind from pursuing its researches. A small degree of penetration in a student will soon enable him to perceive that his adversaries are men of little knowledge, or great prejudice, with very limited capacities, and almost incapable of reflection; without any original thoughts, or indeed thoughts at all, except what they have borrowed from such as have made but few observations of their own, respecting themselves or the universe in general; they are men that are either absorbed in other speculations than those of nature, or who think only by permission; that would believe the legend, and deny the existence of the antipodes if others about them did the same. With them the *vox populi* is truly the *vox Dei*; the only argument capable of convincing them is a great show of hands; and any absurd hypothesis, having the major part of the world on its side, (a thing not very uncommon,) would soon add them to the number of its disciples. I know that in answer to this the opinions of learned men may be quoted, but learning is not always united with discernment or real knowledge, any more than the words of a talking bird, are united with ideas. Learning is a mechanical acquirement that may be posessed by a very silly person; and of this we have numberless instances. With such men reason is useless; they would oppose custom to reason, and authorities to facts. I once had an argument with one of these, a person of extensive learning and uniform dullness, except when relieved at intervals by a most unaccountable, persevering obstinacy. We were speaking of the Moon, which he denied had any influence on the weather. I pointed out to him and even predicted several instances, wherein a change of weather would take place, which most or all of them were verified and I won some trifling wagers from him on this score; but though still vanquished, as Goldsmith says, he would still argue, and with as much obstinacy as if he had never been proved to be in the wrong I then began to appeal to his reason, and asked him, 'If the Moon could move a fluid of such gravity as water, why it might not more easily affect or influence the atmosphere, which was more light and elastic?' He denied that I could prove that it did affect the water, Surely, said I, the tides prove that; this too, he denied. He admitted that it was a strange coincidence of periods, but contended that they might have been as they are, had the Moon never existed. I had some inclination to make him affirm (which I easily could have done,) that day and night, and summer and winter might have been the same as they are, had the Sun never existed; but I was weary of his folly."

Students will readily perceive that no one could be more positive and emphatic in his belief in Astrology than Mr. Wilson. Indeed had he not been a firm believer in that science he would never have compiled, written and published his "Dictionary of Astrology," which work evinces a degree of learning and research that is truly marvellous, and had he had an equally extensive practice in Astrology, he would have been a thorough believer in the "Part of Fortune" the "Twelve Houses" and the "Dragon's Head" and "Dragon's Tail," and the "Essential Dignities," etc.

There are astrologers similar to myself, who may be classed as the "high potency" astrologers, and who believe whatever occurs in the heavens, has a corresponding influence on the earth, and whatever positions the various heavenly bodies assume in the heavens, have a corsponding effect on the earth; and who believe in the principles of Astrology similar to the poet Thomas Niel who wrote the following lines, and which contain more truth than poetry.

"I tell thee,
"There is not a pulse beats in the human frame
That is not governed by the stars above us,
The blood that fills our veins, in all its ebb
And flow, is swayed by them as certainly
As are the restless tides of the salt sea
By the resplendent moon: and at thy birth
Thy mother's eye, gazed not more steadfastly
On thee, than did the star that rules thy fate,
Showering upon thy head an influence
Malignant or benign."

The above lines prove that Mr. Neil was what we might term a "high potency" astrologer.

The poet Dryden may be classed among the high potency astrologers, if we may judge by the following remarks, which he made to his wife, after he had calculated the horoscope of his son Charles. He told lady Dryden that the child was born in an *evil hour*, meaning an evil "planetary hour," which was one of the hours of Saturn or Mars, and as he said "the lord of the ascendant was afflicted with a hateful square of both Saturn and Mars," and being born in the hour of one of those planets made that aspect more *unfortunate or evil.*

Also we may class the poet Goethe among the high potency Astrologers, if we may judge by what he states in his autobiography. He tells us: "My horoscope was propitious; the Sun was in the sign of the virgin and had culminated for the day. Jupiter and Venus looked on him with a friendly eye, and Mercury not adversely, while Saturn and Mars kept themselves indifferent. The Moon alone just full exerted the power of her reflection all the more, as she had just reached her "*'planetary hour.'*"

John Kepler, may also be classed among the high potency astrologers, where he says: "A most unfailing experience of the excitement of sublunary natures by the conjunctions and aspects of the planets, has instructed and compelled my unwilling belief."

Remarks on the Planetary Hours.

The planetary hour is not the ordinary sixty minutes of the clock time, but the period of Sunrise to Sunset, divided into twelve equal parts; each part being a "planetary hour" of that day. From Sunset to Sunrise is also divided into twelve equal parts, and each part is a "planetary hour" of that night.

One of the main reasons why "planetary hours" have been so neglected by modern astrologers, is the difficulty in calculating those " hours," especially in the higher latitudes where the days are very long in the Summer months, (as in England, Scotland, Sweden and Norway,) and where the days are so short in the winter months. Also the difficulty in counting the planets in their proper order, from sunrise of that particular day to the hour and minute the astrologers wish to attend to any important business, or the time a person was born.

I have succeeded in getting up a set of "Tables of Planetary Hours," that by inspecting and knowing the day of the week, month, and the day of the month, and the hour of day, one can easily find which planet rules that particular "Planetary Hour" and see when any planet's hour begins, and when it ends, and by these tables a person can choose "*fortunate planetary hours*" to transact any important business or commence a new undertaking; and can guard against beginning those undertakings *in evil hours*. Not only that, but the student can avoid making the mistakes which were very common, in counting the planets and the hours from sunrise or sunset, to the hour and minute he wishes to calculate them to.

If the student turns to pages 14, 15, 16 and 17 of this volume, he will find an explanation of the origin of the names of the days in the week, and of the order in which they run.

On page 14 he will find a table illustrating why Sunday follows Saturday, and Monday follows Sunday, and so on of all the other days in the week. These days were arranged on the principle of the *first hour* after sunrise of that day, being dedicated to the planet which it is named after, or the planet which rules that day.

We have no historical account of the time when the days were first arranged in the order we now have them. It even goes back long before any written record, or the building of the Pyramids of Egypt, and is even older than the Three Towers of Babylon.

The order of the days and their arrangement into seven, or one quarter of a Moon, or the fourth of a month, so harmonizes with the laws of nature that it has penetrated into every nation that is even half civilized, and has been adopted by those nations in every quarter of the globe. Not only that, but they have been called by the names of the planets, and used by the people in all ages or at least as far back as we have any record.

The Latin and the French languages up to the present day make use of the names of the planets, for all the names of the days of the week, except Sunday.*

As already stated in pages 13, 14, 15, 16 and 17, and illustrated in the Table of Planetary Hours on page 14, that the planet rules the day it is named after, and also rules the first hour after sunrise; that the seven planets have each a day of the week allotted to them, and that the order of the planets are reckoned from the planet Saturn inwards towards the Moon, and the first hour of the day after sunrise is ruled by the planet that the day is named after, therefore on Sunday the Sun rules the first

---

* Whenever I have lectured on the "Planetary Hours," some one of the audience has taken exception to the idea that certain names of the days of the week have been changed and named after some notable General, and will insist that they are named in honor of deities or pagan gods. I cannot bring to mind in which History of England I have seen the names of those pagan generals mentioned, and stated that the names of certain days of the week were called after them. I think it is Lingard in his History of England mentioned "Twi" and stated that Tuesday was named after that General. Mrs. Anna Bowman in her book on Travels in Norway and Sweden gives the account of the church, and the two graves where Thorr and his wife Frea are buried, also states that Thursday and Friday were named in honor of them. "Wolden" or man of the woods, has been named in a number of histories as being a noted General and afterwards became a deity or Saint after his death, and Wednesday was named in honor of him.

Mr. Isaac Sharpless and Professor G. M. Phillips in their astronomy mention that Tuesday, Wednesday, Thursday and Friday are named after four English deities. Nothing could be more ridiculous than that, as the ancient Druids did not have any deities, or Pagan gods, like the Pagans on the northern part of Europe; they were great observers of the laws of nature, and of the heavenly bodies, especially the rising and setting of the Sun, Moon, and the various planets as can be proved by the ruins of Stonehenge, which still remain on Salisbury Plains, Wiltshire, England. No matter what names some of the days of the week are now called, one thing is certain, that in old or ancient languages, as the Latin, the names of the days of the week were all named after the planets, which rule these days, and they were afterwards changed in the modern European languages, such as the German, Italian, English, etc., all of which are corruptions of the ancient Latin.

The following table No. 1, gives the names which the French use at the present day, for the names of the days of the week, and which they have used from time immemorial. The student will see that each day of the week is designated by the French names of the planets which rules that day, except Sunday; and in some way that has got changed, as Soleil is the French name for the Sun. The word Dimanche is supposed to be a corruption of the Latin "Dominica" or the Lord's day, the English still retain the name of Sunday or Sun's day, and the German's Sonntag, or Sunday, for the first day of the week.

The French, during the Revolution, divided the months into three decades of ten days each, and gave the following Latin numerical terms for the names for the respective days of the Decade in the order as given in the 2d Table. But by Napoleon's command this new system was abolished, as it was found to be too artificial for general use, and at variance with planetary laws. The Gregorian Calender was resumed on Jan. 1st, 1807.

TABLE No. 1.	TABLE No. 2.
FRENCH NAMES OF THE DAYS OF THE WEEK.	NAMES OF THE DAYS OF THE DECADE USED BY THE FRENCH DURING THE FRENCH REVOLUTION.
Dimanche.........Sunday.	1st Primidi. 6th Sextidi.
Lundi............Monday.	2d Duodi. 7th Septidi.
Mardi............Tuesday.	3d Tridi. 8th Octidi.
Mercredi.........Wednesday.	4th Quartidi. 9th Nonidi.
Jeudi............Thursday.	5th Quintidi. 10th Decadi.
Vendredi........Friday.	
Samedi..........Saturday.	

The names of the days of the week in the German language, is very similar to that in the English language. They are called Sonntag, Montag, Dienstag, Mittwoch, Donnerstag, Fritag, Samstag. Tag meaning day in German.

hour after sunrise, Venus rules the second hour, Mercury rules the third, the Moon rules the fourth, Saturn rules the fifth, Jupiter rules the sixth, Mars rules the seventh, the Sun rules the eighth, Venus rules the ninth, Mercury the tenth and the Moon the eleventh, as the student will see in the "Perpetual Tables of Planetary Hours, from Sunrise to 2 Hours after Sunset" on page 255, and also in the following table.

> Sun governs the first hour after Sunrise on Sunday.
> Moon governs the first hour after Sunrise on Monday.
> Mars governs the first hour after Sunrise on Tuesday.
> Mercury governs the first hour after Sunrise on Wednesday.
> Jupiter governs the first hour after Sunrise on Thursday.
> Venus governs the first hour after Sunrise on Friday.
> Saturn governs the first hour after Sunrise on Satnrday.

Signification of the Planetary Hours, and what use may be made of Them.

The significance of the planetary hours, and the matters, or kinds of business they rule, and the manner in which they may be used to advantage are clearly explained by old astrologers. I here give their teaching not only because it is curious and interesting, but also because it is based on sound astrological rules and principles.

The Influence of the Planetary Hours of the Sun, Moon and the Five Planets.

The Hour of ♄.

614 In the *Hour of Saturn* take no voyage to Sea, neither take any long journey by land, for crosses will assuredly attend, and small success may be expected; take no medicine, for it will produce harm rather than good, and engage no servants, for they will prove idle, careless and worthless persons; Evil to put on new garments or cut your hair; but this hour is good to buy, or take leases of houses or lands; good to buy any kind of grain, or to dig in the earth, or plow; not good to borrow money in this hour or to lend it. It is an evil hour to fall sick in, for it threatens a long disease and liable to terminate in death.

The Hour of ♃.

615 In the *Hour of Jupiter*, it is good to apply to ecclesiastical persons, or persons in office, and all great or wealthy men such as lawyers, judges, senators, etc., to obtain their favor. In this hour it is good to go out of the house, to commence a journey to have it end with success; good to sow all kind of seeds or to plant; not good to let blood; he that falls sick in

this hour will soon recover; also good to lend or borrow money; not good to enter a ship; not good to buy cattle. This hour is good to propose marriage, or contract matrimony, etc.

THE HOUR OF ♂.

616 In the *Hour of Mars* begin no worthy action, or important undertaking, or great enterprise, for it is a very unfortunate hour, and therefore it is an hour to be avoided; it is ill to take or commence a journey, for you will be in danger of thieves; very ill to take a voyage to sea, and generally evil for all things, especially for surgical operations, etc. It is an *evil hour;* therefore to be shunned as much as possible.

THE HOUR OF ☉.

617 The *Hour of the Sun* is not to be chosen, as it is generally unfortunate, unless in making application, or asking favors of wealthy or influential persons; not good to begin a building, or put on new garments; not good to enter a new house, or remove into a house, for discontent and brawling may then be expected to follow; this hour is good for a man to receive preferment in; not good to court the female sex as they will try to control you; do not pay, or lend money upon on any account; it is also a very critical hour to be taken ill, as the sickness is liable to be dangerous, and violent.

THE HOUR OF ♀.

618 In the *Hour of Venus* it is good to court women, or to begin a journey, but not a long voyage; good to enter upon any play, sport or pastime; not good to let blood; good to go out of a man's or friend's house with success; but not so good to return again to it; but good to enter your own home; good to take medicine; but if a man falls sick in the Hour of Venus, the disease proceeds from self-indulgence, or intemperance, or caused someway by females; this hour is generally good to undertake any business relating to what concerns women, or any delightful actions; not good to begin to make new garments, but singularly good to propose marriage, and contract Matrimony. Good for either men or women to have dealing with females.

THE HOUR OF ☿.

619 The *Hour of Mercury* is very good to deal in merchandise, or buy or sell, or to write letters; to send messengers; to take medicine; to send children to school; to begin a journey; to lend or borrow money; to put forth or bind apprentices; to begin any building; but not good to contract marriage; or to buy houses or lands; or to re-enter your

house after being on a journey, or after going abroad, lest discontent or brawling arise; not good to take or hire a servant; or to redeem a prisoner; but good to plant or graft; and finally good to ask favors from wealthy or prominent persons.

The Hour of ☽.

620 The *Hour of the Moon* is not counted a good hour to buy cattle, especially of the smaller kind; nor to take medicine; or begin any building; not good to lend money; or to make or put on new clothes; it is a good hour to court the female sex; or send children to school; and in some cases to take a journey; or to pursue an enemy, or begin a lawsuit; and to conclude, you may make choice of this hour to leave your native country, (if designed to travel) but choose the hour of Venus to enter your house or return, and to re-enter your own country again.

Remarks on the Planetary Hours

The signification of the Planetary Hours are very ancient and was approved and made use of by the Arabians, and by nearly all the Eastern and Asiatic nations, and are so made use of even to the present day, and they are confirmed by astrologers generally, and by Haly and later authors, and are of great use in all ordinary business; though they are not of that efficacy or influence as the calculations of the movements of the heavenly bodies, for the finding out and choosing a special time to commence any new business or important undertaking, and which time does also sympathize or agree with the horoscope of the native.

By observing the following Tables of Planetary Hours, the reader, even if he knows nothing of Astrology can choose fortunate periods to begin any particular undertaking, or removal, or to commence any important change in his life.*

I have made many thousands of observations and calculated the positions of the planets for the time that people have got married, or made any particular change of their life, such as removal, or going into any new business, etc , and it almost invariably proved the truth of Astrology; for when they have made these changes at unfortunate periods or under what are termed evil aspects, they almost invariably ended unfortunately, or some way disastrously to the parties. But when they made important changes, or commenced new undertakings under fortunate aspects, they generally turned out successfully to the persons who commenced them.

---

* During February 1897 I went to hear a lecture on Astrology in New York City, but as the speaker was taken ill during the lecture I was called upon to continue the subject. When I had finished, the sick man having recovered, he said that if any of the audience would tell him the time they had received a letter, or met a person, or any persons had called to see them, etc.. he would tell them whether the letter contained good or bad news, etc., or whether the meeting of the friend was favorable or not. I was much surprised to learn from the interogators that they all stated that each of the answers the astrologer gave were correct, He did it by calculating the *good and evil Planetary Hours.*

The first time I obtained or acquired perfect confidence in "Planetary Hours" was in the year 1870, when I was practising medicine at Saratoga, N. Y. I had then leisure to calculate each Planetary Hour during the day, so that I could choose fortunate hours to visit my patients, or to change the medicine, etc., or to have them call and see me at my office, I found this method attended with great success, so much so, that the people that I was acquainted with, or knew of me, often made the remark that whenever Dr. Broughton commenced treating any patient, they all began to improve or get well.*

The reason that the influence of the Planetary Hours can be observed and applied to good advantage with sick people, is that generally when a person is in poor health he feels the changes of the weather, currents of air, damp or chilly atmosphere, noises, etc., or anything which disturbs the nervous system more than when in perfect health. He also feels the Planetary Influence in a more marked degree at those times. In short it is the Planetary Influence that makes him sick, and the slighter effects of the planets,, which at another time would only affect his wife; his parents or near relations, or affect his business, will, when he is sick, fall directly on himself, consequently we can more easily notice the effect of the good and evil influence of the " Planetary Hours" on a sick patient, and thus make use of them to benefit his health, or promote his recovery.

The various good and evil planets, in their planetary hours do not act on all persons alike. The positions, the strength, and the various aspects of the planets in an individual's horoscope, have all to be noticed and taken into account when judging the good or evil influence of " planetary hours" on any particular individual.

---

* Should the reader be a physician, and wish to make use of astrology in his practice, I would advice him not to let any of his patients, or even any other physician know, that he has any knowledge of Astrology, or that he is making any use of it in any way connected with his treatment. Of course the prejudice against astrology is dying out, and it is nothing now to what it was 40 or 50 years ago, but even now any physician would find it a great damage to him, if he should let any of his patients know that he is giving any attention to the subject.

At this day religious communities would not expel a Sunday school teacher from the school and church, if it was known that he was studying astrology, and it is even becoming very unpopular to arrest people for practising this science in any part of the United States, or even in England, or other European countries; but the influence that would be brought to bear on the patient's mind, if it was known that the doctor used Astrology in his pratice would be a serions drawback against their recovery, or at least I have found it so in my practise.

I give the following as a sample of what the doctor would have to fight against, if his patients discover that he is studying astrology, even if he cured them, they will be ashamed of themselves, and sorry they ever got well.

Some 30 years ago when I was treating Mr. William Keeny's son, in Lafayette, Jersey City, his mother used to tell me that all the neighbors were talking to her, and wondering how she could sleep in her bed at night. when she had such an impostor, fraud, and humbug as Dr. Broughton, treating her son In course of time, that kind of talk had an effect on her mind, to please her neighbors she changed doctors, but afterwards she was glad to re-engage me, although too late to save her son. The family told all the friends and neighbors that had they not discharged Dr. Broughton, the son would certainly have recovered.

I have found the use of astrology in my practise of infinite advantage, and had I simply practised medicine, and used astrology in a quiet way, no physician would have been more fortunate than myself, in making cures, but people of standing or of any influence in society, are afraid of it being known, that they have an astrologer for a doctor. therefore the advantage the physician gains by being successful in his practise, he loses again through the ignorance and superstition of his patients and their friends. While I was in Saratoga, I did not let my patients know I used astrology in treating their diseases.

For instance the man whose horoscope I referred to on page 222 who had Jupiter so afflicted in the eighth house, would scarcely ever be able to accomplish much, or have any good luck in the "hour of Jupiter," and the hours of Mars and Saturn would be more marked *evil* for him, on account of Saturn afflicting his ascendant, and Mars so afflicted in the 11th house. But as he had the Sun in the midheaven, and also Venus in the 9th house, in its own sign, (Taurus,) in trine to Saturn, in the ascendant, his most fortunate planetary hours would be those of Venus and the Sun.

Possibly the reason that I could notice the marked influence of Planetary Hours, while treating sick patients, is on account of Saturn and Mars afflicting my horoscope in such a marked manner at birth. Mars being in the 6th house, (the house of sickness,) and also being in square to Mercury in the midheaven, and in opposition to the Moon my ruling planet, and also Saturn afflicting my 12th house, (or the house of secret enemies,) in the sign Cancer and the Moon my ruling planet making a conjunction of Saturn. These planetary influences make the evil Planetary Hours of both Saturn and Mars *doubly evil in my horoscope.* Jupiter in the 5th house, and lord of both the 9th and 10th houses, and also lord of the 6th house, and the Moon rising in close trine to Jupiter; and also Venus in the 11th house, unafflicted and lady of the 11th, and the Sun in the midheaven at my birth, makes the hours of Jupiter, Venus, the Moon and the Sun, doubly fortunate for me; and their influence in any business, etc., which I may undertake in their planetary hours, and especially in the commencement of treating the sick.

The reason I have given the planetary hours that would have the most marked effect in the above horoscopes, is that the student may learn to judge for himself what planetary hours will have the most marked effect in any special horoscope he may calculate. He should always bear in mind no matter whether the planet is good or evil, according to these terms in astrology; that planet which is the strongest, and best aspected in any special horoscope is good for the native in that nativity. Therefore it is possible that the planetary hours of Mars, may in certain horoscopes be the most fortunate hours for some persons; especially if they are born under that planet, and it is strong in its own sign, exaltation or joy, in the midheaven, or in good aspect to his ascendant, Sun, Moon, Jupiter or Venus, at these person's time of birth, then the planetary hour of Mars will be the most fortunate for that native to commence any special undertaking or business for himself. But if he wants to deal with other people, or to get the good will of other persons, no matter how strong the planet Mars may be in his horoscope, he must choose the planetary hour of Jupiter, Venus or the Sun, in asking favors or gaining any benefit from others, as he does not know but that the planetary hours of Jupiter, Venus, Sun or Mercury may be the strongest planets in these other person's horoscopes, and therefore these planetary hours are the best for these persons to grant any favors. Besides these hours are generally fortunate and they are the most safe for you to ask favors or benefit from others in, and generally these parties are more likely to grant these favors when they are approached in what is termed good planetary hours, especially if you have fortunate planetary influences operating in your own horoscope at the same time.

Before I noticed the good and evil influence of the Planetary Hours in regard to sick persons, I never had much confidence in them, as I could get no marked effect when I tried to use them in ordinary business, but since 1870 I have been able to notice them much more closely, and with great advantage.

TABLES OF PLANETARY HOURS WHICH COMMENCE ON PAGE 255.

By inspecting them the student will see that the hours are calculated from Sunrise until two hours after Sunset. The first column in each table includes both the commencement of the planetary hour and its end; in all the other columns the hour and minute is printed when a planetary hour *ends*, and the name of the *planet* is printed in that *column*, and the column preceding gives the hour and minute when that *planetary hour commences*. The two hours after Sunset gives the length of the planetary hours of the night, for each day in the year that the Tables are printed for, and therefore any person who wishes to find what particular planet rules before Sunrise, has only to deduct from the hour and minute the length of the planetary hour of the night from the hour and minute given of the first figures printed in the first column of the Table, and count in the order of the planets from the Moon to the planet Saturn. Should the student wish to find what planet rules the hour and the length of the hour after Sunset, he can add the length of the planetary hour of the night to the last column after Sunset, and continue counting the planets from Saturn inward towards the Moon. By doing so he can easily find what planet rules any special hour of the night or early morning.

Near the 21st of March or the 21st of September in any year it is very easy to reckon the planetary hours from sunrise to sunset, also from sunset to sunrise. The student should always bear in mind that the first hour of the day is always ruled by the planet that rules that day; therefore on Sunday near the above dates, the Sun rules from the hour and minute that it rises to one hour after sunrise Venus rules from one hour after sunrise to two hours after sunrise and so on in that order of the planets.

If the student turns to page 258 of the planetary hours where it reads, "on or near the second day of May of any year" he will find that the planetary hours through the day is one hour and ten minutes; therefore he can reckon the hour before sunrise to any part of the early morning by calling each planetary hour fifty minutes, being ten minutes less on the hour, and so on in any of the other tables.

The student should also bear in mind that the last hour of any day is ruled by the planet next preceding the one which rules the following day. For instance on Saturday the last hour of the night is ruled by the planet Mars, and the hour previous to that is ruled by the planet Jupiter, and so on of all other planets and planetary hours of the night.

These tables are in *Local Mean Time* and for latitude 40°–41° North. They are suitable, unmodified, for Philadelphia, New York, Denver and other locations at those latitudes, which are at longitudes divisible by 15. Remember to correct for Daylight. — *Publisher, 2012*

Perpetual Table of Planetary Hours, from Sunrise until 2 hours after Sunset.

Sunday, on or near the 21st of March, of any year.

Sunrise. Sun. A.M.	Venus. A.M.	Mercury. A.M.	Moon. A.M.	Saturn. A.M.	Meridian. Jupiter. M.	Mars. P.M.	Sun. P.M.	Venus. P.M.	Mercury. P.M.	Moon. P.M.	Sunset. Saturn.	After Sunset. Jupiter. P.M.	Mars. P.M.
6.3 to 7.4	to 8.5	to 9.6	to 10.7	to 11.8	to 12.9	to 1.10	to 2.11	to 3.12	to 4.13	to 5.13	to 6.13	to 7.12	to 8.11

Monday, on or near the 22d of March, of any year.

Moon.	Saturn.	Jupiter.	Mars.	Sun.	Venus.	Mercury.	Moon.	Saturn.	Jupiter.	Mars.	Sun.	Venus.	Mercury.
6.1 to 7.2	to 8.3	to 9.4	to 10.5	to 11.6	to 12.7	to 1.8	to 2.9	to 3.10	to 4.11	to 5.12	to 6.14	to 7.13	to 8.12

Tuesday, on or near the 23d of March, of any year.

Mars.	Sun.	Venus.	Mercury.	Moon.	Saturn.	Jupiter.	Mars.	Sun.	Venus.	Mercury.	Moon.	Saturn.	Jupiter.
5.59 to 7.0	to 8.1	to 9.2	to 10.3	to 11.4	to 12.5	to 1.6	to 2.7	to 3.9	to 4.11	to 5.13	to 6.15	to 7.14	to 8.12

Wednesday, on or near the 24th of March, of any year.

Mercury.	Moon.	Saturn.	Jupiter.	Mars.	Sun.	Venus.	Mercury.	Moon.	Saturn.	Jupiter.	Mars.	Sun.	Venus.
5.58 to 6.59	to 8.0	to 9.1	to 10.2	to 11.3	to 12.4	to 1.6	to 2.8	to 3.10	to 4.12	to 5.14	to 6.16	to 7.15	to 8.13

Thursday, on or near the 25th of March, of any year.

Jupiter.	Mars.	Sun.	Venus.	Mercury.	Moon.	Saturn.	Jupiter.	Mars.	Sun.	Venus.	Mercury.	Moon.	Saturn.
5.56 to 6.57	to 7.58	to 8.59	to 10.2	to 11.3	to 12.5	to 1.7	to 2.9	to 3.11	to 4.13	to 5.15	to 6.17	to 7.16	to 8.14

Friday, on or near the 26th of March, of any year.

Venus.	Mercury.	Moon.	Saturn.	Jupiter.	Mars.	Sun.	Venus.	Mercury.	Moon.	Saturn.	Jupiter.	Mars.	Sun.
5.54 to 6.56	to 7.58	to 9.0	to 10.2	to 11.3	to 12.5	to 1.7	to 2.9	to 3.11	to 4.13	to 5.16	to 6.18	to 7.16	to 8.14

Saturday, on or near the 27th of March, of any year.

Saturn.	Jupiter.	Mars.	Sun.	Venus.	Mercury.	Moon.	Saturn.	Jupiter.	Mars.	Sun.	Venus.	Mercury.	Moon.
5.53 to 6.55	to 7.57	to 8.59	to 10.1	to 11.3	to 12.5	to 1.7	to 2.9	to 3.11	to 4.13	to 5.16	to 6.19	to 7.17	to 8.15

Copyright, 1898, by Luke D. Broughton. Entered at Stationers' Hall, London, England. All rights reserved.

Perpetual Table of Planetary Hours, from Sunrise until 2 hours after Sunset.

Sunday, on or near the 4th of April, of any year.

Sunrise. Sun. A.M.	Venus. A.M.	Mercury. A.M.	Moon. A.M.	Saturn. A.M.	Meridian. Jupiter. M.	Mars. P.M.	Sun. P.M.	Venus. P.M.	Mercury. P.M.	Moon. P.M.	Sunset. Saturn. P.M.	After Sunset. Jupiter. P.M.	Mars. P.M.
5.39 to 6.44	to 7.49	to 8.53	to 9.57	to 11.0	to 12.4	to 1.8	to 2.12	to 3.15	to 4.18	to 5.23	to 6.27	to 7.23	to 8.19

Monday, on or near the 5th of April, of any year.

Moon.	Saturn.	Jupiter.	Mars.	Sun.	Venus.	Mercury.	Moon.	Saturn.	Jupiter.	Mars.	Sun.	Venus.	Mercury.
5.38 to 6.43	to 7.47	to 8.52	to 9.56	to 11.0	to 12.4	to 1.8	to 2.12	to 3.15	to 4.19	to 5.24	to 6.28	to 7.24	to 8.20

Tuesday, on or near the 6th of April, of any year.

Mars.	Sun.	Venus.	Mercury.	Moon.	Saturn.	Jupiter.	Mars.	Sun.	Venus.	Mercury.	Moon.	Saturn.	Jupiter.
5.36 to 6.41	to 7.45	to 8.49	to 9.55	to 10.59	to 12.3	to 1.7	to 2.11	to 3.15	to 4.19	to 5.24	to 6.29	to 7.25	to 8.21

Wednesday, on or near the 7th of April, of any year.

Mercury.	Moon.	Saturn.	Jupiter.	Mars.	Sun.	Venus.	Mercury.	Moon.	Saturn.	Jupiter.	Mars.	Sun.	Venus.
5.35 to 6.40	to 7.44	to 8.48	to 9.53	to 10.58	to 12.3	to 1.7	to 2.12	to 3.16	to 4.21	to 5.26	to 6.30	to 7.26	to 8.21

Thursday, on or near the 8th of April, of any year.

Jupiter.	Mars.	Sun.	Venus.	Mercury.	Moon.	Saturn.	Jupiter.	Mars.	Sun.	Venus.	Mercury.	Moon.	Saturn.
5.33 to 6.37	to 7.42	to 8.47	to 9.52	to 10.57	to 12.3	to 1.7	to 2.12	to 3.17	to 4.22	to 5.27	to 6.32	to 7.27	to 8.22

Friday, on or near the 9th of April, of any year.

Venus.	Mercury.	Moon.	Saturn.	Jupiter.	Mars.	Sun.	Venus.	Mercury.	Moon.	Saturn.	Jupiter.	Mars.	Sun.
5.31 to 6.37	to 7.42	to 8.47	to 9.52	to 10.57	to 12.3	to 1.8	to 2.13	to 3.18	to 4.23	to 5.28	to 6.33	to 7.28	to 8.23

Saturday, on or near the 10th of April, of any year.

Saturn.	Jupiter.	Mars.	Sun.	Venus.	Mercury.	Moon.	Saturn.	Jupiter.	Mars.	Sun.	Venus.	Mercury.	Moon.
5.30 to 6.36	to 7.42	to 8.47	to 9.52	to 10.57	to 12.3	to 1.9	to 2.14	to 3.19	to 4.24	to 5.29	to 6.34	to 7.29	to 8.24

Copyright, 1898, by Luke D. Broughton. Entered at Stationers' Hall, London, England. All rights reserved.

Perpetual Table of Planetary Hours, from Sunrise until 2 hours after Sunset.

Sunday, on or near the 18th of April, of any year.

Sunrise. Sun. A. M.	Venus. A. M.	Mercury. A. M.	Moon. A. M.	Saturn. A. M.	Meridian. Jupiter. M.	Mars. P. M.	Sun. P. M.	Venus. P. M.	Mercury. P. M.	Moon. P. M.	Sunset. Saturn. P. M.	After Sunset. Jupiter. P. M.	Mars. P. M.
5.17 to 6.25	to 7.32	to 8.39	to 9.46	to 10.53	to 12.0	to 1.7	to 2.14	to 3.21	to 4.28	to 5.35	to 6.42	to 7.35	to 8.28

Monday, on or near the 19th of April, of any year.

Moon.	Saturn.	Jupiter.	Mars.	Sun.	Venus.	Mercury.	Moon.	Saturn.	Jupiter.	Mars.	Sun.	Venus.	Mercury.
5.16 to 6.24	to 7.32	to 8.39	to 9.46	to 10.53	to 12.0	to 1.7	to 2.14	to 3.22	to 4.29	to 5.36	to 6.43	to 7.36	to 8.29

Tuesday, on or near the 20th of April, of any year.

Mars.	Sun.	Venus.	Mercury.	Moon.	Saturn.	Jupiter.	Mars.	Sun.	Venus.	Mercury.	Moon.	Saturn.	Jupiter.
5.14 to 6.22	to 7.29	to 8.37	to 9.44	to 10.51	to 11.59	to 1.6	to 2.14	to 3.22	to 4.29	to 5.37	to 6.44	to 7.37	to 8.29

Wednesday, on or near the 21st of April, of any year.

Mercury.	Moon.	Saturn.	Jupiter.	Mars.	Sun.	Venus.	Mercury.	Moon.	Saturn.	Jupiter.	Mars.	Sun.	Venus.
5.13 to 6.21	to 7.28	to 8.36	to 9.43	to 10.51	to 11.59	to 1.6	to 2.14	to 3.22	to 4.29	to 5.38	to 6.45	to 7.38	to 8.30

Thursday, on or near the 22d of April, of any year.

Jupiter.	Mars.	Sun.	Venus.	Mercury.	Moon.	Saturn.	Jupiter.	Mars.	Sun.	Venus.	Mercury.	Moon.	Saturn.
5.11 to 6.18	to 7.26	to 8.35	to 9.40	to 10.48	to 11.58	to 1.5	to 2.13	to 3.21	to 4.29	to 5.38	to 6.46	to 7.38	to 8.30

Friday, on or near the 23d of April, of any year.

Venus.	Mercury.	Moon.	Saturn.	Jupiter.	Mars.	Sun.	Venus.	Mercury.	Moon.	Saturn.	Jupiter.	Mars.	Sun.
5.10 to 6.19	to 7.26	to 8.35	to 9.43	to 10.51	to 11.59	to 1.7	to 2.15	to 3.23	to 4.31	to 5.39	to 6.47	to 7.39	to 8.31

Saturday, on or near the 24th of April, of any year.

Saturn.	Jupiter.	Mars.	Sun.	Venus.	Mercury.	Moon.	Saturn.	Jupiter.	Mars.	Sun.	Venus.	Mercury.	Moon.
5.9 to 6.18	to 7.26	to 8.35	to 9.43	to 10.51	to 12.0	to 1.8	to 2.16	to 3.24	to 4.32	to 5.40	to 6.48	to 7.40	to 8.32

Copyright, 1898, by Luke D. Broughton. Entered at Stationers' Hall, London, England. All rights reserved.

Perpetual Table of Planetary Hours, from Sunrise until 2 hours after Sunset.

Sunday, on or near the 2d of May, of any year.

Sunrise. Sun. A. M.	Venus. A. M.	Mercury. A. M.	Moon. A. M.	Saturn. A. M.	Meridian. Jupiter. M.	Mars. P. M.	Venus. P. M.	Sun. P. M.	Mercury. P. M.	Moon. P. M.	Sunset. Saturn. P. M.	After Sunset. Jupiter. P. M.	Mars. P. M.
4.58 to 6.7	to 7.17	to 8.27	to 9.37	to 10.47	to 11.56	to 1.6	to 2.16	to 3.26	to 4.36	to 5.46	to 6.56	to 7.46	to 8.36

Monday, on or near the 3d of May, of any year.

Moon.	Saturn.	Jupiter.	Mars.	Sun.	Venus.	Mercury.	Moon.	Saturn.	Jupiter.	Mars.	Sun.	Venus.	Mercury.
4.57 to 6.7	to 7.17	to 8.27	to 9.37	to 10.47	to 11.57	to 1.7	to 2.17	to 3.27	to 4.37	to 5.47	to 6.57	to 7.47	to 8.37

Tuesday, on or near the 4th of May, of any year.

Mars.	Sun.	Venus.	Mercury.	Moon.	Saturn.	Jupiter.	Mars.	Sun.	Venus.	Mercury.	Moon.	Saturn.	Jupiter.
4.55 to 6.6	to 7.16	to 8.27	to 9.37	to 10.47	to 11.58	to 1.8	to 2.18	to 3.28	to 4.38	to 5.48	to 6.58	to 7.48	to 8.38

Wednesday, on or near the 5th of May, of any year.

Mercury.	Moon.	Saturn.	Jupiter.	Mars.	Sun.	Venus.	Mercury.	Moon.	Saturn.	Jupiter.	Mars.	Sun.	Venus.
4.54 to 6.6	to 7.16	to 8.27	to 9.37	to 10.47	to 11.58	to 1.9	to 2.19	to 3.29	to 4.40	to 5.50	to 7.0	to 7.50	to 8.39

Thursday, on or near the 6th of May, of any year.

Jupiter.	Mars.	Sun.	Venus.	Mercury.	Moon.	Saturn.	Jupiter.	Mars.	Sun.	Venus.	Mercury.	Moon.	Saturn.
4.53 to 6.4	to 7.14	to 8.25	to 9.35	to 10.46	to 11.57	to 1.8	to 2.18	to 3.29	to 4.40	to 5.51	to 7.1	to 7.51	to 8.40

Friday, on or near the 7th of May, of any year.

Venus.	Mercury.	Moon.	Saturn.	Jupiter.	Mars.	Sun.	Venus.	Mercury.	Moon.	Saturn.	Jupiter.	Mars.	Sun.
4.52 to 6.2	to 7.13	to 8.24	to 9.35	to 10.46	to 11.57	to 1.8	to 2.19	to 3.29	to 4.40	to 5.51	to 7.2	to 7.52	to 8.41

Saturday, on or near the 8th of May, of any year.

Saturn.	Jupiter.	Mars.	Sun.	Venus.	Mercury.	Moon.	Saturn.	Jupiter.	Mars.	Sun.	Venus.	Mercury.	Moon.
4.51 to 6.2	to 7.13	to 8.25	to 9.36	to 10.47	to 11.58	to 1.9	to 2.20	to 3.31	to 4.42	to 5.53	to 7.3	to 7.52	to 8.41

Copyright, 1898, by Luke D. Broughton. Entered at Stationers' Hall, London, England. All rights reserved.

Perpetual Table of Planetary Hours, from Sunrise until 2 hours after Sunset.

Sunday, on or near the 16th of May, of any year.

Sunrise. Sun. A. M.	Venus. A. M.	Mercury. A. M.	Moon. A. M.	Saturn. A. M.	Meridian. Jupiter.	Mars. P. M.	Sun. P. M.	Venus. P. M.	Mercury. P. M.	Moon. P. M.	Sunset. Saturn. P. M.	After Sunset. Jupiter. P. M.	Mars.
4.42 to 5.55	to 7.7	to 8.20	to 9.32	to 10.45	to 11.57	to 1.10	to 2.22	to 3.35	to 4.47	to 5.59	to 7.11	to 7.59	to 8.46

Monday, on or near the 17th of May, of any year.

Moon.	Saturn.	Jupiter.	Mars.	Sun.	Venus.	Mercury.	Moon.	Saturn.	Jupiter.	Mars.	Sun.	Venus.	Mercury.
4.41 to 5.55	to 7.7	to 8.20	to 9.32	to 10.45	to 11.57	to 1.10	to 2.22	to 3.35	to 4.47	to 5.59	to 7.11	to 7.59	to 8.46

Tuesday, on or near the 18th of May, of any year.

Mars.	Sun.	Venus.	Mercury.	Moon.	Saturn.	Jupiter.	Mars.	Sun.	Venus.	Mercury.	Moon.	Saturn.	Jupiter.
4.40 to 5.53	to 7.5	to 8.19	to 9.30	to 10.43	to 11.56	to 1.9	to 2.22	to 3.34	to 4.47	to 5.59	to 4.12	to 8.0	to 8.47

Wednesday, on or near the 19th of May, of any year.

Mercury.	Moon.	Saturn.	Jupiter.	Mars.	Sun.	Venus.	Mercury.	Moon.	Saturn.	Jupiter.	Sun.	Venus.
4.40 to 5.53	to 7.5	to 8.18	to 9.30	to 10.43	to 11.56	to 1.9	to 2.22	to 3.34	to 4.47	to 6.0	to 8.1	to 8.48

Thursday, on or near the 20th of May, of any year.

Jupiter.	Mars.	Sun.	Venus.	Mercury.	Moon.	Saturn.	Jupiter.	Mars.	Sun.	Venus.	Mercury.	Moon.	Saturn.
4.38 to 5.51	to 7.4	to 8.17	to 9.30	to 10.43	to 11.56	to 1.9	to 2.22	to 3.35	to 4.48	to 6.1	to 7.14	to 8.1	to 8.48

Friday, on or near the 21st of May, of any year.

Venus.	Mercury.	Moon.	Saturn.	Jupiter.	Mars.	Sun.	Venus.	Mercury.	Moon.	Saturn.	Jupiter.	Mars.	Sun.
4.38 to 5.51	to 7.4	to 8.17	to 9.30	to 10.43	to 11.56	to 1.9	to 2.22	to 3.35	to 4.48	to 6.1	to 7.15	to 8.2	to 8.49

Saturday, on or near the 22d of May, of any year.

Saturn.	Jupiter.	Mars.	Sun.	Venus.	Mercury.	Moon.	Saturn.	Jupiter.	Mars.	Sun.	Venus.	Mercury.	Moon.
4.37 to 5.51	to 7.4	to 8.17	to 9.30	to 10.43	to 11.57	to 1.10	to 2.23	to 3.36	to 4.49	to 6.2	to 7.16	to 8.3	to 8.49

Copyright, 1898, by Luke D. Broughton. Entered at Stationers' Hall, London, England. All rights reserved.

Perpetual Table of Planetary Hours, from Sunrise until 2 hours after Sunset.

Sunday, on or near the 30th of May, of any year.

Sunrise. Sun. A. M.	Venus. A. M.	Mercury. A. M.	Moon. A. M.	Saturn. A. M.	Meridian. Jupiter. M.	Mars. P. M.	Sun. P. M.	Venus. P. M.	Mercury. P. M.	Moon. P. M.	Sunset. Saturn. P. M.	After Sunset. Jupiter. P. M.	Mars. P. M.
4.32 to 5.47	to 7.1	to 8.15	to 9.29	to 10.43	to 11.57	to 1.12	to 2.26	to 3.40	to 4.54	to 6.8	to 7.22	to 8.8	to 8.54

Monday, on or near the 31st of May, of any year.

Moon.	Saturn.	Jupiter.	Mars.	Sun.	Venus.	Mercury.	Moon.	Saturn.	Jupiter.	Mars.	Sun.	Venus.	Mercury.
4.31 to 5.46	to 7.0	to 8.15	to 9.29	to 10.43	to 11.57	to 1.11	to 2.25	to 3.39	to 4.54	to 6.9	to 7.23	to 8.9	to 8.55

Tuesday, on or near the 1st of June, of any year.

Mars.	Sun.	Venus.	Mercury.	Moon.	Saturn.	Jupiter.	Mars.	Sun.	Venus.	Mercury.	Moon.	Saturn.	Jupiter.
4.31 to 5.46	to 7.0	to 8.15	to 9.30	to 10.43	to 11.58	to 1.12	to 2.26	to 3.40	to 4.54	to 6.10	to 7.24	to 8.10	to 8.56

Wednesday, on or near the 2d of June, of any year.

Mercury.	Moon.	Saturn.	Jupiter.	Mars.	Sun.	Venus.	Mercury.	Moon.	Saturn.	Jupiter.	Mars.	Sun.	Venus.
4.30 to 5.45	to 7.0	to 8.15	to 9.30	to 10.43	to 11.59	to 1.13	to 2.27	to 3.41	to 4.56	to 6.11	to 7.25	to 8.11	to 8.56

Thursday, on or near the 3d of June, of any year.

Jupiter.	Mars.	Sun.	Venus.	Mercury.	Moon.	Saturn.	Jupiter.	Mars.	Sun.	Venus.	Mercury.	Moon.	Saturn.
4.30 to 5.45	to 7.0	to 8.14	to 9.29	to 10.43	to 11.58	to 1.13	to 2.28	to 3.42	to 4.57	to 6.12	to 7.26	to 8.12	to 8.57

Friday, on or near the 4th of June, of any year.

Venus.	Mercury.	Moon.	Saturn.	Jupiter.	Mars.	Sun.	Venus.	Mercury.	Moon.	Saturn.	Jupiter.	Mars.	Sun.
4.30 to 5.45	to 7.0	to 8.14	to 9.29	to 10.43	to 11.58	to 1.13	to 2.28	to 3.42	to 4.57	to 6.12	to 7.26	to 8.12	to 8.57

Saturday, on or near the 5th of June, of any year.

Saturn.	Jupiter.	Mars.	Sun.	Venus.	Mercury.	Moon.	Saturn.	Jupiter.	Mars.	Sun.	Venus.	Mercury.	Moon.
4.29 to 5.44	to 6.59	to 8.14	to 9.29	to 10.43	to 11.58	to 1.13	to 2.28	to 3.43	to 4.58	to 6.13	to 7.27	to 8.13	to 8.58

Copyright, 1898, by Luke D. Broughton. Entered at Stationers' Hall, London, England. All rights reserved.

Perpetual Table of Planetary Hours, from Sunrise until 2 hours after Sunset.

Sunday, on or near the 13th of June, of any year.

Sunrise. Sun. A.M.	Venus. A.M.	Mercury. A.M.	Moon. A.M.	Saturn. A.M.	Meridian. Jupiter. M.	Mars. P.M.	Sun. P.M.	Venus. P.M.	Mercury. P.M.	Moon. P.M.	Sunset. Saturn. P.M.	After Sunset. Jupiter. P.M.	Mars. P.M.
4.28 to 5.44	to 6.59	to 8.14	to 9.29	to 10.44	to 12.0	to 1.15	to 2.30	to 3.45	to 5.0	to 6.16	to 7.31	to 8.16	to 9.1

Monday, on or near the 14th of June, of any year.

Moon.	Saturn.	Jupiter.	Mars.	Sun.	Venus.	Mercury.	Moon.	Saturn.	Jupiter.	Mars.	Sun.	Venus.	Mercury.
4.28 to 5.44	to 6.59	to 8.14	to 9.29	to 10.44	to 12.0	to 1.15	to 2.30	to 3.45	to 5.0	to 6.16	to 7.31	to 8.16	to 9.1

Tuesday, on or near the 15th of June, of any year.

Mars.	Sun.	Venus.	Mercury.	Moon.	Saturn.	Jupiter.	Mars.	Sun.	Venus.	Mercury.	Moon.	Saturn.	Jupiter.
4.28 to 5.44	to 6.59	to 8.14	to 9.29	to 10.44	to 0.1	to 1.16	to 2.31	to 3.46	to 5.1	to 6.17	to 7.32	to 8.17	to 9.2

Wednesday, on or near the 16th of June, of any year.

Mercury.	Moon.	Saturn.	Jupiter.	Mars.	Sun.	Venus.	Mercury.	Moon.	Saturn.	Jupiter.	Mars.	Sun.	Venus.
4.28 to 5.44	to 6.59	to 8.14	to 9.29	to 10.44	to 0.1	to 1.16	to 2.31	to 3.46	to 5.1	to 6.17	to 7.32	to 8.17	to 9.2

Thursday, on or near the 17th of June, of any year.

Jupiter.	Mars.	Sun.	Venus.	Mercury.	Moon.	Saturn.	Jupiter.	Mars.	Sun.	Venus.	Mercury.	Moon.	Saturn.
4.28 to 5.44	to 7.0	to 8.15	to 9.30	to 10.45	to 0.2	to 1.17	to 2.32	to 3.47	to 5.2	to 6.18	to 7.33	to 8.18	to 9.3

Friday, on or near the 18th of June, of any year.

Venus.	Mercury.	Moon.	Saturn.	Jupiter.	Mars.	Sun.	Venus.	Mercury.	Moon.	Saturn.	Jupiter.	Mars.	Sun.
4.28 to 5.44	to 7.0	to 8.15	to 9.30	to 10.45	to 0.2	to 1.17	to 2.32	to 3.47	to 5.2	to 6.18	to 7.33	to 8.18	to 9.3

Saturday, on or near the 19th of June, of any year.

Saturn.	Jupiter.	Mars.	Sun.	Venus.	Mercury.	Moon.	Saturn.	Jupiter.	Mars.	Sun.	Venus.	Mercury.	Moon.
4.28 to 5.44	to 7.1	to 8.16	to 9.31	to 10.46	to 0.3	to 1.18	to 2.33	to 3.48	to 5.3	to 6.19	to 7.34	to 8.19	to 9.3

Copyright, 1898, by Luke D. Broughton. Entered at Stationers' Hall, London, England. All rights reserved.

Perpetual Table of Planetary Hours, from Sunrise until 2 hours after Sunset.

Sunday, on or near the 27th of June, of any year.

Sunrise. Sun. A. M.	Venus. A. M.	Mercury. A. M.	Moon. A. M.	Saturn. A. M.	Meridian. Jupiter. M.	Mars. P. M.	Sun. P. M.	Venus. P. M.	Mercury. P. M.	Moon. P. M.	Sunset. Saturn. P. M.	After Sunset. Jupiter. P. M.	Mars. P. M.
4.30 to 5.46	to 7.0	to 8.16	to 9.31	to 10.46	to 0.2	to 1.17	to 2.32	to 3.48	to 5.3	to 6.19	to 7.35	to 8.20	to 9.4

Monday, on or near the 28th of June, of any year.

Moon.	Saturn.	Jupiter.	Mars.	Sun.	Venus.	Mercury.	Moon.	Saturn.	Jupiter.	Mars.	Sun.	Venus.	Mercury.
4.30 to 5.46	to 7.0	to 8.16	to 9.31	to 10.46	to 0.2	to 1.17	to 2.32	to 3.48	to 5.3	to 6.19	to 7.35	to 8.20	to 9.4

Tuesday, on or near the 29th of June, of any year.

Mars.	Sun.	Venus.	Mercury.	Moon.	Saturn.	Jupiter.	Mars.	Sun.	Venus.	Mercury.	Moon.	Saturn.	Jupiter.
4.30 to 5.46	to 7.0	to 8.16	to 9.31	to 10.48	to 0.2	to 1.17	to 2.32	to 3.48	to 5.3	to 6.19	to 7.35	to 8.20	to 9.4

Wednesday, on or near the 30th of June, of any year.

Mercury.	Moon.	Saturn.	Jupiter.	Mars.	Sun.	Venus.	Mercury.	Moon.	Saturn.	Jupiter.	Mars.	Sun.	Venus.
4.32 to 5.48	to 7.3	to 8.18	to 9.34	to 10.49	to 0.2	to 1.17	to 2.32	to 3.48	to 5.3	to 6.19	to 7.35	to 8.20	to 9.4

Thursday, on or near the 1st of July, of any year.

Jupiter.	Mars.	Sun.	Venus.	Mercury.	Moon.	Saturn.	Jupiter.	Mars.	Sun.	Venus.	Mercury.	Moon.	Saturn.
4.32 to 5.48	to 7.3	to 8.18	to 9.34	to 10.49	to 0.2	to 1.17	to 2.33	to 3.48	to 5.3	to 6.19	to 7.35	to 8.20	to 9.4

Friday, on or near the 2d of July, of any year.

Venus.	Mercury.	Moon.	Saturn.	Jupiter.	Mars.	Sun.	Venus.	Mercury.	Moon.	Saturn.	Jupiter.	Mars.	Sun.
4.32 to 5.48	to 7.3	to 8.18	to 9.34	to 10.49	to 0.3	to 1.18	to 2.33	to 3.48	to 5.3	to 6.19	to 7.35	to 8.20	to 9.4

Saturday, on or near the 3d of July, of any year.

Saturn.	Jupiter.	Mars.	Sun.	Venus.	Mercury.	Moon.	Saturn.	Jupiter.	Mars.	Sun.	Venus.	Mercury.	Moon.
4.33 to 5.50	to 7.5	to 8.20	to 9.35	to 10.50	to 0.5	to 1.20	to 2.35	to 3.50	to 5.5	to 6.20	to 7.34	to 8.19	to 9.3

Copyright, 1898, by Luke D. Broughton. Entered at Stationers' Hall, London, England. All rights reserved.

Perpetual Table of Planetary Hours, from Sunrise until 2 hours after Sunset.

Sunday, on or near the 11th of July, of any year.

Sunrise. Sun. A. M.	Venus. A. M.	Mercury. A. M.	Moon. A. M.	Saturn. A. M.	Meridian. Jupiter. M.	Mars. P. M.	Sun. P. M.	Venus. P. M.	Mercury. P. M.	Moon. P. M.	Sunset. Saturn.	After Sunset. Jupiter. P. M.	Mars. P. M.
4.38 to 5.53	to 7.7	to 8.22	to 9.36	to 10.51	to 0.5	to 1.20	to 2.34	to 3.49	to 5.3	to 6.18	to 7.32	to 8.28	to 9.13

Monday, on or near the 12th of July, of any year.

Moon.	Saturn.	Jupiter.	Mars.	Sun.	Venus.	Mercury.	Moon.	Saturn.	Jupiter.	Mars.	Sun.	Venus.	Mercury.
4.39 to 5.53	to 7.7	to 8.22	to 9.36	to 10.51	to 0.5	to 1.20	to 2.34	to 3.48	to 5.2	to 6.18	to 7.32	to 8.28	to 9.13

Tuesday, on or near the 13th of July, of any year.

Mars.	Sun.	Venus.	Mercury.	Moon.	Saturn.	Jupiter.	Mars.	Sun.	Venus.	Mercury.	Moon.	Saturn.	Jupiter.
4.39 to 5.54	to 7.8	to 8.22	to 9.36	to 10.51	to 0.5	to 1.20	to 2.34	to 3.48	to 5.2	to 6.16	to 7.31	to 8.27	to 9.12

Wednesday, on or near the 14th of July, of any year.

Mercury.	Moon.	Saturn.	Jupiter.	Mars.	Sun.	Venus.	Mercury.	Moon.	Saturn.	Jupiter.	Mars.	Sun.	Venus.
4.40 to 5.54	to 7.9	to 8.23	to 9.37	to 10.51	to 0.6	to 1.20	to 2.34	to 3.48	to 5.2	to 6.16	to 7.30	to 8.26	to 9.11

Thursday, on or near the 15th of July, of any year.

Jupiter.	Mars.	Sun.	Venus.	Mercury.	Moon.	Saturn.	Jupiter.	Mars.	Sun.	Venus.	Mercury.	Moon.	Saturn.
4.41 to 5.56	to 7.10	to 8.24	to 9.38	to 10.52	to 0.6	to 1.20	to 2.34	to 3.48	to 5.2	to 6.16	to 7.30	to 8.26	to 9.11

Friday, on or near the 16th of July, of any year.

Venus.	Mercury.	Moon.	Saturn.	Jupiter.	Mars.	Sun.	Venus.	Mercury.	Moon.	Saturn.	Jupiter.	Mars.	Sun.
4.42 to 5.55	to 7.9	to 8.23	to 9.37	to 10.51	to 0.5	to 1.19	to 2.33	to 3.47	to 5.1	to 6.15	to 7.29	to 8.25	to 9.11

Saturday, on or near the 17th of July, of any year.

Saturn.	Jupiter.	Mars.	Sun.	Venus.	Mercury.	Moon.	Saturn.	Jupiter.	Mars.	Sun.	Venus.	Mercury.	Moon.
4.42 to 5.55	to 7.9	to 8.23	to 9.37	to 10.51	to 0.5	to 1.19	to 2.33	to 3.47	to 5.1	to 6.15	to 7.29	to 8.25	to 9.11

Copyright, 1898, by Luke D. Broughton. Entered at Stationers' Hall, London, England. All rights reserved.

Perpetual Table of Planetary Hours, from Sunrise until 2 hours after Sunset.

Sunday, on or near the 25th of July, of any year.

Sunrise. Sun. A. M.	Venus. A. M.	Mercury. A. M.	Moon. A. M.	Saturn. A. M.	Meridian. Jupiter. M.	Mars. P. M.	Sun. P. M.	Venus. P. M.	Mercury. P. M.	Moon. P. M.	Sunset. Saturn. P. M.	After Sunset. Jupiter. P. M.	Mars. P. M.
4.49 to 6.2	to 7.14	to 8.27	to 9.40	to 10.53	to 0.6	to 1.18	to 2.31	to 3.44	to 4.57	to 6.10	to 7.23	to 8.10	to 8.57

Monday, on or near the 26th of July, of any year.

Moon.	Saturn.	Jupiter.	Mars.	Sun.	Venus.	Mercury.	Moon.	Saturn.	Jupiter.	Mars.	Sun.	Venus.	Mercury.
4.50 to 6.3	to 7.15	to 8.28	to 9.41	to 10.53	to 0.6	to 1.19	to 2.31	to 3.43	to 4.56	to 6.9	to 7.22	to 8.9	to 8.56

Tuesday, on or near the 27th of July, of any year.

Mars.	Sun.	Venus.	Mercury.	Moon.	Saturn.	Jupiter.	Mars.	Sun.	Venus.	Mercury.	Moon.	Saturn.	Jupiter.
4.51 to 6.4	to 7.16	to 8.29	to 9.41	to 10.54	to 0.6	to 1.19	to 2.31	to 3.43	to 4.56	to 6.8	to 7.21	to 8.8	to 8.55

Wednesday, on or near the 28th of July, of any year.

Mercury.	Moon.	Saturn.	Jupiter.	Mars.	Sun.	Venus.	Mercury.	Moon.	Saturn.	Jupiter.	Mars.	Sun.	Venus.
4.52 to 6.5	to 7.17	to 8.29	to 9.42	to 10.54	to 0.5	to 1.18	to 2.30	to 3.42	to 4.55	to 6.7	to 7.20	to 8.8	to 8.55

Thursday, on or near the 29th of July, of any year.

Jupiter.	Mars.	Sun.	Venus.	Mercury.	Moon.	Saturn.	Jupiter.	Mars.	Sun.	Venus.	Mercury.	Moon.	Saturn.
4.53 to 6.6	to 7.18	to 8.30	to 9.42	to 10.54	to 0.6	to 1.18	to 2.30	to 3.42	to 4.54	to 6.6	to 7.19	to 8.7	to 8.55

Friday, on or near the 30th of July, of any year.

Venus.	Mercury.	Moon.	Saturn.	Jupiter.	Mars.	Sun.	Venus.	Mercury.	Moon.	Saturn.	Jupiter.	Mars.	Sun.
4.54 to 6.6	to 7.18	to 8.30	to 9.42	to 10.54	to 0.6	to 1.18	to 2.30	to 3.42	to 4.54	to 6.6	to 7.18	to 8.6	to 8.54

Saturday, on or near the 31st of July, of any year.

Saturn.	Jupiter.	Mars.	Sun.	Venus.	Mercury.	Moon.	Saturn.	Jupiter.	Mars.	Sun.	Venus.	Mercury.	Moon.
4.55 to 6.7	to 7.18	to 8.30	to 9.40	to 10.54	to 0.5	to 1.17	to 2.29	to 3.41	to 4.53	to 6.5	to 7.17	to 8.5	to 8.53

Copyright, 1898, by Luke D. Broughton. Entered at Stationers' Hall, London, England. All rights reserved.

Perpetual Table of Planetary Hours, from Sunrise until 2 hours after Sunset.

Sunday, on or near the 8th of August, of any year.

Sunrise. Sun. A.M.	Venus. A.M.	Mercury. A.M.	Moon. A.M.	Saturn. A.M.	Meridian. Jupiter.	Mars. P.M.	Sun. P.M.	Venus. P.M.	Mercury. P.M.	Moon. P.M.	Sunset. Saturn. P.M.	After Sunset. Jupiter. P.M.	Mars. P.M.
5.2 to 6.13	to 7.23	to 8.34	to 9.44	to 10.55	to 0.5	to 1.16	to 2.26	to 3.37	to 4.47	to 5.58	to 7.8	to 7.58	to 8.47

Monday, on or near the 9th of August, of any year.

Moon.	Saturn.	Jupiter.	Mars.	Sun.	Venus.	Mercury.	Moon.	Saturn.	Jupiter.	Mars.	Sun.	Venus.	Mercury.
5.3 to 6.14	to 7.24	to 8.35	to 9.45	to 10.55	to 0.6	to 1.16	to 2.27	to 3.37	to 4.47	to 5.57	to 7.7	to 7.57	to 8.46

Tuesday, on or near the 10th of August, of any year.

Mars.	Sun.	Venus.	Mercury.	Moon.	Saturn.	Jupiter.	Mars.	Sun.	Venus.	Mercury.	Moon.	Saturn.	Jupiter.
5.4 to 6.15	to 7.25	to 8.35	to 9.45	to 10.55	to 0.5	to 1.15	to 2.25	to 3.35	to 4.45	to 5.55	to 7.5	to 7.55	to 8.45

Wednesday, on or near the 11th of August, of any year.

Mercury.	Moon.	Saturn.	Jupiter.	Mars.	Sun.	Venus.	Mercury.	Moon.	Saturn.	Jupiter.	Mars.	Sun.	Venus.
5.5 to 6.15	to 7.25	to 8.35	to 9.44	to 10.54	to 0.4	to 1.14	to 2.24	to 3.34	to 4.45	to 5.54	to 7.4	to 7.54	to 8.44

Thursday, on or near the 12th of August, of any year.

Jupiter.	Mars.	Sun.	Venus.	Mercury.	Moon.	Saturn.	Jupiter.	Mars.	Sun.	Venus.	Mercury.	Moon.	Saturn.
5.6 to 6.16	to 7.25	to 8.35	to 9.44	to 10.54	to 0.4	to 1.13	to 2.23	to 3.33	to 4.43	to 5.53	to 7.3	to 7.53	to 8.43

Friday, on or near the 13th of August, of any year.

Venus.	Mercury.	Moon.	Saturn.	Jupiter.	Mars.	Sun.	Venus.	Mercury.	Moon.	Saturn.	Jupiter.	Mars.	Sun.
5.7 to 6.17	to 7.26	to 8.36	to 9.45	to 10.55	to 0.4	to 1.13	to 2.23	to 3.32	to 4.42	to 5.51	to 7.1	to 7.51	to 8.42

Saturday, on or near the 14th of August, of any year.

Saturn.	Jupiter.	Mars.	Sun.	Venus.	Mercury.	Moon.	Saturn.	Jupiter.	Mars.	Sun.	Venus.	Mercury.	Moon.
5.8 to 6.17	to 7.27	to 8.36	to 9.45	to 10.55	to 0.4	to 1.13	to 2.22	to 3.31	to 4.41	to 5.51	to 7.0	to 7.50	to 8.41

Copyright, 1898, by Luke D. Broughton. Entered at Stationers' Hall, London, England. All rights reserved.

Perpetual Table of Planetary Hours, from Sunrise until 2 hours after Sunset.

Sunday, on or near the 22d of August, of any year.

Sunrise. Sun. A.M.	Venus. A.M.	Mercury. A.M.	Moon. A.M.	Saturn. A.M.	Meridian. Jupiter. M.	Mars. P.M.	Sun. P.M.	Venus. P.M.	Mercury. P.M.	Moon. P.M.	Sunset. Saturn. P.M.	Jupiter. P.M.	After Sunset. Mars. P.M.
5.16 to 6.24	to 7.31	to 8.40	to 9.48	to 10.57	to 0.4	to 1.12	to 2.20	to 3.27	to 4.34	to 5.41	to 6.48	to 7.40	to 8.32

Monday, on or near the 23d of August, of any year.

Moon.	Saturn.	Jupiter.	Mars.	Sun.	Venus.	Mercury.	Moon.	Saturn.	Jupiter.	Mars.	Sun.	Venus.	Mercury.
5.17 to 6.25	to 7.32	to 8.40	to 9.47	to 10.55	to 0.2	to 1.10	to 2.18	to 3.26	to 4.34	to 5.41	to 6.47	to 7.39	to 8.31

Tuesday, on or near the 24th of August, of any year.

Mars.	Sun.	Venus.	Mercury.	Moon.	Saturn.	Jupiter.	Mars.	Sun.	Venus.	Mercury.	Moon.	Saturn.	Jupiter.
5.18 to 6.26	to 7.33	to 8.40	to 9.47	to 10.54	to 0.2	to 1.9	to 2.16	to 3.23	to 4.32	to 5.39	to 6.45	to 7.37	to 8.30

Wednesday, on or near the 25th of August, of any year.

Mercury.	Moon.	Saturn.	Jupiter.	Mars.	Sun.	Venus.	Mercury.	Moon.	Saturn.	Jupiter.	Mars.	Sun.	Venus.
5.19 to 6.27	to 7.34	to 8.41	to 9.48	to 10.54	to 0.1	to 1.8	to 2.15	to 3.22	to 4.29	to 5.36	to 6.44	to 7.37	to 8.30

Thursday, on or near the 26th of August, of any year.

Jupiter.	Mars.	Sun.	Venus.	Mercury.	Moon.	Saturn.	Jupiter.	Mars.	Sun.	Venus.	Mercury.	Moon.	Saturn.
5.20 to 6.27	to 7.34	to 8.41	to 9.48	to 10.54	to 12.0	to 1.7	to 2.14	to 3.21	to 4.28	to 5.35	to 6.42	to 7.35	to 8.28

Friday, on or near the 27th of August, of any year.

Venus.	Mercury.	Moon.	Saturn.	Jupiter.	Mars.	Sun.	Venus.	Mercury.	Moon.	Saturn.	Jupiter.	Mars.	Sun.
5.21 to 6.28	to 7.34	to 8.41	to 9.48	to 10.54	to 12.0	to 1.6	to 2.13	to 3.20	to 4.27	to 5.34	to 6.41	to 7.34	to 8.28

Saturday, on or near the 28th of August, of any year.

Saturn.	Jupiter.	Mars.	Sun.	Venus.	Mercury.	Moon.	Saturn.	Jupiter.	Mars.	Sun.	Venus.	Mercury.	Moon.
5.22 to 6.29	to 7.35	to 8.42	to 9.48	to 10.54	to 12.0	to 1.6	to 2.12	to 3.19	to 4.26	to 5.33	to 6.39	to 7.33	to 8.27

Copyright, 1898, by Luke D. Broughton. Entered at Stationers' Hall, London, England. All rights reserved.

Perpetual Table of Planetary Hours, from Sunrise until 2 hours after Sunset.

Sunday, on or near the 5th of September, of any year.

Sunrise. Sun. A.M.	Venus. A.M.	Mercury. A.M.	Moon. A.M.	Saturn. A.M.	Meridian. Jupiter. M.	Mars. P.M.	Sun. P.M.	Venus. P.M.	Mercury. P.M.	Moon. P.M.	Sunset. Saturn. P.M.	Jupiter. P.M.	After Sunset. Mars. P.M.
5.30 to 6.35	to 7.39	to 8.44	to 9.48	to 10.53	to 11.58	to 1.2	to 2.6	to 3.11	to 4.15	to 5.20	to 6.26	to 7.21	to 8.17

Monday, on or near the 6th of September, of any year.

Moon.	Saturn.	Jupiter.	Mars.	Sun.	Venus.	Mercury.	Moon.	Saturn.	Jupiter.	Mars.	Sun.	Venus.	Mercury.
5.31 to 6.36	to 7.40	to 8.45	to 9.49	to 10.53	to 11.58	to 1.2	to 2.6	to 3.10	to 4.15	to 5.20	to 6.25	to 7.20	to 8.16

Tuesday, on or near the 7th of September, of any year.

Mars.	Sun.	Venus.	Mercury.	Moon.	Saturn.	Jupiter.	Mars.	Sun.	Venus.	Mercury.	Moon.	Saturn.	Jupiter.
5.32 to 6.37	to 7.41	to 8.46	to 9.50	to 10.54	to 11.58	to 1.2	to 2.6	to 3.10	to 4.14	to 5.19	to 6.23	to 7.19	to 8.15

Wednesday, on or near the 8th of September, of any year.

Mercury.	Moon.	Saturn.	Jupiter.	Mars.	Sun.	Venus.	Mercury.	Moon.	Saturn.	Jupiter.	Mars.	Sun.	Venus.
5.33 to 6.38	to 7.42	to 8.46	to 9.50	to 10.54	to 11.58	to 1.2	to 2.6	to 3.10	to 4.14	to 5.18	to 6.22	to 7.18	to 8.14

Thursday, on or near the 9th of September, of any year.

Jupiter.	Mars.	Sun.	Venus.	Mercury.	Saturn.	Jupiter.	Mars.	Sun.	Venus.	Mercury.	Moon.	Saturn.
5.34 to 6.37	to 7.42	to 8.46	to 9.50	to 10.54	to 11.58	to 1.1	to 2.5	to 3.9	to 4.13	to 5.17	to 6.20	to 7.16	to 8.12

Friday, on or near the 10th of September, of any year.

Venus.	Mercury.	Moon.	Saturn.	Jupiter.	Mars.	Sun.	Venus.	Mercury.	Moon.	Saturn.	Jupiter.	Mars.	Sun.
5.35 to 6.38	to 7.42	to 8.46	to 9.50	to 10.54	to 12.58	to 1.0	to 2.4	to 3.8	to 4.12	to 5.15	to 6.18	to 7.14	to 8.10

Saturday, on or near the 11th of September, of any year.

Saturn.	Jupiter.	Mars.	Sun.	Venus.	Mercury.	Saturn.	Jupiter.	Mars.	Sun.	Venus.	Mercury.	Moon.
5.36 to 6.39	to 7.43	to 8.46	to 9.50	to 10.54	to 11.58	to 12.58	to 2.3	to 3.7	to 4.11	to 5.14	to 6.16	to 7.12	to 8.9

Copyright, 1898, by Luke D. Broughton. Entered at Stationers' Hall, London, England. All rights reserved.

Perpetual Table of Planetary Hours, from Sunrise until 2 hours after Sunset.

Sunday, on or near the 19th of September, of any year.

Sunrise. Sun. A. M.	Venus. A. M.	Mercury. A. M.	Moon. A. M.	Saturn. A. M.	Meridian. Jupiter. M.	Mars. P. M.	Sun. P. M.	Venus. P. M.	Mercury. P. M.	Moon. P. M.	Sunset. Saturn. P. M.	After Sunset. Jupiter. P. M.	Mars. P. M.
5.44 to 6.46	to 7.47	to 8.49	to 9.50	to 10.52	to 11.54	to 0.56	to 1.58	to 2.59	to 4.0	to 5.2	to 6.3	to 7.2	to 8.1

Monday, on or near the 20th of September, of any year.

Moon.	Saturn.	Jupiter.	Mars.	Sun.	Venus.	Mercury.	Moon.	Saturn.	Jupiter.	Mars.	Sun.	Venus.	Mercury.
5.45 to 6.47	to 7.48	to 8.50	to 9.51	to 10.52	to 11.53	to 0.55	to 1.57	to 2.58	to 3.59	to 5.0	to 6.1	to 7.1	to 8.0

Tuesday, on or near the 21st of September, of any year.

Mars.	Sun.	Venus.	Mercury.	Moon.	Saturn.	Jupiter.	Mars.	Sun.	Venus.	Mercury.	Moon.	Saturn.	Jupiter.
5.46 to 6.48	to 7.49	to 8.50	to 9.51	to 10.52	to 11.53	to 0.55	to 1.56	to 2.57	to 3.58	to 4.59	to 6.0	to 6.59	to 7.58

Wednesday, on or near the 22d of September, of any year.

Mercury.	Moon.	Saturn.	Jupiter.	Mars.	Sun.	Venus.	Mercury.	Moon.	Saturn.	Jupiter.	Mars.	Sun.	Venus.
5.47 to 6.48	to 7.49	to 8.50	to 9.50	to 10.51	to 11.52	to 0.53	to 1.54	to 2.55	to 3.56	to 4.57	to 5.58	to 6.57	to 7.56

Thursday, on or near the 23d of September, of any year.

Jupiter.	Mars.	Sun.	Venus.	Mercury.	Moon.	Saturn.	Jupiter.	Mars.	Sun.	Venus.	Mercury.	Moon.	Saturn.
5.48 to 6.48	to 7.49	to 8.50	to 9.50	to 10.51	to 11.52	to 0.52	to 1.53	to 2.54	to 3.54	to 4.55	to 5.56	to 6.55	to 7.54

Friday, on or near the 24th of September, of any year.

Venus.	Mercury.	Moon.	Saturn.	Jupiter.	Mars.	Sun.	Venus.	Mercury.	Moon.	Saturn.	Jupiter.	Mars.	Sun.
5.49 to 6.48	to 7.49	to 8.50	to 9.50	to 10.51	to 11.51	to 0.51	to 1.52	to 2.52	to 3.53	to 4.53	to 5.55	to 6.55	to 7.54

Saturday, on or near the 25th of September, of any year.

Saturn.	Jupiter.	Mars.	Sun.	Venus.	Mercury.	Moon.	Saturn.	Jupiter.	Mars.	Sun.	Venus.	Mercury.	Moon.
5.50 to 6.50	to 7.50	to 8.51	to 9.51	to 10.51	to 11.51	to 0.52	to 1.52	to 2.52	to 3.52	to 4.52	to 5.53	to 6.53	to 7.52

Copyright, 1898, by Luke D. Broughton. Entered at Stationers' Hall, London, England. All rights reserved.

Perpetual Table of Planetary Hours, from Sunrise until 2 hours after Sunset.

Sunday, on or near the 3d of October, of any year.

Sunrise. Sun. A. M.	Venus. A. M.	Mercury. A. M.	Moon. A. M.	Saturn. A. M.	Meridian. Jupiter. M.	Mars. P. M.	Sun. P. M.	Venus. P. M.	Mercury. P. M.	Moon. P. M.	Sunset. Saturn. P. M.	After Sunset. Jupiter. P. M.	Mars. P. M.
5.58 to 6.56	to 7.55	to 8.33	to 9.51	to 10.50	to 11.48	to 0.47	to 1.45	to 2.44	to 3.42	to 4.41	to 5.40	to 6.42	to 7.44

Monday, on or near the 4th of October, of any year.

Moon.	Saturn.	Jupiter.	Mars.	Sun.	Venus.	Mercury.	Moon.	Saturn.	Jupiter.	Mars.	Sun.	Venus.	Mercury.
5.59 to 6.58	to 7.57	to 8.55	to 9.53	to 10.51	to 11.49	to 0.47	to 1.46	to 2.44	to 3.42	to 4.40	to 5.38	to 6.40	to 7.43

Tuesday, on or near the 5th of October, of any year.

Mars.	Sun.	Venus.	Mercury.	Moon.	Saturn.	Jupiter.	Mars.	Sun.	Venus.	Mercury.	Moon.	Saturn.	Jupiter.
6.0 to 6.59	to 7.57	to 8.55	to 9.53	to 10.51	to 11.49	to 0.47	to 1.45	to 2.43	to 3.41	to 4.39	to 5.37	to 6.40	to 7.42

Wednesday, on or near the 6th of October, of any year.

Mercury.	Moon.	Saturn.	Jupiter.	Mars.	Sun.	Venus.	Mercury.	Moon.	Saturn.	Jupiter.	Mars.	Sun.	Venus.
6.1 to 6.58	to 7.57	to 8.55	to 9.53	to 10.50	to 11.48	to 0.45	to 1.43	to 2.41	to 3.39	to 4.37	to 5.35	to 6.37	to 7.39

Thursday, on or near the 7th of October, of any year.

Jupiter.	Mars.	Sun.	Venus.	Mercury.	Moon.	Saturn.	Jupiter.	Mars.	Sun.	Venus.	Mercury.	Moon.	Saturn.
6.2 to 6.59	to 7.57	to 8.55	to 9.53	to 10.50	to 11.48	to 0.45	to 1.42	to 2.40	to 3.37	to 4.35	to 5.33	to 6.35	to 7.37

Friday, on or near the 8th of October, of any year.

Venus.	Mercury.	Moon.	Saturn.	Jupiter.	Mars.	Sun.	Venus.	Mercury.	Moon.	Saturn.	Jupiter.	Mars.	Sun.
6.3 to 7.0	to 7.58	to 8.55	to 9.53	to 10.50	to 11.48	to 0.45	to 1.41	to 2.38	to 3.35	to 4.33	to 5.32	to 6.34	to 7.36

Saturday, on or near the 9th of October, of any year.

Saturn.	Jupiter.	Mars.	Sun.	Venus.	Mercury.	Moon.	Saturn.	Jupiter.	Mars.	Sun.	Venus.	Mercury.	Moon.
6.4 to 7.2	to 7.59	to 8.57	to 9.54	to 10.51	to 11.48	to 0.45	to 1.41	to 2.38	to 3.35	to 4.32	to 5.30	to 6.32	to 7.34

Copyright, 1898, by Luke D. Broughton. Entered at Stationers' Hall, London, England. All rights reserved.

Perpetual Table of Planetary Hours, from Sunrise until 2 hours after Sunset.

Sunday, on or near the 17th of October, of any year.

Sunrise. Sun. A.M.	Venus. A.M.	Mercury. A.M.	Moon. A.M.	Saturn. A.M.	Meridian. Jupiter. M.	Mars. P.M.	Sun. P.M.	Venus. P.M.	Mercury. P.M.	Moon. P.M.	Sunset. Saturn. P.M.	After Sunset. Jupiter. P.M.	Mars. P.M.
6.13 to 7.8	to 8.4	to 8.59	to 9.55	to 10.50	to 11.45	to 0.40	to 1.36	to 2.32	to 3.28	to 4.24	to 5.18	to 6.22	to 7.27

Monday, on or near the 18th of October, of any year.

Moon.	Saturn.	Jupiter.	Mars.	Sun.	Venus.	Mercury.	Moon.	Saturn.	Jupiter.	Mars.	Sun.	Venus.	Mercury.
6.14 to 7.10	to 8.5	to 9.0	to 9.55	to 10.50	to 11.45	to 0.41	to 1.36	to 2.31	to 3.27	to 4.22	to 5.16	to 6.21	to 7.26

Tuesday, on or near the 19th of October, of any year.

Mars.	Sun.	Venus.	Mercury.	Moon.	Saturn.	Jupiter.	Mars.	Sun.	Venus.	Mercury.	Moon.	Saturn.	Jupiter.
6.15 to 7.10	to 8.5	to 9.0	to 9.55	to 10.50	to 11.45	to 0.40	to 1.35	to 2.30	to 3.25	to 4.20	to 5.15	to 6.20	to 7.25

Wednesday, on or near the 20th of October, of any year.

Mercury.	Moon.	Saturn.	Jupiter.	Mars.	Sun.	Venus.	Mercury.	Moon.	Saturn.	Jupiter.	Mars.	Sun.	Venus.
6.16 to 7.10	to 8.5	to 9.0	to 9.55	to 10.50	to 11.44	to 0.39	to 1.34	to 2.29	to 3.24	to 4.19	to 5.13	to 6.18	to 7.23

Thursday, on or near the 21st of October, of any year.

Jupiter.	Mars.	Sun.	Venus.	Mercury.	Moon.	Saturn.	Jupiter.	Mars.	Sun.	Venus.	Mercury.	Moon.	Saturn.
6.17 to 7.11	to 8.6	to 9.0	to 9.55	to 10.50	to 11.44	to 0.39	to 1.33	to 2.28	to 3.23	to 4.17	to 5.12	to 6.18	to 7.23

Friday, on or near the 22d of October, of any year.

Venus.	Mercury.	Moon.	Saturn.	Jupiter.	Mars.	Sun.	Venus.	Mercury.	Moon.	Saturn.	Jupiter.	Mars.	Sun.
6.18 to 7.12	to 8.7	to 9.1	to 9.55	to 10.49	to 11.44	to 0.38	to 1.32	to 2.27	to 3.21	to 4.16	to 5.10	to 6.16	to 7.21

Saturday, on or near the 23d of October, of any year.

Saturn.	Jupiter.	Mars.	Sun.	Venus.	Mercury.	Moon.	Saturn.	Jupiter.	Mars.	Sun.	Venus.	Mercury.	Moon.
6.19 to 7.14	to 8.8	to 9.2	to 9.56	to 10.50	to 11.44	to 0.38	to 1.32	to 2.26	to 3.20	to 4.14	to 5.9	to 6.15	to 7.21

Copyright, 1898, by Luke D. Broughton. Entered at Stationers' Hall, London, England. All rights reserved.

Perpetual Table of Planetary Hours, from Sunrise until 2 hours after Sunset.

Sunday, on or near the 31st of October, of any year.

Sunrise. Sun. A.M.	Venus. A.M.	Mercury. A.M.	Moon. A.M.	Saturn. A.M.	Meridian. Jupiter. M.	Mars. P.M.	Sun. P.M.	Venus. P.M.	Mercury. P.M.	Moon. P.M.	Sunset. Saturn. P.M.	After Sunset. Jupiter. P.M.	Mars. P.M.
6.29 to 7.22	to 8.14	to 9.7	to 9.59	to 10.51	to 11.43	to 0.36	to 1.28	to 2.20	to 3.13	to 4.5	to 4.58	to 6.6	to 7.13

Monday, on or near the 1st of November, of any year.

Moon.	Saturn.	Jupiter.	Mars.	Sun.	Venus.	Mercury.	Moon.	Saturn.	Jupiter.	Mars.	Sun.	Venus.	Mercury.
6.30 to 7.23	to 8.15	to 9.7	to 9.59	to 10.51	to 11.43	to 0.36	to 1.28	to 2.20	to 3.13	to 4.5	to 4.57	to 6.4	to 7.12

Tuesday, on or near the 2d of November, of any year.

Mars.	Sun.	Venus.	Mercury.	Moon.	Saturn.	Jupiter.	Mars.	Sun.	Venus.	Mercury.	Moon.	Saturn.	Jupiter.
6.31 to 7.24	to 8.16	to 9.8	to 10.0	to 10.52	to 11.43	to 0.36	to 1.28	to 2.20	to 3.12	to 4.4	to 4.56	to 6.4	to 7.12

Wednesday, on or near the 3d of November, of any year.

Mercury.	Moon.	Saturn.	Jupiter.	Mars.	Sun.	Venus.	Mercury.	Moon.	Saturn.	Jupiter.	Mars.	Sun.	Venus.
6.32 to 7.24	to 8.16	to 9.8	to 9.59	to 10.51	to 11.43	to 0.35	to 1.27	to 2.19	to 3.11	to 4.3	to 4.55	to 6.3	to 7.11

Thursday, on or near the 4th of November, of any year.

Jupiter.	Mars.	Sun.	Venus.	Mercury.	Moon.	Saturn.	Jupiter.	Mars.	Sun.	Venus.	Mercury.	Moon.	Saturn.
6.33 to 7.24	to 8.16	to 9.8	to 9.59	to 10.51	to 11.43	to 0.35	to 1.27	to 2.18	to 3.10	to 4.2	to 4.54	to 6.2	to 7.10

Friday, on or near the 5th of November, of any year.

Venus.	Mercury.	Moon.	Saturn.	Jupiter.	Mars.	Sun.	Venus.	Mercury.	Moon.	Saturn.	Jupiter.	Mars.	Sun.
6.35 to 7.26	to 8.16	to 9.8	to 9.59	to 10.51	to 11.42	to 0.34	to 1.25	to 2.17	to 3.8	to 4.0	to 4.52	to 6.1	to 7.9

Saturday, on or near the 6th of November, of any year.

Saturn.	Jupiter.	Mars.	Sun.	Venus.	Mercury.	Moon.	Saturn.	Jupiter.	Mars.	Sun.	Venus.	Mercury.	Moon.
6.36 to 7.28	to 8.18	to 9.10	to 10.1	to 10.51	to 11.42	to 0.33	to 1.25	to 2.17	to 3.9	to 4.0	to 4.51	to 6.0	to 7.8

Copyright, 1898, by Luke D. Broughton. Entered at Stationers' Hall, London, England. All rights reserved.

Perpetual Table of Planetary Hours, from Sunrise until 2 hours after Sunset.

Sunday, on or near the 14th of November, of any year.

Sunrise. Sun. A.M.	Venus. A.M.	Mercury. A.M.	Moon. A.M.	Saturn. A.M.	Meridian. Jupiter. M.	Mars. P.M.	Sun. P.M.	Venus. P.M.	Mercury. P.M.	Moon. P.M.	Sunset. Saturn. P.M.	After Sunset. Jupiter. P.M.	Mars. P.M.
6.45 to 7.34	to 8.24	to 9.14	to 10.4	to 10.56	to 11.46	to 0.36	to 1.26	to 2.16	to 3.5	to 3.54	to 4.43	to 5.53	to 7.3

Monday, on or near the 15th of November, of any year.

Moon.	Saturn.	Jupiter.	Mars.	Sun.	Venus.	Mercury.	Moon.	Saturn.	Jupiter.	Mars.	Sun.	Venus.	Mercury.
6.46 to 7.35	to 8.25	to 9.15	to 10.5	to 10.56	to 11.46	to 0.35	to 1.25	to 2.15	to 3.5	to 3.55	to 4.43	to 5.53	to 7.3

Tuesday, on or near the 16th of November, of any year.

Mars.	Sun.	Venus.	Mercury.	Moon.	Saturn.	Jupiter.	Mars.	Sun.	Venus.	Mercury.	Moon.	Saturn.	Jupiter.
6.48 to 7.37	to 8.27	to 9.16	to 10.6	to 10.56	to 11.46	to 0.35	to 1.24	to 2.13	to 3.3	to 3.52	to 4.42	to 5.52	to 7.2

Wednesday, on or near the 17th of November, of any year.

Mercury.	Moon.	Saturn.	Jupiter.	Mars.	Sun.	Venus.	Mercury.	Moon.	Saturn.	Jupiter.	Mars.	Sun.	Venus.
6.49 to 7.38	to 8.28	to 9.17	to 10.7	to 10.56	to 11.46	to 0.35	to 1.24	to 2.13	to 3.2	to 3.51	to 4.41	to 5.51	to 7.2

Thursday, on or near the 18th of November, of any year.

Jupiter.	Mars.	Sun.	Venus.	Mercury.	Moon.	Saturn.	Sun.	Mars.	Mercury.	Venus.	Mercury.	Moon.	Saturn.
6.50 to 7.39	to 8.29	to 9.18	to 10.7	to 10.56	to 11.46	to 0.35	to 1.24	to 2.13	to 3.1	to 3.51	to 4.40	to 5.50	to 7.1

Friday, on or near the 19th of November, of any year.

Venus.	Mercury.	Moon.	Saturn.	Jupiter.	Mars.	Sun.	Venus.	Mercury.	Moon.	Saturn.	Jupiter.	Mars.	Sun.
6.51 to 7.41	to 8.30	to 9.19	to 10.8	to 10.57	to 11.46	to 0.35	to 1.24	to 2.13	to 3.2	to 3.51	to 4.40	to 5.50	to 7.1

Saturday, on or near the 20th of November, of any year.

Saturn.	Jupiter.	Mars.	Sun.	Venus.	Mercury.	Moon.	Saturn.	Jupiter.	Mars.	Sun.	Venus.	Mercury.	Moon.
6.93 to 7.41	to 8.30	to 9.19	to 10.8	to 10.57	to 11.46	to 0.35	to 1.24	to 2.12	to 3.1	to 3.50	to 4.39	to 5.50	to 7.1

Copyright, 1898, by Luke D. Broughton. Entered at Stationers' Hall, London, England. All rights reserved.

Perpetual Table of Planetary Hours, from Sunrise until 2 hours after Sunset.

Sunday, on or near the 28th of November, of any year.

Sunrise. Sun. A.M.	Venus. A.M.	Mercury. A.M.	Moon. A.M.	Saturn. A.M.	Meridian. Jupiter. M.	Mars. P.M.	Sun. P.M.	Venus. P.M.	Mercury. P.M.	Moon. P.M.	Sunset. Saturn. P.M.	After Sunset. Jupiter. P.M.	Mars. P.M.
7.1 to 7.48	to 8.36	to 9.24	to 10.12	to 11.0	to 11.47	to 0.35	to 1.23	to 2.11	to 2.59	to 3.47	to 4.35	to 5.47	to 6.59

Monday, on or near the 29th of November, of any year.

Moon.	Saturn.	Jupiter.	Mars.	Sun.	Venus.	Mercury.	Moon.	Saturn.	Jupiter.	Mars.	Sun.	Venus.	Mercury.
7.2 to 7.49	to 8.37	to 9.25	to 10.13	to 11.1	to 11.48	to 0.36	to 1.23	to 2.11	to 2.59	to 3.47	to 4.35	to 5.47	to 6.59

Tuesday, on or near the 30th of November, of any year.

Mars.	Sun.	Venus.	Mercury.	Moon.	Saturn.	Jupiter.	Mars.	Sun.	Venus.	Mercury.	Moon.	Saturn.	Jupiter.
7.3 to 7.50	to 8.38	to 9.25	to 10.13	to 11.1	to 11.48	to 0.36	to 1.23	to 2.10	to 2.59	to 3.46	to 4.34	to 5.46	to 6.58

Wednesday, on or near the 1st of December, of any year.

Mercury.	Moon.	Saturn.	Jupiter.	Mars.	Sun.	Venus.	Mercury.	Moon.	Saturn.	Jupiter.	Mars.	Sun.	Venus.
7.4 to 7.51	to 8.39	to 9.26	to 10.14	to 11.1	to 11.49	to 0.36	to 1.24	to 2.11	to 2.59	to 3.46	to 4.34	to 5.46	to 6.58

Thursday, on or near the 2d of December, of any year.

Jupiter.	Mars.	Sun.	Venus.	Mercury.	Moon.	Saturn.	Jupiter.	Mars.	Sun.	Venus.	Mercury.	Moon.	Saturn.
7.5 to 7.52	to 8.39	to 9.27	to 10.14	to 11.1	to 11.50	to 0.37	to 1.24	to 2.11	to 2.59	to 3.46	to 4.34	to 5.46	to 6.58

Friday, on or near the 3d of December, of any year.

Venus.	Mercury.	Moon.	Saturn.	Jupiter.	Mars.	Sun.	Venus.	Mercury.	Moon.	Saturn.	Jupiter.	Mars.	Sun.
7.6 to 7.53	to 8.41	to 9.28	to 10.15	to 11.2	to 11.50	to 0.37	to 1.24	to 2.11	to 2.58	to 3.45	to 4.33	to 5.46	to 6.58

Saturday, on or near the 4th of December, of any year.

Saturn.	Jupiter.	Mars.	Sun.	Venus.	Mercury.	Moon.	Saturn.	Jupiter.	Mars.	Sun.	Venus.	Mercury.	Moon.
7.7 to 7.54	to 8.42	to 9.29	to 10.16	to 11.3	to 11.50	to 0.37	to 1.24	to 2.11	to 2.58	to 3.45	to 4.33	to 5.46	to 6.58

Copyright, 1898, by Luke D. Broughton. Entered at Stationers' Hall, London, England. All rights reserved.

Perpetual Table of Planetary Hours, from Sunrise until 2 hours after Sunset.

Sunday, on or near the 12th of December, of any year.

Sunrise. Sun. A.M.	Venus. A.M.	Mercury. A.M.	Moon A.M.	Saturn. A.M.	Meridian. Jupiter. M.	Mars. P.M.	Sun. P.M.	Venus. P.M.	Mercury. P.M.	Moon. P.M.	Sunset. Saturn. P.M.	After Sunset. Jupiter. P.M.	Mars. P.M.
7.15 to 8.1	to 8.48	to 9.34	to 10.21	to 11.7	to 11.54	to 0.40	to 1.27	to 2.13	to 3.0	to 3.46	to 4.33	to 5.47	to 7.0

Monday, on or near the 13th of December, of any year.

Moon.	Saturn.	Jupiter.	Mars.	Sun.	Venus.	Mercury.	Moon.	Saturn.	Jupiter.	Mars.	Sun.	Venus.	Mercury.
7.16 to 8.2	to 8.48	to 9.34	to 10.21	to 11.7	to 11.54	to 0.40	to 1.27	to 2.13	to 3.0	to 3.46	to 4.33	to 5.47	to 7.0

Tuesday, on or near the 14th of December, of any year.

Mars.	Sun.	Venus.	Mercury.	Moon.	Saturn.	Jupiter.	Mars.	Sun.	Venus.	Mercury.	Moon.	Saturn.	Jupiter.
7.16 to 8.2	to 8.48	to 9.34	to 10.21	to 11.7	to 11.54	to 0.40	to 1.27	to 2.13	to 3.0	to 3.46	to 4.34	to 5.47	to 7.1

Wednesday, on or near the 15th of December, of any year.

Mercury.	Moon.	Saturn.	Jupiter.	Mars.	Sun.	Venus.	Mercury.	Moon.	Saturn.	Jupiter.	Mars.	Sun.	Venus.
7.17 to 8.3	to 8.50	to 9.36	to 10.22	to 11.9	to 11.55	to 0.41	to 1.28	to 2.14	to 3.1	to 3.47	to 4.34	to 5.47	to 7.1

Thursday, on or near the 16th of December, of any year.

Jupiter.	Mars.	Sun.	Venus.	Mercury.	Moon.	Saturn.	Jupiter.	Mars.	Sun.	Venus.	Mercury.	Moon.	Saturn.
7.18 to 8.4	to 8.51	to 9.37	to 10.24	to 11.10	to 11.57	to 0.42	to 1.29	to 2.15	to 3.1	to 3.48	to 4.34	to 5.47	to 7.1

Friday, on or near the 17th of December, of any year.

Venus.	Mercury.	Moon.	Saturn.	Jupiter.	Mars.	Sun.	Venus.	Mercury.	Moon.	Saturn.	Jupiter.	Mars.	Sun.
7.18 to 8.4	to 8.51	to 9.37	to 10.24	to 11.10	to 11.57	to 0.43	to 1.29	to 2.15	to 3.1	to 3.48	to 4.34	to 5.47	to 7.1

Saturday, on or near the 18th of December, of any year.

Saturn.	Jupiter.	Mars.	Sun.	Venus.	Mercury.	Moon.	Saturn.	Jupiter.	Mars.	Sun.	Venus.	Mercury.	Moon.
7.19 to 8.5	to 8.52	to 9.38	to 10.25	to 11.10	to 11.57	to 0.44	to 1.30	to 2.16	to 3.2	to 3.48	to 4.35	to 5.49	to 7.2

Copyright, 1898, by Luke D. Broughton. Entered at Stationers' Hall, London, England. All rights reserved.

Perpetual Table of Planetary Hours, from Sunrise until 2 hours after Sunset.

Sunday, on or near the 26th of December, of any year.

Sunrise. Sun. A. M.	Venus. A. M.	Mercury. A. M.	Moon. A. M.	Saturn. A. M.	Meridian. Jupiter. M.	Mars. P. M.	Sun. P. M.	Venus. P. M.	Mercury. P. M.	Moon. P. M.	Sunset. Saturn. P. M.	After Sunset. Jupiter. P. M.	Mars. P. M.
7.23 to 8.9	to 8.56	to 9.42	to 10.28	to 11.15	to 0.2	to 0.48	to 1.34	to 2.21	to 3.7	to 3.56	to 4.40	to 5.53	to 7.6

Monday, on or near the 27th of December, of any year.

Moon.	Saturn.	Jupiter.	Mars.	Sun.	Venus.	Mercury.	Moon.	Saturn.	Jupiter.	Mars.	Sun.	Venus.	Mercury.
7.23 to 8.9	to 8.56	to 9.42	to 10.28	to 11.15	to 0.2	to 0.48	to 1.34	to 2.21	to 3.7	to 3.56	to 4.40	to 5.54	to 7.7

Tuesday, on or near the 28th of December, of any year.

Mars.	Sun.	Venus.	Mercury.	Moon.	Saturn.	Jupiter.	Mars.	Sun.	Venus.	Mercury.	Moon.	Saturn.	Jupiter.
7.23 to 8.9	to 8.56	to 9.42	to 10.28	to 11.15	to 0.2	to 0.48	to 1.34	to 2.21	to 3.8	to 3.56	to 4.40	to 5.54	to 7.7

Wednesday, on or near the 29th of December, of any year.

Mercury.	Moon.	Saturn.	Jupiter.	Mars.	Sun.	Venus.	Mercury.	Moon.	Saturn.	Jupiter.	Mars.	Sun.	Venus.
7.24 to 8.10	to 8.57	to 9.43	to 10.29	to 11.16	to 0.3	to 0.48	to 1.35	to 2.21	to 3.8	to 3.56	to 4.41	to 5.55	to 7.8

Thursday, on or near the 30th of December, of any year.

Jupiter.	Mars.	Sun.	Venus.	Mercury.	Moon.	Saturn.	Jupiter.	Mars.	Sun.	Venus.	Mercury.	Moon.	Saturn.
7.24 to 8.10	to 8.57	to 9.43	to 10.30	to 11.16	to 0.3	to 0.49	to 1.36	to 2.22	to 3.9	to 3.55	to 4.42	to 5.56	to 7.9

Friday, on or near the 31st of December, of any year.

Venus.	Mercury.	Moon.	Saturn.	Jupiter.	Mars.	Sun.	Venus.	Mercury.	Moon.	Saturn.	Jupiter.	Mars.	Sun.
7.24 to 8.10	to 8.57	to 9.43	to 10.30	to 11.16	to 0.3	to 0.49	to 1.36	to 2.22	to 3.9	to 3.55	to 4.42	to 5.56	to 7.9

Saturday, on or near the 1st of January, of any year.

Saturn.	Jupiter.	Mars.	Sun.	Venus.	Mercury.	Moon.	Saturn.	Jupiter.	Mars.	Sun.	Venus.	Mercury.	Moon.
7.25 to 8.11	to 8.58	to 9.44	to 10.31	to 11.17	to 0.4	to 0.50	to 1.37	to 2.23	to 3.10	to 3.55	to 4.43	to 5.57	to 7.10

Copyright, 1898, by Luke D. Broughton. Entered at Stationers' Hall, London, England. All rights reserved.

Perpetual Table of Planetary Hours, from Sunrise until 2 hours after Sunset.

Sunday, on or near the 9th of January, of any year.

Sunrise. Sun. A. M.	Venus. A. M.	Mercury. A. M.	Moon A. M.	Saturn. A. M.	Meridian. Jupiter. M.	Mars. P. M.	Sun. P. M.	Venus. P. M.	Mercury. P. M.	Moon. P. M.	Sunset. Saturn. P. M.	After Sunset. Jupiter. P. M.	Mars. P. M.
7.24 to 8.11	to 8.59	to 9.46	to 10.32	to 11.19	to 0.6	to 0.54	to 1.41	to 2.28	to 3.15	to 4.2	to 4.51	to 6.4	to 7.16

Monday, on or near the 10th of January, of any year.

Moon.	Saturn.	Jupiter.	Mars.	Sun.	Venus.	Mercury.	Moon.	Saturn.	Jupiter.	Mars.	Sun.	Venus.	Mercury.
7.24 to 8.11	to 8.59	to 9.46	to 10.32	to 11.19	to 0.7	to 0.55	to 1.42	to 2.29	to 3.16	to 4.3	to 4.52	to 6.5	to 7.17

Tuesday, on or near the 11th of January, of any year.

Mars.	Sun.	Venus.	Mercury.	Moon.	Saturn.	Jupiter.	Mars.	Sun.	Venus.	Mercury.	Moon.	Saturn.	Jupiter.
7.24 to 8.11	to 8.59	to 9.46	to 10.34	to 11.20	to 0.8	to 0.56	to 1.43	to 2.31	to 3.19	to 4.5	to 4.53	to 6.6	to 7.18

Wednesday, on or near the 12th of January, of any year.

Mercury.	Moon.	Saturn.	Jupiter.	Mars.	Sun.	Venus.	Mercury.	Moon.	Saturn.	Jupiter.	Mars.	Sun.	Venus.
7.24 to 8.11	to 8.59	to 9.46	to 10.34	to 11.21	to 0.9	to 0.56	to 1.44	to 2.32	to 3.19	to 4.7	to 4.54	to 6.7	to 7.19

Thursday, on or near the 13th of January, of any year.

Jupiter.	Mars.	Sun.	Venus.	Mercury.	Moon.	Saturn.	Jupiter.	Mars.	Sun.	Venus.	Mercury.	Moon.	Saturn.
7.23 to 8.10	to 8.58	to 9.45	to 10.34	to 11.21	to 0.9	to 0.56	to 1.44	to 2.32	to 3.19	to 4.8	to 4.55	to 6.8	to 7.20

Friday, on or near the 14th of January, of any year.

Venus.	Mercury.	Moon.	Saturn.	Jupiter.	Mars.	Sun.	Venus.	Mercury.	Moon.	Saturn.	Jupiter.	Mars.	Sun.
7.23 to 8.10	to 8.58	to 9.46	to 10.34	to 11.22	to 0.9	to 0.57	to 1.45	to 2.33	to 3.21	to 4.9	to 4.56	to 6.9	to 7.21

Saturday, on or near the 15th of January, of any year.

Saturn.	Jupiter.	Mars.	Sun.	Venus.	Mercury.	Moon.	Saturn.	Jupiter.	Mars.	Sun.	Venus.	Mercury.	Moon.
7.23 to 8.10	to 8.58	to 9.46	to 10.34	to 11.22	to 0.9	to 0.57	to 1.45	to 2.33	to 3.21	to 4.9	to 4.57	to 6.10	to 7.22

Copyright, 1898, by Luke D. Broughton. Entered at Stationers' Hall, London, England. All rights reserved.

Perpetual Table of Planetary Hours, from Sunrise until 2 hours after Sunset.

Sunday, on or near the 23d of January, of any year.

Sunrise. Sun. A. M.	Venus. A. M.	Mercury. A. M.	Moon. A. M.	Saturn. A. M.	Meridian. Jupiter. M.	Mars. P. M.	Sun. P. M.	Venus. P. M.	Mercury. P. M.	Moon. P. M.	Sunset. Saturn. P. M.	After Sunset. Jupiter. P. M.	Mars. P. M.
7.18 to 8.7	to 8.56	to 9.45	to 10.34	to 11.23	to 0.12	to 1.1	to 1.50	to 2.39	to 3.28	to 4.17	to 5.7	to 6.18	to 7.30

Monday, on or near the 24th of January, of any year.

Moon.	Saturn.	Jupiter.	Mars.	Sun.	Venus.	Mercury.	Moon.	Saturn.	Jupiter.	Mars.	Sun.	Venus.	Mercury.
7.17 to 8.7	to 8.56	to 9.45	to 10.34	to 11.23	to 0.13	to 1.2	to 1.51	to 2.40	to 3.29	to 4.18	to 5.8	to 6.19	to 7.31

Tuesday, on or near the 25th of January, of any year.

Mars.	Sun.	Venus.	Mercury.	Moon.	Saturn.	Jupiter.	Mars.	Sun.	Venus.	Mercury.	Moon.	Saturn.	Jupiter.
7.17 to 8.7	to 8.56	to 9.45	to 10.34	to 11.24	to 0.14	to 1.3	to 1.52	to 2.41	to 3.30	to 4.19	to 5.9	to 6.20	to 7.31

Wednesday, on or near the 26th of January, of any year.

Mercury.	Moon.	Saturn.	Jupiter.	Mars.	Sun.	Venus.	Mercury.	Moon.	Saturn.	Jupiter.	Mars.	Sun.	Venus.
7.16 to 8.6	to 8.55	to 9.45	to 10.34	to 11.24	to 0.14	to 1.3	to 1.52	to 2.42	to 3.31	to 4.20	to 5.10	to 6.21	to 7.31

Thursday, on or near the 27th of January, of any year.

Jupiter.	Mars.	Sun.	Venus.	Mercury.	Moon.	Saturn.	Jupiter.	Mars.	Sun.	Venus.	Mercury.	Moon.	Saturn.
7.15 to 8.5	to 8.55	to 9.45	to 10.34	to 11.24	to 0.14	to 1.4	to 1.53	to 2.43	to 3.32	to 4.22	to 5.11	to 6.22	to 7.32

Friday, on or near the 28th of January, of any year.

Venus.	Mercury.	Moon.	Saturn.	Jupiter.	Mars.	Sun.	Venus.	Mercury.	Moon.	Saturn.	Jupiter.	Mars.	Sun.
7.14 to 8.4	to 8.54	to 9.44	to 10.33	to 11.23	to 0.13	to 1.3	to 1.53	to 2.43	to 3.33	to 4.23	to 5.13	to 6.23	to 7.33

Saturday, on or near the 29th of January, of any year.

Saturn.	Jupiter.	Mars.	Sun.	Venus.	Mercury.	Moon.	Saturn.	Jupiter.	Mars.	Sun.	Venus.	Mercury.	Moon.
7.13 to 8.4	to 8.53	to 9.43	to 10.33	to 11.23	to 0.13	to 1.3	to 1.53	to 2.43	to 3.33	to 4.23	to 5.14	to 6.24	to 7.34

Copyright, 1898, by Luke D Broughton. Entered at Stationers' Hall, London, England. All rights reserved.

Perpetual Table of Planetary Hours, from Sunrise until 2 hours after Sunset.

Sunday, on or near the 6th of February, of any year.

Sunrise. Sun. A.M.	Venus. A.M.	Mercury. A.M.	Moon. A.M.	Saturn. A.M.	Meridian. Jupiter. M.	Mars. P.M.	Sun. P.M.	Venus. P.M.	Mercury. P.M.	Moon. P.M.	Sunset. Saturn. P.M.	After Sunset. Jupiter. P.M.	Mars. P.M.
7.6 to 7.57	to 8.49	to 9.41	to 10.33	to 11.24	to 0.16	to 1.7	to 1.58	to 2.50	to 3.41	to 4.33	to 5.24	to 6.33	to 7.41

Monday, on or near the 7th of February, of any year.

Moon.	Saturn.	Jupiter.	Mars.	Sun.	Venus.	Mercury.	Moon.	Saturn.	Jupiter.	Mars.	Sun.	Venus.	Mercury.
7.5 to 7.57	to 8.48	to 9.40	to 10.31	to 11.23	to 0.15	to 1.7	to 1.58	to 2.50	to 3.41	to 4.33	to 5.25	to 6.34	to 7.42

Tuesday, on or near the 8th of February, of any year.

Mars.	Sun.	Venus.	Mercury.	Moon.	Saturn.	Jupiter.	Mars.	Sun.	Venus.	Mercury.	Moon.	Saturn.	Jupiter.
7.3 to 7.56	to 8.46	to 9.39	to 10.31	to 11.22	to 0.15	to 1.7	to 1.58	to 2.50	to 3.42	to 4.34	to 5.26	to 6.34	to 7.42

Wednesday, on or near the 9th of February, of any year.

Mercury.	Moon.	Saturn.	Jupiter.	Mars.	Sun.	Venus.	Mercury.	Moon.	Saturn.	Jupiter.	Mars.	Sun.	Venus.
7.2 to 7.55	to 8.47	to 9.39	to 10.31	to 11.23	to 0.15	to 1.7	to 1.59	to 2.51	to 3.43	to 4.35	to 5.27	to 6.35	to 7.43

Thursday, on or near the 10th of February, of any year.

Jupiter.	Mars.	Sun.	Venus.	Mercury.	Moon.	Saturn.	Jupiter.	Mars.	Sun.	Venus.	Mercury.	Moon.	Saturn.
7.1 to 7.53	to 8.46	to 9.38	to 10.31	to 11.23	to 0.15	to 1.7	to 2.0	to 2.52	to 3.44	to 4.36	to 5.28	to 6.36	to 7.44

Friday, on or near the 11th of February, of any year.

Venus.	Mercury.	Moon.	Saturn.	Jupiter.	Mars.	Sun.	Venus.	Mercury.	Moon.	Saturn.	Jupiter.	Mars.	Sun.
7.0 to 7.53	to 8.45	to 9.38	to 10.30	to 11.23	to 0.15	to 1.8	to 2.1	to 2.53	to 3.45	to 4.38	to 5.30	to 6.38	to 7.45

Saturday, on or near the 12th of February, of any year.

Saturn.	Jupiter.	Mars.	Sun.	Venus.	Mercury.	Moon.	Saturn.	Jupiter.	Mars.	Sun.	Venus.	Mercury.	Moon.
6.59 to 7.51	to 8.44	to 9.37	to 10.30	to 11.23	to 0.16	to 1.9	to 2.2	to 2.54	to 3.46	to 4.39	to 5.31	to 6.39	to 7.46

Copyright, 1898, by Luke D. Broughton. Entered at Stationers' Hall, London, England. All rights reserved.

Perpetual Table of Planetary Hours, from Sunrise until 2 hours after Sunset.

Sunday, on or near the 20th of February, of any year.

Sunrise. Sun. A. M.	Venus. A. M.	Mercury. A. M.	Moon. A. M.	Saturn. A. M.	Meridian. Jupiter. M.	Mars. P. M.	Sun. P. M.	Venus. P. M.	Mercury. P. M.	Moon. P. M.	Sunset. Saturn. P. M.	After Sunset. Jupiter. P. M.	Mars. P. M.
6.48 to 7.42	to 8.37	to 9.31	to 10.26	to 11.21	to 0.15	to 1.10	to 2.4	to 2.58	to 3.53	to 4.47	to 5.41	to 6.47	to 7.52

Monday, on or near the 21st of February, of any year.

Moon.	Saturn.	Jupiter.	Mars.	Sun.	Venus.	Mercury.	Moon.	Saturn.	Jupiter.	Mars.	Sun.	Venus.	Mercury.
6.46 to 7.41	to 8.35	to 9.30	to 10.25	to 11.20	to 0.14	to 1.9	to 2.4	to 2.58	to 3.53	to 4.48	to 5.42	to 6.48	to 7.53

Tuesday, on or near the 22d of February, of any year.

Mars.	Sun.	Venus.	Mercury.	Moon.	Saturn.	Jupiter.	Mars.	Sun.	Venus.	Mercury.	Moon.	Saturn.	Jupiter.
6.45 to 7.40	to 8.34	to 9.29	to 10.24	to 11.19	to 0.14	to 1.9	to 2.4	to 2.59	to 3.54	to 4.50	to 5.43	to 6.49	to 7.54

Wednesday, on or near the 23d of February, of any year.

Mercury.	Moon.	Saturn.	Jupiter.	Mars.	Sun.	Venus.	Mercury.	Moon.	Saturn.	Jupiter.	Mars.	Sun.	Venus.
6.44 to 7.39	to 8.34	to 9.29	to 10.24	to 11.19	to 0.14	to 1.9	to 2.4	to 2.59	to 3.54	to 4.50	to 5.44	to 6.49	to 7.54

Thursday, on or near the 24th of February, of any year.

Jupiter.	Mars.	Sun.	Venus.	Mercury.	Moon.	Saturn.	Jupiter.	Mars.	Sun.	Venus.	Mercury.	Moon.	Saturn.
6.42 to 7.37	to 8.33	to 9.28	to 10.23	to 11.19	to 0.14	to 1.9	to 2.4	to 2.59	to 3.55	to 4.51	to 5.45	to 6.50	to 7.55

Friday, on or near the 25th of February, of any year.

Venus.	Mercury.	Moon.	Saturn.	Jupiter.	Mars.	Sun.	Venus.	Mercury.	Moon.	Saturn.	Jupiter.	Mars.	Sun.
6.41 to 7.35	to 8.32	to 9.28	to 10.23	to 11.19	to 0.14	to 1.9	to 2.5	to 3.1	to 3.56	to 4.52	to 5.47	to 6.52	to 7.56

Saturday, on or near the 26th of February, of any year.

Saturn.	Jupiter.	Mars.	Sun.	Venus.	Mercury.	Moon.	Saturn.	Jupiter.	Mars.	Sun.	Venus.	Mercury.	Moon.
6.39 to 7.34	to 8.31	to 9.27	to 10.23	to 11.19	to 0.14	to 1.9	to 2.6	to 3.2	to 3.58	to 4.54	to 5.48	to 6.43	to 7.57

Copyright, 1898, by Luke D. Broughton. Entered at Stationers' Hall, London, England. All rights reserved.

Perpetual Table of Planetary Hours, from Sunrise until 2 hours after Sunset.

Sunday, on or near the 6th of March, of any year.

Sunrise. Sun. A. M.	Venus. A. M.	Mercury. A. M.	Moon A. M.	Saturn. A. M.	Meridian. Jupiter. M.	Mars. P. M.	Sun. P. M.	Venus. P. M.	Mercury. P. M.	Moon. P. M.	Sunset. Saturn. P. M.	After Sunset. Jupiter. P. M.	Mars. P. M.
6.27 to 7.24	to 8.22	to 9.19	to 10.17	to 11.14	to 0.12	to 1.9	to 2.7	to 3.5	to 4.2	to 4.59	to 5.57	to 7.0	to 8.2

Monday, on or near the 7th of March, of any year.

Moon.	Saturn.	Jupiter.	Mars.	Sun.	Venus.	Mercury.	Moon.	Saturn.	Jupiter.	Mars.	Sun.	Venus.	Mercury.
6.26 to 7.24	to 8.21	to 9.19	to 10.16	to 11.14	to 0.12	to 1.10	to 2.8	to 3.6	to 4.3	to 5.0	to 5.58	to 7.0	to 8.2

Tuesday, on or near the 8th of March, of any year.

Mars.	Sun.	Venus.	Mercury.	Moon.	Saturn.	Jupiter.	Mars.	Sun.	Venus.	Mercury.	Moon.	Saturn.	Jupiter.
6.24 to 7.21	to 8.19	to 9.17	to 10.15	to 11.13	to 0.11	to 1.10	to 2.8	to 3.6	to 4.3	to 5.1	to 5.59	to 7.1	to 8.3

Wednesday, on or near the 9th of March, of any year.

Mercury.	Moon.	Saturn.	Jupiter.	Mars.	Sun.	Venus.	Mercury.	Moon.	Saturn.	Jupiter.	Mars.	Sun.	Venus.
6.22 to 7.21	to 8.19	to 9.17	to 10.15	to 11.13	to 0.11	to 1.10	to 2.8	to 3.6	to 4.4	to 5.2	to 6.0	to 7.2	to 8.4

Thursday, on or near the 10th of March, of any year.

Jupiter.	Mars.	Sun.	Venus.	Mercury.	Moon.	Saturn.	Jupiter.	Mars.	Sun.	Venus.	Mercury.	Moon.	Saturn.
6.21 to 7.20	to 8.18	to 9.15	to 10.15	to 11.12	to 0.11	to 1.10	to 2.9	to 3.6	to 4.5	to 5.3	to 6.1	to 7.3	to 8.5

Friday, on or near the 11th of March, of any year.

Venus.	Mercury.	Moon.	Saturn	Jupiter.	Mars.	Sun.	Venus.	Mercury.	Moon.	Saturn.	Jupiter.	Mars.	Sun.
6.19 to 7.18	to 8.16	to 9.15	to 10.14	to 11.12	to 0.11	to 1.9	to 2.8	to 3.6	to 4.5	to 5.3	to 6.2	to 7.4	to 8.6

Saturday, on or near the 12th of March, of any year.

Saturn.	Jupiter.	Mars.	Sun.	Venus.	Mercury.	Moon.	Saturn.	Jupiter.	Mars.	Sun.	Venus.	Mercury.	Moon.
6.17 to 7.15	to 8.14	to 9.13	to 10.12	to 11.11	to 0.10	to 1.8	to 2.7	to 3.6	to 4.5	to 5.4	to 6.3	to 7.5	to 8.7

Copyright, 1898, by Luke D. Broughton. Entered at Stationers' Hall, London, England. All rights reserved.

ELEMENTS OF ASTROLOGY.

☞ In order to make the foregoing "Tables of Planetary Hours" as perfect as possible, I have added the following four pages, of tables calculated for the middle of every other week; so by comparing the beginning and end of the day, or Sunrise and Sunset in the Tables of Planetary Hours, with the Sunrise and Sunset of the Wednesday of the following week, the student can arrive at nearly the exact minute that the Sun rises or sets in any day of the year. Especially for the years similar to 1897 where the days of the month correspond with the days of the week that the tables are calculated for. If the student inspects the Perpetual Tables, he will see that there are only six minutes difference between the Sunrise on Sunday and Sunrise on the following Saturday. Therefore by the following tables, he can ascertain, within one minute of the exact time of Sunrise and Sunset, or the beginning or ending of any planetary hour, either night or day, for any week in the year.

Table of Planetary Hours from Sunrise until 2 hours after Sunset, for every alternate Wednesday of any Year.

Wednesday, on or near the 31st of March, of any year.

Sunrise. Mercury. A. M.	Moon. A. M.	Saturn. A. M.	Jupiter. A. M.	Mars. A. M.	Meridian. Sun. M.	Venus. P. M.	Mercury. P. M.	Moon. P. M.	Saturn. P. M	Jupiter. P. M.	Sunset. Mars. P. M.	After Sunset. Sun. P. M.	Venus. P. M.
5.46 to 6.50	to 7.53	to 8.56	to 9.59	to 11.2	to 12.5	to 1.8	to 2.11	to 3.14	to 4.17	to 5.20	to 6.23	to 7.20	to 8.17

Wednesday, on or near the 14th of April, of any year.

Mercury.	Moon.	Saturn.	Jupiter.	Mars.	Sun.	Venus.	Mercury.	Moon.	Saturn.	Jupiter.	Mars.	Sun.	Venus.
5.24 to 6.31	to 7.37	to 8.42	to 9.48	to 10.54	to 12.0	to 1.7	to 2.13	to 3.19	to 4.25	to 5.31	to 6.38	to 7.32	to 8.26

Wednesday, on or near the 28th of April, of any year.

Mercury.	Moon.	Saturn.	Jupiter.	Mars.	Sun.	Venus.	Mercury.	Moon.	Saturn.	Jupiter.	Mars.	Sun.	Venus.
5.3 to 6.13	to 7.22	to 8.31	to 9.40	to 10.49	to 11.58	to 1.7	to 2.16	to 3.25	to 4.34	to 5.43	to 6.52	to 7.43	to 8.34

Wednesday, on or near the 12th of May, of any year.

Mercury.	Moon.	Saturn.	Jupiter.	Mars.	Sun.	Venus.	Mercury.	Moon.	Saturn.	Jupiter.	Mars.	Sun.	Venus.
4.46 to 5.58	to 7.9	to 8.21	to 9.33	to 10.45	to 11.56	to 1.8	to 2.20	to 3.32	to 4.44	to 5.56	to 7.7	to 7.55	to 8.43

Wednesday, on or near the 26th of May, of any year.

Mercury.	Moon.	Saturn.	Jupiter.	Mars.	Sun.	Venus.	Mercury.	Moon.	Saturn.	Jupiter.	Mars.	Sun.	Venus.
4.34 to 5.48	to 7.2	to 8.14	to 9.27	to 10.41	to 11.55	to 1.8	to 2.23	to 3.37	to 4.50	to 6.5	to 7.19	to 8.5	to 8.51

Copyright, 1898, by Luke D. Broughton. Entered at Stationers' Hall, London, England. All rights reserved.

Perpetual Table of Planetary Hours, from Sunrise until 2 hours after Sunset.

Wednesday, on or near the 9th of June, of any year.

Sunrise. Mercury. A. M.	Moon. A. M.	Saturn. A. M.	Jupiter. A. M.	Mars. A. M.	Meridian. Sun. M.	Venus. P. M.	Mercury. P. M.	Moon. P. M.	Saturn. P. M.	Jupiter. P. M.	Sunset. Mars. P. M.	After Sunset. Sun. P. M.	Venus. P. M.
4.28 to 5.44	to 6.59	to 8.14	to 9.29	to 10.44	to 11.59	to 1.14	to 2.29	to 3.44	to 4.59	to 6.14	to 7.29	to 8.14	to 8.59

Wednesday, on or near the 23d of June, of any year.

Mercury.	Moon.	Saturn.	Jupiter.	Mars.	Sun.	Venus.	Mercury.	Moon.	Saturn.	Jupiter.	Mars.	Sun.	Venus.
4.29 to 5.45	to 7.0	to 8.16	to 9.31	to 10.47	to 0.2	to 1.18	to 2.33	to 3.49	to 5.4	to 6.20	to 7.35	to 8.20	to 9.5

Wednesday, on or near the 7th of July, of any year.

Mercury.	Moon.	Saturn.	Jupiter.	Mars.	Sun.	Venus.	Mercury.	Moon.	Saturn.	Jupiter.	Mars.	Sun.	Venus.
4.36 to 5.50	to 7.5	to 8.20	to 9.37	to 10.52	to 0.7	to 1.21	to 2.36	to 3.51	to 5.4	to 6.20	to 7.33	to 8.19	to 9.5

Wednesday, on or near the 21st of July, of any year.

Mercury.	Moon.	Saturn.	Jupiter.	Mars.	Sun.	Venus.	Mercury.	Moon.	Saturn.	Jupiter.	Mars.	Sun.	Venus.
4.46 to 6.0	to 7.13	to 8.26	to 9.39	to 10.52	to 0.6	to 1.19	to 2.32	to 3.46	to 4.59	to 6.12	to 7.26	to 8.13	to 9.0

Wednesday, on or near the 4th of August, of any year.

Mercury.	Moon.	Saturn.	Jupiter.	Mars.	Sun.	Venus.	Mercury.	Moon.	Saturn.	Jupiter.	Mars.	Sun.	Venus.
4.59 to 6.11	to 7.22	to 8.33	to 9.44	to 10.55	to 0.6	to 1.18	to 2.29	to 3.40	to 4.51	to 6.2	to 7.13	to 8.2	to 8.51

Wednesday, on or near the 18th of August, of any year.

Mercury.	Moon.	Saturn.	Jupiter.	Mars.	Sun.	Venus.	Mercury.	Moon.	Saturn.	Jupiter.	Mars.	Sun.	Venus.
5.12 to 6.21	to 7.29	to 8.37	to 9.45	to 10.54	to 0.2	to 1.10	to 2.18	to 3.26	to 4.34	to 5.44	to 6.56	to 7.48	to 8.40

Wednesday, on or near the 1st of September, of any year.

Mercury.	Moon.	Saturn.	Jupiter.	Mars.	Sun.	Venus.	Mercury.	Moon.	Saturn.	Jupiter.	Mars.	Sun.	Venus.
5.26 to 6.32	to 7.37	to 8.43	to 9.48	to 10.54	to 0.0	to 1.5	to 2.11	to 3.16	to 4.21	to 5.27	to 6.33	to 7.27	to 8.22

Copyright, 1898, by Luke D. Broughton. Entered at Stationers' Hall, London, England. All rights reserved.

Perpetual Table of Planetary Hours, from Sunrise until 2 hours after Sunset.

Wednesday, on or near the 15th of September, of any year.

Sunrise. Mercury. A. M.	Moon. A. M.	Saturn. A. M.	Jupiter. A. M.	Mars. A. M.	Meridian. Sun. M.	Venus. P. M.	Mercury. P. M.	Moon. P. M.	Saturn. P. M.	Jupiter. P. M.	Sunset. Mars. P. M.	After Sunset. Sun. P. M.	Venus. P. M.
5.40 to 6.43	to 7.45	to 8.48	to 9.50	to 10.53	to 11.55	to 0.58	to 2.1	to 3.4	to 4.6	to 5.8	to 6.10	to 7.7	to 8.5

Wednesday, on or near the 29th of September, of any year.

Mercury.	Moon.	Saturn.	Jupiter.	Mars.	Sun.	Venus.	Mercury.	Moon.	Saturn.	Jupiter.	Mars.	Sun.	Venus.
5.54 to 6.54	to 7.53	to 8.52	to 9.51	to 10.50	to 11.49	to 0.48	to 1.47	to 2.47	to 3.47	to 4.46	to 5.46	to 6.47	to 7.48

Wednesday, on or near the 13th of October, of any year.

Mercury.	Moon.	Saturn.	Jupiter.	Mars.	Sun.	Venus.	Mercury.	Moon.	Saturn.	Jupiter.	Mars.	Sun.	Venus.
6.8 to 7.5	to 8.1	to 8.57	to 9.53	to 10.50	to 11.46	to 0.43	to 1.40	to 2.36	to 3.32	to 4.28	to 5.24	to 6.28	to 7.31

Wednesday, on or near the 27th of October, of any year.

Mercury.	Moon.	Saturn.	Jupiter.	Mars.	Sun.	Venus.	Mercury.	Moon.	Saturn.	Jupiter.	Mars.	Sun.	Venus.
6.24 to 7.18	to 8.11	to 9.4	to 9.57	to 10.50	to 11.43	to 0.37	to 1.30	to 2.23	to 3.16	to 4.9	to 5.3	to 6.10	to 7.17

Wednesday, on or near the 10th of November, of any year.

Mercury.	Moon.	Saturn.	Jupiter.	Mars.	Sun.	Venus.	Mercury.	Moon.	Saturn.	Jupiter.	Mars.	Sun.	Venus.
6.41 to 7.31	to 8.22	to 9.12	to 10.3	to 10.53	to 11.44	to 0.34	to 1.25	to 2.15	to 3.6	to 3.56	to 4.47	to 5.57	to 7.6

Wednesday, on or near the 24th of November, of any year.

Mercury.	Moon.	Saturn.	Jupiter.	Mars.	Sun.	Venus.	Mercury.	Moon.	Saturn.	Jupiter.	Mars.	Sun.	Venus.
6.57 to 7.46	to 8.34	to 9.22	to 10.10	to 10.58	to 11.47	to 0.35	to 1.23	to 2.12	to 3.0	to 3.48	to 4.37	to 5.49	to 7.1

Wednesday, on or near the 8th of December, of any year.

Mercury.	Moon.	Saturn.	Jupiter.	Mars.	Sun.	Venus.	Mercury.	Moon.	Saturn.	Jupiter.	Mars.	Sun.	Venus.
7.11 to 7.57	to 8.44	to 9.31	to 10.18	to 11.5	to 11.51	to 0.38	to 1.25	to 2.12	to 2.59	to 3.46	to 4.33	to 5.46	to 6.59

Copyright, 1890, by Luke D. Broughton. Entered at Stationers' Hall, London, England. All rights reserved.

Perpetual Table of Planetary Hours, from Sunrise until 2 hours after Sunset.

Wednesday, on or near the 22d of December, of any year.

Sunrise. Mercury. A. M.	Moon. A. M.	Saturn. A. M.	Jupiter. A. M.	Mars. A. M.	Meridian. Sun. M.	Venus. P. M.	Mercury. P. M.	Moon. P. M.	Saturn. P. M.	Jupiter. P. M.	Sunset. Mars. P. M.	After Sunset. Sun. P. M.	Venus. P. M.
7.21 to 8.8	to 8.54	to 9.40	to 10.27	to 11.13	to 11.59	to 0.45	to 1.31	to 2.17	to 3.3	to 3.49	to 4.37	to 5.51	to 7.5

Wednesday, on or near the 6th of January, of any year.

Mercury.	Moon.	Saturn.	Jupiter.	Mars.	Sun.	Venus.	Mercury.	Moon.	Saturn.	Jupiter.	Mars.	Sun.	Venus.
7.25 to 8.11	to 8.58	to 9.45	to 10.32	to 11.19	to 0.6	to 0.53	to 1.40	to 2.27	to 3.14	to 4.1	to 4.48	to 6.1	to 7.14

Wednesday, on or near the 20th of January, of any year.

Mercury.	Moon.	Saturn.	Jupiter.	Mars.	Sun.	Venus.	Mercury.	Moon.	Saturn.	Jupiter.	Mars.	Sun.	Venus.
7.20 to 8.9	to 8.57	to 9.45	to 10.33	to 11.22	to 0.11	to 1.0	to 1.48	to 2.37	to 3.26	to 4.14	to 5.3	to 6.15	to 7.27

Wednesday, on or near the 3d of February, of any year.

Mercury.	Moon.	Saturn.	Jupiter.	Mars.	Sun.	Venus.	Mercury.	Moon.	Saturn.	Jupiter.	Mars.	Sun.	Venus.
7.9 to 8.0	to 8.51	to 9.42	to 10.33	to 11.24	to 0.15	to 1.6	to 1.57	to 2.49	to 3.40	to 4.30	to 5.20	to 6.29	to 7.38

Wednesday, on or near the 17th of February, of any year.

Mercury.	Moon.	Saturn.	Jupiter.	Mars.	Sun.	Venus.	Mercury.	Moon.	Saturn.	Jupiter.	Mars.	Sun.	Venus.
6.52 to 7.45	to 8.39	to 9.33	to 10.27	to 11.21	to 0.15	to 1.8	to 2.2	to 2.56	to 3.50	to 4.43	to 5.37	to 6.43	to 7.49

Wednesday, on or near the 3d of March, of any year.

Mercury.	Moon.	Saturn.	Jupiter.	Mars.	Sun.	Venus.	Mercury.	Moon.	Saturn.	Jupiter.	Mars.	Sun.	Venus.
6.32 to 7.30	to 8.27	to 9.24	to 10.21	to 11.19	to 0.16	to 1.12	to 2.8	to 3.4	to 4.0	to 4.56	to 5.53	to 6.56	to 7.59

Wednesday, on or near the 17th of March, of any year.

Mercury.	Moon.	Saturn.	Jupiter.	Mars.	Sun.	Venus.	Mercury.	Moon.	Saturn.	Jupiter.	Mars.	Sun.	Venus.
6.9 to 7.9	to 8.9	to 9.9	to 10.9	to 11.9	to 0.9	to 1.9	to 2.9	to 3.9	to 4.9	to 5.9	to 6.9	to 7.9	to 8.9

Copyright, 1898, by Luke D. Broughton. Entered at Stationers' Hall, London, England. All rights reserved.

The Difference Between Clock or Mean and Solar Time.

The time that I have used in calculating the Tables of the foregoing Planetary Hours from Sunrise until two hours after Sunset, is what is called the *apparent* time, the time given in the Almanac being what is termed the *mean* time. Some modern authors of Astrology appear to think that the mean time must be corrected by applying thereto the equation of time given in the Almanac for the given day.

The old authors of works on Astrology gave what was termed the solar time, or apparent time, but I have not followed the teachings of the old authors in this respect.

The Equation of time, or the Sun's time as shown by a Sun dial, and by setting the clock at 12 noon each day, when the Sun is exactly on the meridian. The Sun's time agrees with the true or mean time only on four days of the year. These are April 15, June 15, Sept. 1st and Dec. 25th. See Table of Equation of Time on next page.

The greatest difference between *Solar* time and *mean* time, occurs on Feb. 10th, when the clock is then 15 minutes fast. On May 14th the clock is 4 minutes slow. On July 25th the clock is 6 minutes fast, and on Nov. 2d the clock is 16 minutes slow.

The reason of the inequality in a solar day, and the mean or sidereal time, is caused by the earth being in perihelion, or nearest the Sun on or near the 31st of Dec., when it moves more rapidly around the Sun than in any other part of its orbit; but when in its aphelion, on or near the 30th of June, it moves more slowly.

The only time it can possibly make much difference in the foregoing Tables, will be near the 10th of Feb., the 14th of May, the 21st of June, and the 2d of Nov.; at each of these times it is possible that the time in the foregoing Planetary Hours may not exactly agree, or the planetary hour may begin and end a few minutes sooner, or begin and end a few minutes later than the time marked in the foregoing Tables, reckoning by clock time, as the old authors used the solar time, and for fear there might be some variation, and the student wishes to make observations as to whether the time agrees in all cases with the Planetary Influences marked in the *planetary hours*, I have inserted a Table of Equation of Time from Jan. 1st to the end of Dec., answering for any year, by the use of which the student can make observations and compare the mean or clock time with the solar time.

For several weeks near April 15th, June 15th, Sept. 1st and Dec. 25th, the tables of planetary hours and the clock time must agree. The student, if he chooses to be very exact, can correct the clock time with the solar time, by *adding* when the clock is slow the number of minutes and seconds marked in the perpetual table of equation of time from April 15th to June 14th, and from Sept. 1st to Dec 24th, and by *subtracting* during the other parts of the year, that is: from Dec. 26th to April 15th, and from June 16th to Aug 31st, he can make observations of the planetary influence, for instance, of Jupiter or Saturn, marked in the table of planetary hours, and see if they agree near the beginning and the end of said planetary hours.

After the student has made a number of observations near the beginning or the end of the Planetary Hours, during or near Feb. 10th, May 14th, July 25th, Nov. 2d, and he finds from experience that the observation and the planetary influence marked in the Perpetual Table of Planetary Hours do not coincide, I would be glad if he would communicate with me; giving the result of his observations. It is only by experiments and observations that we can prove or disprove the Science of Astrology.

The foregoing tables of Planetary Hours from page 255 to 285 are the first tables of that kind that has ever been calculated or published, or at least that I have ever met with. Henry Cooley, on pages 266 and 267 of his "Key to Astrology," attempted to get up Tables of Planetary Hours, but they are practically useless. Therefore this is the first time that it could be tested by observation whether the "Solar Time" or the "Mean or Clock Time" is the proper or right time, that the Planetary Hours ought to be calculated for.

Perpetual Table of Equation of Time.

	Jan. Subt. M. S.	Feb. Subt. M. S.	Mar. Subt. M. S.	Apr. Subt M. S.	May. Add. M. S.	June. Add. M. S.	July. Subt. M. S.	Aug. Subt. M. S.	Sept Add. M. S.	Oct. Add. M. S.	Nov. Add. M. S.	Dec. Add. M. S.	
1	3-45	13-50	12-36	4-1	3-0	2-30	3-28	6-5	0-3	10-16	16-18	10-52	1
2	4-13	13-58	12-24	3-43	3-7	2-21	3-39	6-1	0-22	10-35	16-19	10-29	2
3	4-41	14-4	12-11	3-25	3-14	2-12	3-51	5-57	0-41	10-54	16-29	10-5	3
4	5-09	14-10	11-58	3-7	3-20	2-2	4-2	5-52	1-0	11-12	19-19	9-41	4
5	5-36	14-16	11-48	2-49	3-26	1-51	4-13	5-47	1-20	11-30	16-18	9-17	5
6	6-03	14-20	11-31	2-32	3-31	1-41	4-23	5-41	1-40	11-48	16-15	8-51	6
7	6-29	14-24	11-17	2-14	3-35	1-30	4-33	5-34	2-0	12-5	16-12	8-26	7
8	6-55	14-27	11-2	1-58	3-39	1-19	4-43	5-27	2-20	12-22	16-9	7-59	8
9	7-20	14-29	10-47	1-41	3-43	1-7	4-52	5-19	2-41	12-38	16-4	7-33	9
10	7-45	14-30	10-31	1-24	3-46	0-56	5-1	5-11	3-1	12-54	15-58	7-6	10
11	8-9	14-30	10-16	1-8	3-48	0-44	5-9	5-2	3-22	13-10	15-52	6-38	11
12	8-32	14-30	10-0	0-52	3-50	0-32	5-17	4-52	3-43	13-25	15-45	6-11	12
13	8-55	14-29	9-43	0-36	3-51	0-19	5-24	4-42	4 4	13-39	15-37	5-42	13
14	9-17	14-27	9-27	0-21	3-51	0-7	5-31	4-31	4-25	13-54	15-28	5-14	14
15	9-39	14-24	9-9	0-5	3-51	Subt	5-38	4-20	4-47	14-8	15-18	4-45	15
16	10-00	14-20	8-52	Add.	3-51	0-18	5-44	4-8	5-8	14-21	15-8	4-16	16
17	10-20	14-16	8-35	0-24	3-50	0-31	5-49	3-55	5 29	14-33	14-56	3-47	17
18	10-39	14-11	8-17	0 38	3 48	0-44	5-54	3-43	5-50	14-45	14-44	3-17	18
19	10-58	14-6	7-59	0-52	3-46	0-57	5-59	3-29	6-12	14-56	14-31	2-47	19
20	11-16	13-59	7-41	1-5	3-43	1-10	6-2	3-15	6-33	15-7	14-17	2-18	20
21	11-33	13-53	7-23	1-18	3-40	1-23	6-6	3-1	6-54	15-17	14-2	1-48	21
22	11-49	13-45	7-5	1-30	3-36	1-36	6-9	2-46	7-15	15-26	13-47	1-18	22
23	12-5	13-37	6-46	1-42	3-32	1-48	6-11	2-31	7-36	15-34	13-30	0-48	23
24	12-20	13-28	6-28	1-54	3-27	2-1	6-12	2-15	7-56	15-42	13-13	0-18	24
25	12-34	13-19	6-9	2-5	3-22	2-14	6-13	1-59	8-17	15-49	12-55	Subt	25
26	12-47	13-9	5-51	2-15	3-16	2-27	6-14	1-43	8-37	15-56	12-36	0-42	26
27	13-0	12-58	5-32	2-25	3-10	2-39	6-14	1-26	8-58	16-1	12-17	1-12	27
28	13-11	12-47	5-14	2-35	3-3	2-52	6-13	1-9	9-18	16-6	11-57	1-42	28
29	13-22		4-55	2-44	2-55	3-4	6-12	0-52	9-37	16-10	11-36	2-11	29
30	13-32		4-37	2-52	2-47	3-16	6-10	0-34	9-57	16-14	11-14	2-41	30
31	13-41		4 19		2-39		6-8	0-16		16-16		3-10	31

Different Methods of Measuring Time by the Heavenly Bodies.

Although the earth when in its perihelion travels faster than when it is in its aphelion, yet during both of these periods, it takes the same time to make a revolution on its axis. It has been observed with telescopes when pointed to any particular star in the heavens, that at the end of exactly 24 hours, that star will pass a particular line, across the end of the telescope, and it has been known to do so for several hundred years, without any variation. That time is called "Sidereal, Mean, or Clock Time." But as the earth is moving in its orbit around the Sun it has to travel four minutes more in the 24 hours to reach the same point, and that is called "apparent time;" but on account of the Earth being in its perihelion, it travels faster than at other times and consequently Sun time is not uniform, and time measured in that manner is called "Solar Time" when deducting the four minutes from apparent time. Formerly it was customary to have a "Sun-dial" in each churchyard, to find exactly when the Sun arrives in the "Meridian," and they set their clocks for that time; but since they have been able to measure time more accurately by clocks and by observation of the fixed stars by telescopes. What is called "Sidereal or Mean Time" is the time they now use for measuring the rising, culminating and setting of the Sun.

ELECTIONS, OR CHOOSING A FORTUNATE TIME TO COMMENCE NEW BUSINESS, REMOVAL OR REMARKABLE CHANGES.

621 What is termed an election, is the choosing or selecting a fortunate time to commence an undertaking.

Besides choosing a fortunate planetary hour to commence any new business or undertaking, it is always advisable for the native to have his own nativity calculated, and see first whether he is fortunate in that particular line of business that he wishes to engage in. This can be seen or pointed out by the positions of the planets at the time of his birth. If the nativity denies success in that particular business, it is impossible to be successful by simply choosing a fortunate planetary hour, or making what is termed an election ; still he would be more fortunate by choosing a fortunate hour and making a good election, than he would by commencing the business in a haphazard manner, and without any regard to Planetary Influences.

622 There are special rules in Astrology that have been known and have been acted upon, and continued to be made use of for thousands of years, by almost all civilized nations, although within the last two or three hundred years these rules have been very much neglected by the people in Europe and the United States; yet there are people in these countries who imitate the ancient astrologers, and by doing so, they make themselves ridiculous.

623 The people talk about the superstition of Astrology. But what is termed laying the corner stone of a church, or any other building is *real superstition*. The ancients called it the laying of the first stone, and they chose fortunate planetary influence to do it under, and selected a fortunate time for turning the sod, or breaking the ground previous to laying the first stone.

624 Andrew H. Green imitated the ancients by turning the sod for the commencement of the bridge that is to cross the Hudson River; and Count De Lesseps turned the sod for the commencement of the Panama Canal in Central America, but neither of them attempted to select a fortunate time for that purpose. See page 466* of Appendix.

The following are a few choice rules for the choosing or electing fortunate times for any particular business. These rules are very old and are based on sound Astrological principles.

*Page number added by the Publisher, 2012.

Election for Laying the First Stone of a Building.

625 The old astrologers tell us to begin no building with the Moon in Pisces or Scorpio, having south latitude descending, for if you do it will soon fall. The most fortunate time to begin any new building, such as turning the sod, driving the first pile or laying the first stone, is when the Moon is in Aquarius, or when Aquarius ascends, and the Moon is in good aspect to the ascendant, and the fortunate planets, Jupiter and Venus, are in good aspect to the degree ascending.

Election for Buying or Renting a House, Lands, Tenements, etc.

626 The first thing to be attended to in buying or renting houses, etc., is to make as strong as possible the lord of the fourth house in the nativity, and also the fourth house in the horoscope of the election, together with the Moon; also let the Moon apply by a sextile or trine to the lord of the fourth and the second house in the election horoscope; also let as many of the significators that are lords of the fourth, tenth, first, second and seventh houses, be in reception if possible and in good places, both in the nativity and in the horoscope, and let a fixed sign be on the ascendant of the election.

Election on Removal from one House to Another.

627 The change of habitation, house or lodgings, etc., is best done when the Moon is in a fixed sign increasing in light, and at the same time in good aspect with fortunate planets in the fourth house, or ascendant of the election; the lord of the second house should, if possible, be strong, above the earth, and in sextile or trine to the lord of the seventh and the eighth houses, for that is the place the party must go to have profit or gain, and if the lord of the seventh or eighth houses are afflicted, then he goes or removes to his loss or misfortune.

Election for Entering into new Business, Office or Employment.

628 First, let the Sun or Moon be in their dignities or at least not afflicted by Saturn, Mars or Uranus. Second, let Jupiter be in the ascendant, and the Sun in the midheaven if possible. Third, let the seventh and second houses be strong and fortunate, for one signifies money and the other counsels for the native's assistance; for if these houses are afflicted it shows great damage to the native. Let Jupiter and Venus be strong if possible, and in good aspect in the election horoscope.

Election for Commencing a Trade or Profession.

629 Let the cusp of the tenth house in the nativity be the ascendant in the horoscope of the election, and let the lord of the ascendant and the Moon in the election, not only be free from affliction, but in sextile or trine to the lords of the second and tenth houses, and if possible let the fortunate planets Jupiter and Venus be in the ascendant, or the midheaven or in an angle of the election, and the unfortunate planets Saturn and Mars cadent, or in the third, sixth or twelfth houses.

Election for Marriage.

630 In all marriages the ascendant stands for the man, and the seventh house for the woman; if the fortunate planets are in the ascendant, the marriage is best for the man, but if the fortunate planets are in the seventh house, the woman receives the most advantage by marriage. In all marriages do not let the Moon be combust, that is in conjunction with the Sun, on the marriage day, for that signifies death of the man within two years after marriage; nor applying to combustion or new Moon, for that signifies an ill end for the parties getting married. It is very unfortunate in marriages for the Moon to apply to ether Saturn or Mars, though the aspect be ever so good, as there will be neither peace nor love between them. In all marriages let the Moon increase in light, or be going from the new Moon to the full Moon. Let the Moon be increasing in motion and have no evil aspect to the Sun, nor any aspect at all to either Saturn or Mars. Venus is the one general significatrix, or the chief significator of happiness in all marriages, therefore it is best to let the Moon apply by good aspect to Venus. If the lord of the ascendant is weak, and the lord of the seventh is strong in the seventh house and a commanding planet, and in good aspect to Mars, the woman will domineer over her husband; let not Saturn or Mars be in the seventh house, in any marriage for that makes the woman very ill tempered, and generally have poor health. Also Saturn, Mars or Uranus in the ascendant in a marriage makes the man very cross, ill tempered and generally he has poor health,

631 In choosing an election for the marriage of men, let the Moon and Venus be strong and fortunate, and in good positions in the horoscope, and in good aspect to Jupiter, he being the author of peace and wealth. Also let him be in mutual reception with Venus, and in fortunate aspect to the lord of the ascendant. Let the seventh house and the Moon, and also the ascendant be free from affliction in such

signs as favor marriage, as Taurus, Libra, Sagittary, Aquarius and Pisces. In making an election for the marriage of women, you must notice the seventh house the Sun and Mars, as you did the ascendant, the Moon and Venus for a man's marriage.

Election for Proposing Marriage.

632 In Proposing Marriage do not let the Moon apply to a retrograde planet, no matter whether the aspect be good or evil, or the planet a fortunate or an unfortunate one, unless you wish the engagement to be broken off.

633 If the Moon applies to Jupiter or Venus and they are retrograde, then something occurs to break off the marriage, and both the lady and gentleman are very sorry for it; if to an evil aspect of either of these planets retrograde, then the breaking off of the engagement will be attended with much unhappiness to both parties. If the Moon applies by good aspect to either Saturn or Mars, and they are retrograde, this denotes that the engagement will end in a law-suit, or a breach of promise suit, or one of the parties will go away, and will not return. But if the Moon applies to an evil aspect of either Saturn or Mars, aud that planet is retrograde, then the breaking off of the engagement is certain to result in a law-suit for breach of promise; or should they marry, then a divorce will result, attended with much sensation.

634 In all engagements or promises of marriage, let Venus be in the ascendant, or midheaven, and well aspected, and in some of her dignities. If possible let the Moon be seperating from a good aspect of Jupiter, and making a good aspect to Venus unafflicted, and both direct and swift in motion.

635 Do not let an evil planet be in either the ascendant or seventh house, or in the eleventh or fifth houses. Let Saturn and Mars be cadent, and in no aspect to any planet, and let the Moon have no aspect to an unfortunate planet if it can be avoided.

Election for Introduction to Ladies or Gentlemen.

636 If a lady wishes to be introduced to a gentleman, choose the hour of Jupiter or the Sun, and let the Moon apply by sextile or trine aspect to Jupiter or the Sun, and do not let Saturn or Mars be in the ascendant, midheaven or seventh house.

637 If a gentleman wishes to be introduced to a lady, choose the hour of Venus or the Moon, and let the Moon

apply by good aspect to Venus, and let Venus be in the ascendant, eleventh, tenth or seventh houses, and both Saturn and Mars cadent.

Election for Going on a Journey.

638 In beginning a journey choose that day and hour in which the Moon and the lord of the ascendant are in good aspect in the nativity. Let the eleventh and third houses, with their lords, be fortunate. Watery signs are best for sailing or travelling by water, but fixed signs for inland journeys.

639 Likewise the kind of business must be considered which causes the native to take the journey, for if he goes to a king, president or governor, let the tenth house of the nativity ascend or be on the ascendant of the election, and let the planets that govern the persons he carries the errand to be strong and in good aspect to the lord of the ascendant or the Moon in the election, as the Moon is a general significator of all journeys, and let it be fortunate and free from affliction, and in good aspect with fortunate planets, or let the unfortunates be cadent, but not in the third or ninth houses.

640 The eighth house shows what will happen to the traveller when he comes to the end of his journey, and the seventh house what will happen to him on the day he returns, and the second the profit on his return home; so these houses and their lords must be fortunately placed that success may attend the journey and it end well.

Election for Navigation, or Going on a Voyage.

641 Start on a voyage if you can, when fortunate planets are in angles or in the ninth house, and do not let the Sun or Moon be afflicted by Saturn or Mars, neither let Saturn or Mars be in the third or ninth houses.

642 Never start on a journey in the hours of either Saturn or Mars, for they show either loss, sickness, unhappiness or imprisonment.

643 The Dragon's Tail in the third or ninth houses indicates cheating or robbery on the journey.

644 Do not let Saturn be in the ascendant, nor a Fiery sign on the ascendant, for then there will be a watery sign on the eighth house, and there will be great danger of drowning or the ship going to the bottom, therefore commence your voyage, if possible, in the hours of Jupiter or Venus, and let the Moon apply by good aspect to one or both of these planets.

Election for Collecting a Debt, or Money that is Owing.

645 Be sure to fortify that planet that is lord of the ascendant in the nativity, and also Jupiter, for, he is a natural significator of wealth and substance, and if possible let the lord of the ascendant of the nativity or Jupiter be placed in the second house, or essentially dignified, and in good aspect, and position in the horoscope of election; free from affliction and in good aspect to Jupiter and Venus or lord of the second house. Let the party if possible, go to collect the money in the hours of Jupiter or Venus.

Elections to make Friendship Between Brothers, Sisters, Kindred, Neighbors, etc.

646 On renewing or making Friendship between relations and neighbors; choose a time when the lord of the ascendant in the nativity is in good aspect to fortunate planets in the election, and if you can let it also apply to some good aspect to the lord of the third house in the election, and in good aspect, or in reception, and well posited in good places in the election, either of these planetary influences will make a good election for producing harmony or friendship of brothers, sisters, kindred or neighbors, etc.

647 The same rules will apply for the election of friendship of father, mother, friends, wife, husband, sweetheart or wife's or husband's brothers or sisters, etc. If the student makes use of the fourth house for the father, the tenth house for the mother, the eleventh house for friends, the seventh house for husband, wife, sweetheart or partners, and the ninth house for wife's or husband's brothers or sisters, etc.

Elections for Hiring Servants or Employees.

648 When you hire a servant or an employee, be sure and let the Moon be strong and in good aspect to fortunate planets. Let it also be in good aspect to Jupiter or Mars, if it is a male that you are employing; if it is a female, then let the Moon make a good aspect of Venus and free from all manner of affliction, especially of Saturn or Mars, and let the lord of the ascendant, or of the second house in the nativity, be in good aspect to the lord of the sixth house in the election, or let the fortunate planets Jupiter or Venus, be in the sixth house of the nativity, or in good aspect to the lord of the ascendant, and if possible let the Moon be either in Taurus, Gemini or Virgo.

Some Choice Rules or Aphorisms for Election, Relating to Several Undertakings.

649 In all journeys the greatest affliction of a planet is to be perigrine or out of all Essential Dignities, and retrograde.

650 It is bad in journeys to have Saturn or Mars in the third or ninth house, but much worse to have them, or either of them in the second house.

651 The lord of the ninth or third house in the first, the journey will be successful, and if strong and well dignified and well aspected, all the better.

652 In all journeys look to the Moon, for she is the general significatrix of all journies.

653 The Moon increasing in light and in good aspect to the Sun, assist or help in journies.

654 When a ship sets sail, if Saturn ascends in Pisces, the ship is in danger of being cast away, especially if Mars afflicts Saturn by an evil aspect.

655 If you go to a Prince, King, Governor or President, let a Fiery sign ascend, and let the Sun be in good aspect with Jupiter or Venus.

656 Those who go to war ought to consider coming home safe. To gain this end let the Sun, Jupiter, Venus or Dragon's Head be strong and in good aspect in the ascendant or else they may fail of it.

657 If Saturn be in the ascendant he will be overcome with fear and will not fight but return home again a coward. If Mars is there he will either die in battle or be dangerously wounded. If Saturn and Mars are both in the ascendant, you may be confident that he will never return. If Saturn or Mars or even one of them is in the tenth house, he will be taken a prisoner, especially if the lord of the ascendant is in the twelfth house, and more especially if it is afflicted in the twelfth.

Elections for Duels and Law-suits.

658 Judge the challenger; or the one who commences a law-suit by the ascendant, and so vary the houses accordingly.

659 Judge the opponent by the seventh house, and so vary the houses as before, the tenth being as fourth house, and the fourth as tenth house.

660 It is not good to fight a duel when the lord of the ascendant is in the eighth house, (or house of death,) for then there is great danger of death.

661 The assailant or aggressor, or the one who begins the law-suit, always loses the battle, or suit, if the lord of the ascendant be retrograde or combust or in conjunction with the Sun; but if the lord of the seventh house be afflicted in a similar manner the opponent is beaten. In a duel or battle when the Moon, Saturn and Mars are joined together or in evil aspect, there will be great effusion of blood.

662 If any one goes to a Governor or President, let the Moon be in the ascendant, in sextile or trine to the Sun, in the tenth house in the election. But if one goes to a clergyman, bishop or judge, let the Moon be in good aspect or conjunction with Jupiter, even a square is not so bad, if there is a reception by dignity, between the Moon and Jupiter.

663 If any one goes to see an old man let the Moon apply to the sextile or trine aspect of Saturn, from good places or houses in the election; angles are of the most influence, especially the ascendant or midheaven.

664 In managing business or attending to any of the affairs of women, let the Moon apply by sextile, trine or conjunction to Venus, and do not let Venus be afflicted, if possible.

665 In dealing with book-keepers, printers, publishers or lawyers, let the Moon apply by good aspect to Mercury.

666 If you have dealings with an officer or a soldier, or a machinist, or surgeon, let the Moon apply to a good aspect of Mars; but if you intend to have a surgical operation performed, do not let the Moon apply to any aspect of Mars, even if it is a good aspect, as there will be great danger of fever or inflamation setting in after the operation.

667 If you make an application to a person who deals in old furniture or old books, or anything connected with the occult, let the Moon apply to a good aspect of Uranus.

668 In addition to the above rules, if possible, attend to the business in the right planetary hour, or in the hours of the planets ruling the business or the kind of persons above mentioned, or ruling the persons you make application to.*

---

* The above rules of elections are the most concise and perfect I have ever met with, having been culled from some of the oldest authorities that have written on the subject. In my own practice I have found them reliable, and have put them to the test thousands of times, and especially connected with marriages and business undertakings, where I have been able to observe the time of the event and afterwards notice the result.

On account of the time of marriages being published in the newspapers. I have been able to apply those rules in many thousands of instances, and have observed their effects afterwards.

The next chart of the Heavens that I shall give, is the time of marriage of Mr. Edward and Mrs. Lillie Langtry. The time of marriage was given to the reporters by both parties. By observing the chart the student will see that it was certainly a very unfavorable time judging, by the rules of Astrology, for any person to get married; even the time of that marriage was not as fortunate as that of Nellie Grant, Gen. Grant's daughter, who was married in Washington. D. C.

Mr. Stanley, the African explorer got married under very unfortunate aspects. And he got out of a sick bed to get married. None of these parties have lived happy married lives. Of course each must have had very unfortunate aspects in their horoscope for marriage, and especially Mr. and Mrs. Langtry. The rules and principles of Astrology, when they are violated, are just as absolute in their affliction of pain or punishment, as are any other laws of nature. If these laws are violated, the parties must expect to suffer the penalty.

A short time ago, a lady friend of ours was going to be married, and the time was set on a certain evening; my daughter looked in the ephemeris and saw that the aspect was unfavorable for marriage on that evening, and advised them to change the time. The lady and gentleman went to the minister to appoint another time to be married. The minister pressed them to inform him why they wanted the time changed; after they had told him, they said they thought the minister would never get through laughing. Had the minister gone to any person to talk on religion and had he mentioned the name of Jesus Christ to them, and those parties had commenced laughing, and continued to do so for half an hour or more, it is natural to suppose he would have come to the conclusion that the party had gone insane, or that God would strike them dead for such levity.

From the "New York Recorder" June 20th, 1896.

HOROSCOPE OF EX-GOVERNOR WM. McKINLEY.

Hon. William McKinley was nominated for the Presidency on the evening of June 18th, 1896, and on June 20th the following article appeared in the "New York Recorder," "The Pittsburg Dispatch," and "The Peoria Journal."

"This gentleman, according to his biography, was born Jan. 29th, 1843, in Trumbull Co., Ohio, and according to his description, which was given of him in the various newspapers, there is no doubt he first saw the light about 2 A. M. on that day.

"If so he was born under the planet Mars, in the sign Scorpio, rising, in close sextile to Saturn, with Scorpio on the ascendant, and also Venus rising in the second house. If the above time of birth is correct he had all the planets under the earth, except Mars, when he was born.

"The above horoscope would describe a person near the medium height, with dark hair, slightly full face, high, round forehead, slightly sanguine complexion, and of a rather straight or proud walk. In some respects he has a fortunate horoscope, but has had much to contend with. He has not a strong constitution and there is great danger that he will not live to be old.   *   *   *   He is certainly a person a long way above the average in intellect, and ought to make a very sharp lawyer. He is fortunate in marriage, but unfortunate in children.

"The time when he was nominated was certainly very favorable, the most fortunate for the nomination of a candidate for over 30 years, and I have examined all the maps of the heavens for the times of presidential nominations for more than that period. At the time he received the majority of the votes, 5.17 P. M., June 18th, 1896, St. Louis time, the Moon was in the midheaven, and just making a good aspect of Jupiter, (Jupiter is lord of the ascendant.) Mercury, Neptune, Venus and the Sun were all setting, and Saturn and Uranus rising. It is a much more fortunate time than when Grover Cleveland was nominated, June 23d, 1892, at 0.03 A. M., at Chicago. Also a more fortunate time than when Benj. Harrison was nominated in 1888.

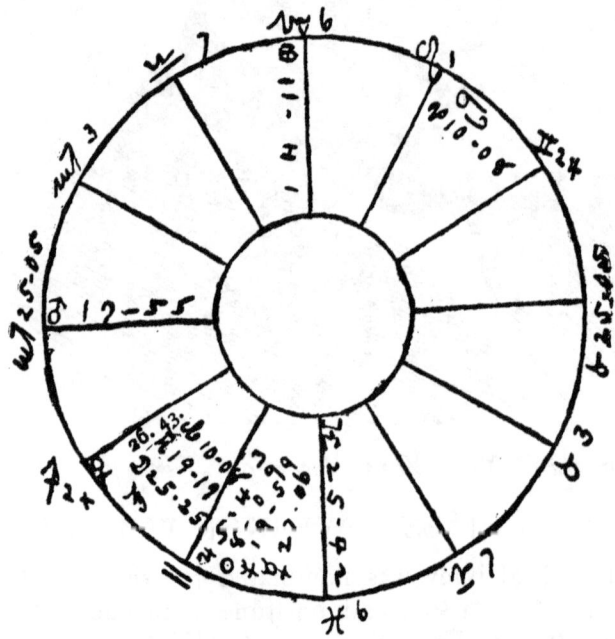

Chart of the Heavens for the Time of Birth of Hon. William McKinley Jan. 29th, 1843, at 2 a. m.

"It was also a fortunate time when the Republican Convention opened, June 16th, 1896, at 0.20 P. M. The time it opened is certainly more fortunate than it will be at noon July 7th, 1896, when the Democratic Convention will open. There is no question in my mind but that Mr. McKinley will be elected President, although he will have a marked evil aspect during the early part of Oct., 1896, but it is more probable he will have poor health, or something may go wrong in the campaign which will almost threaten his defeat. That aspect will be very similar to the one which occured in Grover Cleveland's horoscope in Oct., 1888, which caused his defeat through the British minister at Washington advising Englishmen to vote for President Cleveland, as English interests would be best served by his election.   *   *   *

"Mr. McKinley's horoscope indicates danger of assassination nearly as much as Gen. Garfield's or Abraham Lincoln's. Should he live through the Fall of 1897, there is nothing to threaten his life for some years, but he will have a very troublesome period all the time he is President. I think there is no question but that he will be elected."

[President McKinley's mother died after a short illness, about Dec. 10th, 1897. The evil aspects referred to above, instead of causing the sickness or death of the President, resulted in the death of his mother.]

From the " The Baltimore American," July 26th, 1806.
WHAT THE STARS TELL.

"Prof. Broughton, the Astrologer, says the verdict of the planets, judged by the rules of Astrology, seems to be that the next president of the United States will be the apostle of protection and gold—William McKinley, of Ohio. Mr. Broughton in 1888 predicted the defeat of Grover Cleveland and his election in 1892, and recently has devoted himself to horoscopes of Major McKinley and Mr. Bryan. He consented to make public the result of his researches.

"Here is a chart," said he, "giving the positions of the celestial bodies on Jan. 29, 1843, the day given as the date of birth of William McKinley. After careful study, I have arrived at the conclusion that he was born at about two in the morning, when the Zodiacal sign Scorpio was at the Eastern horizon and Mars was just rising. You will notice that eight of the nine planets were below the Earth, Mars alone appearing above the horizon. This indicates that all Mr. McKinley has gained has been dearly bought, and success has come to him only after many rebuffs and by dint of dogged perseverance. Energy is written in every line of the portraits published of him, and the position of Mars bears the same significance. It is a spur to pride and ambition, forcing him ever onward and to greater heights.

"Intellectually Major McKinley is far above the average. Mercury, the ruler of the mind, being in the intellectual sign Aquarius, and in benefic sextile aspect to Venus, and the Moon in semi-sextile aspect to Venus and Mercury, are all auguries of breadth, depth and height of mental capacity. If I knew nothing of either protection or free trade, and I knew that a man with these horoscopic influences advocated protection, I would be willing to accept his judgment as final. I should say that Mr. McKinley was a logical and forceful speaker, writer and thinker. His career shows that he has been able to impress his followers with his personality, and I am inclined to believe that he will impress the voters in November as few men in history have done. The conjoined strength of Jupiter and the Sun in his horoscope is a potent force for honor. He is an honorable man, if ever man were honorable. There will be a vein of secretiveness in him that will give rise to suspicion, and his enemies may build many stories upon it. Law was undoubtedly an excellent profession for Major McKinley; but as a teacher and writer upon scientific subjects he would have made a successful bid for fame. Probably life would have presented fewer obstacles, had he chosen science, instead of politics, and his path would have been easier as he climbed to success. He has achieved all he has had reason to hope for, and he will not be disappointed in this final stride towards the pinnacle of American ambition.

"Marriage has had a prominent part in the life of Mr. McKinley. Previous to his acceptance of the yoke his heart must have been wrung upon more than one flint-hearted belle, and I fear he carries yet the traces of early shocks of love's battery. The goal passed, and once embarked upon the sea of matrimony, his mate would be, as I understand she has been, a most acceptable *compagon du voyage*. Not many children would come their way, and I fear the close position of the Sun to Jupiter (Jupiter indicating his wife) would wreck her health.

He will not hold money any length of time. Venus in the house of wealth is good; Jupiter, lord of the house of wealth, is another benefit, but Saturn in the house of wealth is evil. He will make and lose more than one fortune.

"Life has had much in it for Mr. McKinley. That he has received more than the average man is due to his perseverance and talent. He must guard his health in October, else he will be ill. Of course, the strain of campaign work will be severe; but, besides that, he will have some complaint affecting the kidneys. Mrs. McKinley may be very ill at that time also."

HON. WILLIAM J. BRYAN'S HOROSCOPE.

"I have not decided upon the time of day Mr. Bryan was born, and have, therefore, only erected a chart for noon of the day given as his birthday—March 19th, 1860. The positions of the planets in this chart indicate a man of many very excellent qualities, but not a man of the caliber of Mr. McKinley. Mercury, ruler of the mind, is in the cardinal sign Aries. Mercury is in square aspect to Jupiter, and in trine aspect to Saturn. Both of these aspects give power, but not depth. I would define Mr. Bryan's mental qualities as moderately strong, ingenious, active and fanciful, though frequently having a sombre cast. He will not leave behind him work that will compare with the solid creations of mental genius brought into the world by Mr. McKinley. Mr. Bryan's clever strokes as an orator must be thoroughly prepared. I doubt their spontaneous creation in the heat of rhetorical picture-building. Judging by this chart, I believe that Mr. Bryan is aiming too high.

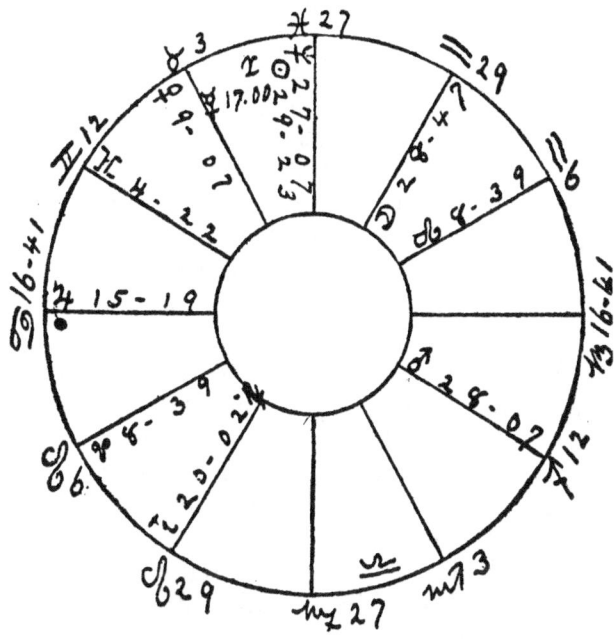

Chart of the Heavens for 12 O'clock Noon, on the Day of Birth of Hon. William J. Bryan, March 19th, 1860. Illinois.

It is true that Jupiter, the great benefic, is in its exaltation; but that and the sextile aspect of Mars and the Moon are not sufficient to raise a man to the presidency. That Mr. Bryan has risen so high in political life can only be explained by the fact that he must have exercised great ingenuity, and his wife must have added not a little to his force. A man without much physical strength can raise great weights by the aid of ingenious contrivances; but his results cannot be compared to those of ingenuity and strength combined. Mr. Bryan has accomplished great results, but I doubt if his results in the coming campaign will be equal to one-half his aspirations.

"Mr. Bryan's married life is too well known for me to remark upon. His wife is described by Mars in Saggitarius. She is taller than he, straight and erect in stature, light or auburn hair; ambitious, proud, but withal a most lovable woman with both eyes on the main chance.

"A comparison of the horoscopes of McKinley and Bryan leads me to one conclusion: The country would fare better under Mr. McKinley than it would under the man from Nebraska. At the time of the election in November, Major McKinley will have several good influences operating in his horoscope, which will aid him greatly. Mr. Bryan will suffer at that time from an opposition of Mars to its own place, and an exact square of Saturn to its own place in his horoscope. These influences alone would indicate Major McKinley's election, even though the horoscopes were reversed and Mr. Bryan's were superior."

THE TWO CONVENTIONS.

"I have here," the Professor continued, "charts erected for the exact minutes the nominations were made in the conventions. McKinley's occured June 18th, at 5.44 P. M., and Bryan's July 10th, at 3.15 P. M. The time of any event in a nation's history can be judged in Astrology the same as if it was a time of birth of a human being—its duration, its influence upon the country, its success or failure, and the collateral parts which bear upon those engaged or ruled by it.

"When Mr. McKinley was nominated, the planets smiled upon the Republican convention. The benefic Jupiter was ruler of the ascending sign Sagittarius. The Moon, ruler of the common people, was approaching a good aspect to Jupiter. Several other good influences are discernable, and all point to success.

"The chart for the nomination of Mr. Bryan is far from good. Mars is lord of the ascending sign Scorpio, and is weakly placed below the earth in a cadent house, and approaching a square aspect of Jupiter. Saturn and Jupiter are in square. The Moon is less than a degree past a conjunction of the Sun which is a very evil affliction, and it is approaching a trine of the retrograde planet Uranus in the ascendant at the time of the nomination, which is another very evil affliction. I fail to find any saving clauses in this review. Mr. Bryan will not retain his following, and his success cannot be found in this chart."

Further Remarks on the Horoscopes of President McKinley and Hon. William J. Bryan, and their Nominations, Written in January, 1898.

The general reader has no idea of the difficulties and obstacles the Astrologer has to overcome in writing or publishing anything in connection with the science or making predictions, as it is next to impossible to get the time of birth of any prominent or leading man or woman. For instance when the Hons. Grover Cleveland and James G. Blaine were nominated and each desiring to be elected President, a newspaper editor of this city made application direct to both gentlemen for their time of birth, but they positively denied any knowledge of the time of day they were born, and said they did not know there was any person living who could tell; yet afterwards Mr. James G. Blaine, when he wished to consult me through a mutual friend, could then give the exact time when he was born, and sent it to me in order that I might erect a proper chart of the heavens.

Within a short time after the nomination of the Hon. William McKinley, a lady friend of mine, and also a relation and intimate friend

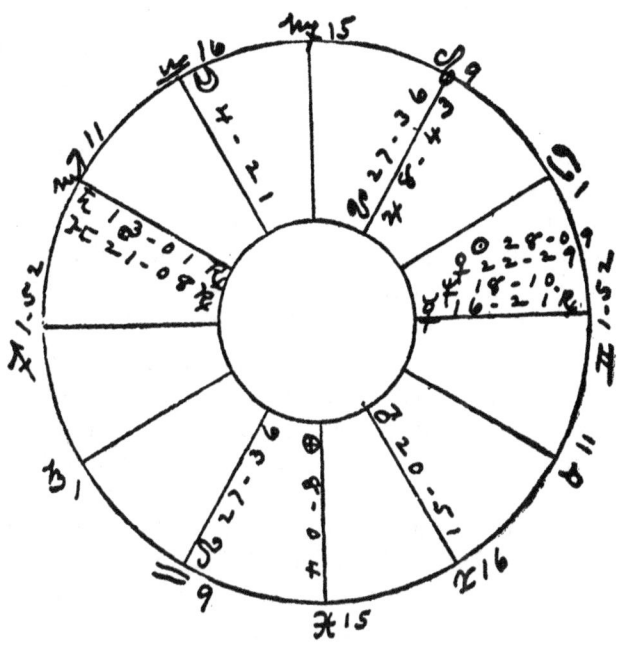

Chart of the Heavens for the Time Hon. William McKinley was Nominated for President, at St. Louis, Mo., at 5.44 P. M., June 18th, 1896.

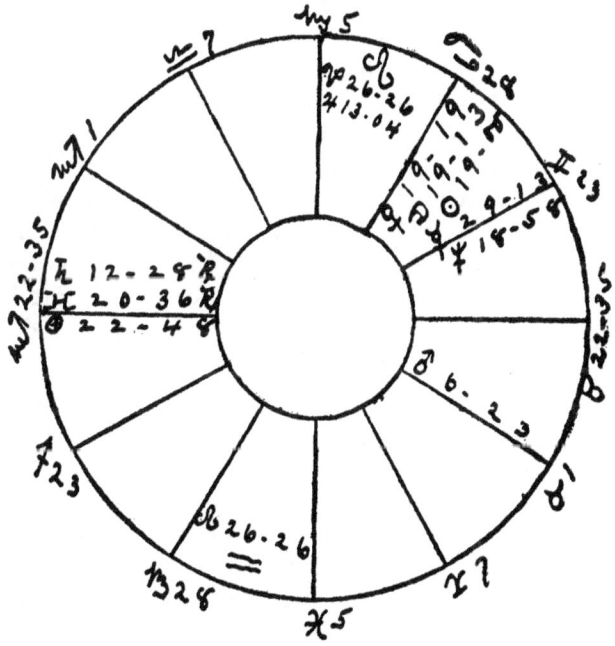

Chart of the Heavens for the Time of the Nomination for the President of Hon. William J. Bryan, at Chicago, July 10th, 1896, at 3.15 P. M.

of Mr. McKinley's private secretary, wrote to the secretary requesting him to obtain Mr. McKinley's time of birth. He wrote back refusing to give it, and stated that a number of people had made application to Mr. McKinley for the same information, but they had all been refused.

When the time of birth is not known, or it has been refused, the only way we have of finding the time in order to erect a chart of the heavens, is to get a good likeness of the individual, and also ascertain the dates of some of the leading events of their life on which to base calculations, and find if the positions of the planets correspond with those events, and also with their personal appearance. By this means I have erected the horoscopes of the Hons. Wm. McKinley and Wm. J. Bryan.

I procured a picture of Mr. McKinley, and looked carefully at it to get some idea of his personal appearance, and then comparing the various positions of the heavenly bodies, for the day of his birth, I found that no other time would answer so well for describing him, as when the latter part of the sign Scorpio was on the ascendant, and Mars a few degrees above the cusp of the degree rising. In that respect he has a horoscope similar to that of Napoleon Bonaparte, who had Scorpio on the ascendant; but in Napoleon's horoscope, Mars, lord of that sign was in Virgo, near the cusp of the 11th house. Napoleon had Jupiter in Scorpio on the ascendant in the same position that Mr. McKinley has Mars, and it is said that President McKinley has quite a resemblance to the "Little Corporal."

In regard to the time of birth of William J. Bryan, I find no position of the planets would so well describe him as near the middle of the sign Cancer rising, with Jupiter in the ascendant, and the Moon, his ruling planet, on the cusp of the 9th house, in Aquarius, in sextile to Mars, just set. In looking at his portrait we find that he has a real Jupiter forehead, with the hair receding from the temples. He has also a Jupiter nose, eyes and mouth. Mr. Bryan is what we term a Jupiter and Moon person, whereas Mr. McKinley is what we term a real Mars man. Of the two Mr. Bryan has a more fortunate horoscope, if we refer to pure luck, and he will meet with fewer reverses in fortune than President McKinley. He has also a mind that spurs him on to great energy and perseverance, although he does not have the depth of intellect of President McKinley; yet Mr. Bryan will come up again, and is bound to make his mark, as he has the Moon in a fixed sign in exact sextile to Mars, the most active and business planet there is in the heavens.

A number of Astrologers were mistaken in predicting that Bryan would be elected, as they thought Mr. Bryan had the most fortunate horoscope of the two, but at the same time they did not take into consideration the time that each was nominated. I predicted and had it published in the newspapers within two days after Mr. McKinley's nomination, that he was certain to be elected, as from the position of the planets I judged his nomination to be more fortunate than any presidential nomination that had been made during the last 40 years, or since I came to this country, and probably there will not be such a fortunate position of the planets at the time of a presidential nomination for the next hundred years as there was when President McKinley received the largest number of votes at the convention in St. Louis. At that time Jupiter was on the cusp of the 9th house, and lord of the ascendant, and the Moon in the midheaven coming to its sextile; these were remarkably fortunate aspects, and had Saturn not been in the 12th house near a square of Jupiter, he would almost have had a walk over, but that aspect caused his party to work hard and spend a great deal of money to secure his election.

Possibly there will never be another presidential nomination made just at the new Moon, as it was when Mr. Bryan was nominated, and if the democratic party at Chicago had had any idea of planetary influence, they certainly would not have nominated a candidate at that unfortunate time, unless they had intended him to be crowned with a crown of thorns, and crucified on a cross of silver.

The old Astrologers have an aphorism which says: "Anything commenced at the New Moon comes to naught." Therefore the democrats could not have chosen a more unfortunate time for the nomination, according to the rules of Astrology. And these rules are like the "Laws of the Medes and Persians which cannot be altered."

In addition to the evil influence of the new Moon at the nomination of Mr. Bryan, the evil planet Saturn was just rising, a little above the ascendant, in almost exact square to Jupiter in the 9th house, and Uranus was in conjunction with the "Part of Fortune" in the ascendant, which are certainly serious afflictions for any public or private undertaking whatever.

It was the want of money that defeated Mr. Bryan, which is shown plainly by the "Part of Fortune" being so seriously afflicted. The Moon was leaving a conjunction of the Sun, and applying to the conjunction of Venus, and all three planets were in trine to Uranus in the ascendant, which indicated that the women would be his friends, and had the ladies had a vote it is possible that Mr. Bryan might have defeated his opponent, but "The Stars fought in their courses against" Bryan.

It is often very difficult for the student to acquire the knowledge of judging almost instantly of two charts of the heavens, and decide which is the strongest and which is the weakest one. Mr. Sibley in his "Illustration of the Science of Astrology," and others have recommended the forming a scale of numbers to measure the strength or debility of planets, aspects, etc.; for instance, a planet in its own sign in the midheaven, they would mark it in strength number 10; and the planet only in its exaltation they would mark 6 or 4, the same in regard to weakness; but the plan that I have generally adopted has been to weigh those different positions of the planets in my mind; by constant practice and experience a person can in time, arrive at a very close judgment in comparing any two charts of the heavens, as to their strength or weakness. For instance, taking the time the Hon. William McKinley was nominated, the Moon was in the sign Libra in the midheaven, applying to a good aspect of Jupiter, lord of the ascendant in a fixed sign, in a fortunate house, afterwards the Moon came to the 11th house, (or house of friends,) and then made good aspects of four planets, that is: Mercury, Neptune, Venus and the Sun, all in the 7th house, and the Moon in the 11th house, indicated that Mr. McKinley would gradually go on gaining friends, and a great many of them, or enough to elect him.

There was one evil aspect, and that was the Moon making an opposition of Mars, but that planet was in good aspect to the four planets in the 7th house.

At the time Mr. Bryan was nominated, Mars, lord of the ascendant was in a cadent house, the 6th, (a very evil house,) and was set, and going lower and lower, and the Moon could hardly have been more afflicted, as it was just the new Moon, and in a very weak house, the 8th, (or house of death) and Saturn, retrograde, just rising, right in square to Jupiter, lord of the 4th, the only planet that was in any way strong. It was a foregone conclusion that McKinley would be elected the moment that Bryan was nominated. Those two charts of the heavens of the nominations of the two presidential candidates, deserve a great deal of study and attention, as they are object lessons to the student, and answer as examples for future nominations.

Some of my readers may say as Mr. McKinley was nominated at such a fortunate time, why should not his administration be equally fortunate? To decide that matter we have to examine the horoscope of William McKinley, and compare it with other horoscopes, and I think if the student compares the horoscope of Queen Victoria with the horoscope of William McKinley, he will find a wonderful difference, as the Queen has Jupiter in a fixed sign in the midheaven, and unafflicted in close good aspect to Mars in its own sign, and the Sun and Moon in the ascendant, and all the planets rising above the Earth except Uranus. We term the horoscope of Queen Victoria, an exceedingly fortunate one, the very opposite to such a horoscope as William McKinley or President Buchanan.

I think the time must come when the leading men in this country will pay attention to the planetary influences in national affairs as was done by leading men in former times in other countries, and that previous to putting any man in nomination for such a high office as president of the United States, they will have some competent Astrologer calculate his horoscope and see whether that individual, if elected, would be a blessing to the nation or a curse. Had the Republicans understood anything about Astrology, they certainly would not have put in nomination and elected a person with a horoscope like the Hon. William McKinley, who has only one planet above the earth, and that the evil planet Mars, neither would the Democrats in 1856, had they any knowledge of Astrology, have put in nomination and elected a person with a horoscope like James Buchanan, who had the evil planet Saturn in his midheaven, and the Moon in the 7th applying to a square of that unfortunate planet. Should the science of Astrology become generally known, and if we can judge anything by the signs of the times, and the trend of events, that day is not far distant, then it will be in the future, as Mr. Ashmond in his translation of "Claudius Ptolemy" states it was in the past, that Astrology "entered into the councils of princes, it guided the policy of nations, it ruled the daily actions of individuals, and physicians who were not well versed in this science were not deemed competent to practice their profession."

HOROSCOPE OF THE SAILING OF THE GERMAN FLEET FOR CHINA.

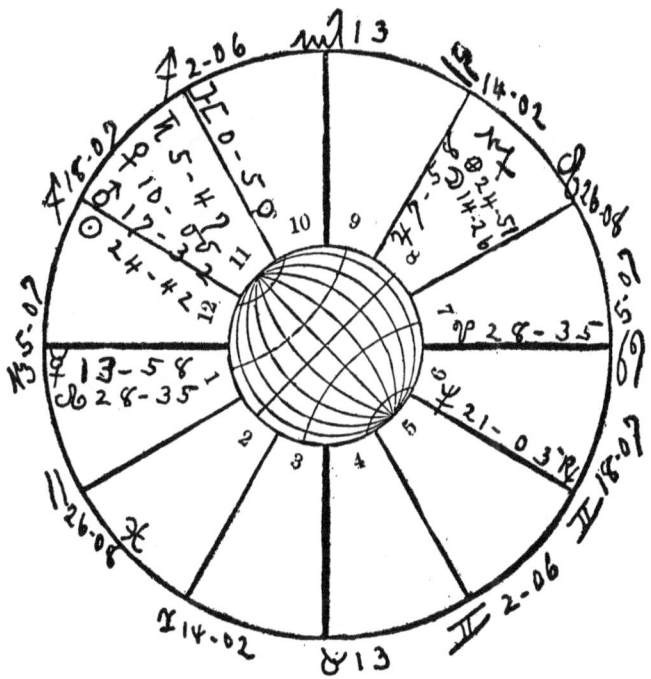

Chart of the Heavens for the Time Prince Henry, Brother of the Emperor of Germany, set Sail from Kiel, Germany, to China, Dec. 16th, 1897, at 9 a. m.

In order to calculate the positions of the signs and planets for the above Chart of the Heavens, the student should read over "Rule to set a Map of the Heavens," on page 142, then procure a map of Germany and look for Kiel Bay, and there he will find Kiel, in a small inlet, 54° north latitude, and near 10° east longitude, from Greenwich, England; then look in an Ephemeris for 1897, and turn to the month of December, and on the 16th day he will find the Sidereal Time is 17 hours and 40 minutes for 12 o'clock noon of that day; he deducts 3 hours from that sum, as it is 3 hours before 12 o'clock noon, which leaves 14 hours and 40 minutes; and in "Dalton's Table of Houses" for latitudes from 22 to 56, he will find on the top line of page 42 that 14 hours and 42 minutes is the nearest to that sum, and a little to the right he will find Scorpio 13°. He places that sign and 13° on the cusp of the 10th house, and then run his finger down the left hand column until he comes to 54, and on a line with that figure, and immediately under 14 hours and 42 minutes he will find the signs and the degrees and minutes for the remainder of the Northern houses; which he will copy into the blank chart. He will then insert the opposite or Southern signs, and their degrees and minutes on the opposite houses.

As Kiel is 10° east longitude from Greenwich, England, the student will multiply that sum by 4, (the number of minutes in time to one degree of longitude,) which makes 40 minutes, which he adds to 12 o'clock noon, and that makes 0 hours and 40 minutes in the afternoon; he then sees how far each planet, the Sun and Moon travels in 3 hours and 40 minutes, and subtracts that sum from the degrees and minutes of each of the planets and Sun and Moon as printed in the Ephemeris for December 16th, 1897, for 12 noon at London, and then insert the remainder of the degrees and minutes, and also the planets and Sun and Moon in the blank chart, and he will find that they correspond, or very nearly, to the above Chart of the Heavens.

If the student turns to page 291 and paragraph 641 he will find "Elections for Navigation or Going on a voyage," and he will see by the above Chart of the Heavens that it was a very evil time to set sail on an important voyage, as the Moon is in the 8th house, (the house of death,) and is just leaving a square of Venus, lady of the 9th house, (the house of long journeys,) and making a square of Mars, lord of the 3d, and also of the 10th house, (house of honor,) and the next aspect it makes afterwards is a square of the Sun in the 12th, and lord of the 8th house. The planet Mercury is in the ascendant, but just leaving a square of Jupiter in the 8th, all marked evil aspects.

There is no doubt that Prince Henry's expedition will prove very disastrous. If the student turns to the horoscope of Emperor William II. of Germany, he will find that the opposite signs of his horoscope are rising in the above election, and that Mercury is in exact opposition to its place at his birth; and the Sun, lord of the 8th house of the election, is in the 12th of the election and is in close conjunction to Venus in the 6th house, in the Emperor's horoscope (or house of sickness,) and is just leaving the square of Neptune, and making a square of Mars, both in the midheaven of the Emperor's horoscope. It will be strange indeed if the voyage does not prove very disastrous to Emperor William and his brother and also to the whole German nation, and that within a short time they will be like the French Republic who sent their navy to seize and possess Tonquin, in China. They were soon very glad to get back to France, and when they did get back, they took the cholera germs with them, which ravaged Marseilles and Toulon, and that epidemic spread over a great part of France, and carried off many thousands of its inhabitants. The expedition also came near making another revolution in France.

When the laws and principles of Astrology become better understood, no government will attempt to send a fleet on an important mission without first consulting the stars. In the East Indies the people pay much more attention to this science than they do in the western countries, they will not even undertake the most trivial matter without first observing the positions and aspects of the heavenly bodies.

CHART OF THE HEAVENS FOR THE TIME OF MARRIAGE OF MR. AND MRS. LANGTRY, ON THE ISLAND OF JERSEY, AT 3 A. M., MARCH 12th, 1874.

In order to calculate the Chart of the Heavens for that time and place, the student should procure a map of France. He will find the Island of Jersey near the northern part of that country, 49° north latitude and 2° west longitude, and if he looks in the Ephemeris for 1874 on the 12th of March, he will find 23 h. and 20 m. sidereal time; from that sum he will subtract 9, which leaves 14 hours and 20 minutes, as it was 9 hours before noon when the marriage occured. In the Table of Houses for London, which is only 2° from that latitude, he will find 8° of Scorpio on the mid-heaven, 29° of Scorpio on the 11th; and 16° of Sagittarius on the 12th; 2° and 18′ of Capricorn on the ascendant, 20° of Aquarius on the 2d, and 8° of Aries on the 3d, which he will fill into a blank chart.

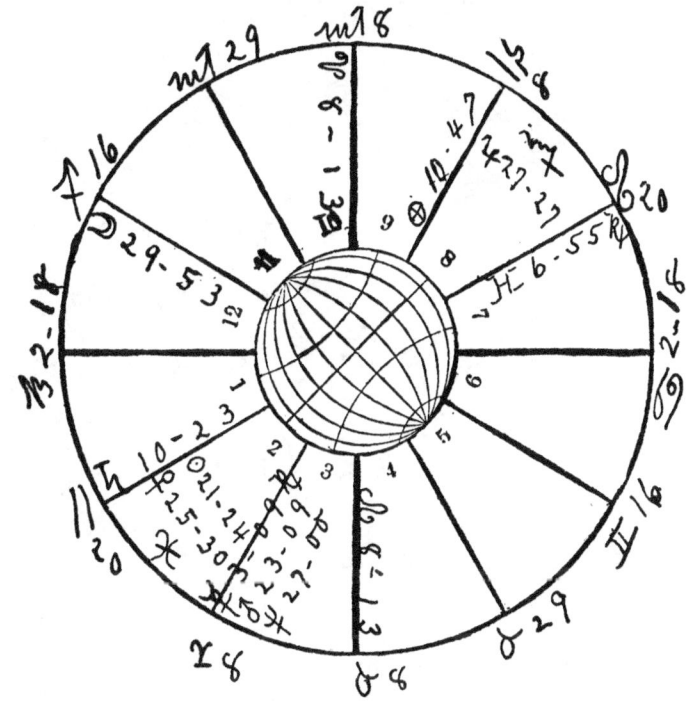

Map of the Heavens, for March 12th, 1874, at 3 a. m., Island of Jersey.

Then insert the opposite signs and degrees and minutes in their proper places. In calculating the longitude of the planets he will see what longitude each planet, and the Sun and Moon is in on that day at noon in London, and deduct one third of the distance they travel that day and one hour over, from the degrees and minutes marked in the Ephemeris, and then insert them in their proper places in the chart. The above he will find is a correct chart of the heavens for the time of their marriage.

The time of marriage is given as 3 o'clock in the morning, but no doubt it was 15 or 20 minutes later or very near half past 3 when they were married, when Saturn was right up in the ascendant, and Uranus in the 7th house near an opposition, only 3° from the aspect and no doubt they separated when that direction came up 3 years after marriage, reckoning a year in time for each degree in longitude.

If the student turns to page 289, paragraphs 630 and 631, he will find that they could not have chosen a more unfortunate time for marriage. The election for marriage referred to in paragraph 630 says: "Let not Saturn, Mars or Uranus be in the 7th house for that makes the woman very ill tempered; also Saturn, Mars or Uranus in the ascendant, makes the man very cross and ill tempered;" it also says: "Let the 7th house and the Moon and also the ascendant be free from affliction in such signs as favor marriage." But at the time of this marriage, Capricorn was on the ascendant and the Moon, lady of the 7th house just

Mrs. Lillian Langtry.

leaving a square of Jupiter, retrograde, in the eighth and making a square of Mercury, retrograde, in the third. The Moon would be on the ascendant when the marriage ceremony would commence, if at 3 A. M.

It has been impossible to get the time of birth from either Mr. or Mrs. Langtry, but if we could get them, there is no doubt both had what we call very evil aspects for marriage in their horoscopes.

Independent of their horoscopes or time of marriage, if we compare their physiognomy and temperaments or even their phrenology by their pictures, one could readily perceive that it was impossible for them to be happy together, as Mrs. Langtry has a peculiar nervous and very fine temperament, and is of a high intellectual order, with refined feelings, whereas the face, chin, and lower back part of Mr. Langtry's head, indicate an entirely opposite nature.

I have referred to this subject, and to the positions of the planets at their marriage, to show that Astrology, phrenology, physiology and physiognomy, all agree when they are properly understood, and also to point out that when a man and woman thus disagree in their married life and separate the latter becomes more or less reckless in her conduct.

I also wish to show how important it is that when a person contemplates marriage, a suitable time should be elected according to planetary influence, if lasting happiness is desired; but if the parties getting married elect an unfortunate time for that event they must expect it to terminate in a similar manner to the marriage of Mr. and Mrs. Langtry.

I have always found that when parties have unfortunate horoscopes for marriage they invariably get married at unfortunate times, unless they employ an Astrologer to calculate a fortunate time for their marriage.

In a horoscope of the time of marriage the ascendant indicates the man and the 7th house the woman. At the time of Mr. and Mrs. Langtry's marriage the evil planet Uranus was retrograde in the 7th house,

Mr. Edward Langtry.

the Moon lady of the 7th house was leaving an evil aspect of one retrograde planet and applying to an evil aspect of another retrograde planet, all indicating that Mrs. Langtry would leave or separate from her husband. She tried several times to get a divorce and finally succeeded in California, but her husband and the English courts never recognized it; but death finally put an end to this ill-starred marriage. In the fall of 1897 Mr. Langtry fell from the gang-plank of a vessel, which accident resulted in insanity and death. The evil planet Saturn in the ascendant in a fixed sign caused Mr. Langtry to be stubborn in opposing her divorce and against recognizing it.

I understand the reason Mr. and Mrs. Langtry were married at such an early hour, was that they wished to start on their wedding tour after the ceremony, and 3 A. M. just allowed them time to take the train or boat.

HOROSCOPE OF VICTORIA, QUEEN OF GREAT BRITAIN AND IRELAND, AND EMPRESS OF INDIA.

Her Majesty was born on the 24th of May 1819, at 4.15 A. M. London, England, at which time 5° of Gemini were rising, and 7° of Aquarius culminating. She was born under the former sign and the planet Mercury in the sign Taurus, in the 12th house, it having no special aspect to any planet; also the Sun and Moon were within orbs of the ascendant, the latter just leaving a conjunction of the former and both leaving a sextile of Saturn, in the sign Pisces in the 11th house, (the house of friends.)

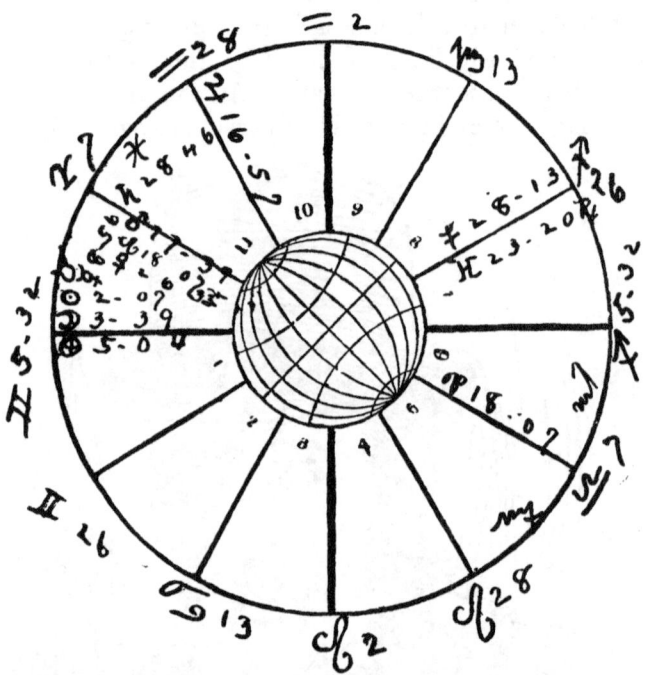

The Queen's Nativity, May 24th, 1819, at 1.15 a. m., London.

In order to get a personal description of the Queen we have to notice Mercury in Taurus, (see par. 129 page 118,) the Sun in Gemini, (see par. 106, page 113,) the Moon in Gemini, (see par. 142, page 120,) and also the sign Gemini, (see par. 15, page 97;) by combining the whole the student will get a very close description of the Queen, especially if he considers the sextile of the Sun and Moon to Saturn, (see par. 216, page 132, and par. 222, page 133;) and can arrive at her personal description, and also her mental qualities.* That which makes

---

* In giving a description of the native, the student should always bear in mind the first rule; Generally the planet which is lord of the ascendant, and the sign it is in, are the main factors for describing the native; the second rule is, the sign on the ascendant; the third, planets in the ascendant, and in aspect to other planets, and also the lord of the ascendant in aspect to other planets; and the fourth, the Moon's, and aspects to other planets. Therefore the above description of Mercury in Taurus, comes near describing the Queen. She would have been quite short, only she has a tall sign on the ascendant, and the Moon and the Sun are both in tall signs, within orbs of the ascendant. If the Sun and Moon had been *in the ascendant* instead of above it she would have been taller and not so stout.

this horoscope so remarkably fortunate is Jupiter in the midheaven unafflicted, in a fixed sign and in close sextile to Mars in its own sign in the 12th; and also to the position of the Sun and Moon within orbs of the ascendant.

Persons born with the Sun, Moon, Jupiter and Mars strong and in good aspect in their horoscope, invariably overcome their enemies, and rise above them, and yet the Queen must have had a number of false friends, as she has Saturn in the 11th house, in square to Uranus on the cusp of the 8th house, (house of death) which has at different times caused her life to be in danger by secret enemies.

The Sun which is the "Giver of Life" in this horoscope, has caused her to live to be an old woman, and should she get past 1898, and especially if she lives by the early part of December, 1899, she may then live some time longer, but 1898 and 1899 will be remarkably trying years, both for her health and constitution, but in a horoscope where the "Hyleg" is so strong as it is in the Queen's, it is very difficult to predict the exact time of death, but during the two years referred to, her vitality will be very seriously tried, also during these two years the English nation will have the world against it, and its enemies will multiply, and many of its supposed friends will turn into deadly enemies.

I shall not enter into any lengthy account of the Queen's horoscope. The main reason I have inserted it is to illustrate four principles in Astrology. The first is honor and wealth; the second a long life; the third marriage, and the fourth children.

The Sun being "Hyleg," strong in the ascendant, unafflicted, and leaving a good aspect of Saturn in the 11th, and Jupiter lord of the 8th,

---

The above positions of the Sun and Moon made the Queen slender when young, but Mercury being in a short stout sign, caused her to become stouter as she grew older. The Sun and Moon so close to the ascendant made the Queen lighter complexioned than she would otherwise have been, if the description had depended only on Mercury in the sign Taurus.

The following which is copied from "Modern Astrology," for Oct. 1896, a monthly periodical published in London, England, evidently shows that the author of the article has not had much experience as an Astrologer; if he had, he certainly would not have made such a mistake. The writer says that:

"If her Majesty is a Gemini lady with both luminaries on the ascendant in that sign, she would to a certainty be a tall dark lady, there being nothing of any consequences to counteract this. If the ideas put forward in The 'Revised Horoscope' are correct, the Queen is a Taurus lady; she answers well to Mercury in Taurus, both in person and mind as well as disposition; if the birth took place at 4.15 a. m., on the 24th of May 1819, the meridian was in 2 degrees and 25 minutes; and by equal division of the sphere, the ascendant would be Taurus 2 degrees and 25 minntes, which will be found to accord with what is known of the lady, better than the horoscope published."

"JARIEL," the Australian Astrologer.

"Jariel" ought to bear in mind that the "equal division of the sphere" or putting the same number of degrees of the signs on each of the 12 houses was discussed and settled over 2,000 years ago, and all nativities are now calculated for the longitude and latitude of the place of birth, by all good Astrologers.

Once while giving a lecture on Astrology, at 814 Broadway, in 1867, the time of birth of a lady born the 24th of May, 1819, at 4.15 a. m., London, was handed in, and I drew the chart on the blackboard, reading it off without any trouble or difficulty, and it appears I gave a very good description of the lady, her marriage, time of marriage, and description of her husband, and time of his death, all appear to correspond exactly. Among other things I stated she would be very wealthy, and ride in her own carriage, and live to a good old age. When I got through I expected the lady to get up and state if what I had said was correct. Instead Prof. Wilson told us it was the horoscope of Queen Victoria I had been reading; I was very much surprised at the accuracy of my reading. Prof. Wilson knew the exact time of birth as she and her guardian consulted him when he was a watchmaker in London. Victoria had not come to the throne at that time, as King William was still living.

strong in the midheaven, and in close sextile to Mars, strong in its own sign, and lord of the 6th, (house of sickness,) indicate that she would live to a great age, and that even although her life has been attempted several times, the "Hyleg" so strong, and Jupiter so strong in the midheaven in close good aspect to Mars, has so changed the bullet's course aimed at her life, that they had no effect on her, and she has never as much as received a wound, only when she fell and hurt her knee.

The Queen's horoscope is exceedingly fortunate for marriage, as Jupiter is lord of the 7th house, in the midheaven, and the Sun first applies to a trine of that planet, and if the student turns to par. 90 page 110, and also par. 21 page 98, he will find that they would exactly describe Prince Albert, her late husband, and also that she would live very happily, and be exceedingly fond of her husband.

Had the Qeen married a second time the marriage would not have been so fortunate, as the second husband would be described by the planet Mars in the sign Aries, in the 12th, an evil house, although that planet being in good aspect to Jupiter, would improve his temper and disposition slightly, but still it would have been an unfortunate marriage, and the Queen would have found a remarkable difference between a Jupiter man and a Mars man for a husband.

On account of the Queen's horoscope being so fortunate for marriage, she appears to have had but little patience or sympathy with women who have what we term unfortunate horoscopes for marriage, and she thinks that when a woman does not live happily with her husband, it is entirely the woman's fault. It is reported that she will not receive a divorced woman at court or in any way recognize her.

If the Queen had as unfortunate a horoscope for marriage as she has for children, she would have much more sympathy with ladies who are so unfortunate as not to be able to live with their husbands. These women might reply to the Queen by telling her it is her own fault she has had so much trouble with her children.

The Queen having the Moon in the ascendant, and it a fruitful planet, particularly as both the Sun and Moon were leaving a good aspect of Saturn in the 11th, in a fruitful sign, caused her to have a large family, but Saturn being in opposition to her 5th house (or house of children,) caused her to have much unhappiness in relation to children. It was reported in the papers that on account of one of the elder sons being turned out of school for bad conduct, Prince Albert, her husband, then in poor health, took a journey to Wales to try and arrange matters, when he caught more cold and brought on gastritis, which resulted in his death.

The Prince Consort died Dec. 14th, 1861,* when the Queen had the Sun right over Uranus's place on the cusp of the 8th house, in exact

---

Prince Albert, husband of Queen Victoria, was born Aug. 26th, 1819, at 6.4 a. m., Saxcoburg-Gotha, Germany.

According to the above time given, he was born under the planet Mercury in the sign Virgo in the ascendant, with 11 degrees of that sign rising, and 6 degrees of Gemini culminating. Mars was 23 degrees in Gemini in the midheaven, almost in exact square to Mercury in the ascendant, and in close opposition to Uranus in the 4th house, and applying to a square of Saturn in the 7th house.

He had a very conflicting horoscope but it indicated a very talented man, and he was very fine looking, so much so that many Astrologers, before they knew the exact time of birth, calcu square to Saturn in the 5th, and Jupiter was also in opposition to Saturn's place. The Queen having her planet in the 12th house (the house of sorrow,) caused her to mourn for a number of years after his death, and would not receive company.

He died rather suddenly. The Queen did not marry under good aspects in her horoscope, as on the day of marriage, Feb. 10th, 1840,

Prince Consort.

the Moon was in Taurus in her 12th house, in square to Jupiter in her midheaven; also making an opposition of Jupiter in Scorpio, and a square of the Sun on that day, which evil aspects had much to do with shortening the life of Prince Albert. Besides, the Prince did not have a long lived horoscope, neither was it a very fortunate one for marriage, although the Queen lived very happily with him.

---

lated his horoscope and supposed him to have been born under Jupiter in Aquarius, but after his death a paper was discovered which gave the exact time of birth as stated above.

The Prince had Saturn in the 7th house (the house of marriage,) and applying by retrograde motion to a square of Mars in the midheaven would indicate that his marriage was not a very happy one to him. The Moon made a square of Jupiter in Aquarius, and Jupiter was lord of the 7th, (or house of marriage,) which would come very near describing a lady like the Queen.

He could not have enjoyed the best of health during many parts of his life, as the ascendant was the giver of life and Mercury so afflicted in the ascendant by a square of Uranus and Mars, and an opposition of Saturn caused his life to be short. He died Dec. 14th, 1861, when the Sun was in exact square to Mercury, and Saturn was just transiting over his Mercury's place in the ascendant, and Jupiter was in the sign Virgo, making an opposition of Saturn's place.

It is a remarkable coincidence that he should die of stomach and liver trouble or **gastritis just** at that time, and all **these planets** afflicting his ruling planet in the sign Virgo, which governs **the abdomen and stomach.**

The above picture gives a typical idea of the features of a person described by Jupiter in Aquarius, and any one who was an artist and understood Astrology might soon after the birth of the Queen have painted almost an exact likeness of the person she would marry, as he would be described by ♃ in ♒ and the sign ♐, and also could have come very close to the time of marriage, as all the planets except one were rising, which would indicate an early marriage.

The following picture of the Queen, taken soon after her coronation, gives a very good likeness of her in her early years, and shows her description as indicated by the Sun and Moon in Gemini, and had the Sun and Moon been lower down in the ascendant, or below the cusp she would have been much taller, slimmer and even lighter complexioned than she is. The second picture (on the opposite page) gives her as

Queen Victoria as she appeared at 20 years of age.

described by the planet Mercury in Taurus, a stout sign, (see par. 578, page 225,) and which shows how she would gradually become an ideal person of the planet Mercury in Taurus in a fixed sign as she grew older.

As I have already mentioned, the Queen has some remarkably evil influences during the next two years, and she would begin to feel them in a more marked manner than she has had it not been for Jupiter coming in good aspect to both the Sun and Moon and her ascendant, which occured in the early part of November, and it will remain in close good aspect to her Sun and Moon and ascendant, until the latter part of August, 1898. It will also form a good aspect of its own place in October, 1898.

If it had not been for the good influence of Jupiter, the Queen and the English nation would have been in serious trouble by the commencement of 1898, as she has both Saturn and Uranus in her 7th house, in opposition to both the Sun and Moon, and they will continue to afflict her during 1898, but the most evil planetary influence is the slow-going planet Neptune which will continue in close opposition to Uranus's place in the 8th house, nearly all of 1898, and the whole of 1899.

The English nation and the Queen will feel the evil influence of Saturn and Uranus in an angle or the seventh house, or Queen's house of enemies, which evil influence will continue for nearly two years. Probably there will be some attempt on her life or she may die very suddenly during these evil aspects.

Queen Victoria as she appears in her 79th year.

It will be next to impossible for the English government to keep out of trouble, and no doubt some of the colonies will rise in rebellion, especially India, and it will be strange indeed, if the nation can avoid being embroiled in war during the next two years.

The Queen also has an unfortunate revolutionary figure for her next birthday, May 24th, 1898, as Jupiter will be in the 4th house, opposite to its position at birth. She will have four planets in the 12th house, (the house of secret enemies,) and Mars an evil planet is almost in the same degree of the sign Aries in the 11th house (the house of friends,) that it was in the 12th house at birth. The Sun is in the 12th and in almost exact opposition to Uranus. She has also two evil planets in the 6th house (or house of sickness,) all indicating that her health will be poor, if she is not dangerously ill during the coming year. Mercury her ruling planet, is almost in the exact position in Taurus that it was at birth, but in the 11th house, instead of being in the 12th as it was when she was born. These aspects and positions of the planets will cause the Queen to have more secret enemies than she has known for a very long time. Her secondary directions are also evil during the coming year. The Moon is making a square of Venus and the Sun is almost in exact opposition to Jupiter's radical place.

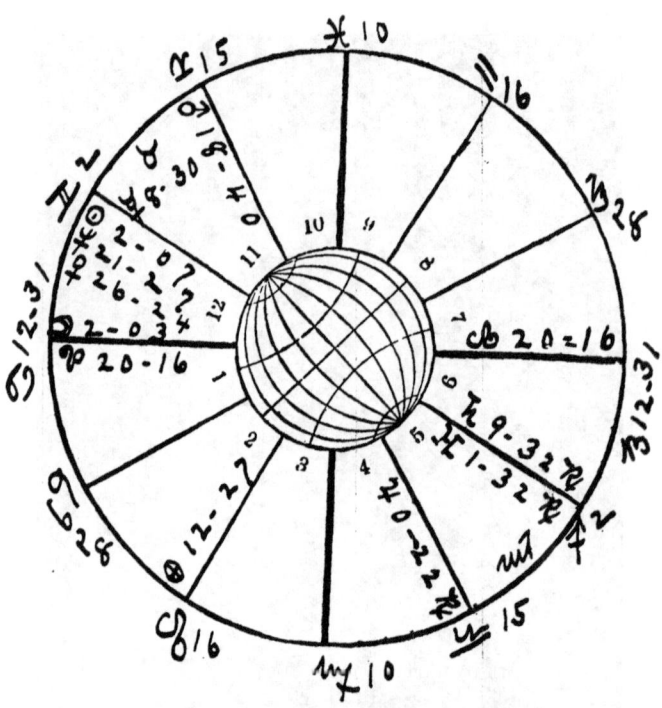

Queen Victoria's Revolution from May 24th, 1898, to May 24th, 1899. Occurs May 23d, 1898 at 6.43 a. m.

If the student inspects the two charts of the heavens, the Revolution figure and the Secondary Directions, he will see that they are not as fortunate as her own nativity was at birth.

THE QUEEN'S REVOLUTION, SECONDARY DIRECTIONS AND TRANSITS FROM MAY 24TH 1898, TO MAY 24TH, 1899.

The Revolutionary figure is a chart of the heavens erected for the exact time that the Sun arrives at the degree and minute that it was in at birth; when that exact moment is ascertained in any particular year, then the student inserts the signs and their degrees and the longitudes of the planets for that time the same as if it was a nativity.

The figure of a Revolution when erected as above described is the horoscope for the year which it is calculated for, and the good or evil aspects in that Revolution have much influence on the native's life for that year. The position and aspects of the planets in the Revolution have also to be noticed in regard to their radical places in the nativity, and in that respect are said to have much influence on the native, and his circumstances for the ensuing year.

The Secondary Directions are calculated by first inserting the signs of the Zodiac and their degrees in a blank chart, the same as they were at birth, then count the number of days from the birthday, that the native is years old, and calculate the longitude of the Sun, Moon and planets for that day, to the same hour and minute of the day, that the native was born; that gives the Secondary Directions for that year.

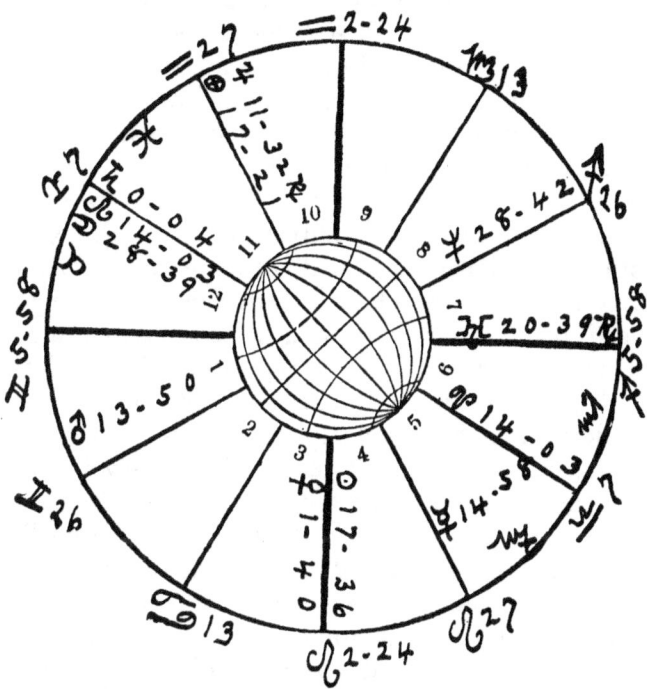

Queen Victoria's Secondary Directions, from May 24th, 1898, to May 24th, 1899.

The number of degrees the Moon is from forming an aspect of a planet, either in the horoscope of Secondary Directions or the Revolution, indicates the number of months after the birthday that the influence of the aspect will be felt, especially if the Moon is travelling at the rate of 12° a day, which corresponds to 12 months of the year. If the Moon is travelling faster, then count a little more than a degree for a month.

This remark applies to the Secondary Directions both in the Secondary Direction figure and to the aspects of the planets to their radical places in the nativity, counting a month for a degree that the Moon is from forming any aspect, which indicates the number of months from the birthday that the influence of the aspect will be felt in that year.

When a Revolution does not harmonize with the nativity it is said to be an unfortunate Revolution for that year; thus, if the sign on the ascendant in the Revolution is in square or opposition to the sign that is on the ascendant at birth, it makes it a very unfortunate Revolution, or vice versa. If the sign on the ascendant is in sextile or trine to the ascendant at birth, and the aspects agree in both the Revolution and nativity, then it is called a good Revolution, etc.

On the whole, the Secondary Directions and the Revolutionary figures are unfavorable for the Queen from May 24, 1898, to May 24, 1899.

The aspects of the planets in their revolution around the Sun which occur in a chart, as in the Queen's nativity, of Saturn and Uranus going through her 7th house, in opposition to the Sun and Moon in the ascendant in 1898 are called "Transits," and the Queen's horoscope has remarkably evil transits during the next two years. They will not only affect her own health and condition, or surroundings, but all those who are subject to or under her. That influence will continue until those evil transits are passed unless she dies in the meantime. In that case for the influence on the subjects we have to notice or look to the aspects in the horoscope of the Prince of Wales, or the horoscope of the heir to the throne, in a similar manner to the Queen's.

For practice the student can compare the two charts of the heavens of the Revolution and Secondary Directions, with the Queen's horoscope, and notice in which month the fortunate or unfortunate aspects will occur, reckoning from the Queen's birthday. He might also procure Raphael's Ephemeris for 1898, and notice in which month the evil transit of Saturn and Uranus will have the most effect, and the time the good aspect of Jupiter will have a modifying influence.

There is in addition to the Revolutionary figures, the Secondary Directions, and the transits, also what are termed "Primary Directions," that is, the aspects of the planets and the Sun and Moon, which occur after or before birth; the former are termed "Direct Directions," the latter, "Converse Directions." For every degree that the planet or Sun and Moon has to travel to complete the aspect is reckoned a year of the native's life. If the student examines the Queen's horoscope he will find that Uranus is 23 degrees and 20 minutes in Sagittarius, and Saturn 28 degeees and 48 minutes in Pisces. Uranus is a little over 5° from a square of Saturn. At 5 1-4 years of age the Queen would feel that evil aspect, and no doubt she was very ill, or there was some serious misfortune in her family at that age; possibly she might have buried a near relation or some other affliction came to her.

These Primary Directions can easily be calculated during the early years of the native's life; but when the native gets older, in order to calculate those directions exactly, we have to draw what we term a "speculum," as these directions, reckoning a degree for a year, do not always correspond with a year of the native's life. When the native arrives at the age of 50 or 60, these discrepancies may in some nativities be considerable.

The Queen will have an evil direction to the Moon during the year 1898, which will very seriously affect her health or cause some other affliction, and as the Moon and Sun are both in Gemini, in the ascendant it will in all probability bring on some serious attack in some way connected with the chest or head near the time when the aspect is complete.

HOROSCOPE OF LILLIAN RUSSELL.

This lady was born Dec. 4th, 1860, at 11.40 P. M., Chicago, Ill. This well-known songstress was born under the planet Mercury, in the sign Scorpio, which it is near leaving and entering Sagittarius, therefore she is described by Mercury in Sagittarius rather than Mercury in Scorpio, as that planet is more than 28° in the sign, and Mercury is also in square to Jupiter, rising. This describes a handsome person as her pictures indicate. She has 12° of Virgo rising, and 10° of Gemini culminating; Saturn is just rising in close opposition to the planet Mars, setting, and both in square to Uranus, retrograde, in the midheaven and applying to a square of the Sun in the 4th house.

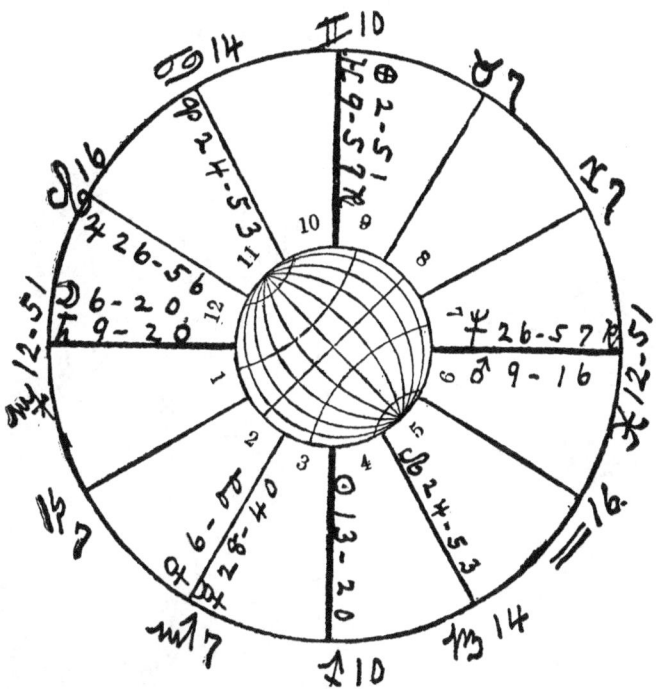

Chart for Dec. 4th, 1860, at 11.40 p. m., Chicago, Ill.

The Moon has just risen in exact sextile to Venus, and applying to an opposition of Mars and conjunction of Saturn, also to a square of Uranus, and the Sun. It is very seldom that we see a horoscope that has so many evil and conflicting aspects as this, especially for marriage or partnership.

In order to describe this lady, both physically and mentally, the student will have to turn to par. 18, page 97, par. 136, page 119, to par. 275, page 139, par. 145, page 120, par. 245 and 246, page 135.

The student may also read Saturn in Virgo, Mars in Pisces, Uranus in Gemini, and the Sun in Sagittarius, as they are all in aspect to each other and the ascendant, also read their square and opposition aspects.*

---

* Mercury in Sagittarius gives brown hair, and I understand that was the original color of the lady's hair.

These numerous squares, oppositions and particularly the sextile of the Moon to Venus, and the Moon rising, has caused this lady to have such remarkable abilities, and to become so well-known, in connection with her musical talents, but still she will not leave a name behind her equal to Jenny Lind, who had Venus in the sign Libra in the ascendant, in her nativity, or of Adelina Patti, who has Venus in Scorpio in the ascendant in her horoscope.

The only other horoscope that I can bring to mind that had so many squares and oppositions was that of Stephen A. Douglass, who was a very talented man, but who met with much opposition through life, and I believe eventually died poor. He ran for President in opposition to Abraham Lincoln, but was defeated. There is much danger that this lady will meet with many oppositions and conflicting difficulties in different periods of her life, and it is very doubtful of her leaving much wealth at her death.

Mr. Harry Braham, First Husband.

Mr. Solomon, Second Husband.

The ascendant, being the giver of life and so afflicted, it is very doubtful of her living to a great age, although it is possible that she might enjoy fair health generally, yet on account of Saturn afflicting Virgo rising, she will at times have severe attacks of illness, chiefly afflicting the abdomen and upper parts of the chest and throat, and will at times be troubled with some slight heart difficulty, as Uranus is in Gemini, in square to the ascendant, and Jupiter is in Leo, afflicting Mercury, her ruling planet, and very probably will die after a very short illness.

The main reason I have inserted this horoscope, is to refer to the marked evil aspects for marriage. In a nativity where there are evil planets in the 7th house, the house of marriage, it is always unfavorable for happiness in married life, and having the planet Neptune in that house is particularly evil, but more especially when Mars is there also in close opposition of Saturn rising. Had the Sun first made the square of Saturn or Mars it would have been much worse for her marriages than it really has been, but the Sun so close to a square of these evil planets has made it bad enough.

Lillian Russell.   Mr. G. Perugini, Third Husband.

In a lady's horoscope she marries the person denoted by the planet that the Sun first applies to by aspect for her first husband. See par. 298 and 299, page 164, also par. 305, page 165. The first aspect the Sun makes in this horoscope is a trine to Jupiter in Leo in the 12th house, (an evil house,) and Jupiter is within 2° of a square of her ruling planet, Mercury. (See picture of first husband.)

The above picture is almost a typical Jupiter in Leo person,* but these two ruling planets being in square to each other, and Mercury retrograde, caused her to leave him. The second aspect the Sun makes is

---

* If the student compares the above picture with Hon. William J. Bryan's, he will see a resemblance, as they are both Jupiter men.

a sextile of Venus, and Mr. Solomon was a real Venus person; Venus being so close to a sextile of the Moon caused her to have considerable affection for him, and the picture of the second husband is almost a typical person described by Venus in Scorpio, both in personal appearance and stature, and it also indicates great reputation for musical talent. For his description the student should turn to par. 123, page 116, and pars. 245, 246, page 135. No doubt there was more harmony between this lady and Mr. Solomon than with her other husbands, but his bad reputation for women finally undermined their happiness.

The third aspect the Sun makes is a sextile of Mars, just setting, near the cusp of the 7th house, and afflicting the house of marriage. The

Reported Fourth Husband.

Lillian Russell.

picture of the third husband indicates a real Mars person. For his personal description the student should turn to par. 103, page 113, par. 259, page 138, and par. 235, page 134. The union with this gentleman was of very short duration as the planet Mars is in the 7th house and so close to an opposition of Saturn within orbs of the ascendant.

The fourth picture shows a person indicated by the planet Uranus in the sign Gemini; for his description turn to par. 58, page 105; but she will not marry him. (See par. 302, page 165.) Should she marry again, the next husband is indicated by the planet Saturn in the sign Virgo, and his personal description would not be anything like the last picture referred to; for his personal description, the student should turn to par. 73, page 107, and to par. 258, page 137, also par. 217, page 133. He will have a peculiar sullen or down look, and not be agreeable in his manners. It is more than probable that this lady will marry a fourth time, and will also separate from that husband, possibly within a year after the marriage. This horoscope is not fortunate for children and certainly she will have only a small family, and these will not be of much comfort or benefit to her, as Saturn lord of the 5th house, (the house of children,) is afflicting the ascendant, but the Moon making a conjunction of Saturn, and at the same time being in sextile to Venus, indicates that she would be very fond of her children, and they would be good-looking.

In early life this lady would be very willful and head-strong, but on the whole good-natured and kind-hearted, except when out of temper; she must have had a number of very severe attacks of illness which seriously threatened her life. One was during her first year, and another at 3 years of age. She had a marked evil time at 6 1-2 years, also at 7 years, 14 years and 21 years. Probably she married the first time when near 18 years of age. Commencing September 1890, and continuing up to the fore part of 1896, she had a number of very evil planetary influences which have caused her serious trouble and unhappiness.

The present year, 1898, will not be a fortunate year, especially May, June, July, August, September and November. The year 1899 will also be unfortunate for her as she will have Uranus afflicting her Moon's place, also Saturn's and Mars' places and in opposition to its own place and a conjunction of the Sun's place in her horoscope. All these are very evil aspects and will afflict her financially and in her health. Uranus will afflict her in a similar manner all through 1899.

If Queen Victoria had a horoscope similar to that of Lillian Russell, she would have much more sympathy and feeling for women who are unfortunate in marriage or compelled to be divorced from their husbands.

I have inserted the foregoing pictures and horoscope of this talented lady to show that when a female has a nativity which is unfortunate for marriage, no matter how attractive she may be in personal appearance, figure or complexion, and no matter how talented a musician she may be, conversationalist or entertainer, yet when it is so evil for marriage, it is an impossibility for that person to retain or live happily with their life's partner. Yet when the horoscope is fortunate for marriage, they live happily even if the lady is old and anything but good-looking.

The same principles apply to those horoscopes of parties who are unfortunate in burying their companions after marriage, whether men or women. In such horoscopes as show the affliction of the life's partner, especially if afflicted in the 6th, 8th or 2d house, no matter how indulgent or careful they are of their partners, those partners are only of short life.

I wish the student to bear in mind that I do not blame Lillian Russell for not living happily with her husbands, because her horoscope shows distinctly that it would be more her husband's fault than her's that she did not continue to live happily with them, and that she is also of an affectionate nature, and ought to live happily with almost any man, if it was not for the evil aspects for marriage in her horoscope.

From Broughton's Monthly Planet Reader, for Dec. 1869.
THE HOROSCOPE OF LORD GEORGE GORDON BYRON.

"There is a name that will survive
Royalty's monumental stone,
And long as history can give
Deserv'd renown, must deathless live;
BYRON, it is thine own."—MIRROR.

"Beautiful stars, in other days,
The prophet's eyes might read your rays,
And tell of many a strange event,
Of warfare and of warning sent."—BYRON.

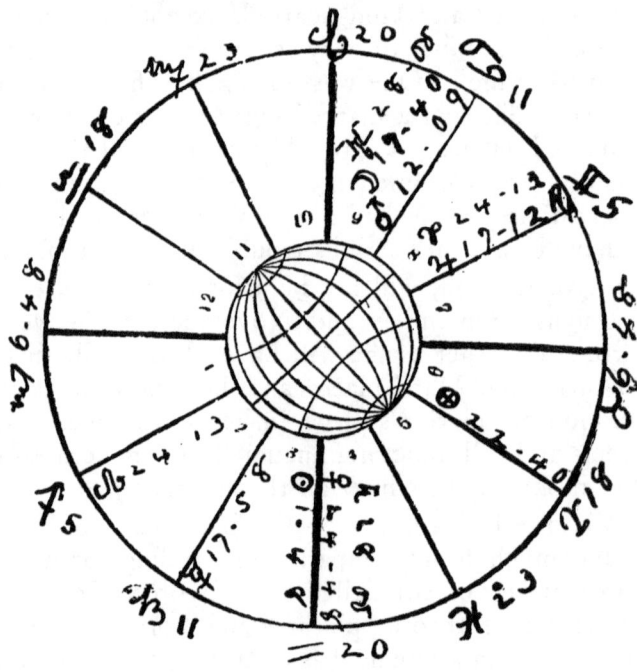

Lord Byron's Nativity, January 22d, 1788, at 1.18 a. m., London.

"Little did Lord Byron think when writing these beautiful lines that years after his death and burial the skill of the 'prophet's eye,' in 'reading the rays of the *Stars*,' should be the only authentic record left to justify his fair name and character; to remove the most ignominious charge of incest, and fix the fabrication of it on the right person, that is Lady Byron.

"The time of birth of this truly noble and most illustrious poet was obtained some years ago, from an authentic source, so that there can be no doubt of its correctness. From what source I received it is of no account to the reader, only I can assure him that I did not receive it from either Harriet Beecher Stowe or Lady Byron. And its perfect agreement with the principally known events of his life exhibits a most remarkable proof of Astrology, by far too strong for the enemies of the science to invalidate.

"Lord Byron was born when 6 degrees of Scorpio were rising, which caused him to be born under the planet Mars, in Cancer, near a conjunction of the Moon, and applying to an opposition of Mercury, which will describe a person near the middle height, well built, light hair and light complexioned, high forehead and oval face.

"The Moon is the giver of life, and being in conjunction with an evil planet, and in opposition to another, and otherwise materially afflicted, indicated a short life, and also the kind of death. But I shall refer to this part of the horoscope afterwards.

"The extraordinary mental qualifications which Lord Byron possessed are most amply demonstrated by the positions and configurations of the Moon and Mercury. The latter planet is the principal ruler of the intellectual faculties, and being free from the affliction of the Solar rays, in the moveable and tropical sign Capricorn, oriental, and approaching a sextile of the ascendant, by which means he may be said to be in a glorious position, contributes, according to the Quadripartile of Ptolemy, to render the mind 'clever, sensible, capable of great learning, inventive, expert, logical, studious of nature, speculative, of good genius, emulous, benevolent, skillful in argument, accurate in conjecture, and adapted to science and mystery.' *

Lord George Gordon Byron.

The page also adds, 'tractable;' but Mercury being in opposition to the Moon and Mars, instead of tractibility, gives hatred of control; inspires the native with the most lofty ideas and aspiring sentiments; gives him originality and eccentricity, with a firmness of mind almost inclining to obstinacy, and which made this illustrious native such an enemy to the track of custom, for which he was so remarkable, and which contributed to form that lofty genius which alike rode in the whirlwind, or sparkled in the sunbeam.

---

* See Ptolemy's Tetrabiblos, page 167, translated from the Greek by J. M. Ashmond, (Edition of 1822.) A work which has stood the test of criticisms of its opponents, for nearly *two thousand years*, and it is likely to be a text book on Astrology for two thousand years to come.

"The disposition and rational faculties are no less plainly described by the position of the Moon in conjunction with Mars; likewise, in a tropical and cardinal sign, wherein she is powerful while Mars is nearly in exact mundane trine to the ascendant. These positions laid the foundation, from the moment of his existence, of that peculiarity of disposition, that keen and cutting vein of satire, that caustic and pointed wit, that extraordinary development of energies, passions and eccentricities, that quick, enterprising and daring mind, and that exquisite taste, talent and sensibility for which he stood unrivalled. But, at the same time that this position of the heavenly bodies gave sentiments of the most perfect heroism and invincible courage, it is to be regretted that it inclined the temper to be both hasty and irascible on the slightest occasion, and to increase the violence of the most powerful passions!

"Mercury, it will be observed, is alone in the sign of the winter tropic, and in semi-quartile to Saturn, which may account for the solitary gloom that so frequently overshadowed his path through life, as well as for that melancholy sadness which tinged some of his brightest ideas, and which actually seems to have embittered the latest hours of his existence.

"Thus it will be observed, from a combined view of the above testimonies, judged according to the established and experimental rules of the astral science, that the nativity plainly demonstrates the illustrious subject thereof to have been endowed with the most extraordinary and stupendous intellect, with a genius and imagination, as far surpassing the common run of poets, as the refulgent rays of the meridian Sun surpass the feeble twinkling of the smallest star that arises in our horizon! Neither is it a trifling proof of Astrology, that his geniture so plainly demonstrate that he was "*born* a poet."

MARRIAGE.

"The Moon first applies to an opposition [the very worst aspect that there is,] of Mercury, in the sign Capricorn; (See par. 306, page 165, par. 137, page 119, par. 290, page 141, par. 283, page 140, and par. 300, page 164.) Therefore, his wife is denoted by the planet Mercury in Capricorn, which will describe a person below the middle height; when young, slender built, dark hair, oval or thin face, and pale skin. Of a quick temper, and at times, ill-natured, peevish, *suspicious* and *jealous*.

"Mercury is in opposition to Mars, [Lord Byron's ruling planet,] and Venus, lady of the seventh house, the house of marriage, is applying to a conjunction of the evil planet Saturn, in the fourth. (See par. 167, page 126.) We seldom meet with a nativity so evil for marriage as this. I have examined over 50,000 nativities myself, and never met with one worse for marriage. However amiable Lady Byron might, at times, have appeared to others, to her husband she would be a perfect she-devil, and could not help it, and it would be just as reasonable to expect the Angel Gabriel to live in wedlock with Satan, as Lord Byron to have continued to live with his wife.*

Lord Byron married Miss Milbanke, Jan. 2d, 1815, when he was 27 years old, while Jupiter was transiting over his midheaven. This ill-starred union did not last quite a year; soon after the birth of their daughter Ida, which occurred on Dec. 10th 1815, Lady Byron returned

---

* Why do not the opponents of Astrology show from the examination of Byron's nativity, that he should have been a fool or a simpleton; and according to the rules of Astrology, he ought to have lived happily and in perfect harmony with his wife? Simply because it is impossible to be done and they know it.

to her father and could not be prevailed upon to go back to "Newstead Abby," Lord Byron's home. The separation brought Lord Byron a great deal of ill-will from different parties, as he writes himself: "I am accused of every monstrous vice, from both public and private rancor."

Lord Byron's horoscope is unfortunate for children, as Jupiter, lord of the 5th house is in the 8th house, (the house of death) which certainly indicates a very small family, and even that small number would not live to be old.

The planet Mars, Lord Byron's significator, being in the 9th house, (house of long journeys) in opposition to Mercury, and both being in movable and cardinal signs, caused Byron to travel a great deal, and to be very unsettled and discontented; also Saturn in conjunction with Venus in the 4th house made his home generally unhappy. It is stated that Lord Byron's father and mother were a very "ill-matched pair," and their ungovernable tempers caused them to separate. Lord Byron's mother returned to her father's home soon after her son's birth.

Whenever Saturn is in the 4th house it always makes much unhappiness connected with home affairs, especially in early life. It also often causes the patrimony to be wasted or squandered, or the property dwindles away; yet Jupiter lord of the 2d house, (house of money,) being in the 8th house, (house of death and wills,) and in good aspect to Venus and Saturn in the 4th house, would indicate that he would inherit a large estate.

Whenever the planet Mercury is in evil aspect to the Moon, (the Moon represents the public,) that native is almost certain to have evil reports circulated about him or her, no matter if they live the life of a saint, and never do an imprudent act in their whole life.

The opposition of the Moon and Mercury was the cause of Byron's lameness, Mercury being in Capricorn which rules the knees, also Saturn in conjunction with Venus, in mundane square to the ascendant, and in Aquarius which governs the ankles and limbs below the knees; no doubt the lameness was brought on by accident which occured at four years of age, when Venus came to a conjunction of Saturn in the 4th, house by direction.

The Moon in the 9th house, (the house of religion,) in opposition to Mercury, caused Byron to rail against the established religion, yet for all that, his ruling planet and the Moon being in the 9th house, (house of religion,) caused him to be of a religious turn of mind, but at the same time he was very much opposed to superstition and to such stories as Adam and Eve in the garden of Eden.

Byron being born under the warlike planet Mars, made him a fighter and of a high temper, and very much opposed to oppression. He died after taking cold while helping to free the Greeks from the oppression of the Turks, when he was 36 years of age, when the evil planet Saturn was transiting over his 7th house, in opposition to his ascendant, and in square to Venus and its own place, and Mars his ruling planet came by direction to an opposition of Saturn's place in the 4th house.

The Moon being the giver of life in this horoscope, and being very much afflicted by an opposition of the planet Mercury, and also besieged between the two evil planets Mars and Uranus. It was impossible for him to have lived to be an old man, even if he had lived a very temperate, quite and uneventful life.

Nearly all the above was published in " Broughton's Monthly Planet Reader," December, 1869, during the time of the great excitement caused by the publication in the " Atlantic Monthly " of the scandal of Lord Byron, as stated by Lady Byron, and written by Mrs. Harriet Beecher Stowe.

Lady Byron reported that Mrs. Colonel Leigh, half sister of Lord Byron, had one or more children to her half brother. The English nation treated the scandal with the contempt that it deserved, by subscribing to, and erecting a statue to Lord Byron in London; that the whole scandal was pure imagination in Lady Byron's own mind, there is no question or doubt, and that it was created by her own jealous disposition. The nativity of Lord Byron proves that it was absolutely impossible for such a disgraceful occurence to have taken place.

Any Astrologer who examines the horoscope of Byron will see at once that it was impossible for any harmony to have continued between his half sister and himself, as the planet Mercury is in the 3d house, (the house of brothers and sisters,) and is almost in exact opposition to the Moon, (the Moon is always the co-significator in a nativity,) therefore it is much more likely that there would be constant unpleasantness or enmity, between Mrs. Leigh and Lord Byron, rather than strong affection or love, and that they would disagree much more when children than the average family of brothers and sisters. In addition to the above testimony Mars, Byron's ruling planet, is applying to an opposition of Mercury, in the 3d house, which shows the very opposite of affection and love between himself and his half sister.

I have inserted the horoscope of Lord Byron chiefly to point out the falsehood of Lady Byron's scandalous report, and also to explain their unhappy married life, according to the principles and rules of Astrology. Also to explain by the same science, that there would be a similar bitter feeling, almost hatred between Lord Byron and his half-sister that there was between him and Lady Byron, as the Moon makes the same aspect, in relation to brothers and sisters, that it did for marriage—that is, the Moon applied to an opposition of Mercury in the 3d house, (the house of relations,) and also to illustrate the unhappiness or even hatred and suspicion which it often produces in families, when parties getting married, disagree and separate.

There is no doubt that the feelings which Lord Byron expressed in his "Farewell to England" has been the sentiment and feelings of thousands of persons who have been divorced from their life partners and that if the method of the Chinese and East Indian people could be adopted of comparing horoscopes before marriage these unhappy unions could be avoided and it would prevent those bickerings, quarrels and separations, and might even be the means of promoting lasting happiness, in families similar to what is stated to exist in the East Indies and China.

In my practice I have noticed that horoscopes indicating unhappy marriages often run in families. When Lord Byron's father and mother quarreled and separated, it is not to be wondered at that Lord Byron should separate also from his wife. Also in the case of Lillian Russell, her father and mother did not live harmoniously, and so I might mention hundreds of other similar cases which have come under my notice.*

Even those men and women who have succeeded in getting divorces, have often expressed their feelings on the subject by saying that if they married a second time they would not go through the anxiety of getting a divorce again, even if they were sure their next husband or wife intended to kill them. Many of these persons who have been uuhappy in marriage and separated, if they had a good command of language, would express themselves in prose in similar words that Lord Byron so elegantly expressed in poetry.†

I have inserted the following poem to show what anguish of mind and heart it sometimes causes both men and women when marriage results in unhappiness and separation, and such separation might all be avoided by the study and application of the principles of Astrology, and following the practice of the people of the East Indies.

That Lord Byron was very much in love with his wife is shown, by the line which says: "I bless thee, I woo thee my wife." What a difference of feeling there is in the above line and the envious, spiteful hate of Lady Byran towards her late husband who had been dead over 50 years. Yet Mrs. Harriet Beecher Stowe endeavored to represent her as a perfect saint. Let us hope that there will be but few such saints in heaven.

---

* In December 1897, a member of the Legislature of Ohio introduced a bill in the Assembly, which if it is passed, would compel every man or woman living in that state contemplating marriage to go before a doctor to be examined to see if there was any insanity, heredity or contagious disease, or any other affliction of that nature in either of the parties.

For my part I do not approve of any of those laws compelling people to do so and so, and inflicting penalties or fines if those laws are not complied with.

Let the people learn that it is to their own advantage and benefit to be satisfied that their life partner is free from all the above complaints mentioned in the aforesaid bill, then it will not require any laws on the matter, they will only need intelligence.

In China and the East Indies and many other countries, the people have learned by experience that it is to their mutual advantage to compare horoscopes previous to getting married, and if they had not proved it, it is unreasonable that the system would have continued for such a long period, and I have no doubt that if the people in Europe and America would follow the same custom, one Court of Justice in New York City would not be turning out divorces at the rate of 15 per day, as I have seen it stated in the newspapers.

It is remarkable that unhappy marriages runs in families; I have calculated horoscopes in some families for the past two or three generations without finding one horoscope in these families where the planets did not indicate an unhappy marriage. It might be as well for these families to discontinue marrying so that the breed might die out, and make room for families who are fortunate in a married life.

---

† When a good Astrologer hears a person speak or sees their style of writing on any subject, he can generally tell the positions of the planets and their aspects in that person's horoscope. One evening I heard Lillian Russell's mother lecture on marriage, she was railing against it, as being nothing but slavery for women.

I knew at once that either she had Saturn or Mars in the 7th house (the house of marriage,) or the Sun first mode an evil aspect of one of these planets for marriage. When I procured her time of birth I found that she had Saturn in the 7th house, and the Sun first made a square of Mars for marriage. No wonder she was opposed to women marrying.

BYRON'S FAREWELL TO ENGLAND.

Oh! land of my fathers and mine,
   The noblest, the best, and the bravest;
Heart-broken, and lorn, I resign
   The joys and the hopes which thou gavest.

Dear mother of Freedom! farewell!
   Even Freedom is irksome to me;
Be calm, throbbing heart, nor rebel,
   For reason approves the decree.

Did I love?—Be my witness High Heaven;
   That mark'd all my frailties and fears;
I adored—but the magic is riven;
   Be the memory expunged by my tears!

The moment of rapture, how bright!
   How dazzling, how transient its glare!
A comet in splendor and flight,
   The herald of darkness and care.

Recollections of tenderness gone,
   Of pleasure no more to return;
A wanderer, an outcast, alone,
   Oh! leave me, untortured, to mourn.

Where—where shall my heart find repose?
   A refuge from memory and grief!
The gangrene, wherever it goes,
   Disdains a fictitious relief.

Could I trace out that fabulous stream,
   Which washes remembrance away,
Again might the eye of Hope gleam
   The dawn of a happier day.

Hath wine an oblivious power!
   Can it pluck out the sting from the brain?
The draught might beguile for an hour,
   But still leaves behind it the pain.

Can distance or time heal the heart
   That bleeds from the innermost pore?
Or intemperance lessen its smart,
   Or a cerate apply to its sore?

If I rush to the ultimate pole,
   The form I adore will be there,
A phantom to torture my soul,
   And mock at my bootless despair.

The zephyr of eve, as it flies,
   Will whisper her voice in mine ear,
And, moist with her sorrows and sighs,
   Demand for Love's altar a tear.

And still in the dreams of the day,
   And still in the visions of night,
Will fancy her beauties display,
   Disordering, deceiving the sight.

Hence, vain fleeting images, hence!
   Grim phantoms that 'wilder my brain,
Mere frauds upon reason and sense,
   Engender'd by folly and pain!

Did I swear on the altar of Heaven
   My fealty to her I adored?
Did she give back the vows I had given,
   And plight back the plight of her lord?

If I err'd a moment from love,
   The error I flew to retrieve;
Kiss'd the heart I had wounded, and strove
   To soothe, ere it ventured to grieve.

Did I bend, who had ne'r bent before?
   Did I sue, who was used to command?
Love forced me to weep and implore,
   And pride was too weak to withstand.

Then why should one frailty like mine,
   Repented, and wash'd with my tears,
Erase those impressions divine,
   The faith and affection of years?

Was it well, between anger and love,
   That pride the stern umpire should be;
And *that* heart should its flintiness prove
   On none, till it proved it on *me?*

And, ah! was it well, when I knelt,
   Thy tenderness so to conceal,
That witnessing all which I felt,
   Thy sternness forbade *thee* to feel.

Then, when the dear pledge of our love
   Look'd up to her mother and smiled,
Say, was there no impulse that strove
   To back the appeal of the child?

That bosom, so callous and chill,
   So treacherous to love and to me;
Ah! felt it no heart-rending thrill,
   As it turn'd from the innocent's plea?

That ear, which was open to all,
   Was ruthlessly closed to its lord;
Those accents, which fiends would enthral,
   Refused a sweet peace-giving word.

And think'st thou, dear object,—for still
   To my bosom thou only art life,
And spite of my pride and my will,
   I bless thee, I woo thee, my wife!

Oh! think'st thou that abscence shall bring
   The balm which will give the relief?
Or time, on its life-wasting wing,
   An antidote yield for thy grief?

Thy hopes will be frail as the dream
   Which cheats the long moments of night,
But melts in the glare of the beam
   Which breaks from the portal of light;

For when on thy babe's smiling face
   Thy features and mine intertwined
The finger of Fancy shall trace,
   The spell shall resistlessly bind.

The dimple that dwells on her cheek,
   The glances that beam from her eye,
The lisp as she struggles to speak,
   Shall dash every smile with a sigh.

Then I, though whole oceans between
   Their billowy barrows may rear,
Shall triumph, though far and unseen,
   Unconscious, uncall'd shall be there.

The cruelty sprang not from thee,
   'T was foreign and foul to thy heart,
That levell'd its arrow at me,
   And fix'd the incurable smart.

Ah, no! 'twas another than thine
   The hand which assail'd my repose;
It struck—and too fatally—mine
   The wound, and its offspring of woes.

They hated us both who destroy'd
   The buds and the promise of Spring;
For who, to replenish the void,
   New ties, new affections can bring?

Alas! to the heart that is rent
   What nostrums can soundness restore?
Or what, to the bow ever-bent,
   The spring which carried it before?

The rent heart will fester and bleed,
 And fade like the leaf in the blast;
The crack'd yew no more will recede,
 Though vigorous and tough to the last.

I wander—it matters not where;
 No clime can restore me my peace,
Or snatch from the frown of despair,
 A cheering—a fleeting release!

How slowly the moments will move!
 How tedious the footsteps of years!
When valley and mountain and grove
 Shall change but the scene of my tears.

The stork on the perishing wall
 Is better and happier than I;
Content in his ivy-built hall;
 He hangs out his home in the sky.

But houseless and heartless I rove,
 My bosom all bared to the wind,
The victim of pride and of love,
 I seek—but, ah! where can I find?

I seek what no tribes can bestow—
 I ask what no clime can impart—
A charm which can neutralise woe,
 And dry up the tears of the heart.

I ask it—I seek it—in vain—
 From Ind to the northernmost pole;
Unheeded—unpitied—complain,
 And pour out the grief of my soul.

What bosom shall heave when I sigh?
 What tears shall respond when I weep?
To my wailings what wail shall reply?
 What eye mark the vigils I keep?

Even thou, as thou learnest to prate,
 Dear babe—while remotely I rove—
Shall count it a duty to *hate*
 Where nature commands thee to *love*.

The foul tongue of malice shall peal
 My vices, my faults, in thine ear,
And teach thee, with demon-like zeal,
 A father's affection to fear.

And oh! if in some distant day
 Thine ear may be struck with my lyre,
And nature's true index may say,
 "It may be—it must be my sire!"

Perchance to thy prejudiced eye
 Obnoxious my form may appear,
Even nature be deaf to my sigh,
 And duty refuse me a tear.

Yet sure in this isle, where my songs
 Have echoed from mountain and dell,
Some tongue the sad tale of my wrongs
 With grateful emotion may tell.

Some youth, who had valued my lay,
 And warm'd o'er the tale as it ran,
To thee e'en may venture to say,
 "His frailties were those of a man."

They were; they were human, but swell'd
 By envy, and malice, and scorn,
Each feeling of nature rebell'd,
 And hated the mask it had worn.

Though human the fault—how severe,
 How harsh the stern sentence pronounced,
E'en pride dropp'd a niggardly tear,
 My love as it grimly denounced.

'Tis past: the great struggle is o'er;
 The war of my bosom subsides;
And passion's strong current no more
 Impels its impetuous tides.

'Tis past: my affections give way;
 The ties of my nature are broke;
The summons of pride I obey,
 And break Love's degenerate yoke.

I fly, like a bird of the air,
 In search of a home and a rest;
A balm for the sickness of care,
 A bliss for a bosom unblest.

And swift as the swallow that floats,
 And bold as the eagle that soars,
Yet dull as the owlet whose notes
 The dark fiend of midnight deplores!

Wife, infant, and country, and friend,
 Ye wizard my fancy no more,
I fly from your solace, and wend
 To weep on some kindlier shore.

The grim-visaged fiend of the storm
 That raves in this agonized breast,
Still raises his pestilent form,
 Till Death calm the tumult to rest.

In the early part of March, 1886, a correspondent signing himself J. J. Y., asked the editor of the New York "World" for some information about Astrology, and received the following for his answer, "In this day and generation, a man who believes that the planets govern our actions should not let any one know it, such an admission is prima facie evidence of insanity or idiocy."

Learned men and editors of newspapers are constantly making remarks similar to the above without bringing a single fact to prove their assertions. In short all the facts that I have gained from experience and inserted in this book, go to prove the very opposite, so much so that I cannot but regard all persons who do not "believe that the planets govern our actions, is prima facie evidence of insanity or idiocy." It certainly proves ignorance or stupidity.

All the nativities that I have given prove this beyond a question, and I am waiting for the enemies of Astrology to prove the opposite. For instance let them produce a horoscope of a person in which the Moon first makes an opposition of Saturn or Mars or even Mercury, like Lord Byron's, and prove that they lived happy married lives, or like Lillian Russell, where Saturn is in the ascendant in opposition to Mars, setting, and prove that they were happy in marriage.

The planets not only have a great influence in controlling our actions, but they control our thoughts and our speech. We have a remarkable proof of this assertion in Lord Byron's "Farewell to England." Had Byron had a fortunate horoscope for marriage how different his "Farewell" would have read.

If Byron had had a nativity like Queen Victoria for marriage, whose Sun made a good aspect of Jupiter in the midheaven, and Jupiter also lord of the 7th house, then instead of railing against his wife he would have been praising her and regarding marriage as the greatest blessing that could come to either man or woman, and like Queen Victoria would not recognize a man or woman who was divorced from their husband or wife.

HOROSCOPE OF THE YOUNG KING OF SPAIN.

Alfonso XIII., King of Spain, was born May 17th, 1886, at 0.30 P. M., Madrid, Spain.

This young King was born with 8° of Virgo rising and 5° of Gemini culminating; Mercury is lord of both the ascendant and midheaven, and is his ruling planet; he has Mars and Jupiter in the ascendant. Mars in sextile to Saturn on the cusp of the 11th house, and Jupiter in close trine to Neptune, and the Sun both culminating.

The Moon is low down in the 3d house, in Scorpio, leaving a good aspect of Mars, and making a good aspect of Jupiter. The student to get a personal description of the young King, should read par. 18, page 97, par. 129, page 118, par. 97, page 112, par. 85, page 109, par. 105, page 113, and par. 247, page 121, par. 225, page 133, par. 214, page 132.

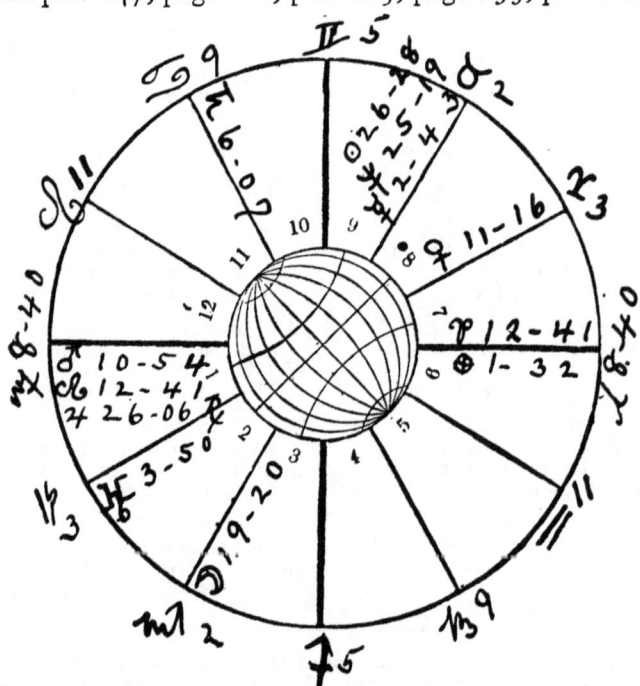

Chart of the Heavens for the Birth of the Young King of Spain, May 17th, 1886, 0.30 p. m., Madrid, Spain.

As Alfonso grows up he will be rather dark complexioned, near or below the medium height, not tall, but have a straight walk, rather high forehead, prominent eyes and nose, fine noble features, and rather handsome, but very likely to get a mark or scar on the face in some part of his life. He will also be very liable to meet with accidents, particularly to the head, face and abdomen. As he gets older he will become quite stout, similar to Queen Victoria, as he is born under the same planet in the same sign, and then he will look much shorter, but will have a very gentlemanly appearance, and like the Queen, he will be very ambitious.

Mars in the ascendant in aspect to Saturn in the 11th house, (the house of friends,) will cause him, when he becomes of age, often to be at

Alphonso XIII., King of Spain, his Mother, the Queen Regent, and his Two Sisters.

war with other nations, but he will generally come off victorious, and gain much renown. His horoscope is fortunate for overcoming his enemies, both in war and diplomacy.

Jupiter in the ascendant in trine to the Sun near the midheaven, makes him very benevolent, kind-hearted and affectionate, especially to friends, for whom he will be willing to make great sacrifices, if they are in need or distress. But Saturn in the 11th house will make his friends very deceitful toward him, and those whom he helps are almost certain to return evil for good, or become enemies. His horoscope in that respect is similar to Horace Greeley, as the late editor had Saturn in the 11th house (or house of friends.)*

He has what we call a very fortunate horoscope, I think equally as fortunate as Queen Victoria's, as Jupiter in the ascendant in exact trine to the Sun and Neptune in the young King's horoscope is equally as strong as Victoria's Jupiter in the midheaven in good aspect to Mars.

Spain will be very prosperous under his reign, and it will become one of the leading nations of the earth before his death. He will have a religious tendency, but will be liberal, or opposed to superstition, and the Catholic Church in his kingdom will undergo reforms during his reign.

The Sun is the giver of life in this horoscope, and its being so well dignified by being near the midheaven and in trine to Jupiter in the ascendant, there is no doubt he will live to be an old man,† the only danger is, he may be killed in war by fire-arms or by accident, but I shall expect them to be only narrow escapes. On the whole, he will enjoy good health, but be liable to suffer from weakness of the stomach, liver and intestines; he will also have some kidney difficulty if he does not lead a temperate life.

He is very likely to marry early in life, and will be very fortunate in marriage. The first aspect the Moon makes is to Jupiter, although previous to that it will make an opposition of Neptune, but the native

---

* Horace Greeley in one of his editorials in the "New York Tribune" advised his readers to assist and help one another. He stated that he had often helped people and lent them money, but it had been his misfortune never to have anything returned to him, except in one instance, when he received $5.00 in a letter from a person he had formerly lent that amount to, and it was so contrary to all his previous experiences that he was astonished, but on looking at the heading of the letter which contained the $5.00, he found it was written in an "insane asylum." So it will be the case of the young King of Spain; if ever he has any borrowed money returned to him, he will know that party has become insane, instead of honest.

† I copy the following remarks of the young King of Spain from the New York Journal of March 9th, 1898.

"Young Alphonso XIII. has all the marks of degeneracy apparent in his features. He has the protruding ears, upon which point of physiognomy Max Nordau lays so much stress; he has a nose flattened at the point, a sloping forehead and a receding jaw, and he talks with a lisp."

I have often observed that the planetary influences are much stronger than hereditary tendencies, as they have already been proved in the case of the young King of Spain.

When it was first cabled over that the young King of Spain was born, it was the general impression that he could not live, having had such a profligate father, who shortened his life by his bad habits. His mother not bearing the best name for virtue and good conduct, and all his relations for several generations had not the best of reputation for correct living, yet when I saw his horoscope, I was convinced that he not only would live to grow up, but live to be an old man, become very powerful as a King, and be equally as successful during his reign as Queen Victoria has been during hers.

When Victoria Alexandria was likely to become Queen of England, the impression was general that she could not live, as all her forefathers had been unfortunate in their married lives, and insanity ran in the family. Her father and most of her relations died young. Her grandfather, George III. was insane for many years, and her uncle George IV. had led a very profligate life, and did not live with his wife, and her own mother did not have the very best of reputation, as King William accused her of not treating her daughter properly. Her great great grandfather and her great grandfather, George I. and George II., had very bad reputations for morality, and yet Queen Victoria has led a very honorable and virtuous life, and has been a pattern for the wives of England.

Such horoscopes as the young King of Spain and Queen Victoria's, appear to defy all hereditary taints, and the planetary influences seems to overcome all degenerating tendencies. No matter what kind of ears, nose and sloping forehead the young King has, he will prove to the sorrow of the Kings and Emperors of Europe the fortunate planetary influences in his horoscope.

never marries the person indicated by the planet Neptune, it will only be a disappointment; very likely to marry when a little over 21 years of age. His wife will be above the medium height, dark complexioned, with dark hair, oval face, high forehead, well built but not stout; a very good carriage and figure, clear or fair skin and handsome features, and somewhat older than himself. For a personal description of the lady the student should see par. 85, page 109, also par. 225, page 133. They will live very happily and both be contented with each other. His wife is likely to live to a good age, but he will outlive her. She will bring him much wealth or territory and influence. His wife will not have a large family of children, probably not more than two or three, of which only one may live, as Saturn is lord of the 5th house, and is in exact opposition to its own sign, and leaving a square of Uranus and making a square of Venus in the 8th house, (the house of death.) She will have more boys than girls.

Spain will be equally as fortunate under the reign of King Alfonso XIII. as that of Great Britain under Queen Victoria, the former having Jupiter in the ascendant, in close trine to the Sun and Neptune, culminating; it is as strong as Victoria's Jupiter in the midheaven, in sextile to Mars in its own sign in the 12th. The Prince was born under Mercury in Taurus, in the 9th house, which is stronger than the ruling planet of Victoria in the 12th house.

The young King generally enjoyed fair health during his early years, but he had an evil time when he was 2 years old, very probably suffered from some severe fever, when Mars came by direction to the ascendant; also another marked evil aspect occured when 7 years old when his life was in great danger. He had a number of evil aspects that commenced about January 1st, 1895. In that year Uranus was transiting over the Moon's place in his horoscope. In January, 1896, Saturn was transiting over his Moon's place which continued to afflict him nearly the whole year. At the same time Uranus came to an opposition of his Neptune and Sun's places, which continued all the year. From May 1st, 1897, to about the middle of November, he had both Uranus and Saturn transiting in opposition to both Neptune and the Sun's places. He and the kingdom of Spain would have felt those evil influences more than they did, if it had not been that during this time, both Uranus and Saturn were in close good aspect to his Jupiter's place in the ascendant, which modified the evil influences and made Spain victorious, but as it was, one misfortune after another befell the nation and colonies, which caused much suffering to both; but those evil aspects have now passed. He has an evil aspect commencing about Feb. 1st, and continuing to the middle of May, 1898. Saturn will be in evil aspect to Mars's place, and afflicting the 4th house during that time, and Spain is likely to be embroiled in serious difficulties, and his own life may be threatened by accident or fire-arms; disturbances and riots, both in Spain and in her colonies, and danger of sickness, accidents or death to his mother is also likely, but after May 1898, the influences gradually improve. He will be very fortunate when he arrives at the age of 22, and Spain will become very prosperous.

HOROSCOPE OF THE MULTI-MILLIONAIRE, JAY GOULD.

This gentleman was born under the planet Mercury, in the last degrees of Gemini, with that sign on the ascendant, and applying to a trine aspect of Saturn, a sextile of Mars, and a trine of Uranus. Six planets were rising. Neptune had culminated, and Saturn and the Moon had set. These positions of the heavenly bodies would describe a person near or below the medium height, slender built, thin face, prominent nose, sunken eyes, of a thoughtful tendency, dark complexion and dark hair. For a personal description of him, see Mercury in Cancer, (not Mercury in Gemini,) as we always describe a person as indicated by the planet in the following sign, or the sign that it is near entering, when it is over 28° degrees in the sign it is leaving. Therefore the student will read for

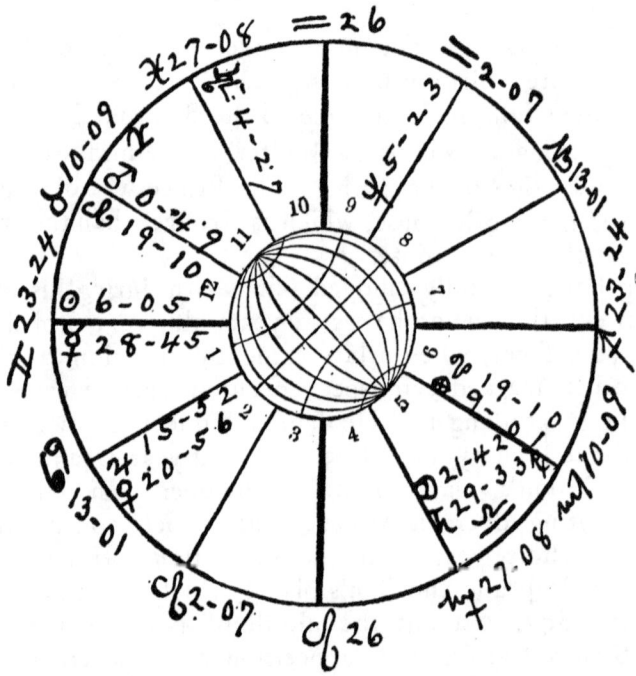

Chart of the Heavens for the Birth of Jay Gould,
May 27th, 1836, at 5.35 a.m., Roxbury, N. Y.

the personal description of Jay Gould, Mercury in Cancer, par. 131, page 118, par. 15, page 97, par. 220, page 133, par. 138, page 134, par. 209, page 132, and also the Moon in the sign Libra, as the Moon is always co-significator in a nativity, and especially in this horoscope, as the Moon is applying to a trine of the planet Mercury, see par. 146, page 120, and by combining the whole, the student will get a very good description, both physical, mental and moral of the late Mr. Jay Gould.

Mercury is near entering a sign in which it has no dignities, but is not otherwise afflicted, so we can not say in this case Mr. Gould was a "very mean little wretch."

One of the main reasons why I have inserted this horoscope is to show the influence of the two most fortunate planets, Jupiter and Venus, in the 2d house (the house of money) unafflicted, except a square of the Moon, which is not counted an affliction; old authors say that that aspect is more fortunate than a good aspect of the Moon to Saturn or Mars. Jupiter is in its exaltation on the cusp of the 2d house in Mr. Gould's horoscope, which makes the money house very fortunate indeed for accumulating wealth, though the close opposition of Mars and Saturn, and the square of the Sun and Uranus, did not make him very particular as to the methods of accumulating it; these evil aspects, particularly the opposition of Mars and Saturn from the house of friends, gave him but few friends who had confidence in him.

No doubt if he had been more honest, and had treated his friends or business associates with a little more consideration, he would have died

Jay Gould.

much richer than he did. Numbers of men have told me they would have nothing to do with him or his stocks under any consideration, for if he learned they were dealing in any securities, over which he had any control, he was certain to try to swindle or ruin them.

It would be very easy for people to become millionaires, (particularly if they were honest,) were they born with Jupiter and Venus strong in the house of money and unafflicted. See par. 2, page 90. One with such a horoscope could not fail to become rich. Mr. Gould accumulated most of his wealth by planning and scheming, and actually robbing others.

There is no question but Mr Gould was one of the smartest men there ever was in Wall Street, his significator, Mercury, is in Gemini in the ascendant, making a trine of Saturn and a sextile of Mars, which made him very smart, a close calculator, and caused him to seldom make a mistake in his calculations.

This horoscope does not indicate one that would live to an old age, as the ascendant is the giver of life, and Mercury is in the ascendant, and in the last degrees of Gemini, in good aspect to the Moon, Saturn and Mars, which would cause him to live to a fair age, but he never would be remarkably strong. No doubt he died from some weakness of the chest or stomach, and suffered from indigestion or liver difficulty.

The horoscope is fortunate for marriage as the Moon first makes a trine aspect of Mercury in the ascendant. Jay Gould and his wife would live rather harmoniously and pleasantly together, but on account of the Moon making a conjunction of Saturn and an opposition of Mars, at the time it made a trine of Mercury, his wife would not live to old age, and he would outlive her; she would have delicate health and seldom be strong.

Mrs. Gould would be near or below the medium height, rather slender when young, but after middle age became slightly full built, oval face, round forehead, rather pale complexion, with brown hair. For a personal description read par. 131, page 118, par. 220, page 133, par. 83, page 109, and combine the whole.

In the horoscope of Mr. Gould Saturn is afflicting the 5th house, and is just leaving a close opposition of Mars in the 11th house; the Moon is separating from a square of Venus, the two planets are not one degree separated; that alone would indicate some scandal or unpleasantness in early life connected with love affairs. If the student turns to par. 303, page 165, he will see the rule for describing the lady a gentleman keeps company with, but does not marry, and for a description of the lady he should read par. 119, page 116.

There is no question but there was some improper conduct on her part, and more than likely a child was born, but that there was no marriage is almost absolute, as the Moon was separating from the aspect of Venus; though possibly the female was made to believe that there was a marriage, as Mr. Gould would not be troubled with very much conscience in such matters, especially in early life.

It does not always imply when the Moon is separating from an aspect of a planet in a male's nativity, even if it is an evil aspect of an evil planet, or that in a female's horoscope, the Sun is separating from an evil aspect of a planet, that in all such cases there has always been some improper condnct between the parties, but it shows strong suspicion. In Mr. Gould's horoscope Saturn is afflicting the 5th house, (the house of pleasure,) in such close opposition to Mars, and the Moon just separating from a square of Venus (the goddess of pleasure,) the aspect is so marked it would show a very strong suspicion, if not an absolute certainty, of improper conduct, even if there had never been a whisper on the subject by any person living.

The Moon in the 5th house, a fruitful planet, and in good aspect to Mercury, indicated he would have a rather large family, and be somewhat fortunate with them, although they wonld cause him at times, a world of trouble, especially in their early years, and also it is very doubtful if his children will be anything like as fortunate as he was on account of the opposition of Saturn and Mars from the 5th house, (or house of children.)

Mr. Gould must have had a great many afflictions in his early life, both from poverty and serious attacks of illness, as all the planets except the Sun that were above the earth at his birth, were evil planets, and Uranus in the midheaven always causes serious misfortunes and unexpected changes to the native in early life ; but those evil influences are indicated in a more marked manner by the close opposition of Saturn and Mars, and those afflictions no doubt had much to do with causing him to be in stature below the medium.

He had marked evil periods at 1, 2, 7, 8, 11, 14 and 15 years of age; each of these times would bring serious illness for himself, and misfortunes for his family, but after that age things would begin to brighten up with him. At 21, 22, 29 and 30 misfortunes would also come, but afterwards prosperity would begin to smile on him.

I explained to several of my pupils Mr. Gould's horoscope, and pointed out the evil aspects for illness, as I deemed it an impossibility for him to live by a certain evil aspect which came up in 1892, as his horoscope did not indicate a long life ; Saturn's transit over the ascendant (the giver of life,) and Uranus over his Sun's place, and in square to its own place, his health began to fail in a very marked degree. These evil influences commenced in Sept., 1890, but they were more marked in the latter part of 1891, and in the spring of 1892, as Saturn was transiting over his ascendant all that time, and Uranus over his Sun's place, but what was most effective in destroying life was when Saturn came to an opposition of the degree ascending by direction, which came up in the latter part of 1892. He died Dec. 2d of that year.

Seven Concise Reasons why Everyone should have a Reading of their Lives, and Strive to Know more of the Science of Astrology.

1. It makes a man or woman acquainted with themselves. It shows them what profession or capacity of life they are best adapted for, and in which they will best succeed.

2. It points out most distinctly the times of prosperity and the times of adversity, thus showing when to push ahead and when to keep quiet.

3. It describes the person you will choose for a wife or husband, and the kind of persons you should choose for friends, and the persons you should avoid who will prove to be enemies.

4. It points out the kind of business or profession you should teach your children for them to be successful.

5. It shows the disease to which the person is naturally subject, also points out the *natural remedy* for such disease.

6. It shows whether a person is liable to accidents or not, and if so when they are in most danger of these accidents.

7. It shows a person what part of the country or world they will be **most prosperous in and enjoy the best health.**

HOROSCOPE OF CHARLES DICKENS.

Mr. Dickens called on Prof. Wilson, an astrologer in London, to have his horoscope calculated, and he afterwards made use of it in one of his novels. Mr. Dickens gave the time of his birth as Feb. 15th, 1812, at 7.50 p. m., Lamport, Hampshire, England.

At the above time 24° of Virgo were rising, which makes Mercury in the sign Aquarius his ruling planet; that will describe a person of medium height, slender built, light brown hair and light complexioned; he had quick eyes, an intelligent look, and was prepossessing in appearance, but as he grew older he became slightly full built. For his personal description and mental abilities see par. 138, page 119, par 18, page 97, par. 140, page 119, pars. 247 and 248, page 135.

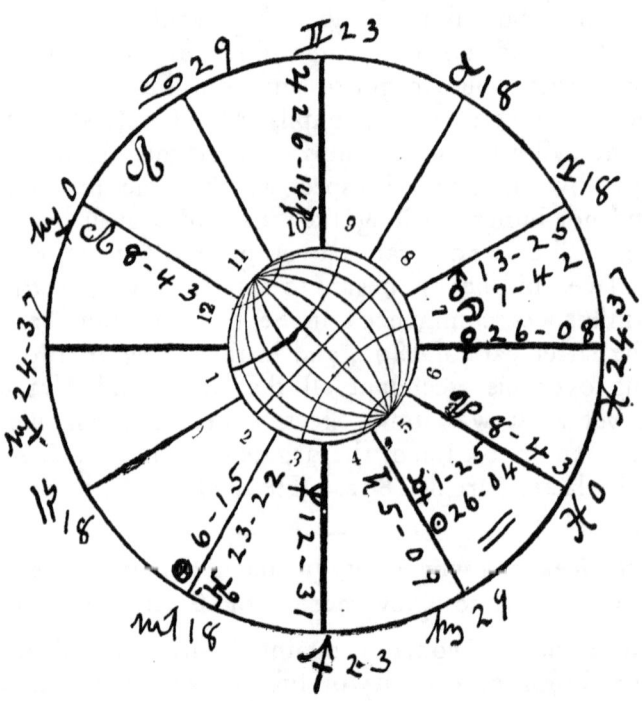

Chart of the Heavens for the Birth of Charles Dickens, Feb. 15th, 1812, at 7.50 p. m., Lamport, Hampshire, England.

What made this horoscope so remarkably fortunate was Jupiter in the midheaven, in the sign Gemini, in almost exact trine to the Sun in Aquarius in the 5th house, (the house of entertainments or amusements,) also Venus in an angle in the 7th house, in its exaltation, just setting, in semi-sextile to the Sun, but in square to Jupiter in the midheaven; a square of Jupiter and Venus is counted a fortunate aspect, rather than unfortunate.)

I have seldom seen a horoscope so fortunate for intellect, and excelling as a writer or speaker; having the Moon in a cardinal sign, Aries, which rules the head, and in an angle in good aspect to his ruling planet Mercury, in a scientific sign, also Jupiter in good aspect in a

Charles Dickens.

scientific sign in the 10th house, gives the highest order of intellect, particularly for scientific subjects, and for being humorous, witty, and sarcastic in his expressions or remarks. These aspects would also cause him to have great ambition to rise in the world, and become prominent and famous.

It would be an impossibility for a person having such a horoscope as Mr. Dickens to remain in obscurity or in low circumstances; he would be certain to rise to prominence and even become wealthy, although he would be a man that would have very extravagant notions, and live in an expensive manner; it would also cause him to be very popular with the people at large and enable him to say and do many things without injury to himself, that would have brought misfortune, if not imprisonment, on any man that had an unfortunate horoscope. Yet the Moon just leaving a square of Saturn would cause him to have much trouble connected with home affairs and domestic life, and even some of his near neighbors would make trouble for him. Mr. Dickens must have had much unpleasantness in love affairs previous to marriage, which would probably delay marriage until 25 years of age. The Moon separating from a square of Saturn, indicates a lady described by that planet in Capricorn that he would keep company with but not marry. See par. 303, page 165, and for a personal description of the lady, see par. 77, page 107; the Moon also made a trine aspect of Neptune, but he would not marry that lady either. See par. 301, page 164.

The next aspect the Moon makes is a conjunction of Mars in the 7th house, and being an unfortunate aspect, and to an unfortunate planet, would not produce much harmony or happiness in married life. See par. 300, page 164. For a personal description of his wife see par. 92, page 111, also par. 127, page 117, and combine the two to describe her temper and her mental abilities. As Venus is in Pisces in the 7th house (the house of marriage,) in square to Jupiter, there would never be much love or happiness between Mr. Dickens and his wife, as it would cause her to be jealous and suspicious of other women. After living together for 20 years, and having several children they agreed, by mutual consent, to a separation. The conjunction of the Moon and Mars in the 7th house, would cause his wife to have a bad temper and make her tyrannical.

The wife's sister, who probably had much to do with their separation, and who afterwards kept house for Mr. Dickens, is indicated by the planet Venus in Pisces in the 7th house, and lady of the 9th house, (the house of the wife's relations.) See par. 127, page 117, also par. 82, page 109 for her description, temper, etc. She would be much more agreeable and pleasant in her manners than his wife.

Although Mr. Dickens had several children born to him, still he would not live harmoniously with them, as the Moon is in square to Saturn, lord of the 5th house, (the house of children,) and they would be of little benefit to him, and very probably he did not reside with them. Mr. Dickens generally would enjoy fair health, but would suffer much from poverty and misfortune in early life, as Saturn is afflicting the 4th house, and especially its being in square to the Moon would make much unhappiness for him in early life, and would also cause much quarreling between his father and mother. He died June 9th, 1870, when Saturn was in the 4th house in almost exact square to his ascendant and his Venus's place, and Uranus was in the 10th house, in almost exact square to Mars.

"There is a tide in the affairs of men which, taken at the flood, leads on to fortune. Omitted, all the voyage of life is bound in shallows and in miseries "—SHAKESPEARE.

Astrology has been accepted and practiced by the greatest and most intelligent minds that have ever lived. The study of Astrology teaches one of the greatest and most universal "Laws of Nature" which no other science does teach.

HOROSCOPE OF GEN. ULYSSES SIMPSON GRANT,

BORN APRIL 27TH, 1822, AT 5.00 A. M., GALENA, ILL.

The time of birth was obtained from Gen. Grant's father, and no doubt it is correct; if so he was born with 3° of Taurus rising, and Venus, lady of that sign, in the sign Pisces in the 12th house, in close good aspect to the Moon in Cancer in the 4th house, and Saturn, Jupiter and the Sun all in the ascendant, which caused him to be born under the four above named planets and the Moon.

They would describe a person near or below the medium height, full built and inclined to be stout, sunburnt or swarthy complexioned, with rather full face, broad forehead, and lightish brown hair.

In order to get a personal description from this horoscope both physically, intellectually and morally, the student should read, par. 14, page 97, par. 127, page 117, par. 143, page 120, par. 69, page 106, par. 105, page 113, par. 81, page 108, and combine the whole; by so doing he will get a very good personal description of Gen. Grant as he appeared in the prime of life. He will also arrive at his disposition and temperament.

What made Gen. Grant so successful in his battles against the rebels was his having three superior planets rising in the ascendant, in a fixed sign, Taurus, and all in close good aspect to Uranus near the midheaven. Venus in its exaltation in close good aspect to the Moon in her own sign, in an angle, contributed also to his success; and what made Gen. Grant so unfortunate in early life and practically kept him almost in poverty up to nearly 40 years of age, was Saturn rising within orbs of the ascendant and above the Sun and Jupiter, at his birth.

If Gen. Washington had had Saturn rising above his Venus in Aries at birth, he would have met with much more misfortune, poverty and distress than he did, especially in early life, and he wonld not have been so successful as a general, but more likely would have been hung as a rebel, as Gen. Washington did not have three superior planets in his ascendant as did Gen. Grant.

Is it not a remarkable coincidence that Gen. Grant and Gen. Washington should both die of throat disease, and each had Taurus on the ascendant which governs the throat, and Gen. Grant had Saturn so seriously afflicting the ascendant by conjunction, and Gen. Washington had Mars in close opposition to the ascendant, which aspect would be almost certain to cause his death by some affection of the throat.

Is it not a strong proof of the truth of Astrology, that Gen. Grant and Gen. Washington should both have been born under the same planet—Venus—and that in both horoscopes Venus should be on the cusp of the 12th house, and that Gen. Grant's Venus should be in a short stout sign, and three planets rising in a short, stout sign, and Washington's Venus in a tall, light, slender sign, and the Moon also in a tall, slender sign, and that the personal appearance of both gentlemen should exactly agree with that indicated in each of their nativities.

There is a rule in Astrology which the student should try and keep in mind, and that is, "When the early degrees of a tall or short sign is on the ascendant, the person is almost invariably short in stature, or at least they are not tall, but when near 20° of a sign is on the ascendant, it is almost certain to give a person of tall stature. But the last few degrees of the sign gives a shorter stature. I have found this almost an invariable rule in Astrology. What made Gen. Grant so original in planning and conquering in battles, was Uranus near the midheaven, in close trine to Saturn, Sun and Jupiter, all in the ascendant. It also made him an original thinker, and not a fighter of battles according to any special military rule; in that respect he was very similar to Napoleon Bonaparte, who was born under Mars in Virgo, near the midheaven, in close trine to Uranus just setting.

Gen. Ulysses Simpson Grant.

Uranus near the midheaven caused Gen. Grant to have a great many ups and downs during his early life, and also caused him many financial losses and misfortunes in the latter part of his life, as it was near a mundane square to the ascendant.

Persons born with Saturn in the ascendant generally have to suffer poverty in their early years and very often are in poor or weak health all through early life. Saturn in the ascendant and Venus in a watery sign in close aspect to the Moon, caused him to acquire the habit of using tobacco and stimulants.

The Moon first made a square of Saturn for his marriage, which certainly in early married life could not have been very fortunate, or conducive to happiness, although being in the ascendant they would become much more attached to each other after middle age. For a personal description of Gen. Grant's wife see par. 69, page 106, also par. 96, page 111, which describes a lady near the medium height, full built, pale complexion, dark hair, and not very refined in appearance or manner.

An evil planet in the 5th house, as Gen. Grant had, is not very good for children; they are apt to be extravagant, if not a source of annoyance to their parents.

It is very seldom that we see a horoscope so strong for overcoming enemies or difficulties as that of Gen. Grant's, with three superior planets in the ascendant in fixed signs; there were very few generals in the army during the rebellion that had stronger or more powerful horoscopes.

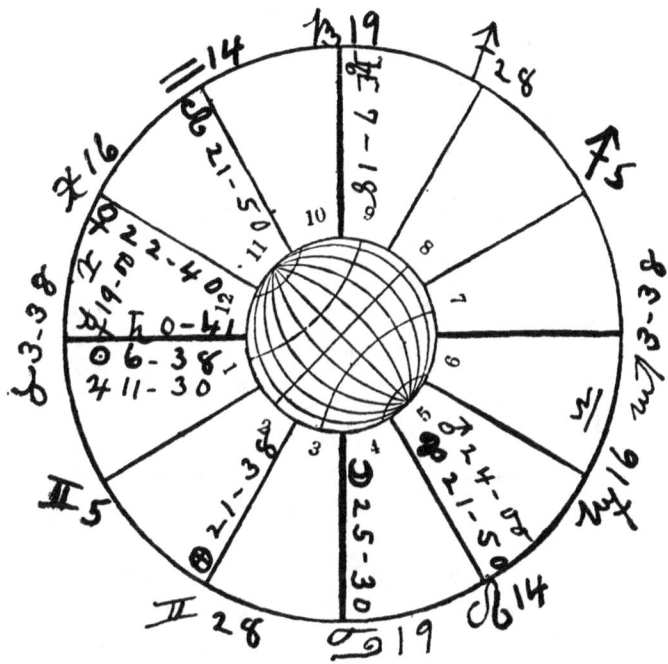

Chart of the Heavens for the Birth of Gen. Ulysses Simpson Grant, April 27th, 1822, 5.00 a. m., at Galena, Ill.

Being born under the planet Venus in the 12th house, (the house of sorrow,) although in good aspect to the Moon, caused him to have periods of worry and despondency, even after he became general, and afterwards President of the United States; and Saturn, lord of the 11th house, afflicting the ascendant, caused him to be exceedingly unfortunate in regard to his friends. He would generally be surrounded by unprincipled people.

The planet Venus in its exaltation rising in close trine to the Moon in the 4th house in its own sign, indicates that Gen. Grant's name will last probably as long as the name of the United States.

"The ruling stars above; by secret laws,
Determine Fortune in her second cause;
These are a book wherein we all may read,
And all should know who would in life succeed."

The history of Astrology is coeval with that of man. It formed the basis of all ancient religions and mythology, and is indissolubly interwoven with the sacred truths of the Christian religion.

346   ELEMENTS OF ASTROLOGY.

From Broughton's Monthly Planet Reader, for Sept., 1861.
HOROSCOPE OF PRESIDENT GEORGE WASHINGTON,
BORN FEB. 11TH, 1732, AT 10 A. M., VIRGINIA.

"He was a man, take him for all in all,
I shall not look upon his like again."—SHAKESPEARE.

"In Mr. Edward Everett's 'Life of Gen. Washington' it states that in the family Bible now in possession of George Washington Bassett, of Hanover county, Virginia, the following entry is found: 'George Washington, son to Augustine and Mary his wife, was born ye 11th day of February, 1732, about 10 in the morning.' And then Mr. Everett adds that he was accordingly born on the 22d of February, new style.

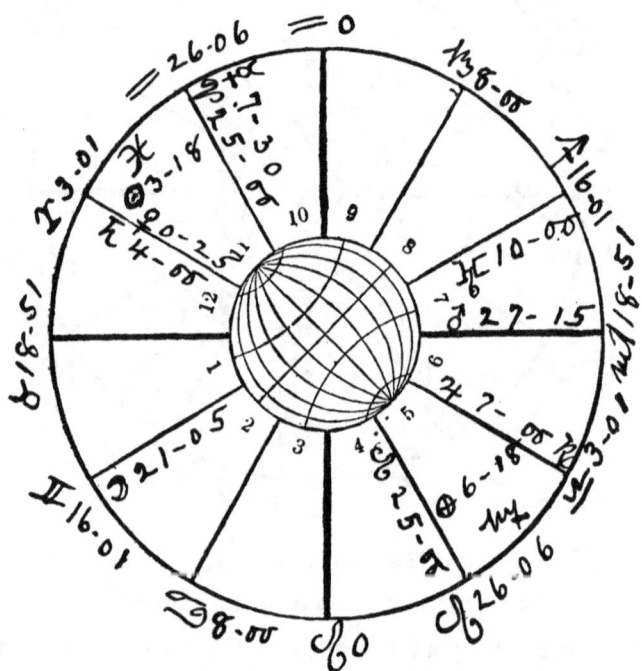

Chart of the Heavens for the Birth of Gen. George Washington,
Feb. 11th, 1732, at 10 a. m., Virginia.

"The above time of birth caused Gen. Washington to be born under the planet Venus, in the sign Aries, with the sign Taurus on the ascendant, and the Moon in Gemini rising, which positions of Venus and the Moon will describe a person of tall stature, sanguine complexion, and the planet Mars in his own sign, just setting would cause him to be of a pensive aspect; also Venus being in trine to Mars, caused him to be rather handsome, and of a noble carriage. He would be of a mild disposition and temper, but firm, yet at times of a very high temper, but it would soon be over. The Moon being in the sign Gemini, the house of Mercury, and Venus his ruling planet, would give him good mental abilities, and a very refined turn of mind. He would have a decided taste for music, poetry, painting, etc. Venus applying to a conjunction of Saturn, and Saturn in sextile aspect to Mercury, and Mercury in trine to Jupiter, would indicate that he would be of a very independent spirit, and whenever he undertook anything, he would scorn to give it up until he had brought it to a final issue. Venus in trine to Mars, would cause him to have a taste for military life, in a just cause, and for gaining knowledge in warlike implements, etc. But Venus applying to a conjunction of Saturn would show that if he had had his choice he would have preferred a retired life, and it would cause him to be of a religious turn of mind. Venus being in trine to Uranus, would show that he was quite original, in his thoughts and actions, and would never be an imitator. The aspects in Gen. Washington's horoscope would indicate that the most remarkable trait in his character would be perseverance.

Gen. George Washington.

MARRIAGE.

"The Moon first makes a square of Venus in this horoscope, and the planet Mars being in the seventh house, (house of marriage) would indicate that the lady he married would be denoted by the above two planets, but chiefly by the planet Venus, which will describe a person about the middle stature, well built, but rather corpulent, round face, good complexion, and dark hair. In temper rather passionate, but soon over. The quality of the mind would be ingenious, active in gaining knowledge; she would likewise be very proud, and of an independent spirit, and rather fond of dress and company.

"The time of Gen. Washington's marriage would be when he was near twenty-seven years of age, while the planet Jupiter was transiting over the 10th house, in good aspect to his own place, and I should say that it would then be a fortunate time for him generally.

"We have not space to notice all the fortunate and unfortunate periods of his life, but might mention that at ten years and again at fifteen years of age were unfortunate periods for him; and also at twenty years of age was another unfortunate period. But the most fortunate period was in 1787 when he had Jupiter passing over the ascendant and over the Moon's place, besides several other fortunate aspects; and then again at fifty-seven years of age, when he was elected President for the first time.

Children.

"Leo, a barren sign, being on the cusp of the 5th house (the house of children) and Virgo another barren sign, being intercepted in the 5th house, and the Moon in Gemini, another barren sign, all would indicate that his wife would not have any children to live.

"On the whole, Gen. Washington's horoscope is one of the most remarkable I have ever examined, and if space permitted to make all the calculations, and trace them through his whole life, and see how they agreed with the events that happened to him, it would go far towards proving Astrology a true science."

For the description of Gen. Washington, First, physically, as indicated by the planets at the time of birth see par. 116, page 115, par. 44, page 102, par. 142, page 120, par. 14, page 97, par. 99, page 112. Second, his mental qualities see par. 138, page 119, par. 86, page 109, pars. 229 and 230, page 133, par. 142, page 120, par. 220, page 133. Third, his temper, etc., see par. 256, page 137, par. 220, page 133, par. 236, page 134. For the personal description and mental faculties of his wife, see Venus in Aries, Mars in Scorpio, and Venus in trine to Mars.

The Sun, lord of the 5th house (house of speculation, etc.,) is in the 11th house in opposition to the Part of Fortune in the 5th house. This caused Gen. Washington to be generally unfortunate in card playing, and he refers a number of times in his diary to his bad luck in gambling. The enduring good name that Washington has received is indicated by Mercury being in a scientific and human sign in the midheaven, unafflicted; also the close trine of Mercury to the planet Jupiter setting; a sextile aspect of both Jupiter and Mercury to Uranus, near setting, and Mars being in its own sign in an angle just setting, also the Moon rising and leaving a good aspect of Mercury and Jupiter, and the Moon not afflicted by any planet.

The Moon in the 2d house, (the house of money,) caused Gen. Washington to be very careful in regard to money matters, and to keep a strict account of his expenses.

Had Gen. Washington studied to be a physician instead of a soldier, he would have left an enduring name, and would have been exceedingly successful in his practice, as is indicated by Jupiter in the 6th house, (the house of sickness,) and in close good aspect to Mercury in the midheaven, and applying to a good aspect of Uranus on the cusp of the 8th house. His very presence in a sick room would have been beneficial to his patients and they would have got well, even if he gave them nothing but cold water. It is very seldom that we see a horoscope so remarkably fortunate for being successful as a doctor.

Mr. Elkanah Watson gives a very interesting account in his diary of his visit to Mount Vernon in 1785. On his journey he had taken a severe cold, it being a harsh wintry day, and he coughed excessively. Washington pressed him to take some remedy to relieve it, but he declined. After retiring his cough increased; Washington during the night entered his bedroom, and came to the bedside with a bowl of hot tea in his hands to relieve his cough.

I give this illustration of Washington's tenderness and kindness to persons when suffering from illness. Had Washington prescribed a bowl of hot tea for himself during his last illness, instead of being treated by the Allopathic doctors, it is probable that he might have lived to witness the prosperity of his country for a number of years longer.

Prof. Draper on William Lilly's Astrology.

On page 183 and 184 of this work under the heading "Medical Astrology," I gave an account of Prof. Draper, of this city, publishing an article in "Harper's Magazine," ridiculing William Lilly and his work on Astrology. I there stated if Dr. Draper had wanted material for a Farce or a Comic Opera for the college students, he need not have gone back two hundred years in search of it. Such material he might have found in his own country and within one hundred years, and in his own system of treating disease, or what is called the allopathic practice of medicine. If not too serious a matter for jest, the last illness and death of Gen. George Washington, and the treatment by the allopathic doctors for croup at that time, would be a splendid subject for an audience of Medical students, and cause them to split their sides with laughter over, if they could only disabuse their minds of the idea that it was a real tragedy. However I give the account of the treatment of Gen. Washington's last illness as published by his physicians and will let the student judge for himself.

Sickness and Allopathic Treatment of Gen. George Washington.

Most of the prominent or wealthy men and women of this country have been helped out of this world by the doctors. I refer to the death of Gen. Washington, Vice-President Hendricks, Brigham Young, Roscoe Conkling and Gen. Grant, and I might mention hundreds of other names. "I could a tale unfold," in the treatment of the last sickness of any of these men, but I will only touch upon the doctor's allopathic treatment of the first named gentleman. I choose this one on account of his name being more generally known than any of the others; and for the reason that there cannot be a question raised in regard to the last treatment of Gen. Washington by the allopathic doctors, as we have the account of it signed by his attending physicians. Also I believe it is not generally known by the people of the United States that Geo. Washington did not die a natural death, but was murdered by his doctors. And bear in mind, in pub'ishing these statements, that I do not refer to the lower class or the most ignorant of the allopathic doctors, but on the contrary to those who are the leaders in this particular practice, and to those who are determined that we shall have no other system of medicine.

Gen. Washington appeared to have had a charmed life until he met with those allopathic doctors. I believe in all the battles in which he was engaged, he never received a wound, and was but seldom ill. During the retreat of Gen. Braddock, there was an Indian who afterwards stated that he (the Indian) took deliberate aim, and shot at Col. Washington, some six or eight different times, and yet he missed him every time, although the Indian was counted a "good shot." Therefore he came to the conclusion that Washington was protected by the *Great Spirit*. But after the allopathic doctors began doctoring him, his charmed life soon vanished from the world.

I copy the last treatment of Gen. Washington from the "*Botanic Medical Reformer and Home Physician*," published by Dr. Henry Hollembaek, in Philadelphia, Pa , Dec 19th, 1840, Vol. 1, No. 7. Dr. Henry Hollembaek was professor of Materia Medica and Therapeutics in the medical college from which I graduated.

I have seen the same report of Gen. Washington's last sickness printed in an English allopathic medical work, and it was there published as a *specimen of the American heroic practice of medicine*. And no doubt the reader will come to the conclusion that it was even more heroic than the treatment of Mr. Maybrick, who died in Liverpool, England; as Mr. Maybrick was under the doctor's treatment for near three weeks before they succeeded in killing him, whereas, Gen. Washington was only under his doctor's treatment for a little over twelve hours. Yet during that short period he was bled copiously at three different times, and once the night before. And they gave him 20 or 30 grains of CALOMEL, 5 or 6 grains of EMETIC TARTAR, besides the blisters and other treatment, enough to kill any man.

The Physician's Report of Gen. Washington's Last Sickness.

"Some time in the night of Friday, the 13th of December, 1799, having been exposed to rain on the preceding day, Gen. Washington was attacked with an inflammatory affection of the upper part of the wind-pipe, called in technical language *cynanche trachealis*. The disease commenced with a violent ague, accompanied by some pain in the upper and fore part of the throat, a sense of stricture in the same part, a cough and a difficult rather than a painful deglutition, which were soon succeeded by a fever and a quick and laborious respiration. The necessity of blood letting suggested itself to the General, he procured A BLEEDER in the neighborhood, who took from his arm in the night, TWELVE or FOURTEEN OUNCES OF BLOOD; he would not by any means be prevailed upon by the family to send for the attending physician till the following morning, who arrived at Mount Vernon at about eleven o'clock on Saturday, December 14th. Discovering the case to be highly alarming, and foreseeing the fatal tendency of the disease, two consulting physicians were immediately sent for, who arrived, one at half past three, the other at four o'clock in the afternoon. In the interem were employed TWO COPIOUS BLEEDINGS, a blister was applied to the part affected, two moderate doses of CALOMEL were given, and an injection administered, which operated on the lower intestines—but without any perceptible advantage, the respiration becoming still more difficult and distressing.

"Upon the arrival of the first of the consulting physicians it was agreed, as there was yet no signs of accumulation in the bronchial vessels of the lungs, to try the result of ANOTHER BLEEDING, when about THIRTY-TWO OUNCES of BLOOD were drawn, without the smallest apparent alleviation of the disease. Vapors of vinegar and water were frequently inhaled, TEN GRAINS OF CALOMEL were given and succeeded by REPEATED DOSES OF EMETIC TARTAR, amounting in all to five or six grains, with no other effect than a copious discharge from the bowels. The powers of life seemed now manifestly yielding to the force of the disorder. Blisters were applied to the extremities, together with a cataplasm of bran and vinegar to the throat. Speaking, which was painful from the beginning, now became almost impracticable; respiration grew more and more contracted and imperfect, till after eleven o'clock on Saturday night, retaining the full possession of his intellect, when he—*expired without a struggle!*"

JAMES CRAIK, Att. Physician,
ELISHA C. DICK, Con. Physician.

If any one can read the above account of Gen. Washington's death *without a struggle*, I give him credit for stronger nerves than I possess. When these doctors put themselves in evidence, and were their own judge and jury and convicted themselves, it is reasonable to suppose they did not make their case any blacker than they could help. On the contrary there is no doubt that "not one half has been told." I have read in several lives of Gen. Washington that "he begged and prayed for the doctors to let him alone, and let him die quietly," and there is no doubt but what they tortured him to death by their bleeding, blistering and poisonous medicines.

Dr. Craik and Dr. Dick published the above report as the regular treatment for Croup, and the abstracting of over a half gallon of blood in twenty-four hours, and the number of blisters and the quantity of poisonous medicines administered in that short time, as in no way extraordinary in treating cases of Croup; yet I cannot but believe if any doctor was to treat a similar disease in that manner at the present day, it would cause a sensation if it was published and the patient died.

Dr. Hollembaek in his comments on the sickness and treatment of Gen. Washington says: "Had the physicians in attendance administered a syrup, the basis of which should have been *Lobelia Inflata*, with a little milder treatment on the *botanic* plan, they would not have deprived that great and good man the pleasure of beholding a little longer the freedom and prosperity of that country for which he had so assiduously labored to achieve. The destruction of such a man as Washington by the means mentioned above, should be indeed, a warning never to be forgotten, and we sincerely hope that our friends and the public will profit by it. We hope this case will prove a warning, not only to the physicians of the allopathic school, but to individuals who may need medical aid. Let them shun this deadly instrument, the *lancet*, also *calomel and all similar poisons*, as they would shun the fatal *sting of that reptile* which has been chosen as the emblem of the allopathic school of medicine, the wily and deadly *serpent*."

What a slaughter of innocents must have occured fifty or one hundred years ago when they were bleeding the patients for every complaint in the nosology of diseases, and prescribing their depleting remedies. Even in my own time and what I have observed of the allopathic practice of medicine, in the words of Hamlet's father's ghost, "I could a tale unfold whose lightest word would harrow up thy soul and freeze thy young blood."

If Prof. Draper had wanted another case for a farce for the entertainment of his college students, the treatment of Mr. Maybrick, Liverpool, England, in 1889, who was supposed to have been poisoned by his wife, would answer his purpose very well. Indeed it is sometimes an impossibility to find out after death whether the patient died from the poisons of the intended murderer or the poisons prescribed by the old-school doctors. We have a remarkable instance in that of Mr. Maybrick, whom his wife tried to poison with arsenic, and whom the doctors finished with their treatment. The doctors in that case ought to have been put on trial for their lives, the same as she was.

I copy the following in reference to the Maybrick case from the New York *World*, September 6th, 1889:

MODERN MEDICATION;
Or, the Allopathic Treatment of Mr. Maybrick.

"The practice of medicine in Liverpool is apparently in a state fully justifying the old definition of a physician as a 'man who pours drugs of which he knows little into a body of which he knows less.'

"During his last illness of something like three weeks, the late Mr. Maybrick took from the hands of his physicians the longest and most incongruous list of medicines, of which public record has yet been made. Here is the catalogue, copied from an English druggists' trade journal:

Morphia suppositories.
Ipecachuanha wine.
Papain and Iridin solution.
Cascara sagrada,
Nitro-hydrochloric acid.
Tincture nux vomica,
Fowler's solution.
Plummer's pill.
Dilute hydrocyanic acid.
Tincture of henbane.
Bromide of potassium.
Antipyrin.
Tincture of jaborandi.
Bismuth.
Sulphonal.
Cocaine.
Nitroglycerine.
Dilute phosphoric acid.
Solution of chlorine, sanitas, glycerine and Condy's fluid as mouth washes.

"This list is justly characterized by the trade journal which published it, as 'a jumble of irrational empiricism,' and the question every physician will ask upon reading it is, "What sort of seventeenth-century quacks are permitted to practice in Liverpool in the last quarter of the nineteenth century?"

Mr. Maybrick was dying of arsenical poisoning, and his doctors helped him to death by drenching him with pretty nearly everything they could think of except an antidote for arsenic. Carminatives, purgatives, explosives and acids were indiscriminately jumbled in the poor man's stomach."

If Mr. Maybrick or Gen. Washington had lived through the sickness referred to, they would have felt the effect of their treatment for a long time afterwards, and might never have entirely overcome the bleeding and poisonous medicine that the doctors gave them. The great French Dr. Brown-Sequard's remedy, *the Elixir of Life*, which made such a great sensation among all the allopathic doctors a few years ago, both in Europe and in America, had to be stopped on account of the great destruction of human life which it caused, and the great number of cripples and permanent invalids which it made.

Dr. Koch's remedy for consumption which made such a sensation all over Europe and America a few years ago, is also a remedy that is very dangerous to human life. Indeed some say that it is more *poisonous than the bite of a rattlesnake*. And besides its being a *quack or secret remedy*, its *curative effects are yet to be proven*.

The late Mr. Pasteur of Paris is reported as saying: "Up to this moment, there has not been a single authenticated cure, not even of lupus. Dr. Bergmann himself has seen a patient suffering from lupus return to his hospital, fifteen days after having been discharged as cured, a severe relapse having occured even within that brief interval. Moreover, there is no real certainty as to the consequences of the treatment. The actions of this medicament is of unheard-of virulence, and the reactions which it brings on are terrible.

No venom from a snake, if administered in such small doses (two-tenths of a milligramme) could cause such results. We have therefore a toxic of such indomitable energy that it may introduce into the organism disorders the consequences of which no one can surmise, and have yet to be studied. You may have seen a report in the medical papers, that albuminuria and hæmaturia have been found in a patient who had been treated for tuberculosis, with very small doses of this lymph. In fact, it is the kidneys that are particularly affected by it."—(New York *Medical Record*, Dec. 27th, 1890.)

I copy the following from the New York *Herald* of March 8th, 1891:

"We all know, now, says Prof. Verneuil, in a recent clinical lecture delivered at the Hotel Dieu of Paris, how prompt was the collapse of this famous discovery, and how much remains to-day of the hopes that had been so lightly placed on a laboratory product, ill defined, untried, badly administered and which, in spite of the guarantee of the government of the German Empire, has produced, since it was foolishly transferred from the guinea pig cage to clinical medicine, nothing but deceptions and disaster. Added to this comes the opinion of Professor Virchow in a paper read before the Medical Society of Berlin, in which he related the results of twenty one post mortems that he had performed of persons who had undergone Koch's treatment. Dr. Virchow declared that the injections increased the number of bacilli and made them emigrate into parts of the body that had not been affected before that, creating in this way a new disease. The Professor adds that the lymph invariably produces intense hyperæmia, which endangers the patient's life. Up to the present time Dr. Koch's treatment has not given a single case of recovery, not only of pulmonary tuberculosis, or even of lupus: *on the other hand it has killed a relatively large number of persons who might have lived a long time.* When we consider that even those who survive the treatment present extremely serious symptoms (intense fever, delirium, albumenuria, hematuria, etc.,) we come to the conclusion that it will be better to wait until Dr. Koch can show the medical world undeniable cases of recovery before resorting to a therapeutical method which so far has only produced disaster. And until a case of authentic recovery can be shown I think it will be better to refrain from speaking of a remedy which all sensible persons have declined to use."

A cure for the Bite of a Rattlesnake.

A short time ago I read in the papers that an allopathic doctor in Australia had discovered a remedy for the bite of a rattlesnake, and the remedy was *strychnine,* to be injected by hypodermic syringes into the patient, supposed to have been bitten by the rattlesnake.

If the patient died, who could tell whether he died from the *bite of the rattlesnake* or from the *poisoning of the strychnine.* This is a real specimen of allopathic practice of medicine.

It is a debatable question in my mind whether the liqour traffic or the allopathic treatment of disease, is the most destructive of human life, and which produces the most misery in all parts of the civilized world.

Who are the Regulars and Who are the Quacks?

The reader may think that I am writing at random and making statements of which I have no proof; but, besides my own observations in regard to the allopathic practice of medicine, I find there are other doctors who have made similar observations. In 1890, S. E. Chapman, M. D., of California, published a pamphlet "Who are the Regulars?" Previous to doing so he sent to the leading physicians in the principal cities of the United States the following letter :

"Dear Doctor : I am a great sufferer from indigestion, and apply to you for a prescription. My appetite is usually good, but a few mouthfuls cause a sense of fullness and repletion, as if I had really eaten a hearty meal. I cannot eat enough to keep me strong. There is more or less soreness in the region of the liver. Bowels usually constipated, with much flatulence of stomach and bowels.

"I don't know but my kidneys are badly affected, for I have soreness and aching in that region, and I pass a good deal of red sand in my urine. Naturally I am of a lively temperament, fond of society, but am now often low spirited. One thing about my case strikes me as being peculiar: I am always worse from 4 to 5 or from 8 to 9 p. m. This I have noticed for years, and it is not imagination.

I am a married man, aged 42, fair complexion, weight 135 lbs, height 5 feet 6 inches, occupation, bookkeeper.

Please send prescription by return mail, and find within post office order for $2.00. Very respectfully, SAMUEL BOYER, Box 26,
Watsonville, Cal."

The above letter was sent to ten of the most prominent allopathic physicians in the United States. I have not space to insert all of the prescriptions that were sent by each of these doctors for the $2.00 received, but will state that they are as opposite as it is possible to make them, and all of a poisonous nature. I will render some of the names of these ingredients into plain English, and let the student judge for himself whether they are at all suitable for the cure of an inflamed stomach, which was diseased by dyspepsia in its worst form.

Take of Compound Tinc. Peruvian Bark.
"   "   Gentian.
Diluted Hydrochloric Acid.
Pepsin.
Subnitrate of Bismuth.
Compound Glycyrrhize powder.
Socotrine Aloes.
Podophyllin.
Sulphate quinine.
Extract of Aloes.
"   " Hyoscyamus.
Lactopeptine.
Pulverized Ipecacuanha.
Extract Nux Vomica.

Extract Hyoscyamus,
Extract Colocynth.
Tincture Nux Vomica, Diluted Muriatic Acid.
Compound Tincture of Peruvian Bark.
Lady Webster's Dinner Pill (these contain two grains of aloes each.)
Salicin.
Sulphate Strychnia.
Sulphate quinine.
Compound Rhubarb pill.
Podophyllin.
Powdered Citrate of Potash.
Powdered Phosphate of Soda.

The above poisonous drugs from the leading allopathic physicians of the United States were all intended for one special disease, which disease was well defined.

Some of my readers may think that the letter was sent only to ignorant allopathic physicians or what are termed quacks, but to satisfy the student's mind on this point I insert the names of the 10 physicians that the letter was sent to.

H. I. Bowditch, Boston.
J. E. Darby, Cleveland.
R. Bartholow, Philadelphia.
Chas. T Parks, Chicago.
Austin Flint, New York.

Isaac N. Love, St. Louis.
W. R. Cluness, Sacramento.
W. F. McNutt, San Francisco.
S. O. L. Potter, San Francisco.
J. T. Whitaker, Cincinnati.

The same letter inclosing the $2.00 post office order was sent to ten leading homeopathic physicians in the United States, and they all prescribed one remedy, and that remedy was not of a poisonous or destructive nature, but was simply lycopodium, and they all agreed on that remedy for that disease, and no doubt if this experiment had been extended to Europe, Asia and Africa, or anywhere else where there are homeopathic physicians, they would have all prescribed the same remedy.

I shall not attempt to decide whether lycopodium is the proper remedy for all the above-named symptoms in a sick patient. I leave that to the homeopathic physicians. I shall only touch upon the *harmlessness of the remedy*. Lycopodium has been used for ages as a menstruum for physicians to make up pills with, on account of its harmlessness, similar to what physicians often use wheaten flour as a menstruum to make up pills. And lycopodium comes as near what is termed "bread pills," without actually being made of wheaten flour, as anything can do.

But what shall we say about the conglomeration of all the allopathic doctors' prescriptions sent to Samuel Boyer, either to kill or cure him? They are as different and as various as it is possible to make them. One would think to read them that instead of being prescribed for one particular complaint, that they were almost a pharmacopœia intended "for all the ills that flesh is heir to," and no two of them alike; and yet the allopathic doctors *harp about the science of medicine. Can there be a bigger farce?* At least the reader must admit that *there is room for improvement*. Is it not time that the government of the United States cried halt! to this kind of doctoring. And like the British Parliament, in regard to compulsory vaccination in England, have an investigating committee appointed to see whether this quackery and destruction of human life shall continue as heretofore.

All practising physicians, especially the allopaths, ought to bear in mind that there are certain conditions of the human system in which drugs have a much more marked, or injurious effect than at other times. To give an illustration all alchoholic beverages have a much more intoxicating effect when taken into an empty stomach than when the stomach is full.

I might give hundreds of examples of drugs prescribed by doctors affecting people seriously, and often destroying life under certain weakened or diseased conditions of the human system.

Sometimes the authorities are forced, although very reluctantly, to take notice of these poisonings after taking an allopath's prescription, but it is only when a patient dies, and there are marked symptoms of poisoning, as the real cause of death. There was a case of this kind published in the "New York Sun" of March 13th, 1898, which stated that Mrs. James L. Carhart of 365 Lexington Avenus, called on Dr. Trumbell W. Cleveland of 45 West 50th Street, on Saturday April 10th, 1897, in regard to her own health.

She had a child six weeks old with her; the doctor asked her about the child's health; she told him that it was quite well, only some slight *bowel trouble*. He advised her to use something to check it; she protested and said that she did not believe in giving much medicine to children so young, but afterwards consented to let the child take it, provided it contained no paregoric; he gave the following prescription, which he said was *very light,* and to be sure that she takes it.

        Salol, xliii. gr.
        Bismuth, sub-carb, ii. drachms.
        Tr. Opii camphor, i. drachm.
        Aqua camphor A. D., iii. oz.

It was to be given a teaspoonful every two hours, and she continued the medicine until Monday, April 12th, 1897, when she sent for the doctor as the child was breathing very heavily. When he came he gave her another prescription, which called for 1 1-2 drachms of resorcin in three ounces of water, the medicine to be given to the baby in teaspoonful doses every two hours, along with the other medicine. This would make the dose of resorcin 3 3-4 grains every two hours.

Mrs. Carhart stated to the District Attorney that in about ten minutes after the first dose the baby gasped, the pupils of the eyes enlarged, and she turned from a pink color to white; she vomited slightly, and there was noticeable the odor of carbolic acid, then she leaned back and seemed lifeless; moaned, began to clutch at her mother's wrist, and soon was in a profuse perspiration, although her hands, face and feet were cold; by this time there was a yellow exudation about the child's nose and mouth, her temples having turned black, and her mouth dark blue.

The doctor came again and administered brandy and nitroglycerine into her arms and thighs by hypodermic injections, which caused the child to scream violently; the mother interceded, but the doctor said, "It is heroic treatment, as brandy burns like fire under the skin." The child continued to breathe heavily, its breathing interrupted occasionally with a scream. Its skin turned yellowish green, mixed with blue, the body was heaving in and out, while her eyes were fixed and her hands useless. The child died on Tuesday evening. The newspapers state that the matter has been under investigation in the District Attorney's office for some ten months. The mother says that the child enjoyed good health previous to taking Dr. Cleveland's prescription, which was "very light." Dr. Cleveland called in Dr. Thompson in consultation, and the newspapers state that Dr. Thompson said in an undertone, "blunder this time." There was no autopsy, and the doctor gave a certificate of death. Mrs. Carhart has consulted a number of other doctors since the child's death, and showed them the prescriptions, and they assert that they were powerful enough to kill a man.

It is but seldom that such instances of poisoning are permitted to get into print or in any way before the public; they are generally kept quiet and the doctor gives a certificate of death, and that ends it.

Of course there will be nothing done to Dr. Cleveland, and the whole matter will be forgotten.

Had the child been treated by a "Christian Scientist," "Mental Healer," "Mesmerist," or a doctor who does not prescribe poisonous medicines, and had died a natural death without any of these symptoms of poisoning, the offender would have been taken out of bed at 12 o'clock at night, if necessary, as a common murderer; the newspapers would have had a full account of it the next morning, and would have let their readers know that the child had died without being poisoned by an allopathic doctor, and the reporters would have given notices that all such disgraceful occurences must be stopped in future and at any cost.

Persecution of Homeopathic and Botanic Practitioners.

During the time bleeding was popular the doctors believed that the patient must be bled in all cases; an instance is mentioned by Dr. Guy of London, in his book on Public Health, where he says one hundred and forty patients were all bled for one disease, and they all died. Dr. Samuel Hahnemann of Germany, old Samuel Thompson of this country, and their followers, suffered martyrdom, nearly one hundred years ago, for opposing these destructive methods in the treatment of diseases.

There were a number of volumes published by Prof. Simpson, of Edinburg, Scotland, Dr. Woods, Dr. Hooker, and others at that time, opposing homeopathy and botanic practice of medicine, which volumes endeavored to prove that the botanic and homeopathic physicians did no good to their patients, but that the disease was constantly increasing until it was too late for the patient to be cured by their own destructive and poisonous medicines, and all kinds of persecutions were resorted to, to break up or put a stop to these two innocent and harmless systems of the practice of medicine.

At the time of the illness and death of Gen. Washington, a doctor who attempted to treat fever or any disease, without bleeding the patient several times, and not using calomel and jalap, emetic tartar, etc., and the patient died, he would be arrested at once and tried for manslaughter.

We have an instance in the trial of Samuel Thompson, who was opposed to bleeding, and taking such large doses of poisonous medicine, which he termed "rats bane."

For years and years the allopathic doctors have been combining and raising money to influence the legislature and have laws enacted to prevent any person from taking care of or prescribing for sick persons, without being a regular graduate, and of their school, and have been doing everything possible to prevent druggists from selling what is called proprietary or patent medicines, which are in almost all cases composed of ingredients that are harmless and not destructive to life or health.

On Feb. 17th, 1898, a member of the Assembly of New York State introduced a bill requiring all patent medicines to have the names and quantities of the ingredients printed in plain English on a label pasted on the bottle, so that every person taking the medicine should know just what they are taking, and which would enable the persons to make up the medicine for themselves. How much better it would be to have a law enacted compelling every physician to have printed or written in plain English the names and quantities of each ingredient in the prescription, on a label and pasted on each bottle or package, so that the patient would know what he is taking, or his friends would know what they are giving him.

Another member introduced a bill which provides, that if a proprietary medicine, which contains certain named poisons in any quantity whatever, no matter how small a quantity, the retailer or wholesaler should affix to the bottle or package, a *poison label in red ink*, specially naming the poison and prominently displaying a picture of a *skull, and cross bones*, together with the antidote for the particular poison so advertised.

Such a bill can only have one of two objects. First, to drive the manufacturers of such proprietary medicines out of the State, which medicines are never known to injure any person to any great extent,* or, Secondly, to blackmail the proprietors of patent medicines, in order to raise money to have the bill killed, either in the Assembly or committee rooms.

The allopathic physicians are trying to have the manufacture of patent medicines stopped, and no druggist permitted to sell anything without a prescription from a physician; they are also trying to have laws enacted to close up all dispensaries or at least to make them so uncomfortable for people who visit them, that they will deem themselves more disgraced than if they were paupers.

Such bills as the above are introduced in State Assemblies, **year after year**, at the instigation of the allopathic physicians.

How much more sensible it would be to have a law enacted that all prescriptions sent out of drug stores should be labeled "poison" in red ink, and also that there should be displayed on the label *a skull and cross bones*, so that people would become more cautious when taking such prescriptions.

A great many sensible people think that physicians have no right to doctor unless they use very dangerous and destructive medicines similar to the prescription of Dr. Cleveland, and that in using them he must be equally as skillful as expert performers in theatres who place a man standing with his arms extended and the expert using long knives and so throwing them that they pin him to the board so he cannot move; or like a man who is a good marksman, shooting a lighted cigar from a man's mouth, or a small ball from his head, and in such actions if the ball or knife went an inch crooked it would be almost instant death.

But after all, times are changing, and it is a good indication that the District Attorney is wakening up, and paying some attention to such cases as the death of Mrs. Carhart's child, even if it is a year after the death occured, If in the future the attention of the District Attorney should be called to all such cases as these, which occur almost daily, he will be kept so busy attending to cases of persons who die of violent deaths after taking prescriptions, that he will not have time for arresting and trying people who treat patients who afterwards die a natutal death.

I have given Dr. Draper a number of cases that would make splendid subjects for a farce or comic opera, and could give thousands of other

---

* The manufacturers or proprietors of medicines have to be doubly careful in regard to the ingredients, as they are awlays aware that the person taking such medicines are very careless as regards the quantity to be taken. If any person dies after taking even a large dose of those medinines, no matter of what disease, the proprietor of such medicine would be liable to be instantly arrested and when all the doctors in the state would combine to have him severely punished, both by fine and imprisonment.

To give an instance of how careless some people are in taking medicines, I will mention a case which came under my observation in England.

A cousin of mine who kept a drug store in Leeds, sold a man a box of pills to act on the bowels, with directions to only take one pill each night, but that same night he took the whole box at one time. The effect was fearful, but not fatal.

Had the man been taken seriously ill, or had he died it would have caused my cousin serious trouble and expense, if not imprisonment. So in regard to any person getting up a patent medicine, if any one is injured by it, even by taking a whole bottle at a time (when directions are a teaspoonful a day,) and the patient dies, the manufacturer of such medicine wonld get into serious trouble, and it would completely destroy the sale of his medicines afterwards.

cases that have come under my notice, if he could dispel from the minds of his audience that they were real tragedies.

I had intended devoting some part of this book to "Medical Astrology," but I find I have not space, but anyone wishing to know something of this science can read the last 12 pages of this book.

THE OBJECTIONS TO THE SCIENCE OF ASTROLOGY ANSWERED.

1. *The Folly and Knavery of its Professors.*
2. *The Uncertainty of the Science itself as manifested by the frequent failure of Predictions.*
3. *The certainty that Astrology must be false, because it cannot be true, and therefore no man of learning and sense would believe in it.*

The first objection contains more truth than real weight or value. Formerly when the science was but little known or understood there were great numbers of impostors, pretending to practice it, but since the people have commenced to investigate Astrology for themselves, these pretenders are gradually going out of that kind of business. Therefore that objection is gradually disappearing, and after a time it will be entirely gone. The faculty of possessing foreknowledge is so predominant in our nature, that the desire to gratify it, when not properly trained or developed, causes it to become really a temptation, and impostors are always ready to profit by it where they can. Wise men who studied the science, although convinced of its truth, were fully aware of its difficulties, and careful how they committed themselves. Fools were not so scrupulous, and impostors thought of nothing but how they could make the most of it. At length things came to such a pass that, as Gasendus remarked, some would "scarcely cut their hair or pare their nails without consulting the Almanac to see what sign the Moon was in." It may not be improper to give a hint relative to impostors of the present day in this city, who charge money for telling that to others, which they do not believe themselves, whose principle aim is to make money out of a science they do not understand, and to laugh at the public while they are robbing them. Wretches like these are infinitely more despicable than the greatest blockhead on earth, who is sincere. Astrology, however, must stand or fall by its own merits or demerits and not by those of its professors. Had the study of Chemistry been abandoned because a set of fools, urged on by knaves, ruined themselves in the pursuit of the universal *Menstruum* or *Potable Gold*, the world would have been deprived of a most useful Science.

The second objection, that is, "The Uncertainty of the Science itself as manifested by the frequent failure of Predictions," seems more plausible, but it is equally applicable to other branches of knowledge, of which the truth is not even disputed. We are, for instance, as little acquainted with the true operations of Celestial Affinities, and the Electric Phenomena of the Planetary Orbs as with the Pathology of the human body, and probably much less, as we have fewer opportunities of investigating them; and I would ask not only the medical man, but any man who has studied nature, whether in the event of a person receiving a wound in the hand or foot, he would require the physician to decide as to it being succeeded by Tetanus. A question like this could only proceed from extreme ignorance, and would be treated as such. Not one in ten wounds, nor do I believe one in a hundred, occasions lock-jaw, and yet the identity of Traumatic Tetanus is as perfect as any other disease in Nosology.

The partial failures of Astrologers necessarily presuppose partial successes. If Astrologers always failed in their predictions, the evidence against Astrology would be strongly presumptive, though not absolutely conclusive, in as much as the properties of matter do not result from man's knowledge of them, but pervades all matter, inherently, prior to man's existence, and are only yet ascertained to a very limited extent. When attempts are made to parallel Astrology with many other sciences, its magnitude and complexity appear so immensely overwhelming, that the wonder turns not upon the failure of its professors, but rather upon their frequent successes.

To those who make the third objection, that is, "The certainty that Astrology must be false, because it cannot be true, and therefore no man of learning and sense would believe in it," I would recommend patience, with the assurance that should they by any accident become men of LEARNING AND SENSE themselves, they will probably change their opinions. Besides, it is but right to inform them, that men of sense often conceal their knowledge and belief from a conviction that FOOLS ARE TOO NUMEROUS AND TOO FORMIDABLE A BODY TO BE TAMPERED WITH. A little investigation, however, will enable them to discover that a number of years back, before the spirit of research had been almost subdued by prejudice, most men of acknowledged ability did BELIEVE IN IT. SIR ISAAC NEWTON, and also the great and ingenious KEPLER,* whose astronomical discoveries and mental acuteness have never yet been surpassed; and the profound and intelligent LOCKE, whose indefatigable spirit of research, may justly shame the brightest genius of the present age, were all well convinced of the truth of Astrology, and not ashamed to acknowledge it. Other names such as Dryden, Richelieu,† etc., of equal celebrity, might be quoted, but no such authority is required to sanction truth, and the expedient is seldom resorted to except with a view to blind the ignorant and give currency to prejudice.

As every age brings improvement, "the Society for the Diffusion of Useful Knowledge" seem to have hit upon a plan of improving this expedient, by circulating their own names to serve for authorities, instead of the names of their PREDECESSORS. I forget who it was that prescribed a list of great men with little minds, as a cure for Hypochondriasis, supposing it must operate upon the Nerves through the medium of the visible muscles. The idea was ingenious, and really when I peruse the "*Diffusion*," and compare the names on its covers with the nonsense in its pages, I am tempted to believe we are in possession of the very desideratum alluded to. Such a stale, commonplace farrago

---

* See page 21.   † See page 22.

of physical absurdities was never before let loose upon the uninformed mass of mankind.

I wish they had given their recipe for making a Universe. That for putting the Planets in motion when they are made is truly admirable. The feat, it appears, is performed by a "PUSH given to them at first, and forcing them onward at the same time that they are drawn toward a certain point," and again we find that this attractive force which draws them toward a certain point, is "the same influence or power that makes a stone fall to the ground." Now of all the PUSHES I have ever observed, the original impulse was but momentary, and although the effect must have remained through all eternity, had there been no obstruction, yet where it is, it must be gradually annihilated. A stone thrown forward, even were there no atmospherical resistance, must proceed in a parabolic curve, the effect of two conflicting forces, viz:—that of the first impulse, and the impeding power of gravitation; but the former being but temporary, and the latter perpetual, the former would be gradually exausted by the latter, and the stone would in a given time remain relatively motionless upon the earth's surface. All that now remains to be ascertained, is the nature of the Society's "*Push*." Is it like other PUSHES likely to be overcome by a contrary impulse and if it be, by what means does it still retain its power unimpaired by resistance, undiminished by gravitation? not to mention the variations at the apsides which can neither be caused by primitive impulse, or uniform gravitation. This to ME would be "Useful Knowledge," and I should be happy at seeing it "diffused" as soon as possible. I must however, caution them that I am not one of those "bipeds" that says "pretty poll, or polly wants a cracker," simply because I hear some one else say so, nor am I to be amused by a NAME or an AUTHORITY, whether of Newton or any one else. I may be wrong in applying to the Society for a reason of their own, which they have not to give, but I mean to have a reason, or the fact itself, if it is one, or nothing. Did it ever occur to those wiseacres, that every distinct body in nature, has like themselves, a will of its own, differing only from theirs, in being directed to much wiser purposes! Could they never find out that the LAWS of nature are the WILLS of nature, exercised for the mutual benefit and preservation of all its component parts, collectively and individually? could they once be made to comprehend this obvious truth it would assist them through many of their difficulties, and among other things, teach them to account for the "*falling of a Stone*, a phenomena which seems to puzzle them extremely; and but for the experience they have to the contrary, "It is," they say, "quite conceivable that a stone might STAND still in the air or fly upwards, or in any other direction; and there would be nothing at all absurd, contradictory, inconceivable or impossible in either of these suppositions, as there would be in supposing the stone equal to half itself, or falling and rising at once," etc. Now, really, how one positive absurdity can be more "CONCEIVABLE" than another, is to ME "INCONCEIVABLE," but this is the inevitable consequence when lawyers and statesmen set themselves up for astronomers, astrologers or philosophers. Art is their proper study. They are ignorant of nature, and should never meddle with her affairs. Every attentive observer perceives that in all bodies, whether organized or not, each part or member is interested, and indefatigable in contributing to the preservation of the whole; that were it not the judicious tendency of all substances towards each other, so as to form one common centre of gravity, this globe would instantly be shattered to pieces; and that to prevent this catastrophe, a stone or any other substance left at liberty, rushes towards the centre, or as it is vulgarly termed, "falls to the ground."

We come now to the choicest morsel of the whole, namely, their "Astrological aphorisms," the major part of which will be found in a work of theirs, called "*Companion to the Almanac*," containing a choice collection of Apophthegms, a smart philippic or two against "*Moon and Star Men*," and "The Nonsense of Astrology," and an oblique hint at the means by which they acquired all this knowledge, which it seems was through having "intelligence and good sense, as lords of their ascendants."

At page 23, we are told, "that the revolution of the heavenly bodies produces the appearances of the seasons and NOTHING MORE." At page 24, the "SEASONS" are left to shift for themselves, and the "Celestial Bodies exert no other influence than that of GRAVITATION upon the earth;" and at page 27, they are all, except one, turned out of office, in consequence of the discovery, that "being all much more remote from the earth than the Moon, they have NO INFLUENCE WHATEVER upon the changes of the Seasons, or upon anything that in any way affects the comfort or the ordinary pursuits of mankind." If any one can reconcile this discordant trash, I should be happy to find myself in the list of his acquaintances. Where were "*Intelligence and Good Sense*" that they did not happen to be "*Lords of the Ascendant*" upon this occasion? I fear we have lost even the Sun in the conflict. He is much more remote from the earth than the Moon," being 400 times her distance—he is one of the OUTS.

I need not insult the reader's understanding by any comment, but pass onward, or rather backward to the story of their conversion, which the reader may find at page 21, and as this is a very curious document, I shall insert the passage, verbatim.

"That the different Phases of the Moon have SOME connection with changes in the atmosphere is an opinion so UNIVERSAL and POPULAR, as to be on THAT ACCOUNT ALONE entitled to attention. No observation is more general, and on no occasion perhaps is the almanac so frequently consulted as in forming conjectures upon the state of the weather, the common remark goes no further than the fact that changes from wet to dry, and from dry to wet, happen at the changes of the Moon; when to this result of universal experience WE add the philosophical reasons for the existence of Tides in the Aerial Ocean, we cannot doubt that such a connection exists, and that the Moon exerts considerable influence upon the currents of the air according to her position. The subject, however, is involved in GREAT OBSCURITY, and is one which can only be elucidated by long and careful observation." (See page 269.)

This is what I have been endeavoring to prove and elucidate in this book, as the foundation of the science of Astrology, or what the Society calls the "Nonsense of Astrology," and when we reflect that "*The Society*" themselves, like the man who had been talking prose all his life and did not know it, have been Astrologers all the time, without having the wit to discover it, the thing seems scarcely credible; but we find the whole is justly attributed to that noted Enchantress, "UNIVERSAL AND POPULAR OPINION," who with all the persevering malignity of a fairy, seems never to have quitted those poor victims of her delusions one moment from that of their birth to the present hour. 'Twas she, who in disguise of the scholastic dogmas, and popular prejudices, first taught them to deny, without having a single fact to disprove the truth of Astrology, and then in the garb of "UNIVERSAL AND POPULAR OPINION," compelled them to believe in it, leaving them to extricate themselves from the *horns* of the *dilemma* as well as they could. In addition to these calamities, they are, through some fatality, always in the wrong, like all other persons who meddle with things they know nothing about, even when they happen to take the right side of a question. The weather does NOT change with the Moon, but four or five days before it, and the period is the longer the nearer the Moon is to the Apogee. That the subject is "*involved in great obscurity*," is owing to meddlesome persons like themselves, who are like the tailless fox in the fable, continually exerting themselves to persuade others into their own condition. It is strange they cannot be persuaded to stick to their LASTS, and remain within the very limited sphere for which nature designed them. Really, men like those who are merely the echoes of others opinions, without possessing one original idea of their own, whose minds are so superficial and unreflecting as not only to be incapable of perceiving Astrological truths, but even the nature and tendency of their own ideas—men like those, should be put under some kind of surveillance, and not allowed to go about filling their own empty phials with other men's compositions, which they have not the skill to analyze, and forcing their contents, dregs and all, down the throats of every one they meet. If they must become teachers of Astrology, (though of this I do not see either the necessity or the possibility,) they should become Wards in Chancery, and pursue their studies under proper tutors provided for them. I think, however, they had better remain as they are, or rather as they were before they became "MOON AND STAR MEN." Pikes like these should remain at home in their native rivers, and not venture to sea. They may shine at the BAR or in the SENATE, where great pretensions and small intellect are much oftener "LORDS OF THE ASCENDANT" than "INTELLIGENCE AND GOOD SENSE," and where, if we may credit Lord Chesterfield, a knowledge of any subject in question, is no more essential than a knowledge of "*Celtic or Sclavonian*," and where he boasted of delivering, with unbounded applause, a lecture on Astronomy, while at the same time he was an "UTTER STRANGER" to that Science. In their own spheres they may be GIANTS, but I am really serious when I assure them they are mere PIGMIES in Astrology.

THE PLANET NEPTUNE

Persons Described by Neptune.

There is less known of the influence of the planet Neptune, in describing the appearance of the native, than any of the other planets, except the asteroids.

The personal description of Neptune in the twelve signs comes very near a combination between the planet Uranus and Venus, and any one reading the description in the twelve signs of the Zodiac of both these planets and combining them in his mind, will come very near the personal description of a Neptune person. Also, if the student reads the conjunctions, squares, oppositions, sextiles and trines of Uranus and Venus, and combines the two in his mind, he will have a very good description, physically, mentally and morally, of the ☌, □, ☍, ✶ and △ of Neptune to all the other planets.

A Neptune person is generally near or above the medium height, inclined to be full built rather than slender, slightly dark complexion, with brown or dark brown hair, rather full face, broad high forehead, quick eyes, rather prominent nose, and of a somewhat commanding appearance; they very often look older than they are; a Uranus person looks older than they are, but a Venus person generally looks younger.

Of color Neptune governs a much darker blue than Venus.

The influence of Neptune in a horoscope is, in some cases, very marked, especially if it is in the ascendant, the 10th or the 7th house; it is most evil in these houses. In the 7th house it causes very unhappy marriages, unless the Sun in a woman's and the Moon in a man's horoscope, makes a good aspect of Venus or Jupiter for marriage.

Neptune's evil directions or transits tell with a vengeance, and if it happens to be transiting over, or in evil aspect to two or three planets in angles, the native feels it in a marked degree, especially if those planets are superior planets, and in fixed signs. Some authors intimate that Neptune is more evil in its transits or directions than either Saturn, Mars or Uranus, as it is so long in transiting or going over any particular part of the horoscope. Neptune travels a little more than 2 degrees and 14 minutes a year; therefore, any person having the Moon 16 degrees, the Sun 20 degrees in any sign, and Saturn, Mars or Uranus 18 degrees in the opposite sign, and Neptune coming in evil aspect to those positions, the evil inflence will be felt for four or five years. The sickness caused by Neptune is chiefly of a nervous tendency and of a depressive nature.

Neptune in the Twelve Houses.

Neptune in the 1st house gives a well made person, a rather full face and forehead, eyes generally a dark blue, full and bright, heavy eyebrows, much hair, clear complexion, short and thick neck In disposition they are void of fear, daring, and of a restless nature; practical, ingenious, intuitive, jealous of those they love, fond of dress and display, worldly wise, and if in ☍ ☿, given to criticising and being criticised. Males who have Neptune in the ascendant are said to be effeminate and debilitated; if Neptune be afflicted, they are given to dissolute habits.

♆ IN THE 2D.—Wastes his wealth through profligacy; and his finances are uncertain.

♆ IN THE 3D.—Long residence in a place, and unexpected removals.

♆ IN THE 4TH.—Unfortunate in home affairs and property.

♆ IN THE 5TH.—Speculations turn out "air castles," and his pleasures and associates are of a low order; the native's children are liable to watery diseases and a poor constitution. If in ♓ in the 5th, he has a craving for drink, which leads to dissolute vices and depraved habits.

♆ IN THE 6TH.—Causes the native to be inclined to study medicine, but is not fortunate with servants, small animals, keeping boarding-house.

♆ IN THE 7TH.—The marriage partner is a most undesirable one, and events inimical to marital felicity are apt to suddenly occur.

♆ IN THE 8TH.—Denotes a peculiar death; if Neptune is afflicted, causes a short illness, watery in character, or may be drowned.

♆ IN THE 9TH.—Peculiar religious views; fond of occultism, mesmerism, astrology, and kindred sciences.

♆ IN THE 10TH.—Great success, with sudden reverses of fortune.

♆ IN THE 11TH.—Low acquaintances and dissolute friends.

♆ IN THE 12TH.—Danger of imprisonment, or confinement of some kind; shrewd and dangerous enemies.

The Aspects of Neptune.

♆ IN GOOD ASPECT ♅.—Fond of making explorations, interested in spiritualism, or an investigator of occult science.

♆ IN GOOD ASPECT ♄.—Speculation, financial success, good hearted.

♆ IN GOOD ASPECT ♃.—Causes the native to meet with unexpected good fortune by speculation, inventions, etc.

♆ AFFLICTING ♃.—Denotes that the native will live upon charity at some period in life, but afterwards become wealthy.

♆ IN GOOD ASPECT ♂.—Fond of the study of palmistry, physiognomy, also ability for physician or surgeon.

♆ IN EVIL ASPECT ♂.—Liability to accidents and changes.

♆ IN EVIL ASPECT ♀.—In a male's nativity it gives large animal propensities, low associations, also disappointment in courtship or marriage. With females, they are liable to lose their virtue early in life, or be untrue to their marriage vows, young females are liable to assault, etc.

♆ IN GOOD ASPECT ♀.—Makes the native refined, fond of paintings and music, and of the occult

♆ IN GOOD ASPECT ☿.—Quick, impressional, practical, ingenious, of good judgment, intuitive and shrewd, very sensitive, and a good judge of human nature.

♆ IN EVIL ASPECT ☿.—Makes a clever deceiver, shrewd, and a good judge of human nature, glibness of tongue. It gives imaginative complaints in the head, excitement, fear, hysteria, nervousness, and in some cases pretended ailments. It also makes pretenders, and if Uranus afflict Neptune, bogus astrologers and clairvoyants.

♆ IN △ OR ✶ ☽.—Fond of travel, and desirous of change, will take unexpected journeys and travel to foreign parts.

THE HOROSCOPES OF PRESIDENT CLEVELAND
AND OF
EX-PRESIDENT HARRISON.

Some time in the beginning of October, 1888, a reporter of "The New York World" was sent to nearly all the Astrologers and Clairvoyants in New York City to try and find out what they had to say about the then-coming Presidential election. He was also sent to consult me, but instead of asking my opinion on the Presidential election, he had me cast his own horoscope. When I had finished reading it, he said he would like to ask me one question, which was that he had bet considerable money that Mr. Cleveland would be elected; should he win his money? I showed him the horoscope of Mr. Cleveland, and told him that Cleveland would be defeated in the coming election; that near the end of October, Cleveland would have a very evil aspect in his horoscope, which would give him a *black eye*, and would prevent his election.

Just about the above-mentioned time, Lord Sackville West, British Minister to Washington, wrote a letter to an Englishman out West, advising all Englishmen to vote for Cleveland, as his election would benefit England. This was one of the means of Mr. Cleveland's not being elected in 1888. On account of Lord Sackville West's indiscretion he got his walking papers to go home.

The above was published in "The New York Sunday World" on the 14th of October, 1888. The reporter also published in the same paper that I charged him five dollars for reading his horoscope, but I was the only one of the Astrologers in New York who gave him anything for his money. That was rough on the other Astrologers, but I suppose the reason he made that statement was because they did not charge him enough for reading his horoscope.* I advised him to *hedge* on his Cleveland election bets, if he did not wish to lose all his money.

On the 10th of July, 1892, appeared the following horoscopes of President Cleveland and ex-President Harrison, in the "New York Sunday Journal." I reprint them *verbatim*. At the end of the horoscopes I shall make a few further remarks.

---

* Charles A. Dana, in "The New York Sun," advises his readers never to pay an Astrologer more than twenty-five cents for casting and reading a horoscope. Mr. Dana is a great stickler for personal freedom of the buyer and seller, not only of labor but of every kind of product. He always insists in labor strikes that if there are men or women willing to do the work at a lower wage, that the strikers have no business to interfere; that every one should be left free to ask what he deems proper for any specific work, and the buyer to offer what he deems proper. In this case it is not the Astrologers who are on a strike for higher wages, but what is termed a "lockout." But if Mr. Dana is determined to fix the fee of Astrologers at twenty-five cents, why not fix it for all other professional services? Why does he not tell his readers not to pay more than twenty-five cents to a lawyer for pleading a case in court, nor more than twenty-five cents to a minister for preaching a sermon on Sunday, nor more than twenty-five cents to a doctor for a professional visit to a patient? Why pin all Astrologers down to twenty-five cents, unless he brings all other professions down to the same level?

Mr. Dana may say he does not believe in Astrology, yet there are people just as wise as he who do believe in it, and consider that an Astrological reading is worth as much as the fee given to a lawyer or a doctor.

HOROSCOPE OF GROVER CLEVELAND.

From "The New York Sunday Morning Journal," July 10, 1892.

In times like these, when every one is excited over the possibilities of the Presidential election, even the most extraneous means may be used to throw light upon the uncertainty. In olden times the Court Astrologer was the oracle, and such an oracle must be sadly needed at Washington.

The Astrologer of to-day is not like his predecessor. He is an ordinary looking man, with his books and mathematical tables about him; in a matter-of-fact, business-like way he talks of the future with the ease of a teacher. The gentleman who was consulted for the information here given would not be considered, out of his office, as differing in any way from his neighbors. A man about sixty, gray, and with a pleasant face and a general appearance of honesty, both in actions and conversation. He has devoted forty years of his life to the study, and seems to be a devout believer in all that he says.

He had the charts all prepared, and from their appearance must have spent some time in studying them; his remarks were to the point, and seemed to be the result of deep thought. He was emphatic in his statements regarding the chances of the two candidates, considered from the Astrologer's point of view, and should he be correct, Mr. Cleveland might take much comfort this summer if he realized the good times ahead for him.

The Professor studied the following chart for a while and then said:

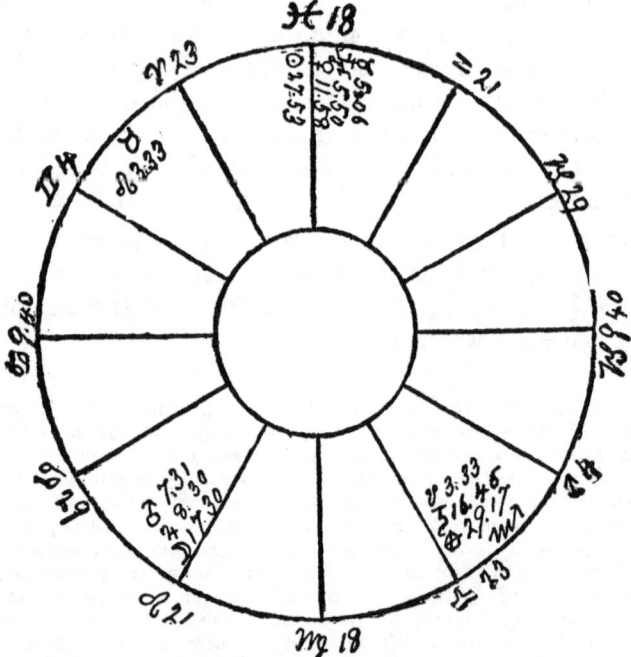

"Grover Cleveland was born March 18, 1837. His biographies do not mention the time of day, but after a careful examination I am convinced that the hour was about 11:30 A. M. He is described by the

Moon in Leo, that orb being at that time afflicted by an evil aspect of the planet Saturn."

The Professor here took down one of his books and read as follows:

"The Moon in Leo describes a person about the middle height, well proportioned, strong, large-boned, sanguine-complexioned, brown hair, large, prominent eyes, and full face, a lofty, proud, aspiring person, very ambitious, and desiring to rule."

The Professor sat back in his chair and looked as though that settled the truth of the matter effectually, and then he went on:

"Mr. Cleveland has four planets in the sign of Pisces, and no doubt they are near the mid-heaven; any person with so many planets in one sign, and in conjunction, is certain to rise and become noted, unless these planets are very much afflicted. He has also the planets Jupiter and Mars in conjunction in the second house—the house of money. This would indicate that he would become quite well to do, though Mars there would make money pass through his hands very easily when he was young.

"The Moon in the second house in evil aspect to the planet Saturn shows that in early life he had many misfortunes, and there was danger even of disgrace.

"Mr. Cleveland is of good constitution, and likely to live to a good age; although he will have several evil influences commence about May, 1895, which will last until the middle of October, 1896. That will be a critical period for him to live through. Should he pass that influence safely there is no serious danger for many years.

"Marriage in Mr. Cleveland's nativity is surrounded by many possibilities; especially was it so in his early life, and difficulties and anxieties from the opposite sex were not the least of his troubles. Mrs. Cleveland is described in his nativity by the planet Mercury; the aspect indicating marriage in Mr. Cleveland's horoscope is not of the best, except for honor and advancement. Mercury near the mid-heaven indicates the popularity of that estimable lady.

"The influences in operation in Mr. Cleveland's nativity this fall are remarkably good; exactly the reverse of those that hampered him in 1888. I am satisfied that he will be elected."

HOROSCOPE OF BENJAMIN HARRISON.

"In Mr. Harrison's biographies the date of birth given is August 20, 1833. The hour is lacking, but after studying the positions of the planets on that day, I am convinced that he was born about 4 A. M. This would indicate that the Sun was the preponderating planet in his horoscope. The Sun in Leo gives the following:

Here the Professor again read:

"The Sun in Leo gives a strong, well-proportioned, and very portly person; sanguine complexioned, light brown or yellowish hair, full face, and large, prominent eyes. There is generally a mark or scar on the face. A very just, upright, and honorable man, who scorns to do any

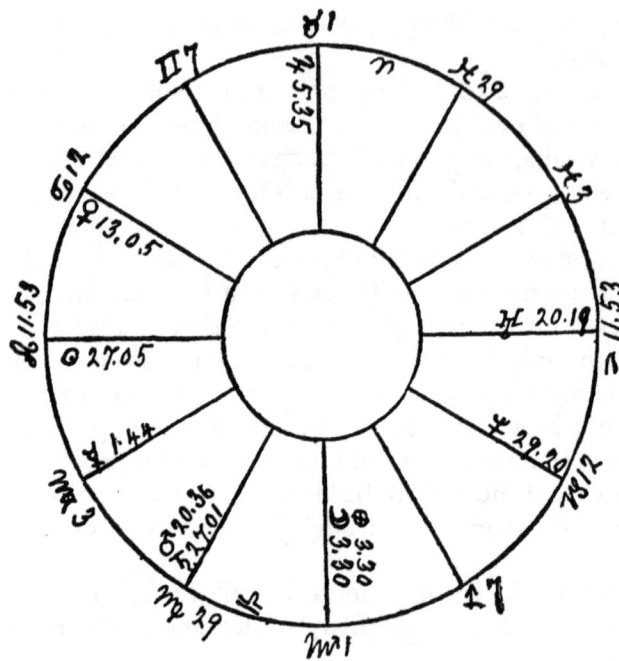

CHART OF THE HEAVENS AT PRESIDENT HARRISON'S BIRTH.

meanness; punctual, faithful to his friends, and magnanimous to his enemies; in short, a right royal disposition; a very ambitious man withal, fond of rule and authority, and given to war, domination and conquest."

The Professor put the book down, and taking up the chart, studied it attentively for some time, and then proceeded:

"The reason of Mr. Harrison's rise to prominence is the position of the planet Jupiter in the mid-heaven of his horoscope, in close good aspect to Mercury; the latter planet is rising in great dignity. Strange as it may appear, there are very few persons born with Jupiter in their mid-heaven. Among these few, Queen Victoria, the Duke of Wellington, and W. W. Astor are numbered. A person having this excellent configuration of the heavens, will in some part of his life rise to prominence and remain prominent.

"A person born with Saturn in that part of the horoscope may rise in life after hard work, but is sure to fall. For instance, the two Bonapartes, Gen. McClellan, and ex-President Buchanan are remarkable illustrations. It may be interesting to know that Worsdale, a very eminent Astrologer of England in the last century, cast the horoscopes of Napoleon Bonaparte and the Duke of Wellington eleven years before the battle of Waterloo, and predicted that if ever these generals met upon the field of battle Wellington would conquer.

But to the matter in hand. In President Harrison's horoscope the planets Saturn and Mars in the house of money would indicate that he had many hard struggles with poverty in his early years. Venus in the house of friends would bring him influential friendships, many of them of the gentler sex. Mercury rising in the ascendant, and in good aspect to Jupiter and the Moon, would give him remarkable intellect, far above the average. When he thoroughly considers a subject he will rarely make a mistake.

"The health and length of life of the President are influenced by the Sun rising in his horoscope. He will live to a good age, and enjoy better health than in his early years. A person indicated by the Sun, as he is, especially when it is so strong, is generally set in his ways and determined to control, making a poor politician.

"The Moon making an aspect of Jupiter in the mid-heaven, would indicate that marriage would be a benefit to Mr. Harrison; he would receive advancement and assistance from the step. He will get along in a rather harmonious manner in married life; the only unpleasantness I see would be over the question of who should rule.

"At the nomination of President Harrison in 1888 it so happened that he had a number of very good influences in operation in his horoscope, and at the same time Cleveland had several very evil ones, particularly in October of that year, about the time when Sackville West wrote the letter advising the Englishmen how to vote.

"At the time of the nomination of President Harrison this year, I find that the Moon was rising, just leaving an opposition of the Sun, and in close square to Saturn in the eleventh, the house of friends. All these influences indicate that when election time comes the President will have been sold out by his friends. I cannot see how he can possibly be elected, unless a miracle occurs. If he should be elected it would bring trouble to the country.

"In addition, the President will have, commencing about the 20th of September of this year, and lasting till after election, several very evil influences, and something will occur about that time which will seriously interfere with his prospects.

"Of the two men, President Harrison has the more fortunate horoscope, yet on account of the evil influences I have mentioned, and the fact that Grover Cleveland will have some exceptionally good influences in his horoscope this fall, among which will be Jupiter in his mid-heaven in exact trine to the Moon, I am satisfied that Grover Cleveland will be elected to the Presidency.

"It is seldom I meet with two nativities that are so strong where the parties are opposed to each other, therefore I expect it to be an exciting election."

A FEW FURTHER REMARKS ON THE HOROSCOPE OF EX-PRESIDENT HARRISON.

The evil planetary influences in ex-President Harrison's nativity in September and October, 1892, had a marked effect, not only in defeating him for a second term, but they also brought misfortune in the loss of his wife. At the time I calculated Mr. Harrison's horoscope for the "Sunday Morning Journal," I expected that there would be a death in his family before the election, but was afraid to mention it, because the aspect might have brought some other affliction. It is sometimes very difficult to tell which way the planetary influence will affect a person.

Before the summer of 1896 Mr. Harrison will have a number of evil planetary influences in his horoscope, which will seriously interfere with his prospects for being nominated a third time, and may also seriously affect his health.

In November and December, 1895, he will have almost as evil an aspect as he had when he buried his wife, his own health will be seriously affected, and possibly another death may occur in his family. February and March, 1896, will bring other evil influences of a similar nature, but in July, 1896, Jupiter will come to his ascendant, which is a very fortunate aspect, yet he will have an evil aspect of Uranus to its own place at the same time, which I think will spoil his prospects for renomination, and the National Convention may act as treacherously as it did to James G. Blaine in 1892. Still, should he get the nomination there will be a fair chance of his being elected, and should they nominate Grover Cleveland for a third term, Mr. Harrison would have a walk-over.

Commencing January 1, 1897, and continuing to the 1st of December, Mr. Harrison will have one of the worst aspects he has had since he was seven years of age, and the chances of his living over that time are very doubtful; still, as his "giver of life" is so strong, there may be a slight prospect of his surviving over 1897. If so, there will be no serious danger of his death until he is about seventy-two or seventy-three years old. Should he possibly be elected President in 1896, it will be just as evil for the United States as was the election of Mr. Cleveland in 1892.

A FEW FURTHER REMARKS ON THE HOROSCOPE OF PRESIDENT CLEVELAND.

For the next few years Mr. Cleveland will have some very evil influences, much worse than those he had in July, August, and September of this year, and they will affect his health in a more marked degree.

It was certainly a serious mistake in the President calling Congress together on the Aug. 7th, 1893, during the time that he had such evil influences in his nativity; the aspects were evil on the day they met, and Congress will be about as submissive, and as much inclined to transact business for the good of the country, as the Long Parliament of England, which finally succeeded in beheading Charles I.

Commencing about the 5th of October, 1893, the influences slightly improve in Mr. Cleveland's horoscope, and continue more favorable until about the 28th of November, when he will have another evil aspect, which will affect his health, and bring him a world of trouble connected with Government affairs, which will continue to the 15th of December; afterwards things look a little more encouraging, and his health improves until February 1st. During February and March he will be very much perplexed in Government affairs; things throughout the country will look gloomy; his health will be poor, and Congress and he will be at loggerheads. After April 1st until the middle of November things will go much smoother, with a much brighter propect throughout the country. His health ought to be quite good, but from Nov. 15, 1894, and continuing until Nov. 15, 1896, he will have some very serious aspects affecting his nativity, very much worse than anything he has had for many years. The most marked evil times will be from Nov. 1st, 1894, to March 20th, 1895. His health will be very poor, and there is great danger that he will be afflicted with rheumatism and dropsy, and heart difficulty setting in. May, 1895, will also be an evil month; then again from the middle of September to November 10th, 1895, and during January, February, March, and April, 1896, and again during September and October, 1896, will all be unusually evil periods.

I shall think Mr. Cleveland a very fortunate man if he lives through these evil influences.

Except from April 1st to Aug. 1st, 1894, and in the spring of 1895, there will be serious disturbances and discontent throughout the country during Mr. Cleveland's administration.

The planetary influences in Mr. Cleveland's horoscope for the next three years, will be similar to those which afflicted Gen. Grant's horoscope in 1873, when he signed the bill which demonetized silver, and which brought such serious disaster and stagnation in business throughout the country in the fall of 1873, continuing for a number of years, and which caused the origin of the "Greenback party."

During 1873, Saturn and Uranus remained in close opposition, and afflicted both Saturn's and the Sun's places in the ascendant of the horoscope of Gen. Grant. As Mr. Cleveland's horoscope has similar aspects, I look for a similar condition of business in the United States while he remains in office.

ESTHER CLEVELAND'S NATIVITY.

The managing editor of the "New York Sunday News," on the evening of the above child's birth, sent to me to have its horoscope cast for the issue of Sept. 10, 1893.

I erected the following map of the heavens, made the necessary calculations, and wrote the following short sketch of the baby's life. I insert it in this pamphlet for the reasons—

First. It being the first President's child born in the White House, its birth is an important event in the history of the country, and it indicates to a certain extent the future of this Government, the condition of the people, and the future prosperity or adversity of the child's father.

Saturn in the mid-heaven, and also the Sun, afflicted by Mars, indicate that both the father and the United States will have to go through a siege of affliction within the next few years. The Sun and Saturn always represent the father in a child's nativity, and the Sun afflicted by Mars in the tenth,* also Saturn afflicting the 10th house, indicate that the father, were he in any ordinary business, would fail or become bankrupt within a few years after the child's birth. Also, they indicate that the father's health will become seriously affected, especi-

---

* The writer in "The Penny Magazine" would say "that the 10th house was fortified by the presence of Mars," but an enemy does not fortify, but afflicts and destroys. Mars being an evil planet, is an enemy.

ally when Mars comes to a conjunction of the Sun by direction, which will be in about one year and nine months, at which time he will come near dying, and will meet with serious afflictions otherwise. Also there will be great discontent and excitement throughout the country, especially as the President will have evil aspects affecting his own horoscope at the same time.

If Miss Esther goes into business, she will often meet with heavy losses, and become bankrupt.

Second. The enemies of Astrology have often made the remark, similar to Mr. Thomas Dick, that "Even though it were admitted that the heavenly bodies have an influence over the human race, yet we have no data whatever by which to ascertain the mode of its operation, or to determine the formula or rules by which calculations are to be made" . . ."and their pretensions nothing short of criminal imposition upon the credulity of mankind." And yet another Astrologer in a New York Sunday paper published Miss Esther's horoscope the same Sunday the one I wrote appeared in the "Sunday News," and we both agreed in all essential particulars. How was that possible if there are no rules or data in Astrology to go by? If the same time of birth were taken to ten thousand Astrologers, they would all agree in the essential particulars in the horoscope, as to the native's personal appearance, temper, mental qualities, marriage, time of marriage, disposition, physical and mental qualities of the husband, and whether a happy marriage or the reverse; children, ailments, sickness, length of life, etc., as ten thousand persons proficient in arithmetic would agree in their calculations in any special sum.

Astrologers are not like doctors, lawyers, ministers, etc., who all disagree with one another, and are always as wide apart in their deductions and conclusions as the north pole is from the south, or the east from the west. It is a common by-word that no two doctors ever agree in their diagnosis and treatment, unless they are Homœopathic or Astrological doctors.

The different religionists have done nothing but disagree and fight with one another all the world over, since Adam's time, and there is nothing so bitter and fierce as a religious war.

The whole stock in trade of a lawyer consists in disagreeing, and in taking a different view on the subject from the lawyer on the opposite side, and he keeps up this disagreement as long as he can, or as long as the money holds out.

The Astrologers compare very favorably with the followers of any of the above professions in the consistency of their deductions. Astrology is an exact science; it is almost impossible for its professors to disagree if the data are correct, and each of the Astrologers is proficient in the science.

Is it not strange that professors of Astrology should be persecuted in all ages? In ancient times they were persecuted as idolaters, because they were supposed to worship the Sun, Moon and Stars; and since the Reformation they have been persecuted as witches and heretics. Yet Astrologers are the only professors who agree with, and do not persecute, each other; and their science is as ancient as any of the sciences.

From "The Sunday News" of September 10, 1893.

THE BABY'S HOROSCOPE.

THE "SUNDAY NEWS" ASTROLOGIST PREDICTS A BRILLIANT LIFE.

A Washington dispatch says: "At 12 noon yesterday (Sept. 9th), Mrs. Cleveland gave birth to a girl baby."

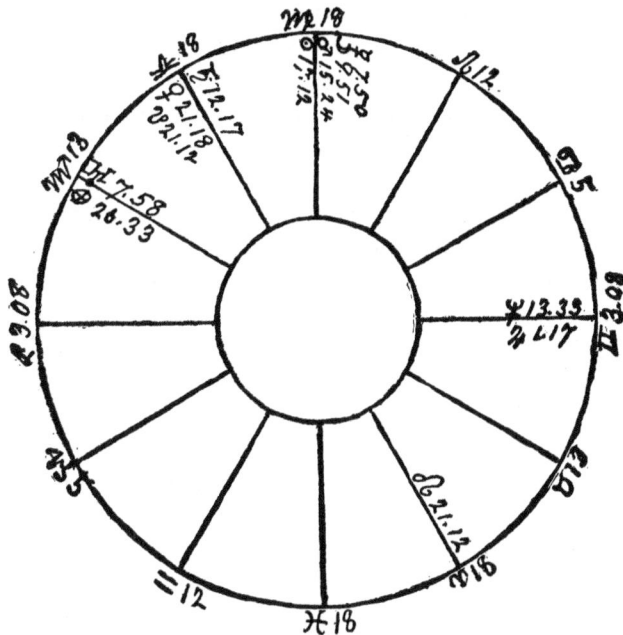

This young lady was born under the planet Jupiter in Gemini, just setting on the western horizon, with 3 deg. 8 min. of Sagittarius rising, and 18 deg. of Virgo on the mid-heaven. In personal appearance she will be similar to her mother. The books say: "Jupiter in Gemini represents a well-made, compact body, above the middle stature, sanguine or rather light complexion, with brown hair; full, expressive eyes, high forehead, the hair receding from the temples, prominent nose, and well-cut features. The deportment is graceful, courteous, gentle, mild, obliging, and good-natured."

In early life she will have delicate health, but the Sun, "the giver of life," being so strong in the mid-heaven, there is but little doubt that she will live to be old, although she will be given up for dead when a little short of two years old, and again when nearly five. At these times she will have a fever or inflammation of the intestines, or may meet with an accident at one or, in fact, at both these times; but there is more danger of real sickness, fever, or inflammation.

The intestines, chest, throat, and kidneys are the parts of her system that are the most likely to become affected, and in any sickness there is danger of these parts of the body becoming deranged. She will have other critical times for health, and will come near dying when 27, 28, and when nearly 30. After the latter age her health will not be seriously affected until she arrives at the age of 57 or 58.

This young lady has a very fortunate horoscope, and is certain to become very noted and prominent; like her father, she has four planets near a conjunction, in the mid-heaven. This is a remarkable phenomenon, and is what caused Mr. Cleveland to be elected President twice. She will arrive at great eminence and marry to great advantage.

This horoscope is remarkably fortunate for intellect, and she will develop into a remarkably smart and intellectual lady, and will be well known for her learning. She will acquire knowledge with great rapidity, and will take to learning as easily as "a duck takes to water." She will excel in languages and mathematics, and become proficient in music, will have a good voice, make an eloquent speaker and a good singer. She will be especially noted for her refinement, intelligence, and good sound common sense.

Ruth's sister will have a vast number of lady friends and acquaintances, and every one will like her. She will be as well known and as much appreciated as her mother. She has a much more fortunate horoscope than Baby Ruth, and will become more popular and more noted than that young lady. She will also marry to greater advantage, and live happier with her husband.

She weds a gentleman indicated by the planets Mercury in Virgo and Jupiter in Gemini. In a great measure he will be similar in appearance to herself, only much larger and taller. At the same time, he will never become stout. The books say: "He will be tall, well built, with dark brown or almost black hair, dark complexion, oval face, high forehead, prominent eyes, and large nose." He will be a fine, handsome-looking man, and be much admired. He will have a pleasing countenance, and an intelligent appearance; be witty, ingenious, and talented, a profound scholar and linguist, and capable of undertaking anything that requires great ability. They will live very happily and lovingly together, as the Sun makes a good aspect of Jupiter in the house of marriage. She is likely to marry only once, and not until she is 24 years of age, and may not marry until 27; but I think she will marry when 24.

Her husband will become very wealthy, and is likely to be a lawyer or hold some high and prominent position under the Government. She stands a much better chance of becoming "the first lady of the land" than her sister does.

She will have a small family of children, not more than three or four, and they are likely to be boys; but there is danger of one-half of them dying in their infancy. She is likely to become a noted authoress, and become very wealthy, and will be exceedingly fond of the curious and wonderful, and will have a liking for spiritualism and magnetism. She will also be very religious.

I should think that any young lady would be willing to spend years in study in order to be able to set up a chart of the heavens, and learn for herself the description of the gentleman she will marry, and whether it will be a happy marriage. It could be learned in a few hours' study and at an expense of twenty-five cents for an ephemeris and a table of houses; besides, it would enable her to point out all the constellations and any planets that may be visible in the heavens; persons not having any knowledge of Astronomy would have to take a few lessons in that science before they could erect a chart of the heavens by means of a table of houses and an ephemeris.

THE HOROSCOPE OF EMPEROR WILLIAM II. OF GERMANY.

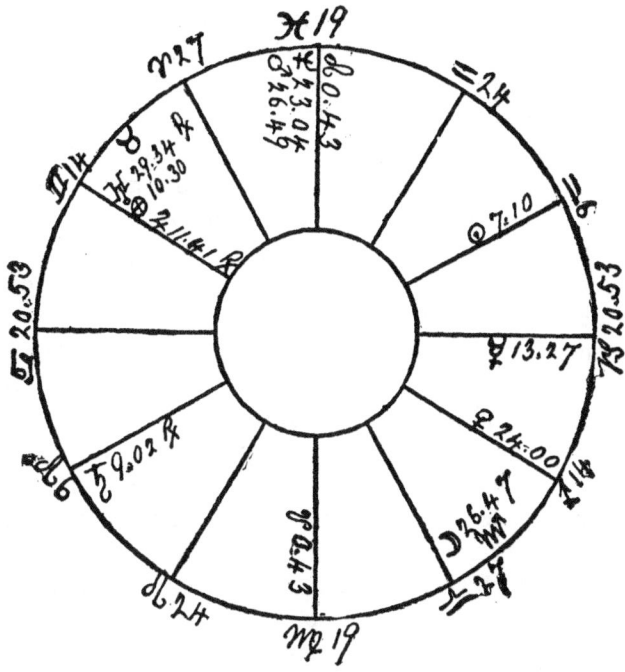

The Emperor was born January 27, 1859, at 2:54 P. M., at Potsdam, Germany. At his birth, 20 deg. of Cancer were rising, with the Moon, his ruling planet, in the sign Scorpio, in the 5th house, in close good aspect to Mars and Neptune in the mid-heaven.

His nativity does not indicate a long life, neither is it very fortunate in money matters, as Saturn is in the 2d house (the house of money) in close opposition (very evil aspect) to the Sun, lord of the 2d, in the 8th house, which indicates that he will be unfortunate in money matters, and is liable to run into debt, and that his substance will be wasted.

The nativity of William II. is rather fortunate for marriage. His wife is indicated by Mars, and being in good aspect to his planet, they will live harmoniously and happily. It is also fortunate for children: one of his sons is almost certain to succeed him as King of Prussia, but the kingdom will be heavily taxed, and be burdened with a large national debt when he comes to the throne.

William I. and the present Emperor both had Mars, the god of war, in the mid-heaven, therefore William II. will not be able to keep out of war any more than his grandfather. But as William I. had a more fortunate horoscope, and his 2d house was not afflicted, he won every war he was engaged in, and received great indemnities; also Mars was in good aspect to Venus, in its exaltation, and the Moon was leaving a good aspect of both, and applying to a good aspect of Jupiter in its own house; all of which indicated that he would increase in substance and power, and arrive at eminence and great honor; but the present Emperor will be unsuccessful in war, and will have to pay indemnities, as he has Saturn afflicting his 2d house in opposition to the lord thereof. These are evil influences especially in money matters.

The aspects in this horoscope, which indicated the present Emperor would arrive at his high position, are that Jupiter (lord of the mid-heaven), is in the 11th house, applying to a good aspect of Saturn and the Sun, and Mars in the mid-heaven in close good aspect to his own planet. These aspects are fortunate in elevating the native to honor; but when evil transits or directions afflict the Sun or Saturn, or both (which govern his substance), the native is liable to heavy losses and disaster.

The Emperor had one of these evil aspects about the 10th or 11th of November, 1892, which caused him a great deal of trouble and anxiety, especially in connection with the Reichstag and government affairs; he felt this evil aspect in a marked degree during April, May, and part of June and September, and will still feel it until the fore part of December, 1893. These evil aspects must have affected his health. But after that date he has favorable influences, and things will be more prosperous both for himself and his dominions; especially commencing in May, 1894, he will have a very fortunate aspect, and will become very popular. Should he commence war at that time with France or any other nation, he will be successful, at least for a time. In July and August, 1894, he will have some difficulty with the Reichstag on account of incurring extra expenses or increasing the taxes; but the latter part of the year 1894 will be a fortunate period. During February and March, 1895, there is danger of his having trouble with the Reichstag on account of the increased expenses of the Government; there is also likely to be a dispute or quarrel with some foreign power, but it may possibly be smoothed over for the time being. He will either be sick during these two months or there will be deaths, sickness, or misfortunes in his family.

During October and November, 1895, he will have evil aspects, which he will continue to feel all through the winter, especially in February and March, 1896. Still he may avoid war.

November and December, 1896, will not pass without his getting involved in war, or some serious disputes, and the whole of 1897 will be a remarkably evil year, during which he is certain to be at war with some foreign nation, likely to be either France or Russia, or both. The German armies will meet with defeat and heavy losses, and will undergo as serious a disaster as France suffered in 1870. There is much danger that the Emperor will not live over 1897; if he does, he is likely to meet with disgrace similar to that of Napoleon at the battle of Sedan.

The Emperor is almost certain to die a natural death, and not be killed in battle. He will suffer with some affection of the head, also of the kidneys and bladder, attended with rheumatism and swelling of the lower limbs; the heart will also become affected.

This horoscope is quite the reverse of that of Jay Gould's, who had Jupiter and Venus in the 2d house, the house of money. He began with nothing, and died worth seventy-two millions; whereas the Emperor of Germany, having his 2d house so much afflicted by Saturn, will either die poor or the nation will be heavily in debt at his death.

THE HOROSCOPE OF THE THIRD FRENCH REPUBLIC.

The Third French Republic was declared Sept. 4, 1870, at 4 P. M., Paris, France.

Thirteen degrees of Capricorn were rising, and 16 deg. of Scorpio were on the mid-heaven; the Moon was just coming to the ascendant and applying to a square of Mercury in Libra, a movable sign; the Moon was also making an opposition of Mars and Uranus, both in the 7th house. The Moon being 17 degrees from an opposition of Uranus, and reckoning a degree for a year, would indicate that the Government of France was in a critical condition in 1888 and '89, when the Boulanger excitement occurred, which came near upsetting the Government. There was another critical time about ten years after the Republic was declared, when the Moon made an opposition of Mars. At that time there came near being a war with Germany.

In the fall and winter of 1892–'93 Saturn was in evil aspect to the Moon's and Mercury's places, both in October and November, '92, and January and February, '93, when the great excitement about the Panama Scandal occurred. In January there was trouble with the laborers and also with the medical students, and riots occurred in Paris.

Saturn was in evil aspect again in July and August, when riots again occurred in Paris, connected with medical students and hospital doctors; and the Siamese excitement, when England threatened France with war.

But, commencing in the middle of December, 1893, and continuing to May 1, 1894, Saturn will be stationary in evil aspect to Uranus's place, Neptune in evil aspect to the Sun's place, and Uranus will be in evil aspect to Venus's place; therefore I look for more excitement and disturbances in Paris, and also in a number of other cities in France, than there have been for a number of years past. I shall deem the Third Republic remarkably fortunate if it can weather that storm.

In the latter part of 1895, and during the whole of 1896, the horoscope of France will be afflicted by Saturn and Uranus transiting its mid-heaven, and either it will be a very stormy period for the Chamber of Deputies, or else the Government will be involved in war. These evil aspects will continue until November, 1897. However, should the Republic survive that stormy period, there is nothing very threatening until February, 1899, at which time there will be severe afflictions for the Republic, which will continue until 1901.

On account of there being so many planets in angles, afflicted in movable signs, it is impossible for the French Republic to last a great number of years, and 1901 is about the limit of its existence. But it may even go under in the fore part of 1894, or the summer of 1895.

When President Carnot of France was assassinated in 1896, the nation was under considerable strain, but finally things adjusted themselves. The government has been put to a decided strain during the latter part of 1897 and the fore part of 1898, in the trial and conviction of Zola, the noted author, and there is really great danger that in 1901 the republic will not be able to weather the storm that will then rise.

APPENDIX.

INTRODUCTORY REMARKS TO A PAMPHLET

ENTITLED

WHY I AM AN ASTROLOGER,

AND A REPLY TO

RICHARD A. PROCTOR'S

ARTICLE ON THE

"HUMBUG OF ASTROLOGY,"

PUBLISHED IN THE "NEW YORK WORLD," FEB. 6TH, 1887, WITH CRITICISMS ON THE "NEW YORK WORLD," MR. PROCTOR, AND JUDGE JOHN JAY GORDON, OF THE COURT OF COMMON PLEAS, PHILADELPHIA, PA.

BY

L. D. BROUGHTON, M. D.

NEW YORK:
PUBLISHED BY THE AUTHOR,
68 SOUTH WASHINGTON SQUARE.

PREFACE.

THE revival of the ancient science of Astrology is now assured beyond a doubt. Twenty years ago when I first commenced publishing *Broughton's Monthly Planet Reader and Astrological Journal*—at that time the only publication of the kind in the world—the word "Astrology" had to be spoken in polite society with 'bated breath; the astrologers were relegated to the category of fools and knaves, and the ministers of the gospel consigned them to the torments and tortures of the infernal regions. The newspapers, lecturers and periodicals of that day mentioned the word "Astrology" only when they wanted to create a laugh, or to hold up its votaries to public ridicule; and I know from dearly-bought experience that astrologers had no more rights, either in the community or in a court of justice, than a "nigger" had "away down South" in the days of slavery. But thanks to the lectures and writings of Professors Tyndall, Huxley and Darwin, the scales are dropping from people's eyes, and they are beginning to find out that the world is governed by *fixed laws*, and that "miracles" are at a discount. Ministers no longer preach sermons against Astrology, and on account of public attention being drawn to the near approach of the *perihelion* of the planets, almost every newspaper, both in this country and Europe, has contained articles advocating the belief in the influence of the planets.

The *London Evening Standard* of July 6th, 1880, in commenting on Mr. B. G. Jenkins' paper on Meteorology and Planetary Influence, read by him before the Dulwich College Geological Club, said:—

" From the lofty heights of modern science we have been accustomed to look down with pity and contempt upon the astrologers of the Middle Ages,—the weak dabblers in science who were foolish enough to believe that the stars had an influence upon man. An allusion to astrologers was always good to raise a laugh at a science meeting, and the astrologers and alchemists were classed together as either dreamers or charlatans. Of late years, however, a certain reaction has set in. The astrologer is becoming rehabilitated very rapidly. The influence of the planets upon the earth is now admitted to be very distinct, and fresh proofs of their disturbing influences are constantly cropping up."

A few scientific men having made observations on the coincidence of Sun-spots with extraordinary features of weather, and also discovering that the Sun-spots were caused by the influence of the planets, and in this way having gradually led the thinking portion of the public to recognize that the master-minds of former generations were not entirely mistaken in tracing the mutations of weather and of mundane events to planetary influence; the day is now fast dawning when Astrology shall again take rank with the physical sciences, and the predictions of the astrologer will go hand in hand with the calculations of the astronomer.

Although the approaching *perihelion* of the planets has not as yet produced any particular famine except in Ireland and certain parts of Russia and Turkey; nor any noted pestilence except the yellow fever in 1878 and 1879 in New Orleans, Granada, Vicksburg and Memphis; the black pest and diphtheria in Russia and part of Turkey, and the cholera in India; yet everyone knows that long droughts are becoming more common; the heats of summer are felt to be more oppressive and destructive to human life,—more people dying from heat in cities with the mercury at 85° than in former years at 95°; *malarial fever* was never before so common among all classes, and steamboat and railroad accidents are almost of every day occurrence. These are some of the effects of our earth not getting its usual share of life and magnetism from the sun, on account of so many of the other superior planets being in their *perihelion* and drawing more than their usual share of life and magnetism from that body.

INTRODUCTORY REMARKS.

Near the first of June, 1886, Mr. Romaine (a complete stranger to me), was sentenced to eighteen months imprisonment in the Penitentiary at Philadelphia, Pennsylvania, solely, so far as I can find out, for practicing astrology. Judge Gordon, when passing sentence on the prisoner, made use of the following words:—"I can conceive of no crime, except possibly low forms of gambling, that is more injurious than the business you carried on."

The general reader will naturally infer, after perusing the above statement, that practicing astrology is a very low business, and that there are but few lines of occupation that can be compared to it, in its degrading effect. That there may be a difference of opinion in regard to the science and practice of astrology is reasonable to expect, but from what cause that difference arises may not be so clear; and it is to make it as clear as possible, and to remove certain erroneous impressions, that I write these Introductory Remarks. The facts and the proofs of the truth of astrology will be given in the Elements of Astrology.

In all nations, both barbarous and civilized, that we have any knowledge of, and in all ages, wherever and whenever there has been a difference of opinion among men, either in learning, science, or religion, those on one side who are in the majority have always claimed the right of imprisoning and putting to death those on the other side who are in the minority, and they have generally carried that assumed right into execution.

The justice or injustice of such proceedings I shall not stop to argue. I only give it as a fact which all history goes to confirm, even up to the present day; and such is likely to be the case as long as the human race exists. I shall bring some very startling evidence in the volume itself. assertion, both in these Introductory Remarks, and in the pamphlet itself. Not only have the minority, or those who are in subjection for the time being, been inprisoned and put to death, but as far as possible they have always been prevented from being heard, either by public speaking, and meetings, or in the public prints;* yet, strange to say, these very persecutions by the majority, instead of accomplishing the object intended, have always had the opposite effect. Hence have arisen such sayings, as "the blood of the martyrs is the seed of the church."

I have divided these Introductory Remarks into sections, in the following order, and for the purpose herewith indicated:

First:—Why I undertook to write this pamphlet.

Second:—The object I hope to accomplish by the present publication.

Third:—An introduction of myself to the reader; a statement of my standing in the society where I have been known for thirty years; also a

---

* See pages 400 and 404.

short description of my parentage, and of what my family has suffered in the cause of good government, and for the cause of astrology; and finally a declaration of the reasons why I became an astrologer.

First:—Why I undertook to write this pamphlet.

To the general reader, the conviction and imprisonment of one person may appear a very slight matter, and not worth troubling one's self about. But it ought to be borne in mind that if one person can be sent to prison unjustly, another may also be sent thither; and finally it may come to the reader's turn himself, to be sent to prison unjustly.

While living under a good goverment, it is very pleasant to think that each individual is protected in his rights, no matter how low or humble he may be.

Let us suppose that one of these individuals finds his property right invaded. What is the course he pursues to gain redress? He applies to the legal tribunals to adjudicate the case, and upon a hearing, it is possibly decided favorably. The sheriff takes the order of the court and proceeds to collect the amount, and if the execution is satisfied, it is well: but if force is resorted to, to prevent the execution, the sheriff calls on a number of citizens who will aid him in securing the injured party's rights. If this should not be sufficient, perhaps, he calls upon the Governor of the State to call out the State troops: and the Governor may even have to call on the President of the United States for troops. And all this may occur to protect one poor individual in his right of property, or his life. This is all very nice in theory, and it is nothing but just that the theory should always be carried out in practice.

In a commonwealth like the State of New York, there may possibly be a dozen murders committed in one year. The county or State goes to a great expense and trouble in arresting the murderers, and in convicting and executing them. All this is done so that each person may know beforehand, if he premeditates committing murder, or indeed any crime, that no expense and trouble will be spared by the county or State in bringing the criminal to justice; and also that each person may know and feel that his life, liberty and property are held sacred. Where legislatures enact good and wise laws, and where there are just and wise judges and legal courts to carry these laws into effect, the commonwealth that possesses them is said to have a good government, and its people are generally happy and prosperous.

On the other hand, let us draw a picture giving the condition of the people where all these things are reversed; that is, where the people are living under a bad government, where bad laws are enacted, and where those laws are executed by unjust judges, and corrupt or biased juries.

I have already supposed that there may be about one dozen murders committed in the State of New York in a year, and that there may be ten or twelve criminals hanged or imprisoned for these crimes in the same length of time. But under a bad government, enacting and executting bad laws, if we can believe history, in a community no larger than the State of New York, there have been thousands and even tens of thousands of innocent persons executed in a single year, and in such an excruciating manner that even to think of their sufferings at the present day, makes our blood run cold. This state of things was continued year after year.

I need only refer the reader to the history of the trials and executions of heretics, witches and wizards, in almost all nations and in all ages. And, as Robert G. Ingersoll has said, there is no doubt but that the authorities would have gone on hanging and burning heretics and witches, even up to the present day, were it not that the number of heretics and witches who seriously objected to being either hanged or roasted alive, gradually became too numerous.

To send even one person to jail unjustly is treading on very dangerous ground. If we may be guided by past history, the sentencing and executing of one heretic, witch or wizard, or, as in the case of Mr. Romaine, the imprisonment of one man for the studying and practicing of a very ancient and useful art and science, may become a most injurious precedent, like that of the first person who was guillotined on account of politics in France, a circumstance which eventually led to the guillotining of Robespierre himself.

Even the conviction of Mr. Romaine of a misdemeanor, and the sentencing of him for felony, is of itself, as they would say in the British House of Commons, a very dangerous precedent. Such proceedings may be compared to a little boy with a lighted match in close proximity to a powder magazine, which may explode it at any moment.

Blackstone in his "Commentaries," in page 60, Book Fourth, says: "To deny the possibility, nay, actual existence of witchcraft and sorcery, is at once flatly to contradict the revealed word of God, in various passages of the Old and New Testament; and the thing itself is a truth to which every nation in the world hath in its turn borne testimony, either by examples seemingly well attested or by prohibitory laws." If it was possible for the legislatures in all ages and all nations (including even the Christian nations), to have been deceived in their belief in witchcraft, is it not possible that all the Christian nations of the present day may equally be deceived in their disbelief in astrology; especially when all these disbelievers are ignorant of even the first A B C of that science.

Mr. Romaine has been tried, convicted and sentenced, and for anything that I know to the contrary, he is now serving out his sentence in the Penitentiary at Philadelphia, Pennsylvania. But I wish to have Mr. Romaine retried in another court, and before another jury; the court to be "Public Opinion," and the jury to be composed of the world at large.

I believe that in reopening a case for a new trial, the lawyers on both sides are sometimes allowed to write out their speeches, and even have them printed, and hand them to the judges to read and study over at their leisure, instead of making any personal argument, or set speech in their presence. I have followed this method in making my appeal to the higher court, in which I hope to have Mr. Romaine's case retried. And if I cannot get a clear verdict in his favor, I trust at least the jury will disagree.

In my pamphlet, I shall only plead Mr. Romaine's side of the case. The other side can be found in all the "Encyclopedias," and "Biographical

Dictionaries," of all the European Languages. It can be obtained in "Appleton's American Cyclopedia," and I might say in nearly every book that treats on the natural sciences, except in those which are specially devoted to astrology. These last named, of course, give Mr. Romaine's side of the question, and to them I refer those readers who may desire a more extensive argument than I can possibly give in this pamphlet, on behalf of astrology. I have in my own possession over fifty different text books on the science of astrology.

Why all the publishers of encyclopedias and dictionaries continue to publish what they know, or ought to know, are falsehoods, in the articles on astrology in their various publications, I shall endeavor to explain, in the latter part of this pamphlet. I shall also give a history of the "Act for the Suppression of Fortune-telling," under which Mr. Romaine was convicted, and a copy of the law itself, which is not very creditable to those persons who were engaged in engineering it through the Pennsylvania Legislature. Also will be found an account of my humble efforts to defeat the enactment of the said bill while it was pending in the Legislature.

Second:—The object I hope to accomplish by the present publication.

If I succeed in getting the jury to disagree, I shall have accomplished a great result. Such a disagreement, like all disagreements of juries, will naturally create discussion, and the discussion will certainly redound to the benefit of astrology. In the forepart of the pamphlet, I compare the calculations in astrology to those in arithmetic, and demonstrate that they are almost equally infallible; but in the latter part of the pamphlet, where I refer to Mr. Babbage's calculating machine, I show that astrology is even more infallible than arithmetic. Consequently, if they send people to prison for practicing astrology, they ought doubly to send them there for practicing arithmetic.

No doubt it will strike the reader as a little remarkable, that astrology should be the only science or art in existence concerning which expert testimony is entirely discarded, and in regard to which only the opinions of men who are the most ignorant of the subject, are entertained. If I can get the public's attention directed even to this point, I shall then not have published this pamphlet in vain. The opponents of astrology meet this point by presupposing that all who give any attention to that science, are either fools or knaves, and therefore their testimony cannot be taken into account.

It may be very puzzling for the reader to understand, how it happens that a person who learns reading, writing, and arithmetic, and who possibly adds a knowledge of chemistry, geography and astronomy, if he stops there, he remains a very sensible and honest man. But if to these acquirements he should add the study of astrology, he then becomes insane, or dishonest. But if we can believe all the Newspapers, Dictionaries, and Encyclopedias published at the present day, such is the fact, whether it can be explained or not. That is one reason why it is almost an impossibility to get anything published in any newspaper in favor of astrology, while anything that is derogatory to that science, can get prominent notice, and almost any amount of space.

Only last March, a correspondent, signing himself J. J. Y., asked the editor of the "New York World," for some information about astrology, and received for his answer the following paragraph:

"In this day and generation a man who believes that the planets govern our actions should not let any one know it. Such an admission is prima facie evidence of insanity or idiocy."

For a wonder, however, the World inserted, the following communication from the writer of these pages:

To the Editor of the World :—

Dear Sir :—Will you please explain why those people who make a lifelong study of astrology, are the greatest believers in it, while those like yourself, who do not know even the A B C of astrology, laugh at and ridicule it? Should it ever be the fortune of "J. J. Y." to study astrology, and prove for himself whether the planets have any influence on the earth and its inhabitants or not, he will exclaim, "What ignorant men the Editors of the World are!" I have made astrology a special study for over forty years; my father made it a study for about forty years; and my grandfather for over forty years, making altogether over one hundred years of careful observation and study, and during that time I have had six children born, and my father had eight and my grandfather had seven or eight born. The exact moment of birth of all these children was noted and all their nativities calculated, all of which have proved the truth of astrology. I have also examined near or about one hundred thousand of other people's nativities, and whenever the time of birth has been correct they have all gone on the side of proving the truth of astrology. I have had also a number of professors of colleges as students, I have had also some of the most learned and wealthy people in the United States and in England as students and patrons.

They are the people who ought to have been able to find out the falsity of astrology. But the fact of the matter is, it is only the ignorant, the insane, and the idiots who do not believe in astrology.

Yours, Respectfully,

L. D. Broughton, M. D.,

March 16th, 1886.   66 West Fourth Street, New York.

In discussing these letters, my son, who assists me in my business, objected to further interest on my part, saying that "I had already suffered enough for astrology, and I ought now to let some one else suffer."

Should the time ever arrive when astrology, like all other arts and sciences, is popularly estimated in accordance with what its friends, and those who are the most experienced, and who possess the fullest knowledge on the subject, have to say about it; instead of being estimated in accordance with the statements of its enemies, and of those who have no knowledge or experience whatever, then the reaction will be remarkable, and the public will begin to find out how much they have been gulled for the last two hundred years, by those pretended scientific men, who give opinions on subjects they know nothing about. New editions of Dictionaries and Encyclopedias and other scientific works will be called for, as the publishers will discover that the present editions have become entirely obsolete.

If the reader accepts the theory that in forming a judgment respecting astrology, we are to be guided by those persons who possess the most knowledge and experience on the subject, in all parts of the world where the science is cultivated, and also that those who possess such knowledge are to be regarded as the true experts of the science; he will likewise perceive, before he concludes these Introductory Remarks, that the standing of the present writer, as an authority on the subject under consideration, is almost unrivalled. In the article which was published in the "New York World," I stated that I had studied astrology for over forty years. During that time I think I have put astrology to the most severe tests, almost every day, which it is possible ever to apply it to. I have also read all the books in the English language, that I could lay my hands on, which have been written for or against the science. After applying the tests for so long a period, extending over successive generations, if I am still deceived, and if my forefathers were also deceived, then I think it is possible to deceive even the very elect. But even supposing that I have been continually deceived, how am I to be convinced of it by persons like Judge Gordon of Philadelphia, who does not even know the first principles of astrology, who never subjected it to a single test, or made a single calculation, and does not know even one solitary fact relating either to the truth or falsity of the science? If sending people to prison, and making "Buncombe speeches," like those of Judge Gordon, is going to convince me, and all other astrologers, that we have been so long deceived, then why did not the hanging and roasting alive of so many millions of heretics and witches in all parts of the civilized world, convince all the remaining heretics and witches, that they were wrong and had been deceived? Judge Gordon's vituperation of Mr. Romaine, and the condemnation of that victim to prison, reminds me of the scolding and whipping of "Topsy," by Aunt Ophelia in "Uncle Tom's Cabin." After Topsy had gone through all the hardships inflicted, she says: "Golly! Aunt Ophelia's whippin' wouldn't kill a skitty."

I think I have made this subject sufficiently plain, and exposed the ignorance of all those who condemn astrology, and persecute astrologers, when they themselves have no practical knowledge on the subject, and have endeavored to prove that it is only the same kind of persecution which harassed Copernicus, Galileo, Samuel Hahnemann, and I might even include all the inventors and discoverers in art or science in former ages. But possibly I might illustrate this point, and make it plainer by one or two anecdotes, which have reference to other sciences or subjects, not at all connected with astrology. In my early years when I was studying Chemistry, if I attempted to argue a point, my teacher would stop me short, by saying:—"You know nothing without experiments," and that has been a lesson which I have never forgotten. If a person can **know** nothing in other sciences, like chemistry, without experiments, then how is it possible for him to know anything in practical astrology, which is a thousand times more intricate than chemistry, without putting it to a single test, or making a single observation.

Another illustration may not be out of place, as it may possibly explain how people, through ignorance, may condemn astrology, on account of its supposed wickedness, similar to the following lecturer on Natural History, who supposed he had a clear case of Natural Theology, or the goodness of God, but which was not proven by experiments and observations.

Some thirty years ago, when I was studying geology in Philadelphia, Prof. Ennis, my teacher gave an account of a man lecturing on Natural History before an audience, among whom there was a person who had traveled in the Arctic Regions. Both the lecturer and the particular listener were known to Prof. Ennis. The former was giving a description of a particular species of deer, which had large spreading horns, or antlers. He was telling how useful those horns were for brushing or scraping the snow from the grass, so that the deer could eat the uncovered herbage at its leisure, and he illustrated his remarks by the motion of his own head, from one side to the other over the desk in front of him. He went on expatiating on the goodness of God in providing the animal with just such horns, in those high latitudes, where the snow covers the ground more than one half of the year, and remarked that if this provision had not been made by an all-wise providence, the deer would all certainly perish of hunger. When this observation was made, the man who had visited the Arctic Regions, burst out laughing. After the lecturer had concluded his discourse, he went to the traveller and asked him why he laughed. The answer was, "that the thing was so good he could not keep from laughing," and added, "do you not know that every year, before the snow begins to fall, that particular species of deer always sheds its horns?"

The above anecdote illustrates what mistakes a man is liable to make when he attempts to speak on a subject or science concerning which he is not well informed. Nothing will, or can, stand in the place of facts, experiments, and observations. Either the lecturer on Natural History in the above anecdote, or the Creator, made a mistake in regard to the use of the horns. But had the lecturer seen the deer, and watched them in the different seasons of the year, he might have observed that they had other methods of brushing the snow off the grass, than by using their horns, to which he was giving such unmerited praise. Had the horns grown on the lecturer's own head, he might have used them for some such purpose, and, like Nebuchadnezzar of old, he could then have eaten the grass at his leisure, even in the middle of winter.

The objections and arguments which the enemies of astrology, and those who are ignorant of that science, bring against it, on account of its wickedness, &c., when they are brought to the test of experiment and observation, are like the horns of the deer, and the falling of the snow. When the snow of purity, truth, and science begins to fall, those horns of arguments and objections, which had stood aloft in ignorance; when they are needed, have already fallen from the deer's head, and lay rotting on the ground.

In the latter part of this volume, I believe I have examined and answered every argument and objection that has been, or can be brought against Astrology, even in the case of twins, or triplets, and also of many thousands of people who are born in one day. Of course the skeptics say that all those persons ought to have the same Nativity, and should experience similar events through life, &c., &c. All such arguments are about as near perfect nonsense as we can find in this world, and the only puzzling part of it is, how any man or woman, outside of an insane asylum, could get such ridiculous ideas into their heads. And yet I cannot remember ever lecturing on astrology without some man or woman getting up in the audience and making just such objections. Only this fall, while giving part of the following pamphlet in a lecture, an old man got up in the middle of the lecture to ask me if he could put a few questions when I got through. But he could not wait until I had finished, and went on to ask the same old stereotyped questions just as if he thought it was a grand new discovery that he had made. The fact being that those very same questions had been asked and answered thousands of years ago, as may be seen by reference to "Ptolemy's Tetrabiblos," and other ancient works on astrology.

Whenever an astrologer is arrested for practicing his profession, all the newspapers, in giving an account of it, have such headings as "An Astrologer who did not know his own Nativity," or "An Astrologer who did not know his own Fate," &c. In answer to those newspaper headings, in the latter part of the volume, I think I have turned the tables on the editors themselves.

THIRD:—An introduction of myself to the reader, a statement of my standing in the society where I have been known for thirty years, also a short description of my parentage and what my family has suffered in the cause of good government, and for the cause of astrology; and finally a declaration of the reasons why I became an astrologer.

Solomon says, "Let another praise thee, yea a stranger, and not thine own self." Were I to consult my own feelings, I should pass by this branch of my topic in silence. But when it comes to matters of persecutions and imprisonment, I think we ought not to stand knocking at the door of modesty, or be guided by the strict rules of etiquette.

In the summer of 1885 I wrote to a friend, who is one of the editors of a leading daily news paper of New York City, stating that I had recently buried my oldest son, and that it had so affected his mother's and my own health, that we had concluded to take a trip to Europe for a change of scene, and in the hope that we might be improved by the ocean voyage, I desired him to give me letters of introduction to persons in London, Paris and Dublin, as we proposed visiting each of those cities. I received the following reply:

New York, July 28th, 1885.

My Dear Doctor:—I enclose a letter to my brother, who has a very good position and large acquaintance in London, and to whom I have often spoken of you. I know no one in Paris, or in Ireland. I am leaving town this afternoon, or I should call and bid your wife and yourself bon voyage in person, and I hope you may have a pleasant journey and a safe return, and complete restoration to health.

I am pained to hear of the death of your son,—which must have been announced when I was out of town. It is a pity such a bright young man, so intelligent, and so amiable as I remember him, should be taken away. Pray accept my very sincere condolence.

Yours, faithfully,

Dr. L. D. Broughton.　　　　　　　　George I. O——."

The following is the letter of introduction.

New York, July 28th, 1885.

Dear David:—This will introduce to you Dr. Broughton, the Seer and Astrologer of whom I have often spoken to you, and who has, for as many as fifteen years been my "guide, philosopher and friend." I shall be very glad if you will do anything you can to oblige him, while in London, and am very sure you will enjoy meeting a gentleman who represents three successive generations of occult intelligence, besides being in his proper person a physician of ability and experience.

Yours, Sincerely,

Geo. I. O——."

I had other letters of introduction to parties in England of a similar nature. I have not given the real name of the above writer for obvious reasons.

Over twenty years ago, a gentleman from the Pacific Slope, was requested to buy a "Raphael's Ephemeris."* He called in vain at most of the booksellers in St. Louis, Chicago, New York, and other cities, and at a shop in Boston, there he got the same answer, "No!" A gentleman who happened to be present, looked up and said, "If you should pass through New York, you can get the work from Dr. Broughton." The gentleman from the West wrote down the address, and while he was doing so, the stranger added, "You call and see the Doctor; you will find him a perfect gentleman, and the best astrologer in America." I never knew who that stranger was. The man from the West started for New York the same afternoon, and on his arrival here, he put his wife in a carriage and sent her to his hotel, while he came direct to my office. He has since brought some of the most prominent people of the United States to consult me, and whenever I, or members of my family, travel in the neighborhood of his relatives or their friends, we are always welcome guests.

Some two years ago, a stranger called to consult me, and while I was making a chart of the heavens for his time of birth, he said:—"Do you know that you are a constant theme of conversation in the capital of

---

Note:—* An Ephemeris is a small book or pamphlet, containing the longitude, latitude, and declination of the moon, and seven of the larger planets, for each day in the year, and also the right ascension, longitude, and declination of the sun, for every day.

Italy." That gentleman I afterwards learned was a sculptor of almost world-wide reputation; he has been the means of sending some of the most wealthy and prominent people of America and Europe to consult me.

A number of years ago I was attending a sick lady in the upper part of the city, and after I came out of her room, her husband requested me to sit down in the parlor. Having asked me about his wife, he said: "Where do you think I first saw your name, and heard people talking about you?" He said, "In Hong Kong, China." He told me that some missionaries had taken several of my publications out there, and that he heard them talking about me, and reading them. People have been recommended to me from all parts of the world, and many have come long distances to see me. Sam. Ward, who died in Europe a few years ago, spoke of me almost everywhere he traveled. When he died I lost a good friend, but a close intimacy has been kept up by some of his relatives.

Among the many friends of the late Gen. John H. Devereux, there was none who felt more grieved to learn of his death than the writer of these pages. During his visits to New York, he often spent a pleasant hour with me in my office. In the fall of 1884 while journeying in the West, I stopped at Cleveland to visit a number of friends, among whom were Mr. Devereaux, who was then President of the C. C. C. & I. Railroad, and Mr. Chas. Lattimere Chief Engineer of the N. Y. P. & O. Railroad, and President of the International Institute for Preserving and Perfecting Weights and Measures. In company with the latter gentleman I called on Mr. Devereaux at his office, during my visit he reiterated a previously made request for me to write his nativity in full as soon as I could spare time. After a pleasant hour spent in conversation, as I was leaving, Mr. Devereaux remarked. "Mr. Lattimere tells me this is your first visit to Cleveland, we do not often do this sort of thing, but we want to make you feel good so you will come again, and that you will remember your visit to our city;" and handing me passes to New York for myself and wife, we parted. The passes were not so much in themselves, but the kindly and cordial manner in which they were so unexpectedly given, left a lasting impression on my mind.

I might here state that Mr. Devereux's nativity was one of the most difficult I ever handled. The positions of the planets were extremely complicated, and he did not know the exact time of birth. Partly on that account, and partly on account of sickness in my family, I had not finished writing it at the time of Mr. Devereux's fatal illness. I should have called to see him at his hotel in New York, on his return from Europe, where he had been to try if the sea voyage would benefit his health, only I was afraid that I might, in his then weak condition, possibly say something which might produce a very gloomy impression on his mind, and thus in some way retard or prevent his recovery. For that reason I denied myself the pleasure of seeing him. Only the night before he died, he said to Mr. Latimere's son, who was attending him, "I would like to have Dr. Broughton's opinion on my case."

After his death, at the request of one of his family, I wrote out a short sketch of his nativity, also giving the aspects in operation at his death.

I have made this part of my Introductory Remarks much longer than I had intended, and will close the subject by alluding to two or three other matters which have reference to myself. I could fill a book of such instances, but as the lawyers say, that would be only cumulative proof.

For a number of years I have been a member of a society called "The Ancient Order of Druids," and after having been elected and serving a term as its presiding officer, I have been elected and re-elected Treasurer every term since. All the Lodges or Groves of that order in the city of New York send delegates to a monthly meeting, which is called the First Grand District, where they transact business for the mutual benefit of all the Groves. I have been re-elected Treasurer for this Grand District" for a number of years, and without opposition.

In the yearly elections of the Grand Grove of the State of New York, for the year 1886, I was unanimously chosen Grand Treasurer for that Grand Grove; and when I was installed, a member belonging to another Grove, was disposed to quarrel with me because I had not asked him to be one of my bondsmen. We have had a Druidic University in the city of New York for a number of years, although not in active operation. I have been re-elected Treasurer every year since it was incorporated.

I was also the Treasurer for the Eclectic Medical Association of the State of New York, for a number of years in succession. Even private persons who have been unfortunate in having their trunks robbed, and from banks failing, have afterwards brought their money to me for safe keeping, and without interest.

I simply mention a few of these circumstances, in order that the reader may have some idea of my standing among people with whom I have associated many years. And yet according to the "Penal Code" of the State of New York, I am classed among "prostitutes," "gamblers," "fortune-tellers," "clairvoyants," and people of "disreputable character," and I am liable at any moment, upon any frivolous complaint, to be arrested, and even without a trial before a jury, to be consigned to prison for six months or required to give bonds to a large amount, that I will discontinue the practice of my profession.

It strikes me as very curious that the people and the law should regard the same things and persons from such opposite standpoints. If these laws were the will of the people, there ought to be no clashing, and the two should run smoothly together. I have reference now to myself and the "Penal Code." There is not a person who knows me, who would class me among criminals, and yet the "Penal Code" does.

No wonder that the hardy toilers called the "Knights of Labor," should be willing to receive all classes of people into their order, either men or women, except liquor sellers, and lawyers. The first rob them of their money and their reason, and the latter of their money, and sometimes of their rights, and their liberties. Next time the "Penal Code" is revised, if the "Knights of Labor" (and they are growing stronger and more numerous every day,) have anything to say in the matter, no doubt the rumsellers, and the lawyers, will be classed with the prostitutes, the gamblers, the fortune-tellers, the clairvoyants, and the disreputable characters. Of course I shall be sorry to keep such company, but if it is the law of the State, I must submit to the inevitable.

But even this is not enough for Chas. A. Dana, of the "New York Sun." In his newspaper, for years past, he has been writing articles and editorials, drawing the attention of the Legislature to the great evil of astrology, and urging that body to enact more stringent laws against the professors of that science. But in the same articles he bewails the radicalism of the New York Legislature, and is afraid that they are too liberal to do their duty. In one instance he says:—"Whatever excuse the ancients had for their belief in astrology, there is no excuse for that belief at the present day."

I have written replies to every article he has published against astrology, for the last ten years, and have taken pains that they should all be handed in to the chief editor of the "Sun," but he has never allowed one of my replies to be published. The "Sun shines for all," but only all on one side of a question, and that must be its own side.

Is Charles A. Dana afflicted with periodical fits of insanity, or with the disease known to physicians as "Monomania?" When persons are so afflicted, there is no knowing when their malady will become dangerous. At one time in his case, it shows itself in a violent hatred to astrology, which, to coin a new word, may be termed "Astro-Phobia." At another time it is a special animosity against the "Fraudulent President." Then it develops itself into a great dislike to "Gen. Grant." At another time it manifests itself in "Addition, Division, and Silence," and "Turn the Rascals out." Now it is incubating itself in the President's Cabinet, and the "Pan-Electric Telephone." But there is no knowing how soon it may switch on to astrology again, and then he will want more stringent laws against that science enacted. Therefore I give the New York Legislature due notice, and they must govern themselves accordingly.

Some of Mr. Dana's attacks on astrology are ridiculous beyond conception. Of course those persons who read them, and do not know anything about the subject, cannot see where the laugh comes in. They remind me of an incident at Saratoga, some time ago. Seeing posters up on the walls stating there was to be a lecture, on a certain evening, against Free Masonry, and being in search of more light, I traveled East to hear the lecture.

No one who is not a Mason can form any conception of what the lecturer had to say about the order, nor what ridiculous mistakes he committed—not knowing what he was talking about. One of the great objections he made against Masonry was that it was a "religion." He said the Masons believed in a "God," they had an Altar, a Bible, and a Hymn book, and if that was not a religion, he would like to know what was. Moreover it was a religion from which "women," "cripples," the "sickly," and "imbecile" were excluded, and he might also have added, that "Free Masons" excluded men like himself, who could not get a "Mason" to vouch for their "honesty," their "good moral character," and for their character as "good citizens."

Is it not strange that men like the above lecturer, supposing them to have only one grain of common sense in their heads, should be going from town to town making fools of themselves, and discoursing on subjects to people who are equally as ignorant as themselves?

Charles A. Dana and others who publish attacks on astrology, are on a par with this lecturer, and their articles are calculated only for persons like themselves, who are altogether ignorant of that science. "Hamlet" must have had such people as Mr. Dana and the aforesaid lecturer in his mind's eye, when giving directions to the "players," says:—"Though it make the unskillful laugh, cannot but make the judicious grieve; the censure of which one, must, in your allowance, o'er weigh a whole theatre of others."

Compared to listening to the lecturer in question, it is even a pleasure to read books which expose "Free Masonry," as those authors sometimes know a little of what they are writing about. But I shall not say one word in defense of men who have, of their own free will, taken a most solemn oath not to reveal certain "secrets," and yet afterwards have broken that oath. Such men at least should not be admitted into the society of really honorable men and women.

To prove how innocent people sometimes suffer, when legislatures commence to enact bad laws, and those laws are carried into effect, I need only refer to the reading of the Bible in the family, (a religious duty which a great many Christian people deem almost indispensable at the present day), but which was at one time regarded as one of the most heinous offences, and if detected was attended with the most severe punishment. I refer the reader to Benjamin Franklin's Autobiography, where he tells us that his forefathers used a Bible fastened under the seat of a four-legged stool, the leaves being held in their place by pack-threads; and that when they wanted to turn a leaf over they had to slide it under the threads. When the family assembled to hear the reading of the Bible, one of them was stationed at some distance from the house, to act as "sentry," and to give warning of the approach of any stranger. If any one appeared, the stool was instantly replaced on its legs, and the family all looked as harmless as doves, as if they had been doing nothing wrong or wicked. Yet those innocent people had been committing one of the gravest crimes known to the law at that time, and if they had been detected in the act they would all have been consigned to the "rack," the "boot," or the "screw," or might even have been roasted alive.

Of the real meaning of such terms as the rack, the boot, and the screw, we can form but a very slight conception at the present day, and it would take up too much space to describe the torture in these pages.

As in Geology, we can often trace an unwritten history of the epochs and ages of the earth by noticing the strata, the rocks, and the fossils, so we can trace the unwritten history of the human race by noticing old ruins, pieces of pottery, medals, and ancient implements of war. We can also find evidence of religious persecution in old buildings, which likewise help us to decipher an unwritten history. Thomas Paxton Hood, in one of his books, gives an account of the tearing down of an edifice in the north of England. In the upper part of that building was found a small room, about three feet wide, between two solid walls, with a secret entrance thereto from above. On a table was found part of a candle, a flint, steel, some tinder and a Bible laid open. Who the owner of those relics was, God only knows. But we can imagine an old man stealing into his little cubby-hole by a secret entrance, beginning to strike his flint and steel together until he procured a light, and then commencing to read his Bible. We can also see in our minds eye, the detectives dogging him at every turn, until at last they have got evidence sufficent to convict him; and then he is lead off to be roasted alive in this world, so as to save him from an everlasting roasting in the world to come. And all for the awful crime of reading the Bible.

If Charles A. Dana had been living in those days, no doubt he would have said that "whatever excuse the ancient Jews had for reading the Old Testament, and the early Christians for reading the New Testament, there is no excuse for their reading either at the present day;" and he would have used the columns of the "Sun" in advocating, and also in pressing upon the attention of the Legislature, the need of more stringent laws against the reading of the "Bible." No doubt he would bewail the liberalism of Parliament, which prevented the full accomplishment of a public duty. The worst of it is, when Legislatures commence to enact laws of this class, they never know where or when to stop. At first they might deem reading the Bible only a slight criminal offence, and enact a law making it a misdemeanor, and if any one was caught after that time reading the Bible, he would be consigned to the common jail for from three to six months. But if there happened to be a judge on the bench who was a bigoted Catholic, like Judge Gordon of Philadelphia, the prisoner might then be convicted of a misdemeanor, and the judge, exceeding his authority, sentence the prisoner to a felon's cell, or the state prison. But still some people might continue reading the Bible, and of course Bible reading must be stopped at any cost. The Legislature goes on enacting more stringent laws, changing the crime of reading the Bible from a misdemeanor to a felony, and from a felony to a capital offence, punishable by hanging. Then, if that does not answer, they resort to the rack, the boot, and the screw.

When they have commenced to make laws against Bible reading, it must be stopped at all hazards, and at any cost. But the worst of it is; the best, the most noble, and generally the most intelligent men and women suffer and are exterminated, while the debased, the bigoted, and the ignorant are preserved to propagate their species. The reader may say I have been drawing on my imagination for the forgoing facts, but I can assure him I have been writing true history, and history that has occured in almost every Christian civilized nation in the world; and the great danger is, that history will repeat itself. But let us hope that the poet will not have to write for the present age what he has written for the past, where he says:—

> "They have used the rack, the boot, the screw,
>   They have kindled high the martyr's fire;
> All has been done, that fiends could do,
>   By malice, sophistry or ire;
> They have burn't the books where truth was laid,
>   They have sunk the writers dungeon deep,
> They have brought a thousand things to aid,
>   To keep the glorious truth asleep."

As one of the almost inspired writers says:—"Truth is mighty and must prevail." For that is a fixed law of nature, "Truth crushed to earth," though it may remain crushed for ages, "will rise again."

I will now give a short account of a few persons who have become interested in astrology, and who have also studied it as a science and labored hard in its cause, and who therefore ought to know something of its truth or falsity. Over twenty years ago, a man that I was slightly acquainted with, came into my office, at 814 Broadway, New York, and after he sat down, he looked around in astonishment at my library, and exclaimed, "Why, you do not believe in Astrology!"

Afterwards I engaged that man as an amanuensis, and to read lectures on astrology for me in public, as he was a very good writer and speaker. He also became a student of mine, studied astrology, took great delight in it, and made rapid progress in the science. After he had remained with me some two years, we parted, and not good friends.

But in going around talking about me to his friends, (and those friends came afterwards and reported it to me), he said: "Dr. Broughton is the best man I ever met in all my life, and I would sooner believe the Doctor's statement on any subject whatever, than I would any other man I ever knew, under oath." I have inserted the above to show, when astrologers fall out, the kind of Billingsgate language they use against each other; and with what black colors they paint each others pictures; and what dirty linen they wash before the public.

I am sorry that Prof. Chaney, (for that is his name), used such harsh language about me. But as Mr. Chaney is a hasty, hot headed man, he spoke it no doubt in one of his excited moments; and as it is near twenty years since the above sentence was uttered, he probably has had time to cool down, and would no doubt now use more sober language when talking about me to his friends. Should Mr. Chaney and I not become reconciled in this world, let us hope that our friendship will be renewed in that "summer land" beyond the grave, unless it be true,—as almost every person believes, even up to the present day, that when a man or woman commences studying astrology, the first thing they do is to sell their souls to the devil. If that be the case, no doubt the devil will hold us both to the "contract," and Mr. Chaney may pass the remainder of eternity in upbraiding me, as being the cause of his having to spend life everlasting in that warm climate, the devil's abode.

If Judge Gordon and the District Attorney of Philadelphia, could only have got some astrologer like Mr. Chaney to lay bare the character of Mr. Romaine, and could then have got some other astrologers to "squeal" about astrology, as the boodle ex-Aldermen Fullgraff and Duffy did about dividing the "boodle;" then, although Mr. Romaine could only be convicted of a misdemeanor, Judge Gordon might, in that case, very easily have passed sentence on him for a capital offence, and consigned him to the gallows.

When I was a little boy, a gentleman named Israel Holdsworth, one day came round getting orders for books to be delivered in parts, or numbers. He came to our weaving shop, where my oldest brother was weaving, and showed him a copy of a book on astronomy. While my brother was looking over it, Mr. Holdsworth made the remark that "Astronomy was a beautiful science, but was nothing to be compared to its sister science Astrology." My brother was taken completely by surprise, but wishing to question Mr. Holdsworth further, he said:—"Why, do you believe in the nonsense of Astrology?" But he soon found Mr. Holdsworth did not even know the first principle of the science.

Mr. Holdsworth afterwards took lessons in astrology from my brother, and they became fast friends. He also brought a number of other students, and they formed an "Astrological Society," and Mr. Holdsworth drew up the rules and by-laws for it. This astrological society was not the only society of the kind in the northern part of England. There was another one that my cousin William Broughton, W. J. Simmonite, Mr. Haywood, and a number of others whose names I have forgotten were members of. I believe they met once a week. Their method of procedure was that a member would give out a time of birth, and the sex. For example:—a male, born Jan. 25th, 1840, at 1:10 p. m., Leeds, England. That would be all they had to go by. It was understood that the child was remarkable for some particular thing, such as a violent death, being crippled, or some special mental or bodily quality. Each member of the society had to write an essay on the childs nativity. He had not only to find out what the child was particularly noted for, from its time of birth, but also if it would die a violent death. They must state what particular kind of death, and at what age the death would occur. A number of those nativities which were the most correctly written were published, and the names of the writers given, in a monthly periodical called the "Scientific Messenger."

We proposed carrying out that idea in the Astrological Society of the city of New York, (of which I was President).

At that time a complete set of back years Ephemerides, or Almanacs, could not be bought at any price. I remember the time when Mr. Holdsworth came to consult my father about republishing a complete set of back Ephemerdes, commencing with the year of 1800 to the year 1850. My father made the calculations for him, how many might be sold in Great Britain and Ireland, and Mr. Holdsworth estimated how much the printing and binding would cost.

The result was that the 50 years Ephemerides were reprinted. It was a "labor of love" on Mr. Holdsworth's part, which cost him and his wife five years of hard work. They kept a book store in Leeds, and lived near by; and while one was attending store, the other was setting the type for the Ephemerides. In that way they kept on until it was completed.

At the time Mr. Chaney left me, the 50 years Ephemerides was out of print. He set to work to reprint it, and continued it from 1800 to the year 1877. When completed, he kindly sent me a copy for myself, and also sent one for my oldest son; and we sold for him several copies at $35 each.

No person who does not understand Astrology and Mathematical Astronomy, can have any idea of the amount of labor it cost to calculate back for 50 or 100 years, the Longitude, Latitude, and Declination of the Moon, Mercury, Venus, Mars, Jupiter, Saturn, and the planet Uranus, to the degree and minute for each day in the year; and also the Longitude, Declination and Right ascension of the Sun, in degrees and minutes for every day for that length of time.

One reason why the work was so long and tedious for Israel Holdsworth, was that he could only procure old almanacs, published by different authors, and he had to rearrange the whole, for the 50 years; besides calculating the Longitude and Latitude of Uranus entirely, for the whole fifty years, as it had never before been calculated.

Mr. Holdsworth in his "Preface" says:—"The scarcity and high price of Ephemerides for past years has been deeply regretted by astrologers generally. Hence, several attempts have previously been made by different parties, but after printing one or two years, they have all abandoned the attempt as too ponderous, or too hazardous a speculation."

Mr. Holdsworth, in some of his calculations had Mr. W. J. Simmonite, who had an academy in Sheffield, England, assist him. Mr. Simmonite, I think, was the most learned and gentlemanly astrologer that England ever knew. He spoke, wrote, and taught eight different languages; besides being a thorough scholar and mathematician. He published a number of astrological works. His "Arcana of Astrology" will be a master-piece of that science for hundreds or thousands of years to come. Mr. Chaney, who republished the Ephemerides, prided himself on his knowledge of Mathematics, and also on having surveyed large tracts of land for the U. S. Government in the far West. He had also been an editor of daily newspapers for years. By profession he was a lawyer, and he had been District Attorney in Iowa, and in Bangor, Maine.

Mr. Chaney's work in republishing the 50 years Ephemerides was not anything so laborious as that of Israel Holdsworth, as it was simply a reprint; though, as he says:—"with over four hundred errors corrected." But from 1850 to 1877, he would have most of the work to rearrange, and would be obliged to make many calculations. But possibly it may be best to let Mr. Chaney speak for himself.

In his "Preface," he says:—"So scarce have Ephemerides for past years become, that they cannot be had for any sum." That was his excuse for republishing them. In regard to his labor, he says:—"I will say in conclusion, that I have toiled very hard the past year and a half, setting type and reading proof, with my mind on a constant strain to detect an error. For months in succession, Sunday as well as week days, I have made an average of fifteen hours daily labor."

Had Mr. Chaney, and Israel Holdsworth, been engaged in Christian work, and labored as hard in converting the heathen, no doubt in this world their name would have been added to the Calendar of Saints, and in the world to come they would wear an everlasting crown of glory. But as they have only been engaged in the work of teaching and spreading the science of astrology, they have received nothing but persecution in this life, and in the life to come, they will be kept warm by an everlasting fire, fumigated with a large percentage of brimstone, and will be entertained with music consisting of weeping, wailing and gnashing of teeth.

While on the subject of Ephemeris, I ought to mention that Raphael, of London, England, has also republished a complete set of Ephemerides from the year 1800 up to the present time; which set is the most complete that has ever been issued in modern times.

The planet Neptune was discovered in September, 1846, and, previous to that date, astrologers had no knowledge of the Longitude of that planet. Consequently they could not calculate its effects in nativities, for persons born before 1846.

A friend of mine asked a gentleman employed in the astronomical department, under the U. S. Government, to calculate Neptune's position from the year 1800 to 1850. I cannot do better than give that gentleman's own words. He says:—"The positions of Neptune, between the year 1800 and the discovery of the planet in Sept. 1846, have never previously been computed, and what I have now prepared is the Longitude for the first and middle of each month for fifty years. For any other planet the work would have been comparatively easy. But as Neptune became known only in 1846, its previous path could only be discovered by special calculation, based upon what is now known of its orbit."

The number of text-books on astrology, published at the present day, is astonishing. There never was a time since the world began, when there were such facilities for studying astrology and becoming familiar with that science. The circulation of English Astrological Almanacs, even in the United States at the present day, is really wonderful. Over twenty years ago, when Mr. Mason Hill started from California and had an order to buy Raphael's Ephemeris for that year, there was hardly one to be had in any store in the United States, from California to the borders of Maine, except those that I imported. At the present day one store in Boston sells more than three thousand of Raphael's Ephemeris every year, and has been doing the same for a number of years.

Twenty five years ago my friends used to tell me that when I was dead astrology would be dead also, as there would be no one left who understood the science; but if we may judge by the signs of the times, when I am dead astrology will then begin to live. Any person who has not given special attention to this matter would be astonished at the amount of literature published at the present day on astrology, in addition to a great number of Astrological Almanacs, which have over 500,060 circulation in England and the United States every year.

"The Prognostic Star Gazer," a periodical published in Boston, Mass., also "The Dreamer," published in the Western States, are both inclined to astrology. "The New York Sunday Mercury," has devoted a column every week, for years, to astrology. "The New York Waverley" devotes two columns every week, and the "Elmira Tidings" also devotes a column every week. And astrological literature in all English speaking countries was never more sought after and bought up than at the present day. In England there are astrological works published every few months for instructing people in that science. And within a very few years any person totally ignorant of astrology (a state of mind which people have specially prided themselves upon of late years), will hardly be tolerated in learned and polite society. And then that condition of things will arrive when there will be too many people who will seriously object to be sent to prison for studying or practicing astrology, the same as there were found too many people who seriously objected to being hung or roasted alive, for being heretics or witches.

Is it not strange that the followers of a religion which was ushered into the world some two thousand years ago, with the "glad tidings of peace on earth and good will towards men," have ever since that time, whenever they have been in the majority, always commenced to imprison, hang, and roast people alive, who were so unfortunate as to be in the minority; and, for no other reason than that they were in the minority.

Orthodoxy has always been the "doxy" of the majority, and heterodoxy has always been the "doxy" of the minority. If we read English History, or, for that matter, the history of any of the Christian nations, we find that whenever by the fortunes of war a change of kings or queens occurred, the religion which was formerly in the minority (or heterodoxy), instantly changed into orthodoxy, and the orthodoxy changed into heterodoxy, and all those who were heterodox had to suffer, like prisoners of war in barbarous nations, until they were in power again, when the turn came again for the former to be imprisoned, hung, or roasted.

Regarding my ancestors and myself, a few words may be interesting.

My maternal grandfather, Benjamin Scott, resided in Wakefield, Yorkshire, England; his parents died when he was very young, and he made his own way in the world; becoming a woolen cloth manufacturer. He was a Jacobite in politics, and suffered much for his support of the "Pretender." My paternal grandfather, Luke Broughton, was a disciple of Nicholas Culpepper. He studied astrology, along with the botanical practice of medicine, and practiced both for many years. In early life he was a manufacturer of cloth. In politics he was a "Tom Painer," the object of which faction was to force an extension of the voting franchise, it being at that time in the hands of property owners only. In that part of England there were over four thousand men who met on moonlight nights to drill on the moors and commons, with the idea of fighting for what they considered their rights. My grandfather was secretary for the companies in his locality, and kept the books of their meetings, with all the names of the members. The government tried in every way to break up these organizations, and to this end the Earl of Cardigan sent for my grandfather and told him the government had their spies, and knew all about their meetings and drilling, and the Earl offered him a large sum in gold, with a position under the government as long as he lived, and a similar position for each son on coming of age, if he would give up the books and leave the organization. My grandfather's reply was that he could not be bought. The result was that a warrant was issued, on the charge of treason, and my ancestor was a fugitive for over ten years, seeing his family only at rare intervals, and then at night. He had so many faithful friends, who kept a sharp look out for government spies, that he was never caught; but his property was confiscated, his business destroyed, and his family reduced almost to poverty. In the latter part of his life he received a small pension from the government, it being recognized that the persecution was far in excess of the offense. On account of the persecution of my grandfather, my father and his brothers had little to do with politics, yet my father came near ending his days on the gallows.

About 1820, the government was determined to crush out all the leaders of reform. It employed spies to go round to entrap all such, by getting them to sign a paper which could be construed into treason. In that part of England twenty eight signed the paper; they were tried, convicted, and all hung on one day. My father was approached, and would have signed it, if it had not been for his father, who gave as a reason that he had suffered so much for politics, that he objected to his sons meddling in such matters. This prevented my father signing it, and being added to the number.

In 1831 and 1832 the people held county meetings all over England, in favor of the extension of the franchise, and the government, to avoid a revolution, granted it. The franchise has since been gradually extended, until now there is almost universal suffrage. If it had not been for such men as my grandfather driving the entering wedge, the people of England would have remained in a condition similar to that of the people of Russia to-day.

My father was the second of three sons, and with his elder brother studied medicine, spending a long period at the Leeds Infirmary; he studied astrology and made use of it in his practice of medicine, but never made a business of it, though he had many students, among whom was the late Thomas Lister of New York, and formerly of Boston. My uncle, Dr. Mark Broughton, was a noted physician and surgeon, and used astrology in his practice, which practice was larger than any other doctor's in that part of England. My aunt, Martha Broughton, was an adept in the science.

My father married Mary Scott, the only child of Benjamin Scott, before mentioned, and had a family of six children, Mathew, Mark, Luke, John, William and Rachel. The first three, which included myself, studied astrology, and continued to use it, both as a business and in private life. My brothers, Mathew and Mark, were expert mathematicians and skilled astrologists; they came to America a few years before I did, and both practiced astrology in Philadelphia. My brother Mark published a monthly periodical for many years, called "The Horoscope;" also an "Astrological Ephemeris."

Probably the incident which had the most influence in drawing me to the science of astrology, was the truthfulness of a prediction made by my father in my horoscope. On account of so many of the planets being afflicted in mute signs, he remarked at my birth, to my mother, that I should not commence to talk till I was about six years of age, and then imperfectly, with an impediment in my speech, till I reached my nineteenth or twentieth year, when I should speak as well as the average person. This prediction was absolutely true, and during my earlier years no one but the members of our family could understand anything I said. Many physicians examined my mouth and larynx, and the diagnoses of the cause of my impediment of speech were as various as the doctors. When I reached my twentieth year, my speech had gradually become natural, and I have since spoken in public.

I commenced to study astrology when I was about eighteen, and have continued in its light ever since. I married at twenty-four, and came to

America two years later; having served my time at weaving, and spent a few years in a chemical laboratory. I settled in Philadelphia, where I graduated at one of the medical colleges and remained about eight years, coming to New York in 1863.* I have always made use of astrology in the practice of medicine, which has been very extensive.

My great desire to spread the truths of astrology induced me in 1866 to lease a large hall at 814 Broadway, for the purpose of giving lectures upon this and kindred subjects. For some years previous I had issued a journal, called "The Monthly Planet Reader," and with these means at hand, I believed astrology would soon reach that position for which my ancestors and myself had labored so long and faithfully. I miscalculated the time, though; the spirit of liberalism was still dormant, and the powers of the religious sects were in too great command of the minds of the people; and although my lectures gave great satisfaction, and were well attended, the cloven foot was soon made apparent. In the same building was the headquarters of a political organization, called the Mozart Hall, which was made up of the Catholic element of the city, and when the object of my meetings became known to its leaders, the whole power of the political machinery was put in motion to crush me. My landlord wanted me to give up my lease, and when I refused, said he would force me out; after that I was subjected to all the annoyances both great and small which it was in the hands of the powerful to inflict upon the weak. My signs at the door were stolen, missiles were thrown down the stairs during the time when people were coming to the lectures; men were sent to roll boxes on the floor above my hall to interfere with the speakers, the owner of the building from whom I leased was caught several times stealing my signs, and when arrested would be immediately discharged on reaching the station house, because of his political power; the only man who did lock him up was Capt. Alex. S. Williams, who also locked up the son-in-law of the landlord on a charge of disorderly conduct, made by my assistant, Mr. W. H. Chaney; Mr. Chaney was arrested for this on a charge of false imprisonment, and spent six months in Ludlow Street Jail, being unable to procure bail. My wife's health and my own being broken down, having buried a very dear child, and being almost ruined financially I gave up the struggle and moved from the place much dissatisfied, and with a poor opinion of the so-called justice meted out to those not having political influence in New York City.

I have in the twenty years which have elapsed since that time, practised astrology in conjunction with medicine, and have three sons and a daughter; three of whom will become astrologers; and while they may not practice it for a living, they will teach it; so that there is no danger of astrology dying out during another generation at least.

---

* As an illustration of ignorance resulting in petty persecution, I might mention that at the college where I graduated, they organized that winter, an Alumni Association. I was elected one of the board of Censors, and signed all the Diplomas, but afterwards when the members discovered that I had studied astrology, nothing would do, but that I must resign, a new Censor was elected in my place, all the Diplomas destroyed, and new ones made out, without an astrologer's signature. A petty persecution occurred to me before I left England. At the church I attended I was a teacher in the Sunday School, and taught writing, drawing, phonography and arithmetic in a night school supported by the church; I was also librarian, all without compensation. When it became known that I was studying astrology, I was told I must give up astrology or resign my positions. I resigned.

Prof. RICHARD A. PROCTOR ON ASTROLOGY.

In the "New York World" of February 6th, 1887, appeared the following article by R. A. Proctor, a popular lecturer on Astronomy. I wrote an answer and sent it to that paper, but the editor refused to publish it; I shall insert it after Mr. Proctor's article, and following will be found my criticisms on Mr. Proctor and the World.

As the press is closed against anything in favor of Astrology and Astrologers, even when in reply to personal attacks, and as the reader has already seen that it was impossible to give public lectures on that science in a city like New York, even though we had a long lease of the hall, and it was entirely under our control for that purpose, there is no other resource but to publish in circular, pamphlet, or book form, everything we desire to place before the public to represent truthfully the Astrologer's side of the argument. It may be very difficult for the reader to believe that a number of printers have actually refused to print any literature on Astrology, even though they were certain of their money, they believing it to be wicked to print such work.

THE HUMBUG OF ASTROLOGY.

PROF. RICHARD A. PROCTOR SHOWS UP THE ALLEGED SCIENCE.—A BELIEF THAT HAS CLUNG TO THE WORLD FOR AGES.—HOW THE WISE MEN OF OLD WERE DECEIVED.—A REFUGE NOW FOR IGNORANT CHARLATANS AND KNAVES.—GROWTH OF AN UNREASONABLE AND FOOLISH SUPERSTITION.

I am often asked, but especially after some notorious astrological charlatan has been exposed, whether it is after all so certain that astrology, universally regarded in old times as a true science, is altogether vain and delusive. Can it be, many have said to me, that all the wise men of past ages, those to whom we attribute so many of the beliefs that to this day we hold sacred, can in this matter of astrology have been wholly deceived? Not only among all the leading races of antiquity, and in all the chief civilized nations, but during periods of time such as no other faith can boast of having swayed, men held firmly to the belief that the stars in their courses foretell, nay, rule, the fortunes of men. The cuneiform inscriptions of Assyria, the hieroglyphs of Egypt, the most ancient records of Persia, India and China, agree in showing that of old all men believed the sun and moon, the planets and the stars, to be as

> Radiant Mercuries,
> Carrying through ether in perpetual round
> Decrees and resolutions of the god.

Nay, throughout the long period, to be measured by thousands of years, when all men held this belief, the most part held what anciently had been the belief of all, that the sun and moon and all the host of heaven are not merely the exponents of the wills of the gods, but are actually as gods themselves. To this day not only are all languages permeated by the expressions belonging to the old astrological teachings, but all the feasts and fasts of the religions of our age, purified though they have long been from Sabaistic beliefs, attest in the clearest way, to the astronomer, their origin in Sabaistic observances. **To this day, Christians and Jews, Buddhists and Mahommetans, regulate their** yearly ceremonial by the solstices and equinoctial passages of the sun, and the weekly renewals of religious observances were derived originally from the moon's motions and were determined by the moon when "new" in her "first quarter," "full" in her "third quarter," and "new" again. Among the Jews and Mahommetans indeed the "new moon" observances and those which formerly attended the rising and setting of the sun are still retained. Astrology, the outcome of those Sabaistic beliefs which were once universally prevalent, had a most respectable origin, and if common opinion could prove any doctrine just, astrology must, it should seem, have been based on truth. Why, then, should it now be held only worthy of belief by the ignorant and silly, and be maintained as true only by rogues and charlatans.

The answer is found in the very circumstances under which of old astrology was believed in. The astrologers of old times were for the most part not only honest men, but men moved by strong religious emotions. They were also by no means wanting in reasoning power. As I pointed out long since in my article on "Astronomy" in the Encyclopædia Britannica, astrology was based on reasoning in old times, and on reasoning which seemed sound and sufficient; it was no mere superstition, and as it was based on reasoning and its supporters honestly explained their reasons for the faith that was in them, we are able not only to understand and in some degree appreciate their doctrine, but also to recognize its utterly groundless nature.

They saw that the sun ruled unmistakably over the day and the year, and they recognized clearly, though they could not explain the matter as science now explains it, that the sun is the life of the earth and of all things in it. Day after day he renewed his victory over Night and brought all things to life after the sleep Night had brought on them. Year after year he renewed his victory over Winter, and brought life into field and forest, so that food and nourishment were provided in due season for men and animals. None could doubt that this orb at least ruled over the fates and fortunes of men and nations. The moon seemed scarcely less obviously a ruling or controlling orb. Even among nations, if such there were, who had never either observed her influence on the tides or heard of it from others, she seemed to have special power. She ruled the night, she measured time for them (nine-tenths of the ancient names of the moon indicated her as "The Measurer," the rest of her names, as Selene, Luna, &c., relating to her light), and pastoral races blessed her as the orb most beneficial, in their belief, to all orders of herdsmen. Can we wonder if, when two of the planets, for the sun and moon were two of the seven planets of ancient astronomy, having thus been recognized as unquestionably ruling men's fortunes in specific ways, the ancients believed that so also must the other seven? And knowing, as we do, how prone half knowledge is to fall into full assurance of faith, can we marvel if ancient astronomers learned to assign special influence to Mercury and Venus, to Mars, Jupiter and Saturn, on the strength of what seemed to them sufficient indications of the specific powers which those planets possessed? We find that they certainly did this; and we can trace quite easily the line of thought by which they were led to their ideas respecting the good or bad, the beneficent or the malign influences which the planets in their belief exerted.

Thus what could be more natural than that Venus, the most beautiful of all the planets to the unaided vision, should have been chosen as the planet of love? Never seen save on the twilight sky, growing more beautiful when she is an evening star as twilight deepens, while as a morning star she "faints in the light that she loves, the light of the daffodil sky," she is the apt emblem, the Cytherean goddess, ruler over love and courtship. And because of her beauty Venus was naturally regarded as a favorite planet—she was the "Lesser Good Fortune," as Jupiter was the greater. Nor was it less natural that Mercury, so hard to detect with the unaided eye, that many astronomers now living have never seen the planet except through a telescope, should be regarded as the planet ruling over all professions and occupations which require craft and subtlety. Neither good nor bad fortune could be assigned to a planet so seldom seen—though when seen in the skies of Chaldea, Egypt, and Greece (as in those of America, by the way) Mercury shines with specially resplendent lustre, insomuch that the Greeks knew him as the Sparkler. What planet but the ruddy Mars could reasonably be regarded as ruling over war and battle? Seen at longer and less regular intervals than any other planet, shining with variable but always with portentous lustre, Mars seemed like the torch of war, waved by the hands of Fate over the nations. Naturally, too, outside his character as planet of war, Mars was regarded as of evil influence; as Venus was the Lesser Good Fortune, so Mars was the "Lesser Ill Fortune," Saturn being the greater. Jupiter's wide circuit and steady light, even surpassing that of Venus in splendor, because seen in the night, whereas hers is visible only in the twilight, suggested power and steady rule for good. So also did his wide orbit, or rather his long period, for of his distance the old astronomers knew nothing. Mars is longer unseen than Jupiter, but the period of Mars's circuit round the star sphere is much shorter, and therefore the old astronomers assigned Jupiter a wider orbit, (or, as they expressed it, a higher sphere), and greater power. To the gloomy Saturn, most beautiful of all planets in the telescope, but saddest and most baleful to ordinary vision and moving still more slowly, in such sort that while Jupiter takes less than twelve he takes nearly thirty years in circuiting the star sphere, yet greater power, but even more malign influence, was as naturally assigned.

Having thus decided on the special influences of their seven planets, the ancients readily formed a system by which, as they supposed, the action of those influences on the fortunes of men and nations might be determined. When they had also learned how to calculate the positions of the planets for any length of time in advance, they believed they had obtained full power of predicting the fortunes of each man, so soon as, having calculated the aspect of the heavens at his nativity, they had learned which planets were most potent in their influence on his fortunes. And with this power of prediction came some power of favoring good fortune and preventing evil; in other words, of ruling as well as reading the planets.

But the very circumstance that astrology, though a superstition, was a very natural and even reasonable superstition in those old days, shows what an unreasonable and foolish superstition it is now. The very fact that the old astrologers were for the most honest, though mistaken, proves that the astrologer of to-day must necessarily be a rogue and a charlatan. For now men know how the sun and the moon produce their effects; they know why Mercury seems shifty, and Venus lovely; how Mars comes to look red and Jupiter bright and Saturn yellow. That a ruddy or ochre tinge in the continents of Mars, never less than forty millions of miles from us, should have anything to do with war and turmoils on the earth, is an idea which none but persons of very weak mind could for a moment entertain. That because Venus travels inside the earth's track, and, therefore, can only be seen during twilight, the loves of our boys and girls, our young men and maidens, aye, and of our men and women who have passed the days of youth, must be influenced by that sister world, never less than 26,000,000 miles from us, is a thought too preposterous to need contradiction. And so with the splendor of Jupiter, the gloom of Saturn, and the swift movements of Mercury. The "astrologers" of to-day either know all this and make a lying pretense of believing in planetary influences, or they are ignorant of it all and make lying pretense to knowledge. Be the case how it may, they must of necessity be lying knaves.

It is the same nowadays with all orders of fortune-tellers, character readers, phrenologists *et id genus omne*. Nothing but the ignorance which mistook itself for knowledge in the wise old times, could justify the claims put forward by men of these classes. In our day there can be none who believe they know how to read the stars, for those who alone know how to calculate the movements of the heavenly bodies, know that the supposed influences of these bodies were purely imaginary, and based on mere fanciful analogies. Among "astrologers" there is no more knowledge of astronomy than there is a knowledge of the physiology of the brain among "phrenologists." The astrologer of old knew all the astronomy of his time; the astrologer of to-day has written himself down a charlatan, and is probably an unscrupulous rascal.

RICHARD A. PROCTOR.

After waiting three weeks and not noticing any reply to Richard A. Proctor, I wrote the following article and took it myself to the editor of the "World," and told him that about one year ago they had published a short communication of mine in favor of astrology, and that I had brought a reply to Mr. Proctor's article. But at the same time I said that possibly they, like the "New York Sun," publish only one side of a question.

After keeping it a few days the article was returned to me with the following note:—

Dear Sir:—I regret to say, that, owing to the pressure upon our space, the manuscript you kindly sent, has not been found available for the WORLD'S columns. It is therefore returned as you requested. Thanking you, I am, yours respectfully,*

JOHN A. COCKERILL,
Managing Editor.

The following is the article which the "World" refused, although they published Mr. Proctor's, which called all astrologers "lying knaves" and "unscrupulous rascals," and the reader ought to bear in mind that no astrologer had attacked Mr. Proctor's reputation or his standing in society.

---

* A friend of mine, a publisher, who has been the editor of a daily newspaper, and who had a knowledge of Astrology, commenced an article in reply to Mr. Proctor, but on hearing that the "World" refused to publish mine, came to the conclusion that it was of no use finishing it. Another gentleman who is a physician in general practice, and has been a professor in two medical colleges in this city, and who has published a number of medical works, also has been the editor of a prominent medical journal for a number of years, and has a good practical knowledge of Astrology, told me that he would have replied to Mr. Proctor, if he did not feel positive that the "World" would not publish his reply, having committed themselves against Astrology; if they did publish it, he feared it would be so garbled that he would not be able to recognize it.

I have been credibly informed that Mr. Elias Colbert, who is editor of the "Chicago Tribune," and who is a good astronomer and astrologer, had to sign a contract before he took his position as editor, that he would not even mention the word "astrology" in the "Tribune." All those persons whom I have talked to about Mr. Colbert, and who are personally acquainted with him, speak of him in the highest terms, both as a gentleman and a man of science. None of those persons even hint that he is either a "lying knave" or an "unscrupulous rascal." Mr. B. C. Murray, an astrologer and editor, and owner of a daily newspaper called the Dennison Gazetteer, Texas, and who has perhaps the largest astrological library in the world, sometimes mentions astrology favorably in his newspaper, but has to do it very gingerly, so as not to injure its circulation.

Some years ago, on the death of a student of mine, Dr. Charles Winterburn, of this city, I wrote an article for the "Truth Seeker," giving an account of him as an astrologer and physician, and Mr. D. M. Bennett told me that he received a number of letters from subscribers, threatening to withdraw their subscription, if any more astrology appeared in the "Truth Seeker." In this enlightened age, we are inclined to believe that there is no prejudice or persecution of either science or religion, and that to meet with it, we must go among the barbarians, or search for it in the history of past ages; but when the professor of one science calls all the professors of another science "lying knaves" and "unscrupulous rascals," and the editors of the newspapers in which these slanderous attacks appear, refuse to publish any reply to such attacks, it looks as if history was repeating itself.

Mr. Proctor ought to remember the words of "Othello" where he says:—"He that filches from me my good name, robs me of that which not enriches him, but makes me poor indeed." I shall reserve my strictures both for the "World" and for Mr. Proctor, until the reader can judge of the refused article itself, by reading it.

REPLY TO MR. PROCTOR.

The article on "The Humbug of Astrology," in the "World" of February 6th, 1887, from the pen of so great an authority on astronomical matters as Richard A. Proctor, must carry with it so much weight that I fear many will not admit the possibility of there being another side to the question, and pass by any attempt to prove the contrary with a smile. Yet the position assumed by Mr. Proctor is not impregnable; as there have been as great men, even in modern times, if not greater, in the science of which he is an able teacher, who have held opposite opinions, on the science of astrology, to those which he promulgates.

The article in question contains several peculiar assertions, and not a few ideas which, viewed from another standpoint, convey an altogether different, and a more logical conclusion; and if we can allow prejudice to remain dormant, for a short time, and judge from an unbiased standpoint, we may with all due respect to Mr. Proctor differ with him, even in so far as to draw a different or even opposite deduction from his own words and arguments.

Mr. Proctor says, "Can it be, many have said to me, that all the wise men of past ages * * * in this matter of astrology have been wholly deceived?" "Not only among all the leading races of antiquity, and in all the chief civilized nations, but during periods of time such as no other faith can boast of having swayed, men held firmly to the belief that the stars in their courses foretell, nay, rule the fortunes of men." Again he says:—"Astrology had a most respectable origin, and if common opinion could prove any doctrine just, astrology must, it should seem, have been based on truth. Why then should it now be held only worthy of belief by the ignorant and silly, and be maintained as true by rogues and charlatans?" "The Astrologers of old times were for the most part not only honest men, * * * they were by no means wanting in reasoning powers," * * "Astrology was based on reasoning which seemed sound and sufficient."

If Mr. Proctor's object had been to lay a firm and solid foundation for the science of astrology, I do not see how he could have chosen more logical and convincing arguments, and yet Mr. Proctor is so wilfully blind as not to see the force of his own words. But as the author of the "Vestiges of Creation," when speaking of his critics in his preface, says:—"It is no discredit to them that they are, almost without exception, engaged each in his own little department of science, and are able to give little or no attention to that vast field outside their department; all beyond is regarded with suspicion and distrust." This is a truth, and almost every man believes his own religion or science to be the only one that is right, and all the others wrong. Even in cases of men of the same profession, each man appears to travel in his own narrow groove, and thinks that men who travel in another path, to use Mr. Proctor's words, are "lying knaves" and "unscrupulous rascals." For instance, the allopathic physicians think that the homœopaths are all dishonest in their practice of medicine, and vice versa. The anatomists, as a rule, do not believe in medicine, neither do the surgeons believe in aught but steel. Mathematicians rarely are metaphysicians, and many botanists do not have any faith in the medicinal effects of herbs and roots. Some persons are born with a natural tendency in some one direction, and sometimes it is as the mind is trained;

some persons are practical, and some are theoretical, and they rarely admit that truth exists outside their own sphere.

To the average person there appears but little difference between astronomy and astrology, the general conclusion being that they both have to do with the planets; and with those persons the opinion of an astronomer is taken on astrology, with full confidence in his ability to pronounce upon that subject. There cannot be a greater mistake. The astronomer's opinion on astrology is of no more weight than a botanist's opinion is on the action of herbs on the human system, if the botanist is not also a physician. Astronomy deals with numbers, and the inanimate laws of nature. The astrologer depends on the long continued observation of the effects of the positions and revolutions of the heavenly bodies on the earth and its inhabitants. Some of the most noted and learned men of the world have been astrologers. The great John Kepler, to whom the science of astronomy of the present day is so much indebted, was a firm believer in astrology. He made many discoveries in astrology, which are almost equal to those he made in astronomy.

Baron Napier, to whom mathematicians are so much indebted for his marvelous discovery of logarythms, used them solely to facilitate his astrological calculations. Flamstead, the first astronomer of the Greenwich Observatory, England, Placidus De Titus, Cardan, Galileo, Bishop Butler, and almost every astronomer of any note in the past, were firm believers and promoters of this seience; of which Mr. Proctor says:—"No one who understands astronomy believes in astrology. The old school doctors used to say that no person who understood anatomy, physiology, chemistry, and materia medica, believed in Homœopathy. Yet Homœopathy lives, and its practitioners are the most intelligent physicians of the present day.

Is it not a strange assertion for Mr. Proctor to make, that all the ancients had upon which to base their belief in astrology, a belief which lasted for thousands of years, was the color of the planets; that men who, Mr. Proctor says, had good reasoning faculties, would cling to a faith which was based on a mere fancied resemblance between the baleful hue of the light emitted by Saturn, and the dark forebodings of a person in despondency?

This assertion on the part of a man who is altogether ignorant of astrology, to account for the faiths of persons who lived thousands of years ago, is rather impertinent, to say the least, when we have the books of those ancient astrologers, which teach the contrary.

It is true that astrology had an honest parentage. Its cradle was the patient observation and experience of the greatest men of all past ages; its boyhood the books containing the experiences and observations of those men, and its manhood was the grandeur of its following and its hold upon their reason, and the facts and experience which went to confirm that reason.

Astrology flourished for ages; and that its growth and power were great, is of itself proof that it was built upon the laws of nature. It continued in power and held its place until the middle of the seventeenth century, when the Protestant Reformation began to be established, (which religion was built upon faith and miracles, and ignored the laws of nature,) when it was suppressed by the religious sects of that period, and placed under the ban of the church, and astrologers were classed and persecuted among the witches and wizards. Since that time every form of divination has been condemned by every one without investigation, except a few followers.

The assertion made by Mr. Proctor, that the reasons which made it possible for men of past ages to believe in astrology are not reasons which can be accepted at the present day, is preposterous; and it is strange that any person outside of an insane asylum should make any such an assertion without proof. The laws of nature have not changed, the condition of our earth in its surroundings and its relations to the other planets of the solar system have not changed, the facts and observations upon which the ancients based their belief, are still the same.

The Ptolemaic theory of astronomy, that the earth was in the centre of the universe, and that the sun went round the earth every day, which caused day and night, was wrong, but the discovery of the Copernican system of astronomy, did not alter the order of things on our earth, day and night, summer and winter, and every law of nature that existed previous to that discovery, remains the same to-day. Those observations and experiences, extending over thousands of years, which the ancients made in astrology and recorded in books, are truths which live to-day.

The ancient practice of medicine was not overthrown by the discovery of the circulation of the blood; religion lived in all its purity, after geology was taught in our colleges, and astrology will live long after Mr. Proctor is turned to clay.

I do not write this reply to Mr. Proctor to convert him to a belief in astrology, and no doubt he regards me as one of the modern heretics who ought to be either imprisoned or roasted alive. There has always been, and must always be, a difference of opinion on science and religion, in order that the world of thought should progress. When every person thinks and believes alike on every subject, and where dogmas and creeds are thrust down people's throats and no questions asked, then we shall revert back to the dark ages and to that conservatism that made this world a hell for Columbus, Galileo, and Copernicus, and all the other heretics either in science or religion.

How much of positive science is known, even in our own enlightened age, that was not known to the ancients? There is very little but theory, and theories which may be overthrown at any time, and yet Mr. Proctor, resting on so insecure a basis, calls all those who are so unfortunate as to differ from him "lying knaves" and "unscrupulous rascals."

Astrology may be dead so far as Mr. Proctor is concerned, but he is not the whole world. There are hundreds of students in astrology in England and this country, and there are hundreds of thousands of firm believers in that science, and the number is constantly increasing. The Almanacs and Ephemeris published every year, by Raphael and Zadkiel of London, and which are purchased by the believers in astrology, number over half a million.

L. D. BROUGHTON, M. D.

66 West 4th St., New York.

The above is a copy of the article, with very slight changes in the wording, which the editors of the "World" refused to publish. Yet they published Mr. Proctor's "Humbug of Astrology," which stated "that the astrologer of to-day must necessarily be a rogue and charlatan." Consequently the astrologers of to-day, according to the ethics of the New York "World," must be tried, convicted and sentenced without being heard in the public press.

This narrow bigotry resembles the intolerance that almost up to the present time prevails in the English Courts, where prisoners of the downtrodden Irish race are prevented from speaking in their own defence; the officers of the court silencing them when attempting to testify. Such oppression frequently came to my personal knowledge, when a resident of Leeds, England.

Had those prisoners been Russians, Prussians or Frenchmen, they would have been heard in their own defence, or the nations to which they belonged would have known the reason why, even if it led to a war.

Had Mr. Proctor published in the "World" an attack on all the physicians, or all the ministers, lawyers, or musicians, or indeed any other profession, (but astrologers,) and called them all "lying knaves" and "unscrupulous rascals;" and had the "World" refused to publish a reply to such falsehoods, and vituperations, even at the present day of intolerance, I cannot but think it would make a sensation, and the "World" itself would lose caste, especially among those persons who had received a liberal education and were inclined to freedom of thought, free speech, and fair play. This intolerance almost equals the Lord George Gordon riots, which were supposed to belong to the past; but the reader has already seen what I have passed through in and for the cause of Astrology in the civilized city of New York, and near the present time.

The Catholics of England, in 1778, petitioned the government to repeal certain unjust penal laws of long standing, which classed popish priests as felons or traitors; also the forfeiture of real estate by Catholic heirs educated abroad; the power which was given to a son or nearest relation, being a protestant, of taking possession of a father's or other relative's estate, who had been Catholics; the depriving papists of the power of acquiring landed property, &c. Parliament heard the petitioners and the repeal was granted. But instead of all classes in England and all religious denominations rejoicing and having bon-fires on account of the repeal of such barbarous and unjust laws, nearly 60,000 persons met in St. George's Fields, London, and walked in procession to Palace Yard, to give force to the remonstrance they were about presenting to Parliament against the repeal of the above laws. The prayer of the remonstrators being rejected, the mob headed by Lord George Gordon gave way to violence. The Catholic chapels and the prisons were forced and set on fire; no less than thirty fires were to be seen blazing at one time. For five days the rabble had possession of London, and nearly five hundred persons were killed or wounded.

I give the above to illustrate how much easier it is to enact than it is to repeal bad laws, when prejudice and ignorance are in the preponderance, and how unreasonable it was for Parliament to have enacted laws granting such unjust privileges and monopolies to such pious christian people as the Lord George Gordon rioters proved themselves to be. No doubt if there were efforts made to repeal the fortune-telling law of Pennsylvania, and to strike the corresponding clause out of the "Penal Code" of New York, Mr. Proctor and the editors of the "World" would be ready to head a riot to oppose such a repeal.

Mr. Proctor says:—"In our day there can be none who believe they know how to read the stars, for those who alone know how to calculate the movements of the heavenly bodies, know that the supposed influences of those bodies were purely imaginary, and based on merely fanciful analogies."

If Mr. Proctor had been laying a wager that he could tell the greatest falsehood, there might be some excuse for writing the above sentence; but he has no more excuse than the Protestants had in the Lord George Gordon riots, in 1778, and it shows an equally vicious disposition on his part.

I suppose Mr. Proctor knows that for ages upon ages the words astronomy and astrology had very nearly the same meaning, and during all that time the calculations in the science of astronomy were made solely for the astrologer, and for him to make his predictions from; or in other words the astronomers were the hewers of wood and drawers of water for astrologers, and the latter were always the advisers and privy counsellors of Kings, Emperors and Pharoahs in ancient times.

When the science of navigation became more developed and better understood among mariners, these calculations were also made for sea captains who took long voyages, as well as for astrologers, and the two sciences, astronomy and astrology, gradually became separated.

No doubt the navigator in ancient times made his own calculations in astronomy, but as navigation and astronomy were developed, the two gradually became separated. Yet the former is dependent on the latter for its gradual perfection, as the astrologer is dependent on the perfection of the science of astronomy for the accuracy of his predictions.

In the dim ages of the past, even before the days of Hippocrates, the botanist and the practitioner of medicine were one and the same person, but as the science of medicine and surgery became more developed and extended in its application, and the science of botany progressed, and new herbs and plants were discovered, these two sciences gradually became separated; and each student studied and extended his own favorite and special science. But the botanists of the present day do not call the physicians "lying knaves" and "unscrupulous rascals." The most learned botanist that I ever knew, who could tell almost every herb and plant which grew in the United States, when we were out together in the fields botanizing, often laughed at the very idea that those herbs and roots could have any medicinal effect upon the human body. When travelling along together we often had this matter up for discussion, but it was imposible for me to convince him of his error as he had no knowledge of diseases or the method of treating them. Had he studied medicine, and had forty years practice, like myself, there would then have been no necessity of any argument to convince him of his error.

Had that botanist called all physicians "rogues and charlatans," he would have manifested a want of good taste equal to that of Mr. Proctor, when he calls all astrologers by such names. He knew as much of the practice of medicine as Mr. Proctor knows of the practice of astrology, and the botanist also believed "that the supposed influence" of the herbs and roots on the human system was purely imaginary, and based on merely fanciful analogies, (such as the signatures of herbs and roots of the ancients, and the supposed magical effects they had on the human system.) That belief of the ancients is no proof that herbs and roots, when they are administered at the present day, have no effect on the bodies of men or women; on the contrary it is presumptive evidence that they not only have an effect now, but that they have always had an effect when so administered, from time immemorial, and will always continue to have an effect to the end of time. But the theories which attempt to account for these effects may change, and may continue to change from age to age. So the belief, for so many thousand years, of the ancients, in the influence of the sun, moon and planets on men and nations, is presumptive proof that that belief was correct, and founded on the laws of nature; and the reader will see in the pamphlet which follows these Introductory Remarks, that there is positive proof that the heavenly bodies do continue to influence men and nations, and indeed all mundane affairs. Instead of Mr. Proctor calling me and all other astrologers "lying knaves" and "unscrupulous rascals," and writing articles in the "World" about what the ancients "believed" or "imagined," I think it would be more becoming in him, as a gentleman, to first produce some tangible evidence or proof of the falsity of astrology and the dishonesty of its professors.

If we can believe the accounts in the New Testament, during Christ's time, in Palestine, the general belief was, that when any person was sick, or afflicted bodily, it was produced by evil spirits or devils entering that diseased person's body; and if they could succeed in casting these devils out, the diseased person instantly became well, and could take up his bed and walk. What the people believed in Christ's time, cannot be taken as proof that there are no diseases in the human family at the present day, but what are produced by evil spirits or devils entering the bodies of those diseased persons? Some kind of diseases have existed in the human family in all ages, and it is only the theory of the cause of those diseases which has changed?

Why does not Mr. Proctor bring arguments to prove that all the diseases of the human body "were purely imaginary, and based on merely fanciful analogies," as the ancients believed that all those diseases were caused by evil spirits entering those diseased person's bodies? and even have the Bible on his side, because it is stated in it that there were persons who witnessed Christ casting out those devils and evil spirits, and the sick becoming well, and the spirits entering into swine; and go on to show according to the scriptures that the doctor "of to-day must necessarily be a rogue and charlatan," and also that they are all "lying knaves" and "unscrupulous rascals?" He can bring much stronger arguments against the doctors, and have stronger reasons for calling them vile names, than he can possibly bring against astrology or astrologers.

Mr. Proctor's "facts" and "reasoning" not only apply to doctors and astrologers, but to almost every other profession that is practiced at the present day; and I am not defending astrologers alone, but I am actually defending all other professional men from being called "lying knaves" and "unscrupulous rascals," even including Mr. Proctor himself.

Let us take another illustration, to prove my assertion. There is about the same relation between acoustics and music, as there is between astronomy and astrology; and it would be just as reasonable for Mr. Proctor to have said:—That all music was an ancient "superstition," and that the musicians "of old times were for the most part not only honest men, but men moved by strong religious emotions," and that music, "though a superstition, was a very natural and even reasonable superstition in those old days, this fact shows what an unreasonable and foolish superstition it is now." "The very fact that the old" musicians "were for the most honest, though mistaken, proves that the" musician "of to-day must necessarily be a rogue and a charlatan;" as the ancients believed in the "music of the spheres," the singing of angels, and the magic charm of sound, &c., &c. And the ancients had practically no knowledge of the science of acoustics, or not near as much as they had of astronomy. Consequently, according to Mr. Proctor's reasoning, all the musicians of the present day must be much more ignorant of acoustics than the astrologers are now supposed to be ignorant of astronomy; and he would also say that :—" Those who alone know how to calculate the" vibrations of sound, "know that the supposed" musical notes, "were purely imaginary, and based on merely fanciful analogies," and that the musician of to-day "must of necessity be a "lying knave" and an "unscrupulous rascal," as he could prove it by the science of acoustics. Mr. Proctor might with just the same reasoning and propriety have used all the above expressions against musicians, as he has against astrologers, although he might not have the least taste or skill for music himself, any more than he has for the science of astrology; in short he might not be able to perceive any difference when listening to the tunes of Yankee Doodle and Old Hundred. Yet music is built upon the science of acoustics, as astrology is built upon the science of astronomy.

I am aware that there is a vast difference between music and astrology, and between acoustics and astronomy, but bear in mind I have only used them as comparisons, and to show that the only way to prove or disprove the falsity of music is by music itself, and by music of the present day, and not by what the ancients knew about music, or by what they knew of the science of acoustics, or the calculation of sound vibrations. So the truth or falsity of astrology can only be proved or disproved by astrology itself of the present day, and not by what the ancients believed or did not believe about astrology, or the brightness, color, or quick movements of the planets, and Mr. Proctor may yet find that the astrologers of to-day know better how to calculate the movements of the heavenly bodies than he knows himself.

When an astrologer erects a horoscope, or map of the heavens for any person's time of birth, he calculates the exact position of all the signs of the Zodiack on each of the cusps of the twelve houses, to the degree and minute, for the exact longitude and latitude of the place where the person was born. He also calculates the daily and hourly motions of the sun, moon, and of all the larger planets; also the longitude, latitude, right ascension, and declination of the moon, and seven of the larger planets, and the right ascension, declination, and longitude of the sun. Also the meridian distance, the semi-diurnal, or semi-nocturnal arcs; the oblique ascension or descension, and the distance from the preceding, or the succeeding cusps of the houses, of the sun, moon, and all the larger planets. When the astrologer has made all these calculations, he has has only laid the foundation, or drawn a speculum of the person's nativity; and when all this is done, the main or most important part of his calculations is yet to commence, such as the transits, (or the movements of the heavenly bodies, as Mr. Proctor calls them,) and the directions, both secondary and primary, and converse and direct, the parallels, and rapt parallels, &c., &c. Yet Mr. Proctor says (heaven save the mark!) that the astrologer of to-day cannot calculate the movements of the heavenly bodies. I mean to say that if any person were to offer Mr. Proctor a million dollars to calculate a nativity properly, with all the transits and directions, and read it off, he could not do it, with all his pretended knowledge of the science of astronomy, and his "calculation of the movements of the heavenly bodies." I very much doubt whether he even knows the meaning of one half of the scientific terms which I have just used, let alone making the astronomical calculations referred to.

It may be asked, why does Mr. Proctor make such statements about astrology and astrologers, when he knows them to be untrue. The fact of the matter is, Mr. Proctor is a Catholic, or at least a particular friend of mine, an editor, told me that he heard Mr. Proctor say himself that he was a Catholic, and he being of that religious denomination, like Judge Gordon of Philadelphia, regards all astrologers as criminals, even without a shadow of proof that they have committed any crime, either against God or man.

In view of the fact that Mr. Proctor is a devotee of that most superstitious of all Christian beliefs, that of the Church of Rome, the severity of his denunciation of superstition in his attack upon astrology is not a little singular. But what else could be expected from a votary of a church notoriously opposed to all progress and reform, a church that burned alive John Huss, (even when he had a safe conduct to his trial,) and also thousands of other good men and reformers, and which also perpetrated the terrors of the Inquisition.

Is it not a little singular that astrologers are "lying knaves" and "unscrupulous rascals" only in Christian countries, and even in those Christian nations only within the last two hundred years? In all other civilized countries, (and which cover more than three-fourths of the globe,) they have always been looked up to, and held in the highest esteem from time immemorial, even up to the present day. I shall bring some remarkable facts to prove this assertion in the volume which follows. And as Mr. Proctor says:—"The cuneiform inscriptions of Assyria, the hieroglyphs of Egypt, the most ancient records of Persia, India, and China, agree in showing that of *old, all men believed the sun and moon, the planets and the stars, in their courses foretell, nay, rule the fortunes of men.*" Is it not strange that in all those nations astrology is studied, even at the present day, by the most learned and intelligent people of those nations, and put to the test every day by thousands of people, and relied on as a science by hundreds of millions of people in their every day life, and has been for thousands of years;—that those people have never discovered that the astrologers are "lying knaves" and "unscrupulous rascals," while in Christian countries, where the practice of astrology is almost a lost art, and out of the vast number who now treat this ancient science with supercilious ridicule, there is not one in a thousand who know distinctly what it is he laughs at, and yet astrology has sustained a most conspicuous part throughout the history of the world? Are ignorance and want of practical experience the tests by which Christian people prove or disprove everything? I will defy Mr. Proctor to find a single astrologer even in those Christian countries, who has had any practical experience in that science, but what holds astrology in as high esteem as he, or any other astronomer holds astronomy. Does this not prove, as "Hamlet" says:—"There is something rotten in the state of Denmark?"

But what is the cause of all this change in Christian nations, which, as Mr. Proctor says:—"proves that the astrologer of to-day must necessarily be a rogue and a charlatan?" Is it, as Mr. Proctor says:—"now men know how the sun and the moon produce their effects; they know why Mercury seems shifty, and Venus lovely, how Mars comes to look red, and Jupiter bright, and Saturn yellow."

Does Mr. Proctor or any other astronomer know all those things? If he does, why is it not made known or published? I should like to be informed myself in all those matters. But the fact of the matter is, that those astrologers of old knew as much about those things as Mr. Proctor, or any other astronomer of the present day. The ancients had their theories about those "effects," and Mr. Proctor has only theories, which theories may be upset any day. But suppose we did "know how the sun and moon did produce their effects," or how "Venus looks lovely, Mars red, Jupiter bright, and Saturn yellow," (which I totally deny,) that would have nothing to do with upsetting the science of astrology. It might possibly help to explain some things we do not now understand, and, of course, place that science on a firmer foundation than it ever had before.

If Mr. Proctor did not happen to know everything, and I was not "ignorant and silly," and a "rogue and charlatan," it might be possible for me to explain to him how astrology fell into disrepute in Christian nations, and more especially within the last two hundred years. But the reader of these Introductory Remarks may not be so wise and know every thing, like Mr. Proctor, and may possibly not be in the condition of the man whom Solomon speaks of, where he says:—"seest thou a man wise in his own conceit, there is more hopes of a fool than of him." And Solomon does not appear to have a very high opinion even of a fool, where he says:—"Though thou shouldest bray a fool in a mortar among wheat with a pestle, yet will not his foolishness depart from him."

Therefore as it may possibly be interesting for the reader to know how it came about, that astrologers who had been held in the highest veneration for thousands of years in all civilized nations, and have always been the counsellors and advisers of Kings, Queens, Emperors, Sultans and Pharoahs, have changed of late years in Christian countries into "ignorant charlatans," "lying knaves" and "unscrupulous rascals," I will endeavor to explain to the best of my ability, although it may not be very flattering to either Mr. Proctor, Judge Gordon, or even to those Christian nations which have enacted laws against astrologers and astrology.

I shall divide these explanations into three parts or sections. 1st. The Christian Religion. 2d. The Reformation and Witchcraft. 3d. The change from the Ptolemaic system of astronomy to the Copernican system.

First.—The Christian Religion.—The Christian religion was entirely unique at its commencement, nothing ever being like it before, or can be compared to it since. Its very inception was a miracle, and it appeared to consist of nothing but miracles, saints, and relics, for over a thousand years, and the laws of nature were entirely ignored by its followers, who were a class of people entirely separated from their fellow beings, and who were a kind of a cross-breed between the socialist and anarchist of the present day, and if we can believe the New Testament, the laws of nature were either entirely suspended, or else they were terribly out of joint, and went limping along similar to a man with a long leg and a short one. The conception of Christ was a miracle. His birth was another. His whole life appeared to consist of nothing but miracles; such as turning water into wine, walking on the water, stilling the storm, feeding thousands with five loaves and two fishes, raising the dead, healing the sick with the touch, casting out devils, and even those devils talking to Christ after they were cast out, &c., &c. Christ's death was a miracle, and His resurrection, and His eating and drinking afterwards with his disciples, were all miracles, and His ascension into heaven was another miracle. Consequently such occupations as those of doctors, astronomers, astrologers, farmers, and even fishermen, who had to depend on the laws of nature in order to successfully carry on their business, were all played out; but as the people could not continue to subsist upon miracles, or rather provisions miraculously produced, all those employments gradually came into use again. But as the early Christians believed that by praying to Christ, Virgin Mary, or some other saint, or by possessing some "relic," the laws of nature could easily be changed in their particular cases, the science of astrology, which is entirely built upon those laws, has never been fully recognized by the people professing the Christian religion, as it has been by all the other religions, (whose creeds did not consist of miracles,) and all other civilized nations, but Christian, in every other part of the inhabited globe. Those Christians that profess a religion which consists of the greatest amount of superstition, similar to the Roman Catholic religion, love astrology about as much as the devil loves holy water; hence when bigoted Catholics like Mr. Proctor or Judge Gordon have a chance to show their venom and hatred against an astrologer, they never let the opportunity slip.

Not only Catholics, but all ministers of the gospel are specially opposed to the science of astrology, and deem it specially wicked to even desire to know anything of our prospects for the future, and any person giving way to such a weakness was placed in the catalogue of those persons whom Christ speaks of when he says that:—"whomsoever looketh on a woman to lust after her, has committed adultery in his heart already." Some thirty years ago there was not a Sunday passed, in a city like New York or Philadelphia, but what some minister was preaching about the wickedness of astrology or fortune-tellers, in short it was a constant text or theme for a sermon, similar to "If a man gains the whole world, and lose his own soul," or "Go and sin no more," &c., &c. But ministers no longer preach sermons against astrology, and we are gradually coming back to the laws of nature. Miracles and relics of saints are held at a discount, thanks to the lectures and writings of such men as Profs. Tyndall, Huxley and Darwin, who are teaching the people that the world is governed by fixed laws, and that the condition and happiness of man is improved by understanding and obeying these laws; and on account of the perihelion of the superior planets, a great number of the newspapers, both in this country and Europe, have articles on the influence of the planets, as for instance:

The *London Evening Standard* of July 6th, 1880, in commenting on Mr. B. G. Jenkins' paper on Meteorology and Planetary Influence, read by him before the Dulwich College Geological Club, said:—

"From the lofty heights of modern science we have been accustomed to look down with pity and contempt upon the astrologers of the Middle Ages,— the weak dabblers in science who were foolish enough to believe that the stars had an influence upon man. An allusion to astrologers was always good to raise a laugh at a science meeting, and the astrologers and alchemists were classed together as either dreamers or charlatans. Of late years, however, a certain reaction has set in. The astrologer is becoming rehabilitated very rapidly. The influence of the planets upon the earth is now admitted to be very distinct, and fresh proofs of their disturbing influences are constantly cropping up."

Second.—The Reformation and Witchcraft.—Besides the "creeds" and "dogmas," the practical part of the Catholic religion consisted of good works, and a life of purity and celibacy, which were necessary for a person to perform miracles, their souls to be added to the calendar of saints, and parts of their bodies to serve the purpose of relics. The reformation changed all this, faith was put in the place of good works and purity, marriage was substituted for celibacy, witchery took the place of miracles, and everything which had the appearance of the supernatural or of mystery was classed under the name of witchcraft, except that miraculous change of heart which was necessary to get "religion," or be converted from evil ways. Man had nothing to do with the laws of nature, neither had the laws of nature anything to do with man.

"In Adam's fall,
We sinned all."

Consequently before man was converted he was under the power of the devil, and after he was converted, he was controlled by the grace of God. Within the last twenty years, when ministers were giving notice of religious meetings, they would invariably say:—"The Lord permiting," or "The Lord willing." It was blasphemy to even suppose that man was subject to natural laws, and years ago, every one was accused of witchcraft who attempted to trace those laws, or tried to find out their effects, and to calculate them in a person's nativity was equivalent to sinning against the Holy Ghost, which is never forgiven either in this world or in that which is to come. To be accused of witchcraft was certain to be followed by conviction and execution. The injunction given to the ancient Jews in the Old Testament, "Thou shalt not suffer a witch to live," was carried out to the letter, not only against witches, but also against astrologers, by the Protestant Reformers in all Europe, and in some parts of America. In some countries in Europe there were persons employed as detectives, whose special business it was to hunt up witches and bring them to justice; they were called witch finders, and very few supposed witches or astrologers escaped them, especially when put to the torture. This persecution has continued almost to the present day. Even within the last twenty years a satirical writer in New York, who was known by the name of "Doesticks," wrote a book pretending to give an account of all the Fortune-tellers, Clairvoyants, Spiritualists and Astrologers in this city; and he called his book "The Witches of New York." Under the belief, no doubt, that the Devil cannot be painted too black, he appears to have told as many lies about them as he could well put together. Only a few years ago the "New York Sun" gave an account of a woman in the Eastern States who had made a prediction in regard to the election of Gen. Garfield. The "Sun" did not say whether the woman was a fortune-teller, Gipsy, clairvoyant, spiritualist or astrologer; it simply stated that she was a "witch," and that term appears to cover everything of that nature.

When I was attending Medical College, the Prof. of Anatomy, in giving a description of the eye, remarked that if we were in doubt as to the name of a disease of the eye, we could call it Ophthalmia, as that meant simply disease of the eye, and covered everything else. In this way it has been the custom to class all forms of divination under the term witchcraft, and astrologers and fortune-tellers of every kind have continued to be persecuted as such.

An old author has said that "a miracle is legitimate witchcraft, and witchcraft is an illegitimate miracle." To make it plainer it might be said, that the turning of water into wine by Christ was a miracle, but if any other man did the same thing, it would be witchcraft, and up to a few years ago, he would have been persecuted as a wizard.

Is it not strange that astrologers who have been observers and students of the laws of nature for thousands of years, and are, as a rule, not believers in witchcraft or miracles, or in fact anything supernatural or contrary to the laws of nature, should have been called witches and persecuted as such by the persons who are the only advocates of, and believers in witchcraft and miracles?

We have a similar paradox or circumstance in the practice of Medicine. Paracelsus, who lived in the early part of the fifteenth century, commenced his career by publicly burning the works of Galen, (who was an astrologer, and taught the use of herbs, roots and barks in medicine,) saying that "Galen did not know as much as his shoe latchets." Paracelsus was the first of the school of mineral medicines, who commenced to treat every disease with that class of drugs; and as mercury was mainly employed by them, the German name of which was Quacksalver, they were called Quacks, and those who used herbs and roots were the regular physicians. Now fashion has changed so much that the herb doctors are called Quacks, and the others who use the Quacksalver, the regular physicians.

If the Christian religion were the most perfect religion on the face of the earth, then we might wink at some of its miracles and superstitions, and at its ignoring the laws of nature, but if we can be guided by past history, the opposite is much nearer the truth. Except within the last hundred years, whenever and wherever the Christians have gained a foothold in any civilized or partly civilized nation, they have always reduced that nation to barbarism, and it has reverted to the condition of the dark ages, and often to slavery of the most degrading nature. It is only since the human mind has thrown off some of the superstition of the Christian religion, and discarded miracles and relics, and returned to the investigation of the laws of nature, and at the same time been guided by knowledge and science which sweep away all superstition and witchcraft, (all of which by the scientific mind, are now classed with the hobgoblins of the past,) that there has been any real improvement in the condition of man in Christian nations. Even now if it were not for the influence of the liberal minded inhabitants of those countries, some of those Christians would be ready to cut one another's throats, and persecute each other as of old, if they happened to differ in their beliefs. The Lord George Gordon riots may be taken as an example; and it is the same in every place where Christians are away from liberal minded people.

Many writers in referring to the Christians and their religion, away from civilization, say that it forms a very poor comparison to any other religion, even in the cradle of Christianity. Bayard Taylor in his " Lands of the Saracens," speaking of the Christians in Jerusalem, page 79, says:

"Whatever good the various missions here may, in time, accomplish (at present, it does not amount to much), Jerusalem is the last place in the world where an intelligent heathen would be converted to Christianity. Were I cast here, ignorant of any religion, and were I to compare the lives and practices of the different sects as the means of making my choice—in short, to judge of each faith by the conduct of its professors—I should at once turn Mussulman. When you consider that in the Holy Sepulchre there are *nineteen* chapels, each belonging to a different sect, calling itself Christian, and that a Turkish police is always stationed there to prevent the bloody quarrels which often ensue between them, you may judge how those who call themselves followers of the Prince of Peace practice the pure faith he sought to establish. Between the Greek and Latin churches, especially, there is a deadly feud, and their contentions are a scandal, not only to the few Christians here, but to the Moslems themselves. I believe there is a sort of truce at present, owing to the settlement of some of the disputes—as for instance, the restoration of the silver star, which the Greeks stole from the shrine of the Nativity, at Bethlehem. The Latins, however, not long since, demolished, *vi et armis*, a chapel which the Greeks commenced building on Mount Zion. But, if the employment of material weapons has been abandoned for the time, there is none the less a war of words and sounds still going on. Go into the Holy Sepulchre, when mass is being celebrated, and you can scarcely endure the din. No sooner does the Greek choir begin its shrill chant, than the Latins fly to the assault. They have an organ, and terribly does that organ strain its bellows and labor its pipes to drown the rival singing. You think the Latins will carry the day, when suddenly the cymbals of the Abyssinians strike in with harsh brazen clang, and for the moment, triumph. Then there are Copts, and Maronites, and Armenians, and I know not how many other sects, who must have their share; and the service that should be a many-toned harmony, pervaded by one grand spirit of devotion, becomes a discordant orgie, befitting the rites of Belial.

A long time ago—I do not know the precise number of years—the Sultan granted a firman, in answer to the application of both Jews and Christians, allowing the members of each sect to put to death any person belonging to the other sect, who should be found inside of their churches or synagogues. The firman has never been recalled, though in every place but Jerusalem it remains a dead letter. Here, although the Jews freely permit Christians to enter their synagogue, a Jew who should enter the Holy Sepulchre would be lucky if he escaped with his life. Not long since, an English gentleman, who was taken by the monks for a Jew, was so severely beaten that he was confined to his bed for two months. What worse than scandal, what abomination, that the spot looked upon by so many Christians as the most awfully sacred on earth, should be the scene of such brutish intolerance!"

I give the above as a specimen of Christianity in its simplicity and purity, when removed from liberal minds and infidel influence. As for the Mohammedans, they are believers in astrology, consequently they are all "lying knaves" and "unscrupulous rascals," and cannot be compared to their neighbors, the Christians in Jerusalem.

A missionary who was trying to convert a Mohammedan to the Christian faith, was asked by the mussulman what Christianity taught. The Christian said:—"It teaches the doctrine of a future life, and peace and good will on earth." The mussulman answered that his religion taught of a future life also, and as for the peace and good will, if it were not for the Mohammedans the Christians would murder each other over the sepulchre of the founder of their religion.

Third.—The change from the Ptolemaic to the Copernican System of Astronomy:—Claudius Ptolemy lived about one hundred and fifty years previous to the time of Christ. He was an astronomer, astrologer, and knew all of the geography of his day. The system of astronomy which was known by his name was in vogue for thousands of years previous to his time. He was a compiler, collecting and embodying in his works all the knowledge of these sciences that then existed; and Ptolemy's Tetrabiblos contains all the rules of astrology that had been laid down during the centuries before his time, and is to-day to the astrologer what the Bible is to the Christian. Up to a very late day his astronomical and astrological books were bound in one volume, as there was very little use for astronomy except in the practice of astrology.

When the change from the Ptolemaic to the Copernican system of astronomy occurred, many believed that Ptolemy's system of astrology was swept away also, but this was wrong and only the result of a want of knowledge. All the calculations that were made under the Copernican system were the same as those made under the old system, such as the calculation of eclipses, the revolutions of the heavenly bodies, etc., the difference being that there was more accuracy in the modern method; but by whatever method calculations are made in astronomy the result is the same in astrology, and the astrologer of the present day makes his calculations similar in every respect to those that were made when they wrote the "hieroglyphics of Egypt, the cuneiform inscriptions of Assyria, and the most ancient records of Persia, India and China."

I have at the present time Tate's Astronomy and Hackett's Astrology, both bound in one volume, and even if the Copernican and Newtonian systems were overthrown and replaced by some other system of astronomy, Hackett's Astrology with all its calculations, would remain true, no matter by what system they were computed. The angles of geometry and mensuration are true to nature whether they be calculated by simple arithmetic or the higher mathematics. Therefore the reader will see the foolishness and illogical conclusions of Mr. Proctor when he says.—"The very fact that the old astrologers were for the most part honest, though mistaken, proves that the astrologer of to-day must necessarily be a rogue and a charlatan," and yet he does not in his article bring a single fact to prove that the old astrologers were mistaken.*

As there appears to be a difference of opinion, either real or imaginary, on the subject of astrology, between Mr. Proctor and myself; and as the newspapers will publish only his side of the question; and as I have the utmost confidence in the principles which all astrologers claim as the truths of that science, I believe this question can only be settled so far as Mr. Proctor is concerned, on the public rostrum, with an intelligent and critical audience for judges. Although the chances are that those judges will be biased against astrology, because of previous education, yet it seems to me the most fitting place for investigating truth or exposing error. I therefore request Mr. Proctor, in the most kind and friendly manner, to meet me in public discussion on the following question:—"Are the principles of astrology true, and can they be borne out by, and in accordance with, the laws of nature and reason."

Mr. Proctor is a public lecturer and has been in practice as such for years, and nearly all the audience will be more in sympathy with his side of the question. Yet, while I possess none of his advantages and am not a fluent speaker, I will allow him his choice to either lead or follow me in the discussion, and he may choose the length of time to be occupied, provide that each shall have the same length of time. He shall also elect whether the discussion shall occupy one evening or more. I will bear half the expense of hall rent and advertising.

The conditions I shall insist upon in these discussions, are:—There shall be at least four nativities read off before the audience, two by Mr. Proctor and two by myself. In those that are to be read by me the exact time of birth shall be vouched for, or sworn to, and selected by a committee; one half of this committee to be named by Mr. Proctor, and one half by myself. Mr. Proctor must, from the date of birth of the two nativities which fall to his lot, give descriptions of the persons physically and mentally; give all the good and evil periods of life, marriage and children, and the outlines of their lives or natural tendencies.

If it be true, as Mr. Proctor says, that "the astrologers of to-day make a lying pretence of believing in planetary influences," then he can sketch off the outlines of a person's life as well from a piece of blank paper as I or any other astrologer can from a chart of the heavens erected for the moment of birth.

Mr. Proctor may say that it is all nonsense and a waste of time to have a discussion on astrology, as it has already been exploded. The

---

* I have not produced any facts to prove the truth of astrology in this article, because Mr. Proctor has not given any facts to prove the falsity of that science; the proofs I have to offer will be found in the pamphlet which will follow. All that Mr. Proctor appears to have done is to show the universality of astrology and the general belief in it in all civilized nations up to a recent date; probably he has brought as strong arguments in that direction for the truth of astrology as I could have done. Where he gets his logic from, in trying to prove a science or any subject false at the present day, which was true at its commencement and continued so for thousands of years; or that it could be reasonable then and not now, is hard to understand. If the astrologers of to-day are ignorant and dishonest, why were they not so thousands of years ago? And yet Mr. Proctor vouches for "the astrologers of old times" being "honest men," and "by no means wanting in reasoning power." Let us hope that if Mr. Proctor should in future publish another article on the "Humbug of Astrology," he will first learn something of its principles, and remember that none should condemn who do not understand.

same remark might just as truly be made of mesmerism, phrenology, homœopathy, and hundreds of other subjects that live after they are said to have been exploded. The great misfortune is, that all of these sciences have been exploded by persons who are as little posted on them as Mr. Proctor is on astrology.

Every science is gradually built up from facts which are gathered from observation and experiment, sometimes extending over hundreds of years; these facts are afterwards generalized and classified according to certain rules, principles or laws, and when these rules, principles, and laws harmonize and are verified by other experiments and observations, then it is called a science. Every science must stand on its own merits; one science cannot be proved or disproved by another; it is impossible to prove or disprove, English grammar by the rules of arithmetic, and no man can prove or disprove astrology by astronomy, no matter how learned he may be in the latter science; nor can he prove or disprove phrenology by anatomy, or homœopathy by allopathy. Very often one science will throw light upon another; for instance geology may throw some light upon astronomy, but it is impossible to prove or disprove astronomy by geology, although they both have a relation to the planets, geology treating specially of our planet, and astronomy of all the planets and stars.

If I have made any proposition which Mr. Proctor cannot accept, then I trust he will signify to me either privately or in the public prints on what terms he is willing to meet me for the purpose of having a fair and searching examination of principles which I regard as truths in astrology. I will concede anything he may ask, except the public tests of nativities, as these I consider the most important proofs which can be brought for or against astrology.

After Mr. Proctor has made use of such expressions in the public prints in referring to myself and all other astrologers, there is one of two things he must do: he must either meet me or some other astrologer in public discussion on astrology, including the public tests I have before referred to, or he must make apology in an equally public manner over his own name. It will not do for him to say that I am beneath his notice, as the reader can see from what I have related in these Introductory Remarks that my standing as a physician and a gentleman is equal to Mr. Proctor's.

Possibly it will be best to insert in this reply to Mr. Proctor one or two anecdotes which illustrate the errors he has fallen into in attacking astrologers and astrology.

Dr. Caldwell, a professor and prominent physician of Philadelphia, gives an account in his autobiography of an incident which occurred while he was traveling in England. In journeying by stage from Liverpool to Birmingham, while on the outskirts of Liverpool, he noticed a large mansion with beautiful grounds, which were decorated in various places with fine statuary. This statuary attracted his attention to a degree which led him to enquire whom the place belonged to; a fellow passenger told him that it had been the residence of the late Dr. Salmon. Dr. Caldwell knew Dr. Salmon as the proprietor of a medicine, called the Balm of Gilead. Caldwell commenced a tirade against Salmon, using epithets similar to "fraud," "impostor," "prince of quacks," etc., but no reply was made by his fellow passengers. He noticed that they all looked towards a lady dressed in deep mourning, who was in the coach. When the coach neared Birmingham, all the passengers had left it except the lady in mourning and himself, and, American like, he tried to introduce himself, enquired if she had far to go when they reached Birmingham, and concluded by asking her name. She said, "I am Mrs. Salmon, and I live in the house just outside of Liverpool." Dr. Caldwell was taken by surprise and began apologizing, but she stopped him by saying, "You need not apologize; if you had known my husband as his friends and I knew him, you would have spoken differently, and would have held a different opinion of him from that you expressed when passing my house." Dr. Caldwell afterwards became well acquainted with Mrs. Salmon, and he says that it was a lesson to him never to condemn any one without previous knowledge of his character.

If Mr. Proctor had become acquainted with a number of astrologers, possibly he would hold a different opinion of them to what he expressed in the "World." For instance, Mr. John Ledbetter, who died in Brooklyn a short time ago, spent forty-five years in the study and investigation of astrology, and has left several volumes in manuscript as the fruits of his labor. He invented a planisphere to facilitate his calculations in the science, yet he never made a dollar from the practice of astrology. His former employers, who are wholesale jewelers in this city, speak of him in the highest terms as an honorable man and a man of learning. I could give a number of names of men living who are students of astrology, and who have devoted years to its investigation, but on account of the prejudice against that science they would not wish their names to come before the public.

A number of years since a physician entered the office of Dr. Cox of Philadelphia, and picking up a work on the Homœopathic practice of medicine, which lay on the desk, looked at it a moment and threw it down, with the contemptuous exclamation:—"Humbug! humbug!" Dr. Cox looked at him in surprise, and asked:—"Do you know anything of Homœopathy?" The visitor replied, "No! but it is all humbug and nonsense!" Dr. Cox said, "Well I do not know anything of Homœopathy myself; but who must I believe; you, who admit that you do not know anything of the subject, or my son, who has graduated from a Homœopathic College and is using Homœopathic medicines every day in his practice? And he tells me it is not all humbug."

In seeking knowledge or information of any science or profession, is it not best to be guided and advised by those who are the most informed, and have had the longest experience in that science or profession, rather than to take the opinion of one who simply reasons on general principles and who has had no practical experience. It was such men as Richard A. Proctor, and their reasoning without knowledge, which caused all the sufferings and hardships of Galileo, Columbus, and I might say of all the reformers, discoverers, heretics, and witches who have been persecuted for the last thousand years.

I once heard Mr. Proctor say in one of his lectures on Astronomy, in New York City, while speaking of the perihelion of the superior planets, that even if the Science of Astronomy could be used in making predictions of earthquakes and of the periods of epidemics, it would depreciate in the estimation of scientific minds, and everything which had a tendency to develop astronomy in that direction ought to be discouraged. I beg to differ with him on this point; I do not think it can lower the dignity of any science to make it more useful and add to the happiness of man.

I think I have proved by the various rules and principles of Astrology in a number of horoscopes in the foregoing pages, and have shown clearly that if the science of astrology were put into every day use, as Mr. Proctor says it was of old, fully fifty per cent of all the sickness, poverty, misery, and hardships of the people of the present day would be done away with.

I also propose to show that thousands of people are murdered every year, and some of them in a most barbarous manner by physicians, on account of a want of knowledge of astrology.

I ask Mr. Proctor to come before an audience and prove, if he can, the falsity of a science which for thousands of years was in every day use, "*not only among all the leading races of antiquity and in all the chief civilized nations, but during periods of time which no other faith can boast of having swayed.*" If he can do this, and yet be uninformed of the practical application of that science, I shall give him credit for being a remarkably smart man.

As I have said before, I request Mr. Proctor to meet me in a public hall to try and accomplish that most difficult task, or else make a suitable apology. He might as well attempt to prove that all the astronomers of the present day, in all civilized nations on the globe, are deceived when making their calculations for the captains of vessels; and those captains are equally deceived when making use of those calculations to find out the locations of their ships at sea; or in other words, the astronomers and mariners are gulling each other, or are combined together to gull the people, and have been doing so for hundreds of years; as to say astrologers have been "making a lying pretense of believing in planetary influence," and have been doing so for ages.

Why should Mr. Proctor say that the astrologers who calculate the movements of the heavenly bodies have been "making a lying pretense of believing in planetary influence," and at the same time not say that the captains of vessels have been making a lying pretense of calculating the longitude and latitude of the ships at sea? Does not the astrologer make his calculations as carefully as a mariner makes his? Only those of the astrologer are much more intricate, and even more difficult. And yet captains of large ocean steamers are held in the highest respect, and are deemed men of great responsibility, while astrologers are "lying knaves" and "unscrupulous rascals."

> "Strange such a difference there should be
> 'Twixt tweedledum and tweedledee."

Instead of Mr. Proctor calling all astrologers vile names, it would have been more logical and convincing to the readers of the "New York World," if he had taken the time of birth of some well-known person, such as General Washington or General Grant, and shown that the rules and principles of astrology were not borne out in those nativities. He must know that one clear case of that kind would do more to sink astrology into oblivion than all the Billingsgate language he could hurl at its votaries. Why has this not been done? I leave the reader to draw his own inference.

To make this matter plainer, I will go into a few particulars of the science of astrology.

The path in the heavens in which the Sun and planets appear to travel, when viewed from the earth, is called the ecliptic, or zodiac, and it is divided into twelve parts, each of which is called a sign of the zodiac. These signs are classed or grouped together according to the influences they possess, and are known as tall, short, stout, slender, dark and light signs, etc. When a child is born, if a tall sign be rising and the moon and the planet which has dominion over the sign rising be both in tall signs, that child when it has reached adult life will be tall, no matter how short the parents were. The same rule applies, if the signs which have control are short, dark or light, stout or slender, no matter how the parents are formed. Persons are invariably formed as the planets indicate, even when the planetary influence has to overcome hereditary or parental tendencies.

General Washington was born under the planet Venus, which was situated in the sign Aries, a tall, slender, light sign; but having Taurus, (a stout sign) on the ascendant, he became rather full made after middle age. General Grant was born under the planet Venus, but Venus was in the sign Pisces, which is a rather short and stout sign, and having Taurus, (a short sign) on the ascendant, it was an impossibility for him to be tall and slender like General Washington, even if General Grant's parents had both been tall and slender.

Nothing but the science of astrology can account for the great difference in children of the same family, some tall and light complexioned, others short and dark; and though the believers in heredity think that in such cases one child will take after the father, another after the grandmother, or even further back, it can be demonstrated that those children owe their appearance and tendencies to planetary influence.

While a student of astrology, many times have I said to parents whose child's nativity I was calculating: "Why! you have made a mistake in the time; this would indicate a light complexioned child, while you are both dark;" But the answer would always be: "Yes, the child is light complexioned and has light hair." Believers in heredity would say that the child took after its great-great-grand-parents, or some of its fore-fathers who lived before the flood.

I defy Mr. Proctor to bring a single instance to contradict these laws and principles in astrology. He might just as well try to prove that twice two are five.

I shall bring one more illustration and with it close this reply to Mr. Proctor.

In all nativities the seventh house or Western Horizon is called the house of marriage, and as there are good or evil planets placed therein, so will marriage be more or less fortunate or unfortunate. In the horoscope of a female, the planet to which the sun first applies by aspect will describe the husband, and if the aspect be a benign one, and to a fortunate planet, it will indicate an excellent man, and happiness in marriage life; if it be a malign aspect and to an evil planet, and evil planets be in the seventh house, it will be impossible for husband and wife to live together in a happy manner. We have a remarkable proof of Astrology in Queen Victoria's nativity, wherein the sun first applied by good or trine aspect to Jupiter, which was in Aquarius, Prince Albert being exactly described by Jupiter in Aquarius, and the happiness of their married life is too well known to need comment.

In the horoscope of a male the rule applies the same, except that the first aspect of the moon to a planet is taken instead of the sun's first aspect. Lord Byron's nativity is a remarkable example of the influences of the planets, in causing unhappiness in his married life. The moon in his nativity first made an opposition of Mercury in Capricorn, an evil aspect, and an evil planet. His married life is well known.

I defy Mr. Proctor to produce one instance or nativity, where the rules and principles in astrology which I have mentioned are not apparent in every day life. If he says he can do so he simply proves himself to be a "*lying knave*" and an "*unscrupulous rascal,*" and "*makes a lying pretense of*" NOT "*believing in planetary influence.*"

Since Richard A. Proctor published the "Humbug of Astrology," in which he called all Astrologers, "silly charlatans, lying knaves, rogues, and unscrupulous rascals," in the New York World on Feb. 6th, 1887, there has been a considerable change in the opinion of some of the editors, and the people connected with that paper; some of them have not only become converts to the science of Astrology, but have even investigated and studied it to a great extent.

Mr. T. E. Wilson, the librarian of the New York World, on Feb. 2d, 1894, when Mr. A. N. Doerschuk, of Kansas City, wrote to him to find who was the best astrologer in the United States, directed the letter to O. D. Bragdon, an astrologer in Boston, Mass., regarding him as the best; but Mr. Bragdon forwarded the letter to me. I have since learned from a pupil of mine that Mr. Wilson has given considerable attention to Astrology and regards it as a true science.

Mr. Jonas Whitley, one of the present editors of the New York World, has also read much on the science of Astrology, and when he graduated at the College of New York the thesis which he handed to the officers of that institution was entirely on the science of Astrology. Besides the New York World of late has given considerable space to articles on Astrology, and to publishing horoscopes. See page 50.

From "The New York Morning Advertiser" of October 4, 1893.

AT PROCTOR'S TOMB.

Impressive Ceremonies Mark the Re-interment of the Astronomer's Body in Greenwood.

The memorial in Greenwood Cemetery, which has been provided mainly through the efforts of George W. Childs, of Philadelphia, is of Quincy granite, a great bluish block, which is beautifully polished. It is eight feet high and five feet wide. One inscription tells that "Richard A. Proctor, Astronomer, was born in Chelsea, England, on March 23, 1837, and died in New York City, on Sept. 12, 1888, aged 51 years." On a polished face on the reverse side of the vase, in script, is the epitaph especially written for it by Herbert Spencer. It reads: "On public as on private grounds, Professor Proctor's premature death was much to be lamented. He united great detailed knowledge with broad general views in an unusual degree, and while admirably fitted for a popular expositor, was at the same time well equipped for original investigation, which, had he lived, would have added to our astronomical knowledge. Professor Proctor was also to be admired for his endeavors to keep the pursuit of science free from the corrupting and paralyzing influence of State aid."

Mr. Herbert Spencer ought to add that people differing in opinion from Richard A. Proctor on a scientific subject he called "charlatans, unscrupulous rascals, and lying knaves."

The public may say I am going too far in following Mr. Proctor to the grave, but I believe, as Lord Byron says, "Nothing is worse than a lying tombstone."

In ancient Rome, when a noted general returned, after making great conquests abroad, and paraded through the streets, the populace clapping and shouting his praises, there was always a person appointed to ride before him to tell of the hero's faults and shortcomings; and I think it would be a good thing to have a corner on a tombstone to describe the faults and shortcomings of those who have departed this life.

Had any Astrologer ever attacked Mr. Proctor, in any shape or form, there might have been some explanation, but not an excuse, for his falsehoods against the professors of that science. When I think how many Astrologers have had to suffer years of imprisonment, insults, and disgrace on account of men like Mr. Proctor telling such untruths about them, and men who stood far higher in honesty and principles, and even in scientific ability, than Mr. Proctor, no wonder that I feel justified in using strong language against such scientific "witch finders."

Some years ago I attended a course of lectures on Astronomy by Prof. Proctor, given in Chickering Hall, New York. He said: "Even if epidemics could be foretold by means of Astronomy it would degrade the science by making use of it for any such purpose."

Why did he not go further, and say it would degrade Astronomy to make use of it for the purpose of navigation, or for the guidance of travelers in their journeys over the deserts of Africa, or the prairies of America? It never degrades any science or any person to become useful.

Had not Astronomy become so perfected as to be used for such purposes, the Astronomers of the present day would be persecuted far more than the Astrologers. Formerly the Astronomers made their calculations only for Astrologers, to enable them to make predictions. They were the hewers of wood and drawers of water for the Astrologers.

TO THE READER.

Part of the ensuing pages have been inserted in preceding parts of this book, under the heading, "History of Astrology by its Enemies," but I think it advisable to reprint the following arguments in favor of Astrology for two reasons: first, that the theme would not be complete without them, and second, that the reader can appreciate and understand the arguments much better than when reading the "Brief History of Astrology, by Its Friends and by Its Enemies." If he has also studied the science he can enjoy the ridiculous statements that the Rev. Thomas Dick, William and Robert Chambers, and Richard A. Proctor have made use of in vilifying Astrology and Astrologers.

It certainly must appear very strange to the student that men of learning such as they, should expose themselves to ridicule and contempt. There might be some excuse if they were missionaries talking to the natives of the islands of the Pacific Ocean, or in New Zealand, Australia, or to the people living in the wilds of Africa. Then they could use such expressions and arguments without any fear of contradiction; but in a land of freedom and liberty, where a majority of the people can read and write, and study Astrology for themselves, and where thousands of text-books are printed and published on that science, these writers must appear contemptible and absurd in the extreme.

It is remarkable that the publishers of the leading encyclopoedias should continue to treat the science of Astrology with such disfavor, when Astrology is so well known and understood, and when there are men, both willing and able, to write articles on the science for these publications, who can treat it in an intelligent manner, so as to be interesting to the general reader. Certainly if an Astrologer reads the statements and arguments printed under the head "Astrology," at the same time knowing them to be entirely false, they reduce the value of other parts of the encyclopoedia in his estimation.

If the writers of each article had produced a single argument that Astrology was false or not worthy of serious attention, it would be a different matter. For instance, if they were to bring forward the horoscope of Gen. Washington, and prove from the time of his birth and the position of the planets that he ought to have been a short, stout person, dark complexioned, with dark hair, and also that the planets indicated that he would be a person of shallow brain and remain in obscurity; or could they prove from the time of birth of Gen. Grant, that he should have been a tall, slender, light complexioned person, and that as a business man he would be remarkably fortunate, but as a soldier a mere numbskull, then they might have some excuse for such articles on that science in the encyclopoedias. But every one who has a slight knowledge of the science knows it is impossible for such writers to bring proof or facts of that description against Astrology.

The articles in the encyclopoedias above referred to evince a strong prejudice against Astrology, especially when it is well known that the science can be taught the same as the science of arithmetic, or any other science. This prejudice and bias against Astrology from reading such books becomes more marked in such cases as that of Mr. Robert Bonner's "New York Ledger," whose editor in replying to a question sent to that paper by Kate Kellwood, said: "Fortune-telling by cards, by casting nativities, or by any other method is utterly false, *and an insult to the Majesty of Heaven*."*

---

* There are two classes of writers and lecturers in the community. One follows the method which I have adopted in the "Elements of Astrology," by trying to teach and explain the science or

Is it not strange that two-thirds of the inhabitants of the world at the present time are insulting the Majesty of Heaven almost every day of their lives, and have been doing so for thousands of years, if we can believe the people who have lived in China, Japan, Turkey and the East Indies, and almost all other countries except in Europe and America? Even in Europe and America people who insult the Majesty of Heaven are constantly increasing in number of late years. The Majesty of Heaven may possibly think that remaining in ignorance is more insulting to its dignity than studying the laws of the universe and of natural philosophy, especially when the said Majesty has endowed man with an intelligent mind, capable of cultivation, and has placed him in a world governed by laws and whose advancement in happiness consists in learning and understanding these laws, and decreed that the more ignorant he is of them the more sorrow and affliction he has to suffer and endure.

The late Mr. Wells, former editor of the "Phrenological Journal" published by "Fowler & Wells," goes one better than Mr. Robert Bonner's journal in his answer to a correspondent, who wrote asking the editor about the science of Astrology and the influence of the signs of the Zodiac. Mr. Wells, in answering the inquirer, wound up his article by stating that "no one practised Astrology *except designing villains*." I took the "Phrenological Journal" in my hand and went to see Mr. Wells in his office, thinking that perhaps the statement was a misprint or a mistake, but the editor certainly proved himself very ungentlemanly, if not a "*designing villain*," in replying to my question. Mr. Wells afterwards, in answering another question on Astrology, sent by a correspondent to the "Journal," concluded his article by stating that "no one consulted Astrologers except thieves and prostitutes."†

How Mr. Wells found out what kind of people consulted Astrologers it is difficult to understand; perhaps he took it for granted that the same class that consulted Phrenologists also consulted Astrologers, and knew them to be such by his dealings subsequently with them in their different lines of

---

subject so the people can understand and judge for themselves whether it is true or false. The other class of teachers are those who try to keep people in ignorance and will not permit them to investigate for themselves, if they can prevent it.

These persons generally are of shallow brain and have but little understanding, and actually believe that if they do not know anything on any special subject that nobody else does, and it is not worth learning. They are like the fox with the sour grapes, or like the fox that had lost its tail, and endeavored to persuade all the other foxes to have theirs cut off.

Sometimes these people get their eyes open, and then they become enthusiastic over sciences or subjects which they did everything possible to crush Prof. Chaney was one of those persons, but after he was convinced of the truth of Astrology, he has devoted the remainder of his life to teaching and promulgating the science. Robert G. Ingersoll was one of those teachers, who regarded Astrology as being reduced to the level of the Christian religion, yet he has of late changed his mind, and no doubt we will soon hear him giving lectures on Astrology.

No one could have been more opposed to it or tried harder to ridicule Astrology in some of his lectures than Mr. Ingersoll, and yet we find in an article by Prof. McDonald in the March number of the "20th Century Astrologer" of 1898, reports Mr. Ingersoll as saying :—"I have never given much attention to the study of Astrology, but personally I have received great benefits from my horoscope. I can say little of it as a science, yet in many ways I have been influenced by it. I am glad to acknowledge myself a debtor to what, if the world was not so busy, I should be glad to study more carefully."

How much more it would have been to the credit of Robert G. Ingersoll had he studied Astrology more carefully before he began ridiculing it so outrageously in some of his public lectures, especially in the lecture which he gave on John Kepler, who discovered the first three laws of astronomy. There are thousands of other learned and scientific men like Robert G. Ingersoll, who would have a different opinion of Astrology, if they would only study it more carefully.

---

† I have been creditably informed that Fowler & Wells now keep a number of astrological works for sale in their phrenological rooms. Either these phrenologists have changed their opinion in regard to astrologers and those who consult them, or else they have placed themselves in a very unfavorable light by encouraging people to become "designing villains," and trying to lower the standard of honesty and morality in the community.

business or occupations; but even if such was the case, he could not know that no other kind of persons consulted Astrologers.

If the statement of Mr. Wells is correct, the standard of morality, virtue and honesty of nearly three-fourths of the present inhabitants of the globe must be at a very low ebb, or else people who have lived in different parts of the East must tell a great many falsehoods when speaking of the manners, customs, beliefs and religions of its inhabitants. The Sultan of Turkey has his Astrologers in constant attendance, and besides nearly all the inhabitants are firm believers in the science; yet if anything is stolen in Turkey, the first remark the people make is, "There has been a Christian around here." In the East Indies and many other parts, the people who have resided there speak with emphasis of the honesty and virtue of both the men and women, as contrasted with the virtue of the inhabitants in most of the Christian countries. From China and Japan we have the same reports, but when the missionaries go to these countries and teach the Christian doctrines, then dishonesty and licentiousness spring up, because the people are taught by the missionaries that no matter how many sins they commit, if they repent they are foregiven and go to heaven.

In the East Indies and China, the people consult the Astrologer on every kind of business. They not only compare the horoscopes of young men and women previous to marriage, but even will not take a boarder into the house without first consulting an Astrologer; and yet honesty and virtue appear to stand on a much higher plane than honesty and virtue in any Christian country, whose people are unbelievers in Astrology, and are taught from childhood that Astrologers are "designing villains," and that Astrology "is utterly false and an insult to the Majesty of Heaven."

The people in these Eastern countries, before the Christian missionaries go there, are taught that whatever sins or crimes they commit, they have to pay the penalty for, either in this life or in some future life. How much more sensible would it have been for Mr. Wells or Mr. Robert Bonner to have told their correspondents to investigate Astrology for themselves, and be guided by such investigation, and if true and not contrary to the laws of morality, patronize it and defend it, but if false and degrading to human nature, discard it.

When these Christian people attempt to investigate Astrology, either in this country or in Europe, they try every way possible, by manufacturing all kinds of lies that they can possibly invent, to misrepresent it, and think they are serving God by so doing. As an illustration I refer the reader to page 439 of this book, where the "Penny Magazine," of London, pretends to refute the science of Astrology. The remarks which the writer makes use of when pretending to read the horoscope of a person born in London, June 13th, 1842, at 12 noon, is one tissue of lies from beginning to end, as any person who has studied Astrology, or even has read this book through so far, can easily prove for himself. For instance, all text-books on Astrology, when describing a person born under the planet Mercury in Cancer, agree in the statement that he is small, ugly, ill-natured, and a deceitful little wretch, and very often given to drink; and yet the writer of the "Penny Magazine" makes the native of a most admirable fancy, and a great elocutionist, ingenious and studious, all of which is entirely contrary to the rules of the science. Also the books teach that Mars afflicts any part of the nativity wherever it is situated, and it never "fortifies the midheaven" or any angle of the horoscope.

Astrology, if submitted to any fair and honest test will always come off victorious. That is the reason why these Christian people continue to tell lies about it, imagining it is opposed to their religion.

DISCUSSIONS IN FAVOR OF ASTROLOGY

AND

ASSERTIONS AGAINST IT.

FIRST—ARGUMENTS IN FAVOR OF ASTROLOGY.

In a world of perpetual change and bewildering uncertainty, which so materially affects the destiny of every human being, what mind alive to its own welfare can lull itself to sleep, and calmly commit its destiny to the ocean of chance? The drunkard, in a fit of intoxication; the lunatic, in the violence of disease; the idiot, in his imbecility; or the superstitious devotee enveloped in the mist of fanaticism, may unconcernedly revel on the brink of a precipice; *but the man of mind, alive to the necessary connection between cause and effect, and their unavoidable influence upon his own welfare,* will, in the language of Scripture, "ponder the path of his feet," or he will practically exclaim, "So teach us to number our days that we may apply our hearts unto wisdom."

Reader, what is meant by the word "ponder?" What is meant by the phrase "teach us to number our days?" Were they inserted in the Bible as jests upon human frailty, or as sober and practical realities? *Is nature governed by laws? Are those laws discoverable? Is the mind of man capable of applying them to advantage?* Astrology says Yes! and it offers at the same time to demonstrate to every sincere and competent inquirer the truth of its affirmation.

Those who have studied the science of Astrology, and ought, therefore, to be considered capable of judging, assert and maintain that it is a *science,* that is, a *system consisting of principles and rules which may be learned;* and history shows us that it is no recent upstart, but that it has been *studied, practised, and relied upon as a science from time immemorial;* and although there are no records in existence, that I am aware of, denoting where, when, and by whom Astrology was demonstrated *not* to be a science, yet it is somewhat strange to find that in an article published in the "New York World" on February 6th, 1887, by Professor Proctor, which he designated "The Humbug of Astrology," he says "that the Astrologer of to-day has written himself down a charlatan, and is probably an unscrupulous rascal, and a lying knave."

It often happens in arguments, as in the fortunes of war, that when an enemy has fired off all his ammunition, and has nothing left to defend himself, instead of yielding gracefully and admitting that he is beaten, he degrades himself by throwing "mud" and "dirt" as a last resort. Calling names is the weakest of all arguments. But a sensible man will stick to his principles and his science, and defend them with honest and legitimate means.

The Astrologer, even while being called these hard names, may be a person of learning, and have the capacity and industry to master Geometry, Astronomy, Trigonometry, and the whole circle of sciences; he may be perfectly honest and established in a reputable line of business; be a good neighbor and an honorable citizen, and yet if he practice

Astrology, that is, if he honestly follows his profession, he is called the vilest names by those who call themselves scientists, but who know nothing of the principles and science of Astrology.

In reflecting upon the application necessary to be able to practice Astrology, and the persecution it meets, no wonder that its ill-remunerated adherents write such verses as these:

> "Why do I stretch the chain of space,
>   Or scan the stars' irradiancy,
> While scientists their "wisdom" join
>   To dub these labors "vagrancy?"
>
> "Why seize the compasses and rule
>   In Euclid's musty books to dabble,
> While others with one-tenth the toil,
>   But smile and fatten on the rabble?"

Among the opponents of Astrology, so far as my observation goes, there is one remarkable fact, that not one of them so much as understands the first principle upon which it is founded! They presume to offer an opinion upon a subject with which they are entirely ignorant— a subject which they have never studied, nor applied so much as one scientific test. They are generally so ignorant as to confound it with Necromancy, Sorcery, Witchcraft, Interpretation of Dreams, Gypsy Fortune-telling, Clairvoyance, Soothsaying, and a host of other such etceteras.

Frequently their opposition is so wide of the mark as to be merely a disbelief in some undefinable chimera of their own imagination, which has no more to do with Astrology than a Chinaman has to do with enacting the laws that prohibit his immigration into this country. What can be more absurd than such conduct as this? What would a society of chemists, or surgeons, or mathematicians think of an uneducated peasant confronting his supercilious opinions with their analyzations, classifications, and demonstrations? They would pity his ignorance, sneer at his presumption, and treat his interference with contempt. The opponents of Astrology, although favored by popular ignorance and prejudice, are viewed by the experienced with the same disgust.

Astrologers may be persecuted for a time, as astronomers and all other scientists have suffered in their time. After Galileo had been compelled, at the peril of his life, to subscribe to the quiescence of the world, he exclaimed, "Still it moves." The puny arm of man may be raised against the heavens, but the influences of the Pleiades cannot be bound, neither can Arcturus be stayed in his course.

Against Astrology we sometimes hear a little in the shape of argument, but nothing that ever affects its truth or validity as a science. One argument adduced by some of its most enlightened opponents is, that "Astrologers often err in their predictions," and to the truth of this objection every Astrologer must bow. But, at the same time, we must not allow a particular exception to usurp the place of a general rule; we must not allow a local detail to circumscribe a universal truth. The partial failure of Astrologers necessarily presupposes partial success. If Astrologers always failed in their predictions, the evidence against

Astrology would be strongly presumptive, though not absolutely conclusive, inasmuch as the properties of matter do not result from man's knowledge of them, but, on the contrary, these attributes of matter pervaded inherently prior to man's existence, and are only yet ascertained to a very limited extent.

When attempts are made to parallel Astrology with many other sciences, its magnitude and complexity appear so immensely overwhelming that the wonder turns not upon the failures of its adherents, but rather upon their frequent successes. If the shoemaker be sometimes deceived in the quality of a handful of leather, why should we marvel at the Astrologer's occasional misjudgments, when his materials are worlds, suns, and systems? If the shoemaker sometimes misfits his customer, after careful measurement of so small an object as the human foot, why be surprised at the errors of the Astrologer, who has to gauge the heavens? However often the shoemaker may err, where is the man to denounce the craft as useless, false, and not strictly based on scientific principles? Not only are the shoemaker and the Astrologer at times similarly erroneous in their practice, but such is the case with every art, every science, and every professson on earth. If, therefore, the occasional errors of Astrologers be admitted as conclusive against Astrology as a science, all other sciences, so called, are equally open to the same objection—all sciences are false. The chemist, the mathematician, the architect, the painter, the divine, the lawyer, the newspaper editor, the photographer, the legislator, the shoemaker, and the Astrologer may all shake hands together and mutually exclaim, "We are brethren all."

Unless it can be demonstrated that Astrology is false, and not in accordance with the laws of nature, its professors ought not to be called "charlatans" and "unscrupulous rascals and lying knaves" by persons who are altogether ignorant of that science. It indicates an ignorance and prejudice that will not be believed one hundred years to come. The people in those days, when reading the history of the present time, will look back to the persecutions of Astrologers, the Botanic and Homœopathic physicians, the Socialist and the Spiritualist, as we look back to the persecution of the "Witches," "Heretics," and "itinerant Preachers," who lived two hundred years ago, and which the Poet Whittier describes in his Poem entitled

THE PASTORAL LETTER.

Oh, glorious days, when church and state
   Were wedded by your spiritual fathers,
And on submissive shoulders sat
   Your Wilsons and your Cotton Mathers.
No vile "itinerant" then could mar
   The beauty of your tranquil Zion,
But at his peril of the scar
   Of hangman's whip and branding-iron.

Then wholesome laws relieved the church
   Of heretic and mischief-maker,
And priest and bailiff joined in search,
   By turns, of *Papist, witch and Quaker!*

The stocks were at each church's door,
  The gallows stood on Boston Common,
A Papist's ears the pillory bore,—
  The gallows-rope, a Quaker woman!

Your fathers dealt not as ye deal
  With "non-professing" frantic teachers;
They bored the tongue with red-hot steel,
  And flayed the back of "female preachers."
Old Newbury had her fields a tongue,
  And Salem's streets could tell their story
Of fainting woman dragged along,
  Gashed by the whip, accursed and gory.

And will ye ask me, why this taunt
  Of memories sacred from the scorner?
And why with reckless hand I plant
  A nettle on the graves ye honor?
Not to reproach New England's dead
  This record from the past I summon,
Of manhood to the scaffold led,
  And suffering and heroic woman.

SECOND—THE ASSERTIONS OF THOSE WHO OPPOSE ASTROLOGY.

These include all those who write for Encyclopœdias, editors of newspapers, especially of religious periodicals and scientific books, except text books on Astrology.

Why publishers should continue to engage men to write on the subject of Astrology in the above named books, whose only qualification is their ignorance of that science, is impossible to understand, especially when there are so many Astrological almanacs and monthly Astrological periodicals, as well as a number of Astrological text books, the authors of which are well qualified to write for any of the various "Encyclopœdias."

Surely if the publishers of the above named works desired to impart the truth to their readers on this science, there are a number who understand Asrology whose services could be procured.

Any one understanding Astrology, and reading the articles printed under the words "Astrology," "Horoscope," etc., in the Encyclopœdias now published, would naturally arrive at the conclusion that the writers had gone through a civil service examination in the science of Astrology, and those who could answer the fewest questions had been selected, or those who were most prejudiced against the science had been chosen to write the articles.

Chambers, in their "Information for the People," commence their article on Phrenology with these words: "It has of late been customary for the conductors of popular cyclopœdias to admit articles on Phrenology; but in most if not all the instances in which this has been done, the articles were the composition of persons who denied that phrenology was a true system of mental philosophy, and whose aim rather was to show its want of sound foundation than simply to present a view of its doctrines. In every one of these instances it was afterwards successfully shown by phrenological writers that their science had been misrepresented, and its doctrines challenged on unfair grounds, so that the articles in question might as well not have been written, in so far as the instruction of candid inquirers was concerned. We have resolved to eschew this practical absurdity, by presenting a view of Phrenology by one who believes it to be the true system of mind."

Yet these publishers, in their work called "Chambers' Encyclopœdia," have followed the same erroneous plan in their article on Astrology which they condemned in others as being wrong in treating the subject of Phrenology. They have employed a person who was altogether ignorant of Astrology. and at the same time prejudiced against it. This writer, under the title "Astrology," goes on to make the following false statements:

"Belief in Astrology is not extensively professed in any Christian country, though a few solitary advocates have from time to time appeared. But it still holds sway in the East, and among the Mohammedans wherever situated. Even in Europe, the craving of the ignorant of all countries for divination is still gratified by the publication of multitudes of almanacs containing Astrological predictions, though the writers no longer believe in them."*

---

* It might have been just as well for the morals of the community if Messrs. Chambers had not mentioned the last named fact, when they say "that the authors no longer believe in them." In this sentence they refer to the Astrological Almanac published by John Partridge, in London, England, which, while he was living, had a very large circulation. After his death, by some means that I do not recollect, the Baptist Missionary Society of London, procured the Almanac and continued its publication. It sold at that time for what was considered a high price, viz., 2s. 3d. (54 cents) per copy. The society sent Bibles and missionaries to the benighted heathen with the profits of this Astrological Almanac. This equals the statement of Fred Douglas in the narrative of his life where he says "that during the time of slavery in the South, the slaveholders sold men to build churches, they sold women to send missionaries abroad, and babies to send Bibles to the savages in Africa." But only think of it, those pious people went into the business of *fortune-telling*, which they did not believe in, in order to save souls. It is almost incredible. The Missionary Society bought the right of publishing the Astrological Almanac either from the widow or the executors of John Partridge about the year 1830, and they discontinued publishing it only when it did not pay.

Raphael, and also Zadkiel, both of London, seeing an opening for an Astrological Almanac, each started one nearly at the same time, and both almanacs, being well written by persons who understood and believed in Astrology, soon took the place of John Partridge's.

These two almanacs are still published, and they have a circulation at the present time of near half a million. There has never been an Astrological Almanac published except by those pious religious people referred to by William and Robert Chambers, that the authors were not firm believers in Astrology.

If it were discovered that one minister of the Gospel in the whole world had been preaching a religion that he did not believe, it would be too sweeping an assertion to say that all ministers were frauds, and that all religions were false. These pious people were not Astrologers, did not know anything about it, and did not believe in it. They only published the almanac to raise money to convert the heathen and send Bibles and missionaries to them, and I do not see why Astrologers and Astrology, should be blamed for what they did. *It is misrepresenting Astrology and challenging its doctrines on unfair grounds.*

I have a number of John Partridge's almanacs that were published after it fell into the pious people's hands, and I intend at some future time to publish some of the predictions and remarks they contain. There is material enough in them to make a first-class comic opera, and I have no doubt it would take wonderfully.

Had either William or Robert Chambers known anything about Astrology they would have seen that those zealots did not know the first A, B, C of the science, therefore could not believe

How Messrs. Chambers found out that the writers of Astrological books and almanacs "no longer believe in them" they do not inform us. But what should we think of any writer or publisher making use of such remarks about professors of another science or religion except Astrology? What would be thought of a professor of chemistry, astronomy, or any of the sects of the Christian religion who should make such uncharitable accusations? It is reasonable to suppose the writer would find himself, figuratively speaking, in a hornet's nest.

But even in the last fifty or seventy-five years there has been a remarkable change in all the encyclopædias and biographical dictionaries, or works that have anything to say on the subject of Astrology. All of the works at that time which mentioned the word Astrology or Astrologers could not find epithets severe enough in condemnation of both. The Astrologer was called a "fraud," "impostor," "ignoramus," "charlatan," and a number of names of that description, especially when they spoke of William Lilly, John Gadbury, and others. The people who consulted them were called their "dupes," even when the people were the kings and queens and members of Parliament of England. When they spoke of that science they stated that Astrology was exploded, condemned, "put under ban of the law," etc.

But in all the new Biographical Dictionaries, under the name William Lilly they do not even mention that he was a "fraud" or "impostor." And under Astrology in the new Encyclopædias they do not even mention its being "exploded," or that it is an "ancient superstition." At the same time, they do not offer any apologies for having previously made use of those expressions in former editions. Even Chambers will soon be compelled to change the wording of the article on Astrology in their Encyclopædia.

I propose shortly to publish a pamphlet showing how the scientists and writers of the works above mentioned are evoluting out of their own "ignorance" and "superstition" when treating on those subjects. I have every reason to believe it will be as interesting as anything published in the latter part of the nineteenth century. Professor Richard A. Proctor, when he published his "Humbug of Astrology" in the "New York World," knew at the time that he was uttering untruths and falsehoods. The "World" would not publish my reply, but I published it in a pamphlet entitled "WHY I AM AN ASTROLOGER." Even Mr. Proctor could not help admitting that the science of Astrology was as ancient as any on the face of the earth, and "that all nations which had attained any advance in civilization were firm believers in it." As he says himself, "the cuneiform inscriptions of Assyria, the hieroglyphs of Egypt, the most ancient records of Babylon, Persia, India, and China, agree in showing that of old all men believed that the *Sun aud Moon, the planets and the stars foretold, nay, ruled the fortunes of men and nations.*"

---

in it, and published the almanac because they could raise money by it. If those pious missionary people had to go into the counterfeiting business in order to raise money to spend in saving the souls of the heathen, that would be no valid reason for condemning all good money. Neither should Astrology be condemned because those hypocrites counterfeited it.

THOMAS DICK ON THE ABSURDITY OF ASTROLOGY.

In a work published in England by Thomas Dick, about 1830, and which has gone through a great many editions, called "The Improvement of Society by the Diffusion of Knowledge," in Harpers' edition, published in New York in 1839, on page 31 he says:

"The planetary bodies, indeed, may, in certain cases, have some degree of *physical* influence on the earth, by virtue of their attractive power, but that influence can never affect the operation of moral causes, or the qualities of the mind. Even although it were admitted that the heavenly bodies have an influence over the destinies of the human race, yet we have no data whatever by which to ascertain the mode of its operation, or to determine the formula and rules by which calculations are to be made, in order to predict the fates of nations, or the individual temperaments and destinies of men; and consequently, the principles and rules on which Astrologers proceed in constructing horoscopes, and calculating nativities, are nothing else than mere assumptions, and their pretensions nothing short of criminal impositions upon the credulity of mankind."

It is difficult to understand what Mr. Dick meant when he said "we have no data whatever by which to ascertain, or to determine the formula or rules by which calculations are to be made, in order to predict the fate of nations or the individual temperaments and destinies of men." Did Mr. Dick write this sentence in pure ignorance, or was it a deliberate falsehood on his part? He must have known that there were thousands of Astrological works published in different parts of Europe, which give the data and formula for making the calculations and predicting the fate of men. In other words, did he believe that because he had never read and studied those books no one else has ever done so? There are hundreds of thousands of men who have read these works, if he has not. I have read and studied scores of different text books on Astrology myself, and have quite a library of such books, all in the English language.

Some years ago a prominent member of the Parliament of England (I think it was Lord Brougham) rose in the House of Commons to reply to a question, and said "that he had never seen, read, or heard that there was a periodical published called 'The London Journal,'" yet at that time that Journal had a circulation of over three hundred thousand, the largest of any paper in the world. His answer produced roars of laughter, as there were but few people in England at that time who had not read or knew something about "The London Journal." Suppose this member of Parliament had said "that any one who had read or seen "The London Journal" was a criminal impostor, who wanted to impose on the credulity of mankind; he would then have placed himself in the very position that Mr. Dick placed himself when he wrote the book "On the Improvement of Society by the Diffusion of Knowledge," and which ought to have read, "Diffusion of Falsehoods."

It is astonishing how far prejudice will go against certain sciences, literature, and religions, when the teaching does not coincide with their particular class of reading or study. For instance, the Allopathic doctors will not read or pay any attention to anything that is published in Homœopathic, Botanic, or Eclectic works. They say it is not "official" unless it is published in their own literature and text books. They do everything possible to crush out all systems of medicine except their own, and call all other schools of medicine "quacks and frauds." They tell me, as they have told hundreds of others, that "we are going to have only one sect in medicine," and they use the same means which the people formerly used when they were determined to have only one sect in religion.

It is the same in regard to scientists; they will not notice or recognize any kind of knowledge or learning unless it is published in their particular kind of literature. They are like the General, who, while burning the Alexandrian Library, said "that if what is in those many thousands of volumes is in the Koran, it is of no use, as we have it in the Koran; and if it is not in the Koran, then it is false, and ought to be burned."

Even in this small pamphlet I have given some of the rules and data by which to make the calculations that are used by Astrologers, and how to make predictions, and I am not the only Astrologer in the world. Not only that, but there have been Astrologers ever since the dawn of civilization. Even at the present day three-fourths of the inhabitants of the world are believers in Astrology, and use it in their every-day life.

Mr. Dick also says, "The planetary bodies may have some physical influence on the earth." Does he not know that even thousands of years ago that influence was known and recognized? We read in Job xxxviii, 31, "Canst thou bind the sweet influences of the Pleiades, or loose the bands of Orion? Knowest thou the ordinances of heaven? Canst thou set the dominion thereof in the earth?" In those days planetary influence was universally recognized, and to doubt it was almost equal to doubting the existence of the sun.

Even Thomas Dick admits that Astrology was taught and recognized in ancient times by every nation on the face of the earth that had attained any degree of civilization. Although he does not bring a single fact nor argument against Astrology, he admits its universality when he says :

"Notwitstanding the absurdity of the doctrines of Astrology, this art has been practised in every period of time. Among the Romans the people were so infatuated with it that the Astrologers, or, as they were then called, the *mathematicians*, maintained their ground in spite of all the edicts of the emperors to expel them from the capital; and after they were at length expelled by a formal decree of the senate, they found so much protection from the credulity of the people, that they still remained in Rome unmolested. Among the Chaldeans, the Assyrians, the Egyptians, the Greeks, and the Arabians, *in ancient times, Astrology was uniformly included in the list of the sciences*, and used as one species of divination by which they attempted to pry into the secrets of futurity. The Brahmins in India, at an early period, introduced this art into that country, and, by means of it, have rendered themselves the arbiters of good and evil hours, and of the fortunes of their fellow-men, and have thus raised themselves to great authority and influence among the illiterate multitude. They are consulted as oracles, and, like all other impostors, they have taken great care never to sell their answers without a handsome remuneration.* *In almost every country in the world this art is still practised,* and only a short time has elapsed since the princes and legislators of Europe were directed in the most important concerns of the state by the predictions of Astrologers. In the time of Queen Catharine de Medici, Astrology was so much in vogue, that nothing, however trifling, was to be done without consulting the stars. The Astrologer Morin, in the seventeenth century, directed Cardinal Richelieu's motions in some of his journeys, and Louisa Maria de Gonzaga, Queen of Poland, gave 2000 crowns to carry on an edition of his *Astrologia Gallica;* and in the reign of Henry the Third and Henry the Fourth of France, the predictions of Astrologers were the common theme of court conversation. Even in the present day, and in the metropolis of the British empire, this fallacious art is practised, and its professors are resorted to for judicial information, not only by the vulgar, but even by many in the higher spheres of life. The extensive annual sale of more than 240,000 copies of 'Moore's Almanac,' which abounds in such predictions, and of similar publications, is a striking proof of the belief which is still attached to the doctrines of Astrology in our own age and country."

If we had wanted some person to give Astrology a special "puff" in some modern newspaper, as an advertisement, I do not see that we could engage a man better adapted to do it than Mr. Thomas Dick. He says, "Notwithstanding the absurdity of the doctrine of Astrology, this art has been practised in every period of time." And yet he does not give a single fact, argument, or reason why it is absurd. Is Astrology only absurd to those who know nothing about it? Possibly that is the reason why those people ignorant of Astrology write as they do when treating on that subject.

All persons, before they learn geography, think it quite absurd that the earth is round. It takes a long time to convince them that it is not flat like a pancake. Every one has very crude ideas about astronomy, and thinks many things in connection with that science are erroneous, until he becomes better acquainted with the stars and planetary bodies including the sun and the earth.

Even those who have been taught that the world was created in six days as described in the first chapter of Genesis think that geology is very absurd, and it takes time to convince them that it took thousands of years for the earth and its inhabitants to be developed to their present state of perfection.

Possibly if Mr. Dick and Professor Richard A. Proctor had been taught Astrology in their early years, it might not appear quite so absurd

---

* Are doctors, lawyers, ministers, and followers of other professions impostors, because they receive a remuneration for their services? All writers against Astrology harp on that subject. According to their notion Astrologers are the worst people in the world, and are the only people who must work for nothing, and if they want anything for their services, they are impostors!

to them. It frequently happens that the absurdity of a thing exists only in the minds of the ignorant. At least, a comprehensive knowledge of any science ought to make one more charitable to the unlearned. It is difficult to believe that any one who has received a liberal education would stoop so low as to call those who differ with him in opinion on scientific subjects "criminal impostors," "unscrupulous rascals," "charlatans," and "lying knaves."

In regard to the people of Rome being so infatuated with the Astrologers, and protecting them in spite of the edicts of the Emperors and the Senate to expel them, they still remained in Rome, unmolested. Are we to understand from Mr. Dick's remarks that the people of Rome protected their *mathematicians,* or Astrologers, when they knew them to be frauds and impostors, similar to what they might have protected thieves, murderers, bandits, or pirates, knowing them to be such? Or did the Romans protect the Astrologers because they knew them to be innocent of any crime, and only persecuted by the Emperors and Senate for some reason of their own, the same as we read in history of the British Government persecuting the Roman Catholics, and driving them out of the British Islands, and at other times persecuting the Presbyterians, Nonconformists, and Puritans, and driving them to the wilds of America.

The reason why the Roman citizens protected the Astrologers was, that they knew they were a benefit to the community, and had great influence over the people, and the Astrologers prevented the Emperors and Senate from making slaves of them. That is the reason why the rulers wanted to drive the Astrologers out of the capital.

If the Astrologers had been driven out of Rome, would it have made them any worse citizens than the Pilgrim Fathers who were driven out of England on account of adhering to their religious belief?

There are two orders of nobility in America. One is, when a man can trace his ancestry back to the landing of the Pilgrim Fathers at Plymouth Rock, after they were expelled from the British Islands; the other is, when a man can say his grandfather fought in the Revolution, and helped to drive the English from this country. Even if the Astrologers had been driven out of Rome, their descendants might have been proud in tracing back their ancestry to that epoch, the same as the English are proud when they can say their ancestors came over with William the Conqueror.

It is strange that what is considered in connection with the Pilgrim Fathers as a badge of honor, is regarded in connection with Astrologers as a stigma of disgrace.

The people of Rome must have regarded the Astrologers as equal if not superior to other citizens, and of great service to the community, which made them disobey the laws of the country in protecting, and not assisting the authorities in driving them out of Rome.*

---

* The main reason why I have criticised Mr. Thomas Dick's "Absurdity of Astrology" in preference to other authors who have written against that science, is because the British Parliament granted him £5,000 (equal to $25,000) on account of the religious vein which runs through all his works, and the great amount of supposed good his "Improvement of Society by the Diffu-

PENNY MAGAZINE'S REFUTATION OF ASTROLOGY.

In the "Penny Magazine," No. 736, published in London, England, may be found an article on Judicial Astrology, being, as the author imagines, a refutation of that science, which, however, we now take the liberty to tell the writer we consider so much beneath a refutation that it goes far to establish the truth of Astrology. It appears from the general disrepute in which Astrology is held by some people, that any snarling cur has a right to give it a bite, and every ass a kick, with impunity, because it does not happen to be the fashion of the day.

We shall give a few extracts from the article in question, considering this the shortest and most proper method of showing the writer's falsehood, and his inability to perform the task he has so inconsiderately undertaken:

"Even the disbelief in Astrology, which is now so generally prevalent in society, is rather to be considered the effect of education than a firm conviction of the mind, resulting from investigation and inquiry."

We may state that we are also of the same opinion. Here is a plain confession that the general disbelief in Astrology, in the community at large, is to be considered chiefly as the effect of prejudice, and not from any conviction of mind arising from inquiry and proper investigation; that is, they are disbelievers simply because they have been taught that Astrology is not true, and that it is not the fashion of the day to believe in it; not that they know any just cause or impropriety in the science,— and thus relying upon other persons' judgments, they renounce the science without they, themselves, knowing anything of its principles, or of its truth or falsehood. This alone is one proof of the verity of the science. If Astrology were false, an investigation of its laws would, of itself, be sufficient to condemn it. But, instead of this being done, we find it set down for falsehood by persons altogether unacquainted with its principles.

---

sion of Knowledge," "Celestial Scenery," etc., had done, and which gave him the name of "The Christian Philosopher." I believe he is the only author the British Government ever honored or recognized in such a substantial manner. Yet if I went through the whole of his works I would find them just as full of falsehoods and misrepresentations as his "Absurdity of Astrology." I have read nearly all of them.

I cannot understand why the British Government thus honors one author, even if his works were perfection itself, while they are doing everything possible by all kinds of persecution to suppress or destroy other authors. I refer to a noted writer, whose name I do not wish to mention, but who is an Astrologer and an author of Astrological books. The authorities in England have broken into his house numbers of times, and carried off everything he used in his business or in making his calculations to enable him to publish his works, in the same manner that the authorities in this country carry off faro tables and other gambling instruments, "sawdust" circulars, etc., from gambling houses.

The only way the Astrologer could circumvent the authorities was by making a friend of his landlord, whose name was Mr. Lord, and who permitted him to label all his books, globes, and mathematical tables and instruments "This is the property of Mr. Lord." Then the authorities dare not take them. Yet that man was placed at the mercy of his landlord, who could have carried off all his goods at any time, and without a moment's notice.

Astrology has prospered in England, and in every part of the world, in spite of all this kind of persecution; yet its enemies tell us that it has been exploded, and that there is nothing in it.

In a free and civilized country such as England is at the present day, why should some authors be thus honored and rewarded, and others persecuted and imprisoned? As the poet says—

"Strange that such a difference there should be
'Twixt tweedledum and tweedledee."

440   APPENDIX.

The writer of the article goes on to say:

"Yet the practice (since 1611), I fear, has fluctuated rather **than decreased."**

Here is another strong evidence in favor of Astrology, that it has withstood the prejudice of centuries and the censure of ages. Had Astrology been false and based in error, it would have fallen by its own weapons, and time alone would have proven sufficient to consign it to oblivion; yet we find quite the reverse of this to be the case, and that in late years it has rather increased than otherwise.

The writer then proceeds, in No. 744, to erect a figure or map of the heavens, which he has been pleased to style a Nativity, all of which, however, is mere supposition.

But, in order to show the reader the writer's inability to accomplish the task he has so ignorantly undertaken, we might mention that the figure or map of the heavens is, in many respects, very incorrect. For instance, in the longitude of Jupiter there is an error of four degrees and three minutes; in Saturn, of three degrees and three minutes; in Mercury, of three degrees and seventeen minutes, and in Venus, twenty minutes. The Part of Fortune is also placed in the wrong part of the figure; and the planet Uranus is not in the figure at all. A pretty commencement this is, for a critic to come before the public, with the intention of refuting the science of Astrology—a person altogether ignorant of the common rules or the simple elements of the science. It appears that the erection of a map of the heavens is not so easily accomplished as this would-be critic would lead us to believe.* We shall now proceed

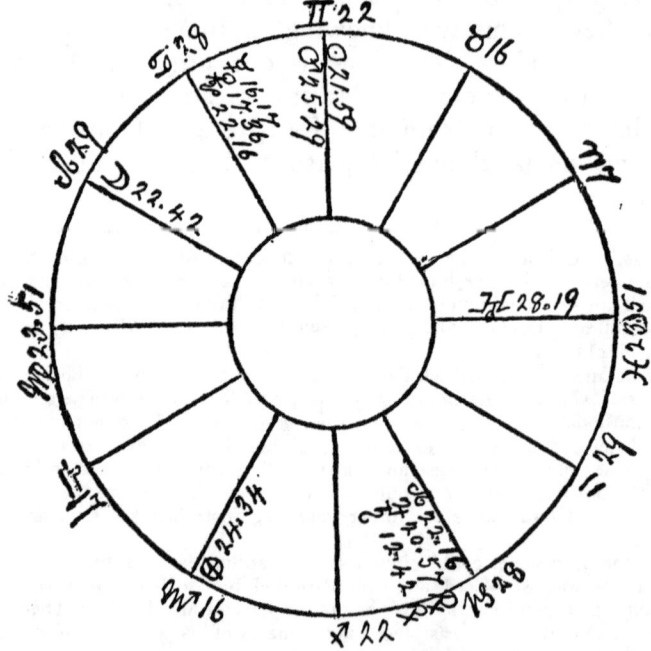

---

* The time the writer erected his supposed horoscope was June 13, 1842, at 12, noon, London, England. I here insert the chart of the heavens for the above time, corrected, and the planets in their proper places, with the planet Uranus and the Part of Fortune inserted, so that the reader can see for himself. I do this to show that I do not want to take any advantage of the writer's ignorance of mathematics, but would rather give him all the aid possible to expose Astrology. I am always willing to "help a lame dog over a stile"—it is my nature. As the planet Neptune was

to give the writer's judgment, or, more strictly, his nonsense, on this supposed nativity:

"The sign Virgo, ascending, makes ingenious and studious persons, and Mercury, the lord of the ascendant, being located in the mid-heaven, and the lord thereof, declares the native to be of a most admirable fancy and great elocution; and as he is also in good aspect of Venus, and in reception of the Moon, the person born under his rule will become a most accomplished orator, and be famous as a divine or philosopher. Venus in the tenth, denotes that the native will be greatly beloved and esteemed, and that he will marry honorably, and gain great eminence and renown. But 'our life is of a mingled yarn.' The Dragon's Tail portends, when located in the tenth house of the Nativity, a fatal end to the honor of the native; and when Mars is posited in the tenth house, being lord of the eighth (as is the case in this figure), he declares death to the native by the sentence of a judge. This would be, indeed, a most inglorious termination to a career which promised, at the outset, to be so resplendent; but hope gleams on the horoscope from one of the most brilliant constellations. The Moon is entering into a conjunction with Cor Leonis, 'the Lion's Heart,' which gives her a greater degree of strength than any other accidental circumstance. And the mid-heaven, well fortified (as in this case) by the presence of Mars and the Sun, not only gives eminent honor, but such as shall be durable, though it may be subject to interruptions. We may there ore hope that the native, even though sentenced by a judge, will be spared from an untimely fate.'

The writer then goes on to say, that nothing can be properly ascertained except by calculating the figure. We, however, have neither time nor space to pursue further this truly *logical* and *scientific* jargon From beginning to end it is one continued scene of confusion and misrepresentation, and clearly shows that the writer is entirely ignorant of Astrology, and unacquainted with the principles by which its professors are guided. Had the writer possessed the slightest knowledge of the rules of Astrology, he would have seen that the figure neither "declared the native to be of a most admirable fancy," nor of "great elocution;" and Mercury having no aspect to the Moon, "the person born under his rule" would neither "become a most accomplished orator," nor "be famous as a divine or philosopher;" but, on the contrary, that he would have seen quite the reverse was shown; and that Mercury in Cancer, in opposition (a very evil aspect) to Jupiter, would denote a person of mean abilities, and one of an evil and dissipated character. But in order to show the reader how far the above critic is wide of his mark, we will insert below a few rules from our Astrological books; *rules that we have to go by in our every-day practice*, and then the reader will see what sort of an ORATOR, or DIVINE, or PHILOSOPHER the above critic's HERO would make:

"The Complete Dictionary of Astrology," by James Wilson, Esq., London, England, page 148, says:

"Mercury in Cancer gives a short squab figure, bad complexion, sad brown hair, thin face, sharp nose, and small eyes; a dishonest, ill-natured, deceitful wretch, and one who is generally given to drinking."

"Astronomy and Elementary Philosophy, by Placidus de Titus, an Italian Monk, translated from the Latin, by E. Sibly, London, England, 1789, Vol. I, page 55, says:

"Mercury in Cancer personates a low or short stature of body, of an ill complexion, dark hair, thin face, sharp nose, small eyes; a mere dissembler, sottish, light-fingered, ill-natured, unless the Moon or Jupiter be in good aspect to Mercury."

In the above Nativity the Moon has no aspect to Mercury, but Jupiter is in opposition to it, which makes it all the worse.

---

not discovered in 1842, he could not have inserted it, but its longitude on June 13 of that year was eighteen degrees and thirty-eight minutes in Aquarius, in the 5th house, and was at that time in opposition to the Moon and in trine to the Sun.

"The Prognostic Astronomer; or Horary Astrology," by Dr. W. J. Simmonite, Leeds, Yorkshire, England, 1854, page 10, says:

"Mercury in Cancer personates a low or short stature, dull complexion, sad brown hair, thin face, sharp nose, and small eyes; and in disposition dissembling, sottish, thievish, except Mercury happens to be in good aspect to the Moon and Jupiter. But if Jupiter be in Virgo or Gemini, then the native is a vagabond, etc."

"New and Complete Illustration of the Occult Sciences," by E. Sibly, M. D., F. R. H. S., London, England, 1807, page 375, says:

"Mercury in Cancer personates a low or short stature of body, of an ill complexion, sad brown hair, thin face, sharp nose, and small eyes; and in disposition a mere dissembler, a sottish kind of pot-companion, and light-fingered; also an ill-natured person, unless the Moon and Jupiter be in good aspect to Mercury."

"The Complete Arcana of Astral Philosophy," by W. J. Simmonite, A. M., M. B. A., London, England, 1847, Vol. I, page 71, says:

"Mercury in Cancer gives a short, squab figure, bad complexion, sad brown hair, thin face, sharp nose, small eyes; dishonest, deceitful, and given to drinking."*

I do not think the writer for the "Penny Magazine" could get much wider of the mark even if he tried. I have inserted the above Astrological Rules, in order to show the reader what kind of an *accomplished orator, divine,* or *philosopher* the above writer's hero would be, and partly to refute the accusations brought against Astrology (by its enemies) that there are no rules, data, or system in that science, but that it is all *imagination,* as Thomas Dick falsely states.

If the writer had known anything of the rules of Astrology, he would have known that the "mid-heaven would not be fortified by the presence of Mars," but that both the Sun and the mid-heaven would be afflicted by its presence. Mars, like Saturn, being an evil planet, does not fortify, but afflicts wherever it is situated in a horoscope.

Venus in the 10th house would have nothing to do with the native's marriage, or he "marrying honorably, and gaining great eminence and renown." Venus in the mid-heaven, in conjunction with Mercury, would cause him to have a number of female friends, very much like himself, and be fond of music and the fine arts, but he would probably steal both the music and the pictures.

In a man's nativity we always look to the planet that the Moon first applies to by aspect, also the 7th house and the lord of the seventh, to describe the wife and the kind of marriage. The Moon first makes a sextile of Mars in the mid-heaven in Gemini in this horoscope, which describes a tall, slender, proud and straight-built, dark-complexioned lady, with brown hair. But so far from giving him "eminence and renown by his marriage," it would be quite the reverse, as his wife would bring him nothing but misfortune, and break him up in his business, on account of Mars afflicting the 10th house, and the Sun in the 10th.

William Lilly's Introduction to Astrology by Zadkiel, Bohn's edition, London, England, page 302, says:

---

* I could copy from twenty or thirty other authors, all describing Mercury in Cancer, but it would be almost a repetition of the above, and I think I have given enough to show that the writer is perfectly ignorant of the subject, and has not consulted a single text-book on Astrology: if he had he would not have made such glaring blunders. I am disposed to believe that he is publishing his own horoscope, as it would describe just such a person as the writer in the "Penny Magazine," and that is one reason why he tried to make it appear so favorable, to flatter his own vanity. But I must leave it to the reader to decide the question whether it is his horoscope or not.

"Mars in Gemini describes a person who is unfortunate, living in a mean way, generally shifting here and there, leaving debts unpaid, and exercising her wits for her livelihood; in short, a *chevalier d'industrie*, or mere swindler."

Also, Mars being in close square to Uranus, in the 7th house (the house of marriage), would cause her to be tyrannical, extravagant, and to have a terrible temper, in short, a regular Tartar. Also, Jupiter, lord of the 7th house, being retrograde, in opposition to Mercury and Venus, and applying to a conjunction of Saturn, would show that she would elope with another man, indicated by Saturn in Capricorn.

Therefore this native "marrying so honorably and gaining great eminence and renown," would come to a most disastrous end. Truly this "Refutation of Astrology" is a "mingled yarn" of misrepresentations and falsehoods, and of which the writer ought to be ashamed; but no doubt it is an exact description of his wife, if the time given is his own time of birth. Had he been versed in Astrology he would see that the Dragon's Tail is not afflicting any planet, and is not in the 10th house, but on the cusp of the 11th, consequently could not declare "death to the native by the sentence of a judge," unless the judge made as many mistakes as the writer in "The Penny Magazine."

If he be surprised (as he scornfully says) how one Astrologer could look in the face of another without laughing, I am truly astonished that he, presumptuous as he is, could come before the public with such preposterous untruths. I may justly say, in transposition of the words of Byron:

"If Ptolemy, when his works were ended,
Had heard this blockhead prate before him,
To us his works had ne'er descended;
In furious mood he would have torn 'em."

Although I have endeavored to be as plain as possible in attacking every argument brought forward by the above writer in his "Refutation of Astrology," yet I am aware that my remarks will not be understood and appreciated by the general reader as they are meant to be, unless he has some knowledge of that science.*

But the most flagrant and absurd part of this farce is, that it emanates from the "SOCIETY FOR THE DIFFUSION OF USEFUL KNOWLEDGE."†

---

* If Astrology were one-quarter as well understood as arithmetic, the writer of the "Refutation of Astrology" would become the laughing stock of the whole civilized world.

Similar to Rev. John Jasper, when he preached his sermon "The Sun Do Move." Yet two or three hundred years ago the Rev. John Jasper's belief was universal, and for any one known to believe differently it was certain death or long imprisonment. Even Galileo, at seventy years of age, in 1634, was sentenced to an indefinite term of imprisonment by the Inquisition because he said the Sun did not move. He had to adjure, by oath, on his knees, that the Sun did move, in order to be liberated.

The reason why the Reverend gentleman got himself and the Bible laughed at so extensively, was that he tried to prove his science by the Scriptures, as if the Bible were a text-book on astronomy. Nothing could be more absurd.

There is no doubt that two or three hundred years hence belief in Astrology will be universal, and any one disbelieving in it will be considered behind the age, and laughed at like the Rev. John Jasper in his sermon on "The Sun Do Move."

† A society that many of the wealthy classes of England belong to, which publishes a vast number of books, chiefly of a moral, religious, and popular science nature. Any respectable person can become a member by paying a yearly donation, and members can buy books published by the Society, in any part of the British dominions, at 25 per cent. off.

One would think that a society of that character would engage the most talented writers that

Now, had the Nativity of some well-known character (as Lord Brougham, the Duke of Wellington, George Washington, etc.) been selected, and have proven that the rules had failed, or were not borne out by facts, it would have done more to condemn Astrology than if volumes had been written against that science. *Why has this not been done? Why is it not done?* Simply because it cannot be done. The reader may rest assured that it either cannot be done, or, if it can, the enemies of Astrology have not *brains* sufficient to do it. I think that one plain fact of this nature would be worth more, and would do more, to disprove Astrology than if a folio volume were written against it. My limits will not allow of saying more at present; I however consider that I have sufficiently shown the falsehoods of the article in question, and the writer's inability to disprove the rules of Astrology. I hope, should he at any future time be disposed to take up his pen against this science, he will first learn something of its principles, *and know that none should condemn who do not understand;* and I hope he will remember

"Nothing to extenuate, or set down aught in malice."

On a fine starlit evening, returning from Yonkers, my wife wished me to point out the various constellations and planets then visible. A friend with us, noticing that I was familiar with the heavenly bodies, asked if I was an Astrologer. I answered yes, and had some conversation with him on the subject. My friend, some time afterwards, heard the minister of his church saying how wicked it was to consult Astrologers, and that the science was false, asked, "Do you, of your own knowledge, know that Astrology is false?" He answered, "I do not." My friend continued: "I have an acquaintance who understands Astrology, and he says it is true. Which must I believe?"

---

could be had, or money could hire, to write for or against any subject, but the reader can see how deficient the writer in "The Penny Magazine" has been in his knowledge of Astrology.

I might go on answering scores of other writers who have published articles in refutation of Astrology; some have published whole volumes against it. They have brought God, the Bible, Jesus Christ, and every "thing that is in heaven above, or in the earth beneath, or in the waters under the earth" against it; and everything that could be raked up out of their own imagination. But I ask only one question in all these matters, that is, *Is it true?* Truth is irresistible, and every thing that is *not true* vanishes before it like *vapor* in broad daylight. Truth is mighty and must prevail.

All these writers against Astrology are generally so shallow and nonsensical that it is not worth while answering them. Even the article in the "Penny Magazine" was not worth answering, but the "Society for the Diffusion of Useful Knowledge" gave it an *eclat* which caused me to notice it. In all the writings against Astrology that I have met with, there is one concurrent fact which runs through the whole of them, and which stands out prominently; that is, they are all intended to keep people who know nothing about it in ignorance of it. If the writers of these articles knew the first principles of the science they would stop writing against Astrology, and write in favor of it.

A prominent divine in England, who had written article after article in refutation of Astrology, after thinking the matter over carefully, came to the conclusion that if he only had a knowledge of the subject, he could write against it with more effect. So he commenced to study it for that purpose, but there is where he made his great mistake, for, instead of continuing to write against it, he published one of the best text books we have on that subject, called "Butler's Astrology." I refer to Bishop Butler of the Episcopal Church of England. Therefore, if you wish to write and talk against Astrology, the less you know about it the better, and you will always find that the people who are as ignorant as yourself will agree with you, and they are in the great majority in all Christian countries.

You must never study Astrology if you do not want to be convinced of its truth, and become a convert to that science.

Note continued from "To the Student," page ix.

I should not have taken any notice of the Stationers' Company buying the right to publish John Partridge's Almanac and Ephemeris from his widow, if William and Robert Chambers had not referred to it in their Encyclopœdia with the sole object of degrading Astrology and Astrologers.

To convince the student that Astrologers had nothing whatever to do with the publication of that Almanac and Ephemeris after John Partridge's death, I cannot do better than quote a prediction from Mr. Partridge's Almanac during the time he was publishing it, and also one or two predictions from the same Almanac during the time it was published by the Stationers' Co. But before doing so I think it might be interesting to the reader to insert a passage from the Almanac and Ephemeris of Mr. Francis Moore, the Almanac which Rev. Thomas Dick refers to as having a yearly sale of 240,000 copies, and at the time when there was probably not more than 500,000 inhabitants in London. Then the reader can judge of the merits of the Almanac and its author, and I think he can readily perceive that Mr. Moore was well informed on the science of Astrology, especially in that branch, called "Mundane Astrology," and which branch is chiefly made use of in Astrological Almanacs. On page 14 in his prediction for the Spring quarter of that year which occured for the longitude of England on March 20th, at 51 minutes past one in the morning, he says:

"The ground of all predictions is referred to Comets, and great conjunctions of the two Superiors, Saturn and Jupiter; and also of Saturn, Jupiter and Mars, in cardinal signs, and in angles of the heaven, near eminent fixed stars, but in the very beginning of Aries, chiefest of all. Now he that would discover the active, and turbulent years before they come, and when great and eminent things shall be transacted, or mankind suffer by some uncommon calamity or plague, scarcity, inundations, fire or War, he must first observe the place of the Comet, what Kingdom it afflicts, and also what princes' nativity it afflicts, also what kingdom or city it is vertical to, and of what nature this Comet is, whether Saturnine, Martial, etc., and in what year it doth afflict any of those countries or persons; and secondly, let him observe at the entrance of every year, how the Sun, Moon or Mars, behold the place of the conjunction by Quartile or opposition, and if near any violent fixed star; as also what eclipses fall in or near those points or parts of Heaven, and how Saturn and Mars do govern or afflict at those times, and in what part of the scheme they fall, as well as in what part of the Zodiac. Likewise the eclipses ought to be considered with the comets also, and in particular how they stand or are affected in their declinations, for I esteem that to be one of the most considerable incidents that doth or can attend them in this circumstance; and then lastly, when you have considered all these particulars carefully, make use of the ingress of the Sun into the sign Aries to guide and direct you in your judgment in the discovery of what is most remarkable and likely to happen, in that or any other year. Besides these things there are the transits of Saturn through the twelve Signs, by which means, he does afflict divers Countries and Kingdoms, by his conjunction every thirtieth year, and by his opposition every fifteenth year. He is just entering Cancer, (Saturn entered Cancer the 24th of April, 1768,) those Kingdoms and Countries under that sign, and many others will be found uneasy and out of order, during his transit through that sign, and that indeed seldom fails, without something remarkable to prevent it, as I could show you by going backwards, with history in one hand, and an ephemeris in the other."

I have copied the above from Moore's Almanac for 1768, for two purposes; the first to show there is little wonder that the almanac attained an annual sale of two hundred and forty thousand copies, not by appealing to the ignorance and superstition of the people then living, according to the inferences of the Rev. Thomas Dick, but by appealing to the knowledge and intelligence of the public.

The second purpose the student will readily perceive, is that he could not understand intelligently the reading of the two horoscopes inserted on pages 145 and 150, the first for the time of the Inauguration of President McKinley, and the second for the time the extra session of Congress met at Washington on March 15th, 1897, at 12 o'clock noon, without first having had an explanation of the principles and rules of what is termed "Mundane Astrology," and I find it impossible to include them in the present volume on account of devoting so much space to "Planetary Hours," etc.

The second almanac which attained the next largest circulation was that of John Partridge; the right of publication was afterwards bought from his widow. I make the following quotation from his remarks on the eclipses which occured in 1768; on page 38 he says:

The Eclipses for the Year 1768.

There will be five eclipses to the inhabitants of this globe, two of the greater luminary, the Sun, and three of the Moon; they will happen in the following order:

The first visible in England, is but a partial eclipse of the Moon, on Monday, the 4th of January, which begins at 3 h. 12 m. and 57 s. in the morning. The second is an invisible eclipse of the Sun on the 19th of January, at 18 m past six at night, but it is a great and visible eclipse in *North America*. The third is a great and total eclipse of the Moon, and visible throughout all Europe, on the 30th of June, which begins at 2 h. 2 m. and 25 s. in the morning. The fourth is an invisible eclipse of the greater luminary, the Sun, on the 14th of July, near 2 in the morning, but to those who sail on southern seas it will be a visible eclipse. The fifth and last is of the Moon, total and visible, on the 23d of December, which begins at 1 h. 17 m. and 45 s. in the evening.

After stating the above calculations, Mr. Partridge remarks on the above eclipses, page 39:

"It is observed that Eclipses of the Sun or Moon have very rarely, if ever, happened in any age, when they were not attended with considerable effects, according to the magnitude thereof, which may be easily proved if we do but look back, and consult antiquity or the histories of former ages. It is the opinion of the learned Pencer, who says: 'What shall I say? Or why shall I trifle away my time against such as deny the influence of the heavenly bodies? Or what shall I say concerning the eclipses of the Sun and Moon? Are we ourselves, rational men, ignorant that eclipses of the Sun and Moon, and the radiations, and the aspects of the other planets are concomitant and assistant with those eclipses, their good or bad aspects, each to the other? Do we not know their significations in all ages have been ominous, and have caused men's minds to be terrified by a secret and occult sense of the miseries and calamities these eclipses did presage,—to be near at hand, or immediately to follow after the same.

"It is the judgment of several learned and experienced authors, that an eclipse of the Sun or Moon in the signs of either Cancer, Scorpio or Pisces, (the Watery Triplicity,) is very ominous. The first eclipse occurs in the 13.25 of Cancer, in the eighth house, the most evil part of the whole heavens. It doth usually presage deaths, destruction of the common people; many various and groundless fears and rumors, false intelligence, frequent risings, or seditious conspiracies, unexpected mutinies in many countries, especially those under the aforesaid triplicity,—expectations of sudden wars, and the spirits of men generally perplexed with the affairs of the present times. I really wish that our sins and impieties do not hinder our welfare this year, but if we expect any deliverance from the evils the Celestials seem to forbode us, let us not so highly prize the things of the world, and grind the faces of one another, as is usual in these days. I wish the following rule was better observed, and put into practice. No man must do that in his own property or profession which may hurt another man's. And we must so use our own as we may not offend and injure our neighbor; let us therefore as we have occasion, do good to all men, as the apostle speaks, Gal. vi. 10; but how adverse and contrary the practice of these times is to this heavenly rule, I need not here remember; we now cry, 'Every man for himself, but God for us all;' but as one has well inverted it, 'That where every man is for himself, the devil is for all.' One of the greatest miseries this nation groans under, is depopulation; but sure there is a woe to them that join house to house, and lay field to field, till there be no place, that they may be placed above in the midst of the earth, Isaiah v. 8. How many houses, nay almost towns, that I know of, are depopulated and ruined of late years.

"Nay doth not the poor smart the most of all by this sore evil? viz.: The industrious poor, that would live by their own works and endeavors, how many of them are utterly ruined and spoiled thereby, and several are forced to flee into other parts of the world for harbor and a poor habitation. How doth the city sit solitary that was full of people? How is she become a widow? Lam. i. 1.

"I heartily wish we may all of us shake off those vipers, those great enemies and curses of sin and oppression, as the forestalling of markets, and the engrossing of provisions into private hands before they are exposed to sale, whereby the industrious poor are greatly oppressed; if we I say, could rid the nations of these enormities, that abound in this land, then shall that of the prophet be undoubtedly verified, and made good unto us. Then shall we have no cause to fear the face of the greatest oppressor, depopulators and racking landlords."

I have given the above lengthy extract from John Partridge's Almanac for 1768, to show that at that time, the publisher was a firm believer in the Science of Astrology, and understood the science; also to show that he was a believer in the Bible, as a pious strain appears to run through all his writings. In England the tax-ridden people complained of the same unjust taxation and oppression, that the American colonies were suffering from, and which resulted in the Revolution of 1776, and that in those days there were the same racking landlords, trusts and speculators and moneyed men forestalling the market of wheat and other eatables of the poor as they are at the present day. It is very probable that the pious strain of the author of the Almanac, and the large profits from its sale were the reasons which induced the Stationers' Company to purchase the right of publication from Mr. Partridge's widow. I have not been able to find in what year that pious company bought the right to publish the almanac, but it probably was near 1792 or 1793, as I see the predictions in those years did not require an Astrologer to write them, and they gradually became worse from year to year.

I will here give two predictions that were made in Partridge's Almanac in 1833, and any person can readily perceive that those who wrote them were ignorant of the science. One was the prediction for the month of June, 1833, which says: "Many of our political clergy expose themselves to the just animadversions of the public; let such beware, or they may find, perhaps, when too late, that they had better have kept within the province of their calling, when all thoughtful men would respect them."

The next prediction which I here insert was for the month of November, 1833, which says: "Great and important things are now or will ere long be under consideration; I wish it may be for the good of the English nation. The western parts of this kingdom send bad news from the watery element, of boisterous storms and tempest, proving very prejudicial to the adventurers thereon."

They generally have bad weather near the British Islands in November, every year, and that is the month in which the greatest number of suicides are committed in England on account of the gloomy and depressing weather.

The two above predictions were all that was published for the months of June and November in Partridge for 1833. The predictions for the other months, and other years are similar in every way.

I do not think that Astrologers ought to be blamed for those pious persons making the above predictions, as they had nothing to do with publishing such almanacs, and especially Partridge's almanac in 1833, as it is evident from the reading that the persons who wrote them had no knowledge whatever of Astrology. Therefore William and Robert Chambers and all such revilers against Astrology ought to put the saddle on the right horse's back.

I refer the reader to page ooo, for further information on this subject.

One of the main reasons why I inserted the two lengthy predictions from the almanacs of 1768 was partly on account of their being so many eclipses in that year, and also its being a year in which really the American Revolution commenced.

Knight in his history of England when writing the events that occured in 1768, in Vol. v., page 123, says: "The imposing of duties in America on glass, red and white lead, painter's colors, paper and tea, form the prologue to the tragedy of the American Revolution." The student will remember that nearly all the assemblies in the colonies, passed resolutions repudiating those duties, and Knight says: "Lord Hillsborough, Secretary of the Colonies, was directed to require in the King's name that these be rescinded, and if they refused, immediately to dissolve them." And on page 125 he says: "The King on opening Parliament on the 8th of November 1768, spoke in severe terms, of the proceedings in North America."

In John Partridge's account of the various eclipses which occured in 1768, that of the Sun on the 18th of January, although invisible in England, he says: "*It is a great and visible eclipse in North America.*"

There was an unusual number of eclipses during that year, there being **five in all.**

The student should bear in mind that the large number of eclipses of 1768, were not the only cause of the Revolution of 1776, although they were the cause of "the prologue to the tragedy of the American Revolution." The real cause was the planet Uranus entering the sign Gemini, which sign rules the United States. On the 25th of June, 1774, Uranus entered Gemini, but it only reached 2°.22′ on September 19th, and then it retrograded and re-entered the sign Taurus, December 1st, 1774. But during the short time Uranus was in the sign Gemini, the American Congress met at Philadelphia on the 5th of September, and the delegates to that Congress from Virginia were Col. Washington, Peyton Randolph, Richard Henry Lee, Patrick Henry, Richard Bland, Benjamin Harrison and Edmund Pendleton. The Congress passed a Declaration of Rights addressed to the King, and recommended a suspension of all commercial relations with the mother country and adjourned to meet May 10th, 1775.

Uranus re-entered the sign Gemini, on the 8th of April 1775, and the Battle of Lexington was fought on the 19th of April, 1775. Uranus continued in the sign Gemini until July 15th, 1781, when it entered the sign Cancer. Lord Cornwallis surrendered to General Washington at Yorktown on Oct. 19th, 1781. Butler in his history of the United States, on page 154, says: "The war was virtually closed with the surrender of Cornwallis, occasional skirmishes alone indicated its continuance."

Uranus retrograded into Gemini on the 25th of January, 1782, and remained there until May, 1782, but during these three months that Uranus was in Gemini, its influence was still felt, and we read in "Butler's History," on page 154, "The treasury was bankrupt, commerce destroyed, business neglected and the army unpaid. Congress was powerless, for its jurisdiction was undefined or disputed. Under these circumstances, the troops, the great bulk of whom were encamped at Newburgh on the Hudson, became restless, impatient and finally mutinous, and failing to obtain relief from Congress, besought Washington to make himself king and manage affairs after his own judgment. To prevent a mutiny, Washington called a meeting of the generals to arrange some method of pacification." The meeting was called and General Gage was elected chairman.

Gen. Washington in opening the meeting took his spectacles from his pocket, to enable him to read his speech, remarking in his quiet way; "I have grown gray in your service, and now I am growing blind; but I never doubted the justice of my country, or its gratitude." No stroke of oratory could have moved so many hearts, as did this unaffected language of Washington. (Norton's "Life of Washington," page 515.)

A preliminary treaty of peace was signed at Paris, November 30th, 1782.

I find in the list of eclipses, both of the Sun and Moon, from 1850 to 1898 inclusive, there are only five years in which five eclipses occur in one year, and each of these periods were attended with remarkable events or occurences in different parts of the world. I have not space to enumerate them all or the years in which they occurred, but there is no doubt that the great number of eclipses in 1768, had a great deal to do with England losing her American colonies; but it is not altogether the number of eclipses that occur in a single year, it depends chiefly if those eclipses are what are termed *total*, or they occur, as Francis Moore says, "in vertical places in the heavens or in prominent positions in princes' horoscopes."

From 1850 to 1898 inclusive I find that there are four of those years that have six eclipses, the last year was in 1880, and the year following was remarkable for the large increase of sickness and epidemics, and the great number of accidents, inundations, cyclones and misfortunes of almost all kinds, so much so that the "New York Herald," near the end of the year devoted a whole page of that paper reciting the various misfortunes that had occured in 1881, and there scarcely was a day in the whole year, that there was not some serious accident or misfortune, such as shipwrecks and other disasters and calamities. Cholera was epidemic in almost all parts of Europe, especially in Egypt and France, particularly at Marseilles and Toulon.

The time previous to 1880, when six eclipses occured in one year, was in 1870, and the most remarkable event of that time was the war between Germany and France which commenced in July, 1870, it was a terribly destructive war, both to life and property, and Louis Napoleon met with his Waterloo, and surrendered to the Emperor of Germany at Sedan, September 1st, 1870. Paris also capitulated to the German Army after being besieged for a long time, and a great Revolution occured in that city afterwards called the "Commune." The Empire of France was abolished and a Republic was inaugurated. Alsace and Lorraine were ceded to Germany, besides France paying a heavy indemnity.

The great fire in Chicago occured in 1871, which was soon after followed by the great fire of Boston; but the planet Uranus, not afflicting the sign which governs the United States, this country was not specially afflicted with any other serious calamity or political disturbance.

The time previous to 1870 when six eclipses occured in one year was in 1859. On the 16th of October in that year, John Brown, with 21 associates, seized the United States Arsenal, at Harper's Ferry, intending to arm therefrom such slaves as would join them. He held the position for two days, but no slaves came, and his adherents were captured, tried, and executed. " This was the prologue to the tragedy of the rebellion of the Southern States."

But as I stated above the great number of eclipses in 1768, was not the only cause of the Revolution in 1776, but the main cause was the planet Uranus entering the sign Gemini. So the extraordinary number of eclipses in 1859 was not the only cause of the commencement of the rebellion of the Southern States, but as in the case of the rebellion of the American Colonies against the mother country 84 years before, or one revolution of that planet, when it re-entered Gemini on the 8th of April, 1775, and the battle of Lexington was fought April 19th, 1775, and the revolution lasted until Uranus left that sign and entered Cancer; Lord Cornwallis surrendered to General Washington at Yorktown, October 19th, 1781. Uranus left Gemini July 15th, 1781.

Uranus again entered the sign Gemini the second time in the history of the United States, on the 12th of March, 1859, which was the main cause of the excitement and hanging of John Brown, and the commotion in the Southern States on account of the "slavery question," caused by the Abolitionists in the North. Uranus turned retrograde on the 15th of September, 1859, and continued retrograding until the 10th of February, 1860, and it retrograded almost out of the sign Gemini, which caused the commotion to almost die out, but on that day Uranus turned direct and continued in the sign Gemini until the 25th of June, 1865.

The Civil War commenced with the firing on Fort Sumter, April 13th, 1861, when the war-like planet Mars, formed a square of Uranus in Gemini; and the war was practically ended, by the surrender of Gen. Robert E. Lee to Gen. Grant, April 9th, 1865, when Uranus was just leaving Gemini.

In 1852 was the next previous period when we had six eclipses in one year; in that year there was great excitement caused by religious disputes, (and even riots) between the Catholics and Protestants, especially in Philadelphia. In that year the United States was on the point of war with Great Britain on account of the "fishery question," but it was settled in the following year. There was also much excitement over the "slavery question," the North being very much incensed because of the fugitive slave law, and the passage of the Kansas-Nebraska Bill, which nullified the "Missouri Compromise;" the bill was introduced into the Senate by Stephen A. Douglass, which was violently opposed by the North.

In 1851 about six hundred adventurers, familiarly known as "Filibusters," undertook to annex Cuba to the United States. Led by General Lopez, they landed on the Cuban coast, but were captured, and the leaders were shot without any interposition on the part of the United States government. Their execution created great sympathy throughout the civilized world.

There was also some trouble caused by the Mormons in Utah; but the planet Uranus not being in the sign Gemini, but Neptune only afflicting that sign by a square from the sign Pisces, the government was enabled to settle it without war or revolution.

There will be six eclipses in 1898, as follows: a partial eclipse of the Moon, Jan. 7; a total eclipse of the Sun, Jan. 22; a total eclipse of the Moon, July 3d; an annular eclipse of the Sun, July 18th; a partial eclipse of the Sun, Dec. 13th, and a total eclipse of the Moon, Dec. 27th.* There has not been a year in almost a century in which there was such marked phenomena, of total or annular eclipses, and I look for some remarkable events,

---

* In counting back for a period of nearly fifty years, I find the highest number of eclipses that occured in one year was six, and the lowest number two, the average is a little over three in a year. But in looking back for a long period, I have not found any year where there was more than six eclipses. The eclipse of the Sun is counted the most evil in its influence, and a total eclipse of the Sun is the most evil, but the influence chiefly depends on whether the eclipse falls vertical over any particular country, or in any sign which rules any particular nation ; or whether it falls in any marked evil position or place in the King's, Queen's, Emperor's or Czar's horoscope ruling any particular nation.

To prove that nearly all the Eastern Nations regard eclipses of the Sun as portending calamity and disaster, even up to the present day, I copy the following from the "New York Evening Sun," Dec. 29th, 1897:

"The State Department at Washington, has received by mail from Charles Denby, the United States Minister to China, a copy of an official decree issued by the Emperor setting forth the ancient superstition of the Orientals that the eclipse of the Sun portends disaster.

The eclipse will occur on the first day of the 24th year of the reign Kuang Hau, and the Emperor is filled with forebodings as to its effects. In view of the troubles which have beset China the predictions contained in the decree are remarkable. The decree is as follows :

"According to the Chun Chiu (Spring and Autumn annals) it has been stated that an eclipse of the Sun on the first day of the year betokens an impending calamity, hence the Sovereigns of every dynasty which has preceded us has always made it a point, whenever an eclipse of the Sun is prognosticated, to undergo self-abasement and humble themselves before heaven in order to avert the wrath from above.

"In the case of our own imperial dynasty, for instance, during the reign of their Majesties Kang Hsi and Chen Lung (1662-1794,) there were observed two eclipses of the Sun, which fell each on New Year's day; and now, according to the Board of Astronomy, the first day of the 24th year of our reign (Jan 22d, 1898,) there will be yet another eclipse of the Sun We are filled with forebodings at this news, and hasten to seek within ourselves for signs which may have thus brought upon the land the wrath of high Heaven.

"We further command that the ceremonies of congratulation usually held on New Year's day in the Taiho Throne Hall to be curtailed, and only ordinary obeisances be made, the place being changed to the Chien Tsing Throne Hall. The banquet usually given to the clansmen on New Year's day must be stopped, and when the eclipse occurs let all members of the court wear sombre garments and assemble in the inner place before the altar set up to Heaven to pray for forbearance and mercy to the country at large.

"This is as far as we shall concern ourselves to show our desire to propitiate high Heaven, but as her Majesty the Empress Dowager is an elder and senior, it is but right that the full ceremonies be observed in paying the court's obeisances on New Year's day to her Majesty. Let all the Yamens concerned take note."

The fact that the eclipse which takes place on the 22d of January, 1898, occurs on the Chinese New Year's day, will have no more effect than if it had occured on any other day of the year.

calamities and disasters occuring during the year 1898, but of what nature it is difficult to say without close calculations.

The two evil planets, Saturn and Uranus, will be near a conjunction in the sign Saggitarius, in opposition to Gemini, which sign rules the United States, and remain in that sign the whole year, excepting when Uranus retrogrades into Scorpio on the 5th of July, but re-enters Saggitarius again on the 10th of September. Mars comes to the opposition of both of these planets in the month of July, 1898. Also the planet Neptune is now in the sign Gemini, and afflicting the United States, and remains in that sign until the end of 1900. It is unreasonable to expect 1898 will close without some serious misfortune or calamity afflicting this country. There certainly is much danger of war with some other nation, and there is no doubt that during 1898 there will be some disastrous war in some other country equal to the Franco-Prussian War of 1870, and that Germany will be involved and will meet with serious affliction or disaster. It will be curious if all these nations ruled by the sign in which the total eclipse of the Sun on Jan. 22, 1898, occurs keeps out of war during 1898 and 1899. The time Prince Henry, brother to the Emperor of Germany, set sail from Kiel, Germany, for China, Dec. 16th, 1897, at 9 A. M., was a remarkably evil period, and he is certain to meet with serious disaster and misfortune. See chart of the heavens for that date on page ooo.

In tracing back the periods when Uranus was transiting through the sign Gemini, which rules the United States, and when six eclipses occured in one year, there is another part belonging to "Mundane Astrology," which I would like to have introduced here but could not do it without danger of confusion to the student or the general reader. I refer to *Comets*. Francis Moore says in his almanac of 1768: "The ground of all predictions is referable to Comets and great conjunctions of the two superior planets, Saturn and Jupiter." [Uranus was not then discovered.]

Noah Webster, the author of "Webster's Dictionary, in his History of Epidemics and Pestilential Diseases," attributes the cause of those devastating calamities, cyclones, earthquakes, and volcanic eruptions, to the influence of Comets; he says in tracing back through history for a period of over two thousand years, whenever these phenomena and disastrous events occured they have always been preceded or accompanied by Comets.

The great disasters and misfortunes which overtook the Christians in their wars with the Turks, whenever a Comet appeared, induced the Pope of Rome to direct prayers to the Almighty beseeching him to avert their baleful and calamitous influence. The Pope also anathematized a

---

First: Had the eclipse occured in the sign which governs China, that nation might then have felt its evil influence in a marked degree.

Second: Had it taken place in an angle in the Emperor's horoscope, especially the ascendant or mid-heaven, or

Third: Had it fallen on, or near the Sun or Moon's place, or in any evil position in his horoscope, then not only the Emperor, but the whole Chinese people would have felt its influence and it would cause some calamity or disaster to afflict that nation.

But China will feel some of its evil influence, as I find that this eclipse commences in the north of China, which is in the line of its central track, and it will be seen to great advantage throughout the whole of China, and in some parts of that country it will be vertical, and these parts will feel its influence the most.

There is more danger that Arabia, Russia, Turkey, Prussia, Poland and Sweeden, will feel more of the evil influence of this eclipse than China, as it falls in the sign of the Zodiac which governs these countries. It will also be visible in all these countries except Sweeden, and if it happens to afflict the horoscopes of the rulers of those countries then they will feel its effect all the more. England will feel its evil influence in a marked degree, as the sign Aquarius, the sign in which the eclipse occurs, rules the affairs of State of that nation.

It is very foolish for the "Emperor of China to command his subjects to wear sombre garments, and to assemble before the altar set up to heaven, and pray for forbearance and mercy during the time of the eclipse," as it will have about as much effect as the "Pope's bull against the Comet." The Emperor should command his people, to prepare to meet, or combat the disaster that is impending over them.

Comet which made its appearance in the early part of the 15th century, which has always been referred to as the "*Pope's bull against the Comet.*" It is evident that four or five hundred years ago that nearly all Professors of the Christian religion regarded Comets as threatening great calamities or disasters which caused them to pray to God to guard them against or avert their evil influence.

I shall only refer here to four Comets which of late years have appeared. One Comet appeared in 1852, which had in its previous visit to our solar system divided into two, and the parts were one and one-quarter millions of miles from each other, on this their second visit. Another one, appeared in the Fall of 1858, which many believe to this day, presaged the war of 1861. I remember distinctly walking out on the hills at Frankford, near Philadelphia, and observing the Comet when it was setting in the West after the Sun, its nucleus just above the horizon, and its tail extending to the meridian. It was to me an awful and grand sight. There was another Comet that appeared in the early part of 1861.

Another remarkable Comet made its appearance before the commencement of the Franco-Prussian War in 1870.

When we look back through history and observe these various phenomena in the heavens and their effect on the earth and its inhabitants, is it any wonder that we should exclaim in the language of Shakespeare, "Can such things be and overcome us like a summer cloud, without our special wonder?"

I do not see why such men as Richard A. Proctor should call persons who pay attention to these subjects, "silly, ignorant rogues, charlatans, unscrupulous rascals, and lying knaves," especially when we can find by calculations the time these eclipses, and other phenomena occur, and as John Partridge says: "They may be easily proved, if we do but look back and consult the history of former ages."

I can only answer such men as Prof. Proctor, in the words of Hamlet, when he says: "There are more things in heaven and earth, Horatio, than are dreamt of in your philosophy."

"To the Student," continued from page xii.

There are a great number of people like Prof. Roeback, who undertake to advertise themselves extensively as Astrologers, when they do not have the remotest idea of even the meaning of the word "Astrology." To explain I will give an instance: My brother, M. A. Broughton, came from England to New York, and shortly afterwards went to Philadelphia; while there he got several orders to write nativities, but having left his books and ephemeris in New York, he called upon Dr. Roeback, and requested the privilege of copying the planet's places of certain years and days from Roeback's Ephemeris. My brother had one of his own ephemeris with him which he had published in England, and explained to Dr. Roeback what he wanted. Roeback replied by saying: "That is all humbug; that is no Astrology," and showed him a small almanac, such as is published by patent medicine men, and said: "This is the real Astrology." It is astonishing what harm such men as Dr. Roeback can do a science which they pretend to follow or practice, especially that of Astrology, of which so few persons have a knowledge.

I do not wish to say a word against clairvoyants, palmists, mind-readers, phrenologists, spiritualists and card-cutters, as I believe a number of them are honest in their calling. But at the same time these professions have nothing whatever to do with the science of Astrology, although they are often classed as Astrologers.

Note continued from bottom of page 34.

* We have another remarkable instance of the power of hypnotism in that of **Mr. Nelson M. Weeks**, superintendent of a Sunday-school in Hackensack, N. J., over Miss Aimee Smith, who was a teacher in the same school and also organist in the church. The newspapers state that at an evening sociable Mr. Weeks tried his mesmeric influence on Aimee and she easily became under his control, so much so that after a while the people in the room begged of him to bring her out of the hypnotic state ; but it appears that the influence continued, even when she was not hypnotized, and afterwards they were often seen together by neighbors and friends, until finally she was taken suddenly ill and afterwards died, it was supposed of poison, in the Victor Hotel, near 26th Street and Third Avenue, New York, March 8th, 1897, where they had registered as man and wife. Mr. Weeks after calling a doctor departed.

Neither Harry Hayward nor Mr. Weeks are what are termed professional magnetizers. I have seen a number of remarkable instances of hypnotic power of one person over another in public lectures and museums, by professionals, in New York and other cities, by both ladies and gentlemen who make it a business to train themselves to hypnotize people. These facts prove beyond a question that there is some remarkable influence or secret power which one person has over another. This influence is brought to bear in relieving pain and suffering in sick people, and even curing disease, which goes under the various names of mind-healing, Christian science, mesmerism, hypnotism, clairvoyancy and massage, and nearly one-half of the people in the cities, if not in the country towns, are firm believers in one or the other of those various isms or so-called sciences, and make use of them in curing nervousness and other complaints.

Note continued from bottom of page 41.

† The reader may be so interested in the lawsuit referred to on page 41, that he may wish to know how we finally came out of those persecutions.

In the $100 damages, which the jury awarded Mr. James McDermott while Mr. Chaney was confined in jail, Chaney and his lawyer made a plea for a new trial, but the judge reserved his decision. Mr. Chaney went down to the City Hall and saw the clerk of the court every day, except Sunday, for about six weeks, and each day received the same answer from the clerk of the court, which was, that the judge had not *yet rendered his decision*; finally he was told that the judge had rendered a decision, and that he was to have a new trial, but he was to make application within a month from the time the decision was rendered, the month having already expired. Mr. Chaney became so disgusted with New York Court proceedings, that he gave the matter up in despair of ever having a new trial, and said: "It's no use attempting to do anything with such a corrupt judiciary." The reader ought to bear in mind that this was during the regime of William M. Tweed, and at the same period referred to by the Rev. Henry Ward Beecher, when he said: "That the judges of New York City were so corrupt that they actually stunk."

The following is a specimen of Mr. Chaney's writing, and a sample of editorials written by a Western Editor during the forties and fifties, and is a true account of what we had to endure at 814 Broadway, New York, which at the time was thought to be the centre of the Metropolis of the Western Hemisphere. So far as my memory serves me, it is strictly true, even to the letter, yet I was sued for libel by Alexander Eagleson for printing it in the "Planet Reader." The part of the article that Mr. Eagleson's lawyer construed as libelous was, where it states, "the landlord seems possessed of a mania for sign-stealing." Mr. John Townsend, Eagleson's lawyer and also lawyer for Mr. James Gordon Bennett, of the *New York Herald*, stated in his argument, when pleading for heavy damages before the jury, "that it was plainly a libel, that Mr. Eagleson had only stolen Dr. Broughton's signs, and that he had not gone from one end of Broadway to the other stealing all the signs he could lay his hands on, and carting them off," he gave as a precedent, that a "certain gentleman had got heavy damages against a newspaper which stated that the gentleman had been going around stealing bread, and all that they could prove against the defendant was 'that he had stolen one loaf.'" The jury brought in a verdict against me for six cents damages, and six cents costs.

I might here remark, that previous to becoming acquainted with me, Mr. Chaney had looked upon Astrology with supreme contempt and derision, and thought a person of ordinary intelligence, or who could read and write, could have no faith in the science. The first time he came to visit me, looking at my library, he remarked: "Why, you don't believe in Astrology?" After becoming acquainted with me the whole current of his life was changed, and he has devoted over 30 years to the study and investigation of that despised and persecuted science.

The following is copied from Broughton's Monthly Planet Reader and Astrological Journal, for April, 1867.

UNPARALLELED OUTRAGES—RELIGIOUS MEETINGS BROKEN UP BY ROWDIES—PERSECUTION AGAINST ASTROLOGY—SPECIMENS OF NEW YORK JUSTICE—BY W. H. CHANEY.

"I shall now devote my life to Astrology, and come what may, never shrink from being its defender."

Such was the remark we made to Dr. Broughton last October, after having become thoroughly convinced, not only of the truthfulness of Astrology, but that it was the most precious science ever made known to man.

"You will find that you will have enough to do, then," replied the doctor, quietly.

He had seen service as an apostle in the cause; had been driven out of Pennsylvania by the passage of a law punishing with imprisonment any one who should presume to practice the celestial science, and he knew that the life of an Astrologer was anything but pleasant. Well, we have had six months experience, and though not very brilliant, we propose giving it to the public.

After forming the resolution aforesaid, we made arrangements with the Doctor to live in his family, lecture for, and study with him. We gave the first course of lectures upon Astrology ever delivered in this country, and on each occasion Dr. B. examined one or more Nativities before the audience, giving most wonderful tests of the accuracy with which the events of life can be calculated by a knowledge of the influence and movements of the heavenly bodies. For a time the undertaking went on swimmingly, and we began to boast of victory.

"Don't be too sanguine," quoth the Doctor, "for you and I have some evil aspects approaching which will be likely to tell against us."

The beginning of the year proved that he was right. All hands ill and hard times generally. Then the *Herald*, the "satanic press," commenced its villainous abuse of "814 Broadway." The place was styled the "Ghoul's Garrett," and all who came here denominated as infidels and blasphemers. As for ourselves, we were described as "the chief ghoul of the den," "a played-out bruiser," and a "used up prize fighter," together with other expressions equally flattering, and charteristic of a journal whose proprietor has been cowhided through the streets, on sundry occasions, on occount of the eloquence of his language applied to gentlemen who never injured him.

As might be expected, these puffs of the "satanic," brought a class of rowdies to disturb our lectures, and for some weeks our prospects looked gloomy enough. This was the beginning of trouble.

On the 11th of February, the owner of the premises, evidently anxious to drive the Doctor away, commenced stealing his signs, placards, bulletins, door-plates, etc., which were placed at the door. In vain the Doctor remonstrated. The landlord seemed possessed of a *mania for sign stealing*. He is a queer genius, and as the public may be interested, as well as posterity, in knowing who he is, we will say that the first two letters of his name is—Alexander Eagleson, and his place of business is No. 43 Fourth Avenue.

When Eagleson had stolen "in the neighborhood of twenty signs," as he admitted to police officer Waldron, of the Broadway squad, Dr. B. procured a warrant and had him arrested. He was taken before Justice Dodge, of Jefferson Market Police Court, and—*promptly discharged!* Three hours later, Eagleson stole three more signs. The Doctor persisted in putting down others as fast as they were stolen, and Eagleson persisted in stealing them as fast as put down. This made lively times in the sign business.

On the evening of the day when he was so *honorably* acquitted by Justice Dodge, Eagleson stole another sign, making the fourth for that day. This time the Doctor concluded to try and capture the stolen property. But Eagleson is a very enterprising man, and a firm believer in the maxim—"hold fast all you get." So, doubling his fist, when the Doctor approached, he let fly, and the next moment there was an Astrologer rolling on the sidewalk. Nothing daunted, the Doctor came to time, slightly under the influence of Mars, yet restrained from committing murder through the benevolent Jupiter.

"Why don't you sue me again before Judge Dodge?" sneered Eagleson.

To make a long story short, the Astrologer persevered, called in the aid of a policeman, and finally the sign stealer and sign was captured, taken to the station house and locked up for the night. Next morning charges of theft, and assault and battery, were preferred, and upon hearing the evidence, Justice Dodge bound him over to the Court of Sessions. This was on the 12th of March, but from that day to this (April 29th), not a word more has been heard about it.*

Before Sol had culminated in the midheaven, on the day Eagleson was bound over, his son-in-law, a simple-minded youth, with more brass than brains, allowed himself to be persuaded into trying *his* hand at sign stealing. The alarm was sounded by the boy on watch, and then the excitement commenced. The Doctor started at a 2.40 gait, without waiting for his hat, while we followed at a more dignified pace.

"Stop thief! Stop thief! Stop thief!"

Men ran; boys yelled; women screamed; dogs barked. Down Broadway ran the thief to Tenth street, then across to Fourth avenue, then down to the Bible Honse, when he dodged into the place of Eagleson and locked the door.

The crowd gathered, blocking up the sidewalk, every one asking—

"What is it? What is it?"

We happened to be blessed with a pretty good pair of lungs, and having learned to speak in the open air by "stump speaking in the west," very obligingly informed the crowd it was nothing only that Eagleson and his thievish hirelings had been stealing Dr. Broughton's signs. Each new arrival repeated the inquiry, and being a very good natured man, we answered the question over and over again.

---

* When Mr. Eagleson was bound over to appear at the Court of Sessions, Justice Dodge told me that we would be notified when to appear against him, but we never were, although Mr. Chaney and my wife went to the District Attorney's office a number of times to make inquiry when we were to appear in court, and each time they were told that we would be notified. Mr. Eagleson was discharged, because we did not appear against him as complainants, as we were not notified, and I was arrested and had to give heavy bail, and was sued for $10,000 damages, for false imprisonment.

Several policemen collected and demanded admission. But the thief refused to unlock the door. He then went into a back room, out of sight, and the next moment such a chopping, hewing and slashing, we never heard. Of course he was not chopping up the sign—"no, I guess not"—he was only getting some wood ready for building a fire next morning. He's a very innocent youth—the landlord's son-in-law—he is.

About this time two smart looking citizens forced their way through the crowd and asked the officers if they wanted any help. The officers began to explain how matters stood, when Eagleson himself came up and ordered everybody away from his premises, cursing, swearing and blaspheming in a style that would have put to blush even a "plug ugly."

"That's the man who stole Dr. Brougton's signs yesterday, and slept in the station house for it last night!" we exclaimed, pointing to the sign-stealer.

This enraged him beyond description, and had we been within his reach, it is not likely that we should have lived to write this article. As it was, he gave vent to his insane wrath by pushing the two gentlemen before alluded to, notwithstanding they had exhibited their badges as detectives.

"I don't care a G—— D——n who you are!" shouted the infuriated sign-stealer, giving them a violent push backwards.

Half a minute later the sign-stealer might have been seen walking in the direction of the Station House, politely attended by two detectives. He was taken before a magistrate, "*and on account of his well-known respectability, instantly discharged!!!*" But the crowning act of his effrontery is yet to be told. He preferred a complaint against the detectives for arresting him, and on the examination boasted that he was worth $135,000. He also availed himself of the opportunity to state under oath that "Dr. Brougton's principal business was to blaspheme against God?"

But we must return to the crowd in front of the Bible House. When Eagleson was arrested, his hopeful son-in-law, having got his *wood chopped for morning*, unlocked the door, and in a voice tremulous with emotion on account of his wife's father being again brought to grief, so soon after having passed a restless night in a thief's cell, bitterly exclaimed:

"Now let him go," pointing to the retreating figure of his unhappy father-in-law; "you got the wrong man—I'm the man, gentlemen."

"He's arrested for assaulting an officer," replied one of the policemen, "and now we want the man who stole the sign."

"There's no sign here," added young hopeful, "and I forbid you searching for it unless you have a warrant."

But we felt sure that we could identify the relics of the sign if allowed a glance at the young man's pile of kindling wood, and by request of the officers we went in.

"Who are you? Go out o' here!" cried the industrious wood chopper.

The officers concluded that we had better go out, and not feeling inclined to contest the point, we amiably assented. We had not taken two steps towards the door before the wood-chopper seized us by the collar. It must have been a comical sight, he a "feather weight," pulling away at our 180 lbs. *avoirdupois*. We thanked him for his polite attentions, assuring him that we could go very well without his assistance. But he was too much of a gentleman not to lead us to the door, and by a gentle push, hinted that our company was not agreeable to one of his caliber of brain.

The next act in the drama, which is still in danger of becoming a tragedy, was for the Doctor to sue Eagleson in the Supreme Court, for five hundred dollars damage on account of stealing his signs, service of which was made March 22d.

Then came a change of programme. Evidently disgusted with the slow progress he was making to put down Astrology by stealing signs, he abandoned that mode of attack. Under pretence of leasing to the Fenians, as a drill room, the floor over the one occupied by the Doctor, on the night of that day that Eagleson was sued for five hundred dollars, there came such a motly crowd, Rag, Tag and Bobtail, as has not been seen since the days of Falstaff, and tumbling, swearing, thundering up the stairs, under the leadership of the eminent wood-chopper, they piled into the rooms overhead.

Fenians? It is a base slander against men who have devoted their lives for redressing the wrongs of the oppressed, to charge upon them such outrageous acts of cruelty and barbarism as have been perpetrated here for the last three weeks. No, they were not Fenians, but loafers, vagrants, thieves and pickpockets, gathered up from the slums of the city, and ripe for any outrage, provided they were filled with bad whiskey. Fenians, indeed! We venture there is not a Fenian in the United States who would not scorn to associate with such rowdies, much less be a party to their acts of infamy.

It was evident that the wood-chopper had found his level at last, and he was in his glory. Not satisfied with the infernal din made by himself and motly crew, simply because Mrs. Broughton pushed the door to a little, so that she could see down the stairs, he broke out—

"The fust one that shets that door agin, I'll cut their G—— d——d head off!"

He might have spoken more grammatically and less profanely—but what can be expected from a wood-chopper?

Shortly after, Mrs. B. went again to look down the stairs for the Doctor, when the wood-chopper hurled a piece of board at her head, which would no doubt have caused her death had it hit her.

But we need not dwell upon the details of this series of outrages which have been continued to the present writing. In vain we have appealed to the officers of the law for protection. We were all under evil aspects, and no one would do anything.

One evening they came as usual, but remained until nearly two o'clock in the morning. Several times during the night they tried the doctor's door, making threats like this:

"Let's break down the door and bring out the d——d sons of b——s!"

Of course there was no sleep for the doctor nor his family, for we were all in momentary expectation of being obliged to defend ourselves with our lives against a horde of drunken rowdies. Mrs. B. had been suffering from poor health all winter, and now, so great was the shock to her nervous system that her senses wandered and her life was in peril.

One day after the persecutions had been contined for a week, the wood-chopping son-in-law had the impudence to speak to Mrs. Broughton upon the subject. He evidently came as a spy, to find out what he could, yet was weak enough to let out what Eagleson and the "Satanic" will not thank him for.

"O, 'twont cost my father-in-law anything," exclaimed the simpleton, "for he's done jest as Bennett's lawyers told him to, and they'll pay all damages."

We will not pretend to say whether the fellow lied or not; but if he did lie, it is a remarkable coincidence that *Galbraith*, who has office in the *Herald* building, answered to the case in behalf of Eagleson. If the wood-chopper told the truth, then it looks very much like a conspiracy on the part of the

"Satanic" and sign-stealer to either break the Doctor down, or "blackmail" him into buying peace from them. They may succeed in accomplishing the former, and if there should be no change in the administration of justice in the city, they probably will, but the Doctor will never pay one penny of blackmail, not even to save his life.

During this "reign of terror," Mrs. Broughton had been the greatest sufferer. Being obliged to keep her bed a great portion of the time; no rest at night; and the demoniacal noises and threats so preying upon her that her reason failed at times, when she would utter cries and shrieks enough to drive mad those who heard them. We remember her words on one occasion:

"O, God! the blood is running down my neck! help! help! help! *

One night the Doctor was obliged to get her out of bed and take her to a friend's house, fearing the most serious consequences unless he did so.

On the 4th April Dr. B. sent the following notice to the landlord, which explains itself.

814 BROADWAY, NEW YORK CITY,
April 1st, 1867.

ALEXANDER EAGLESON—

SIR :—On the 23d ultimo, two of your workmen were seen to enter the water-closet on the second floor of these premises, where they remained for a short time, apparently having no particular errand there. But soon after, on trying my pumps, no water could be obtained, nor have we been able to obtain any since.

When this visit of your plumbers to the water-closet on the second floor, and the discovery soon after that my supply of water had been cut off, are taken in connection with your stealing my signs; your assaulting me upon the street, your arrest and confinement in the station house, your son-in-law threatening to cut my wife's head off, and his hurling a piece of board violently at her head, one of your plumbers striking her with a stick, the violence and outrages of the drunken rowdies who nightly assemble in your rooms over my head, their stealing my lamp and letter box, their breaking down my gas brackets, their stealing my bell-cord and tassel; their breaking up my Sunday night meeting—when all these things are considered in connection with your savage persecution, such as would disgrace any outcast from society, unless he could boast, as you do, of being worth $135,000, every unprejudiced mind must conclude that you sent your plumbers upon an errand of mischief, duly instructed to cut off my supply of water.

But whether it is true or not that you sent them, being deprived of water is a serious damage to me, for which I shall be obliged to look to you for satisfaction, unless you remedy the mischief so that I can obtain water through my pump without delay.

The reply to this notice was an impudent letter, received April 6th, enclosing a trumped-up account of $53.10, not one penny of which is due from the doctor to him, either in law or equity.

---

* There is one part of the report of what we had to endure at 814 Broadway, which Mr. Chaney left out and which I now insert in this note. For months every night or rather morning during the time the meetings overhead were breaking up, and these rowdies were coming down stairs, they would stop at our landing and use all kind of vile language, threatening to break into our apartments and drag us out, and push against the door with such violence, that we expected every moment it would give way and they would break in.

While these things were going on outside the door, Mr. Chaney and I were stationed inside, each with a large axe (such as are used by lumbermen to chop trees) held over our heads. I gave Mr. Chaney directions that if they broke through, I would take the first man, he must take the second, and I the third, etc. Had they broken in we would have sold our lives as dearly as possible.

We had the door propped and barred by a ladder and planks, and protected every way possible, besides it being locked and bolted. There was no going to bed for us until after all those rowdies were gone, which was generally from two to three, and sometimes four o'clock in the morning.

My wife being of a nervous temperament and the noise frightened the children, making them scream, she often became delirious under this excitement, and imagined the rowdies, that the authorities had engaged to annoy us had succeeded in breaking into our apartments, and were murdering her husband, children and herself. Hence at these times in her sleep, she would often use the expressions that Mr. Chaney has above related, and would attempt to get out of bed to run away.

I give the above in explanation of my wife's say in her sleep: "Oh God! the blood is running down my neck," etc. If I did not do so some of my readers might think that Mr. Chaney had been calling on imagination for material for his unparallel outrages, etc.

April 9th the Doctor sued him for damages done to his business by the drunken rowdies aforesaid, their breaking up his lectures, etc., laying his claim at five thousand dollars, which will not make Dr. B. whole, even if he recovers the full amount.

On Sunday evening, April 14th, we were advertised to lecture on "Creation." As usual, the wood-chopping son-in-law came with his hireling horde, and after continuing their noisy demonstrations for half an hour, headed by the wood-chopper, they came down stairs and into the hall where we were lecturing. This was part of their system of annoyances, running out and in, and disturbing us by groans, interruptions, and so forth. We had hitherto borne it with christian fortitude, but on this occasion our patience gave way.

Quietly asking the audience to excuse us for a moment, we walked to the other end of the hall and ordered the wood-chopper out. He refused to go. We said he should. He swore he wouldn't. We could not afford to waste time in argument with the fellow, and so we took him by the collar. He doubled his fist. We smiled derisively and said "go." He commenced going. He was terribly disgusted, but kept going. Our argument was irresistible, and he continued to go. When half way through the ante-room he proposed to go himself if we would let him alone. We remembered his courtesy the day *he* escorted *us* to the door, and not liking to be outdone in politeness, even by a wood-chopper, we merely replied by tightening our grasp. He continued going, and his legs had to hurry to keep up with his body. When he was fairly beyond the outer door, we released our hold, but instead of returning thanks for our civility, the unmannerly fellow actually struck and kicked at us in a most furious manner. He had probably eaten something for dinner that laid hard on his stomach.

We returned to the hall and resumed our lecture, as though nothing had happened. For a brief space of time all was quite overhead, and then the noise began again. People passing through Broadway would stop and listen, wondering if a pandemonium had been opened upon that fashionable thoroughfare, for this was the third Sunday evening the outrages had been kept up.

When a crowd of some hundred and fifty had been gathered, two policemen went up to the pandemonium and arrested the wood-chopper and three of his rag-tags, the others having made their escape by being down in our meeting, where they remained very quietly. The rag-tags gave the names of John Boyce, John Bowie and James Loomis, at the Station House, and together with the wood-chopper were locked up for the night.

Next morning the case came before Justice Dodge. His Honor listened to the complaint of the officers who made the arrests, and to the doctor's account of the long continued outrages, and after rebuking the wood-chopper and his rag-tags sharply, he threatened to send them to the Island, if they repeated the offence,. They were *honorably discharged!!!*

The reader may imagine that we have been amusing him by giving a sensational romance ; and we admit that it seems impossible for our account to be true, But if it is false then we are liable to heavy damage, and to imprisonment, for uttering a malicious libel. We have given real names, and some of the parties are well known in the city. Will they prosecute us? We dare and defy them to do so. Our own name heads this article and we take all the responsibility of the publication. We have had ten years experience as a practicing lawyer, and more than ten years as editor and author. Therefore we pretend to know the law, and we not only know the facts, but **can** prove a majority of them by more than a hundred witnesses.

The doctor has expended fully two thousand dollars in the purchase of improvements on his premises, making other improvements and advertising his business as a Physician and Astrologer. The lease has two years more to run, and now when he is just ready to realize some return for his outlay of money, he is compelled to encounter these fiendish persecutions, not for any wrong committed, for he would never harm any one, but simply because he is an Astrologer, and Astrology is not popular.

Are we going back into the dark ages again? It really seems so, when there is no redress by law for such outrages, committed upon the most public street of the metropolis of a continent. The doctor and his family may be murdered here—we may share the same fate, for we are determined to defend Astrology to the last—but this record shall live after us, a monument of lasting disgrace to the Empire City."

SUPPLEMENT.

"THURSDAY, APRIL 18th.—The reign of terror still continues. Last night we attempted to lecture, and as usual, James McDermott commenced his outrageous noises above us. Sometimes we were obliged to pause for a minute, on account of the thumping, pounding and boisterous noises overhead. The wood-chopper brought a speaking trumpet with him, and while others were stamping and running about, he continued to sing, evidently holding the trumpet near his mouth, so that the harsh, metallic detonations sounded more like shrieks from the damned than a human voice.

The police were sent for and once more the wood-chopper came to grief, being obliged to pass the night in the Station House. This morning he was taken before Justice Dodge, and once more, *honorably discharged!!!*

Mrs. Broughton is lying very low, with symptoms of brain fever. The noises last night nearly drove her distracted. I hear her groans of anguish while I write, and at the same moment I hear the voice of James McDermott overhead, and hear him stamping and pounding on the floor.

When will this "reign of terror" cease? Verily, the doctor was a true prophet when he said we should find plenty to do in defending Astrology. But we shall not give up yet awhile. Astrology is undergoing its fiery baptism, and this is no time for turning recreant to the cause."

I have inserted the above article, written by W. H. Chaney, and published in the "Planet Reader," April, 1867, to prove to the reader what Astrologers had to suffer thirty years ago. But there has come a change over the whole community since that time, and if the change continues, there is no doubt that a few years hence the ministers of the Gospel will be preaching Astrological sermons on Sundays in the various churches and saying, "That Jesus Christ was an Astrologer, and that he taught Astrology to his Apostles," and for once they will actually preach the truth, because if we can believe the apocrypha to the New Testament, it is there stated that Christ learned the various significations of the planets and the signs of the Zodiac, and the sextile, trine, square and opposition aspects; and even a number of passages in the New Testament goes to prove that he had a general knowledge of the signs of the Heavens. See Matt. xvi., 2 and 3.

Astrology was just as true thirty years ago as it is to-day, and as it will be thirty years hence. It is not Astrology that changes, but public opinion. At the present day I think it would be very difficult for the judges of the various courts, even in New York City, to prostitute the law in their courts as they did in 1867, without attracting the attention of the community.

In regard to Alexander Eagleson, and his son-in-law, James McDermott, I am of the opinion that they were simply the cat's paw in these persecutions, and the real monkey that used their hands to pull the chestnuts out of the fire was no other than James Gordon Bennett, proprietor of the New York Herald, as at that time the Herald was devoting two or three columns every Monday morning to reporting, or rather misrepresenting, the Sunday meetings at 814 Broadway, and even the reporters of the Herald would bring rowdies with them to create disturbances and break up the meetings. In the latter part of these persecutione James McDermott came to me in my office and told me, that James Gordon Bennett's lawyers had deceived his father-in-law in telling him that they would protect him in stealing my signs, and said he had a right to take them, and had a right to make all the disturbance that Mr. Chaney has enumerated in the foregoing account of these persecutions; and that he and his father-in-law were getting tired of it. I told McDermott all we wanted was to live peaceably.

It certainly was a bitter pill for Mr. Eagleson and his son-in-law, to spend a number of nights in the prison cells. In the lawsuit in which they sued me for $10,000 damages, Mr. Eagleson and Mr. McDermott had been attending court over two months, every day except Sunday, before I was notified by my lawyer, Charles Spencer, (as I had moved and Mr. Spencer did not know my address.) After I was notified they had to attend every day for six or seven weeks, as the late Judge McCunn was on the bench, and he only tried about one law-suit a month. A number of names that were on the docket were called off before the court commenced, and each had to answer to their name and say "Ready." The witnesses in my case had to attend court nearly two months before it came to trial. I believe it was tried before Judge Garvin.

Besides entering suit for $500 against Mr. Eagleson, I also entered suit for $5,000, and afterwards for $10,000 damages, but it was impossible to get any of these cases in court.

There is no doubt the persecution we had to endure was the means of shortening my wife's life, who has now lain in Greenwood a number of years. Had these persecutions occured in Cuba, Armenia, or in the Island of Crete, the newspapers in the United States would have had long accounts calling them religious persecutions and they would have wanted the United States Government to send men-of-war to stop such astrocities; but as they occured in the Metropolis of the Western Hemisphere, it was all right and we got all we deserved. Not a newspaper in the country referred to them except the New York Herald. Any reader that is interested in such literature may refer to the "Herald" published in 1866 and 1867. It is strange what venom the religious community displayed fifty or seventy five years ago, against Astrology, and its professors. There is no doubt that James Gordon Bennett was influenced by the Catholic clergy, the Herald being a Catholic paper.

It is strange what a change in regard to Astrology has come over the community and the editors of the New York Herald since 1867. One of the former editors of that paper has since studied Astrology under my tuition, and has written and published much in the various newspapers and periodicals on the science of Astrology, and is a firm believer in it, and is practising it publicly. Even Mr. James Ingston one of the present editors of the New York Herald has studied the science and has just published a book on Astrology, calling it the "Gospel of the Stars, or the Wonders of Astrology." The introduction to which is written by the chief editor of the Herald, Rev. George H. Hepworth. In reviewing that book in the Herald, they praise it by saying, "that it is the best book that has ever been published on the Science of Astrology." Of late years Mr. Ingston and "Asræl" have published much on the Science of Astrology in the Herald. Mr. Ingston has even made application to myself for articles on

that science for that paper, which were furnished him and were published.*
Who knows but the present James Gordon Bennett may become an Astrologer, and have to go through the same kind of persecutions that I had to endure. Saul of Tarsus, according to the New Testament spent most of his time in persecuting the early Christians, and yet afterwards became one of the greatest advocates of Christianity, under the name of Paul the Apostle and had to endure persecutions for Christ's sake.

Near the time the above persecutions were going on at 814 Broadway, Prof. Henry Holembæk, who was at that time Mayor of Burlington city, New Jersey, and was Professor of Materia Medica, at the Medical college where I graduated, made me a friendly visit and in talking on the subject of medicine and Astrology, made the following remark, "I do not believe in Astrology, but I respect you all the more for believing in it, because you stick to Astrology, when it is clearly to your disadvantage to do so."

No one could have been more opposed to Astrology than Prof. Chaney, before he became acquainted with me. He had the impression that the science had been entirely exploded, and that any person who could read and write could not possibly believe in Astrology. The first time he came into my office, he looked at my library and made the remark, "Why, you don't believe in Astrology!" But becoming acquainted with me changed the whole current of his life, and he has spent the last 30 years in reading, investigating, writing and lecturing on that subject, and no doubt he will continue to do so as long as he lives. He has published a number of books and pamphlets on the Science of Astrology, besides editing monthly periodicals that treat altogether on that subject. He has also published an Astrological Ephemeris of his own calculating besides republishing White's Ephemeris from 1800 to 1875.

---

* Mr. James Ingston in his book on the "Wonders of Astrology," on page 30, tells us:

"The services which a skilled Astrologer can render are various. He can tell those who consult him the fortunate and unfortunate periods of their lives, whether wealth or poverty will be their lot, whether they will be happy or unhappy in their married life, whether they will have children or not, whether they will be successful or unsuccessful in speculation, whether they will obtain legacies or marriage portions or not, whether they will have strong or weak constitutions, whether they will be subject to diseases, and if so, of what nature, whether they will have many or few enemies and friends, whether they will quarrel or live peaceably with their neighbors and kindred, whether they will travel much or little, whether they will be in peril while traveling or not, whether they will be successful in intellectual or manual labor and whether they will live to a good old age or not. But this is not all. The astrologer can tell what trade or profession is most suitable for a person and what likelihood there is of success therein; he can tell what manner of man a woman will marry and what manner of woman a man will marry, and whether the two will live happily together or be sundered by separation or divorce; he can also tell whether the life as a whole will be prosperous and happy or sad and unfortunate. The character, temperament and intellectual tastes he can describe with a precision that will astonish those who have been led to believe that star-readers are impostors and that Astrology is an invention of the devil.

"Young girls who desire to know their fortune in marriage, young men who are undecided as to what profession or trade they shall adopt, fathers and mothers who are anxious as to the education and health of their children, all, who are worried about money matters, the sick, who would fain know whether they will recover their strength and the strong, whose duty it is to ascertain whether any disease threatens them in the future—all these may rest assured that they will find comfort in astrology. Aye, and so may all others, who honestly desire to know what the future has in store for them. In the heavens is mapped out the entire life of every human being with all its joys and sorrows, all its tragedies and successes, all its incidents and changes both grave and trivial, and the story there told in seemingly unintelligible language can be made clear to any one who cares to hear it."

Had there been such men as Mr. Ingston and "Asræl" editors of the New York Herald in 1866 and 1867, I do not believe that Mr. James Gordon Bennett could have influenced them to write such articles against me and Astrology, as appeared in that paper during these years; no amount of money that Mr. Bennett might offer could have induced them to so prostitute their talents and principles.

If the reader wishes to know what a change has come over the community in thirty years, let him turn to the files of the New York Herald published in 1866 and 1867, and read the "reports?" of the meeting at 814 Broadway, also to page 43 of this volume, and read what the detective wrote to my patron after he had been robbing my mail.

Lord Beaconsfield had a saying: "The unexpected always happens." Who would have thought, 30 years ago, that the editors of the Herald would have become Astrologers?

Note continued from paragraph 624, page 283.

In these days the people never think of choosing a fortunate period for laying the first stone, or as the newspapers call it, the "corner stone," and which is often anything but the *first stone*. All they attend to is making speeches, singing and praying; especially if the building is intended for religious purposes, and they never trouble themselves to choose fortunate planetary influences, and good planetary hours for laying the first stone.

Some years ago I read an account in the New York Sunday papers of laying the "corner stone" on Saturday afternoon of what was intended to be a large church. That same day I went to see where the church was to be situated; when I got there I found the church was more than half built and the builders had left one corner, so that the person appointed to lay the stone in that corner could say he laid *that corner stone*; but instead of it being the *first stone* of that building, it came nearer being the last.

When I read in the newspapers, the accounts of laying corner stones, it is impossible to avoid smiling to think how people have perverted the meaning of laying the first stone. But it becomes truly laughable when we read the account of Andrew H. Greene going in a coach with a spade to about 70th Street, in New York and "turning the sod" where it is intended to commence digging for the foundation of the Bridge to cross the Hudson River, and then driving to the Ferry and crossing the River to Weehawken, turning another "sod" there, and then driving home. Had Andrew H. Greene calculated the movements of the heavenly bodies, and chosen the most propitious time for turning these sods, it is possible they might have commenced building the bridge before this time.

We have another curious instance of Count De Lesseps, coming to this continent from France, and turning the first sod of the Panama Canal, on the Atlantic side, then riding by railway over to the Pacific coast and taking a steam tug to the place of the other end of the intended canal. But the sea being boisterous it was impossible for him to land, so he procured some sand and turned it over instead of the "sod," on the steamer's deck; that was supposed to be the commencement of the digging of the Panama Canal. He certainly must have chosen a very evil time to turn the "first sod," as the canal is not yet completed, and is never likely to be, and all those who had anything to do with the digging of the Canal, are either in prison or disgrace, or came to misfortune, besides bringing the whole French nation into disgrace and financial loss, and numbers of the most active men in the undertaking fled their country or committed suicide to avoid imprisonment.

These things remind us so much of the imitation of monkeys, repeating things they see their masters perform, that it is possible in some future age, the readers of the history of these days will actually say, that the people who lived in the last decade of the 19th century were a species of monkeys.

The various religious sects of the present day, all unite in talking and preaching about the ignorance, superstition and wickedness of Astrologers; but where can the student find such unadulterated ignorance and superstition as that of Andrew H. Greene, and Count De Lesseps, turning the first "sod" and the religious people laying the corner stone of a church that was more than half built.

There is no doubt that more than nine tenths of all the present religious ceremonies have had a similar origin as "turning the sod" or laying the first stone of important structures, and these religious ceremonies have in time been changed into singing, praying and speech making, instead of calculating and observing the movements of the heavenly bodies, to find when is the most fortunate time to commence these undertakings.

As what is termed laying the corner stone, is generally anything but the first stone, I have seldom made an astrological calculation in relation to the laying of these stones, or what is sometimes thermed "turning the sod." But I was interested in, and noticed the time of laying what is called the "corner stone" of the "School of Theosophy" by the Theosophical Crusaders who went around the World, spreading their new doctrines in every country they travelled through. On their return to the United States they stopped at Point Loma, San Diego, California, and Mrs. Katherine Tingley of New York, laid the corner stone of their new School of Theosophy, at or very near 2.45 P. M., Feb. 23d, 1897. I calculated the chart of the heavens for that time, and for the longitude and latitude of Point Loma. I find it would have been quite a difficult task for them to have chosen a more *unfortunate period* for that purpose. There is no question that the School of Theosophy will never be finished.* At the time the first stone was laid, twenty six degrees of Cancer was on the ascendant, in the horoscope, and the Moon, lady of that sign, was just leaving a conjunction of Saturn and applying to a square of Jupiter and the Sun, which were almost in exact opposition from the 3d house, to the 9th house (the house of science and learning.) Should the College building ever be completed (which is almost an impossibility) and should they commence to teach Theosophy, there will be nothing but quarrels about what they shall teach and what they shall not teach.

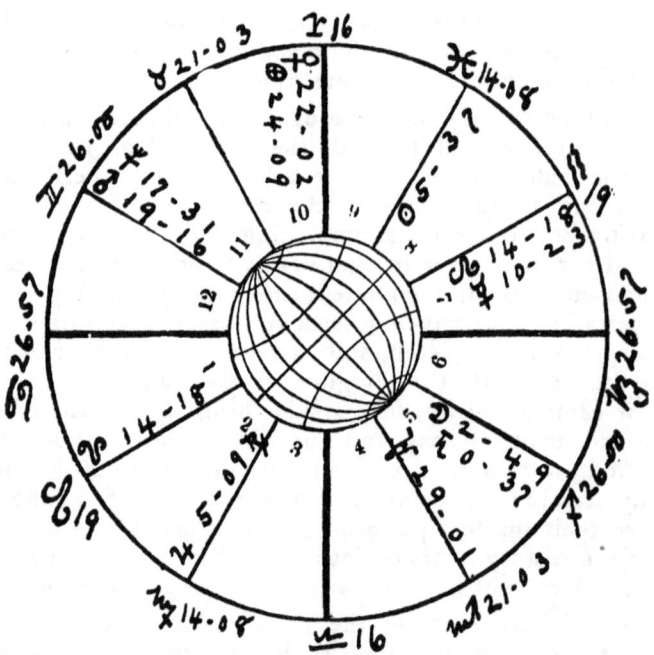

Chart of the Heavens, February 23d, 1897, at 2.45 P. M. when the Corner Stone of the School of Theosophy was laid, at San Diego, California.

The above is the chart of the heavens of the laying the first or corner stone for the school of Theosophy and on page 289 are given the Astrological rules and principles for laying the first stone of any special building.

---

* The above was written and in type several months before I saw the article in the New York Sun, referred to on page .

How to Calculate a Horoscope for Point Loma, San Diego.

662 If the student is not in regular practice in erecting charts of the heavens, for any longitude or latitude; he had better read over again very carefully "Rule to Set a Map of the Heavens," on pages 142, 143, 144, 145 and 146, before attempting to calculate the foregoing chart of the heavens, and after he has refreshed his memory, then he must get "Raphael's Ephemeris" for 1897, and look for the 23d of February of that year, and on a line with it, under the heading of "Sidereal Time," he will find 22 hours and 14 minutes; he will add the 2 hours and 45 minutes to that sum making in all 24 hours and 59 minutes. As 24 hours completes the day, he will reject the 24, and look in the table of houses, for the latitude of Point Loma, San Diego. In order to do so he will have to get a geography of the United States, which contains a map of California, and look for the latitude of Point Loma, San Diego, and he will find it is near 33 north latitude. The only table of houses that I know that is printed for every even degree of north latitude from 22 to 56 is that of Joseph G. Dalton's.

663 Then look in Dalton's table of houses for 59 minutes on top line of the 4th page, and in the last set of columns of that page, on the top line of that table, he will find 58 minutes and 57 seconds; and on the right of these figures in the top column he will find ♈ Aries 16°, which he will place on the cusp of the 10th house, and then if he draws his hand down on the left hand column, until he gets to figure 33; then carry the figure on that line until he gets to the last right hand column of the page he will find 21° and 3′ of ♉ Taurus, which he will place on the cusp of the 11th house; and on a line with the last figures he will find 26° 0′ of ♊ Gemini in the next column, which he will place on the cusp of the 12th house, and next on that line 26° and 57′ of ♋ Cancer, which he will place on the ascendant or the first house; in the next column he will find 19° of ♌ Leo, which he will place on the 2d house, and on the last column, he will find 14° 8′ of ♍ Virgo, which he will place on the cusp of 3d house; and then he will commence to copy the southern signs and the degrees and minutes on the opposite houses in the blank chart.

664 After the student has inserted the 12 signs in the blank chart, he will get his map of California again, and look for the longitude of Point Loma, and he will find it near 117°, west longitude from Greenwich, England; he will then take that 117° and multiply it by four, as there are four minutes in time, to one degree of longitude, which makes 468′; he divides that 468 by 60, the number of minutes in an hour, and it gives 7 hours and 48 minutes; therefore the longitude of Point Loma is 7 hours and 48 minutes earlier in time than London, and the student must make his calculations for the longitude of the planets and the Sun and Moon which occurs in London at 12 o'clock noon, as if they were 4 hours and 12 minutes, A. M. at Point Loma. In addition he must add the 2 hours and 45 minutes, (as the corner stone was laid at 2 hours and 45 minutes in the afternoon;) to the 7 hours and 48 minutes making 10 hours and 33 minutes. He must then calculate how far the

Sun and Moon and planets will travel in 10 hours and 33 minutes, and add that sum to the longitude of the planets and Sun and Moon given in the Ephemeris on Feb. 23d, 1897, at noon in London.

665 The easiest way to make these calculations is to see in the Ephemeris how far each planet travels in 24 hours, and divide that sum by 2 to find how far they travel in 12 hours, and add the remainder to the longitude of the planets as they are printed in the Ephemeris, and then deduct the distance that each one will travel in one hour and a half, and the student will get very close to the exact longitude of each planet.*

If the student turns to page 288 paragraph 625, he will find the "Election for laying the first stone of a building," and will there see that the old Astrologers had serious objections to the Watery triplicity particularly to Pisces and Scorpio; but Cancer is objectionable, because it is unsafe to erect a building on the water. Cancer, Scorpio or Pisces on the ascendant, or the Moon in these signs, (particularly Cancer as it is a moveable sign) is very evil for laying the first stone. The rule is to have the Moon, either in a fixed sign, or have a fixed sign on the ascendant and the Moon in good aspect to that sign. But if the student turns to the chart of the heavens for the laying of the first stone of the School of Theosophy, he will find Cancer is on the ascendant, and the Moon lady of that sign is within 2° of the conjunction of Saturn; also just leaving a conjunction of Uranus, which are two very evil afflictions to that luminary.

The old authors on Astrology all agree that a planet or the Moon leaving a conjunction, square or opposition of one or more evil planets in a horary question, laying the first stone, or in a nativity, is more unfortunate or weaker than a planet applying to an evil aspect, as they say that the Moon or the planet leaving the evil aspect is so completely saturated with the evil influence of the planet that it is leaving, that it takes it a long time to overcome that influence. They compare it to a miller whose clothes and everything about him gets so impregnated with flour, that if he leaves the mill, it takes a long time for him to get rid of it; it has so penetrated into his clothing.

In all charts of the heavens, the old Astrologers say: whether in a time of birth, or a question, or laying the first stone of a building never have the Moon afflicted. They say: It is better to have the lord of the ascendant afflicted than the Moon." The Moon is not only afflicted in the foregoing horoscope, but it is also lady of the ascendant, which causes it to be doubly afflicted. The Moon after leaving a conjunction of Uranus and Saturn is making a square of Jupiter, lord of the 9th, (house of science and religion,) and also a square of the Sun, and the Sun and Jupiter are in exact opposition. The Moon is also making an opposition of Neptune and Mars. The only good aspect the Moon makes is a sextile of Mercury, but Mercury is setting. It is a particularly evil horoscope for the laying of the first stone, as Venus, although in the midheaven, is seriously afflicted on account of being in its detriment and in square to the ascendant. The ancients say, "let the fortunate planets, Jupiter and Venus be in good aspect to each other or to the degree ascending." Jupiter could hardly be more afflicted, and has no aspect to the ascendant, and Venus is in square to the degree ascending.

---

* There is no doubt the stone was laid within a very few minutes of 2,45 P. M., as I asked a gentleman who was present at the laying of the corner stone, and he told me when he arrived at the gate of the grounds he looked at his watch, which he set by Standard or San Francisco time, and it was 25 minutes to three; and he calculated it would take 10 minutes to walk the short distance, and for Mr. Hargrove to deliver the speech which he made previous to laying the stone.

What a pity it is that people do not pay attention at the present day to these rules and principles which have been known and used to such great advantage by the ancients for thousands of years.

My father had a saying that "experience is a dear school, but fools will learn at no other." Unfortunately there are some people who will not even learn at the school of experience, and those fools are generally known by the name of "Christians."

I learn from the newspapers that the School is going to be completed, and used as a Sanitarium. The building will be unfortunate as a Sanitarium, and the patients who attend there are more likely to die than to get well, as Jupiter, lord of the 6th, (the house of sickness) is in close opposition to the Sun in the 8th, (the house of death,) and the Moon, lady of the ascendant makes a square of both. The building will not be a paying institution as a Sanitarium, as the Sun, lord of the 2d house, (the house of money) is so afflicted by the opposition of Jupiter, lord of the 6th and 9th houses, (the houses of science and sickness.)

The following appeared in the "New York Sun," Tuesday, Dec. 28th, 1897, under the head of "Theosophists all Awry."

"There is, in the words of one of the 'advanced enthusiasts of the Theosophical Society, a violent row' in the organization, manifesting itself, both here and abroad. It is said to be due to dissatisfaction with Mrs. Kittie Tingley, the head of the esoteric body here. There are people who do not wholly approve of Mrs. Tingley's high place in the society, and according to the story, their number is growing so fast that already two esoteric Presidents have resigned, and the resignation of a third is expected.

"The information received yesterday from London included a strong intimation of the intention of one of the other European Presidents to resign shortly. Complaints are made that the society in this city no longer studies Theosophy, and that it has been converted into a charitable organization, the work of which is carried on in the name of the 'International Brotherhood League.'

"Mrs. Tingley's pet project, the 'School for the Revival of the Lost Mysteries of Antiquity,' it is said, has so far fallen into desuetude that the building which was only just begun at Point Loma, near San Diego, Cal., is to be completed and turned into a Sanitarium by Dr. Loren A. Wood, formerly of Westerly, R. I., to whom it has been turned over. Dr. Wood was on the recent crusade of the Tingley Theosophists. Mrs. Annie Besant's proselyting here last spring has begun to tell. Branches of the Society in different cities have deserted the body whose esoteric head Mrs. Tingley is, and have joined themselves to that fostered by Mrs. Besant. The branch at Lynn, Mass., Mrs. Tingley's former home, has gone over to the Besant enemy."

In ancient times the people not only chose the most propitious times according to the planetary influences for "turning the sod," laying the first stone, or driving the first pile for the erection of important structures, but they actually built those structures on the principles or order of the planetary system.

For instance there is a model made of the Tower of Babylon in the National Museum, at Washington, D. C., which if the student examines he will find the walls of the first story were painted black, the color of Saturn, the second a deep orange, the color of Jupiter; the third, red, Mars's color; the fourth gold, the Sun's color; the fifth white, the color of Venus; the sixth blue, the color of Mercury; the seventh silver, the Moon's color. A picture of which the reader will find on page   .

There is a printed page pasted on the model which states that the "Tower of Babel" was originally painted these colors when first built. Not only that, but in late excavations in that country they have discovered two other structures, one underneath the other, and near where the Tower of Babel stands at the present day, each of these structures were built with seven stories, similar to the Tower of Babel. The deepest or most ancient of these buildings had been the most perfect in its architecture and construction.

There are cuneiform writings on these structures, giving certain astronomical calculations which prove beyond question, that the most ancient of these structures is over 9,000 years old, or more than 3,000 years older than the Mozaic History of the Creation of the world.

TOWER OF BABEL, OR BABYLON.

(FROM THE BIBLE—GENESIS, XI., 1-9.)

And the whole earth was of one language and of one speech. As they journeyed from the East they found a plain in the land of Shinar and dwelt there. And they said one to the other: Go to, let us make brick and burn them thoroughly, and they had brick for stone and slime they had for mortar. And they said, Go to, let us build a city, and a tower, whose top may reach to heaven, and let us make us a name, lest we be scattered abroad upon the face of the whole earth, and the Lord came down to see the city and tower the children of men builded. And the Lord said, let us go down, and there confound their language. So the Lord scattered them abroad from thence upon the face of all the earth, and they left off to build the city. Therefore is the name of it called Babel, because the Lord did there confound the language of all the earth, and from thence did the Lord scatter them abroad upon the face of all the earth.

Description of the Tower of Babel.

The drawing on the opposite page is from the model of the Tower of Babylon in the National Museum, at Washington, D. C., and copied from the New York Sunday Journal of October 17, 1897. The model was made by Mr. Palmer, and conforms to the theory of the Tower by Sir Henry Rawlinson, the great Orientalist, who gives the dimensions of the Tower as follows:

"The first was a stage or platform of crude brick raised a few feet above the level of the plain. The first story of the Tower or basement was an exact square of 272 feet each way, and 25 feet in perpendicular height; the second story was 230 feet each way, and 26 feet high; the third story was 180 feet square each way, and 26 feet high; the fourth was 146 feet square, and 15 feet high; the fifth 104 feet square, and 15 feet high; the sixth 62 feet square and the 7th, 20 feet square, and both were 15 feet high.

"Concerning the origin of the "Tower of Babel," little is known save from the Bible. The historian Herodotus mentions it, and there are also certain cuneiform inscriptions on some of the bricks which give the name of Nebuchadnezzar as the person who finished the building of the Temple. These inscriptions state that it was commenced by a former king, but that king never finished it. It was said to have been built in honor of the Babylonian god, called Nebo or Nabu. There were seven stories of this temple; each story was painted a particular color, each color being governed by one of the seven planets. The lowest story was painted black, the color of Saturn; the next story above was painted a deep orange, the color of Jupiter; the next red, the color of Mars; next the Sun, a golden color; next white, Venus' color; next Mercury's color, blue; and the top story the Moon's color, a silvery or kind of glistening color."—*New York Journal.*

The above colors are those which are said to be ruled by the planets at the present day in the books of "Modern Astrology." The Tower gives the color of Venus as white, but in books of Modern Astrology the color given is light blue or light sky color; all the other colors correspond or nearly so. In Raphæl's Horary Astrology, on page 53, the colors there given as ruled by the planets, are as follows: That of Saturn rules black; that of Jupiter green spotted or ash color; Mars red or scarlet; Sun saffron or yellow; Venus lightish blue; Mercury gray or buff-color; Moon white or cream, but the Moon also governs silvery or glistening color; these colors of the planets vary somewhat when they are in different signs of the Zodiac, and it depends on what sign the planet is in in regard to the various shades, and it also depends on what house it is in, as that sometimes varies the shade or color that the planets rule.

There is no doubt that all of these stories dedicated to their respective planets, were commenced when these planets were in the most fortunate positions in the Zodiac, and in good aspects to other planets, especially to what are called the two fortunate planets, Jupiter and Venus.

The Tower of Babel may have been used as a fortification against the enemies of the Babylonians, as the extra Tower built on the top of the seven stories, which is shown in the small cut underneath the large picture, and which was afterwards added to the top of the original Tower by some Babylonian king whose name is not mentioned; this appears to be indicated by the top Tower, and it also might have been used as a lookout for watching the approach of enemies of the Babylonians.

Antiquity of Astrology Proved by the Tower of Babel.

The ruins of the ancient "Tower of Babel" prove unquestionably that Astronomy and Astrology were well understood and practised over 9,000 years ago, and that the people conducted their business and controlled the various events of life by the principles and rules of these sciences. It is also stated that the bricks that the Tower of Babel was built with, even at this day, are in a good state of preservation, or at least people who have been to Babylon and examined them make this statement, and it is more than 4,000 years since the latter building was finished by Nebuchadnezzar. Were bricks that buildings are now made of exposed to the action of the weather, either in England or the United States, only for a few hundred years, they would crumble to dust.

Continued from page 174.

I wish the reader to understand that I have no particular spite against the editor of the New York Times, as I honestly believe that he is not any more prejudiced against Astrology than most editors in New York, only he happened to lay himself open to criticism at the present time, which has caused me to give more attention to him than to other editors.

Had Mrs. Maud S. sent her daughter's time of birth to an editor of almost any other newspaper in the United States, or for that matter to any newspaper in Europe, they would have given her a similar answer to the one she received from the "New York Times," * and no matter how much these editors might differ in politics, or on the labor or money question, they would all agree that calculating horoscopes was a "debasing superstition" and whould have expatiated on the "harmful influence" on children's minds" of such calculations. If she had sent her daughter's time of birth to all the Christian Ministers in Europe and America, no matter how much they might quarrel or disagree on religious doctrines, or of the meaning of any passage of the Old or New Testament, they would have been unanimous in saying that calculating horoscopes was a debasing superstition, and in denouncing the Astrologer as an impostor or a fraud, and in consigning him to everlasting torment. It would have been the same if she had sent the time of birth to any lawyer, or judge on the bench in any Christian country of the world, no matter how much they might differ on law points, quarrel and call each other hard names, they would all have been of one opinion on the merits, or rather the demerits of Astrology; and no matter how many times the judges reversed each other's decisions on other matters they would have all decided alike when it came to their judgment on Astrology.

I will even go further and state that if Mrs.' Maud S. had sent her daughter's time of birth to the doctors of the United States, Canada or Europe, they would all, with very few exceptions, (and those exceptions are doctors who are now using Astrology in the practice of medicine,) if they had answered her letter have agreed that Astrology was a "de-basing superstition," no matter how much they quarrel among themselves, and call each other quacks, frauds and impostors on account of their not agreeing on any particular school of "pathy." Yet, if Mrs. Maud S.'s daughter had been taken sick, and she called in twenty or thirty of those same doctors, each and every one of them would have diagnosed the case differently, and each would contend that she had a different disease or complaint, and no two of them would have agreed in the treatment of any one symptom, and each would have put her under different, or almost opposite treatment, and diet, and it would have been the same if those twenty doctors had all graduated from the same college, and had been taught by the same professors, and yet we talk about the science of medicine.

But if she had sent her child's time and place of birth to twenty different Astrologers, they would have all agreed, or come very near agreeing in regard to the child's diseases or complaints in the different periods of her life, and the parts of the body which would be affected at those times, thirty or forty years before these periods of sickness would take place.

---

* Although when the Editor of the New York Times, was writing the criticisms on Astrology, the New York Sunday News was publishing three or four columns of horoscopes each Sunday; the Pittsburg (Pa.) Dispatch from twelve to fourteen columns each week; the Pittsburg Leader three; columns; the Cincinnati Inquirer about six columns; the Louisville Courier Journal three columns; the Illustrated American was publishing two pages; the Manchester Mirror (N. H.) was publishing three columns; the Harrisburg (Pa.,) Telegraph one column per week. Besides there were a number of other papers publishing horoscopes, during 1893, 1894, 1895 and 1896.

If Mrs. Maud S. had sent the time of birth to all the Astrologers in the world, and those Astrologers had studied the science so as to be proficient, and had sufficient practice in reading nativities, these horoscopes of the girl would have agreed in almost every particular; the same as if a thousand painters had painted the likeness of the girl, or a thousand photographers had taken her picture with their cameras, those pictures would have agreed with each other; one might have given a darker or a lighter shade to some particular part, or made some particular feature come out a little more prominent in one picture than in another, but any number of persons who had looked at the whole of them and had known the girl, would have said each was a true picture. Had Mrs. Maud S. sent her daughter's time of birth, and named the place where she was born, also the race, to a thousand Astrologers, (if that number could be found) each and every one would have drawn or calculated exactly, the same chart or map of the heavens; or if she had the map of the heavens calculated by some Astrologer and then sent a copy of the same map to the nine hundred and ninety-nine, and not have stated when or where she was born, those thousand Astrologers would each give the same reading, almost word for word. Some of them might dwelt a little more on one particular part of her personal description or on some particular feature of her mental or moral character, or the special diseases she would be most liable to, and they might have varied slightly in regard to her future husband, her married life, her children, domestic happiness, or unhappiness, business, etc. But any person who was acquainted with the girl, after they read her horoscope, would all say, that this is the horoscope of Mrs. Maud S.'s daughter, and not the horoscope of any other person, unless that person was born at or near the same time, and in or very near the same place, and in that case the only difference would be in the parentage, heredity, environment, surroundings or training, and education.

We cannot overcome or change the planetary influence at the time of birth. To give an illustration, when the position of the planets in horoscopes are evil or unfortunate for any particular mental quality, say music, no amount of education or training in music will ever make a musician of that person. It is the same when the planets are evil in regard to any other faculty or quality of the mind or body. You might as well attempt to teach a person to see, who is born blind, or to hear, who is born deaf.

Therefore the reader will at once see the great advantage the study of Astrology will be to the whole human family, and especially to the young of both sexes. Three fourths of the rising generation are put to trades, occupations and professions for which they are altogether unfit, and in which it is impossible for them ever to make a success.

Most of the misery, poverty and degradation is the result of these mistakes, and they could be avoided by having the child's horoscope calculated by a competent Astrologer, and by following his advice and instructions.

To give an illustration and proof that all Astrologers agree in the principles and practice of Astrology, I copy the following from an article in the "Penny Magazine," New York, for May, 1897, called "READING THE STARS," by "Azrael," a former pupil of mine, and who was formerly one of the editors of the *New York Herald*. He was also at one time, on the *Evening Telegram*. On page 20, he says: "Given the birth hour, and the place of birth of any individual anywhere, a qualified Astrologer will, without peradventure, delineate his or her nature and characteristics and the leading events of his or her life without important error. And if the same data be presented to different Astrologers in New York, London, Calcutta or Melbourne, every one of these will give the same facts exactly, only clothed in different language. Just as any such Astrologer will take a horoscope, or chart of the heavens already cast, knowing nothing but the sex and race of the person, and will read off therefrom the nature, ability, propensities intellectual qualifications and major events of the life, from the relative positions and configuration of the planets, as though it were an open page in a known language."*

"In a brief and superficial article little more can be said. But this I say; that Astrology, as a science and an art, is true; that it can do what it promises; that it will submit to any conceivable test; that it is not contrary to free will, nor to true religion, nor to exact science; that it is the most fascinating of studies, and absolutely the most valuable and useful to mankind of all the arts."

I have given the above as an example of the experience of an Astrologer who has only had a few years practice in this fascinating science. If "Azrael" lives, his interest in Astrology will increase as he grows older.

Astrology is the only science or knowledge in which the opinions of those who are the most ignorant on the subject are accepted. In all other sciences or professions the opinion of those who have had the most experience and practice carry the most weight, and is generally the most convincing to all sensible persons. Even in the practice of medicine, a science in which there are so many different systems or "pathies," and which changes almost as often, as the fashion in ladies' bonnets and dresses, those physicians who have the most practice, have the most attention paid to them, and can charge the highest fees. An uncle of mine, Dr. Mark Broughton, at a trial in the York Assizes, in England, was the means of saving a young woman from being executed, by being able to swear that he had more than forty times the number of accouchements than the doctor on the opposing side. That evidence decided the jury in bringing in a verdict of not guilty. But had the jury known that my uncle made use of the science of Astrology in his every day practice of medicine, it is more than probable the opposing lawyer would have taken exceptions to his evidence, and asked the judge to rule out his testimony.

It must appear to the reader, that if all doctors had to agree to study Astrology, instead of agreeing in condemning it without any knowledge or

---

* As "Asreal" says given the time and place of birth, the sect and race of the individual to any number of Astrologers, they will all read the horoscope nearly alike, only clothing it in slightly different language. Any number of persons who study the science of Astrology will express themselves in a similar manner as "Azrael." This cannot be said of any other of the learned professions.

About two years ago a reporter of "New York Press," went around to a number of clairvoyants, fortune-tellers, card-cutters, mind-readers, spiritualists, palmists, phrenologists mesmerists, etc., (all of which he called "Astrologers,") in New York City, and that paper devoted nearly a whole page to the interviews, and because the professors of these various "isms" did not all agree exactly in their statements, the "Press" insisted they should all be arrested and sent to States Prison. Had the same reporter gone to all the different trades in New York, such as shoe-makers, hatters, tailors, shirt makers, underwear and stocking makers, and paid each $5.00, and because they did not all make him a hat, a pair of shoes or a shirt etc., would the reporter claim all the followers of these trades were impostors, and declare that they shou'd be sent to States Prison. There is more difference between the various systems of what is called fortune tellers than there is in the above named different trades.

The editor of the "Press" knows that there are numbers of people who have gone around to different doctors, and all of the same school, (Alopathy,) and yet these doctors give the patient a different disease, and they all prescribe different and opposite treatment and medicine, and yet they are all taught in the same schools and have the same text books to go by. This has been tried over and over again by "Nellie Bly" and numbers of others.

What a wonderfully happy family we have of the professors of ths Christian religion and yet they all have the Bible for a text-book, and Christ for their guide, and constantly consign each other to eternal torment, and would have gone on burning one another alive at the stake even to the present day, if it was not for the infidels stopping them. The lawyers, judges and legislators are no better, and the politicians are the worst of all.

evidence on the subject, it would produce more harmony among them, and there would be fewer systems of the practice of medicine, and the number of patients who come to untimely deaths would rapidly decrease.

Some years ago there came into existence several new games, which attracted public attention, and for a time they were the *fad* for almost everybody. One was the "Fifteen puzzle," another the "Cows in the clover," and the third was putting the "Pigs in the Pen." The latter so absorbed the public mind, that even a majority of the Senators, at Washington, if we can believe the daily newspapers, spent most of their time in the Committee rooms in trying to solve this puzzle, instead of attending to their duties for which they were receiving large salaries.

I know people who spent months trying to solve the "fifteen puzzle," and could not do it; others tried to put the "Pigs in the Pen" in as few seconds as possible. If they learned to solve the "Fifteen puzzle" every time, what good would it have done them, or would it have been any advantage to them. Yet I am not aware that there was a single newspaper, or minister of the gospel, or lawyer, judge or legislator, that ever uttered a single word against people spending their time in such useless occupations, or about such studies being a "debasing superstition," or about the "mournful incompletensss of modern civilization." Yet it will not take any more study, or as much time to become a fair Astrologer as it did to solve the "Fifteen puzzle." When the student has studied Astrology, he has learned something that will be of every day use to himself, and to his friends or acquaintances, as long as he lives, and will do more to enlarge and develop his mental faculties, than any other study he could be engaged in, and it will be the means of bringing more happiness, and avoiding more misery than anything else, to say nothing of the profit or money it may bring them, notwithstanding all the abuse and malicious slander that the editors of the *New York Times*, and other newspapers may heap upon it in addition to the slanders that nearly all Christian Ministers of the Gospel have piled on it and its professors, and the laws which the Legislatures in Christian countries have enacted to crush it, its advocates and its practitioners.

Their object is to keep the people in ignorance but my desire is that the reader apply himself with all diligence, in learning to erect a chart of the heavens for any geographical latitude and longitude, and for any year, month, day of the month, and hour and minute of the day, and learn to read it like reading a book. It is to enable the student to calculate charts of the heavens, and to read them, that I have published the "*Elements of Astrology*." and to enable him to prove for himself, by his own horoscope and those of his friends, the truth or falsity of the science, and not let the ministers of the Gospel, newspaper editors, lawyers, doctors, judges or encyclopædias form his opinions for him; but learn to judge on all these matters for himself; he no doubt then will find that all these men know less about the various religions, sciences, politics and laws that they are preaching, writing, and talking about, and in which they differ so widely than they do about Astrology, which they are so unanimous in condemning. I will conclude this section in the words and advice of Longfellow:

"In the world's broad field of battle,
  In the bivouac of life
Be not like dumb driven cattle,
  Be an hero in the strife.

The lives of great men all remind us
  That we can make our live's sublime,
And departing leave behind us
  Foot-prints on the sands of time.

Foot-prints that perhaps another
  Sailing o'er life's solemn main,
A forlorn, shipwrecked brother,
  Seeing shall take heart again.

Let us then be up and doing,
  With a heart for any *fate*,
Still achieving, still pursuing,
  Learn to labor, and to wait."

READ AND REFLECT.

Of all sciences which have at any time engaged the attention of the world, there is not one of which the real or assumed principles are less generally known, in the present age, than those of Astrology. Among a thousand persons who now treat the mention of this ancient science with supercilious ridicule, there is scarcely one who knows distinctly what it is he laughs at. Such contented ignorance, in persons, too, sufficiently informed in other respects is the more extraordinary, since Astrology has sustained a most conspicuous part throughout the history of the world, even until comparatively recent days. In the East, where it first arose, at a period of very remote antiquity, it still, even now, holds sway. In Europe, and in every part of the world where learning had "impressed the human soil," Astrology reigned supreme until the middle of the 17th century. It entered into the councils of princes it guided the policy of nations; it ruled the daily actions of individuals, and physicians who were not well versed in this science, were not deemed competent to practice their profession. All this is attested by the records of every nation which has a history.

—:o:—

ASTRO-MEDICAL BOTANY,

OR THE

Ancient Botanic Practice of Medicine Revived

BY

Dr. L. D. BROUGHTON, 68 So. Washington Square, N. Y.

Graduate of the Eclectic Medical College,

OF THE STATE OF PENNSYLVANIA,

AND

Editor of "The Eclectic Medical Record," of the State of N. J.

Invalids whose afflictions have been pronounced incurable by the old school practice, have been perfectly restored to HEALTH by Herbs under planetary influence. The Art has been supposed to be lost, but its restoration is certain, since minerals and other unnatural remedies have sent multitudes to untimely graves. *Ignorance*, which always goes hand-in-hand with blind, heaven-defying *prejudice*, may stand aloof. Planetary influence over vegetation has Bible authority, the laws of Nature, and the practice of the greatest physicians the world ever knew; such as *Hippocrates, Galen, Culpepper, &c., &c.* Astrology and Medicine were ever connected by the master minds of honest philosophy and medicine in by-gone days.

The Opinions of Eminent Ancient Physicians

Hippocrates, the father of medicine, "declares that the man who did not well understand *Astrology*, was rather deserving to be called a *fool* than a physician."* *Galen* "declared Anatomy to be the right eye of physic and *Astrology* its left; for such is the *influence* of the *sun*, *moon* and *stars*, especially the *planets* upon the human body, or terrestrial bodies." *Culpepper*, in his *British Herbal*, says: "that those who study *Astrology*, are the only men who are fit to study physics, *physic* without *astrology*, being like a lamp without *oil*." In short it is impossible for any physician to foretell the various changes of diseases, the "crisis," or "climactric periods," etc., etc., without a knowledge of Astrology. When every child is born, the *germs* of the various or different diseases, it will suffer from through life, and the parts of the body which will be affected, are impressed on it by the heavenly bodies, and can be foretold or pointed out by the *Astrologer*. Also the different *moles*, *marks*, or *scars*, which any person may have in any part of their body. And the physician who undertakes to treat a difficult case of sickness without any knowledge Astrology, is equally as criminal as the captain who should attempt to guide a vessel across the Atlantic without a knowledge of Astronomy or Navigation. And the time will come when this will be the general opinion formed by the public of physicians who are ignorant of Astrology.

The following Questions may be correctly ascertained by the science of Astrology, in conjunction with Astro-Medical Botany:—If the sick party will recover or die of the present sickness; if recover, the time they will begin to amend; what part of the body is afflicted or diseased; what has been the cause of the sickness; when the sick person has had any particular changes, either favorable or the reverse, also what kind of *Treatment* and *Medicine* would be best adapted for the sick person. All these points can be definitely ascertained by the above named Sciences; either by personal application, or by letter from the sick person, stating the correct time and sex and place of birth, and without any other question being asked of the sick party.

N. B. All forms of Nervous and Chronic Diseases successfully treated by Electricity, Nature's true remedial agent.

Ladies suffering from Prolapsus Uteri, Leucorrhœa and other Uterine complaints, immediately relieved and speedily cured.

A lady in attendance to wait upon ladies, if the patient desires it.

Rheumatism, Piles, Paralysis, Epilipsy, Obstructions, Dyspepsia, Pleurisy, Opthalmia, Aphonia, Amaurosis, etc. etc., speedily yield to this method of treatment when skillfully administered. Cases invited that have been pronounced incurable by the regular practice

---

*HIPPOCRATES further says, "It is the best thing, in my opinion, for a physician to apply himself diligently to the art of FOREKNOWLEDGE, (or Astrology); for he who is master of this art, and shows himself such among his patients, with respect to what is present, past or future, declaring at the same time wherein the patient has been wanting, will give such proofs of a superior knowledge in what relates to the sick that the generality of men will commit themselves to that physician without any manner of diffidence · add to this, the cure will be best performed by one who knows beforehand what will happen in diseases. It is, indeed, impossible to recover every sick person, or else this would be better than the foreknowledge of what is to happen; and, therefore, since mankind die, some -of the vehemence of the d sease—before the physician is called, others immediately after; some living one day, others a little longer, before the physician has time to set himself by his art against the particular disease,—knowing, therefore, the nature of such diseases, how far they exceed the power of the body, or how far there may be anything divine in them, he ought also to study THE ART OF FOREKNOWING THEM, for by this means he will be justly admired and esteemed a good physician ; add to this, that, as to those who are to recover he will be better able to preserve them in a proper manner, as his intention or advice in every step is founded upon a long view beforehand ; and, whether the patient lives or dies, his foreknowing and declaring himself, shall exempt him from all blame." This is a splendid piece for those who condemn Astrology to consider; but Astrology is out of fashion, and unpopular, so physicians will blunder and kill as many patients as they cure, and the Lord will be credited for taking the patient out of this wicked world, when, in reality, it is the physician who has murdered the patient on account of his ignorance of Astrology, or foreknowledge.

P. S. The Doctor will be most happy to give any applicant all the desired information concerning every known disease, at his office,

68 South Washington Square, New York.

ASTROLOGY AND MEDICINE.—The Prognosis of Disease.

The "London Medical Press and Circular," November 7, 1877, in a leading article upon the "Prognosis of Disease," said:—

"Remarkable is the fact that the study of prognostics should be so neglected at the present day, when we reflect how much this department of medical science was cultivated at a very early period in the history of medicine. Some have gone so far as to say that the science of prognosis has advanced little since the time of Hippocrates; and certainly, if we compare its progress with that which has been made in diagnosis, in pathology, and in therapeutics, we must admit that it has been comparatively at a standstill. For one work that is written on prognosis, there are a thousand on the subjects just mentioned. We are as well acquainted as most people with the medical publications of the last half-century, and yet, so meagre is our literature, that we cannot call to mind a single work that has been entirely devoted to the consideration of a department of medicine which is of the first importance, and the state of which is the best test that can be afforded of the general progress of the healing art. We need scarcely remark that the prognosis of disease is one of the chief goals to which all our other medical studies should eventually lead, and the chief criterion by which the public estimate the scientific value of medicine, and the skill and ability of the practitioner. A correct prognosis involves a correct diagnosis, a correct pathology, a correct estimate of the value of the therapeutic agents at our disposal, and a due consideration of the constitution of the patient, his mode of life, his surroundings, &c. The greater perfection of medicine as an exact science would be unattainable without a much more perfect knowledge of prognosis than we now possess, and in this respect prognosis stands on a higher footing than even treatment, or the combined knowledge of anatomy, pathology, diagnosis, therapeutics and chemistry.*

"One case of typhoid fever, for example, terminates unfavorably, another to all appearances running in a very similar course ends in recovery. In the former case the conditions which regulated the progress and termination of the disease, were such that it was a physical impossibility for recovery to have taken place, while in the other case it was likewise, and for the same reason, a physical impossibility for death to have taken place. One of the difficulties therefore, we have to overcome is that of discerning what these conditions are."

Thus we see the helplessness of the medical profession in regard to prognostics. The wisdom of Hippocrates and Galen is set at naught in this matter, and the fact is *concealed* that they taught that Astrology must be studied by physicians, before they can be safely trusted to arrive at a correct prognosis, and to employ

---

*From "New York Herald" of November 27, 1878.

"GREAT DISCOVERY IN CHEMISTRY.—At the last sitting of the French Academy of Sciences, a very remarkable communication was read from Mr. Norman Lockyer, which, if correct, will entirely overthrow all the theories of Chemistry at present accepted. In a series of investigations extending over some years, into the nature of the spectra of the sun and other heavenly bodies, and of different simple bodies at various degrees of temperature, Mr. Lockyer has arrived at the conviction that all the elementary bodies recognized by chemists are neither more nor less than hydrogen at various degrees of condensation. According to Mr. Lockyer, the stars which are the hottest, contain either pure hydrogen or the most elementary substances. The sun consists of a mixture of various elements, while the colder heavenly bodies, such as Saturn, Jupiter and Mars, show the most complex compounds. The startling nature of the announcement excited great astonishment, as it is utterly opposed to the scientific notions of the chemistry of the present day, and very naturally makes us think that the ancient Astrologers were not after all such visionaries as they have generally been considered."

Mr. Edison has just electrified the world with his marvellous invention of bottling sounds with his Telephone, and before we get over the astonishment, here steps forward Professor Hughes, who announces the discovery of the Microphone, which is the offspring of the Telephone, and which has the power of magnifying the sound of a fly's footsteps until it seems like the tramp of a race-horse. We see therefore that "the music of the spheres" may not be an astronomical myth after all. Who knows but that by the aid of a sufficiently sensitive Microphone, the minute beatings of the heart, the flowing of the blood through the smallest blood vessels, the expansion of the lung tissue, and even those subtle transitions of brain or nerve substance, each producing, in health, its own peculiar audible sound or harmonious rythms, and in disease, each member or organ of the body emitting its own peculiar discordant vibration—I say, who knows but by this valuable discovery of the Microphone, and by going back to the only true system of medicine, or the ancient Astrological practice of Hippocrates and Galen, that more progress will be made in a few years in diagnosis and prognosis of diseases, than has been made in the last two thousand years.

the appropriate remedies in the treatment of the cases submitted to their care. Dr. Watson, of London, who wrote a work on " The Medical Profession in Ancient Times," (1856, page 169), testified to the fact that Galen advocated the Hippocratic doctrine of critical days, and "attempts to support it on grounds purely theoretical, and drawn from the periodical changes in nature, or *the influence of the stars*." It is also concealed, but it is nevertheless true, that Galen admonished his contemporaries "not to trust themselves to that physician (or rather pretender) who is not skilled in Astrology."

The chief (astrological) method of forming a judgement of the violence and magnitude of a disease, or whether it is curable or fatal, is by inspection of the scheme of the heavens, erected for the moment of *birth* of the patient, if it can be procured, for sickness very seldom happens but through some malignant directions of the luminaries, or of the ascendant to the body or aspects of the malefic planets (Mars, Saturn, and Uranus).

We know that the moment of birth is a consideration above all others, but if the figure of birth cannot be had, or if it be not exact, and rectified by events, then in this case the figure for the decumbiture, or the time when the patient is first taken sick, must be procured and used in its stead.

If physicians of this day were to study Astrology in connection with medicine, as Hippocrates, the father of medicine, taught and practiced, it would enable them to determine why in one case " it was a physical impossibility for recovery to have taken place, while in the other case it was likewise a physical impossibility for death to have taken place." The occurrence of the crisis, and the nature of the prognosis can be foretold with scientific precision, by watching the motion of the moon, and her configuration with the sun and planets in the sick person's nativity, or, if that cannot be obtained, a map of the heavens taken for the time the patient is first taken sick, or the time he first sees his physician.

The following are some of the aphorisms of Cardan relating to medical astrology :

'In sickness, when the Moon applies to a planet contrary to the nature of the distemper, especially if it be a fortune, the disease will be changed for the better.

"When the Moon at the decumbiture, or first falling sick, shall be under the beams of the Sun, or with Saturn, Mars [or Uranus,] if the party be old, even her conjunction with Jupiter, Venus, or Mercury, is not without peril.

"Saturn causes *long* diseases ; Mercury, varying ones ; the Moon, such as return after a time, as vertigoes, epilepsy, etc.; Jupiter and the Sun give *short* diseases ; but Mars, the acutest of all.

"When the Moon is in a fixed sign, physic works the less ; and if in Aries, Taurus or Capricorn, will be apt to prove nauseous to the patient.

"In purging, it is well that both the Moon and the lord of the ascendant be descending and under the Earth ; in vomiting that they ascend.

"When at the beginning of a disease the luminaries are both with the infortunes, or in opposition to them, the sick will hardly escape.

"With respect to *fevers*. When the Sun is afflicted in Leo, mischievous fevers are threatened. It will be a *fatal* time to suffer *amputation,* or lose any member, when the Moon is under the Sun's beams and opposed by Mars.

"When you think to do good to your eyes, let the Moon be fortunate, increasing in light, and by no means in a sign of earthly triplicity."

"A physician is nature's helper, or at least he ought to be. Whosoever would help nature, must of necessity be well acquainted with her laws. A little communication or understanding of her laws will instruct him in the way and manner the Almighty governs the world. Wisdom instructs her children in the knowledge of time, for there is an appointed time for everything under the sun. If, then, when a disease seems extremely dangerous, you would make an essay to relieve languishing nature, do it at the time when the Moon passes by the body or good aspect of Jupiter or Venus ; then is the patient in a condition to receive help. You can sooner lift up a living man with one finger than a dead man with both hands ; a bird, whilst it has wings can fly, but cut off the wings, and hang a couple of stones on its legs, and it cannot. Even so the good aspects of the Moon to Jupiter and Venus are like wings to conduct the man from sickness to health. The bodies and aspects of Saturn and Mars to the Moon are like stones to weigh him to the grave.

'The aspects of the Moon to the planets are always to be noted, for they will produce something, either favorable or unfavorable to the sick; but upon critical and judicial days the influence of the Moon's aspects to the planets or the Sun are much more marked, for you will find this a certain truth, even as certain as the existence of the Sun, that when the Moon passes by the body of Jupiter or Venus, or their aspects, especially their good ones, if they be not lords of death, she remits the most desperate symptoms in sickness, and gives the sick some ease; as also the Moon to the bodies, or any evil aspect of Saturn or Mars, exasperates a disease, and dispels the most hopeful symptoms.

For the Cure of any Disease take these Rules.

"First determine what the disease is.

"Second, consider what is the author or cause of it; and that you may know if you notice or consider what planet governs that disease.

"Consider whether it be caused by the sympathy or antipathy of the planet; and that you may know this (which is the whole key of physic), consider first whether the planet afflicting governs the part afflicted; and if he has any dominion in that part of the body he causes it by sympathy. One example will clear all:—Suppose the disease is in the bones, spleen, etc., if Saturn be the cause of it, it is by sympathy, because he governs those parts; and so of the other planets.

"If the disease be caused by antipathy, consider what part of the body any planet afflicts, either by his presence or aspects; and then, secondly, consider what planet governs that part. If the planet afflicting be an enemy to that planet governing that part, then the disease is caused by antipathy. As is the disease so is the cure.

"If by antipathy, then apply those medicines proper to the place affected and governed by the afflicting planet; then the cure is by antipathy. Suppose Saturn afflicts some part the Moon governs, here the disease is cured by antipathy, because Saturn is an enemy to the Moon; to cure which, apply herbs, roots, etc., to the part affected and governed by the Moon, because they are antipathetical to the disease caused by Saturn.

"If the disease is caused by his sympathy, then must you apply medicine proper to the parts affected, or disease affecting and governing by that planet afflicting; here is cure by sympathy; here the planet that kills or strikes is repelled, or is beat with his own weapons.

"One thing more let me tell you, and I will tell you but the truth. The old astrologers say if Saturn afflicts, Jupiter helps more than Venus; but if Mars afflicts, Venus helps more than Jupiter. Let them say so still; but make use of that fortune which is strongest. A rich friend may relieve your wants, a poor friend cannot—he may wish you well, but cannot help you. But suppose you dare not wait until the Moon comes to the good aspect of Jupiter and Venus, administer your medicine when she is in the place where one of them was at the decumbiture. If you dare not wait until that time neither, for delay is dangerous in acute diseases, be sure you place one of those two in the ascendant when you administer the medicine.

"The place and state of the planet from which the Moon is separated at the decumbiture, and the condition of the planet also, is to be heeded.

"If you please to observe the state of that same planet, by it you may know the state of the sick, and what the cause of the sickness is.

"When you have done so, it is your wisest way to consider to what planet the Moon applies; and then do but view what sign that planet is in, what his conditions be, whether he is benevolent or malevolent, whether he is masculine or feminine, diurnal or nocturnal, hot, dry, cold, or moist, what part of the body he governs, and what disease he signifies.

"Consider whether the planet the Moon applies to be in an angle, in a succeedent, or in a cadent house; and when you have done so, do but consider what the house he is in signifies, and what members of the body he governs; and then take but a little notice whether the planet joys in the house or not. That you may not be mistaken therein, I will inform you in what house every planet takes his delight, as being suspicious, even amongst astrologers, more are ignorant of it than know it.

1. The Sun delights in the 4th, 9th and 11th houses.
2. The Moon rejoices in the 3d and 7th houses.
3. Saturn rejoices in the ascendant, 8th and 12th houses.
4. Jupiter rejoices in the 2d, 9th and 11th.
5. Mars rejoices in the 3d, 5th and 10th.
6. Venus rejoices in the 5th and 12th.
7. Mercury rejoices in the ascendant and 6th.

"Consider whether the planet the Moon applies to be direct or retrograde, swift or slow in motion, oriental, occidental, or combust; whether fortunated or unfortunated by other planets.

"When you have done so, it is your wisest way to consider whether the afflicting planet be in its own house or exaltation, or other essential dignities, whether he be in planet's of good terms or evil; for if a good planet has got an ill planet in his term he will order him. In one word, consider whether the threatening planet has power to execute his will or not.

"First, take notice that the significators of diseases are to be taken under these two denominations—1, General, or more principal; 2, Particular, or less principal. The general or more principal are these—The Sun, the Moon and the ascendant. Of these, the Sun is principally to be looked to in chronic diseases, the Moon in acute.

"Significators particular, or less principal, are these—
1st. The lord of the ascendant.
2d. The 6th house.
3d. The lord of the 6th house.
4th. The planet in the ascendant or 6th house.
5th. Saturn and Mars, for they naturally hurt the body, whatever the matter or disease is.

"The 6th house and its lord, and the planets in it, if there be any there, best describe the nature of the disease usually, nay always, if they afflict either of the luminaries, or the lord of the ascendant.

"Consider what configurations the lord of the ascendant, the 6th and 8th houses, have one with another; and amongst the rest, do not forget the lords of the 7th and 12th houses, and I will give you my reason why.—The 7th, because he opposes the ascendant, he assaults life openly; and the 6th, 8th, and 12th houses have no affinity at all with the ascendant, but signify the loss of life.

"Partile aspects are far more strong and prevalent than platic.

"You must always consider that the 6th and its lord signifies the sickness; the 7th, the physician; the 8th, death; the 10th, the medicine; and the 4th, the end of the disease."

Hippocrates (and be it remembered that he and his followers for centuries were heathens) held that life could be prolonged just so long as the vital forces were capable of resisting disease or natural decay, and no longer, and that so long as the "hyleg" (giver of life) remained strong, so long the person would live, medicine or no medicine. They maintained that while the "giver of life" is strong and unafflicted, death would be a physical impossibility, pills and drugs to the contrary notwithstanding.

He also taught (vol. i. p. 360): "The physician must be able to tell the antecedents, know the past, and foretell the future. Must meditate these things, and have two special objects in view, with regard to disease, namely: to do good or to do no harm. The art consists in three things—the 'disease' (its nature), the 'patient' (his constitutional maladies and natural ability to resist disease), and the 'physician.' The physician is the *servant* of the art, and the patient (not the medicine administered, chiefly,) *must combat the disease along with the physician.*

Has Hippocrates' doctrines and teachings been "exploded long ago"? Modern medical works speak of him as the "father of medicine."

In his day it was the custom of the physician to erect a map of the heavens of the birth of the patient, to determine what the patient's *constitutional* diseases were likely to be,—what portions of the system were indicated as being weak by the position of the planets at *birth*,—each zodiacal sign governing certain portions of the body, as Aries, the head; Taurus, the throat; Cancer, the chest; Libra, the kidneys, etc.

Another map of the heavens was erected for the date of the beginning of the disease, to ascertain what planets are transiting through the patient's ascendant (house of life—the sign ascending in the east at birth) or over the *places* of the Sun, Moon or other planets at birth, to ascertain the *nature* of the disease, and the *parts* of the body where the disease was *located* at that *time*.

For example: the cold, phlegmatic Moon located at birth in the sign Cancer, (the breast) being transited by the *cold* Saturn, would be likely, in a *weak* constitution to produce a cough, or some other chest disease, produced by the concentration of too much *cold* in the breast at *this time*. Mars transiting the same place instead of Saturn, if afflicted, might produce measles, inflammation of the lungs, or fever, or some hot disease of his nature in the sign Cancer. In a *strong* and *healthy* constitution, these transits are but seldom serious, and sometimes are but hardly noticeable until the person is advanced in life.

Physical harmony and perfect development in all particulars, comes of *planetary harmony* at the time of birth, and from harmony, inharmonious results cannot come.

When people are ignorant of those planetary laws governing our nature, the mistakes and wrong conclusions they often arrive at are innumerable; especially are those (sometimes fatal) mistakes liable to occur in calling in or changing a physician, or in prescribing medicine for a very sick patient. For instance, a medicine is prescribed, or a physician is called to attend a patient at the first stages of a disease, (when a transit is just commencing and not yet complete), and the patient grows worse on his hands, or while taking that medicine, the physician is dismissed for supposed incompetency, or the medicine is changed because it is imagined to be making the patient worse. Just at the time when, astrologically speaking, the planets transiting have reached a degree of longitude occupied by the Moon at birth, another physician is called, or another medicine is tried (just as the transiting planet is passing off the place transited), and the patient at once begins to improve (the planetary *cause* now passing off), the last physician, or the last medicine is accredited with the cure, by both the patient and his friends.

Not so, says the astrologer, for the first physician may be far the better man, more prudent, painstaking and philanthropic; or the first medicine might have been much better for the patient and the disease, but unfortunately for the physician, or the medicine he was then using, the physician by being dismissed, or the medicine by being changed a little too soon to reap the benefit of the planetary *separation*, which benefit accrues to the latter, unmerited.

There are times, or rather certain positions of the planets, when to change the physician or medicine, or to perform a common surgical operation is certain death to the patient.

By astrology only are these phenomena elucidated and logically explained. Without astrology man treads, as it were, in the dim twilight of ignorance, or as Culpepper says, "medicine without astrology, is like a lamp without oil." Man's constitution is surrounded by and interwoven with subtle laws, which cannot be violated with impunity, or without him suffering the consequences.

It is known to all who have studied their influences, that the numerous diseases afflicting mankind, are caused by the planetary bodies; and by observing the different significators in a nativity, the nature of the disorders to which the constitution is predisposed may be ascertained, and this fact once known, the cure is half effected.

But it must be understood, that success in curing the disease depends greatly on the time when the treatment is commenced. There is a period when no disease can be combated, when it has obtained the mastery, and the physical energy and vitality is so lessened and reduced as to be beyond human power.

I have made these numerous quotations from the writings of Hippocrates and other ancient physicians, to show the reader that the ancients were not so ignorant in the most important branches of medicine as physicians are at the present day. These observations which they had made on prognosis and diagnosis of disease, in connection with planetary influence, had been continued for hundreds or thousands of years; and the perfection at which they had arrived in astro-medical botany, and in prognosing disease, by the positions and aspects of the Moon and planets, was so marvelous, that it will require hundreds of years of patient application and observation of planetary influence in disease, for the physicians of the present and coming generations, to arrive at anything like the perfection attained by our forefathers two thousand years ago.

If, in publishing this circular, I have succeeded in drawing the attention of even a few practicing physicians, so that they will commence to investigate this ancient and only true system of medicine, as I and my forefathers have done, its main object will be accomplished.

The study of the stars has always been pursued in all ages. The astrologer and philosopher have ever occupied prominent places among men. At the present time, the astrologer who has studied the science and read the books of the old masters of the art, cannot be otherwise than a learned man, and capable of giving to the world much that is useful, interesting and exciting. The realms of the past, the present and the future are constantly before his vision, and with magic power, lessons of wisdom are imparted with almost entire accuracy.

To those entirely unacquainted with judicial Astronomy or Astrology, it will, perhaps, be necessary to state that it is a science based upon mathematical calculations, deductions being made from the daily configurations and aspects of the planetary orbs, and has no connection with the various methods of fortune telling by cards and other methods of divination imposed upon the public.

The desire to penetrate the future is common to all, it is born with our birth and implanted in us for a wise purpose and the signs of the heavens interpreted by a skillful professor are the only true means of attaining it.

There is nothing repugnant to virtue, morality, or the laws of the Deity in the study or application of astral science to the benefit of mankind; it is perhaps the most ancient of all sciences, and has been studied and venerated by literary men from time immemorial.

A nativity is a scheme or diagram of the heavens at the time of birth; from this, deductions can be made regarding duration of life, sickness, accidents. mental qualities, disposition, the profession or employment most suitable, description of person of wife or husband, children, reputation, friends, enemies, wealth, prosperity or adversity, honor, etc., etc.; and by computing the planetary motions termed TRANSITS, OR ARCS OF DIRECTION, the periods are foretold when changes for good or evil may be expected, and the various future events of life ascertained. From this diagram of the heavens, the road to health and happiness so far as attainable in individual cases can be pointed out.

Parents knowing the planetary influences existing at the birth of their children, are enabled so to direct their education as to be of incalculable advantage to their future interests in life.

By Horary Astrology, may be determined the result, success or failure of any intention, event or undertaking, such as speculations, investments, co-partnerships, lawsuits, courtship, marriage, making purchases or sales, rise and fall of the grain or stock market, mortgages, hiring houses or lands, commencing business or journeys, obtaining employment or office, the most profitable quarter to reside in for the pursuit of health or wealth, recovery of debts, situation and health of absent friends, lost property, mining interests—in short there are no transactions in life which may not most certainly be determined when the inquirer sincerely desires information. This knowledge of the future is invaluable to the trader, farmer, merchant and speculator.

L. D. BROUGHTON, M. D.,

President of the International Astrological Society, located in the City of New York,

Editor of "Broughton's Monthly Planet Reader and Astrological Journal," Etc.,

Respectfully announces to his friends and the public in general, that he is permanently located at 68 South Washington Square, New York. where he will be happy to receive all those who may favor him with a visit. His scientific and literary attainments as an Astrologer makes it an object for the public to consult him upon the various contingencies and events of human life.

The most sensitive need have no hesitation in seeking for information upon any matter, as the Doctor pays the most scrupulous regard to the feelings and interests of those who consult him, his sole aim being to advise with sincerity, and in all cases the most inviolable confidence is observed.

CONSULTATION FEE—Ladies $1 to $3; gentlemen $3 to $5. Office open day and evening.

Persons residing at a distance, can consult the Doctor by letter, enclosing $2 and stamp. Send date and place of birth, hour and minute if possible; if hour and minute are not known send a description of person, height, weight, color of hair, complexion, etc., and state time of some events such as sickness, etc., and if married, give date of marriage, as this assists the Doctor in finding the true time of birth.

THE OPINION OF THE PRESS.

WONDERS NEVER CEASE.—We understand that Dr. L. D. Broughton of this city has a method of telling any person's disposition and character by the position of the planets at the time of birth, and also that he can tell any person's past, present and future destiny by the revolutions of the Heavenly bodies, and with as much certainty as an astronomer can tell when it will be Summer and Winter by the revolution of the earth around the Sun; and that he can tell whether any person will become wealthy, and what kind of business they will succeed the best in, and what they are best adapted for; also the description and disposition of any person's future wife or husband, and if they will live happily in a married life, etc., etc.

Should this fact be thoroughly established by trial and experience, we think that it will be one of the greatest sciences of the age; for if people could tell for certain what is likely to happen to them, they might guard against misfortune very much, so as not to feel its influence in its full force, just in the same manner as we can guard against the cold and inclemency of Winter by providing suitable clothing, food, fire, etc., and if we knew when our most fortunate times were coming, we might improve them very much. As Shakespeare says:

" There is a tide in the affairs of men
Which taken at the flood leads on to fortune,
Omitted, all the voyage of their life
Is bound in shallows and in miseries."

We would say to all our readers, call on or send time and place of birth to Dr. Broughton, and give him a fair trial, and then you can prove for yourself whether there is any truth in this science or not. His charges are very moderate.—*Philadelphia Evening Reporter.*

To the opponents of Astrology I have not one word to say in defense of this science, but to those who are unprejudiced and wish to learn the truth, I will here offer a few suggestions which may assist them in investigating this subject.

That the heavenly bodies, that is, the stars, Sun, Moon, and planets, have an effect upon this earth and its inhabitants is as self-evident a truth as that they have an existence. The ebbing and flowing of the tides prove this, as well as the periodical returns of heat and cold, light and darkness; these are some of the most prominent influences by which the truths of Astrology become manifest, and planetary influences are being universally felt and admitted, and its periods are accurately calculated and known. Thus far, at least, all men and women are astrologers, but most of them are like the man who had been talking prose all his life and did not know it.

The opponents of Astrology tell us that this science has been exploded, but when or where the explosion took place, or who heard it, "deponent sayeth not," simply because they do not know and never will.

Twenty-five years ago I stood, as it were, alone, and almost the only advocate and defender of this science on this continent, and the reader of this day would not believe the amount of persecution I had to endure; but within the last twenty years there has been a great change in public opinion in regard to the science of Astrology and its professors.

The scientific men and savans, both in Europe and this country, have begun to give attention to this ancient science, and have come to the conclusion that our forefathers for hundreds of years past, were not such fools after all as they have taken them to be.

One of the prominent lecturers who have drawn attention to this subject, in his lectures and publications is the English astronomer, Mr. Richard A. Proctor, who in his book called *Myths and Marvels of Astronomy,* on page 7, says:

"The Moon, as she circles around the earth exerts a manifest influence upon terrestrial matter—the tidal wave, rising and sinking cinchronously with the movements of the Moon, and other consequences depend, directly or indirectly upon her revolution around the earth. The Sun's influence is still more manifest, being the greater light which rules the day, rules the seasons also—and in ruling them provides the annual supply of vegetable food on which the very existence of men and animals depend, if these two bodies, the Sun and Moon, are thus potent, must it not be supposed that the other celestial bodies exert corresponding influences. The Sun is second only to the Moon in tidal influences. We know also that his position as fire, light, and life of the earth, and its inhabitants, is due directly to the tremendous heat with which the whole of his mighty frame is instinct."

And the same author goes on to say, on page 15:

"The seasons of our earth, are affected by the condition of the Sun in the matter of spots—for instance, it has been found that years, when the Sun has been free from spots, have been warmer than the average. And that the Sun's spots wax and ware in periods of time which are manifestly referable to the planetary motions. Thus the great solar spot period lasts about eleven years, the successive spotless epochs being separated on the average by about that time; and so nearly does this period agree with the period of the planet Jupiter's revolution around the Sun, that during eight consecutive spot periods the spots were most numerous when Jupiter was nearest to the Sun. Seeing then that the Sun's spots manifestly affect the weather and the seasons, while the planets rule the Sun's spots, it is clear that the planets really rule the seasons, and again, seeing that the planets rule the seasons, while the seasons largely affect the well being of men and nations (to say nothing of animals), it follows that the planets influence the fate of men and nations (and animals)."

This is positive proof of the influence of the planets on the earth and its inhabitants.

Dr. Knapp, of Chicago, Illinois, has of late years drawn special attention to the *perihelion* of the superior planets, and the remarkable effects which have been produced on the earth in droughts, pestilence and famine, and which have always occurred at those particular periods when those planets were in their *perihelion*.

The effects which have been produced upon the earth by those superior planets being in their nearest position to the sun, appears to outweigh all other natural causes in producing those various epidemics, at those particular epochs, and no wonder that the effect should be marvelous when we consider the Sun as the great source of light and heat to our earth, and so many of those planets which are so many thousand times larger than our earth, and while in their *perihelion* being so many millions of miles nearer to the Sun, and drawing from that source so much more of its light, heat and magnetism than their usual share or allotment, and leaving our earth so much less than its natural share, that the effect should be that our atmosphere becomes "muggy" and the sky loses its natural healthy blueness, the sun almost covered with spots, harvests fail, and pestilence should stalk through the land at those particular periods.

During the fifth century, at one of those *perihelion* of the superior planets, there was an epidemic caused by it, which carried off over fifty millions of the people during that time.

I have not space in this pamphlet to notice the different *perihelions* that have occurred since the Christian era commenced, and therefore refer the readers to the writings of Dr. Knapp, who has calculated all the *perihelions*, and who has taken note of all the epidemics for the last two thousand years, and has shown clearly that there has not been any epidemic of any note, during all that time, that has not occurred during the *perihelion* of one or more of the superior planets.

B. G. Jenkins, F. R. A. S., of England, in an article published in *The Pall Mall Gazette*, London, says:

"The reason why people of the present day do not believe in planetary influence are two-fold—first, it is held to betoken ignorance and superstition; points on which educated people are very sensitive, and secondly, they cannot imagine how such tiny objects can affect their great globe, unconsciously forgetting that our earth among the planets is as a pea among cannon balls. From a lengthy study of this subject, I can come to no other conclusion than that the planets of the solar system are intimately connected with the phenomena or what takes place on this earth, and I shall, in as few words as possible, lay before the reader my reasons for such a conclusion."

Mr. Jenkins goes on to cite the different periods at which cholera was pervalent, from 1816 to 1861, and he noticed that the outbreak occured about every seventeen years, which periods were alternately the maximum and minimum of the Sun's spots. He further says;

"Certainly the Sun spots could not have produced the cholera, for there was a great outbreak when they were very plentiful, and next when they were very few, but that there was a connection, I felt convinced, and that they were both in the nature of cause and effect."

Further on, he says:

"I suggested, in a paper I read at the time before the Royal Historical Society, that the cause was probably to be found in the influence of the planets. I noticed the number of periods in which cholera broke out, but meanwhile I worked at the Sun's spots, and was rewarded by finding that the average period of the phenomena or magnetic storms or auroral periods was eleven and one-ninth years, the period of Jupiter's animalistic year. I then turned to terrestrial magnetism, and found that the needle of the compass, at London was moving east up to 1580, and west till 1816, and east ever since. The outbreak of the plague directed my attention to that subject; as the magnetic poles advance the epidemics accompanied them.

On calculating back, I found that the line which is now passing across Russia, and causing diphtheria, pestilence, famine, etc., must have passed over that region five hundred years ago; this will take us back to the middle of the fourteenth century, and with similar magnetic conditions we have similar epidemics."

THE BLACK DEATH.—We know this plague devastated Europe more or less the two centuries thereafter, culuminating in the great plague of London in 1665. It occurred to me that the planet Neptune might be the cause of the movement of the magnetic pole. On examining the movements of that planet and its orbit I found that the movements of the needle varied in accordance with those of that planet, while it makes three revolutions. The magnet makes an eccentric circle around the pole of the earth; this eccentricity I found was due to some influence at the maximum of about 80 years. On examining the movements and position of Uranus, which planet completes its revolution in 84 years, I found that they were such as to account for the anomaly.

In conclusion, Mr. Jenkins agrees with Dr. Knapp of Chicago, that within the next seven years, commencing with 1880, there will occur that which has not happened before for hundreds of years. All the superior planets will be at or near their nearest point to the sun, called the perihelion of the planets; therefore we may expect extraordinary magnetic phenomena during the next seven years. Great plagues will manifest themselves in all their intensity, commencing about 1878 and ending about 1886 or a few years later.

I copy the following from the *New York Sunday Mercury*, June 27, 1880:

"There occurs a conjunction of Jupiter and Saturn about every twenty years. A conjunction took place in 1822, another in 1842, and another in 1861. Another conjunction will occur in 1881, and another in 1901; and the two planets will make their commensurate perihelia in 1915.

"Jupiter will make his perihelia in October, 1880; Mars will follow a year hence, on May 28, 1881; Neptune, a few months later; Urauus, in the spring of 1882; and Saturn in the autumn of 1885. In other words all the great planets are rapidly approaching the great central luminary. Great drifts of sun-spots consequently shoot athwart his disk. The earth feels the reactive effect of the solar disturbance. Rain is withheld; springs are dried up; grass is withered; crops are ruined, and gaunt famine stares us in the face. With the unpleasant experiences of the past, and the, probably, near future before us, the subject of the striking coincidences of planetary perihelia and pestilence, will be likely to receive more respectful attention from astronomers and medical men than it has been accorded in the past."

Although it is reasonable to expect that the *perihelion* of the superior planets, (which phenomenon commences in the latter part of this year, 1880, and lasts until the end of 1885), will have a similar effect, and which effect is felt a few years before the first *perihelion*, and also for a number of years after the last *perihelion*, on the earth and its inhabitants, in droughts, epidemics, pestilence and famine, that they have had in former ages, yet it is unreasonable to expect that their influences will be felt as much as formerly in cultivated and civilized countries. For instance, the improvements in ship building, navigation, canals, and railways will prevent famine from becoming very prevalent in any one civilized country, as those improvements in travel can take the surplus of eatables from more fortunate localities; as the crops have never been known to fail in all parts of the world alike, or to the same extent at one time. As an instance, the famine in Ireland and the large crops in America in 1879, enabled us to give or send some of our surplus to that famishing country.

The improvements in the supply of fresh water, and good sewerage, and the sanitary conditions of large towns and cities, have also, in a great measure prevented the spread of epidemics such as cholera, yellow fever, etc., from one city to another, except in those places where the water, drainage, and sanitary conditions are bad.

For instance, although the yellow fever was very prevalent in the Summer and Fall of 1878, in New Orleans, Grenada, Vicksburg and Memphis where the drainage and water were unhealthy, and although numbers of people stricken with yellow fever fled to Philadelphia, New York, and other cities where numbers of them died, yet that fever did not become epidemic or contagious in those cities.

Nearly a hundred years ago Dr. Rush and Dr. Caldwell, both of Philadelphia, Pa., became almost bitter enemies in their discussions and arguments as to whether yellow fever was epidemic or endemic. Dr. Caldwell took the endemic side, and Dr. Rush the epidemic. Dr. Rush argued that if they could keep the yellow fever from being imported into Philadelphia they would never have any there. Dr. Caldwell argued that if they had plenty of fresh water in Philadelphia, and kept the streets and sewers clean, they would still have no yellow fever there, even if it was imported. The facts have proved since, that Dr. Caldwell was right, as they have never had yellow fever epidemic in Philadelphia since they stopped using the well water; and the purer water of the Schuylkill has been used for drinking and cooking purposes, and also in quantities to keep the streets and sewers clean. The same may be said of New York, since they have used the water of the Croton River, and the same principle applies to other cities in the Northern States.

Although all those improvements in the sanitary condition of cities have greatly improved the health of the people living in them, and in preventing the development and spread of those various epidemics, yet we cannot prevent altogether those peculiar conditions of the atmosphere which are the main secondary causes of those epidemics, and which are produced by planetary influences.

Sometimes some simple-minded physician, who perhaps has discovered a remedy for some special disease, and which in most ordinary cases appears to have a beneficial effect in curing or alleviating that disease, yet when applied in those cases produced by telluric influence appears to have no effect whatever. I might instance a certain doctor, who went to New Orleans in the Fall of 1878. during the yellow fever epidemic in that city, with a peculiar patent bedstead to be in some way used in curing that fever; yet when applied there, and in that particular condition of the atmosphere, had no effect, and he soon became a victim to the yellow fever himself.

I might also instance here a certain doctor who went from the United States to Russia, with a certain plant which he deemed a positive cure for diphtheria, a disease which has become epidemic in that country of late through telluric influence, and although there has been a number of diphtheria patients placed under his care, yet according to the report every one of them has died while under his treatment, and he may in time become a victim to his own infatuation.

I mention these few instances to illustrate my point, that all doctors ought to study those peculiar planetary influences which cause the various epidemics: then they would not be so likely to lose all faith in some good remedy for some special disease; which might be good in all ordinary cases of that disease, but of no use when applied under those special telluric influences and conditions. A fire engine might be very useful in quenching a fire in an ordinary building, but of no use whatever when a prairie is on fire, in a very hot and dry season.

The ancestors of Dr. Broughton have made Astrology, in connection with medicine a special study for a number of generations, and the Hippocrates practice of medicine has been taught, from father to son, in their family during that time.

Dr. Broughton has also had a large practice in Astrology and Medical Botany, for over 25 years, in England, Philadelphia, New York and Saratoga Springs; he would be happy to treat any patient who has not found relief from any other system of practice, at his office and residence,

68 South Washington Square, New York.

He can also be consulted by letter enclosing $2, giving time of birth of patient, also when first taken sick, etc.

Incurable cases solicited and cured or money returned.

BROUGHTON'S

Monthly Planet Reader

AND

ASTROLOGICAL JOURNAL.

This periodical commenced April 1st, 1860, and continued to Dec., 1869; all the back numbers are bound in one volume, price, by mail, $1.00. It contains nearly 300 pages, and was devoted to the illustration and defence of Astrology, besides a great deal of very curious information regarding the science of Astrology and the occult. It contains a great number of horoscopes of leading generals who fought in the Rebellion, and of presidents of the United States. Among others the horoscopes of Gen. George B. McClellan, General Winfield Scott, President Buchanan, President Lincoln, Gen. Grant, Louis Napoleon Bonaparte, Gen. John C. Fremont, Stephen A. Douglass, Hon. John Bell, The Prince of Wales, Charles Dickens, Lord Byron, Hon. William H. Seward, Gen. Burnside, Gen. Giuseppe Garibaldi and Gen. Washington, with charts of the heavens for the same.

It also contains a colored chart illustrating Astro-Phrenology and a guide for students for that science, besides other interesting matter.

About the author:

Luke Dennis Broughton was born in Leeds, England, on April 20, 1828, at 10 am. He died in New York on September 22, 1899.

By any standard, the true Pioneer of Astrology in America.

His ancestors for several generations back had been interested in astrology, and his own father had taught it to him. He emigrated to the U.S. from England about 1854, settling in Philadelphia. There, he studied medicine and took his degree from the Eclectic Medical College of the State of Pennsylvania. He practiced homeopathic medicine for the rest of his life, using astrology as an aid to diagnosis and treatment.

George J. McCormack (AFA Bulletin, 5:11, 28 October 1943) says, "On March 3, 1860, the State legislature in Harrisburg, Penna., a bill was introduced to suppress 'fortune telling' of future events and any form of advertising concerning the same. That proposed legislation was instrumental in causing reactions that prompted Dr. Broughton to start a crusade in defense of serious astrology. Within a month he issued the first number of his *Monthly Planet Reader and Astrological Journal*."

This periodical seems to have been successful. But anti-fortune telling legislation was passed by the Pennsylvania legislature in 1861, and in 1863 Broughton suspended and left Philadelphia for New York City. A year later he resumed publication and continued the periodical until the end of 1869, when agitation against astrology reached the point of violence in that city. Thereafter he operated less openly but continued his studies, practice and teaching until the end of his life. At some time in his later years he was President of the Astrological Society of America.

While still in Philadelphia, he had predicted that Lincoln would lose the 1860 election to Stephen A. Douglas. The election was a 4-way race, and in fact Lincoln only received 39.7% of the popular vote. But he was high man (Douglas was No. 2 with 29.3%) and received 180 of the 303 electoral votes. Broughton stated following the election that he had taken the evil aspects in Lincoln's nativity (he used a chart with Saturn rising in Sagittarius) to refer to his prospects for gaining the presidency, whereas he should have realized that they referred to what would take place after the election.

When time came for the next election, the Oct-Nov-Dec 1864 issue of his Monthly Planet Reader and Astrological Journal led off with an article by Broughton entitled "The Nativity of Abraham Lincoln President of the United States" in which he correctly forecast the re-election of Pres. Lincoln, but added, "I might here state, that shortly after the election is over, Mr. Lincoln will have a number of evil aspects afflicting his nativity (I do not think that any of these will begin to be felt until the election is past.) they will then be in operation in Nov. and Dec. of this year. During these months, let him be especially on his guard against attempts to take his life; by such as fire arms, and infernal machines."

In the spring 1865 issue he added the further prediction: "Some noted general or person in high office dies or is removed about the 17th or 18th (of April)." As it turned out, Lincoln was shot on April 14 and died the next morning. This prediction enhanced Broughton's reputation considerably, but may well have hurt him eventually. For, by putting him in the public eye, it made him an obvious target for opponents of astrology and culminated four years later in attacks against his lecture hall, the sacking of his home by a mob, and the suppression of his magazine, as mentioned above.

In fact, for the last forty years of his life he suffered much persecution for his practice and teaching of astrology (see his book *The Elements of Astrology* for details). Adding to his misfortune, his branch of medical science (homeopathy and naturopathy) increasingly fell into disrepute during the latter half of the nineteenth century, so that the two intellectual disciplines to which he had devoted his life were both out of the main stream of American thought. Towards the end of his life, he found some consolation in the fact that the overall acceptance of astrology by the public had increased significantly during that period.

In retrospect, Dr. Broughton was undoubtedly the foremost American astrologer of the 19th century. He established the first major astrological journal, he achieved considerable fame, he was an effective teacher, and he wrote an excellent treatise on astrology. He is also said to have been the first to call attention to the "20 year cycle" of U.S. presidents dying in office. His most famous pupil was Professor Chaney.

— Quoted with permission from *Astrological Pioneers of America*, by James H. Holden and Robert A. Hughes, AFA, Tempe, AZ, 1988. The book is dedicated to the memory of Dr. Broughton.

Better books make better astrologers.
Here are some of our other titles:

AstroAmerica's Daily Ephemeris, 2010-2020
AstroAmerica's Daily Ephemeris, 2000-2020
  - *both for Midnight. Compiled & formatted by David R. Roell*

Al Biruni
The Book of Instructions in the Elements of the Art of Astrology, *1029 AD,*
  translated by R. Ramsay Wright

David Anrias
Man and the Zodiac

Derek Appleby
Horary Astrology: The Art of Astrological Divination

E.H. Bailey
The Prenatal Epoch

Joseph Blagrave
Astrological Practice of Physick

C.E.O. Carter
The Astrology of Accidents
An Encyclopaedia of Psychological Astrology
Essays on the Foundations of Astrology
The Principles of Astrology, *Intermediate no. 1*
Some Principles of Horoscopic Delineation, *Intermediate no. 2*
Symbolic Directions in Modern Astrology
The Zodiac and the Soul

Charubel & Sepharial
Degrees of the Zodiac Symbolized, *1898*

H.L. Cornell
Encyclopaedia of Medical Astrology

Nicholas Culpeper
Astrological Judgement of Diseases from the Decumbiture of the Sick, *1655, and,*
  Urinalia, *1658*

Dorotheus of Sidon
Carmen Astrologicum, *c. 50 AD, translated by David Pingree*

Nicholas deVore
Encyclopedia of Astrology

Firmicus Maternus
Ancient Astrology Theory & Practice: Matheseos Libri VIII,
c. 350 AD, translated by Jean Rhys Bram

Margaret Hone
The Modern Text-Book of Astrology

Alan Leo
The Progressed Horoscope, *1905*
The Key to Your Own Nativity, *1910*
Dictionary of Astrology, *edited by Vivian Robson, 1929*

William Lilly
Christian Astrology, books 1 & 2, *1647*
  The Introduction to Astrology, Resolution of all manner of questions.
Christian Astrology, book 3, *1647*
  Easie and plaine method teaching how to judge upon nativities.

George J. McCormack
A Text-Book of Long Range Weather Forecasting
  With Foreword by David R. Roell, Astrology At Our Feet

Jean-Baptiste Morin
The Cabal of the Twelve Houses Astrological
  translated by George Wharton, edited by D.R. Roell

Claudius Ptolemy
Tetrabiblos, *c. 140 AD, translated by J.M. Ashmand*

Vivian Robson
Astrology and Sex
Electional Astrology
Fixed Stars & Constellations in Astrology
A Beginner's Guide to Practical Astrology
A Student's Text-Book of Astrology,
  Vivian Robson Memorial Edition

Diana Roche
The Sabian Symbols, A Screen of Prophecy

David Roell
Skeet Shooting for Astrologers

Richard Saunders
The Astrological Judgement and Practice of Physick, *1677*

Sepharial
The Manual of Astrology, the Standard Work
Primary Directions, a definitive study
Sepharial On Money. *For the first time in one volume, complete texts:*
  - **Law of Values**
  - **Silver Key**
  - **Arcana, or Stock and Share Key** — *first time in print!*

Zane Stein
Essence and Application, A View from Chiron

James Wilson, Esq.
Dictionary of Astrology

H.S. Green, Raphael & C.E.O. Carter
Mundane Astrology: *3 Books, complete in one volume.*

If not available from your local bookseller, order directly from:
The Astrology Center of America
207 Victory Lane
Bel Air, MD 21014

on the web at:
http://www.astroamerica.com

www.ingramcontent.com/pod-product-compliance
Lightning Source LLC
Chambersburg PA
CBHW081754300426
44116CB00014B/2111